D0848637

ON SUNSET BOULEVARD

ON SUNSET BOULEVARD

THE LIFE AND TIMES OF BILLY WILDER

by ED SIKOV

NEW YORK

DECATUR PUBLIC LIBRARY

DECATUR, ILLINOIS

WITHDRAWN 791.43023
W

THAT OLD GANG OF MINE

Words by Billy Rose and Mort Dixon Music by Ray Henderson Copyright ©
1923 by Bourne Co. Copyright renewed Extended term: Bourne Co., Ray
Henderson Music and Olde Clover Leaf Music All Rights Reserved International Copyright Secured Used by Permission ASCAP

Academy Awards® Photographs Copyright of the Academy of Motion Picture Arts and Sciences

Copyright © 1998 Ed Sikov

All rights reserved. No part of this book may be used or reproduced
in any manner whatsoever without the written permission of the Publisher.
Printed in the United States of America. For information address
Hyperion, 114 Fifth Avenue, New York, New York 10011.

DESIGN BY DOROTHY S. BAKER

Library of Congress Cataloging-in-Publication Data

Sikov, Ed.
    On Sunset Boulevard : the life and times of Billy Wilder / by Ed
Sikov. — 1st ed.
       p.   cm.
    Filmography: p.
    Includes bibliographical references and index.
       1. Wilder, Billy, 1906–   . 2. Motion picture producers and
directors—United States—Biography.   I. Title.
PN1998.3.W56S55   1998
791.43'0233'092—dc21
    [b]   98-23504
                                                                  CIP

DECATUR PUBLIC LIBRARY

FEB 0 1 1999

DECATUR, ILLINOIS

ISBN 0-7868-6194-0

FIRST EDITION

10 9 8 7 6 5 4 3 2 1

PREFACE

In real life, most women are stupid—and so are persons who are
writing biographies of Hollywood celebrities.

—Billy Wilder

don't go to church," the sneering floozy announces to Kirk Douglas in
Billy Wilder's *Ace in the Hole*. Then she explains why: "Kneeling bags
my nylons." The floozy is married, her husband is dying at the bottom
of a dank pit—a collapsed cave into which he has ventured to steal
sacred Indian relics. Douglas, an ambitious and self-serving reporter, keeps
him trapped there to enhance the drama and advance his own career. Sight-
seers show up, sniffing thrills. A traveling carnival arrives on the scene
complete with a Ferris wheel and junk food stands. Newspaper readers
across the country shiver at each day's breathless account of the rescue
operation until the trapped man stops breathing and the excitement dies
with him. Douglas nearly strangles the floozy with a ratty fur stole, and
she responds by stabbing him in the gut with a pair of scissors. After a
period of slow, degrading bleeding, he keels over, slamming headfirst onto
the floor, and dies, his empty eyes staring in close-up into the camera.

Wilder wrote, produced, and directed *Ace in the Hole* in 1951. It was
his most personal movie to date, and it bombed—badly. American audiences just weren't willing to see themselves exposed in the most searing,
caustic light he could shine at them. They'd bought Fred MacMurray as a
greedy strangler in *Double Indemnity*, Ray Milland as a sullen terminal
drunk in *The Lost Weekend*, and Gloria Swanson as the crazy has-been
movie star in *Sunset Boulevard* who shoots a young screenwriter in the
back and lets him bleed to death in her Beverly Hills swimming pool, but
they drew the line at the corrupt, self-hating journalist and his slut (who,

by the way, simply walks off into the dust at the end and never pays for her crime).

With our national spirit growing ever more poisonous in the final, hissing years of what was once billed (proudly) as the American Century, Billy Wilder's morbid cinema takes on a richer burnish. Our cynicism has grown rootless. His was always romantic. Our national strain of self-loathing is inescapable in the 1990s—even the average television laughs have a bitter bite, and the best cartoons are surly—and as a result Wilder's sour comedies and harsh, morally compromised dramas now ring truer than ever. In the quaint-seeming past, Wilder offered sharp refreshment from Hollywood's egregious gladness—the flood of sappy endings in which nice peoples' lives worked out just fine. With a series of toxic antidotes, Wilder hit at some deeper, more depressing truths. He offered shots of acid in place of bromides, leering smirks instead of contented smiles. Even his blockbuster comedies *Some Like It Hot* and *The Apartment* are tinged with meanness. Astoundingly, he almost always got away with it. But not even Wilder, the master cynic, could foresee the kicker. The big joke is, with each passing decade Wilder's acerbic tales only seem more tender. At the end of our vicious and exhausted century, Wilder's nastiness has taken on a kind of romantic poignance. His movies are shockingly delicate.

There was always decency there, even if no one could ever quite grasp it for good. There was love, however uncertain or tentative. Sometimes there was hope, of a sad sort. But there was never sloppiness. Wilder crafted his movies in a classical and beautiful way. They are structured, refined. His rhythmic words matter as much as his understated images. Because his bitter jokes were composed with virtuoso care, they have become reassuring. The fact that Wilder got it so right for so long is itself a profound solace, even if the relentless proof he offers of life's rottenness never fails to haunt and dishearten. Wilder's is a world of cheaters and jerks, bitches and whores; a diseased world; an ugly one. He looks at humanity and he is sickened by it, in part because of his own complicity.

It isn't as if Wilder remained an unsung outcast in his own time, a lone artist rubbing against the grain of his culture. On the contrary. His knack for tapping and expanding a vast public's limited imagination made him a very rich man who boasted a slew of handsome gold trophies to go with his museum-quality art collection. He was an uncommonly successful, unrepentantly commercial Hollywood director, a genius at making corruption marketable. Except for *Ace in the Hole*, Wilder's films hardly ever found critical and commercial disfavor until the final few (and ironically, two of those box office duds are among his most sweet-tempered pictures). With hit after hit, he prospered. An outsider when it came to sentiment, he was always an inside player. Never did he pit himself against the system—not in his first job (as an editor of crossword puzzles for a Viennese scandal sheet); not as a hungry young screenwriter in Berlin making the rounds of cafés, smoking and looking for work; not as a multimillionaire director in Hollywood hanging around Romanoff's puffing cigars, drinking martinis, and insulting his competition. Wilder adapted—wherever he landed, whatever it took. At an early age he learned to work the system, in middle age he became it, and he hung on as long as he could, to his own enormous benefit.

Because he wrote all the films he directed, Billy Wilder's body of work is unparalleled in the American cinema. Nobody else's career lasted as long. No one else wrote and directed a more accomplished string of hits. Sturges and Welles burned out. Chaplin felt no compulsion to keep working all the time. Hitchcock, Ford, and Hawks didn't write their own material; Spielberg, Scorsese, and Coppola don't either. Wilder personally wrote every word of every film he directed, though always with a teammate. Blending story and image with rare taste and intelligence, the refugee director learned to speak the subtle, supple language of American filmmaking perfectly, though always with an accent.

And he lasted. His movies still hold up, some better than ever. Wilder's artistic stock would be higher if his visual style had been more ostentatious, but his goal was never to dazzle his audience with pretty pictures. His visual gestures are too intimate and self-effacing. Now, in our gaudier, more kinetic era, Wilder's camera style seems so restrained as to be invisible, but that is simply because he never clobbered anyone with it.

On Sunset Boulevard is the story of Billy Wilder's life in motion pictures. It focuses on what he achieved on-screen and how he came to achieve it. It is an unauthorized biography. When Jack Lemmon called Wilder to ask whether he should grant an interview to me, Wilder said bluntly that the idea of sitting through an interview made him want to throw up. Funny, I felt the same way. The fastest, funniest, meanest mind in Hollywood, he has been ridiculing friends and enemies in three languages for most of his ninety-two years, and frankly I wasn't certain I could withstand his legendary assault. When he declined my repeated requests for meetings, lunches, and tours of art galleries in which I promised not to bring even a piece of paper or a pencil, I confess to feeling as much relieved as disappointed.

Still, writing about Billy Wilder's extraordinary life has been the greatest honor of my own. I hope to have done him justice.

July 1998

PART ONE

1906–1933

1. FROM KRAKÓW TO VIENNA

There is the low-bred and the high-bred. And if the low-bred has
the impertinence to come distastefully close, what can he expect
but to be bitten?
—Countess Johanna Franziska von Stoltzenberg-Stoltzenberg
(Joan Fontaine) in *The Emperor Waltz*

On June 22, 1906, in the Galician village of Sucha Beskidzka, south of
Kraków, Eugenia Wilder went into labor with her second child. Her
husband, Max, ran a small café at the Sucha railroad station, one of
several along the Vienna–Lemberg line. The Wilders didn't live in
Sucha, a tiny nothing of a town. They were there because Max was checking up on business, his wife and infant son, Willie, in tow. They didn't live
much of anywhere, really, though Kraków was more or less their home
base. Max was trying to work his fledgling business into something sus-
tainable, and he and his young family had to spend a few days here and a
few days there while Max nursed the business along. At the end of June,
there happened to be Sucha Beskidzka, where Genia gave birth to another
boy. She and Max named him Samuel.

The Wilders were German-speaking Jews living among Poles and Gypsies in an absurdly overstretched empire run by a dynasty of Roman Catholic Austrians. (After young Samuel grew up and became a famous film
director in Hollywood, the world forgot that he and his family used to
pronounce their name in German, too. It didn't start out sounding like the
comparative form of *wild*. Billy's name used to rhyme with *builder*, however accented the rhyme may have been. And it began with the sound of a
v.) Galicia was poor, peasant country with scattered dirt farms and isolated
villages; the locals spoke Polish. The Hapsburgs, seated in imperial splendor
well on the other side of the Carpathians, had pocketed an immense swath
of land north of the mountains when Poland was partitioned in the late
eighteenth century. They called their new trophy Galicia, a Latinate cor-

ruption of Halicz, the title of an ancient Hungarian duchy. Along with their vast new territory, the Hapsburgs took on a huge number of new subjects— Poles, Ruthenes, Silesians, Gypsies, Ukrainians, and Jews, the latter constituting about 9 percent of Galicia's population. Some of the Jews spoke German; some spoke Polish; most knew Yiddish. It was a destitute area, agrarian and superstitious, and outside of Kraków there was little in the way of education and culture. Vestiges of an old *szlachta*, or gentry, survived, but even the landowners were in tatters. As one historian describes them, "In Galicia even the *szlachta* was poor."

Eugenia's middle-class mother had imagined better things for her daughter than this, but then she'd probably imagined a more suitable match than Max Wilder. In the eyes of his wife's family, Max was a bit of a peasant himself. Like Genia, he was not a dirt-poor Galician. He was, however, a Galician. Max was from Stanislawczyk, much farther to the east, in the part of Galicia dominated by Ruthenes, and the farther east one hailed from, the further down the scale he was thought to be. Across the mountains to the southwest, in Vienna, the social ideals of which Genia's German-speaking family had adopted, *anyone* from Galicia was suspect. Max, like many Galician Jews, aspired early on to leave his eastern Galician heritage behind him. He'd been named Hersch Mendel Wilder at birth, late in the spring of 1872, but he soon adopted the regal name Maximilian—to make himself more of an Austro-Hungarian, to fit in with a better class of people. A tall, good-looking young man with clear brown eyes, who tried earnestly to shed the mud and sweat of eastern Galicia in favor of the more dignified and sophisticated west, Max affected a Kaiser Wilhelm mustache to go along with the emperor's dead brother's first name.

Max Wilder had been working as a headwaiter in a Kraków restaurant when he met Eugenia Dittler, a dark-haired, energetic, quick-witted girl in her late teens. She was from Zakopane, a small mountain town ninety kilometers south of Kraków. Her mother owned and operated a resort hotel, the Zent'al, in nearby Nowy Targ, which was the next-to-the-last stop on the railway line that took people into the mountains for some beneficial high-altitude air. The hotel was small, consisting of only nine rooms and a single bathroom, but it was reasonably successful, and Genia's mother had reason to be proud of it. Genia herself was no simple peasant girl from the mountains. By the time she turned up at Max's restaurant, she'd already spent five or six years in New York City, where she had lived with her uncle, a jeweler named Reich, and his family on Madison Avenue. Genia's extended holiday in America was part of her mother's ongoing effort to raise her standing in life, to expose her to a more refined world than the one into which she was born. Why she went back to Zakopane is unclear. Her father was dead, her mother had remarried a man named Baldinger (who proceeded to widow her a second time), and Genia, having tasted a better future, set her heart on finding her way back to the United States, where she thought she could really get somewhere.

She married Max in 1903 when the railway café idea seemed a good bet: from Vienna through Pressburg, Brünn, Mährisch-Ostrau, Kraków, and Lemberg, came a steady flow of customers. The couple trouped from town to town, managing the growing chain of little snack bars, and in 1904 they had their first child. By the end of June 1906, they were an itinerant family of four.

Following Jewish custom, the baby, Samuel, was named for someone dead. He and his brother, Wilhelm, were each given the name of a deceased grandfather—Max's father was a Wilhelm, Genia's was a Samuel—but Genia had little intention of saddling yet another son with a moribund past. So she began calling him Billie, after Buffalo Bill. He may have been born in a dust speck of a Galician outpost, but Billie was her American boy.

Wilder's only memories of Galicia were of his grandmother, the last observant Orthodox Jew in his family. He visited her in the mountains every summer. He slept in her bedroom with her, and Wilder remembered that every night before going to sleep, his grandmother checked under the beds to make sure there weren't any burglars lying in wait.

Nowy Targ was a remote village in a severe, unforgiving land, and Jews weren't held in the highest regard. Most Galician peasants lived in one-room huts with earthen floors. Barnyard animals strolled in and out at will. Being middle class, the Wilders were outsiders already. Being Jewish, they were set doubly apart from their Polish neighbors. Violence against Jews was scarcely unheard of in these parts—"The Jew will buy the entire countryside, and you'll be working on your knees," a peasant newspaper *Zwiazek Chlopski* in western Galicia had written only a few years earlier. "Shun the Jews. Pull yourselves together. Save every penny and learn." In 1898, there was a wave of anti-Jewish tumult in western Galicia, with mobs setting fire to Jewish-owned businesses, attacking Jewish houses with rocks, assaulting synagogues during Friday night services. Maybe Billie's grandmother knew what she was talking about.

The critic and historian Verlyn Klinkenborg reports that "Lion Phillimore, a traveler who toured the Carpathians about 1911, remarked of the Poles that 'their only oppressor was their own will-lessness. It was a blight lying on the face of the country.' " It was with this very population that young Billie Wilder saw his first business opportunities. Even as a child, Billie developed the skills necessary to parlay other people's ignorance into personal gain. He became a pool shark.

The Wilders settled in Kraków. With two young children and an ambitious wife, it became increasingly difficult for Max to manage all of his little businesses, so he consolidated his resources and opened a four-story hotel and restaurant at the base of Wawel Castle near Jagiellonian University, Poland's oldest educational institution. He called his venture Hotel City, giving it an English name to make it seem all the more twentieth-century. In addition to its guest rooms, Hotel City featured a full-service restaurant, an outdoor terrace, and a gaming room with billiards as well as tables for card playing. Max dressed for work in a cutaway and striped trousers. Billie dressed in children's play clothes and played the role of an average five- or six-year-old, but only as long as it took for him to snooker strangers into playing three-cushion billiards. The regulars set up the bets with each hapless newcomer. Tiny Billie did the rest, with the adult winners paying the child off in candy. (Stories like this led his second wife, Audrey, to remark, "Long before Billy Wilder was Billy Wilder, he behaved like Billy Wilder.")

Always a fast learner, Billie moved on to outright thievery and was soon enjoying the easy money to be gained by swiping the waiters' tips off the tables when nobody was looking. Then the waiters caught him. "They beat the shit out of me," Wilder recalled. Upon seeing his child being thrashed by his own staff, Max became enraged and demanded to know why the waiters were pummeling the boy. They informed him that his son was a crook, after which Max beat Billie himself for good measure. "I learned many things about human nature," Wilder once said of his life at Hotel City—"none of them favorable."

Max's power over Billie didn't last very long. There comes a point when sons see their fathers as being, having been, or on the road to becoming pathetic, and they discover with a nasty jolt their own fate—to carry on the tradition themselves. Wilder's epiphany came early on when he found out that Max had been nothing more glorious than a waiter at the time of his parents' marriage. It was one of the great disheartening jolts of his childhood. Billie uncovered the drab fact on Max and Genia's marriage certificate, which listed the groom's profession. He was jarred, amazed, and more than a little disgusted.

Kraków was the ancient capital of Poland, a center of learning and culture where Jews could mix more readily with the Poles than they could in the countryside. After all, the Jew and the Pole shared a common pessimism, a joint appreciation of the brutal fact that nothing was ever likely to come of anything. At the time, this was especially true in regard to the institutions of government. Hardly anyone respected the imperial bureaucracy in Vienna, where, in classic Viennese fashion, scandal after scandal had succeeded in whittling away the mammoth empire's confidence in its leaders. Franz Josef still cut an impressive figure, and his subjects continued to mourn the late Empress Elisabeth's assassination. ("Sisi" was knifed to death in 1898 by a meddling anarchist—an ugly, gratuitous murder.) But the empire itself was increasingly the object of ironic contempt. Everyone knew that the never-ending territories of greater Austria-Hungary were desperately bloated, profoundly unrelated, and utterly unmanageable, and fewer and fewer people took anything related to the Hapsburgs with quite the same degree of seriousness and respect they once would have granted willingly.The Hapsburgs' institutions still stood and functioned; they were powerful but hollow. Government buildings were inscribed "*K. u. K.*"— *Kaiserlich und Königlich*, Imperial and Royal—leading the acerbic writer Robert Musil to coin the name *Kakania* to describe Austro-Hungarian society. As no one failed to notice, *Kakania* meant more than just *Kaiserlich und Königlich*. The Hapsburg's fine empire had degenerated into kakaland.

Still, the existence of Austria-Hungary as a political entity was, as the old expression had it, good for the Jews. Franz Josef himself was excellent in this regard. The anti-Semitic Karl Lueger had to be elected mayor of Vienna five times before the emperor allowed him to take office. For the Jews in outlying provinces, there was an important practical consequence of Franz Josef's friendliness: as long as the emperor kept his empire alive, the Jews could get out of Galicia. Between 1891 and 1914, 320,000 Jews emigrated from Austria-Hungary to the United States; 85 percent of these Jews were from Galicia. The Jewish population of Vienna rose as well. In 1880 Jews made up 18 percent of the population in the capital; by 1910 it was 23 percent, with most of the newcomers arriving from Galicia. The exodus was motivated to some degree by fear, but it was also driven by hunger—mercantile, social, financial ambitions. In the words of the historian William O. McCagg, "This was flight upwards as well as out."

The Wilders liked to think of themselves as moving up in the world, Genia in particular. She saw a wider, richer future than the one she inhabited. Her dream of America never left her, and she instilled it in her sons. She and Max were newspaper readers—keen on current events but more or less disinterested in fiction. Billie's aunt, however, introduced the boys to the works of Mann, Dumas, and Zola, and their uncle steered them toward Zionism. Genia's tastes veered more toward popular culture—specifically, anything to do with America. She had been to Coney Island as a child. Now, as a young mother stuck in an outback of the empire, she loved to tell her two boys about the bizarre sculptures of aborigines that lurked outside the doors of cigar shops—big, imposing, expressionless chiefs holding tomahawks and wearing headdresses and war paint. Once, in New York, she had gotten hopelessly lost and only found her way back home when she recognized the familiar wooden savage on the corner.

From his mother, young Billie learned to tell a tale. You begin with the plausible and move on from there; when the actual event pales, you change it. And you never tell the same story twice. As told by Wilder, his life was a series of themes and variations, with heavy accent on the variations and little attention paid to inconsistencies. No one knows, for example, when his family moved from Kraków to Vienna. None of his biographers agree, least of all Billy. According to the entertainment writer Maurice Zolotow (who conducted extensive interviews with Wilder in the mid-1970s), the Wilders left for Vienna when World War I broke out and Kraków was evacuated. Wilder later reported that he "was brought as a kid of two and a half years old to Vienna, and I went there to grammar school, and then to high school." In the late 1980s, Wilder spent several months recounting his life with a German writer, Hellmuth Karasek, at which time he revealed that he and his parents had moved to Vienna in 1910. Another writer, Kevin Lally, took his information in large measure from Karasek and agreed that by 1910 the Wilder family owned a house in Vienna's First District. But according to Lally, the family shifted back and forth between Vienna and Kraków until 1914, at which time they moved to Vienna permanently.

None of these stories seems to be true. According to an array of hotel registration forms unearthed by a particularly dogged Austrian journalist and film historian named Andreas Hutter, Max Wilder made a number of business trips to Vienna between 1910 and 1916. Over and over, Max stayed in hotels. (He favored the Hotel Dungl on Gluckgasse.) Unless Genia kept throwing her husband out, how likely is it that Billie's father would have paid for all these hotel rooms if he already had an apartment in the center of town? These records have convinced Hutter that the Wilders actually lived in Vienna no earlier than 1916, two years after the war began.

The precise time of the Wilders' move to Vienna was probably not as crucial to the course of Billy's life as the migration's effect on the boy, the war's impact on his family, and the ringing novelty of his new life in the heart of a crumbling empire. Wilder recalled the day the war began, a scorching August day in 1914. The family was still in Kraków. Wilder remembered his father cutting off the café band to announce the assassination of Ferdinand in Sarajevo. In this version, the Wilder family set off for Vienna quickly in a rented horse-drawn carriage because the trains were too crowded. Never mind that the assassination occurred on June 30, not in August, and the fact that it took another month before war was declared.

Wilder never chronicled this migration as a single set of recordable facts. He also recalled spending the summer of 1914 with his grandmother. It was still an unusually hot season, he remembered, and he liked to spend his time sitting inside her cool, dark room in a Thonet rocking chair. In this version, it was Grandmother Baldinger who found the horse and carriage that set them on course toward Vienna, and as they packed their belongings onto the carriage, Billie, then eight years old, demanded that they take the rocking chair along with them. His grandmother put the problem to him tersely: she made him choose between the chair or the grandmother. Billie picked the chair. The old lady swatted him.

Whenever the Wilders actually left Kraków, the turmoil of wartime spelled the end of Hotel City. Max lost his business, and when the Wilders arrived in Vienna he had to start virtually from scratch yet again. The family did, however, have enough money to afford a nice middle-class apartment at Fleischmarkt 7 in the First District. Dominated by the immense Stephansdom, the crowning symbol of Viennese Catholicism, the First District is the heart and lungs of the city. In fact, deep in Stephansdom's crypt lie urns containing the disembodied guts of various Hapsburgs. One could scarcely be closer to the empire's bowels than to live only a few blocks north on Fleischmarkt. Next door to the Wilders' was an old inn, the Griechenbeisl, with its exterior sculpture of the legendary Viennese bagpiper who'd passed out in a drunken stupor during the plague of 1679 and been hurled into the plague pit, where he awoke, startled and surrounded by rotting corpses. He responded by playing a little tune on his bagpipes, a resurrection commemorated by the sculpture.

A few blocks in the other direction on Fleischmarkt lay the old Jewish district, the Judenplatz, and the narrow streets surrounding it. Regarded in the most positive light, the area had been populated by Jews since the thirteenth century. On the other hand, the Jews of Vienna had become so successful by the fifteenth century that they were all thrown out, except for the three hundred people the Viennese burned alive in 1421. At Judenplatz 2, a memorial plaque commemorates this triumph. Commissioned in 1491, the relief depicts the Baptism of Christ in the river Jordan, the stream that cleans away evil. As the Latin text of the relief tells us, the evil in question was personified by the Jews, whom the Viennese rightly punished for their misdeeds by incinerating them. By the early twentieth century, the Jews had returned to the Judenplatz, but it was no longer a strict ghetto. They were integrated into the rest of Vienna, or so they thought.

Ornate, courtly, formal beyond caricature, religious, cosmopolitan, and stretched and torn by the first global war—this was the Vienna into which the Wilder family moved and the neighborhood in which they lived. Max had new business opportunities, Genia had a good address, and Willie and Billie had the streets of Vienna to prowl. (Willie was now eleven, Billie ten.) They were practically within spitting distance of the ancient emperor, Franz Josef, who fortunately managed to die soon thereafter, thus providing Billie with an imperial spectacle the likes of which he had never imagined. It was rainy and cold on November 21, 1916, the day of the funeral. Franz Josef died eleven days earlier at eighty-seven years, sixty-eight years of which had been spent on the throne. Knowing that no impresarios in the world could put on a better show than the Hapsburgs, Max took his sons to the second floor of the Café Edison on the Ringstrasse to watch the funeral cortege. Wilder recalled that his father stood him on a marble table near the window. They waited a very long time, but eventually the procession appeared, everyone dressed in black. One by one, Max introduced the players: the German crown prince; the Bavarians; the Saxons; the Bulgarians; the Turks. Finally came the coffin of Franz Josef, followed by the new emperor, Karl, and his wife, Zita.

One aspect of the spectacle made a particularly vivid impression on young Billie: "Amid all of the black splendor there was one point of white—a bright, radiant phenomenon: a figure of light signaling the future in all of the darkness." Crown Prince Otto, more or less Billie's age, was clad in pristine, fairy-tale white, his helmet topped by a feather. "He was my dream prince," Wilder later recalled. "I became one with him, I took his place." It was a magic moment of the sort that can only occur as a delusion. It goes without saying that Billie Wilder was not the crown prince of the Hapsburgs, but the harsher fact was that he wasn't even an Austrian, the fact of which no Austrian could lose sight. Billie was a Jew from Poland. He was an immigrant, one of the many thousand foreign Jews who crammed themselves into Vienna as war refugees. Austria was—and still is—a Roman Catholic country, and a deeply conservative one at that. Its citizens, subjects of a rigid empire, were—and to some extent still are—obsessed with social standing. Wilder's low position in Austrian society would bother him for the rest of his life. He was just another Polish Jew, and neither he nor they would ever let him forget it.

In 1860, there were about 6,200 Jews in Vienna. By 1870 there were 40,200. By 1900 there were 147,000. The rich ones built great mansions on the Ringstrasse—the Wertheims, the Todescos, the Epsteins, the Ephrussis. There were Rothschilds living in a French-style palace on the Heugasse. Industrialist-financier Karl Wittgenstein lived in splendor, raising a family of rich overachievers that included Ludwig, a philosopher, and Paul, a one-armed concert pianist. Jews achieved fame in less monetary ways as well. Theodor Herzl, though born in Budapest, lived and worked in Vienna. Sigmund Freud lived on the Berggasse. In the formerly anti-Semitic areas of Josefstadt and Neubau, rising young Jews like Stefan Zweig were beginning to settle—perhaps because the Second and Ninth Districts had too many other Jews. Most of the new immigrants from Galicia, meanwhile, lived in poverty in the areas of Leopoldstadt and Brigittenau. Billie and his family were far luckier. They had a First District address and all the amenities that went along with a middle-class lifestyle. The lobby of their apartment building was graced with tasteful blue tile work, and while the apartment itself wasn't grand, it was clean, bright, and comfortable. But the Wilders still weren't Viennese.

In the fall of 1916, Billie's parents sent him to his first Viennese school—the PrivatRealgymnasium Juranek, a public school. Most of the boys at Juranek were recent immigrants from Czechoslovakia, Yugoslavia, Hungary, and Romania. According to Wilder, this grammar school was "actually more of a franchise of the foreign legion, suited for slightly retarded or hard to handle students." But unlike the other kids, Billie had his *ausländisch* difficulties built directly into his own name. In German, a *Wilder* is an uncouth foreigner, a barbarian. (In a slightly different sense, a *Wilder* is also a lunatic. *"Er tobt wie ein Wilder"* means "He was raving like a psycho.") Billie may not have been the incorrigible, unruly child he likes to paint himself as being, but the Juranek was without doubt not one of Vienna's finest academies for boys.

All the elements of Billie's adult personality were in place at ten, though they still took an awkward, childlike form: he was restless, easily bored, prone to pranks; a quick and incisive reader; a dicey student who excelled when he cared to and defaulted when he didn't. He hated math and science, a fact reflected in his grades, but he loved history (a fact *not* reflected by his grades). He liked literature and languages, too—German and Latin were his strongest areas. "At the age of ten we had a choice of two of the dead languages," he recalled. "Greek or Latin. I chose Latin." When he was thirteen the boys were asked to choose between English and French: "I chose French, naturally—*la langue diplomatique.*" It was a disaster. Young Billie Wilder appeared to have only the weakest ability to speak a foreign language.

By 1917, the war was going very badly, at least as far as the Austrians were concerned, and Vienna was spiraling downward into a state of near-extreme deprivation. Like many youths his age—and many adults, too—Billie was pressed into service cleaning streets, shoveling snow, and collecting garbage. Max was in the reserves doing guard duty, while Genia worked with the Austrian Red Cross. Billie got used to waiting on food ration lines. He would return home with three potatoes. Still, Willie and Billie had an easier time of it than the adults. "We were flexible," Wilder recalled. "You'd go out to the country and grab a couple of eggs and things like that. You went into the swapping business—I'll give you my watch for a half a ham, or whatever." At the time, of course, he blamed the English. The little soldier of the Central Powers proudly wore a lapel button inscribed *Gott Strafe England* ("God Punishes England").

On the day the war ended, November 11, 1918, Billie was in school. As he walked home to Fleischmarkt he watched mobs forming in the streets—looting, pulling down royal statues, tearing down any *K. u. K.* insignia they could find. Austrian soldiers, faced with the escalating chaos, quickly changed into civilian clothing to avoid being attacked.

The empire was no more. From being the seat of a multinational, imperial conglomerate of 56 million people, Austria was reduced to a single small country of 7 million. Three million of those 7 million people were now living in Vienna. What had once been a sophisticated world capital had suddenly become a cramped backwater, and the infamous cynicism of the Viennese now had catastrophic recent history to back itself up. The sense of irony Wilder gained, the bemused bitterness on which he built his life's work, no doubt found its roots in the heart of a twelve-year-old who watched, at close range, as an empire fell into dust and, thanks to the all-but-pointless war, took countless lives with it.

By the age of fifteen, Billie Wilder was tough—a redheaded, wiry, muscular kid who stood at five foot ten and liked to show off his strength. He played soccer; he skated; he skied; he played hockey; he rode a bike. He stole a motorcycle—a Zündapp—and rode around Vienna until he ran out of gas. He is said to have moved on to stealing cars, though this is a bit suspect. In any event, young Billie was periodically truant from school, and he was well on the way to earning a solid reputation as a delinquent. He saw his first Egon Schiele nude while in grammar school—"pornography, we called it"—and on at least one occasion he blamed the possession of this Schiele reproduction for getting him thrown out of one school and dispatched to the foreign legion.

That detail is improbable. More plausible, though perhaps only in degree, is the story of the first whore in Billie's life. She's said to have lived near the family's apartment on Fleischmarkt, and she gave young Billy some small change to take care of her hideous dachshund while she was busy with a customer. The vile dog had a temper, barking and biting whenever it pleased, and one day the police showed up while the whore was tricking, arresting her and leaving Billie with the dog. How he got rid of it is anyone's guess.

Sex, nature's way of torturing teenage boys, was now beginning to work its rotten charms on Billie. There is the beloved story about a chum whose father walked in on him while he was jerking off and announced that if he did it fifty more times he'd die. Terrified, the boy ceased the practice—but only for the following day or two, at which point he just couldn't take it anymore and stroked again to full fruition. Shadowed by a sense of his own impending doom, the boy began marking off each session on a sheet of paper, tabulating his orgasms like a World War I dogfighter putting notches on his plane, except of course that in his case he was his own victim. At first, Wilder said, the boy beat off only twice a week, then only once a week. Finally, he hit the forty-nine mark. According to Wilder, "He wrote a farewell note to his parents about how he had fought against it; now he would be going to his death, and he asked their forgiveness." Sliding the letter under his parents' bedroom door, he returned to his room and masturbated himself to death—not the death of body and soul, but the death of his belief in his father: "And from then on, he never believed another word his father told him." The boys' room of the Privat-Realgymnasium Juranek was set ablaze by the tale.

Billie's own family life was troubled in ways both typical and particular. The twenty-four-volume standard edition of the collected works of Sigmund Freud attests to the daily derangement of Viennese family life in the early twentieth century, a quiet frenzy of deceit, repression, and melancholia from which the Wilders were hardly immune. Max was always on the make with some failed business scheme. He imported Swiss watches but knew nothing about them. The business failed. He bought a trout hatchery. His knowledge of the spawning habits of fish was equally limited, and the business collapsed. Max was, as Wilder described him later, "a dreamer and adventurer who searched his whole life after something without exactly knowing what it was." He played a powerful role in Billie's life: Max's son knew with increasing self-assurance that his father was really very weak.

Deceit was no stranger to the household. Wilder tells the story of the time he was playing soccer after school—with rocks, one of which went crashing through the window of a neighborhood shop. Billie, always enterprising, quickly struck a deal with the shopkeeper. If Billie paid for the damage, the owner would keep it a secret from his parents. Billie then explained to Max and Genia with great earnestness and enthusiasm that he was going to learn typing and stenographic skills at school—for a small fee. Thrilled with Billie's newfound interest in schoolwork, they were only too glad to give the boy the money he needed, and Billie successfully faked them out by refraining from rock-soccer during the time he was supposed to be getting his typing lessons. Then one Sunday, Max had some business work to do, and since it was Sunday his secretary wasn't available. After taking shorthand (meaningless doodles), Billie was asked to type the correspondence. A guilty look, a glance of paternal disappointment, but no punishment; by that point Billie was observant enough to understand that Max often went to the racetrack instead of his office. A workable family dynamic: if the son didn't rat on the father, the father wouldn't rat on the son.

There was a much more serious bit of information about Max that Billie supposedly kept from his mother as well. It is a tale of such stupefying deception and backdoor domestic intrigue that the offhand way Wilder discusses it is all the more pathological. Wilder told Hellmuth Karasek that one day he accidentally found in the mail an invitation, addressed to his father, from a boarding school. It seems that Max was being invited to a party for one of his sons—a third son, one Genia didn't know about. There was something bothersome about this, said the adult Billy, so he took the invitation out of the mail and gave it to his father later on the sly. Max looked at Billie, Billie looked at Max. No one said a word, and that is the end of the story. None of the volumes of material written about and by Billy Wilder ever mentions his half-brother again.

Less extreme tales of Billie's teenage years depict Billie dumping out a bottle of his father's best wine in order to get the deposit on the bottle, and conspiring with a friend to steal some valuable stamps from a decrepit and half-blind philatelist. "But he was not as old and not half as blind as we had believed, and he caught us," Wilder remembered, though he was quick to note that he and his friend escaped before the old man could call the cops.

Distant from his father and treating his mother with filial bemusement, Billie does not appear to have been terribly close to his brother, either. In the hundreds of interviews Wilder gave over the years, Willie's name hardly ever surfaces. Of anyone in his family, he got along best with Genia's brother, David Baldinger, who trained as an engineer and fought in Haller's Army during the war in an effort to gain independence for Poland. Baldinger then moved to Lodz and, later, Israel. Uncle David steered Billie away from Wagner toward Greek and Jewish classics—the Maccabees, Bar Kokhba, maybe *Oedipus*. . . . When his uncle realized that Billie was *still* a lot more interested in Austro-German and American popular culture he was very disappointed, though he and Wilder stayed in touch even after Baldinger moved to Israel.

Judah Maccabee may have sparked the heroic dreams of Jewish boys for thousands of years, but for daring, glamour, and heroism, Douglas Fairbanks held a more intense appeal to Billie Wilder. Once World War I was over, American movies came flooding into Vienna, and Billie began spending an increasing amount of time in darkened theaters. The Wiener Urania was a regular hangout, as was the Rotenturm Kino, located only a block or two from Fleischmarkt. Whenever Billie failed to show up at home, Genia would send Willie out to find him. The Rotenturm Kino was one of the first places he looked. Watching films may have been the only time Billie sat still.

Wilder has said that he liked to watch Tom Mix, Hoot Gibson, and William S. Hart, and to a certain degree he probably did, but it was Fairbanks who really did it for him. Fairbanks wasn't just handsome and heroic. He was *funny*—a dashing, romantic leading man who was as much a master of the subtle smile as of a sword or knife. Billie found in the cinema what countless other restless, drifting adolescent boys have found: a better version of themselves in a better vision of the world.

This was especially true in postwar Vienna, where Billie, despite his street smarts and ingratiating personality, was still very much an outsider. Anthony Heilbut, the historian of the Austro-German Diaspora in America, makes the point that many of the German and Austrian Jews forced out of their countries by the Nazis had a particularly visceral love of popular culture, and he links this appreciation of movies, sports, and popular music to their nature as outsiders. He quotes the politician Walther Rathenau (Jewish, gay, and, in 1922, assassinated) as observing that early in the life of every German Jew there comes a signal moment when "he realizes he is a second-class citizen." The Wilders' realization became concrete in 1920. The empire's collapse left certain practical matters to be resolved, not least of which was the question of citizenship. After 1918, residents of the old empire were given two options: they could become citizens of whatever new country had been fashioned from the former crown land in which they had lived, or, if they spoke German or Hungarian, they could become citizens of the new republics of Austria or Hungary. Max Wilder chose the latter course, and in 1920 he applied for Austrian citizenship. His request was summarily denied.

The official response he received is chilling in its bureaucratic clarity. August 20, 1920: "The claim of acknowledgment of Austrian nationality is dismissed because Mr. Max Wilder was not able to bring proof that he belongs to the German majority of the population of Austria according to race and language." The Wilders may have spoken German, but they would never *be* German, nor would they be Austrian.

Movies were a visceral link to a better, more egalitarian world. There were social benefits as well. Billie, increasingly obsessed with sex, fell hard for a girl named Greta, whom he met while playing tennis in the park. Wilder was still almost completely inexperienced, so he asked his friend Egon for advice, Egon having claimed to have earned a case of the clap at the age of eleven. (It was later revealed to have been measles.) Egon gave Billie some wise advice: take her to the movies. And when the lights go down, go for it. Cleverly, Billie took Greta to a film called *Storms of Passion* starring Asta Nielsen, and at an opportune moment, he reached between her legs. Greta, startled, screamed so loud that the lights were turned on throughout the theater; when an usher found them, Billie's hand was pinned between Greta's bony knees.

It was a shame that something so simple would turn out to be such a disaster, though Billie, of course, would eventually earn millions of dollars and six Academy Awards chronicling people's sexual catastrophes. For the time being, however, he was a ripe teenage boy with too much energy and too few chances. At school he sat looking out the window for hours—years, actually—trying to peer into the windows of the fleabag across the street, a crummy lodging house of the sort the Viennese called a "hotel by the hour." Billie was fascinated by the Hotel Stadion—its appeal was obviously more intense than math or geography—and he spent much of his school day getting to know the Stadion's cast of characters and their habits. Billie noticed, for example, that nobody ever carried a suitcase in; they weren't staying long enough to need supplies. Soon Billie was an expert at who was who, which ones were the working girls, and which of their clients were married—they were the nervous ones. He reported: "I thought to myself 'Patience, patience. Right after graduation I'll go to the hotel with "Red Fritzi" or whatever her first name was.' And so it happened. A couple of days after graduation, I went to her. We negotiated quickly over the price and marched into the hotel and straight to the front desk where I, with the sangfroid of an experienced Casanova, registered us as Mr. and Mrs. Finsterbusch," which supposedly was the name of Billie's French teacher.

For a man who went on to write any number of films that dealt either directly or indirectly with prostitution, this was literally a seminal event. If it actually happened, it took place in July of 1924. More certain is the fact that Billie took his *Matura*, or exit exam, from the PrivatRealgymnasium Juranek on July 4. He passed. Billie Wilder got B's in German and Latin and a surprising A in math, but he nearly flunked French. After eight years of school in Vienna, Billie Wilder still had little facility with foreign languages.

The Wilder family, meanwhile, was heading into rougher financial waters. The circumstances aren't entirely clear, but Max's inability to keep a business running led to the family's having to move out of their Fleischmarkt apartment and relocate in the distant Nineteenth District, where they found an even smaller place at Billrothstrasse 15. Willie had already moved out—he was living in London—and Billie was ready to be on his own as well. He may have spent the summer on Billrothstrasse, but by fall he was ready to go to work and live on his own.

In regard to his college education, Wilder claimed to have entered the University of Vienna to study law and to have dropped out after a single semester, but there is no record of Samuel Wilder's ever having matriculated at the University of Vienna, let alone attending it. (And the Austrians, like their German brothers and sisters, are adept at keeping records.)

Wilder's tale involves Genia's long-standing wish for Billie to become a lawyer and Billie's failure to comply, and it is compounded in the Zolotow version by an ill-fated romance with a whore. Zolotow finds in Wilder's putative decision to drop out of college the seeds of his entire psychopathology, a theory that enraged Wilder no end. Wilder made the mistake of telling Zolotow about a girl he'd been interested in—a girl named Ilse. She worked at a record store on the Ringstrasse, the story goes, and Wilder, who was becoming interested to the point of obsession in American jazz, is said to have taken her on dates to the dance halls on Kärntnerstrasse. He wrote poetry to Ilse and even dreamed of marrying her and moving to the United States and starting a family. Zolotow reports that Billie registered for the university and began attending classes in September, information evidently supplied by Wilder himself. By December, the story has it, Billie quit school, stopped seeing Ilse, and moved out of his parents' apartment. Willie Wilder, interviewed by Zolotow, said that he had no idea what happened to change Billie's life in this way, and Zolotow concludes that it was all because Billie discovered Ilse was turning tricks on the side. The revelation allegedly caused him to fall into despair and abandon his studies, destroying his faith in all women as an extra measure of drama. It is Ilse, Zolotow concludes, who lies behind every hard-bitten, lying, cheating slut in Billy Wilder's film career.

"No! Bullshit! Total bullshit!" was Wilder's emphatic response to Zolotow's theory. "My God!" he told critics Joseph McBride and Todd McCarthy in a 1979 interview. "In my youth in Vienna, sex was far less prevalent. I never slept with a hooker in my high school days, (a) because I couldn't afford it, and (b) because I was scared shitless. In those days, the idea of gonorrhea and the fear which it struck—no kid would have." Wilder's explanation, of course, stands in thorough contradiction to the Red Fritzi–*l'affaire Finsterbusch* tale he told a decade later. While one can well understand Wilder's fury at seeing his life and work reduced to a failed romance with a Viennese whore, it is a conclusion he wrought himself, having supplied Zolotow with all the raw material.

In any case, Wilder himself admitted to Andreas Hutter that in fact he never studied law.

What he did do was to begin learning a few words of English by memorizing the lyrics to the latest jazz hits, though he had no idea what the words actually meant. Music, not Ilse, was Billie's real passion. Nothing was more appealing to the excitable, fidgeting eighteen-year-old than the rhythmic agitations of American jazz. Vienna was just beginning to bring in jazz records—perhaps to the very store in which the possibly fictitious Ilse worked—and Billie started collecting them. He snapped up Paul Whiteman's "Japanese Sandman" when it came out and anything else he could find. He was rapidly becoming a proficient dancer as well. What better way was there to burn up all that excess energy and meet girls at the same time? But what on earth was he going to do for a job?

2. DAREDEVIL REPORTER

Mr. Boot, I'm a $250 a week newspaperman. I can be had for
fifty. I know newspapers backward forward and sideways. I can
write 'em, edit 'em, print 'em, wrap 'em, and sell 'em. I can handle big news and little news. And if there's no news, I'll go out
and bite a dog. Make it forty-five.
                  —Chuck Tatum (Kirk Douglas) in *Ace in the Hole*

Billie Wilder was no longer a child, if indeed he'd ever been one at all.
He was eighteen years old, tall and lean and sporting an adult smirk.
He was scarcely about to continue living with his parents in the depressing *Ausland* of the Nineteenth District. Quiet suburbs were not
his style, nor was the prospect of taking the first dumb job that came his
way. Restless and eager to get out of the house and live on his own, back
in the heart of Vienna, Billie set out to find work that would engage him.
But what could he do with a high school diploma and a lackluster academic
record? Sure, he loved movies, and yes, he thought he could write, but the
Austrian film industry was small, scarcely big enough to offer him even an
apprenticeship. Inspired by an American newsreel, he found himself considering a career in journalism. He liked the way the young reporters
dressed.

There were several highly respected newspapers in Vienna—the conservative *Neue Freie Presse*, the progressive *Arbeiter Zeitung*—but Billie had
no training as a reporter, and he wasn't likely to convince anyone to hire
him simply on the basis of his aggressive, prickly charm. There was *Die
Fackel* (*The Torch*), Karl Kraus's magazine, but Kraus was a high-class,
one-man show, and he would never have hired a fast-talking and utterly
inexperienced eighteen-year-old jazz fan. Kraus was the undisputed master
of the Viennese feuilleton—a beautiful, fiery essay / prose-poem / polemic.
Kraus's play of language was dazzling, and better still, Kraus was supremely nasty. He was bilious and respected very little about the Viennese,

so naturally the Viennese adored him—except, of course, for those he mauled.

But there were two new tabloid papers, the daily *Die Stunde* (*The Hour*), and its sister publication, a weekly theater magazine called *Die Bühne* (*The Stage*), both run under the corporate umbrella of Kronos Verlag. Started up in 1922 by a shady Hungarian named Imré Békessy, Kronos Verlag was on the cutting edge as far as Viennese journalism was concerned: Békessy's papers peddled scandal, crime, sports, movie reviews, theater reviews, and snappy personality profiles. If any newspaper had a job opening, it would be one of Békessy's. So in December 1924, eighteen-year-old Billie Wilder wrote a letter to the editor of *Die Bühne* begging him kindly to reveal the secret of what a guy had to do to become a reporter. Billie particularly wanted to know how to become an *American* reporter, by which he meant either a Viennese correspondent for an American newspaper or just a Viennese reporter who acted like an American. As a jumping-off point for his planned career as a press hound, he even offered to work for *Die Bühne* for free, if only the editor would take him.

Sadly, he could not. Just before Christmas, in a published response addressed to Billie S. Wilde [*sic*] of the Nineteenth District, *Die Bühne* told the aspiring cub, "We cannot employ anyone without salary, because that isn't permitted by the company. But if you want to get acquainted with journalism, you may come in from time to time. Conditions in America are very difficult, which we know all too well. Reporters are crucial to American newspapers, and it isn't easy to compete with a whole troop of those clever boys. Without perfect knowledge of English, you can't get anywhere in German newspapers either. Many thanks for your best wishes!"

It was a setback, but not a major one; Billie was not so easily dissuaded. *Die Bühne* and *Die Stunde* were too appealing as potential employers. When *Die Stunde*'s reporters covered crimes, they included the dirty details other papers demurely glossed over. They covered sports, which Billie adored. And they were full of photographs. While the other Viennese newspapers still depended on sketches and drawings to illustrate their stories, *Die Bühne* and *Die Stunde* were pioneering the use (in Austria) of photojournalism with captions—direct images unmediated by an artist's imagination, with just a few descriptive words to nail down the facts. This was exactly the kind of tough, modern paper Billie wanted to join.

None of this was what Genia had in mind for her second son. As Wilder describes it, his parents' dreams were typical for their class—the first son is the doctor, and the second is a lawyer, "or at least one of them is a dentist and the other an accountant." In the Wilders' case, none of it worked out, at least as far as Genia was concerned. Willie took a job in

New York in a company that made ladies' handbags. As for Billie, he saw plainly that his father couldn't support him anymore, and besides, he craved independence.

Years after the fact, Wilder would tell and retell the story of how he was hired by the theater editor and chief drama critic of *Die Bühne*, Hans Liebstöckl. Fifty years old then and one of Vienna's leading theater critics, Liebstöckl wrote not only for *Die Stunde* and *Die Bühne*, where he was soon to become editor in chief, but also for the more respectable daily paper *Wiener Tagblatt*. According to Wilder's tale, one of his high school teachers, Alfred Spitzer, encouraged him to be a writer and, after Wilder's graduation, gave Billie a letter of introduction to the esteemed Herr Liebstöckl. A cleaning lady was mopping the floor in the lobby, Billie said, when he wandered through the seemingly empty office building. She jutted her thumb in the direction of the second floor. Gasping sounds were heard as Billie approached a closed door. Opening it, he discovered a panting, beet-faced Liebstöckl sticking it to his disheveled secretary and, soon thereafter, all too conveniently, offering Billie a job to keep his mouth shut.

Wilder was never one to pass up the chance to embellish a tale, especially when it involved a penis being inserted into or withdrawn from an orifice. He particularly loved the Liebstöckl story. But as Wilder finally confessed to Andreas Hutter in 1990, he got his first job from Maximillian Kramer, the games editor: "I made up crossword puzzles. That was the beginning of my career as a journalist."

He published his first piece of reportage in *Die Bühne* on January 22, 1925—a profile of Hungary's greatest actress, Sari Fedak. She was the divorced wife of the playwright Ferenc Molnár, and the rumor was that she was currently having a torrid affair with none other than Imré Békessy. (Eagle-eyed Viennese wags hadn't failed to notice that photos of Sari Fedak were showing up with great regularity in both *Die Stunde* and *Die Bühne*.) But even after he cut his teeth on his publisher's girlfriend, Wilder was still not promoted to first-string reporter, so he spent most of his first few months at *Die Bühne* editing crossword puzzles and writing short reviews of amateur theater, opera, and dance. In March, *Die Bühne* paid a dividend to the Wilder family when Genia successfully solved one of her own son's puzzles and won, as her prize, a bunch of bananas.

For his short writing efforts, Billie was paid "space rates." He only earned money when he got something into print. Wilder quickly learned to be pragmatic, understanding that he had to connect with both his readership and his bank account. It was a talent that would serve him well once he got into the film business.

By May, it was clear that Billie needed to earn more money than he could possibly make doing short pieces for *Die Bühne*, which only came out once a week. So Billie began writing for the daily *Die Stunde* as well. He wrote at night and handed in his copy at ten in the morning, when the paper went to press; by noon, his articles for *Die Stunde* were in print.

He tells of waiting in the café across the street from police headquarters, playing pool or chess while waiting for the day's horrible crimes to unfold. The reporters on the crime beat had an agreement with the police: a red light installed in the café flashed whenever the cops had something juicy for the boys of the press. Dead bodies in the Danube, suicides at the Sacher, Lippizaner stallions led away by crafty cabdrivers—these, supposedly, were the seedy, everyday horrors that served as Billie's bread and butter. "I was doing some reportage of a criminal nature. I would do the dirty work," he said. Wilder's crime reportage may have been repellent, but it doesn't appear to have been terribly extensive; the number of crime stories Wilder actually wrote is much lower than he remembered. After painstakingly going through volume after dusty volume of *Die Stunde* looking for articles by Billie Wilder, Andreas Hutter found only a single signed article covering a crime. Then again, as another one of his colleagues from the *Die Stunde* days remembers, Billie liked to go around the office telling his colleagues that "his mother woke him up every morning with the instruction, 'Get up and write some anecdotes.' "

Some of Wilder's peers recalled him as being an industrious young reporter who often stayed in the office until 2:00 A.M. or later. On the other hand, one of Wilder's old friends, Anton Kuh, once remarked that "Billie always had an alibi. Whenever there was something going on, he had an alibi. He was born with an alibi, and as a consequence, he was never there when anything happened." Békessy's assistant, Ludwig Hoffenreich, remembered Wilder as being "extremely lazy" (an unduly harsh assessment, given that no one else has ever described this agile, work-obsessed, notoriously antsy man as "lazy"). But even Hoffenreich was quick to add that when he *did* write, the results were marvelous.

Wilder himself once acknowledged that his reputation among his peers was spotty. Young Billie earned a nickname among his fellow reporters. In Viennese dialect the word is *Schlieferl*—in English, "the bootlicker." In the eyes of his fellow journalists, Wilder displayed a tendency to curry favor whenever necessary—to get ahead by whatever means he could find. It's not a stretch to think of Billie Wilder as an opportunist, but then his ambition was powerful, compulsive, and enviable, and he always had the talent to back it up. As for his relationship with his bosses, Wilder reported that he finally won Hans Liebstöckl's grudging respect, but only after a lot of effort and one particular turn of phrase. After some minor famous fat man died, Billie closed his obituary with the line "May he become as light as the earth."

At *Die Stunde*, Wilder soon began covering sports. He found two experienced sportswriters to serve as his mentors—Maximilian Reich and Aurel Föld. They taught him how to create atmosphere, how to be lively and easy to read, and how to write in a breezy but elegant style. Wilder's were snappy, clever, discursive essays—sports feuilletons. (In a feuilleton, the writer's feeling about his subject mattered more than the subject itself.) Wilder covered not only athletic events, but he also wrote profiles of the leading athletes of the day—soccer, tennis, and biking stars.

The copy room in which Wilder worked was also used by a man named Friedrich Porges, who wrote the film columns for both *Die Stunde* and *Die Bühne*. Porges had been a scriptwriter and director of early Austrian and German silent movies; more recently, he had been the editor of the Berlin paper *Der Montag Morgen*, after which he returned to Vienna to edit *Die Bühne*'s cinema section. It was thanks to Porges that Billie Wilder first witnessed the daily, grinding hell of making a motion picture. One day in August 1925, Porges assigned him to write a piece on the filming of Robert Wiene's *Der Rosenkavalier*, then in production in Vienna. Eager to finally see filmmaking at close range, and fascinated by the idea of meeting the director of *Das Kabinett des Dr. Caligari*, Billie set out to interview Wiene. He didn't get very far. Wiene was frantic, the production chaotic, and none of the reporters who were seeking interviews got anywhere. There was, Billie learned, a lot of waiting. "This is no profession for me," an exhausted Wiene told the bored and frustrated journalists at the end of the day; "It's awful." Billie was most impressed. Hoffenreich remembered Wilder telling him, "Film is the future—one has to do it. You can make money with it."

Making money, or better *keeping* money, wasn't easy in Vienna in the 1920s. Inflation was rampant, and the nation was still struggling to recover from the war and the ensuing collapse of the empire. In another article for *Die Stunde*, Wilder wrote with sick, funny irony about the current state of Vienna's economy, using its best-known pawnshop as his focal point. "The size of a city's pawn industry enables one to conclude something about its citizens' pecuniary state," Wilder began. "The Dorotheum, the main office of our pawn industry, is an impressive business with four floors, eight staircases, countless corridors, and some one hundred rooms." But, he went on, so many people were hawking so much of their patrimony that the Dorotheum had to add a whole new layer: "Yes, a fifth floor, in order to store your winter coat or your fifteen-volume edition of Meyer, which your grandfather's father bought in the good old days. A few more years of restoration and Vienna will give the Old World its first skyscraper."

Billie is said to have met and interviewed Cardinal Pacelli, later Pope Pius XII. He also maintained that he met and interviewed Ferenc Molnár on the outdoor terrace of a country hotel, where Molnár was repeatedly interrupted by an aggressive chicken. The irritated playwright kept kicking it away and ultimately threatened to cook it. As another old friend put it, "Billy Wilder wants his biography to be as original as his movies." The most outrageous story concerns the breathtaking day Billie interviewed Sigmund Freud, Richard Strauss, Arthur Schnitzler, and Alfred Adler; the tale appears in nearly every profile of Wilder ever written. For a Christmastime article on the rise of Fascism, the story goes, Billie was dispatched to the four internationally renowned men's houses to get their impressions of the newly rumbling Right. Strauss, it's said, told Billie that he rather admired Mussolini and believed that Austria needed precisely such a man to set the nation on the correct course. With a few good quotes in his notebook, Billie proceeded by trolley to Schnitzler's house, where the grand old man of Austrian letters told him that he believed Mussolini wouldn't last very long because the Italians, like the Viennese, were too wedded to their own passions and wouldn't tolerate any degree of rigid discipline in the long run. Adler, who lived in a large apartment on Nussdorferstrasse, turned out to be a fat man who wore a pince-nez; he rambled on and on about Mussolini's inferiority complex, the existence of which was self-evident to Adler. "Strauss and Adler talked their heads off," was how Wilder described it later. Finally, Billie showed up at the door of Sigmund Freud's home and office at Berggasse 19 and asked to see the doctor. The founder of psychoanalysis appeared with a napkin tucked under his chin—Billie had interrupted his lunch—and when Billie handed him his business card, Freud summarily threw him out. He didn't like reporters.

Wilder finally admitted in 1990 that these four interviews did not, in fact, take place on a single day around Christmastime. He kept insisting, however, that he really did speak to all four men, though on different occasions.

Friedrich Porges may have given Billie his first film-related writing assignment, and Reich and Föld were his sports mentors, but it was still another writer and editor, Karl Tschuppik, who became Wilder's greatest influence—his first role model. Tschuppik was something of a bohemian who became editor in chief of *Die Stunde* in 1923, but he'd written and edited for better, more respected papers earlier in his career. Billie began frequenting the same cafés as Tschuppik—the Atlantis, the Central, and the Herrenhof—and he ingratiated himself with Tschuppik's circle of friends, including Klaus Mann, Joseph Roth, and Anton Kuh. Kuh, the incarnation of what the Viennese call a *Kaffeehausliterat*, was a writer who essentially lived in cafés and did most (if not all) of his writing there. To say that he lived in the cafés is not entirely hyperbolic; Kuh rarely had his own place, tending instead to stay in hotels. Kuh was also, in Andreas Hutter's words, "the most successful scrounger in the Café Herrenhof and the Café Central." In return for a little cash, Kuh would stage extemporaneous performances on a variety of themes—politics, literature, the arts. He was always terribly funny and quick on the trigger with clever remarks. He was Billie's sort of man.

During this time, Wilder made another new friend—Laszlo Löwenstein, a Hungarian actor known for his sharp wit and buggy eyes. "Laczy" and Billie made a good team, and together they formed a kind of impromptu cabaret act for their pals at the Café Herrenhof, including Tschuppik, Alfred Polgar, Franz Werfel, and Max Prel. The son of a rabbi, Löwenstein was obsessive on the subject of theater. He'd begun his career in drama as a claqueur, a professional applauder hired to get the audience up to speed, but by 1925 he was getting some pretty good acting roles. Round and puffy-faced with a set of dark, haunted eyes and a notoriously nasal voice, Laczy was hardly a handsome leading man. But he had an extraordinary stage presence and could turn himself into whomever he wished, as long as he had an audience. He and Billie quickly hit it off. Constantly ribbing each other and everyone else, the two young cutups were always good for an obscene rhyme, a hilarious pun, or a malicious remark about some idiot they both despised. Until Laczy developed a fierce drug habit later in his life, they stayed good friends.

In early November 1925, Billie got himself into a bit of a jam—a minor if sticky jam, one that most writers find themselves in at some point or another. It occurred because he interviewed another writer. When Dr. Hans Fulda picked up *Die Bühne* and read what he supposedly said, he was appalled, and he fired off a hostile letter to Liebstöckl: "In the last issue of your esteemed newspaper *Die Bühne* . . . it is reported that I said things 'about myself.' The literal reproduction of transitory answers to transitory questions cannot, of course, be demanded. But it cannot be indifferent to me if your Mr. Contributor places remarks into my mouth that in both tone and content are strictly contrary to my nature and views." Billie was snidely contrite. He responded defiantly and with characteristic humor: "Dearest Dr. Fulda! I admit the possibility that of the many witty and striking things you said, just a few casual and unessential remarks stuck in my ear. Will you forgive that? Your very devoted, Billie."

Wilder had already developed an eye for ironic black comedy, as evidenced by a squib he wrote in December 1925: "A suitable Christmas present for 12- to 14-year-old boys," the piece was called, and it had to do with the advertisement Billie had seen posted on a billboard under a trolley bridge: "Machine gun, in good working order, as a Christmas present for 12- to 14-year-old boys," it said, giving a telephone number to call for more information. "Oh, by today it has certainly been sold already," Wilder wrote. "On Christmas Day little Wotan Wotawa will play with his

Christmas present and his father will buy him ammunition for New Year's Eve. Symptoms of the time—the little one gets a machine gun and makes himself independent."

By the beginning of 1926, Wilder was a seasoned newspaperman—he learned fast—and he was given a plum assignment: an interview with the film star Asta Nielsen. A World War I pinup girl who managed to attract both French and German soldiers alike, Nielsen still had star power. She could, in the words of the critic and film theorist Béla Balázs, "suggest obscene nudity with her eyes, and she can smile in a way that would oblige the police to ban the film as pornography." It was Nielsen's face, after all, that had shined on the screen while Billie's hand was clamped firmly between his date's legs. The only trouble was that Nielsen generally refused to grant interviews even if she was allowed to read them before publication. Wilder cornered her at the Raimund Theater, where she was currently appearing, and waited in the coatroom with her husband, Gregory Chmara. "Like a schoolgirl," he wrote, "she sits down at the table while Chmara's hand caresses her hair. (The two love each other like seventeen-year-olds.) I am brief. Asta Nielsen answers quickly and precisely. She speaks with a foreign accent, almost like an Englishwoman, but fluently and easily understood. 'So you left film forever?' 'No—I left it because it had no new, true tasks for me. But I will belong to it again if it becomes an art. For me, film and theater are the same. I am loyal to myself.' Asta Nielsen, the world's greatest film actress, will not appear again on-screen for a long time. The many thousands who could admire her ingenious art will become hundreds. And that, I think, is a shame."

While Billie was gaining a foothold in the world of Viennese journalism, he was also moving around Vienna. In his seventies, Wilder blamed his chronic backaches on his youthful transience: "It is all the result of those hot nights in Vienna when I was screwing girls standing up in doorways—and sometimes, alas, no girls, just doorways." In March, Wilder moved out of his furnished room and began living in more respectable Viennese hotels—first at the Prager Hof and then at the Österreichischen Hof at Fleischmarkt 10, just a few doors down the street from his family's old apartment. He was where he once thought he wanted to be, and he was finding that it wasn't enough. Vienna was an irrelevant backwater, driven by the same intrigues and pretensions it had under the Hapsburgs but without any of the gaudy power to justify it. He was getting bored.

Vienna was still, however, the world capital of rumors. By 1925, the whispers that swirled around town concerning Imré Békessy, his newspapers, the police, and the state prosecutor were becoming considerably more audible. The word was that Békessy had a penchant for blackmailing people, and the habit had finally attracted the attention of the authorities. Banks and cafés were Békessy's prime targets. Békessy threatened to expose the banks' illegal business dealings unless they put ads in his papers or simply paid him off. As for the cafés, Békessy had set up an informal system of restaurant criticism: *Die Stunde*'s photographers went around Vienna taking pictures of new cafés and then turning the pictures over to the head of advertising at the paper, Eugen Forda. If the cafés put ads in Békessy's papers, his roving critics would give them a good write-up. If they refused, they got panned. For a city propelled by its *Melange und Strudel*, this was hot news.

From the Olympian heights of *Die Fackel* as well as from his lecture stage, the journalist-lecturer Karl Kraus stepped up his attacks on Békessy, whom he despised. With characteristic wit and malevolence, Kraus called the Hungarian immigrant a "Budapestilence." *Die Stunde* was nothing more than a "daily inbreeding of stock exchange and brothel." To Kraus and his many fans, Békessy and his writers were foisting upon Vienna a "journalism of glutton and sweet-tooth." In short, Békessy was a panderer, and a foreign one at that. In a November 1925 lecture, Kraus turned yet again to the subject of Békessy, who was now beginning to resemble a hounded rat in the public eye, and delivered his soon-to-be-famous imperative: "Imré Békessy is a scoundrel. . . . Out of Vienna with the scoundrel!"

For the most part, Billie found an alibi, watching from a safe distance as the scandal unfolded—as safe a distance as the offices of Békessy's company allowed. But he did play a minor role. Ernst Spitz, another *Die Stunde* writer, accused Wilder of having an active part in the blackmailing business by way of the so-called café tax. Wilder, said Spitz, was one of the reviewers who reported favorably on new cafés in exchange for a payoff to Békessy. For Békessy and his boys, this was merely a form of ad sales, albeit an illegal one; Austrian law covered the crime with a fine of between 3,000 and 30,000 kronen. According to Spitz, *Die Stunde*'s advertising manager, Eugen Forda, used to personally pay Billie a little extra for his good reviews. In addition, Spitz charged Wilder with engineering his firing from *Die Stunde*. Spitz claimed that he told the management of *Die Stunde* that he had heard blackmailing rumors against one of the assistant editors, Ladislaus Frank, little knowing that blackmailing was actually an integral part of the Békessy publishing empire. The other editors decided to fire Spitz, and they gave Billie the task of finding an acceptable pretext. Békessy then called Spitz into his office, where his secretary read a report—penned by Billie—that accused Spitz of making ugly and derogatory remarks about his colleagues. Spitz realized that he'd been set up, and he was forced to leave the paper that day.

Békessy refused to pay Spitz the severance pay that was due to him, so

Spitz went to court to retrieve it; he also made the incident public by writing an article about it called "Békessy's Revolver," by which he meant none other than Billie Wilder. He won his lawsuit and enraged Billie. When Andreas Hutter asked Wilder about his encounter with Spitz, Wilder replied bluntly: "I remember him as a mean and totally untalented asshole." As for Békessy, Wilder recalled that he "knew that Békessy was an unscrupulous scoundrel, but my principal worry was not to sit in judgment but to feed myself and have a roof over my head."

In addition to his forays into café-tax-collecting, Billie was also given the job of writing puff pieces about various politicians whose favor Békessy needed to curry; the mayor of Baden, for example, earned at least one friendly article by Billie. But Wilder's journalistic tastes were running in a much different direction. In early April, he wrote a disturbing but hilarious article about current social and moral conditions in Vienna, using the then-current craze for commercial hunger-strikers (*Hungerkünstler*—literally, "hunger artists") as his theme. Four years earlier, in his short story "Ein Hungerkünstler," Franz Kafka reported that the starvation-as-entertainment craze had vastly diminished in Prague, but apparently it was still going strong in Vienna in 1926. Wilder had no need to write social satire. He simply reported some bitterly funny news.

> The man is called "Nicky." Today, at exactly 6:00 P.M., he will climb into the glass case. University professors, doctors, an expert commission, and a notary will be present during the festive sealing. The scene is the L. W. Olympiasaal in the Rothgasse. A huge cube has been standing there for a few days, three meters at the edges, completely covered with glass, above which is only a fine wire grating. In the glass case, a bed. Shelves with 300 bottles of mineral water and 3000 Kedive cigarettes, a table with a ventilator on it, an electric heater, a radio with headphones and a speaker, books about occultism and theosophy, some volumes by Rabindranath Tagore, a perfume sprayer, a wash tub, and even a "private" area. Around the glass case is a barrier. The audience will be able to see Nicky from all sides. . . . The sealing occurs tonight. Admission is one shilling. It will be a smash. A man sitting 45 days long with an empty stomach in a glass case: that's a feast for the Viennese.

In early April 1925, an all-female swing band swept into Vienna from England by way of Berlin. Billie was there to meet them when their train pulled in:

> Out of the train from Berlin, which arrived today before noon at the Westbahnhof, stepped thirty-two of the most attractive legs. Their owners, delightful ladies, were wearing fashionable traveling outfits. . . .

These are the charming Lawrence Tiller Girls from Manchester. Everybody is pleased as punch, chirping and giggling. You don't know where to look first. Sixteen of the most splendid girls in the entire world, one more beautiful than the other. These figures, these legs, these tiny faces, and so well-bred—aristocratic, so to speak. . . . Sixteen girls, sixteen questions. Let's go! Hilda is always tilting her head. "Do you believe in love at first sight?" "If I'm looking at you, yes!" Olive has wonderful teeth. "What do you think about short skirts?" "If you have great legs like Flossie, Vera, Molly, Marjorie, Mabel, and Maisie, then the shorter the better!" Joyce is laughing seductively. "Bernard Shaw? No idea. Don't know him." Flossie is serious: "Do you know *Hamlet?*" "Yes, a good piece. Why doesn't this Shakespeare guy write shows?"

Billie filed it all away for future reference.

In June of 1926, two completely unrelated events occurred more or less simultaneously to propel Billie Wilder out of Vienna. Imré Békessy, having been warned that his arrest was imminent, fled Austria for Bad Wildungen in Germany, and the American bandleader Paul Whiteman showed up in Vienna on a European tour. By the beginning of June, everyone in the offices of Kronos Verlag knew that their boss was in deep, possibly abysmal, trouble, and that their own jobs were in grave jeopardy. Billie was certainly not exempt. His writing career was flourishing, but if Békessy's papers were forced to close he'd be back to square one. Who in Vienna would hire the very reporters who'd been collecting the café tax? Enter Paul Whiteman and his band.

Vienna had its share of Whiteman fans, but Billie Wilder was a fanatic. He had been collecting jazz and swing records for years, he knew the songs by heart, and he couldn't get enough of them. There was a jittery quality to jazz that appealed to Wilder's naturally overstimulated mind and soul. You could dance to it, too. And Paul Whiteman was the best, most famous jazz bandleader in the world. His recordings of "Whispering" and "Japanese Sandman" were hugely popular all around the world; each sold a million copies. His music *moved.* It was most emphatically *not Viennese.* It was purely, loudly, at times even raucously *American.* It was Whiteman, after all, who had commissioned George Gershwin to write "Rhapsody in Blue" in 1924, the New York premiere of which shook musicians and listeners alike around the globe.

"Rhapsody in Blue" was a major factor in getting the tour organized. It had become immensely popular all over Europe, and audiences specifically wanted to hear Paul Whiteman conduct it. Not only was Whiteman's concert at Royal Albert Hall on April 11 sold out, but London papers reported that five thousand more people had tried, and failed, to get tickets. (This prompted one London paper to call Whiteman "the Mussolini of jazz.") The band stayed on in England and Scotland until June, playing the Kit Kat Club almost every night, with the Prince of Wales a regular patron. Offstage, Whiteman was a man who liked to have a good time—an excessively good time. He was a heavy drinker and an even heavier eater. He and his trumpeter once drank a case of champagne a night for nineteen nights. Solo, Whiteman himself drank a hundred pint bottles of beer in a single sitting.

In June, the band left England for the Continent. A general strike in England had forced the cancellation of several concerts, giving the band some time to rest, relax, and consume a lot of food and drink in Vienna. The group on tour included a total of fifty people—Paul and twenty-eight other musicians, about a dozen wives, and even some children. Wilder has always liked to tell the story of how he discovered that Whiteman and his party were in Vienna: ace reporter that he was, Billie was doing his usual snooping around at the best hotels to see who was in town. One can picture him strolling up to the concierge at the Hotel Sacher and asking his buddy if anyone of note had just checked in. There he is, sitting at a café across from the Opera, making notes about anyone arriving at the Imperial with an especially majestic array of trunks. And here he comes, into the Hotel Bristol, where a porter pal reveals that none other than the great American bandleader Paul Whiteman had registered that very morning. Billie rushes back to the office, where he pitches a story idea to Békessy, who hadn't fled yet: Billie would bring the work of some Viennese musicians to the king of jazz himself and record his opinion. Three hundred words, Békessy told Billie, and no more. So Billie and a photographer go back to the Bristol and present Paul Whiteman with two new songs written by the composer Robert Katscher—"*Wenn der Weisse Flieder Wieder Blühn*" ("When the White Lilacs Bloom Again") and "*Madonna, Du Bist Schöner als der Sonnenschein*" ("Madonna, You Are Lovelier Than the Sunlight"). Whiteman loves Billie, loves "Madonna," buys the rights, gives Billie an exclusive interview, turns the song into one of his most successful recordings, and accepts Billie's offer to show him around the best nightspots in Vienna.

It's a fine tale, but not a true one. Franz Lehár, the king of Viennese operetta composers, knew precisely when Paul Whiteman and his immense entourage were arriving in Vienna and arranged to give them a not-so-secret welcoming luncheon in Paul's honor. And Robert Katscher needed no intermediary. Katscher was at the train station along with Billie and a host of other reporters when Whiteman and his party arrived in town on June 12. Whiteman had already purchased "Madonna."

Still, Billie *was* disarmingly charming as far as Whiteman was concerned, and Billie did write a series of very favorable articles about the band, jazz, and why they mattered. Unlike the other reporters who met Whiteman at the station, Billie Wilder knew what he was talking about. More important, he was so *chutspadiche* that he became the bandleader's favorite Viennese host. Franz Lehár may have known Vienna's best and brightest people, but Billie knew where to get the best food and drink late at night. Wilder's knowledge of jazz was extraordinary, his memory for facts superb, his command of Vienna's culinary hot spots unparalleled. His knowledge of English was limited almost entirely to fragments of jazz lyrics, and he had the guts to throw them willy-nilly into the conversation whenever things got dull.

The day after Whiteman and the band arrived, Billie published a glowing appreciation, not only of Whiteman's music but of Whiteman himself: "You add the most delightful mustache imaginable," Wilder wrote, "an entirely charming double chin, two gentle, child's eyes in a good, broad face, a massively graceful, tall stature slovenly but respectably dressed, and you have—Paul Whiteman." He was a fat man with a cartoonishly open and jolly face. In fact, his band's logo was a drawing of Whiteman's head— a big, long moon of a face decorated with a tiny mustache formed by two spiky lines drawn out from under the nose.

Having found this funny, tall, and yet somehow elfin guide who always made him laugh, Whiteman didn't want to let him go. He offered Billie the chance to accompany him on the next leg of his tour—to Berlin. It mattered not a whit that Billie had never been to Berlin; he scarcely needed to inform Whiteman of his own ignorance. The publisher of "Madonna" agreed to pay Billie's expenses and a small stipend. With Békessy himself about to skedaddle out of town as fast as his corrupt legs and bank account permitted, there was really no reason for Billie to stay in Vienna. He asked his editors at *Die Stunde* for a three-day leave of absence and said farewell to his mother and father.

Ludwig Hoffenreich and a secretary from Kronos Verlag accompanied him to the train station. They brought with them a going-away present— a wreath fashioned from a string of Viennese knockwurst. They wanted their gift to be practical as well as ridiculous, for after a year and a half of steady work as a reporter, a train ticket to Berlin was essentially the only worthwhile thing that twenty-year-old Billie Wilder possessed.

3. JUST A GIGOLO

God wants me to go to Berlin.

—Peter Hannemann (Johannes Riemann)
in *Der falsche Ehemann*

left Vienna and went to Berlin like a schmuck," Billy Wilder once declared to Garson Kanin. At the time, however, he probably didn't feel so schmucky. The means of financing Wilder's trip to Berlin remain murky, but the outcome is a sure bet: he left Vienna for good. Whoever it was, somebody else paid for Billie Wilder's ticket to Berlin. "Madonna"'s publisher has been credited, but Wilder once said it was Whiteman's own money: "I persuaded him to buy me a train ticket to Berlin, where he was going to play, and I would write a review of his concert in my newspaper in Vienna that would have never paid for me to go there. So I went to Berlin for a two- or three-day trip, but I didn't come back." What did it matter if the portly bandleader paid an ambitious young writer for a series of good reviews? Billie's editors at *Die Stunde* had more troubling ethical lapses to worry about, and Wilder himself had little intention of returning to Vienna anyway.

Upon his arrival in Berlin, Billie quickly learned that he was not Whiteman's only champion in Germany. He had to share nightclubbing duties with the violinist Fritz Kreisler, who was almost as big a Whiteman fan. Kreisler had actually been in the audience at the world premiere of "Rhapsody in Blue" in New York. Better still, he knew his way around Berlin, whereas the twenty-year-old Billie was a complete stranger in the immense, harsh city.

The Berlin papers treated Whiteman well, at first. The popular *Berliner Zeitung am Mittag* welcomed the entourage by hiring a plane to give them an aerial tour of the city. The concerts themselves played well enough, too, but Whiteman's American jazz wasn't nearly as well received as it had been in Vienna. Jazz was popular in Berlin—there were about nine hundred dance bands in Berlin in those years. Oscar Joost, Teddy Stauffer, and Bernhard Etté were the kings of modern German dance music. But German jazz wasn't the genuine article—the lampooning caricaturist George Grosz once described it as nothing more than a deranged rendition of Viennese salon music—but it was German jazz that Berliners wanted to hear. As a result, Berlin's music critics weren't as wild about Whiteman's music as either the Viennese or the British. The conservative papers in particular were outraged by everything jazz represented, calling it "a shriek from the jungle and a proof that American civilization is basically Negroid."

Billie, on the other hand, was ecstatic. "Whiteman Triumphs in Berlin" was the title of the story he filed for *Die Stunde*. Perhaps because of the questionable funding of his trip to Berlin, Wilder has been described as Whiteman's publicist, but that's not fair. Billie's review was a rave, but it was an intelligent one, written with style and verve—a visceral appreciation of what Whiteman achieved onstage: "His body vibrates, his double chin waddles, the mustache jumps, the knee trembles—rhythm personified." Billie reported to his readers that "Rhapsody in Blue" was a sensation in the United States, an attempt to use the rhythms of American folk music in a modern way. "If Whiteman is playing it, then it's a big artistic thing," Billie explained. The critic concluded with a youthful polemic: "For jazz? Against jazz? Most modern music? Kitsch? Art? Need! A necessary blood transfusion for an atherosclerotic Europe."

Wisely, Billie had spent time during his last hectic days in Vienna securing a letter of recommendation from a Dr. Krienes, the Vienna correspondent for Scherl, the Berlin newspaper conglomerate. Armed with the Whiteman connection as well as Krienes's letter, he managed in short order to sell a personality profile of Whiteman to the *Berliner Zeitung am Mittag*, known in Berlin shorthand as the *B.Z.*, which boasted a much more sophisticated audience than *Die Stunde* had in Vienna. After a few days, Whiteman moved on—first to Paris, then back to the States, where Calvin Coolidge invited him to the summer White House in upstate New York. Twenty-year-old Billie, meanwhile, was left homeless, friendless, and unemployed in Berlin.

But Wilder already had the skills it took to survive in the crusty city, a classic *Berliner schnauze* foremost among them. Translating literally as "Berlin lip," *Berliner schnauze* describes the sarcastic, urbane way that Berliners deal with the world they inhabit—"a natural propensity for the ironic put-down or send-up." Billie's sneering *schnauze* had already been formed in Vienna (if not in Kraków), but it worked even more self-assuredly in Berlin. A harder-edged, far less formal city than staid, old, waltzy Vienna,

Berlin was a speedy, anxious place packed with speedy, anxious people. The playwright and journalist Carl Zuckmayer once said that Berliners talked about their city as though it was a highly prized woman: "We called her proud, snobbish, nouveau riche, uncultured, crude. But secretly everyone looked upon her as the goal of his desires. Some saw her as hefty, full-breasted, in lace underwear; others as a mere wisp of a thing, with boyish legs in black silk stockings. The daring saw both aspects, and her very reputation for cruelty made them the more aggressive. To conquer Berlin was to conquer the world." Having started out in Berlin by selling cocaine on the streets, Zuckmayer knew what it took to lose one's virginity there. "Berlin tasted of the future," Zuckmayer wrote, "and that is why we gladly took the crap and the coldness."

Hard, smoky, and driven, Berlin was Billie's kind of town. Robert Lantz, whose father knew and worked with Wilder in Berlin, remembers Billie as having been "a real snotty Berliner—and I mean that in the most complimentary sense." Berlin was a city of Jews. Its spirit was profoundly Jewish. As Peter Gay writes, "The idea of a Berlin-Jewish symbiosis" is "the only dogma that Jews, philo-Semites, and anti-Semites of all descriptions hold in common." Cynical, critical, jokey, nihilistic, and not a little morbid, the spirit of Berlin resonated with Billie Wilder. In a way, by moving to this harsh and intimidating city, this young foreigner was coming home.

Berlin wasn't the kind of city that gave transplanted foreigners any quick hugs to make them feel better about themselves in the morning. Still, it was a city of readers, and a young reporter looking for work could find considerably more opportunities than he had in Vienna. By the end of the 1920s, the city boasted more papers than any other city in the world. There were 149 of them by 1930, and they covered all constituencies. Twenty of the daily papers ran two editions; *Tempo* ran three. Nearly four hundred magazines were published in the city. In addition, Berlin had about sixteen thousand cafés, bars, and dance halls. As far as the cafés were concerned, there was a style and price range for everyone. For upper-level film people, there was Anna Maenze's in Augsburgerstrasse; Ernst Lubitsch was a regular there before he moved to Hollywood. For actors, there was the Weinstube von Schwannecke or the bar at the Eden Hotel. The comedian Max Pallenberg and the actor Fritz Kortner liked the Eden, along with the novelist Erich Maria Remarque. Foreign press people gravitated toward the Adlon. Highbrow writers (like the movie-hating Alfred Döblin and his clique) preferred the Café Adler. Erich Kästner, who wrote the best-selling children's novel *Emil und die Detektive*, was fond of the Café Leon, while at the Jockey one might see Max Liebermann, Jean Cocteau, Ernest Hemingway, or the racy cabaret and film actress Marlene Dietrich.

Then there was the Romanisches Café, a "horrible, inhospitable, neo-Romantic pile" with a "harshly lit interior divided into two rooms and a gallery." The writer Anton Gill describes the cavernous place as being constantly full of "bearded men in tweed jackets and bow ties and plump or slinky women with bobbed hair smoking cheroots and waving long fingers heavy with rings." The Romanisches was a bohemian café with bare tables—lots of them—on which patrons doodled on paper napkins while lingering over breakfast. For the most ragtag among the Romanisches crowd, Gill points out, two raw eggs in a glass might well have served as the only meal of the day.

The Romanisches was located on Auguste-Viktoria-Platz across from the Kaiser-Wilhelm Gedächtniskirche (Kaiser Wilhelm Memorial Church). Inside the café, a hierarchy prevailed: on one side was the so-called swimming pool section for top-notch regulars like Emil Orlik and George Grosz. On the other side was the "paddling pool" for writers and poets—Bertolt Brecht could be found there, along with Heinrich Mann. In the middle, a flight of steps led to a balcony area with chess tables. The place was over-scaled, like a train station—a thousand customers could drink coffee, smoke cigarettes, complain, and ridicule their friends, all at the same time in the same establishment. Eccentricities were not only tolerated but encouraged. Grosz, indeed, was known to show up dressed as an American cowboy, complete with boots and spurs. In short, the Romanisches Café was pure spectacle. Billie loved it.

If the memoirs of Wilder's old friends can be trusted, Billie turned up at the door of the Romanisches Café soon after arriving in Berlin and asked the establishment's porter to announce him to a man he didn't know. Paul Erich Marcus, a stockbroker turned journalist, was writing for the prestigious *Berliner Börsen Courier* (signing his articles "Pem"). The porter told Marcus that there was a young man outside who wished to speak with him, and "then the shy young man was standing at our table. 'My name is Billie Wilder, actually Samuel Wilder. I've come from Vienna—Kraków, actually." Marcus asked, pleasantly but with some confusion, what he could do for the tall, slim, redheaded stranger. Billie replied, "If you'd invite me for a cup of coffee, for instance." There was a moment of awkwardness (as well there might have been), whereupon another fellow sitting at Marcus's table asked Billie what else they might do for him. "Tell me where I'm going to sleep tonight," said Billie.

According to Marcus, Billie spent his first night in Berlin on the sofa of Marcus's furnished room, though a more likely time frame is that they met after Wilder's meal ticket, Paul Whiteman, left town. In any event, Billie had not a mark to his name when he moved to Berlin, he had nowhere to stay, and he had nothing to return to in Vienna, either. In mid-July, *Die*

Stunde's corrupt advertising manager, Eugen Forda, was arrested over the blackmailing business, and the following day Billie's friend and editor, Karl Tschuppik, resigned from the company. This was no small scandal—Forda was sentenced to three months of hard labor. Kronos Verlag was sold almost immediately, and although its newspapers continued to be published by the new regime, most of Billie's colleagues quickly departed. (Imré Békessy turned up in Paris for a year or two but eventually landed back in Budapest, where he resumed his publishing-blackmailing operations; he ended up committing suicide in 1951.)

Tschuppik and Anton Kuh followed Billie to Berlin, along with a number of other *Die Stunde* refugees. They joined the seventy thousand Austrians, mostly Viennese, who were then living in Berlin. As usual, there were cafés open and waiting for them: the most influential Austrian émigrés tended to frequent the Wienlokal Schwannecke on Rankestrasse or the Mampestuben just off the Kurfürstendamm (that's where Tschuppik and Kuh gravitated, along with theater critic Alfred Polgar; Kuh, of course, kept mooching). Billie preferred the manic Romanisches.

After spending any number of nights on the couches of his new friends, Billie found himself a furnished room on Viktoria-Luise Platz, so tiny it had only enough space for a bed. Billie was thrilled to have it, though, even if the toilet next door ran constantly and kept him awake with the sound of gushing water. He consoled himself by imagining that it was a beautiful waterfall. Work dripped as well. From the Berlin offices of *Die Stunde* and *Die Bühne*, Wilder won the odd assignment, but Erich Leimdörfer was already their permanent Berlin correspondent, so Billie could take only the assignments Leimdörfer didn't want. Still, he managed to land and publish an interview with Cornelius Vanderbilt III. Playing smart, Wilder casually asked the multimillionaire how much money he had on him at the time. Vanderbilt confessed that he had only a few coins. When they went out for lunch, the American robber baron stiffed Billie for the price of a few *buletten* and some beer.

From his arrival in June through mid-autumn of 1926, Billie managed to win some assignments as a crime reporter for the *Berliner Nachtausgabe*, a Scherl-owned paper. But Billie found it harder to make a go of it as a journalist in Berlin than he had in Vienna. As the Hungarian film director Géza von Cziffra observed, "Berlin newspapers were edited differently than *Die Stunde*. Most editors didn't want to have anything to do with Billie. They said he wasn't serious." When Billie found work in 1926, it was piecemeal and freelance. He always needed money, and characteristically, he always needed attention, if not approval. In later years Wilder told a story about how he tried to trick his mother into thinking that he'd made a quick success of himself in Berlin, when in point of fact he was still a nobody long after he should have turned into a fledgling someone. He wrote to Genia, so the story goes, and told her that he'd changed his first name—to Thornton. To prove his point, Billie enclosed a series of clippings about his new novel, *The Bridge of San Luis Rey*. His mother then went out and bought the book, saw the author's photo, and made light of her son's lie by saying, "That other fellow Wilder, I never really liked his stuff very much." As usual, the Thornton story is probably a thoroughgoing fraud, but it still hits at the truth: Billie was desperate. By the end of 1926 he was a gigolo.

He was standing on Potsdamer Platz, penniless—and coatless, too. A chilling autumn rain was pouring down on him, and his knees rattled from the cold. A voice yelled out from behind him—"Hello, Billie!" The greeting came from a French dancer he knew by the name of Robert. They'd met in Vienna. Robert was currently dancing at the Hotel Eden—he was a performer, not an *Eintänzer*, or dancer for hire—but he suggested to his freezing, starving young friend that Billie get a job there. The hours were from four-thirty to seven in the early evening and from nine-thirty at night to three in the morning. The pay wasn't great—five marks a day plus tips—but it was more than Wilder had to his name. Billie scurried over to the Eden, applied for a job as an *Eintänzer*, got the job, found some dry clothes, and began dancing for money with lonely old ladies. He started work in the late afternoon of October 15.

"Since I was a gifted enough dancer and I was in a difficult period, I acted as a dancer-gigolo," Wilder said. "But it wasn't as romantic as it sounds, because I was gathering evidence to write a series of articles on what it's like to be a gigolo in Berlin in 1926 and '27. My reporting caused a small scandal with its look at a very old theme. Obviously the children's films of today are much more daring than these revelations, which had nothing indecent. But for the age it was new and interesting." Wilder did gather evidence, and he did write the articles, but he was aided immeasurably in this project by having danced with a moderately famous poet's wife. Klabund (aka Alfred Henschke), who was also a novelist and composer of erotic cabaret songs, had tuberculosis, and his shortness of breath prevented him from dancing with his wife, the actress Carola Neher. So they picked Billie out of the crowd and paid him to do the dancing. Billie seemed like a nice young man, and after striking up a conversation with him, Klabund asked him what his real profession was. When Billie told him that he was a writer, Klabund suggested writing the series, and it was Klabund who facilitated Billie's publishing his work in the *B.Z.* They struck up a friendship, in part because Klabund had a morbid sense of humor that Billie appreciated. (The consumptive writer titled his 1922 novel *Spuk*—a play on the German words for *ghost* and *sputum*.)

The scene in the dance hall was grim. Eight gigolos sat at a table in a room full of dance-hungry women and, sometimes, their decrepit husbands. For formality's sake, the boys would ask the ladies if they'd like to dance, even though it was the ladies who controlled the transactions by way of their purses. According to Wilder, of course, the older and fatter the women, the higher the tips. Billie must have danced with some pretty fat women: in his first ten days he earned four hundred marks (about $100)— more than an assistant editor at a Berlin newspaper earned in a month. On a particularly good day—a day full of especially ancient and obese women, no doubt—he made as much as a hundred marks. In fact, of course, they weren't all old, fat, or feeble, as Wilder himself wrote at the time:

> I dance with young ones and old ones; with very short ones and women who are two heads taller than I am; with pretty ones and less attractive ones; with very slim ones who are drinking dieter's tea; with ladies who send the waiter to me and enjoy the tango with closed, enraptured eyes; with wives—chic ones wearing black-rimmed monocles, while their husbands, themselves unable to dance, are watching me; with embarrassingly clumsy travelers for whom a trip to Berlin without 5:00 o'clock tea seems senseless; with splendid strangers, who divide their stay in Berlin between hotel room, hall, and ballroom; with ladies who are there day after day, whom one doesn't know where they come from or where they go; with a thousand types.

In one of his articles, Billie chronicled the evening he spent dancing with two all-too-tireless young sisters under the watchful eyes of their parents. After dancing with both girls for hours, alternating one with the other, they finally reach their limit and prepare to leave. The father slips Billie a tip: "I feel something in the palm of my hand—paper. They're already in the cloakroom. I put my hand in the trouser pocket and run, red as a freshly boiled crayfish, straight ahead into the men's room, lock myself in and, with two fingers, pull the thing out of the pocket. A five mark bill."

At one point, Billie found that he'd earned four hundred marks in ten days and immediately spent three hundred. He bought a portable record player, fifteen records (Whiteman, Hylton, the Revelers, Whispering Jack Smith), a new suit ("dark blue, finely-made, double-breasted, six buttons, broad trousers, the most modern"), three ties, four shirts, and a pair of black shoes. The record player was not only for personal use; Wilder also moonlighted as a private dance instructor. After a girlfriend named Margerie came back from New York and taught him the new American dance craze, the Charleston, the two of them hired themselves out as coaches. They carried the record player to their clients' apartments, and while Margerie worked on the husbands, Billie worked on the wives. There has never been any evidence that Billie Wilder ever sold a woman anything more lurid than a dance, though he did report that one of his customers at the Eden insisted that he accompany her home at 3:00 A.M., with all the attendant implications. In a rather obscure exchange, the woman attempted to elicit from Billie a brief explication of the life and work of Immanuel Kant, a question from which Wilder took umbrage. He felt as though he was being tested on something, and he resented it. Swathed in ermine, she had treated him to a nine-course meal complete with a bottle of Veuve Cliquot: "In between, we dance. She does not say a word. She must think: 'I rented two legs because I just wanted to dance, but their owner is an idiot.' " They climb into a waiting taxi, the woman tells the driver to take them to Kantstrasse, and at her door, she asks him to tell her about the philosopher. He responds by saying, "Of course, Madame—he is a Swiss national hero." This was not the answer she wanted, apparently: "She twists her mouth, lifts her hand and caresses my cheek, like a poor crazy child. Then she steps into the house and locks the door behind herself. I put my coat collar up and walk down the street."

Wilder always loved to talk about the sex he enjoyed in his youth, and if the mood was right he'd admit to sex with prostitutes, but he never suggested that he found himself on the receiving end of any money. Nonetheless, hiring himself out as a kind of pleasure machine for women struck a nerve. Wilder enjoyed trading on the stories of his experiences as an *Eintänzer*, but at the time it was probably not quite so amusing for him to feel like a whore.

Billie worked as a gigolo for about two months, until December 1926, whereupon he resumed hustling as a writer. He began publishing his gigolo stories in the *B.Z.* in January 1927 and even sold one to *Die Bühne* back in Vienna as late as September. He wrote:

> It's unbearably hot. My collar is weak as a pudding and completely soaked through with sweat, and my arms hurt. The two bands up there are playing without stop. On the dance floor, seven meters long and barely five broad, there are thirty couples. . . .
>
> It's icy cold in my room. From tomorrow on it has to be heated, at least a little bit. It isn't at all pleasant to have to wash up half naked, to knot your dinner jacket's bow tie with frozen fingers. From 7:00 to 10:30 I have a break. Only apparently, for I have to spend this time changing the suit I wore at the tea dance into the dinner jacket, and to also change my shirt, shoes, socks, and tie. No, it has to be heated tomorrow, by all means. People like us can afford that much, can't we? . . .
>
> 10:30 in the hotel dance hall. There are already guests. The good

tables are reserved for theatergoers. Ladies in silver evening dresses with hairdos smelling of burned hair. Gentlemen in evening suits examining the prices on the wine list through their monocles. The round lady at the corner table lays her hand sensitively on her eyelids. . . . I sit down in some corner. Three waiters around me. The first is shoving the complete menu under my nose, the second the wine list; the third puts a vase with flowers on the table. "Please, are you waiting for someone, sir?" "Well, no—I'm just the new dancer."

Wilder reports that in addition to dancing at the Eden, he also "served as a tea-time partner for lonely old ladies" at the Hotel Adlon. Both venues were attractive not only for the wages but also for the connections one might make. These were posh places frequented by upscale people who could help Billie get a better job. If Klabund could help Billie publish his stories, maybe some of the foreign journalists at the Adlon or the film and theater crowd at the Eden might help him as well. Even if nothing else came of it, the hustlers got something to eat. As Walter Reisch once relayed, "The Hotel Eden was an international center for movie people. . . . One had to have impeccable manners. That was the way you got your dinner, a few drinks, a cigarette, and a little salary, too."

The gigolo articles were a big hit, at least as far as the Romanisches crowd was concerned. Besides being closely felt and beautifully written, they were sufficiently outré to pique the interest of sophisticated Berliners who prided themselves on knowing and seeing everything worth knowing and seeing in town. In a café where a famous artist/caricaturist could show up dressed as Jesse James without anyone batting an eye, this was an accomplishment. Billie earned enough from the gigolo articles to pay off some of his debts, and they also served to get him more work at the Ullstein publishing company—the publisher of the *B.Z.* He soon began writing for Ullstein's *Mittagsblatt* and, later, for the company's new afternoon paper, *Tempo*. The latter had Billie's personality even before Billie got there: "It was a tabloid," writes Peter Gay, "racy in tone, visual in appeal, designed to please the Berliner who ran as he read." As a result, *Tempo* quickly earned a nickname that might as well have described Billie himself: "*Die jüdische Hast*"—"Jewish haste," or as Gay more precisely defines it, "Jewish nervousness."

Perhaps owing to his friendship with Paul Erich Marcus, Billie also landed a job as a reporter for the *Berliner Börsen Courier*. One of his coworkers from those days, Hans Sahl, describes Billie as a lean young rake "who, with his hat tilted on his head and hands in the pockets of his pants, was already playing the American while we still hadn't discovered America at all." Writing for the *Börsen Courier* was a good gig for a young reporter.

In fact, it was *too* good for Billie. "I was not very serious," he later admitted. "I drank too much in Berlin. Once I didn't show up at the editorial offices for a whole week because I went to Hamburg with a girl I was in love with. When I came back, I was fired." His editor at the *Börsen Courier* was Emil Faktor, a man who was obsessed with films and theater and might have appreciated Billie's similar interests, if only Wilder had played his cards right. Faktor's daughter recalls the situation a little differently than Wilder does, but the result remains the same: "I remember that my father sacked Billie Wilder for sloppy writing."

In fact, Billie's writing at the *Börsen Courier* was anything but sloppy. He wrote with precision, wit, and a palpable love of language. In one piece, he expressed his profound dismay at certain changes being wrought in his favorite hangout: "Cafés have something of the nature of a well-played violin. They resonate, swing with, and give off a certain color of sound. Years of the shouting of regular guests has placed their fibers and atoms in a special way, and, wonderfully, the timbers, paneling, and furniture vibrate in the rhythms of the patrons' lives. On the smoky walls, a decade's worth of evil, poisonous thoughts have laid themselves down as a shining golden lacquer—the richest patina." Billie is then horrified to see that the women's lavatory attendant is busily cleaning the floor, wiping away all his favorite jokes and bits of small talk: "Women are guilty of this, believe me—women, with their terrible lack of historical sense." In another piece, Billie asked a professional witch what her clients wanted from her: " 'Mostly death and ruin,' she says with a friendly smile. 'Loss of wealth, disgrace, light damage. For this one I wish business fraud, for that one an unimportant but troublesome skin disease. The wishes of my female clientele are often very detailed—loss of jewelry, loss of hair, rapid weight gain. These are the things that sell well.' "

Late in Billie's tenure at the *Börsen Courier*, he crossed a line that had to do neither with drunken lateness nor sloppy writing. In his role as court reporter, Wilder wrote a story about the unusually stiff sentence handed down to a man who'd been convicted of stealing a bunch of empty egg crates. The incident had occurred around the Jewish holiday of Sukkoth, the harvest festival, a time when observant Jews build small wooden canopies called sukkahs in their yards and use them to celebrate the season's bounty. In his coverage of the sentencing, Billie couldn't resist making a smart remark: perhaps the convicted thief was hoping to build a sukkah with his stolen egg crates. Billie's joke went flat as far as Emil Faktor was concerned, and Wilder felt that Faktor's rage resulted from Billie's having called attention to Jews at a time when assimilated Jews (at least those like Faktor) did not wish to draw attention.

One rarely thinks of this hard-bitten man as a versifier, but during his time in Berlin he even managed to get a piece of poetry into print. He'd fallen in temporary love with a Revue Girls dancer named Olive Victoria, and he commemorated her in a poem. In what may be just another version of the *Börsen Courier* disaster, Wilder is said to have spent the night with Olive, after which he fell asleep on the job the following day and was summarily fired. In any event, Olive bit the dust as far as Billie was concerned, but her poem landed in the July 1927 issue of *Revue of the Month*. It was called "The Fifth from the Right," and the accompanying photo showed a line of Revue Girls with an arrow pointing straight to the heroine of the piece.

From then on, Billie worked consistently as a newspaper writer—without getting fired for drinking, absenteeism, sloppy writing, or offensive remarks about Jewish petty thieves—until 1931. He also wrote for the upscale literary journal *Der Querschnitt* (*Cross Section*). He was intrepid, conversational, likable, fearless. As his friend Walter Reisch recalled, Billie Wilder had "a fantastic knack for getting interviews," though precisely how fantastic is uncertain. "For instance," Reisch reported, "the richest man in the world was Sir Basil Zaharoff—he sold arms to governments, to the Fascists. Nobody ever saw this man. Billie found out he was going to make a two-hour stopover on the train in Vienna. He walked right onto his train and got the interview." In reality, Zaharoff was in Monte Carlo, not Vienna, and Billie never interviewed him. With an advance of 1,000 marks, Billie's editors at the *B.Z.* sent him to the Riviera and the Adriatic coast to do some travel reporting. He was expressly assigned to write an article on system gamblers in Monte Carlo, so in addition to his expense account, the paper gave him 5,000 marks with which to bet. Billie proceeded to lose it all in two days playing *chemin de fer*. It was on this trip that Wilder may or may not have gotten as far as actually *seeing* Sir Basil Zaharoff, who may or may not have owned the casino, but he returned to Berlin without a story. (Billie did, however, write an anecdotal piece about Sir Basil, which he published several years later in *Der Querschnitt*.)

Wilder did return to Vienna in June 1927 to write about the daring aviators Chamberlin and Levine. Billie would have been there to greet them upon their record-breaking, post-Lindbergh arrival from New York, but they crashed in Germany and never made it.

Anecdotes continued to be Billie's stock-in-trade. He was still taking Genia's morning advice, as he would do compulsively for the rest of his life. Erich Maria Remarque, for example, is said (by Billie) to have told Wilder over lunch that he planned to leave his editorial job to write a realistic war novel, and Billie advised him against it on the theory that nobody wanted to read that kind of thing anymore. Using Wilder and

Wilder's friends as his chief source (and who else but Billie Wilder would have served as Wilder's friends' chief source?), Maurice Zolotow reported two versions of another remarkable encounter between Billie Wilder and the man who wrote *All Quiet on the Western Front*: either Billie had been caught fucking the first Mrs. Remarque and ended up being horsewhipped by an outraged Erich, or else Billie had been caught fucking the first Mrs. Remarque and the two men had duked it out until they drew blood. Neither story is true, Wilder made sure to tell Kevin Lally. In fact, Wilder insisted, he never even met the lady!

Billie did meet and interview the American child star Jackie Coogan, however. It wasn't the little boy who intrigued Billie but rather his parents. His reporter's instincts aroused by the funky smell of deceit, Billie started asking the Coogans nosy questions—such as, "Who is handling this child's money?"—and was summarily booted out of the room. Wilder wrote the story anyway, packing it with suggestions about financial impropriety, and indeed Coogan's savings were eventually wiped out, his parents having grossly mismanaged his income. In late 1927, Wilder landed an interview with Fyodor Chaliapin, the *basso* Caruso. Billie also claimed to have sat behind the notorious Prince Youssopoff, the leader of the group that killed Rasputin, at a play, the subject of which was Rasputin. The prince's response: he didn't much like it.

A more vital encounter took place at the Romanisches Café, where Wilder became friendly with the most famous newspaperman in Europe. Egon Erwin Kisch had a regular table at the Romanisches—yes, they called it the *Tisch von Kisch*—and it proved to be a popular destination for newcomers to Berlin. Here one could find Kisch and his circle of brilliant, verbal men: Fröschl, the editor of the *Berliner Illustrierten*; Jacobsohn, the founder of the highly respected *Weltbühne*; and, eventually, young Wilder. "Kisch used the Romanisches like you or I would use a hotel," an associate once recalled. This alone would have endeared him to young Billie, but Egon Erwin Kisch boasted what may well be the single best journalist's tale in the world:

The year was 1914. The location: Prague. After one of his soccer teammates failed to show up for a Sunday game, Kisch, the team's captain, discovered that his player had a very good excuse: a group of imperial soldiers had whisked him away from his locksmith shop and forced him to unlock the secret apartment of a highly respected army officer, Colonel Alfred Redl. It took three hours, and they found women's blouses, silk stockings, cosmetics, a lot of perfume, but no evidence of any women. Having lost his interest in the soccer game, Kisch took the story, ran with it, and scored a cleaner goal than he could ever have imagined. By the following day, the young reporter not only had dug up most of the pertinent facts but had outfoxed the imperial censors by planting a false story with which he hoped to spring the truth. As he reported to his readers, "We have been requested by official sources to deny the rumors particularly current in military circles that the General Staff Chief of the Prague Corps, Col. Alfred Redl, who the day before yesterday committed suicide in Vienna, has betrayed military secrets and has spied for Russia." Prague's censors fell for it, believing that Vienna had authorized the denial. Kisch, meanwhile, sent the full story to a paper in Berlin, and before too long the whole word knew that the highly decorated Colonel Redl financed his extravagant tastes by selling secrets to the Russians.

The Colonel Redl affair was a signal event in Austro-Hungarian history, for it provided an instant allegory in 1914: under the trappings of imperial formality and respectability lay debauchery, deceit, corruption. And Egon Erwin Kisch was the man who exposed it. Kisch's triumph had not been simply a matter of being in the right place at the right time, though he had certainly been there. It was Kisch's uncommonly brilliant strategy for unfolding the tale, outwitting the government, and revealing the truth to his readers. Like any journalist in middle Europe, especially one from Vienna, Billie Wilder had known and respected the name of Egon Erwin Kisch since he was a boy. Now, at the *Tisch von Kisch* in the Romanisches Café in Berlin, Billie could actually smoke and drink coffee with the man. So he did.

Kisch's continuing talent as a newspaperman was his knack for getting to the emotional heart of the story as well as its facts. Wilder learned from him. "Nothing is more imaginative than matter-of-factness," Kisch wrote in the opening pages of *Der rasende Reporter* (*The Breakneck Reporter*, 1925). "Egon Erwin Kisch formed a completely new kind of journalism," Wilder once explained. "His reporting was built like a good movie script— it was classically organized in three acts, and it was never boring for the reader." For his part, Kisch was charmed by the brash young writer from Kraków and Vienna. They shared a love of sports, a sense of humor, and a sure appreciation of the value of scams in the service of a higher truth. In addition to enjoying coffee and bull at the Romanisches, Kisch and Wilder sometimes lunched together in the Austrian restaurant Mutzbauer on Marburgerstrasse. Kisch even helped Billie find a better furnished room in Kisch's own building, where he lived with his girlfriend, Gisela Liner. As Wilder recalled: "He lived on the third floor of a tenement in the Bayrisches Viertel at Güntzelstrasse 3. By chance, he'd heard of a furnished room just below him on the second floor. I visited him very often in his apartment above me. His wife, 'Gisl,' cooked wonderfully for us. Kisch was completely crazy about soccer. Between two armchairs was the goal. I had to be the goalkeeper, and with an old, moldy tennis ball, Egon always shot in on me." (Actually, Wilder is wrong on one point here. Kisch never married Gisela Liner. When asked why not, Kisch had a stock reply: "I know her too well—she's not a nice person.")

Writing for the movies had been an idle dream in Vienna. But in Berlin, the second largest filmmaking city in the world, Billie could dream about concrete jobs. For the first year and a half or two years of his life in Berlin, though, dreaming was as close as he got; actual screenwriting assignments were entirely out of reach. A man of eclectic tastes, Wilder offered various memories of his first screenplay sale. "We were young and dreamed of writing screenplays," he once told two French interviewers. "It's typical. People always think that beyond their own vocation they're also suited to become filmmakers. Hairdressers and chambermaids don't escape the rule. Movie fans all believe they can put together a film. One day, in the Romanisches Café I met a man who worked for a photographic magazine of the *Coronet* type. He asked me if I wanted to write a screenplay. It was in 1927 to 1928, just before the appearance of sound (in Europe, at least, since in America it had already appeared). I said: 'I've never written a screenplay.' " In this tale, the other man—Robert Siodmak—told Wilder that he, Siodmak, was going to do the directing himself, and what's more, he had an uncle who owned a camera. "We wrote a very dilettante script which represented, if you wish, the New Wave or the Neorealism of the age and which was called *Menschen am Sonntag* (*People on Sunday*). The director was Siodmak. The only one who knew his trade was the cameraman. We immediately got work with Ufa and we started to write films for the stars of the time: Lilian Harvey, Willy Fritsch. . . . We also worked for Erich Pommer's productions."

Not so fast, Billy. In fact, by the time Wilder wrote *Menschen am Sonntag* he had already ghostwritten a large number of screenplays and treatments—at times he's claimed as many as 150—as well as one signed script that was filmed and bore Billie's name as its sole screenwriter. Wilder's first professional screenwriting efforts do appear to have resulted from chance encounters at the Romanisches, but they occurred long before Robert Siodmak came along. Wilder had met a number of working screenwriters at the Romanisches as well as at the newspapers for which he wrote. While working at *Tempo*, for instance, Wilder met the scriptwriter Hans G. (Jan) Lustig, who served as the paper's cultural editor. He already knew Walter Reisch, who was hacking out a career with some of the smaller studios. Anton Kuh, Billie's friend from Vienna, had written Lubitsch's *Maria Stuart*. Adolph Lantz, the father of agent Robert Lantz, also helped Billie to find screenwriting work; whenever Wilder would run into Robbie Lantz in later years, he always made it a point to introduce Lantz by saying, "His father gave me my first job."

There was another important contact for Billie in those years—an eccentric genius who was to German-language screenwriting what Egon Erwin Kisch was to journalism. Many mornings at 7:30 A.M., Billie Wilder turned up at the Café Kranzler, conveniently located near the zoo train station where Wilder could pick up copies of Viennese newspapers the minute they were unloaded. One of the Kranzler regulars was Carl Mayer, who had penned a string of German cinema's most influential and artistically consummate films: Wiene's *Das Kabinett des Dr. Caligari* in 1919 and *Genuine* in 1920; Lupu Pick's *Scherben* (*Shattered Fragments*) in 1921 and *Sylvester* in 1923; Murnau's *Der Letzte Mann* (*The Last Laugh*) in 1924 and *Tartüff* in 1925. Walter Reisch reported that the morose Mayer got a real charge out of young Billie. This must have been quite a trick, for Mayer was not a happy man. Born in the Austrian city of Graz, Mayer spent his childhood in provincial plenitude. His father was a rich businessman—until he decided to master the elusive but infallible trick of system gambling. Herr Mayer then sold off everything he owned and rushed to Monte Carlo. When he returned to Graz a few months later, he was destitute. Distraught and humiliated, he turned his sixteen-year-old son Carl as well as Carl's three younger brothers into the street. Then he killed himself. Shocked into premature adulthood, Carl made his way in the world by singing in choirs and playing bit parts in peasant theaters. Billie Wilder was the only one who could ever get a laugh out of Carl Mayer.

Wilder had good reason to respect Mayer and learn from him. Mayer was a creative perfectionist with a biting sense of irony. His scripts had a paranoid streak, a keen sense of impending disaster, but they were also sensitive and honest in their depiction of everyday cruelties. The German film historian Klaus Kreimeier describes it best: "Mayer was a politically thoughtful and socially conscious artist par excellence. He was an observer who understood how to think with his eyes. He could transpose what he saw and thought into 'speaking' film images, because the camera was not just a helpful optical device for him but an extension of his senses and his mind." One can well imagine a twenty- or twenty-one-year-old Billie strolling up to Carl Mayer one day at the Kranzler, working hard to strike up a casual conversation with Germany's most infamously depressive screenwriter, and revealing a sharp and appreciative command of what Mayer had written for the screen.

Géza von Cziffra, who had been working in films since 1923, also claimed to have helped launch Billie Wilder into the scriptwriting business. According to this sporadically reliable source, von Cziffra made it a point to introduce Billie to the head of the European Film Alliance, Friedrich Zelnik, in the hopes of generating some writing work for his young friend. But despite sharing a common background in Kraków, Wilder and Zelnik took an instant dislike to each other and it never got any better. According to von Cziffra, Billie's theory was that "two Jews from Kraków understand each other only in Kraków. In foreign countries they are antipodes." Von Cziffra continues: "When I told Zelnik what Wilder said, he asked me, astonished, 'What does *antipode* mean?' Then it was clear to me why the two of them didn't understand each other."

With his growing list of connections, not to forget his talent and spiny ambition, Billie found his way into the ghostwriting racket. Berliners had an unpleasant term for ghostwriters: they called them *Neger*—niggers. Many of the scripts Wilder wrote as a *Neger* were for Curt Braun, whom Wilder calls a "walking script factory," and the writer-director Franz Schulz. When employed by Schulz, Billie would head over to Schulz's apartment near Bayrischen Platz at 9:00 A.M., where he would remain, without food, for the rest of the day. Schulz, a notorious skinflint, would take himself out for a hearty lunch, leaving the starving Billie to work alone. On one occasion, Billie couldn't stand it anymore and fixed himself a healthy liverwurst sandwich in Schulz's kitchen, an offense for which Schulz made a point of bawling him out. (By the way, according to Wilder, it was really Franz Schulz who'd had the affair with Mrs. Remarque; Wilder knew this to be true because Schulz turned up for work one morning with a pair of black eyes.)

Of more far-reaching consequence was the fact that Wilder met Joe Pasternak, who managed the Berlin office of Universal along with Paul Kohner. Impressed with the personable and amusing young man, Pasternak hired Billie to be a tour guide for the Hollywood director Allan Dwan and his wife, a former Ziegfeld showgirl, who were traveling through Germany on their honeymoon. Dwan paid Wilder the equivalent of fifty dollars a week plus expenses to show him the best sights in Germany. Wilder, of course, knew nothing about Germany outside of Berlin. This was scarcely a problem for Billie, who simply bought a Baedeker guide and memorized as much as he could. Soon, however, Wilder realized that Dwan and his wife were much more interested in drinking than sight-seeing; Prohibition was still very much in force in the States. Dwan introduced Billie to the martini, they'd get tanked, and then they'd go touring. Hamburg, Cologne, Heidelberg . . . It was all very pleasant. In Heidelberg they found a fascinating castle, the history of which Billie, bored with Baedeker, proceeded to embellish with a wild tale of intrigue involving a crazed baron and—what story would be complete without her?—a slut. Dwan may have had a martini or two that day, but he wasn't so sloshed that he missed overhearing a real guide recounting the real, if dull, facts of the castle. Billie was instantly fired.

Wilder has never been known as a heavy, problem drinker, and he was certainly no match for Dwan, who, when he gave Billie his discharge, is said to have announced his own personal rule of thumb: "Never trust a son of a bitch who doesn't drink." Pasternak later reported that Dwan had called him hysterically from Heidelberg and berated him, not just for hiring a liar as a guide, but also for hiring a liar-guide who put the moves on his pretty new wife.

Wilder could take getting fired by Allan Dwan in stride. By that point he was working more or less steadily as a journalist, and he was finding work as a script ghostwriter as well. The consequences of making an enemy of a powerful Hollywood director didn't strike him as anything to worry about. After all, Billie was no longer a stranger in Berlin. He was twenty-two years old, and he had business contacts that were beginning to pay off. He was earning a little money, and if he didn't have enough—and he *never* had enough because he always spent more than he had—one of his innumerable café buddies would always spot him. He may even have bought his first artwork around this time—a poster called *La Goulue* by Toulouse-Lautrec. "I just wanted to have something on the walls," he said much later. He paid about eight dollars for it. "Of course it was way above my means," he noted, "but it was huge and it covered a lot of wall space." He also claimed to have bought himself a car—an old tan Chrysler with a rumble seat. It had taken some time, but Billie was making himself at home in the tough, frantic city he loved.

In late autumn of 1928, Max Wilder arrived in Berlin for a visit with his son. The details of this trip are unclear. Max was on his way to the United States for a visit with Willie; or Max was on his way back from a visit with Willie; or Max was on his way to emigrate to the States along with Genia (who, in this version, saw no need to accompany Max to say good-bye to Billie before leaving for America). What's certain is that Max was not in good shape, physically or financially. Billie could see clearly enough how poor his father's health was, but even when Max was suddenly stricken by severe and inexplicable stomach pains, Billie did not fully appreciate how gravely ill his father was. He died in Billie's arms in the ambulance. They never even made it to the hospital.

The date was November 10, 1928. Billie certainly did not have enough money to send Max's body back to Vienna, so he buried his father in a city and country in which his father had never lived. The Jewish cemetery in Weissensee records the vital facts of Max Wilder's life: his name was Hersh Wilder, he was born on June 2, 1872, and he died on November 10, 1928. The cemetery lists Max's occupation as merchant, and his address as Kyffhäuserstrasse—the street on which the hospital was located.

Billie tried, as usual, to borrow some money—this time for a funeral—but he had no success. He didn't even have enough money to call Willie in New York. It was one occasion when none of Billie Wilder's many friends and acquaintances helped him. When kaddish was said over his father's grave, Billie and the rabbi were the only people to utter it.

4. IN THE FOG OF THE METROPOLIS

Film is not a career for grown-ups.
    —Willy II (Willi Forst) in *Ein blonder Traum*

oneliness, depression, anxiety, despair—these emotions were as deeply
ingrained as Billie Wilder's sex drive, and, like sex, they often served as
the setup for a punch line. Throughout his life, whenever this private,
withholding man actually talked about being morose or suicidal, the
chances were great that he was priming the pump for a joke. For example,
he used to spring a much better story about his first screenplay sale than
the dull one he told about *Menschen am Sonntag*. This one is a tale of
chance, lust, and desperation. Several familiar themes reappear—not the
least of which is his sad state of mind at the beginning of the tale. He is
still living in the tenement on Viktoria-Luise-Platz. He's depressed—a struggling young writer whose dreams of working in the German film industry
are being stifled. Nobody wants to hire him; he's got stacks of unsold
scripts all over his room; he's poor and miserable and the toilet keeps
running. One awful night, Billie is awakened from the sound sleep of the
despondent by the sound of a man pounding on the outer door of the
apartment building. It's Heinz, the bruiser boyfriend of the landlady's
whorish daughter Lulu. Or maybe her name was Inge. Anyway, Heinz is
robust. He owns or manages a lesbian nightclub called the Silhouette, and
he has a bad temper. Inge/Lulu, in a panic, comes knocking on her friend
Billie's door and begs for assistance: "Help me! It's Heinz trying to break
in! He's going to kill us!"

Billie, rousted from sleep, opens the door, and in walks Lulu's customer,
buck naked and holding his clothes under his arm. Lo and behold: it's
Galitzenstein, the president of Maxim Films! What luck! Lulu exits.

Making pleasant conversation, Galitzenstein asks Billie kindly to lend him a shoehorn. Billie tells him that not only will he give Galitzenstein a shoehorn, he'll do him one better: he'll give him a marvelous film script. Galitzenstein offers to set up an appointment with his temporary host, but Billie will have none of it, and, to the sound of a frenzied Heinz shrieking that he will cut the throat of any man who fools around with Lulu, Galitzenstein makes a prudent decision: he purchases Billie's script right there on the spot for 500 marks, cash. A little later, Billie runs into Lulu outside the can, but Billie is only moderately appreciative: "Thank you for sending me Galitzenstein," Billie says to the two-timing whore, "but he is a small-time producer. Next time, please—Erich Pommer!"

In an astonishing coincidence, when fortune smiled on a youthful and depressed Billie Wilder, it once again took the form of an old, rutting goat. More likely, Wilder's screenwriting career began over coffee and cigarettes at the Romanisches Café, though long before Siodmak showed up. Wilder worked, smoked, and relaxed there (in his life the three enterprises have been more or less synonymous) from his earliest days in Berlin. He took along his portable typewriter and banged away on script ideas and news-paper articles amid the din of a thousand clever coffee drinkers. By the beginning of 1929, he was anything but a stranger in Berlin.

Joe Pasternak and Paul Kohner soon forgave Billie his excesses with Mr. and Mrs. Allan Dwan, especially after Carl Laemmle, the head of Universal Pictures in Hollywood, sent two gifts to his staff in Berlin: Laemmle's nephew Ernest, who wanted to learn how to direct a motion picture, and an over-the-hill western star named Eddie Polo, who wanted to continue earning a living. Appalled, Pasternak and Kohner found them-selves desperate. They needed something—or someone—to keep Uncle Carl happy, and they needed him quick, so they recruited their eager young friend Billie Wilder to write his first screenplay.

Years later, Kohner admitted that, yes, it had actually been his idea to hire Wilder to write the Eddie Polo script, having known Billie from (where else?) the cafés. Oddly enough, Pasternak, too, claimed full credit, telling Maurice Zolotow that Billie had "borrowed a thousand marks from me, and in order to get my money back I put him on the Eddie Polo picture. Wilder had lost all his money in a poker game with me and some others." Pasternak added a final damning critique of his old friend: "He was a terrible poker player in those days."

The story Billie concocted for Eddie Polo was close to his own soul. It was about a reporter who doesn't know exactly what he's doing but does it so fast that everything works out fine. The film is called *Der Teufelsreporter* (*The Daredevil Reporter*). Its working title had been *Im Nebel der*

Grossstadt (*In the Fog of the Metropolis*)—but *Der Teufelsreporter* was more to the point, though *Im Nebel der Grossstadt* was retained as a sub-title. Polo begins *Der Teufelsreporter*, Billie's only signed silent film, as a lowly typist at the *Rapid Journal*, though he might just as well have been a crossword puzzle editor in Vienna. Like anyone with any sense, he's frantic to become a reporter. While the rest of the editorial staff is away, Eddie and a boy-apprentice named Max are left to manage the office. (Polo's character's name in the film is actually "Eddie Polo.") When a group of American girls arrive in Berlin, Eddie, seizing his chance, decides to interview them himself. He's late for the train, but he runs after the girls' open-air bus and conducts his interviews from the running board. Paunchy Eddie, sliding toward sixty, is not the speediest runner in the world; lucky for him the girls are on the slowest bus in Berlin.

Alas, a complication: the girls' hatchet-faced chaperone is really part of a gang of kidnappers. Beautiful Miss Bessie, the girls' naive teacher, sus-pects trouble and slips Eddie a note asking him to watch out for them. Eddie doesn't know what to make of this, and he jumps off the bus and lands almost immediately in the arms of the other kidnappers. Jonas, the chief gangster, decides to get rid of Eddie, so naturally he puts him in an insane asylum. ("He thinks he's being pursued," Jonas explains to the eager psychiatrists.) Eddie escapes from his padded cell and hurries back to the newspaper office with his story, which his grateful editor splashes all over the front page. Eddie is now a hero. Jonas, meanwhile, has spirited the girls away to an island in the Havel River. Their fathers in New York have received ransom notes informing them that they must pay up by the fol-lowing day or else. (One measure of the film's slapdash quality occurs when the gangsters yank the schoolgirls roughly off the bus. Two of the obviously inexperienced young actresses can be seen giggling in the background as they await their turn to be roughly manhandled.) An increasingly titanic Eddie finds the hideout by jumping out of windows, skipping across the roofs of moving cars, and hopping from the rumble seat of one onto the back bumper of another. The decidedly middle-aged Polo performs his stunts gamely, but he's not quite able to achieve the right action-hero dex-terity. It's one thing when he commandeers a roadster. It's quite another when he single-handedly fights off seven or eight armed thugs.

In any event, Max calls the cops and Eddie saves the girls. With his two weapons—a telephone in one hand and a revolver in the other—he holds the kidnappers at bay while phoning in his story. The kidnappers have insured that Miss Bessie and the girls won't escape by stripping them down to their underwear, a fact revealed when Eddie pulls open the door and holds his hands over a cop's eyes while taking a good long look himself.

In a final stroke of fantastic luck he falls in love with Miss Bessie and proposes to her in the final fifteen seconds of the last reel. The whole thing takes all of sixty-five minutes to play out.

As Andreas Hutter points out, the hero of *Der Teufelsreporter* is more Billie Wilder than Eddie Polo. Perhaps for this reason, Wilder himself hates the film, hates his screenplay, hates the whole package: "It was bullshit, absolute bullshit," Wilder snarled to interviewers Joseph McBride and Todd McCarthy in 1979. "The leading man was an old Hungarian-American cowboy actor by the name of Eddie Polo and he was already by that time seventy-five." (He was fifty-four, but who's counting?) Wilder's scorn for his German scripts is curious; it points to his deeply held self-contempt. His judgments are harsh, and in terms of his own early films he wants to make sure he's the first to level them. In the 1990s, when another interviewer asked him about his German screenplays, Wilder was equally, gripingly dismissive: "Do I have to talk about them? They were all lousy."

Lousy or not, *Der Teufelsreporter* was a landmark: it was Billie Wilder's first signed script, and it opened on June 19, 1929, at the Schauburgen Theater in Hamburg. But Billie was scarcely ready to quit his many day jobs on the strength of an Eddie Polo picture he probably didn't like even at the time. Wilder was still a devil's reporter himself, and he continued plugging away at celebrity interviews and anything else that came along. For the *B.Z.*, Billie described some location shooting for Marlene Dietrich's latest film, *Das Schiff der verlorenen Menschen* (*The Ship of Lost Souls*), directed by Maurice Tourneur. For *Tempo*, Billie commented on a popular soft drink. Someone he knows, Wilder wrote, "is drinking Coca-Cola, which tastes like burnt pneumatic tires. But it's very refreshing. [Billie's friend] is crazy about Coca-Cola—he's just drinking his fourth glass. If somebody is wild about Coca-Cola, you can bet your last pair of pants that he's an American. And if he's pouring four glasses into himself, he's surely a tired American."

Billie commemorated Klabund's *yahrzeit*, the anniversary of his death, in *Tempo* as well. Wilder's friend and early mentor (the one who inspired him to write his gigolo articles) died of tuberculosis in 1928: "He was holding a handkerchief before his caved-in mouth and coughed. 'It's nothing,' he said, and it really was nothing. Just a tiny red spot. He died of it."

One of Billie best stories, published in *Der Querschnitt* in April 1929, was a profile of a difficult Viennese-born film director who had earned an international reputation as a capricious, profligate, and eminently Teutonic mad artist. In 1929, the man who called himself Erich Oswald Hans Carl Maria von Stroheim—the son of an Austrian count and a German baroness, a decorated war hero who stormed into battle on horseback in the Bosnia-Herzegovina war and emerged with sixteen inches of lead in his body—was living in Los Angeles and honing his reputation as a monster. (No one knew it at the time, but von Stroheim's self-generated biography was a rock-bottom fraud. He was Jewish, in fact, the son of a man who made straw hats, and never saw battle. He made up the "von" as well.) As far as German film audiences were concerned, the Berlin premiere of von Stroheim's *Greed* in mid-May 1926 had helped von Stroheim's villainous reputation immeasurably. Berliners greeted the picture with a violent display of hissing, whistling, and foot stomping at the city's largest theater, the Ufa-Palast am Zoo. The situation deteriorated at the second night's performance to the point that the screening had to be halted halfway through when outraged patrons demanded refunds and created a mob scene the likes of which Berlin moviegoers had never seen before. (*Greed* showed up later in repertory theaters, but it never found wider distribution in Germany.)

Von Stroheim, both the monster and the man, appealed greatly to Billie Wilder. Billie had given *Greed* a decidedly mixed review when he saw it at a Berlin repertory theater back in July of 1928. Referring to *Greed*'s outrageous premiere, Wilder wrote: "None of the old indignation about this cruel, naturalistic representation of human baseness is felt anymore. One follows, with a depressing feeling, this description of human beings that constantly offers the seamier side of the usual onscreen fate. But it's also one-sided and full of meaningless symbols." Still, Billie found one element of *Greed* impressive because of its intensity and urgency: "an agitating portrait of a woman's soul, in which the greed for money awakens all her bad instincts. . . . It's not relaxing to watch this movie, but it's still a delight, even if it's of a different sort than usual."

But now, Billie was just coming off his own first go-round with moviemaking, and von Stroheim's troubles struck a more resonant chord. Von Stroheim was simply called "Von" in Hollywood, Wilder wrote, adding that the Americans pronounce "Von" like *one*. Why *one*? Wilder explained that this was because Hollywood studios can only make *one* movie with von Stroheim; afterward, they go bankrupt. "That's the great thing about von Stroheim—for fifteen years they've gone bankrupt over him. Still, they keep him—the way one keeps cactuses and decadent greyhounds. . . ." Wilder continued: "*Greed* was given exactly one day at the Ufa-Palast. There has never been such a film scandal before in Berlin. People were taken aback—he was five years ahead of us. Quite independently from the Russians, he filmed in the Russian style even before the Russians did. He anticipated something like montage. He filmed associatively. And he unmasked reality for the first time: this is the way a wedding really is; this is the way a funeral really is. George Grosz types stand there, their brutal thoughts visible on their foreheads. Von Stroheim enthralls them."

Billie made special note of von Stroheim's latest film, *Queen Kelly*, which starred the glamorous and fabulously successful Gloria Swanson: "La Swanson is playing the madam of a brothel; the movie will be great." On this point, Billie's prediction proved to be far off the mark. Plagued with production and financing problems, *Queen Kelly* was never finished, let alone released, though a small amount of impressive footage finally saw the light of day in 1950.

Wilder's appreciative interest in crazy Erich von Stroheim and his over-produced masterpieces stood in marked contrast to his opinion of the movies being made in Berlin at the time. Von Stroheim was mad, but he had guts. Most so-called directors were either gutless hacks or, like Murnau and Lubitsch, had already moved to Hollywood. "It was a shallow time in German pictures," he said. "The big companies that were making pictures—they were kind of lost in schmaltz." Still, there were so many production companies and, theoretically, so many opportunities for young writers that Billie kept pursuing his nascent career as best he could. Dominating his dreams was the gargantuan Ufa, where most of the action took place. With over a thousand employees and an enormous annual production slate, Ufa was the biggest film company outside of Hollywood. Its extensive business offices were located in Potsdamer Platz, Kochstrasse, and Dönhoffplatz, while its vast production facilities lay outside of Berlin in the suburbs of Babelsberg and Tempelhof. There were many smaller studios in Germany, too, but the fantastically powerful Ufa remained at the top of the heap, largely because Ufa, like the big Hollywood studios, had a firm grip on exhibition. The company owned a large number of theaters and thus maintained control over its own built-in market, and the smaller studios had trouble competing.

By the time Wilder was in a position to sell his own scripts, some of the artistic wind had been taken out of Ufa's sails, thanks to the German economy as well as shifts in popular tastes. As the film historian Thomas Elsaesser describes it, German cinema of the mid-1920s was a paradox— "a financial disaster and a filmmakers' Mecca." Fighting against competition from Hollywood, Ufa attempted to limit film imports; the German domestic market was so lucrative that Ufa wanted to protect it for itself. At the same time, the head of production at Ufa, Erich Pommer, embarked on a series of ambitious prestige pictures that brought German filmmaking to new levels of art and bankruptcy: Murnau's *Der letzte Mann* (1924) and Fritz Lang's *Metropolis* (1925–26) foremost among them. Immoderately beautiful and expensive, *Metropolis* in particular put an unbearable strain on Ufa's financial resources, and Pommer's artistic ambitions were largely to blame (though he was a handy scapegoat as well). Pommer had a nose for superb talent, and as the critic Stefan Grossmann put it at the time, "as we all know, a good nose is sometimes worth more than a good head for figures."

In 1925, Ufa signed a contract with Paramount Pictures and Loews, Inc. (the parent company of MGM) as part of a loan arrangement to the tune of $4 million. Highly problematic for the Germans, the so-called Parufamet agreement forced Ufa to open up its theater chains to imported Paramount and MGM films to the point that as many as 75 percent of the films shown in Ufa's ninety-nine theaters had to be from Hollywood. At the same time, only twenty Ufa films could be released in the United States every year, but even then this small selection of films was released solely at the discretion of Paramount and MGM executives. If Ufa's movies were not to Hollywood's tastes, then Hollywood was under no obligation to release them. Most were not.

By 1926, the double-barreled disaster of the Parufamet contract coupled with the commercial failure of *Metropolis* brought Ufa back to the brink of bankruptcy. When *Metropolis* was in its sixth month of production, Pommer left for Hollywood; Lang's gargantuan film wouldn't be released for another year. In the mid-1920s, Pommer had championed German national cinema as a distinct alternative to Hollywood, and yet he also believed that this native German cinema could compete (to however limited a degree) with American films on American soil. Part of the huge expense of such films as *Die Nibelungen, Der letzte Mann, Tartüff, Faust,* and *Metropolis* was supposed to be offset by American box office returns, but the returns never materialized. So Pommer left Germany for Hollywood. He produced two films in the States: *Barbed Wire,* a love story between a French peasant girl and a German prisoner of war, and another wartime romance—*Hotel Imperial.* In the latter film, an Austrian officer falls in love with a chambermaid in the Polish town of Lemberg, then under Russian occupation.

In the meantime, in the politics of the film industry and German national political circles alike, talk began to turn to the question of why Germany was being forced to suffer humiliation after humiliation at the greedy hands of other, more prosperous nations. Hollywood was rolling in profits; Ufa's losses ran at about $12 million per year. Creditors demanded a solution, and they found one—in the wax-mustachioed form of Alfred Hugenberg, a sort of Nazi Rupert Murdoch, who owned a newspaper chain, a news service, and an ad agency. (True, Hugenberg was the leader of the German National People's Party, not the National Socialists, but he allied himself with the Nazis, and he was most reactionary politically.) Backed by Ruhr financiers, Hugenberg purchased the troubled Ufa and assumed direct control. He did not, however, turn the studio into a propaganda source—not yet, anyway. What he did do was make speeches, including this one in 1928: "We shall form a united front if we can only let the iron clasp of our philosophy pull us together and in its embrace melt down everything that is soft and fluid in us and recast it as stone. Anyone who would stand in our way will have to step aside or be melted down, too."

Hugenberg promptly renegotiated the Parufamet contract to much more favorable terms for Ufa. Pommer returned from the United States and, under the watchdog general-producership of Ernst Hugo Corell, reassumed his position as head of production. From Hollywood, Pommer brought back to Germany a new appreciation of the commercial value of popular culture. Pommer continued to make grade-A motion pictures, but they were no longer of the radical sort. Pommer's tastes had veered away from overtly arty projects like *Metropolis* toward broader, more crowd-pleasing entertainments.

For aspiring young filmmakers watching from the sidelines as German cinema appeared to decline, the time was right to offer a challenge, both financially and aesthetically. Some of these youthful cineasts wanted to use the cinema the way von Stroheim did, only cheaper. They wanted to get right to the hot heart of life. They were going to show Berliners how they *really* lived. Billie and his café friends spent a good deal of time talking about the problem, and they concluded that in order to experience the reality of city life in Berlin—no, not merely experience it, but *film* it (and therefore experience it on a higher plane)—one had to go to the parks on a Sunday. Berlin was grimy, but it was also a city of green. The Berliner Forst, the banks of the Havel River and the Tegeler See; Treptower Park, the Spree, Köpenick; the immense Grunewald and the Schlachtensee; the Nikolassee and Wannsee . . . To the north, south, east, and west of their dirty, industrial city, Berliners could find earthly, urban-idyllic solace, and if they didn't want to travel far they could just stroll through the lovely Tiergarten in the center of town.

At the time, Ufa was churning out an array of pictures, from elaborate costume dramas and escapist comedies to lower-key dramas about city life and ersatz documentaries known as "cross-section" films. Erich Pommer was making more fluff than he had made before, but he was also helping to spur a broad push toward a kind of street realism. Even Joe May, one of Ufa's most commercially minded, crowd-pleasing directors, had moved into a gritty urban phase with his 1928 big-budget production of *Asphalt*. A decade earlier, May had directed a 20-million-mark extravaganza called *Das Indische Grabmal* (*The Indian Tomb*), a huge production featuring tigers, turbans, and what looked like the entire Indian subcontinent, but now May deferred to the zeitgeist and made a melodrama of the streets. His film opened with a printed intertitle: "Asphalt—pavements—the pounding of muscle and sweat and iron to make a path for man: a smooth path—an asphalt path—feet—wheels—the rumble and roar, the hiss and shriek, the clangor and clamor of a city—moving—endlessly flowing—like life itself."

Cross-section films were, if anything, even closer to the pavement. They were compilation films fashioned out of vignettes of what was (or at least could be passed off as) the common man's common life. Cross-section movies were scarcely limited to Ufa and Germany. All over Europe, directors were trying to capture the flavor of industrialized urban life through montage. Alberto Cavalcanti's Parisian *Rien que les heures* (1926), Dziga Vertov's Soviet *The Man with the Movie Camera* (1928), and Joris Ivens's Dutch films *The Bridge* (1927) and *Rain* (1929) were conscious attempts both to stylize the documentary form and to make the form more real— to bring out the essence of urban reality by splicing fragments of it together creatively on film. Cross-section films were doing just fine at the box office, too. Urban audiences from Paris to Moscow absolutely loved seeing themselves on-screen.

Berlin's first entry in the cross-section genre was *Berlin: Die Sinfonie der Grossstadt* (*Berlin: The Symphony of a Great City*) in 1927. The inspiration had been Carl Mayer's. Mayer had grown weary of fiction and he was bored with studio filmmaking. He wanted to write something harder—something that cut through the fakery to expose the real. The *Kammerspielfilme* he pioneered—the small, closely observed dramas like *Genuine, Die Hintertreppe, Scherben, Sylvester,* and *Vanina*—were no longer interesting to him. So he began writing a movie in and of the streets of Berlin. Karl Freund shot it, Walter Ruttmann edited it, and like so many of Mayer's works, *Berlin* was both an artistic and financial triumph. The ensuing gush of money attracted the attention of other film producers, as money tends to do. After all, cross-section films, as the critic Siegfried Kracauer noted, "could be produced at low cost, and they offered a gratifying opportunity of showing much and revealing nothing." (Kracauer is typically bitter and remarkably unperceptive on this point.)

Structurally, the films were *supposed* to be loose. What might seem to be a mistake in a tightly planned, slickly photographed fiction film could come across as a fortuitous accident in a fake documentary—a glimpse of real life in all its messy glory. Ruttmann, Ivens, Vertov, and Cavalcanti were genuine documentarians, but Ufa's producers knew a good thing when they saw it, and they began gluing together cross-section films with abandon. They even threw in random stock footage—anything, as long as it played. In fact, in 1929 Ufa went so far as to produce several cross-section films composed entirely of clips from old romances and adventure films. Applauded not only by audiences but, even more importantly,

also by the tight-fisted producers who gave out writing and directing assignments, cross-section films were all the rage in 1929. Wilder and his
café pals figured (correctly) that they could make one, too. Billie would
write it.

It was a diverse little group. Moritz Seeler, thirty-five years old, had
founded the avant-garde theater group Junge Bühne in 1921. Seeler had
mounted productions of Brecht's *Baal* and Arnolt Bronnen's *Patricide*, but
now he wanted to be a movie producer. Robert Siodmak, twenty-eight,
was the son of a furrier-banker from Galicia, though he'd actually been
born in Memphis, Tennessee, during one of his father's business trips. Siodmak had been a stage actor and a translator of silent-movie intertitles, and
he'd also worked as a film editor and an assistant director. Currently working as an ad man for the magazine *Neue Revue*, Siodmak also had some
family connections he wanted to mine: his uncle, Heinrich Nebenzahl, was
a film producer who specialized in action-adventure movies.

Curt Siodmak, twenty-seven, was Robert's younger brother, a fledgling
reporter. Eugen Schüfftan, thirty-six, was much more experienced than anyone else in the circle, having invented a method of process photography
that used mirrors to mix live action, front projection, and miniatures. The
system bore his name—the Schüfftan Process—and was used to magnificent
effect in the groundbreaking, bank-breaking *Metropolis*. More recently,
Schüfftan had created the special effects for an Ufa film called *Narkose*,
featuring a flashback sequence gorgeously contained in a single drop of
water. Edgar Ulmer, twenty-five, had worked as a production design assistant on Murnau's elaborate Hollywood film, *Sunrise*; he'd also done set
designs for Max Reinhardt as well as for some low-budget Universal Pictures westerns. And to complete the team, Schüfftan brought in a good
little gofer: a former music and law student who had been trained as a
cinematographer in Paris and had worked as the cameraman's assistant on
Dietrich's *Ich Küsse Ihre Hand, Madame* (*I Kiss Your Hand, Madame*).
Fred Zinnemann was all of twenty-two years old.

A frightening amount of creativity and ambition was sitting around
those café tables weighing forth on the subject of how to make the movie,
but the group still didn't have a director. So through the agency of Moritz
Seeler, Billie met with a man named Rochus Gliese, who could legitimately
claim to have designed both *Der Golem* and *Sunrise*, the latter assignment
having garnered him one of the first set of Academy Award nominations
for scenic design. Gliese had directed films before, too, including *Der verlorene Schatten* (*The Lost Shadow*) and *Komödie des Herzens* (*Comedy of
the Heart*, cowritten with Murnau). Flattered by the attention Billie and
the others showered upon him, Gliese agreed to direct the film, with Robert
Siodmak serving as his assistant.

This was a talented group of filmmakers—so talented that they never agreed on anything. They battled at the time, and the skirmishes continued in their memoirs and the many subsequent interviews they gave after reaching fame and fortune independently of one another. For example, who paid for *Menschen am Sonntag*? Pick your answer: Robert Siodmak said he asked for a loan of 5,000 marks from Uncle Heinrich; Wilder and Siodmak both said Nebenzahl came through with the cash; Curt Siodmak said no, Nebenzahl only gave them fifty marks. Curt himself claimed credit for providing most of the money. The film had a budget of 9,000 marks (about $2,500), and according to Curt, he financed most of the film himself because he had just sold a book to the newspaper *Die Woche* for 12,000 marks. Edgar Ulmer, on the other hand, always said that *he* paid for most of it with his recent Hollywood windfall. Wilder, meanwhile, reported that he sweet-talked some guy he met on Friedrichstrasse into paying for the balance left after Heinrich Nebenzahl's advance.

Who wrote *Menschen am Sonntag*? Curt Siodmak: "I was trying to find a story that could be made into a film Robert could direct—his most ardent wish. A writer can get a break by writing a successful story or a book. But how does a director get his chance? He first needs a 'vehicle,' a story, which I hoped to supply for Robert, since he was brother, father figure, and family to me." Robert Siodmak: Curt never wrote anything down and Billie Wilder only wrote a single gag. Edgar Ulmer: "Billie Wilder did not write a true script. We would have one drink in the tavern and say, 'Next Sunday we will do this and this.' We had a plot thread and defined characters. Our main weapon was that each person was responsible for his own part—even the assistant, Zinnemann, could join in the conversation." Curt Siodmak: "Robert reluctantly put my name on the credits, but in such small lettering that it seems to underline Billie Wilder's name—'After an idea by Curt Siodmak.' For Robert, one Siodmak's prominence in the film business—his—was quite sufficient. He never lost that obsession of sibling rivalry to the end of his life."

Here is the actress Brigitte Borchert on the subject of the script for *Menschen am Sonntag*: "Nothing written ever appeared. Often, we had to wait a long time in the morning in an outdoor restaurant between the railway station and the Wannsee swimming pool until the gentlemen of the shooting team worked out the day's scenes at the next table. They also debated during the many involuntary pauses that occurred because we could only shoot in sunlight. Even during the shooting, [Robert] Siodmak would shout instructions to us, things that had come to him in a flash."

The only member of the *Menschen am Sonntag* creative team to avoid seizing credit after the fact was Fred Zinnemann, who claimed that his own job was mainly to carry the camera around for Eugen Schüfftan and stay out of trouble. Zinnemann described Billie Wilder, most recognizably, as having been "a highly strung young man" who (like everyone else in the production with the notable exception of himself) was as good at causing problems as he was at solving them. According to Zinnemann, Siodmak, Wilder, and the rest of the production team were forced to travel to the locations on public transportation because none of them owned cars and it cost far too much to hire them. (What happened to Billie's old Chrysler? you may well ask. He may not have owned it yet.) This presented its own set of problems, especially when the filmmakers got into one of their frequent tiffs on a Berlin bus: "In the evening, Billie and Siodmak took the exposed negative to the laboratory to be developed. One day they got into an argument and walked angrily off the bus, leaving the negative behind them—three days' work which was never seen again and had to be reshot."

One thing everyone agrees on is that Rochus Gliese quit in disgust soon after the production commenced because of Robert Siodmak's relentless nagging. Siodmak proudly took full credit for Gliese's departure: "Gliese shot so much film on the first day that I threw him out," though the real chronology was more on the order of two weeks. Gliese's exit, of course, enabled Siodmak to seize the reigns himself. As Wilder put it, "Robert was the director for a very simple reason: when kids play football on a meadow, the one who owns the football is the captain—and he owned the camera." The uppity Siodmak then said something obnoxious to Mrs. Edgar Ulmer, and before anyone knew what happened, the huffy Ulmers were on a boat heading for the States. Moritz Seeler, too, got so sick of the rampant ineptitude, ill feelings, and chronic shortage of funding that he left the film as well.

A happier portrait of *Menschen am Sonntag*'s production comes from a published contemporary account written by a freelance reporter for *Tempo*. In an article headlined "*Wir von filmstudio, 1929*" ("We of the Film Studio, 1929") Billie Wilder set forth the filmmakers' ambitions and dreams. Trying to think up a title, Wilder noted, they considered *Sommer 29 (Summer, '29)* and *Junge Leute wie alle (Young People, Like Everybody)* but finally settled on *So ist es und nicht allers (It's Just Like This and Not Otherwise)* on the theory that this was exactly what they were trying to do with the film and that they should state their goals up front. They wanted to make their movie as realistically and simply as possible— no fake drama, just real life. There would be no Russian lieutenants or female spies—just average Berliners:

> The five people in this movie—that's you and me. God may punish us, but our waiter is a good guy who lives in Neukölln. God may punish

us, but our heroine types on a typewriter and doesn't own a pink divan on which she, deceiving spy that she is, elicits the fortification plans of Przemysl. Yes, strong action is missing—obvious conflicts and the devil knows what else. And we hope so. We have evaded all the worn-out turns and stayed on our entirely unused, terribly deserted path for many miles: the road sign says 'Real Life' . . . After the weekend is over, our boys are standing in front of a suburban cinema without seeing it. Behind them, a poster shouts, "Weekend magic." This is the dissonance we want to show—between this weekend movie inside and the Sunday which our five real people have actually experienced.

Four weeks from the publication of the article, Wilder confidently reported, their film would be completed.

Billie was premature. *Menschen am Sonntag* ended up taking nine months to film and edit. In a later account of the production, this time for the newspaper *Montag Morgen*, Wilder recounted the process of selecting their "five real people." In their honest effort to capture real life, they actually had the nerve to cast five real people: "At first, we thought about young actors," Wilder reported, "but the people had to be genuine. We searched. Seeler found a taxi driver, Erwin Splettstösser—taxi number 1A10088—in front of a Kurfürstendamm bar. He was immediately cast. We found Freulein Borchert buying records. She was difficult to persuade; her family thought we were white slavers. In spite of that, she came to the test shoot on Thielplatz. Christl Ehlers also showed up; she had experience already, having once been an extra for Dupont. She also gave us her word of honor that she was on familiar terms with Lupu Pick's cinematographer." They met von Waltershausen by chance and found that he was perfect for the part of the traveling wine salesman.

Wilder acknowledged in the *Montag Morgen* account that the script (the treatment, really) was only seven pages long. He also admitted that the banker who financed the film did so in part because he believed in their success (according to Billie, 3 percent) and partly because he thought he would end up with an incredibly cheap movie (97 percent). The actors received ten marks per day. According to Wilder, they spent only a single day filming inside a studio; the rest was shot on the streets, in the parks, and at the lake.

Weather was an incessant problem, and everyone became more and more nervous—not least of all the financiers. Still, the squabbling consortium finished making its gutsy little movie, only to discover to their great chagrin that nobody wanted to see it. "We project it for the gentlemen of the big film companies. No one takes us seriously. The head of distribution swears that after thirty years' experience, he will resign his job if this film even receives a premiere somewhere—not to speak at all of a success."

Finally, however, a Ufa executive named Hanns Brodnitz bought the distribution and exhibition rights to *Menschen am Sonntag* and booked its premiere at Ufa's own theater on the Kurfürstendamm, a venue that specialized in quirky experimental films.

If the film's premiere was any indication, *Menschen am Sonntag* was poised for blockbuster success, a development that was completely unexpected as far as the filmmakers were concerned. After the first screening, the audience applauded so enthusiastically and ceaselessly that an amazed Moritz Seeler pulled an even more amazed Robert Siodmak onto the stage for a bow. "I locked myself in the toilet and cried with relief," Siodmak later said.

Deft, funny, and tender, *Menschen am Sonntag* opened on February 4, 1930. Its first-night success was not a fluke. The film was an instant hit, as Berliners saw themselves reproduced on-screen in gently satirical form. Ordinary alienated citizens meet for a few moments on the beach or in the park. Their encounters are wistful, more or less empty, and eminently recognizable to tens of thousands of alienated Berliners. The opening titles announce the film's governing philosophy: "In this film, five young people play the roles that they live in real life. A taxi driver, a salesgirl, a girl from a record store, a traveling wine salesman, and a model. When the film was finished, the stars went back into the nameless crowd from which they came."

Siodmak's camera records, as best it can, a sense of unmediated humdrum—people hopping trolleys, doing their nails, smoking cigarettes on the sidewalk, riding in cars. A father washes his infant. Street cleaners sweep horseshit off the pavement. When characters speak (in the form of printed intertitles), they don't sound at all glamorous: "Of course she has to see the Willy Fritsch film," the cabdriver complains, referring to his girlfriend's love of the popular German star. "Well, at least for my sake Garbo's coming next week."

As part of the wider *Neue Sachlichkeit* movement in German filmmaking (translating directly as the new matter-of-factness), *Menschen am Sonntag* meanders along without any apparent narrative drive. Incidental observations take the place of story structure. For instance, a man walks into a drab apartment, sits down at the table, and stubs his cigarette out on a plate. He pours himself a beer, drinks it, and reads the paper while, in the background, the faucet drips. Siodmak cuts back and forth between the man, the dripping faucet, and a woman lounging on a daybed; the man goes to an armoire and takes out a jacket; the woman goes to the same armoire and takes out her clothes, and in both cases the armoire door swings open after they leave and they have to return to shut it—the kind of purposeful accident that cross-section films depended upon to achieve a sense of inescapable quotidian misery. Nothing happens; that's the point.

After its dreary urban opening scenes, a title card appears: "*Alles zieht ins Grune*"—"everything moves into the green"—at which point traveling shots roll the collective vision forward and outward, rapidly transporting both characters and audience into the parks. Crowds of Berliners stream into the woods and onto the beaches, where a peculiar sort of love may bloom. In one scene, the camera follows the romantic pursuits of a young couple in a park. "Romantic" may be too mild a word; the encounter looks more like seasonal rutting. The male chases the female for a little while, after which they meet, embrace, and almost kiss. She runs away; he follows. She lies down against a rock. He touches her hair. She reaches for his face in what looks like a hostile gesture, then smooths it out and relaxes into an embrace. The camera tilts up to the treetops, and after a long pan around the upper reaches of the black-and-white greenery, it tilts back down again to reveal a pile of garbage. Only then does it pan back to the couple lying together on the ground. After another discreet tilt up again to the treetops, the camera returns to the couple just as the man is readjusting his tie. The woman, meanwhile, is lying on the ground looking nothing other than freshly screwed, at which point Siodmak cuts to a close-up of her batting eyes. She reaches under herself and pulls out a pinecone. They laugh, brush the dirt off their clothes, and head back to join their friends and resume their typical day.

Maurice Zolotow reports that the woman pulls an empty sardine can out from under her ass, but even Billie Wilder was never that crude—at least not at that point in his filmmaking career.

5. TAKING OFF

Don't blame me—I'm not an executive, I'm just a writer.
—Joe Gillis (William Holden) in *Sunset Boulevard*

On the shocking strength of *Menschen am Sonntag*'s success, Robert Siodmak landed a scriptwriting job at Ufa, tapped personally by the head of the studio's story department, Robert Liebmann. In addition to his managerial role, Liebmann was a most successful screenwriter himself. In fact, Liebmann was even more successful than Liebmann; everyone at the Romanisches knew that in addition to hiring screenwriters to write their own scripts, Liebmann hired ghostwriters to write under the eminently bankable name "Robert Liebmann." This incensed Billie Wilder no end. There was work to be had, he wasn't having it, and there was Liebmann stealing credit for work he never did. To top it off, Liebmann wouldn't deign to hire young writers because he was afraid of the competition; so said Billie.

Synchronized sound had arrived in Germany, and movie characters suddenly had to have clever things to say as well as do. Never before had there been a more urgent demand for screenwriters. In 1929, the German film industry produced 210 silents and 14 sound films; one year later, 111 sound films stood in contrast to 75 silents (and of those 75, 15 were postsynched for sound). And the scale of Ufa's productions seemed, to Billie at least, to be skyrocketing. *Menschen am Sonntag* had been cheap. It tried to be realistic, it worked, and the film made money. But Ufa's leaders were eager to produce ever more extravagant productions, even if the interior world of the films was brutally realistic. According to Wilder, "Ufa started concentrating on films like *The Blue Angel* that cost ten times as much as the little silent pictures that we did. And so we had to go back to what the studios thought had a chance to make some profits. Our idea of doing pictures on a slightly higher level fell on its face." Wilder may have been disgusted with Ufa's way of doing business and making art, but he still wanted to write for the movies. (And no, *Menschen am Sonntag* is not on a slightly higher level than *The Blue Angel*.) Despite his involvement with a film that was still running on the Kurfürstendamm—and would continue to run for a total of six months—Billie couldn't find any scriptwriting work. That is, until he pushed Liebmann's button one day at the Romanisches Café.

Wilder, Siodmak, and others have all recounted the tale of how thoroughly and indelibly Billie impressed Robert Liebmann—not with his scriptwriting abilities, but with his exasperating chutzpah. It's one of the few stories on which everyone agrees, so it actually appears to have more than the usual basis in fact. "One day Billie Wilder was inveighing loudly against Liebmann, whom he did not know. He declared that Liebmann didn't give young talents any work. At this, a big, dark man in front of him turned around, fixed the impudent Billie in the eye, and said, 'My name is Liebmann. Come into my office tomorrow.' " In one variation, Liebmann appears as a fat man who adds a fillip to Billie: "If you're only one percent as talented in writing as you are in shooting off your mouth, I might give you some work." Whether he was fat or not, Liebmann had but one working eye; the other was glass.

Wilder's first assignment was to write a short film with Robert Siodmak—*Der Kampf mit dem Drachen, oder: Die Tragödie des Untermiesters* (*The Fight with the Dragon, or: The Tenants' Tragedy*), the surreal story of which runs more or less like this: a renter living in a furnished room goes berserk and his landlady drops dead. The inimitable Felix Bressart plays the crazed tenant, and Hedwig Wangel is the eponymous dragon-landlady. Bressart is held accountable for the death, but he's found innocent by a jury of his peers, all of whom are equally tormented by fierce, fire-breathing landlords. Handing short subjects to promising but unproven talents was not uncommon at Ufa. The risk wasn't nearly as great as it would be with a full-scale feature. After all, the worst the young filmmakers could do was to make an unwatchable twelve-minute movie. But even with a twelve-minute short subject there was more than enough room for dissent and subsequent backbiting. Curt Siodmak still insists that the idea for *Der Kampf mit dem Drachen* was his and his alone. Billie Wilder, he says, had nothing to do with it. (One notes a certain pattern here as far as Curt Siodmak is concerned.) In any event, Ufa's executives were impressed enough with *Der Kampf mit dem Drachen* that they gave Robert Siodmak his own production unit, and he took Billie along. They were to report directly to the great Erich Pommer.

An anxious, chain-smoking firebrand, Pommer demanded the full attention of everyone who worked for him. Like any producer with an obsessive personality, Pommer worked intimately and tenaciously on several films at once. He always had an array of projects in the works, but what set him apart was his world-class good taste. He was driven—fiercely—to produce art through commerce. "Please invent something new," Pommer had told the makers of *Der letzte Mann*, "even if it's crazy!" "Pommer was not a man to have soft moments and make big friends," Wilder recalled. "He was a very sober, very talented man—but there were no laughs there." One can imagine the stale air in Pommer's office, with Pommer and Wilder working hard to outdo each other with the smoking. According to Curt Siodmak, Billie couldn't sit still in Pommer's office, but then Billie couldn't sit still anywhere. Pacing, snapping his fingers, sitting for a moment, pumping his leg, hopping up again and pacing—this had been characteristic of Wilder since childhood. For Billie, the fact that Pommer was head of production at Germany's largest studio did not mean that he had to sit sedately in his chair and act cowed. Walter Reisch, to whom Billie introduced Pommer to the eventual success of both young writers, once said that of all the scripters under his command, Wilder was Pommer's favorite: "Billie was the life of the party. Pommer adored him, always had him around, always listened to him."

Apart from his intense, somber personality, Pommer had a nasty little habit: he liked to entice his fledgling writers with a stack of silver coins he kept on his desk. Whoever thought up a good idea got a coin tossed at him. Curt Siodmak reports, not surprisingly, that Billie was very good at Pommer's game: Wilder was "a very quick thinker [with] the will to win. He was always the first one to shoot out an idea, never stopping his marching up and down. And there's this world-famous man, Pommer, throwing him another coin. And Billie—he doesn't even break step, he just keeps up his marching and catches the coins so we don't stand a chance. And that pile of coins, it finished in Billie's pants."

Mostly, Billie spent his time working at home, rather than catching Erich Pommer's spare change. Like almost all the other Ufa writers, Billie had no office at the studio. There was no Writers' Building, as there was on all the big lots in Hollywood. Billie worked in his apartment, though he did go into the office frequently to meet with Pommer. When his scripts were finished, he dropped them off at one of Ufa's Berlin offices, from which messengers spirited them out to the production facilities at Babelsberg and Tempelhof. Some of these scripts bore Wilder's byline; some were ghosted. One of these ghosting assignments was the fluffy *Ein Burschenlied aus Heidelberg* (*A Student Song from Heidelberg*), starring Willi Forst. It was a romance—an American girl, a German boy—and the screenplay was eventually credited to the Viennese writer Ernst Neubach. No matter; Billie Wilder was writing movies for Ufa.

He was lucky to be employed in any capacity. In January of 1930, Germany's unemployment rose in a single month from 1.5 million to 2.5 million. The effects of the Wall Street crash were harsh and immediate, and Germany was especially vulnerable because of its history of trade and credit after World War I. An inordinate number of foreign loans were still outstanding. When the American stock market crashed, Germany's many creditors called in their loans, and an enormous amount of capital went sailing out of Germany in exceedingly short order. The impact on the German people was swift. Tent communities sprang up in the woods outside Berlin—the very woods that were so idyllic in *Menschen am Sonntag*. Now they were squatters' camps. In town, too, there was a looming shadow of despair and futility. Stephen Spender was living in Berlin at the time, watching the dark parade. He describes the city's mood: "When we were sitting at the Romanisches Café, [a friend] said to me one evening, 'There isn't a girl sitting in this place who hasn't scars on her veins in an attempt to commit suicide.' "

In September, when elections were held, Germany got a big surprise. The National Socialist Party, which had held only 12 seats in the old Reichstag, had entered the election confident of winning as many as 50 more. The Nazis ended up winning 107. With curious speed, the Nazi Party had suddenly become the second largest party in Germany. Only the Social Democrats held more power. Just as Billie's screenwriting career was taking off, about 6.5 million Germans decided to vote for the candidates of Adolf Hitler.

Because of the world-altering social, artistic, and political forces under which Wilder became a filmmaker, countless interviewers asked him later to discuss the ways in which he was influenced by life and politics in Berlin. Characteristically, he denied anything trite. For instance, Wilder met Brecht in Berlin, he reported, but wasn't at all affected by him. Weimar culture in general held no particular appeal for Billie, except for the Bauhaus architecture and design he grew to adore. Wilder was always a newshound, and he maintained strong opinions about world politics throughout his life, but he rarely stuffed them into his movies. If one searches his German filmography for manifest evidence of current events and politics, one searches almost completely in vain; the Nazis play not even a covert role. "If there was any influence on me in those days," Wilder once said, "it must have come more from American books and plays I read [in translation]. One of the most popular writers was Upton Sinclair. I read him, and Sinclair Lewis,

Bret Harte, Mark Twain. I was also influenced by Erich von Stroheim and by Ernst Lubitsch. . . . I don't believe I have been influenced by the cynicism of the times or even shown any of it on the screen."

Still, it's curious that *Menschen am Sonntag*'s quiet, understated vision of middle-class anomie gave way to the bizarre inspiration of Wilder's next signed feature-length screenplay, a thriller called *Der Mann, der seinen Mörder sucht*. The title translates directly as *The Man Who Sought His Own Murderer*, but *The Man Who Tried to Have Himself Killed* hits closer to the point. Billie wrote the film with Ludwig Hirschfeld and the Siodmak brothers. It's the story of a depressive little man whose attempt to shoot himself to death is foiled by the sudden appearance of a burglar. Poor, shnooky Hans Herfort (Heinz Rühmann), having fallen into despair, decides to end it all by shooting himself. In fact, he has already raised the loaded gun to his temple in the first shot of the film—we simply assume he has good reason to do so—at which point he is surprised by the rude arrival of a thief. Hans convinces the intruding criminal, Otto Kuttlapp (Raimund Janitschek), to do the job for him. It's a prudent business deal for Otto, actually, for an insurance company will have to pay out 15,000 marks to Hans's beneficiary if Hans is killed, and Otto will only get sentenced to three short years in prison. Otto agrees to become Hans's beneficiary; all he needs to do to collect the money is to murder him, preferably when he least suspects it.

Paranoia reigns. When Hans hears a champagne bottle pop open in a nightclub he immediately thinks he's being shot. In the final scenes of the film, as Hans and his girlfriend, Kitty, engage in an epic screaming match (with Hans rushing around the house clutching his head and shouting "*Nein! Nein! Nein!*"), a genuine killer named Jim attacks the hysterical, bespectacled loser—first with a knife and then with a bomb. Hans and Jim toss the smoking explosive back and forth as Hans and Kitty resolve their quarrel. Then the building blows up. Debris rains down across the screen, and when it clears, Hans and Kitty are wearing wedding outfits amid the rubble. The bombed-out house serves as their chapel while a chorus of gangsters—conducted by the film's composer, Friedrich Holländer, wielding a knife and a revolver—sings a little ditty under a banner marked "Unity Makes Strength." In the final moments of the comedy, Holländer pronounces Hans and Kitty husband and wife and joins them together with a pair of handcuffs.

Twentieth-century history might suggest that a proto-film-noir musical-comedy about suicide and a murder contract would have been a big Weimar-era hit, but in fact the opposite was the case. *Der Mann, der seinen Mörder sucht* bombed badly. Erich Pommer appears to have sensed its dicey commercial prospects soon after the film was edited, for he took the unusual step of ordering a preview, which occurred on January 17, 1931. Hoping to salvage the film from what appeared to be a complete disaster, Ufa released it in two versions—one running ninety-eight minutes, the other a mere fifty-two minutes long. (The fifty-two-minute version was retitled *Jim, der Mann mit den Narbe*, or *Jim, the Man with the Scarf*.)

Wilder, the Siodmaks, and Hirschfeld hadn't thought up this morbid farce entirely by themselves. They based their script on a play by Ernst Neubach, who himself had been inspired by the Jules Verne story "The Tribulations of a Chinaman in China." Holländer, who was making quite a name for himself as a songwriter for cabaret and film—he'd just written the songs Marlene Dietrich sang in *The Blue Angel*—wrote two acidic, cabaret-style numbers for this distressed comedy. *Der Mann, der seinen Mörder sucht* is literally a dark film; its cinematography is elegantly gloomy, with a few sharp spots of glaring light piercing through an otherwise sooty image. Robert Siodmak said, years after the fact, "We thought it was monstrously funny and split our sides while writing it. Erich Pommer liked it too, but the audience didn't. It was far ahead of its time." But actor Heinz Rühmann put it best: "We amused ourselves so much with our own gags that we often had to stop the takes for laughing. When the film got to the cinemas, nobody laughed anymore."

One reason audiences rejected *Der Mann, der seinen Mörder sucht* was that Rühmann tended to play brave little German burghers, and audiences simply wouldn't accept him as a morbid schlemiel who can't even kill himself properly. On the other hand, the Berlin correspondent for *Variety* dismissed the film for reasons having little do to with Rühmann. He called the car chase sequence "a bad copy of old American comedies," though it's far too nightmarish and distorted to be a contemporary imitation of Hollywood. But Wilder, Hirschfeld, and the Siodmaks had the last laugh, since *Der Mann, der seinen Mörder sucht* has inspired four (extremely loose) remakes: Rudolph Maté's *D.O.A.* (1950), Eddie Davis's *Color Me Dead* (1969), Rocky Morton and Annabel Jankel's *D.O.A.* (1988), and Aki Kaurismäki's *I Hired a Contract Killer* (1990).

Der Mann, der seinen Mörder sucht failed, but Billie certainly did not. He worked steadily in this period—and not with Robert Siodmak, for whom he had developed a certain antipathy: "Siodmak and I did not get on very well. I was very suspicious of him. He was a very good director—but not the most trustworthy of persons." Billie didn't need Siodmak anymore. In the single month of March 1931, three films made from Wilder's scripts were released: *Ihre Hoheit befiehlt* (*Her Highness Orders*), *Seitensprünge* (*Escapades*), and *Der falsche Ehemann* (*The Wrong Husband*). Billie wrote *Ihre Hoheit befiehlt* with two collaborators—Paul Frank and Wilder's sometime boss, Robert Liebmann. Not uncommonly, Ufa produced two versions of the film simultaneously—one in German, the other in French. The popular Willy Fritsch starred. Fritsch was a Jazz Age romantic comedian, German-style—a "likable, nervy, go-getter type." Fritsch was accompanied by two leading ladies, one for each language—Käthe von Nagy for the German release, Lilian Harvey for the French. *Ihre Hoheit befiehlt* is a piece of musical comedy fluff. As Wilder once summed it up, "Little does the handsome soldier know that the little peasant girl at the fair is really a countess, and little does she know that the handsome soldier is really the crown prince." And that pretty much describes it, though she's actually a princess not a countess, he's a soldier not the crown prince, and she knows his identity almost from the start. *Ihre Hoheit befiehlt* is a charming little film, utterly without pretension to greatness and quite entertaining. Rights to the film were soon bought by Fox and remade in Hollywood as *Adorable*, thereby giving Billie Wilder his first American screen credit.

Seitensprünge (for which Wilder received only story credit) concerns a married couple (Oskar Sima and Gerda Maurus) who go to a nightclub and meet Carlo and Lupita, a pair of Spanish dancers (Paul Vincenti and Jarmila Marton). Each couple tries to figure out what's wrong with their marriage; fully disappointed at every turn, they go back to each other in the end. *Der falsche Ehemann*, on the other hand, bears Billie's name. It was his second script with Paul Frank, and it stars Johannes Riemann in a dual role—Peter, the lethargic inventor of the sleeping tonic "Somnolin," and Peter's energetic twin brother, Paul. Peter is facing ruin. His wife goes off with a repulsive violinist, and Somnolin doesn't work, so Paul intervenes. First, Paul rescues the business by changing the name of Somnolin to "Energin"; now it sells. Then, through a series of convoluted adventures, he convinces Peter's wife to love him again, and she returns.

Audiences loved it. *Der falsche Ehemann* takes one ridiculous turn after another, and much of it is unapologetically silly slapstick. At the same time, there's a distinct sense of world-weariness behind the frantic comedy. Love in *Der falsche Ehemann* is characterized almost entirely in terms of paranoia, jealousy, and bitterness. When a champagne bottle pops open, for instance, the violinist naturally thinks that he is being shot by the jealous husband. Even the happy ending is sour. Peter reunites with his wife, drinks a healthy dose of Energin, grabs her, shakes her violently and shrieks at her in a rage, whereupon she drops to her knees in a swoon of reignited passion. Peter looks directly at the camera and declares, admiringly, "What a tonic!"

Billie's next script is one of his best from the period: an adaptation of Erich Kästner's children's classic, *Emil und die Detektive* (*Emil and the Detective*). Directed by Gerhard Lamprecht, the film premiered on December 2, 1931. Although it was Billie's second solo screenwriting credit, he based his script not only on Kästner's best-selling book but on Kästner's own screenplay, which the novelist had written in collaboration with Emeric Pressburger. Kästner complained afterward that he and Pressburger made the mistake of finishing their draft too quickly; their efficiency left Robert Liebmann with extra time on his hands—time to hand the screenplay over to Billie for a complete rewrite. In Kästner's view, Wilder "embellished the story and vulgarized it. There was trouble. There was a fight. There were referees. There were compromises." A nasty if ordinary argument took place, at which point the film's producer, Günther von Stapenhorst (in accord with Lamprecht and Liebmann) promised to give screenplay credit not only to Wilder but to Kästner and Pressburger as well. The promise wasn't kept, and Kästner joined the international ranks of annoyed novelist-screenwriters. Kästner is said never to have forgiven Wilder; Wilder claimed he never even met Kästner. He and Pressburger remained friendly.

Unlike the novel, Billie's script begins in a classroom with Emil standing at a blackboard. He draws a diagram and explains to his fellow students the design of the movie we are all about to see. Formally but charmingly, he introduces the film's characters—his own mother and some of the kids he meets on the streets of Berlin, all of whom are sitting proudly, like celebrities, in the classroom. "So, now we will begin," Emil announces pedantically, and the tale unfolds. The only purely self-conscious scene in Wilder's career, the classroom prologue was never filmed.

Following the novel closely but not exactly, *Emil und die Detektive* is the story of a valiant boy from Neustadt (Rolf Wenkhaus) who is sent off to Berlin to visit his grandmother and his cousin "Pony" Hütchen. Emil's widowed mother (Käthe Haack) gives him 140 marks to give to Grandma and puts him on the train, where, in his compartment, a fellow passenger (Fritz Rasp) kindly offers the child a cigarette. Emil refuses, at which point the stranger politely offers candy. Emil takes it. What Emil doesn't know is that the candy is laced with a powerful hallucinogenic drug.

This may have been Billie's addition, one of the points on which Kästner accused him of vulgarizing everything. In the novel, Emil merely falls asleep on the train. In the film, Emil passes out and enjoys a terrifically trippy dream. Beginning with a hilarious special-effects shot of the nefarious candy-proffering stranger—now reduced to a pair of fake, bugged-out eyes peering through a newspaper—the sequence moves on to become a late-Expressionistic montage complete with a cigar, fireworks, a shot of Emil reeling back in terror, superimpositions of smoke and sparks, and a shot of Emil hanging on a balloon and being lifted away. He floats over the town; there's a tower with a policeman; the policeman reaches out and the tower explodes; Emil falls onto the floor clutching his head in agony. When he wakes up, the money is gone and so is the man with the funny candy.

Thus in Wilder and Lamprecht's adaptation, the little boy arrives in Berlin not only robbed but violently ill. As a children's novel, *Emil und die Detektive* works because its boy-hero is unusually clever and competent despite his age—with the single exception of his deception on the train. There, Emil loses his guard and falls asleep, thereby letting himself get robbed by a stranger. The screenplay's candy device solves the problem. By forcing the child to take a very strong, very dangerous, and obviously quite illegal drug, the film fixes the novel's one notable lapse in judgment. Wilder and Lamprecht's Emil is not an irresponsible boy. Instead, he loses the money only because he's essentially tortured into doing so.

After drugging the hero, Wilder and Lamprecht return *Emil* to Kästner's original plot. In Berlin, Emil spots the thief on a streetcar and follows him to a café. Thanks to Emil's own criminal past, he's afraid to call the police. (Emil and his friends have defaced a noble work of public sculpture back home, but in a very minor way—thus the nightmare's inclusion of the policeman and tower, though one can scarcely ignore the psychoanalytic suggestions of the dream). So instead of finding assistance through law, Emil's solution comes in the form of a gang of Berlin street kids. They follow the thief into a hotel. Disguised as a porter, Emil gets into the man's room, but the money doesn't turn up in his briefcase as Emil had hoped. The next morning, a hundred or so children follow the man to a bank, where he tries to change a hundred-mark bill. Emil can prove that the money is his because he had fixed it to his pocket with a pin, and he points to the hole in the bill. In a fabulous conclusion, the man turns out to be a wanted bank robber, and Emil gets a reward of a thousand marks, which he uses to buy his mother a new hair dryer for her beauty salon.

One cannot ascribe anything about *Emil und die Detektive* to Wilder alone; one imagines that Gerhard Lamprecht, one of Germany's most successful directors, had some input as well. But the film does feature certain incidents that reflect Billie's personal sensibility. For instance, when Emil arrives in Berlin, he meets a street-smart boy who can't stand the way Emil looks and immediately turns him into a Berliner by unbuttoning Emil's shirt at the collar and folding the collar out over Emil's jacket, thereby making the *Ausländer* less of a rube. When Emil tells his troubles to his new friend, the boy responds by turning himself into a little Billie Wilder: he paces. *Violently.* The boy even paces himself right off the screen—first to the right, after which he crosses to the left and goes completely out of the image. Only then does he return and agree to help Emil.

The premise of *Emil und die Detektive*, both the novel and the film, stands on the fact that these street kids, eight to twelve years old, run completely on the loose in Berlin. Moreover, these boys are not above pulling deceits of their own, including, in Wilder's adaptation, an attempt to dose the thief with the same hallucinogenic drug that was used to such sickening effect on Emil. The thief asks the hotel to awaken him at 8:00 A.M., and, before going to bed, he puts his jacket outside to be cleaned. A not-so-innocent child then rifles through the pockets with no qualms about the legality of the operation, and he finds remnants of the poisoned candy. Emil waits outside the room and spikes the man's morning coffee with the candy and, for good measure, puts some in his water, too. Much to Emil's dismay, however, the man only uses the water to gargle, and he doesn't even touch the coffee.

The novel concludes with a triple moral. When each character has been asked what he or she has learned, Emil responds that you can't trust anybody, his mother says that you can't allow children to travel alone, and Grandma has the last word: you should only send money through the proper channels—the post office. Billie Wilder's Emil, on the other hand, ends up by squaring off in a fight with his best friend over a girl—a brazen child who then announces with a flourish that she wants to have both of them at the same time.

By the end of 1931, Billie Wilder could say without any fear of contradiction that he was a big shot. He was finally making good money. He was consistently employed. He knew all the players, and indeed he was one himself. Billie should have been floating on air, but he wasn't. He didn't have the temperament. Wilder could be the life of the party, of course, but as Paul Kohner described him, "Already in Berlin he was a man who has suffered and knows everything. Yes, he seemed to know everything about everything. And only twenty-five—it was not to be believed. As we say, he was *mit allen Wassern gewaschen, und mit allen Hunden gehetzt.*" (He'd been washed in all the waters and chased by all the dogs.) This sense of dissatisfaction might have had to do with his raging ambition, but it was an ambition that could not be sated by mere professional success. His nagging doubts were not about jobs or friends. They were about the way the world worked, or didn't. Billie Wilder had a sort of heartburn of the soul. He looked at life, and no matter what he did, no matter how many friends he had or how many screenplays he sold, on some level he just couldn't stomach it.

It was around this time that Billie Wilder saw a rising young British director on the lot at Ufa. Alfred Hitchcock, in his early thirties, was making a name for himself as the methodical director of a spate of breathtakingly unmethodical thrillers. Wilder recalled that Hitchcock was at Ufa to shoot the English-language version of a German film, but it's more likely that he was preparing to direct *Mary*, the German-language version of *Murder*. Whatever the reason for Hitchcock's trip to Berlin, Wilder made a note of his presence. Here was a man who made the films he wanted to make. Here was a director who made films audiences wanted to see. And Hitchcock was a man whose career was bound by no nationality or language. Billie spoke no English, but then Hitchcock spoke little German, and yet there he was at Ufa, directing a movie with an efficient, careerist passion that Billie strongly admired.

Beginning with his next film, *Es war einmal ein Walzer* (*One Upon a Time, a Waltz*), Billie found himself writing a string of musicals, a genre for which he had no love. Directed by Viktor Janson, it was the first of two operettas Wilder wrote for AlthofAmboss Film A.G. (Aafa). An heir and an heiress, perennial favorites, are the film's central characters, but in keeping with the zeitgeist, they're both bankrupt. Rudi Möbius, heir to an on-the-skids Berlin banking family, is all set to marry the heiress Lucie Weidling across the border in Austria. She's also poor. But everything goes wrong in Vienna and they fall in love with two other people, both of whom are as cash-starved as they are. The four principals travel to Berlin, with Lucie's mother, a notary, and an assessor named Pfennig in hot pursuit. It all works out when they decide to open a Viennese-style café in the otherwise unused and empty family bank.

According to Wilder, it was a sorry time for screenwriters. With alarming regularity, they had to force-feed seven or eight songs into the stories they were trying to develop. The composers had their own ideas, as did the lyricists, not to mention the directors. Often, Wilder observed, the songs "only interfered with the development of the story and unnecessarily held it up." For *Es war einmal ein Walzer*, at least, the great Franz Lehár wrote the score, and the leading lady was the sprightly young Hungarian soprano Marta Eggerth. Miss Eggerth recalls Billie as a very pleasant young man—not a troublemaker at all, but charming and cooperative, friendly and helpful on both of the films he wrote for her. (She also appears in *Das Blaue vom himmel.*) He used to show up on the set every day, she remembers, and he was especially helpful in terms of helping her with her dialogue. Since German wasn't her first language—and since she was playing someone from Vienna—she found certain words next to impossible to say convincingly. "Whenever I had difficulties with this or that German word," Eggerth reports, "Billie wrote other words for me which were easier to pronounce."

An Ufa musical-comedy about a former circus acrobat named Jou-Jou was next—*Ein blonder Traum* (*A Blonde Dream*). Wilder wrote the script with his friend Walter Reisch, working mostly in Reisch's apartment near the Olivaer Platz. Directed by Paul Martin, the film stars Willy Fritsch, Willi Forst, and Lilian Harvey. Forst had been Wilder's friend from his Vienna days, and now that Wilder was earning good money in Berlin, he and Forst would meet regularly over a good meal at the Austrian restaurant Mutzbauer. Forst, Wilder, Géza von Cziffra, the actors Hubert von Meyerinck and Hans Heinrich von Twardowsky, and a pilot named Ernst Udet—all enjoyed a regular lunch table in the Mutzbauer, where they could feast on decent schnitzel and *taffelspitz* and obscure Viennese idioms to their hearts' content.

Fritz Lang frequented the Mutzbauer as well, as did Wilder's old Hungarian friend, the café cutup Laczy Löwenstein. In fact, it was over a Mutzbauer table that Lang convinced Löwenstein, now called Peter Lorre, to star in his new thriller, *M*. In an odd twist to the Imré Békessy scandal, Lorre, who had been traveling back and forth between Berlin and Vienna throughout the mid- to late-1920s, had become friendly with Karl Kraus, the "lecture ape" who scourged Békessy. In the years since Billie left *Die Stunde*, the bilious Kraus had not been satisfied with his archenemy Békessy's mere exile and had written a scathing play based on the old scandal—*Die Unüberwindlichen* (*The Unconquerable*). Kraus himself offered the leading role to Lorre, whom he had met at the Café Central. Lorre played it: the piggish Barkassy, a corrupt newspaper publisher who plays footsie with Vienna's bankers.

Lorre, thanks to *M*, was becoming an international star. Billie, meanwhile, was stuck writing operettas and jamming the best story ideas he could think of into a string of songs written by other people over whom he had no control. *Ein blonder Traum* is such a film. It isn't a bad film—in fact, it's quite lively and a lot of fun—but it can be said literally to have given Wilder the Willies. Not only did Willy Fritsch and Willi Forst star, but they also appeared as Willy I and Willy II, window cleaners from the firm "Blitz-Blank." *Ein blonder Traum* is a Depression comedy. The Willies live in two abandoned railroad cars in the outskirts of Berlin. They can afford nothing better.

The two men kid each other and brawl like overgrown boys; *Ein blonder Traum* is the first of Wilder's many buddy movies. Willy I says to Willy II in one of the opening scenes, "I dreamt you were with my Erna." "Funny you dreamt that," Willy II replies. "What did you want with Erna?" says Willy I; "I was looking for you," Willy II replies. The scene ends with the two pals wrestling on the ground, rolling over and over on each other and enjoying themselves immensely. All remains fine until the day the Willies go to clean the windows of the American embassy, where they meet Jou-Jou (Lilian Harvey), who immediately comes between them.

Indeed, they meet this beautiful blonde dream in a most dreamlike way: one of the Willies drops his sausage in the window and Jou-Jou's little dog eats it.

Ein blonder Traum was a top-drawer production. Forst, Fritsch, and Harvey were all immensely popular Ufa stars. Not only was Harvey (in Zolotow's phrase) "the Ginger Rogers of Germany," but to top it all off, she was Erich Pommer's favorite actress. She was also his girlfriend. Because of the three actors' popularity as well as Harvey's relationship with Pommer, the pressure on the two screenwriters must have been very great. The first draft Wilder and Reisch submitted did not meet Pommer's expectations on any level—particularly in terms of its unresolved romance, or, rather, the nature of the romance's resolution. Wilder and Reisch wanted Jou-Jou to be unable to make up her mind between the two Willies, thereby leaving the resolution up to the men, who deal with the dilemma by abandoning the woman and resuming their lives as bachelors. As Zolotow describes it, the Willies were originally scheduled to exit the film together, riding away on bicycles in the rain. Pommer didn't like this idea very much, but Harvey herself was irate. The magnetic, appealing star had no inclination to let herself be ditched by *two* men, let alone one, so Pommer ordered a rewrite, at which point Billie is said to have solved the problem by dreaming up the dog and using it as Willy II's consolation prize.

That, at least, is what Wilder told Zolotow. In point of fact, however, in the film itself the dog has nothing to do with it. *Ein blonder Traum* ends with a film producer, Mr. Merryman, showing up (since he's an American, his production office is in the embassy!) and offering to hire Jou-Jou, but only as a back-row chorus girl. Willy II then intervenes on behalf of his best friend, altruistically yielding Jou-Jou to Willy I. Jou-Jou herself would gladly have moved to Hollywood if Willy II didn't proceed to give Merryman a host of reasons why he shouldn't hire her. The window washer's concluding advice to the Hollywood producer is magnificent: "*Film ist kein beruf für erwachsene leute,*" he tells Merryman—"Film is not a career for grown-ups." Because of Willy II's uncommon shrewdness and knowledge of the Hollywood system, Merryman instantly offers him a job as his assistant. His chief task: to talk would-be starlets out of their Hollywood dreams. The dog stays in Berlin. It's the Austrian Willy, Willi Forst, who ends up heading to Hollywood—alone.

Ein blonder Traum has been all but forgotten; even in Germany it's not well known. The influential sociopolitical critic Siegfried Kracauer dismisses this good-natured satirical comedy for being not only pap but politically offensive pap at that; Jou-Jou, Kracauer writes, is nothing more than "a living projectile in a tent show." What's worse, according to Kracauer, is that the film only works by "pretending that the underprivileged themselves were fully satisfied with their lot." But Kracauer misses entirely the cruel ironies of the film. *Ein blonder Traum* is a satire, not a naive romance. For example, a derelict of the philosophizing type—his nickname is "*Vogel-scheuche*" ("Scarecrow," played by Paul Hörbiger)—lives with the Willies on the outskirts of town, and he sings a sad song concerning the advisability of death: once you're dead, he sings directly to the camera, a black crow firmly planted on his knee, you won't have to pay rent anymore because you'll have your own hole in the ground. The two Willies' friendship is given a sour spin when Willy II sees that Willy I's window-washing ladder is badly splintered and in danger of collapsing under him—and because of the sexual tension introduced by Jou-Jou *he doesn't tell him.* Of all the operettas Billie Wilder wrote in Germany, *Ein blonder Traum* is by far the edgiest and most politically conscious—a brittle, cynical comment on what Berlin audiences knew to be their own grim social reality in 1932.

Despite his success, Billie was not yet finished writing scripts for films in which his name was nowhere to be seen in the credits. Paul Martin directed Wilder's script for *Der Sieger* (*The Victor*) in 1932, but Robert Liebmann and Leonhard Frank got all the credit. It was, in Klaus Krei-meier's words, an "ode to a con artist": a lowly postal worker loses his savings at the races "but wins the heart of a billionaire's daughter." Wilder then traveled to Vienna with one of his closest friends, the writer Max Kolpe, to put together a script for an Austro-German company, Lothar Stark G.m.b.H. The project, the first of two musical comedies for Lothar Stark, was called *Scampolo, ein Kind der Strasse* (*Scampolo, a Child of the Streets*). Based very loosely on a play by Dario Niccodemi, *Scampolo* was both written and filmed in Vienna, though Wilder and Kolpe had already returned to Berlin by the time filming began. Wilder had met Kolpe at the Romanisches Café in 1930, and they hit it off quickly. Like Reisch, Max Kolpe was able to work with the ever-fidgeting Billie without being driven to distraction. Then again, like Reisch, Kolpe was Billie's close friend before he had to write a script with him.

Scampolo (Dolly Haas) is a poor young orphan living on the streets of Vienna. She's boyish, with a short haircut and a striped sailor's shirt, and she looks to be about sixteen years old. What little money she earns comes from running errands, one of which is to pick up some cash from a deadbeat named Maximilian. (Curiously, Niccodemi's play does not contain a character by that name.) The fellow has no money, but he does have good manners, he presents himself elegantly, and he's also very kindhearted, so despite the difference in their ages—or perhaps because of it—Scampolo immediately concludes that he is the man of her dreams. In addition to his other debts, Maximilian owes his boardinghouse several weeks' worth of back rent. There's a board next to the door on which the landlord has written the names of all the deadbeats. Herr Wilder and Herr Kolpe are each listed as owing two weeks' worth, along with someone named Wachsherr (a play on the film's composer, Franz Wachsmann). In an effort to earn a living, Maximilian sets himself up as a language teacher. "The most important word in French is *l'amour*; in English it's *the money*; in Spanish it's *el torero*," Maximilian teaches. A better joke is this: Scampolo appears to have learned a few handy phrases from her new friend, a talent she reveals when she tries to communicate with an old man on the street: *"Parlez-vous français? Do you speak English? Hispano-Suiza?"*

Niccodemi's original Italian realism yields in Wilder and Kolpe's adaptation to a strange kind of naturalistic farce. For instance, the street urchin hears about a great stock market tip through her unlikely association with the head of a bank, a wealthy sugar-daddy type named Phillips. Of the three older men in Scampolo's life, only Phillips really comes on to her romantically; hence he bears the brunt of the filmmakers' distrust. Wilder's early canine theme reappears along with the accompanying sausage leitmotif when Max yells at Phillips for buying Scampolo a set of beautiful and very feminine clothes. Max compares Scampolo to a little pet: a poor man has a dog, he explains, and then one day a rich man shows up and gives his sausage to the dog and spoils it, with all the attendant complications.

Scampolo premiered in Vienna in late October (under the title *Um einen Groschen Liebe—For a Penny Love*); it opened four days later in Berlin. German critics gave *Scampolo* a hard time, but audiences liked it, if box office figures are any indication. By that point, the second Wilder-Kolpe collaboration was in front of the cameras at Aafa-Film's studios—*Das Blaue vom Himmel* (*The Blue of the Sky*). Directed by Viktor Janson, it was yet another in the seemingly endless string of operettas, this one only eighty-two minutes long. Anni Müller (Marta Eggerth) finds a job in the token booth of an *U-bahn* station. Hans Meyer (Hermann Thimig), an airmail pilot, uses this subway station, too, and on Anni's first day of work he shows up at the token booth and promptly stiffs her for the price of a token.

Das Blaue vom Himmel is without a doubt the least plausible of Billie Wilder's screenplays, a fact that becomes idiotically clear when a thunderstorm forces Hans to crash-land near a tree in the woods—the very tree under which Anni has taken shelter after leading an impromptu marching band out of the subway and into the forest. (Don't ask. The event is entirely unmotivated, except, of course, by the need to do a musical number.) Lo and behold, Anni and Hans fall in love. But there's trouble already. Anni works underground during the daytime, while Hans works in the skies at night. Thus they have only ten minutes in the morning and ten minutes in the evening to see each other—hence the song *"Einen Tag möchte ich bei Dir sein"* ("One Day I'd Like to Be with You"). Meanwhile, Anni's love interests multiply when the head of a cigarette factory—where the marvelously named Tabu-Cigarettes are made—meets and falls in love with her. Her allure is scarcely surprising, especially since Eggerth's Anni is clad in a series of exceptionally tight, gauzy outfits that do not appear to have the beneficial support of slips and bras.

Das Blaue vom Himmel reaches its ridiculous conclusion when Anni, unbeknownst to Hans, convinces the cigarette magnate to hire Hans to do skywriting for Tabu. First he writes "Tabu," and then, when the executive tells him how he got the job, he jumps into his plane, takes off, writes *Ich liebe Dich Anni!* in the heavens, lands the plane in the middle of a Berlin street, picks up an overjoyed Anni, and together they fly, all to the cheering of the crowd. Whenever Wilder insisted that his German films were all lousy, *Das Blaue vom Himmel* must have been near the top of his mind. "Yes," Marta Eggerth admits, "the story of *Das Blaue vom Himmel* was maybe not the greatest, but in those days they built the story around my voice, so to speak, and for this purpose it was charming and—more importantly—the public loved it. What else can one ask of a movie? It sold tickets." She goes on to make a charming observation: "If Billy Wilder said that he did not like to write operettas, I can only say what a pity, because, frankly, in his American films I can spot the music even in his dialogue."

One amusing footnote to *Das Blaue vom Himmel* is that Billie's script ran afoul of the Berlin censors, who initially prohibited the film from being shown to adolescents on the grounds of the adverse effect it might have had on their moral development. The implication was one that Billie would favor in later years: the censors were particularly upset by the sequence in which Anni pays a visit to the Tabu head's office and, in the eyes of the censors, acts like a prostitute. After an appeal by Aafa-Film, the censors approved the film with only one deletion—Anni's provocative line, "Sure, you're interested for one night, huh? And by tomorrow morning you would have forgotten me, and that's right."

With all of these steady writing assignments Billie was now making a very good living. He gave up his old Chrysler for a blue, two-seater Graham Paige convertible. (It might go without saying, but it's worth saying anyway: Billie Wilder liked to drive very fast.) He moved out of his little furnished room in Kisch's building on Güntzelstrasse and found himself a new apartment in a stylish, Bauhaus building—the Sächsichen Palais on Sächsischestrasse. He could afford to furnish his new digs in style as well, so he began buying modern pieces, some of which were designed by Mies van der Rohe and Le Corbusier. He'd picked up these tastes in part from his coscreenwriter Max Kolpe, whose brother was a Bauhaus architect. Billie began to collect art, too—mostly prints and posters. He spent money on good food and at tony restaurants. And for the first time in his life, his income enabled him to exercise fully his most extravagant sartorial impulses. Billie became a clotheshorse, a passion he maintained for the rest of his life. In addition to sporting expensive silk shirts and ties and custom-tailored suits, Billy took up an odd new affectation: he began carrying a walking stick. It proved to be an excellent prop. Not only did it lend him an eccentric, Stroheim-like effect, but it was something he could wave and jab in the air, wildly and unpredictably, whenever his incessant pacing wasn't enough.

Now separated from Gisela Liner's home cooking and *haimish* evenings playing living-room soccer with Kisch, Billie consoled himself by going to the finest spots in Berlin. Wilder generally demonstrated an extraordinary capacity for food, but now the food was the best in town. He began wearing hats, both indoors and out, to cover his bright red curly hair. He took vacations at the posh Hiddensee island spa or at Heringsdorf. On one occasion, he went to Hiddensee with Franz Wachsmann, *Scampolo*'s composer, together with Wachsmann's married mistress. When the woman's husband suddenly showed up unannounced, she and Billie exchanged rooms to maintain the charade. Morally loose and temperamentally on edge, Berlin had taken Billie in completely. As Peter Gay puts it, "Berlin was the city where mobile men came to rest." Billie Wilder was at home there.

He was twenty-six years old.

The writing assignments kept coming. German box office receipts remained high despite the rising stench of German political life. As Klaus Kreimeier dryly describes it, "German workers, provided they were not in the direst poverty and totally demoralized or had not been pulled into the maelstrom of politics as pickets or strikebreakers or foot soldiers of the SA or 'Iron Front,' poured into movie theaters in droves." It was in this context that Billie and Max Kolpe produced their third script together: *Madame wünscht keine Kinder* (*Madame Doesn't Want Children*). Kolpe (who later changed his last name to Colpet and worked with Marlene Dietrich as her composer) noted in his memoirs that he and Billie went on vacation together every year to a resort island off the coast of Rügen (on the Baltic Sea). Typically for Wilder, they worked while relaxing. Kolpe described one of these holidays: "We were only a few kilometers out of Berlin when Billie turned to me and asked, 'Have I recovered yet?' He proved how quick-witted he could be when a policeman stopped us in a village because he had been speeding. It's true—we were really tearing along in his convertible. But Billie not only admitted that the cop was right but also declared, with the world's most self-evident expression, 'I'm sorry, but this is a new American model. It only drives fast.' The policeman nodded, aghast, and put his ticket pad back in the pocket of his uniform. We slowly drove away."

Directed by Hans Steinhoff, who had also directed *Scampolo*, *Madame* concerns the flighty, modern Madeleine (Liane Haid)—she's crazy about tennis, and she certainly doesn't want to have any kids. Her husband, on the other hand, is a pediatrician named Felix (Georg Alexander). Felix loves children and wants to have one of his own. What a dilemma. Madeleine's tennis partner (Willi Stettner) takes her side; Felix launches a relationship with his former girlfriend, Luise (Lucie Mannheim); Madeleine gets jealous; Madeleine agrees to be a good wife and have kids.

Madame wünscht keine Kinder wasn't a pleasant experience for Billie, who found himself working once again with a Nazi. Steinhoff, who went on to make the slavishly Naziphilic *Hitlerjunge Quex* ("*Quex*," the Hitler Youth), distinguished himself not only for being a Fascist but also for being a criminal of the sort that, in Wilder's eyes, was even more damnable: "He was a turd, that Steinhoff—a man without any talent at all. He was a Nazi, a hundred percent. There were many Nazis who had talent. I would never say that Leni Riefenstahl had no talent. That was certainly a great thing she did with *The Triumph of the Will*. But I say Steinhoff was an idiot—not because he was a Nazi, but also because he was a terrible director." (Just to dispense with Steinhoff: *Hitlerjunge Quex* was one of the most effective propaganda films of the Third Reich. The tragic but inspiring story of little Heini Völker, whose nickname is "Quex," the movie traces the boy's moral development from a sad-sack son of a Communist to a proud member of Hitler Youth. It concludes with Heini getting stabbed to death by a leftist. As he dies, the first few bars of the Nazi "Youth Song" rise from his lips. The Nazi flag takes Heini's place on the screen, at which point Steinhoff cuts to columns of Hitler Youth marching into glory. The film's director was swiftly appointed head of the film division of the Reichs-jugendführung, but, as it must to all men, death came to Hans Steinhoff. The actor Hans Albers took credit for it. "He's the biggest asshole of the century!" Albers raged to Géza von Cziffra in the 1930s. "He's also a pig. One fine day I'm going to kill him." In the spring of 1945, with the war all but over, Steinhoff boarded the last Lufthansa flight out of a besieged Berlin in an attempt to flee to Spain, but the plane crashed and Steinhoff was killed. According to news reports, the plane had been shot down by Russian troops, but as von Cziffra writes, "Albers knew better: 'That wasn't the Russians—that was me.' ")

In 1932, however, the National Socialists were a political party like any other, albeit a violent party full of thugs. Adolf Hitler was a politician, and fewer and fewer Germans saw anything wrong with him. In March, Hitler won over 11 million votes to Hindenburg's 18.6 million, but because there was no clear majority, the election had to be run a second time. Hindenburg did win his majority in April, but Hitler gained 2 million votes in the process. As William Shirer writes in his classic history, *The Rise and Fall of the Third Reich*, "Political power in Germany no longer resided, as it had since the birth of the Republic, in the people and the body which expressed the people's will, the Reichstag. It was now concentrated in the hands of a senile, eighty-five-year-old President and in those of a few shallow, ambitious men around him who shaped his weary, wandering mind."

Still, life and work continued for Billie Wilder. What else was there to do? Besides, Billie lived in a city of Jews and commerce and vibrant culture and every form of entertaining depravity—the German city Hitler hated most. So many of the Jews and leftists who escaped the Nazis as refugees have reported that they didn't see the threat until it was too late that to make the point in any more detail would be redundant—except for this analogy: if the American religious right were to assume great political power in the South and Midwest, New York and San Francisco would be the last cities to feel it, and the natives would probably keep right on eating, drinking, and working until moments before the cataclysm.

In much the same way, Hitler remained a dark abstraction for Billie Wilder and his filmmaker friends through most of 1932. There were more pressing concerns—like writing scripts. *Was Frauen träumen* (*What Women Dream*) came next. Directed by Géza von Bolvary, the film takes its title from the name of a rare perfume that sells only three bottles every year. Its story is reminiscent of Ernst Lubitsch's *Trouble in Paradise*, which was released in October of 1932. When the haunting scent of *Was Frauen träumen* is found on a stray glove left in a jewelry shop after a heist, it becomes the only clue to the identity of a notorious jewel thief who's been running around town swiping only the best and most expensive gems. Other than the audience, which witnesses one such crime in the film's opening moments, only the mysterious Herr Levassor (Kurt Horwitz) knows the criminal's identity. Levassor has been following the thief and paying for the stolen jewels. The task of solving the mystery falls to the ridiculous detective Füssli, played with comically understated madness by Billie's old friend Peter Lorre. *Was Frauen träumen* marks the only time the two café buddies ever worked on the same film.

Because he takes the youthful form of Peter Lorre, Füssli is a round little man with a puffy face and a nasal voice who nonetheless remains happily, winningly unaware of his own essential ugliness. He's goofy—even strangely lovable, as long as one keeps a secure distance. Füssli's talents for detective work are minimal, as evidenced by his inability to extract himself from the pair of handcuffs with which he repeatedly toys. ("Did you arrest yourself?" he's asked; "No," he answers in Lorre's familiar twang, "I invented a new pair of cuff links.") Still, Füssli's instincts as a human bloodhound remain relatively intact. When he learns that the crime's only clue is a rare fragrance, he enlists the aid of his friend Walter König (Gustav Fröhlich), who works in a perfume shop. Walter has kept receipts from the three buyers of the perfume Was Frauen träumen, and, eliminating the first two as suspects, they trace the third to an address: Room 88 of the Hotel Atlantic. There, in the lobby, Füssli stands eagerly by the elevator door smelling various men and women as they emerge.

The thief is actually the elegant nightclub star Rina Korff, played by the statuesque, patrician Nora Gregor (who is best known for her role as Christine in Jean Renoir's *The Rules of the Game*) Unbeknownst to Füssli, Walter solves the mystery almost immediately and, in the process, becomes dazzled by Rina. He knows that the police are in hot pursuit of her, so despite the fact that she is guilty of a series of serious crimes, he spirits her away to safety in the backseat of a cab. They light cigarettes and talk. "Why are you helping me?" Rina asks. Walter remains silent. "I like you, too," she says.

Walter eventually asks her why she steals, and Rina answers: "I need it. It's exciting. It's like you smoking cigarettes." Like the central characters in Lubitsch's *Trouble in Paradise*, neither Walter nor Rina finds anything morally troubling about stealing expensive jewelry. Rina takes a similarly liberating attitude toward Walter's own apartment. Although he tries to sequester her elsewhere, she ends up lounging on his daybed, having stolen his keys and let herself into the flat in his absence. The inept Füssli shows up—he and Walter are next-door neighbors—and, blissfully ignorant of the fact that Rina is the woman he's trying to find, the two of them sing a song at the piano, Füssli bouncing idiotically up and down on the piano bench as he sings.

Rina, meanwhile, busies herself stealing Füssli's wallet, his watch, his jewelry, and even his gun. She then graciously offers Füssli one of his own cigars, which he happily accepts. "I'm the perfect thief!" she laughingly tells the detective. Füssli jokingly arrests her, saying "And I'm the perfect detective!" They both laugh, though only Rina has a reason to do so.

By the end of 1932, Billie Wilder was in love. To hear him tell it, there was never any lack of available women, but this one was a cut above the rest. The others were casual; Hella Hartwig was a serious romance. He met her at a Berlin party. She was a dark-haired beauty with huge eyes and dark eyelashes who, according to Zolotow, looked like Hedy Lamarr. Hella wore her hair cut short in the latest Berlin fashion. She was not especially cultured—discussions of art and literature went nowhere—but like Billie, she loved sports, dancing, skiing, and jazz. Better still, Hella was very wealthy. Her family owned a big drug company in Frankfurt an der Oder, and she drove her own car—a blue Lancia. Wilder explained the attraction: "I liked her. She liked me. We went out together. We made love. No, she did not talk like Claudette Colbert."

According to Wilder, Hella's family didn't much like him, and they certainly didn't think he was suitable marriage material. According to Wilder, this was fine with him because he had no intention of marrying Hella anyway. As a matter of fact, he didn't intend to marry anyone.

One of the couple's pastimes was to go to Walter Reisch's apartment on Sundays and play dominoes until midnight, at which point Reisch's girlfriend made liverwurst and salami sandwiches. A dozen or so people were there each week. Wilder once went so far as to say that dominoes-and-liverwurst was his favorite sport in Berlin. For Billie, life was humming. He was earning 5,000 marks for each script he wrote, and he was living and working exactly where he wanted—right in the middle of everything.

With his newfound money, Wilder began collecting stamps in addition to his growing stash of posters and lithographs by such artists as Toulouse-Lautrec, Paul Klee, and Ernst Ludwig Kirchner. With his English silk shirts and ties, American hats, and of course his threateningly operative walking stick, Billie Wilder was quite the young man about town. "At night we went to the El Dorado, which was rebuilt in 1972 for the movie *Cabaret*. Or we went to the Silhouette, the famous lesbian nightclub. Today there's so much talk about cocaine, but Berlin was the big cocaine city then." Indeed, the Silhouette was notorious, and Wilder liked to go there. (Whether or not it was still owned or managed by the strong-armed Heinz, Lulu's enraged boyfriend in the Galitzenstein story, is another matter entirely.) A narrow, dark bar on Geisbergstrasse, the Silhouette featured more than its share of alluringly modern attractions: a gigantic bouncer named Jonny, a black waiter or two, boys in drag, Conrad Veidt, Marlene Dietrich, and on and on. Wilder and Marlene hit it off right away, Dietrich being a jazz fan who particularly admired Whispering Jack Smith. Marlene also admired Claire Waldoff, who no doubt was a frequent guest at the Silhouette. Supposedly the first woman in Berlin to have her hair bobbed, she was one of Dietrich's vocal coaches as well as her lover. She was also a cabaret star in her own right, however unlikely her appearance: short and chubby with flaming red hair. Waldoff appeared wearing an Eton collar and tie, which as Anton Gill points out was "all that remained, together with a tartan scarf, of the full Eton suit the police had refused her permission to wear." (Berlin law forbade women to appear in public dressed as men after 11:00 P.M.)

Waldoff, Dietrich, and the rest of the lesbians at the Silhouette were all part of Wilder's scene in those days—or more accurately, he was part of theirs. The appeal was unmistakable. In the words of Robbie Lantz, they were "ladies who carried a bit of the gutter with them," a trait to which Wilder was always attracted. Billie enjoyed life on the transgressive fringes of society even if he had no urge to participate in the transgressions himself. Still, even though he liked the Silhouette, he *loved* the Romanisches Café and continued to make it his second home. By the beginning of 1933, Wilder could well afford more expensive places like the Adlon or the Kempinski, and he did frequent these classy places and others. But for Billie, the almost exclusively male camaraderie at the Romanisches had no equal. Paul Erich Marcus remembered that Wilder, along with Robert Siodmak, still hung out at the Romanisches despite their upward mobility: "They were eating in more pretentious restaurants—the Stöckler on the Kurfürstendamm, the Horcher or the Schlichter on Lutherstrasse—but the twilight surroundings of the café, its magic, still attracted them more."

Late in 1932, Wilder and Walter Reisch wrote another script for Erich Pommer—*Der Frack mit der Chrysantheme (Tailcoat with a Chrysanthemum)*. A sartorial *La Ronde*, it was the story of a suit of clothes passed along from one person to another that ends up as a scarecrow standing in a field of corn. But the film was never made—not in Germany, at any rate. In January 1933, while on a ski vacation at Davos, Billie and Hella were skiing the Parsenn one morning and stopped at a chalet halfway down for lunch. While eating a meal of sausages, potato salad, and mulled wine, they heard the announcement over the radio that Hindenburg had just appointed Hitler to be chancellor. "I think it's time to leave," said Billie; "I'd like to have some coffee and some pastry first," replied Hella. Billie claimed he had to explain what he meant.

They returned to Berlin, and Billie sold his belongings in very short order. For safety's sake, he converted his deutsche marks into dollars—he had $1,000—and prepared himself emotionally as well as materially to become a refugee. "It wasn't my idea," he later said; "It was Hitler's." In one account, Wilder allegedly gave part of his art collection "to an Aryan friend in case I should ever come back," but after the war his so-called friend denied knowing anything about it.

Hitler's rise was swift; Wilder's paranoia was, if anything, even swifter, but neither precluded a good meal. On the night of February 27, he and Hella were dining at a fine restaurant when they looked out the window and noticed that the Reichstag was on fire. According to one account, Hella's father sped them to Zoo station the following morning and they took the train to Paris. More likely, it took a few more days. "It wasn't easy," Wilder later said, "because many people wanted to go, and many wanted to sell as fast as possible as much as possible." In yet another version of the story, he remembered the moment at which he decided to leave Germany. It wasn't in Davos, nor was it at the Adlon or the Kempinski, but rather on an ordinary street on an otherwise forgettable day in Berlin: "One day I watched them beating an old Jew on the Zinnstrasse in broad daylight. Nearly thirty SS men. Strong guys. Butchers. They were writing '*Judengeschäft*' [Jewish shop] on a store window when they saw the old man with his hat, long whiskers, and coat. They battered him mercilessly. And I was just standing there, completely helpless, with tears in my eyes and my fists clenched in my pockets. The next day was the Reichstag fire."

The Nazi threat was scarcely theoretical at this point. Many (if not most) of Wilder's friends and colleagues were either Jews or leftists. Egon Erwin Kisch was quickly arrested along with many other Communists, but thanks to the intervention of the Prague Parliament, Kisch was released and deported to Czechoslovakia. Wilder never saw his friend again. (Kisch survived the war in South America and Mexico; he then returned to Prague, where he died in 1948.)

Robert Siodmak's new film, *Brennendes Geheimnis* (*Burning Mystery*), made its all-too-appropriate premiere the night of the Reichstag fire. Everyone thought it was a funny coincidence, but, less amusingly, the film disappeared from the screens three days later and Siodmak found himself hunted by storm troopers.

Wilder had given up his luxury apartment at the Sächsischen Palais and spent his final days in Berlin in a room at the Hotel Majestic on Brandenburgischenstrasse, where he was awaked one night around 4:00 A.M. by two detectives knocking on his door. Wilder said he panicked, having been browsing through an anti-Hitler pamphlet as bedtime reading, but it had fallen between the bed and the wall and the detectives didn't see it.

Circumstances once again forced Billie Wilder to beat a hasty retreat from a city he loved, where he had worked hard to establish himself, and where he had innumerable friends. This time, however, most of the friends were running with him. But unlike many of them, Billie made a shrewd choice. He did not escape to another German-speaking country, where, with reasonable speed, he could have found his way into a relatively secure position. No, Billie's survivor's instincts had never been sharper. He was paranoid, and correctly so. Those of Wilder's friends who fled to Vienna and Prague were, in his view even at the time, all too shortsighted. Billie spoke no English, but he could understand French well enough so he opted for Paris.

Wherever they were headed, Jews and Communists left Berlin as fast as possible. Many if not most of Wilder's friends and colleagues left on or around the same time: Kolpe, Reisch, Marcus, and both of the Siodmak brothers; Lustig, Liebmann, Schüfftan, Holländer, and Wachsmann; Remarque, Berger, Pasternak, and Kohner. Producers and directors, writers and actors, musicians and editors—Ufa was immediately decimated, much to the Nazis' joy. Erik Charell, Paul Czinner, E. A. Dupont, and Leopold Jessner fled. The director Joe May, one of Ufa's top moneymakers, ran for his life, along with his wife, the glamorous actress Mia May. So did Ernö Metzner, Max Ophuls, Richard Oswald, Erwin Piscator, Max Reinhardt, Hans Richter, Fritz Lang, Leontine Sagan, Hanns Schwarz, Wilhelm Thiele, and Robert Wiene. Erich Pommer, Josef Somlo, Heinrich Nebenzahl, Seymour Nebenzal, Hermann Millkowski, Felix Joachimson, Arnold Pressburger, Gregor Rabinowitsch bailed out as well. Screenwriters Vicky Baum, Bruno Frank, Hans Wilhelm, Friedrich Kohner, Robert Thoeren fled. Cameramen Günther Krampf and Franz Planer, composers Hanns Eisler, Werner Richard Heymann, Walter Jurmann, Bronislaw Kaper, Hans Salter, and Kurt Weill—all escaped. Actors Peter Lorre, Gitta Alpar, Albert Bassermann, Elisabeth Bergner, Ernst Busch, Ernst Deutsch, Therese Giehse, Alexander Granach, Fritz Kortner, Szöke Szakall, and Conrad Veidt left Germany. Cabaret writers and performers ran as well: Kurt Gerron, Valeska Gert, Paul Graetz, Fritz Mehring, Paul Morgan, Rudolf Nelson, Kurt Robitschek, Oskar Homolka, Paul Lukas, and Mischa Spolianoky joined the fifty thousand other people who fled Germany in 1933, and they were lucky to have had the chance. Carola Neher, Klabund's widow, chose to go in the other direction; she moved to the Soviet Union and died in a gulag in 1936. Most of these refugees found safer ports of refuge in the 1930s. Some did not have the foresight. Robert Liebmann stayed in Paris until he was rounded up when the Nazis seized control of France. They murdered him in a death camp.

With the departure of these artists an entire way of life disappeared. "What happened to the novelists?" asks Robert Lantz. "Alfred Knopf's whole publishing house was built on German novelists of the period. What happened? How could this have been? *Where? What?* It's a most peculiar thing. In the world of music it is almost more astonishing, because in Berlin, on any one evening—like tonight, a normal Tuesday evening—there were more first-rank conductors performing on a routine evening in Berlin than now exist in the entire world. What happened? Where is everybody? When you really break a heart, people die. It wasn't just a phase. If you break the spirit, it dies. And that's what happened in Germany."

Despite the fact that Hermann Goering was appointed president of the Reichstag at the end of August, Wilder later reported with characteristic irony that regardless of the elections, the street fighting, the demonstrations, and the hideous rhetoric, he and his friends didn't take the Nazis very seriously until the end of 1932: "But what happened then was one of the little caprices of mother history." Wilder's description of the Reichstag fire is equally classic: "The son of Hindenburg was involved in some kind of monetary scandal, and in order to blow out that fire, Hindenburg demoted the liberal chancellor, General Schleicher, and appointed Mr. Hitler out of nowhere. Mr. von Hindenburg was slightly gaga at the time. He was promised the constitution would stay the way it was and you could vote for different parties. But to grab all the power, Mr. Hitler got hold of a young Dutchman who was slightly out of his mind, locked him up in the Reichstag, and started the fire there. And Mr. Hitler said, 'You see what the Communists have done? There will be no other parties—only the National Socialist party.' "

At a party given for Ernst Lubitsch in December 1932, the journalist Bella Fromm asked the visiting director why he was no longer working in Germany. Lubitsch replied, "That's finished. I'm going to the United States. Nothing good is going to happen here for a long time. The sun shines every day in Hollywood."

Unlike Lubitsch, Billie had no international career to support him. He was long gone from Berlin and eking out an impoverished existence in a fleabag Paris hotel when *Was Frauen träumen* enjoyed its gala premiere, specially timed to occur on April 20, 1933, the night of Hitler's forty-fourth birthday. But by then, of course, the name of Billie Wilder had been deleted from all the prints.

6. ESCAPE

Paris is for lovers. Maybe that's why I stayed only thirty-five minutes.

—Linus Larrabee (Humphrey Bogart) in *Sabrina*

F rantic, frightened, and prudent, the two refugees arrived in Paris. Hella is said to have brought along as much jewelry and as many furs as she could manage as well as a stock of gold coins. Billie, on the other hand, had a single suitcase. He kept the $1,000 tucked away in his hatband.

Then again, maybe not. Walter Reisch recalled that he, not Hella, was Billie's traveling companion: "Hitler took over Berlin in January of '33. A few days later Wilder and I left for Paris." Sports, not housing or employment, was their primary concern: "Our first stop when we got off the train was not at the producer's office. Our first stop in Paris was at the Stade Roland Garros to see a French-English tennis match. That was the most important event when Hitler came to power." Wilder told a *Playboy* interviewer in 1960 that he carried with him only "one suitcase and a bunch of rolled-up canvases," checking them at the station and rushing off to catch Fred Perry and Bunny Austin in the Davis Cup. Billy revised the story later, declaring that he couldn't have carried any rolled-up canvases because he hadn't owned any. He told others over the years that they were posters, not paintings, and that his passport was Polish, not Austrian.

The precise details don't really matter. The salient point is that Billie Wilder demonstrated unusual prescience by leaving Berlin for a non-German-speaking country on drastically short notice, and he arrived in a strange city with $1,000 and a few friends. His nationality was a matter of opinion, which wasn't at all surprising, since that had been the problem all along.

As always, Wilder had read up on Paris and knew enough of the lay of the land to find a hotel room without too much difficulty. Armed with a list of what Zolotow colorfully describes as "rather louche hotels which weren't too serious about making you register," Billie found "a fleabag on the Boulevard Raspail," the key feature of which was its view of a Montparnasse cemetery. He quit the place the same day and checked into the ever-so-slightly more respectable Ansonia, a tawdry residential hotel that had become temporary headquarters for some of the many recent German exiles who were showing up in Paris. The French called them *apatrides*, people without a country. A whole group of them moved into the Ansonia. Friedrich Holländer was there, as was Franz Wachsmann and his wife, Alice. Wachsmann had arranged and conducted Holländer's score for *The Blue Angel*. The talented composer's film career was just taking off when he was beaten up by Nazi thugs on a Berlin street—a good incentive for him to leave Germany with the rest of Ufa's Jews.

Peter Lorre took up residence at the Ansonia as well. "It was located on the rue de Saigon, one of these little streets between l'avenue Foch and l'avenue de la Grande-Armée," Wilder recalled. "No one had much money, but life was cheap. On the street corner there was a restaurant, the Select, with a *prix-fixe* menu of seven francs. We would leave our napkins on the rack to pick them up in the evenings. Very petit bourgeois."

Billie moved into a room on the third floor of the dank hotel. "The rooms are small but dirty," Holländer wrote in his memoirs—"dirty but cheap." Depression and despair ran rampant in what Holländer describes as this "nest for the expelled, refuge of the expropriated, holding tank, transition camp, hotbed for all kinds of premature births—of ideas for the future to suicide plans." If the Ansonians weren't lying in their beds asking themselves what the hell they were going to do next, they were at the Select or the Brasserie Strasbourg across the street from the hotel; and if they weren't there, they were "preparing their tea, eggs, or morphine injection on a small gas cooker in their rooms."

Holding no work permit, Wilder couldn't write screenplays under his own name. To compound his difficulties, his spoken French may have been rather good (he'd evidently been practicing since his brush with flunking in high school), but because he thought in German, he still had to write in German and then translate everything into French. Billie nevertheless managed to maintain the air of a bon vivant, at least in public. He was, after all, in Paris, and he might as well have a good time. Holländer reports that he was struck by Wilder's ability to pull off an elegant demeanor in the face of near-abject poverty. While the others were huddling over their cookers, Billie was heading out on the town, "as if thoroughly convinced that new money could only come if the old stuff was gone." "What does he know?" Holländer asks. "He knows that he has a brilliant little head that he takes care of like the head of a brilliant pin whose worth lies in the future."

Lorre, his wife, Cilly, and the Wachsmanns lived upstairs on the fifth floor. Max Kolpe, Jan Lustig, and Paul Erich Marcus each lived on the first. Kolpe had the biggest room, so when the émigrés got together to scheme for the future or bemoan the past, they often met there. Bitching was an essential activity. They all resented the émigré upper crust, who shunned not only the Ansonia but the Ansonians and (in Holländer's memorable phrase) their "suspect smell of paltriness." The director Joe May and his wife, Mia, for instance, had rented a villa at the edge of the Bois de Boulogne. According to Holländer, the Mays were on the pretentious side. In Germany, Joe May directed extravagant blockbusters under the banner of his own production company. It is only a slight exaggeration to call him the Weimar Steven Spielberg. Lang and Murnau made expensive art films, but May kept pulling in the crowds for over fifteen years with a string of big entertainments. Mia May, too, was no struggling refugee but a movie star in her own right. Though they were now refugees, the Mays didn't share any of the financial anxieties that plagued the other refugees. Mia, according to rumor, managed to smuggle her jewelry out of Germany by embedding them on the shell of her pet turtle, Cleopatra, who, following contemporary fashion, was already sporting enough costume jewelery that the border guards didn't notice the real ones. Fritz Lang, meanwhile, was ensconced at the luxurious Hotel George V.

While the "emigrants deluxe" were wining and dining and keeping up appearances in Paris, the Ansonians weren't as lucky. Some days they all just stayed in bed. It wasn't just a kind of bohemian narcolepsy, but also a healthy form of hibernation, a protective coma in response to an unbearable trauma. Billie, of course, was too restless to sleep all day. His was a more public hibernation—he needed to be out to be calm. Despite the presence of Hella (whose existence in France is given further support by Holländer, though in his account she's merely Billie's nameless girlfriend), Billie was known to head over to the Avenue Wagram, where a red-haired whore nicknamed *die Spinne* (the Spider) entertained him—at a special discount rate for émigrés. She may have been cheap, but *die Spinne* didn't shove Billie and her other clients out the door too soon. She didn't mind just lounging around listening to them go on and on about their own woes and regrets and the beautiful city from which they ran. As Holländer put it, "One could lie beside her all night long and tell her about the Bayreuth-erstrasse and the Grunewaldsee."

Equally productive were the days the melancholy crew spent hatching movie ideas. Meeting in Kolpe's room, the émigrés tried to figure out a way to make a movie and have someone else pay for it. One idea had to do with a crazed sex killer. Wilder, Lustig, Kolpe, Lorre, Holländer, and Wachsmann were sitting in Kolpe's room one day struggling to figure out a plot for this opus. "I've just figured out the problem in your script," Lorre suddenly shouted. "The character of our sex killer is lacking something essential—loving-kindness! Now if *I* were to play this role, this figure would have something universal, something popular—something that appeals to the common man with his childlike mind, namely . . ." Lorre didn't get an enthusiastic reception, and he didn't react well: "It doesn't matter to you if I play him or not! Then naturally *I don't have to!*" And he didn't, because the film—like most of the other failed projects dreamed up at the Ansonia—was never made.

Another project did progress all the way from inspiration to celluloid. Billie wrote it and, having no other choice, codirected it as well. *Mauvaise Graine (Bad Seed)* is a film about mobility, the way the world looks from a moving camera. The story concerns a young man's undying urge to keep himself from getting stuck in one place. Henri Pasquier will do anything to keep moving, including grand larceny. In Wilder's view as well as that of his protagonist, the worst thing in the world is to have your wheels taken away from you; the freedom-loving Henri steals other people's cars so he can stay mobile. Wilder's own restlessness propels his story, and his time at Ufa instilled in him a love of the moving camera. *Mauvaise Graine*'s plot may be about a rich young man's descent into a life of crime, but its real subject is the pure, formal beauty of traveling shots—buildings, cars, trees, people, all sailing across the screen in an endless flow of motion. The first image in Billy Wilder's career as a director is that of a spinning tire; the film ends with a moving shot of rolling waves, the camera hurtling forward, skimming the water toward an indefinite goal.

Sparked by the young refugee's own fidgety, unsettled life in the Ansonia, and driven by his hot ambition, *Mauvaise Graine* pieced itself together by circumstance. There's a catch-as-catch-can quality to the work, just as there is with *Menschen am Sonntag*, but Wilder and his codirector, Alexandre Esway, turn this piecemeal filmmaking style to their advantage. Where strict narrative formulas and studio-quality visuals would have been (had there been more time, money, and equipment), spontaneity and a sense of unsteady life appear.

Wilder pulled the script together with two other Ansonians, both friends from Berlin—Jan Lustig and Max Kolpe. (The three writers had some help from Claude-Andre Puget). Like Wilder, Lustig had been a newspaperman in Berlin and had written scripts for Ufa. Knowing that they wouldn't be likely to have the money to build extensive sets, they devised a screenplay that, like *Menschen am Sonntag*, could be filmed mostly outdoors at public locations that would entail no cost, while the indoor sequences could be shot using cheaply constructed sets that required nothing exceptional in the way of decoration. The idea was to tell the story of an irresponsible youth, the bad-seed son of a wealthy Parisian doctor, who falls into a life of crime after his father sells his car out from under him. There would be a girl, of course, and some comic sidekicks; there would be some kind of chase; they'd go to the south of France and film some sequences there; they would try to find financing.

According to Kolpe, "Everything looked perfect." At first. These were eager, ambitious young men—professional schmoozers. They knew how to talk a good game, at least enough to convince other people that the project was professional enough to film. But the realities of picture making struck quickly in the form of a producer who was eager not only to sign onto the project but also to finance it, with a certain string attached: Monsieur Gaillart of the Panthéon Filament Company expressed interest in financing a film as long as his wife played the lead. Wilder and Esway got as far as giving the would-be starlet a screen test, but according to Kolpe she was terrible. The financier threatened to withdraw his support if she didn't win the part. Disgusted, Wilder was willing to say *auf wiedersehen* to the financier, the wife, and the certainty of the production and start again from zero, but the other two producers were eager to make the film at any price and gave their go-ahead, sending the others into panicky despair. "One seldom saw a sadder bunch trotting along the banks of the Seine back to the hotel," Kolpe later recalled.

There was another problem as well: as ambitious as Wilder was, a deep insecurity about actually directing *Mauvaise Graine* kept nagging at him. He knew he could write, but the technical complexities of directing terrified him. Had he and his cowriters found someone else to direct it, Wilder would gladly have yielded the authority. But he and his Ansonia neighbors were accent-bearing refugees from Berlin. They were nobodies in the Paris film community, and *Mauvaise Graine* was scarcely a hot property. If *Mauvaise Graine* was to be made at all, it seemed, Billie would have to direct it.

So the moment a potential codirector appeared on the scene, Wilder agreed. Alexandre Esway was as much of a nomad as Wilder, and he had what the French film historian Jean-Pierre Jeancolas generously called "an elusive personality." Born in Budapest (probably), Esway had already spent some time in both London and Berlin before arriving in Paris in 1931 or 1932. By the time he met Wilder, he'd already directed *Taxi for Two* (Britain, 1924), *Children of Chance* (Britain, 1931), and *Shadows* (Britain, 1931), and codirected *Le jugement de minuit* (1932), and *Une vie perdue* (1933). Wilder brought Esway onto the project to provide stability and expertise, but there was another payoff, too, for it was Esway—perhaps on the basis of his having actually had some directing experience—who convinced a new producer, Edouard Corniglion-Molinier, to finance the film. Within a matter of days, the previous producer and his wife disappeared, Corniglion-Molinier agreed to pay for the film, and the ingenue role (albeit a criminal ingenue) went to Danielle Darrieux, who, at seventeen, knew precisely what she was doing in front of a camera, having already made seven films since the age of fourteen.

"I directed it with another cineaste and I don't remember how we found the money," Billy told critic Michel Ciment in an interview in the early 1980s. M. Corniglion-Molinier was doubtless more memorable at the time. A World War I flying ace who had made a great deal of money and owned a film production facility in Nice, Corniglion-Molinier found the project appealing and marketable enough to finance, but he was shrewd enough to keep a tight rein on the budget. According to Wilder, not only did they have to improvise much of the filming, but "for lack of money we couldn't use rear projections—the camera and the projectors were placed on a truck and it was rather dangerous." *Mauvaise Graine* is far better for it; rear projection would have looked considerably worse than the vertiginous sweep of a moving camera. When shooting moved to the south of France, the filmmakers didn't even have enough money to afford hotel rooms. Still, *Mauvaise Graine* benefited from its own adversity, just as *Menschen am Sonntag* had. There's an electric quality to the location shooting—a sense of experiment and play. In fact, as Wilder has been the first to note, *Mauvaise Graine*'s ellipses, jump cuts, and ingenuously shaky camerawork look ahead to *Breathless*.

For the story of *Mauvaise Graine*, Wilder and his cowriters constructed a tale of youthful exuberance that leads, paradoxically, not only to catastrophe but to freedom. An opening title tells us that "Happy people don't have stories. This isn't entirely true—Henri Pasquier is very happy, but the one thing he needs is a new car horn." Henri (Pierre Mingand) is rich, young, and supremely irresponsible. Wilder and Esway introduce him roaring through the streets of Paris at high speed, the camera mounted on the back of Henri's car as it flies around curves, into and out of a traffic circle, and finally—in a rapidly edited sequence of shots—careening into a garage and nearly running down several bystanders. In short order, Henri picks up an attractive young woman and sets up a date with her for later that day, but when he arrives back at his father's office to beg some money, he discovers that his father has sold the car and rendered him not only immobile but bourgeois. "It's time for you to go out and get a job," Dr. Pasquier (Paul Escoffier) demands, and Henri is suitably appalled: "And go work in some office earning a thousand francs a week?"

An intertitle announces, "One Parisian out of eight has a car. Henri Pasquier is now one of the other seven." Wilder and Esway cut to an expressionistic comedy montage of Henri walking, dejected to the point of a nightmare; superimposed onto his image are spinning steering wheels, rapidly advancing clocks, speeding cars, and Henri's own close-up, staring forward as if caught in the mind-controlling stare of Dr. Caligari himself. It's a funny sequence, but a fairly obvious one, nothing a second-tier Ufa director with a glancing familiarity with *Metropolis* and a taste for pastiche couldn't have produced. More sophisticated is the way Wilder and Esway handle the moment at which Henri decides to become a car thief. They don't bother to show it. Henri is standing on the sidewalk, looking absently at his reflection in a store window. In the reflection, a car pulls up at the curb, and a man gets out and heads into the building, at which point Wilder and Esway pan from the window to the car itself just as another car pulls up alongside. Cutting back and forth from Henri to the car keys left in the ignition to the men in the other car, Wilder and Esway elide the actual moment of Henri's decision to steal the car, preferring instead to present an extreme long shot of Henri driving away from the camera after the fact. Given the absolute wordlessness of the sequence, together with the clarity and impact of its visuals, it's impossible to believe (as so many critics still do) that Wilder became a director simply to protect his screenplays. As much as Wilder himself claimed to have detested the overwhelming responsibilities of directing it, *Mauvaise Graine* is the work of a visual stylist, not a wordsmith.

With the camera mounted on the back of the stolen car, Wilder and Esway force their audience to experience this crime as a form of liberation. The long-take shot of Henri picking up the young woman in the park is as fluid and elegantly simple as anything Murnau and Karl Freund achieved in the controlled conditions of a studio. The audience comes as close as possible to experiencing the pickup from Henri's point of view: the car swings around a curve; we see the woman in the far distance; as she gets closer, she walks toward the car; the car stops and she gets in, and the car takes off again. Wilder and Esway don't make the obvious cut right away, either. They don't cut in to conventional, predictable close-ups or medium shots of the two characters, but instead they keep the shot going as the car sails around a traffic circle in a graceful spin of motion.

Thieving isn't particularly a problem for Wilder. As with *Was Frauen träumen*, there's no sense of any real wrongdoing as far as grand larceny is concerned. If anything, auto theft is presented as a comic triumph, a redistribution of wealth from those who cannot fully appreciate their cars to those who do. The gang of thieves into which Henri falls are all winning, likable characters, with the notable exception of the boss of the operation

(Michel Duran), whose greatest crime in Wilder's view is that he treats his employees badly. The gang members, on the other hand, are thoroughly appealing, from the beautiful and clever Jeannette (Darrieux) and her boyish brother, Jean-le-cravatte (Raymond Galle), to the drunken, outrageously attired Zebra (Jean Wall), and the Franco-African mechanic Gaby (G. Heritier). *Mauvaise Graine* never bothers to question the morality of their livelihood, let alone censure them for it. In fact, Jean-le-cravatte compounds his grand larceny with petty crimes by stealing every tie he sees (hence his nickname), an activity the film treats as harmless fun. The only force of moral reaction comes in the form of Henri's scowling, killjoy father.

When Henri sends Jean-le-cravatte to Dr. Pasquier's apartment to collect his belongings, Henri kills time by stealing a convertible coupe. When the gang swipes the car of a ridiculously short man who sets his hat on the dashboard, they leave the poor man's hat parked in its place at the curb. Breaking the law isn't the problem. Boredom is. When Jean-le-cravatte and Henri steal yet another car, Jean breathlessly says to his new friend, "Isn't this incredible? Doesn't it thrill you? Is your heart palpitating?" "You mean you don't feel any fear?" Henri asks, and Jean, reiterating Henri's own terror of settling into bourgeois conformity, responds, "You know, pal, what really scares *me* is working in an office."

Mauvaise Graine does work itself around to some vague recognition of the illegality of car theft, but only to the extent that the story needs a climactic scene. Henri does conclude that his devil-may-care life is out of control, but even this revelation occurs not because of a moral awakening but rather because the likable Jean-le-cravatte is shot to death—by the police. The boss, tired of Henri's egalitarian attitudes toward the gang's profits (Henri having forced the boss to share more of the loot), sends Henri and Jeannette to the south of France on an errand and sabotages their car, after which Henri and Jeannette decide to begin a new life together abroad. Henri returns to Paris to pick up Jean-le-cravatte, but the police raid the garage and mortally wound Jean. Wilder and Esway handle the raid itself in a style bordering on farce—the Keystone Kops were only nominally less competent—thereby undercutting whatever moral force the law represents. But the directors shift the tone suddenly when Jean is wounded, making the scene in which Henri takes the dying Jean to his father's office the only harsh scene in the film. Yet even here, Wilder and Esway don't descend into sentimentality. They block the scene in such a way that Henri stands slightly to the left, the boy's body lies on a table in the center, and the doctor stands in front of the corpse with his back to the camera. Cutting back and forth between Henri and Dr. Pasquier, Wilder and Esway never include a shot of the dead boy's face—it's all between Henri and his father.

When Dr. Pasquier sends his son away for good there's barely a trace of emotion.

Henri's reunion with Jeannette, filmed in a series of extreme long shots, has a similar affective distance. Jeannette's reaction to her brother's death is thoroughly restrained. Wilder and Esway are eager to get the couple onto the ship, toning down the emotional resolution of the narrative in favor of motion—the look of the waves, the size and form of the ship as it sets sail. The camera is still in motion at the end of the film, tilting down from the ship to the rippling waves in the wake of the speedboat in which the camera has been set. We're moving, too. The camera is even more restless than any of these unsettled characters; it has a drive of its own, distinct from the restlessness of Henri and Jeannette. They remain on the ship we've left behind as Wilder and Esway's camera speeds us out on the water toward nothing in particular.

Mauvaise Graine didn't open until the summer of 1934, long after Wilder had left Paris. In the meantime, Billie was still killing time at the Ansonia, and it still wasn't good enough. Having white-knuckled his way through the filming of *Mauvaise Graine*, he decided that he didn't have the resilience to be a film director. Writing in cafés and hotel rooms, taking potshots at fools over coffee and cigarettes—these were his talents. Worrying about whether actors would remember his dialogue, whether a sudden cloud would spoil the light, the camera jamming, transportation, sound conditions on the location, a little wind in the microphone—these were not simple irritants. They were hell, and he vowed he would never direct another motion picture again.

He did, however, keep writing scripts and sending them to his upscale Ufa friend Joe May, who had left his transitional Paris villa and moved to Los Angeles to become a producer at Columbia Pictures. One of these screenplays, called *Pam-Pam*, was the blueprint for a musical, the setup of which had a familiar ring. *Pam-Pam* was the story of a runaway youth—a girl this time—who lives in an abandoned Broadway theater and joins a gang of criminals—counterfeiters rather than car thieves. Together they put on a show. Billie already had his first Hollywood credit—Fox had remade *Ihre Hoheit befiehlt* in the spring of 1933 as *Adorable* with Janet Gaynor. Despite the fact that he was just another German-speaking Jew pacing around a none-too-elegant refugee hotel in Paris, there was still the chance that *somebody* in Hollywood might recognize his name and see the talent it represented.

Pam-Pam may not have been the most inspired of Wilder's creations, but it worked—at least to the extent of winning him his first Hollywood deal. In December, May cabled Wilder in Paris with the news that the producer Sam Briskin at Columbia was ready to buy *Pam-Pam* as a story idea. The studio would pay him $150 a week to write the screenplay. More important, Columbia would pay for his ticket—one-way only—from Paris to Los Angeles. Having no particular reason to stay in France, Wilder took the offer. Genia, having remarried earlier that year, was living reasonably comfortably in Vienna with her new husband, a businessman named Siedlisker. The Nazis' power was expanding, and for Billie, there was no safety in returning to a German-speaking city. The already infamous book burning took place in Berlin in May 1933, with the works of Jewish writers like Heine, Marx, Freud, and Zweig, gay writers like Magnus Hirschfeld, and leftist writers such as Mann, Brecht, Remarque, and Sinclair tossed gleefully in a heap and set ablaze. By mid-October it was a crime even to buy these books in Germany.

As for Billie's career, the French film establishment wasn't scrambling to hire him as a screenwriter, and he had no intention of trying to put together another film for himself to write and direct in France. Willie, on the other hand, was in the States (albeit on the East Coast), and he seemed to be making a go of it. Wilder hadn't seen his brother for twelve years, but at least he would have somebody to meet him on his arrival in a new country. According to Wilder, Hollywood was his goal all along; it had simply been a matter of getting there. Other Austro-German émigrés hadn't rushed to the United States right away, since they thought they'd return to Germany eventually, if later rather than sooner. Billie, on the other hand, didn't care if he returned. He obtained a temporary visa, arranged to stay with Willie and his family in a New York suburb, and wrapped up his life in Paris. Hella would not be accompanying him.

On January 22, 1934, Billie Wilder set sail on the *Aquitania*. He chose a British ship so he could work on his English, having learned little more than a few foul phrases to complement the jazz lyrics that kept buzzing in his brain. He took with him a few American novels he'd bought at an English-language bookstore on the Place de l'Opéra—Hemingway's *A Farewell to Arms*, Lewis's *Babbitt*, and Wolfe's *Look Homeward, Angel*—and, reportedly, a mere eleven dollars in cash. More valuable, though, was the relentless nervous energy he carried with him wherever he went. He paced his way across the Atlantic.

PART TWO
1934–1941

7. TO HOLLYWOOD

Scene B-8. Interior. Iscovescu's Room. Iscovescu is pacing the floor restlessly, cane in hand. As he passes the washstand, his eyes fall on something. He stops. A cockroach is crawling down the wall on its way to a haven behind the blotchy mirror. Iscovescu raises his stick.

ISCOVESCU *(to the cockroach):* Where do you think you are going?! You're not a citizen, are you? Where's *your* quota number?!

He smashes the cockroach with his stick.

—*Hold Back the Dawn*

It is a fantastic commentary on the inhumanity of our times that for thousands and thousands of people, a piece of paper with a stamp on it is the difference between life and death." This is the moral judgment of the journalist Dorothy Thompson, writing in the late 1930s. It was too late to save most of these countless thousands by then. Billie Wilder arrived in the United States in 1934 armed with foresight, a few dollars, a six-week job on the other side of the continent, and a piece of paper with a stamp on it. He was lucky to get into the United States when he did. Characteristically, he made the right choice and survived. Others delayed, gambled, settled. They denied the threat, relaxed their guard, and suffered for it.

Willie Wilder, materially in better shape than his younger brother, was living in spare middle-class comfort in Baldwin, New York, one of a string of suburbs that bulge and spread along the south shore of Long Island. Apart from offering his younger brother a few days' bed and board, Willie also had the fraternal pleasure of introducing Billie to Manhattan, the concrete mirage Genia had been bubbling about all those years—the sheer immensity of the city and the vigorous stability it represented. Dreams, loves, crimes, scams, talents, possibilities: Billie, of course, had seen it all before. As Lotte Lenya recalled of her own introduction to New York, "We had no first impressions, for we had all seen the movies of von Sternberg and von Stroheim." The difference was that now Billie could actually smell it for himself.

In spite of the Depression, Willie had made a good life for himself in the States, fashioning purses. Willie had a family as well, a wife and son, and his brother saw that the steady hum of daily life in the States could be most appealing, given certain adjustments. (Hollywood, not Baldwin; movies, not purses; lots of women, not a wife.)

For Wilder, the new world represented a triumph of liberal democracy. True, the rich were earnestly attempting to dismantle Roosevelt's New Deal and thinking up new ways to smash the unions, but then again the rich weren't Nazis and the United States wasn't likely to turn fascist, at least not literally. There were certainly stray swastika-scrawlers lurking around Yorkville and the other German neighborhoods of greater New York, murmuring of the Fatherland's new dawn, but generally they knew enough to keep a fairly low profile. Jews, meanwhile, were everywhere. It was just like Berlin, except that here nobody had to run for their lives. On the streets of New York, in theaters and stores, in the business world, even in the circle of advisors to the president, American Jews were thriving. They were famous for their control of the American film industry: Mayer and Thalberg at MGM; Cohn at Columbia; the Warner brothers; Zukor at Paramount; the amazing Goldfish, now Goldwyn, one of the two driving forces behind United Artists' independent productions; Nicholas Schenck, the other driving force. . . .

On the other hand, Hollywood's top directors weren't Jewish, Lubitsch being a key exception (and he had already earned an international reputation by the time he got to Hollywood). There weren't too many Jewish stars, either—the Marx Brothers, Paul Muni, Al Jolson. But behind the scenes, there were as many Jewish writers in Hollywood as there had been at Ufa. Some of Hollywood's most successful screenwriters were Jews: Ben Hecht, Samson Raphaelson, Herman Mankiewicz, S. J. Perelman, Morrie Ryskind, Sidney Buchman, Jules Furthman, George S. Kaufman. Billie was eager to become one himself. What he didn't already know about Hollywood screenwriting he could learn. And he could bluff his way into anything.

He had a very long train trip to think about it. None of his earlier migrations could compare. Kraków is 200 miles from Vienna, and Vienna is 320 miles from Berlin. From Berlin to Paris is roughly 550 miles. But from New York to Los Angeles by train is well over 2,500 miles. The Twentieth Century took him to Chicago—when he got to work at Columbia Pictures he'd hear about the John Barrymore comedy they were making about that train—and the Chief took him the rest of the way to California. It took fifty-five hours from Chicago on the Chief, which already had a reputation as "a rolling boudoir for film celebrities." The route took him straight through the heart of the American West—Dodge City, Zuni,

Canyon Diablo, Pisgah—speeding through flat, corny plains and empty, dusty deserts until he reached Los Angeles.

Joe May himself met Billie downtown and took him back to his house in the Hollywood Hills. The Mays were no longer on quite such a high financial horse. They arranged with Billie the terms of his room and board—it would be seventy-five dollars a week, half of Billie's salary.

He immediately found that his daily routine was far from glamorous, and it offered more than its share of humiliation. Scriptwriting in a foreign language was lonely, exasperating work, especially for a writer who worked best and most comfortably in collaboration. Moreover, Columbia was still a second-rate studio, albeit a large and successful one. Its fortunes began to rise dramatically even during the few weeks Wilder was there, owing to the phenomenal success of the studio's new comedy, *It Happened One Night*, which had just been released. But Columbia's head, Harry Cohn, was an infamous penny-pincher, crass even by Hollywood standards. Cohn had recently redecorated his office to resemble that of the cartoonish Italian dictator, Benito Mussolini. He already had the matching temper.

Columbia didn't maintain a stable of stars, writers, and directors as the bigger studios tended to do. Instead, Cohn struck deals to borrow stars from elsewhere—for *It Happened One Night*, Clark Gable came from MGM and Claudette Colbert from Paramount. Cohn hired most of his writers on a film-by-film basis as well. Columbia wasn't alone in this practice. In November of 1933, MGM copied the miserly Cohn and began hiring writers on a per-project basis and firing them as soon as their work was done, and the trade papers predicted (wrongly, as it happened) that staff writers would eventually be eliminated entirely. It was for this reason, among others, that Hollywood writers began leaving the producer-dominated Academy of Motion Picture Arts and Sciences in 1933 and joining the more radical and rambunctious Screen Writers Guild. Hollywood's producers were enraged, including the otherwise benign Irving Thalberg. Darryl Zanuck, taking it further than most others, was quoted as saying, "If those guys set up a picket line and try to shut down my studio, I'll mount a machine gun on the roof and mow them down." This is the community into which Billie Wilder walked in 1934.

On his first day on the Columbia lot, when May introduced him to Sam Briskin, Cohn's right hand, Briskin was visibly shaken when he realized that the studio's newest screenwriter barely spoke English. He angrily dispatched the embarrassed immigrant to the Writers' Building in short order.

Billie was better off working on *Pam-Pam* at the Mays' house, by himself. He received some translation assistance from an American who spoke German, while an old friend from Vienna, Reginald LeBorg, tutored him in English. Six weeks later, he turned in his first draft. It impressed nobody, and *Pam-Pam* died.

One wonders whether anyone ever had any real intention of making *Pam-Pam*, or whether Joe May simply took the first available opportunity to finance yet another Jewish refugee's passage out of Europe using a tiny sum of corporate funds that would never be missed. According to Wilder, *Pam-Pam* "never got beyond a draft of a screenplay, with no final dialogue or anything like that. It did not work anyway, even if it had been in perfect English. They liked the original story, but they did not like what I did with it. It's forgotten." But what could May have expected from a writer who didn't even speak the language in which he was required to write? In his dealings with Briskin, May either covered up the fact that Wilder spoke only German and French, or else he lied outright.

In any event, at the end of the appointed six weeks of *Pam-Pam* neither May nor Briskin had anything more to offer at Columbia. There was now the visa problem to contend with. Since Wilder had entered the United States with a specific job and the job was now over, the American immigration service required that he leave the United States and reenter it on a new visa. (Either that or his tourist visa simply ran out; the circumstances of Wilder's emigration are murky.) As far as money was concerned, Billie had only what he'd earned for *Pam-Pam*—the portion he didn't hand over to Joe May for the rent. He had no permanent residence and no sponsor willing to sign on as his financial supporter should he become completely indigent.

Billie headed to Mexicali, a pungently squalid border town whose American sister city had the equally failed-festive name of Calexico. Thanks to the 1928 DeSoto coupe he managed to acquire with what remained of the *Pam-Pam* proceeds, getting down to Mexicali was not a problem. Getting back into Calexico—that was the trick.

The stream of immigrants trying to squeeze their way into the United States was growing, but the immigration department's control over the flow remained tight. Historians disagree violently on this point, but certain facts are clear: the Immigration Act of 1924 established national quotas for immigration, the Depression served to reduce the number of immigrants, and the national quotas were not filled through most of the 1930s, despite the urgency with which the Jews of Austria and Germany needed asylum. In 1930, under pressure from restrictionists in Congress, the State Department began to enforce the so-called public charge clause in the Immigration Act: "If the consular officer believes that the applicant may probably be a public charge at any time, even during a considerable period subsequent to his arrival, he must refuse the visa." This effectively cut immigration by 90 percent in the first five months. Anyone who knew Billie Wilder knew that he wasn't likely to sit still long enough to become a burden on the state. But to the American Immigration Service, an unemployed writer who spoke very little English would not have been the most promising candidate for a residency permit.

In 1933, fifty thousand refugees left Germany. Many headed for the United States. In April 1934, following President Roosevelt's personal directive, the State Department called on its consuls to give refugees "the most humane and favorable treatment under the law." Still, in 1934, only 13.7 percent of the quotas for Austrians and Germans were filled. In 1935, the number rose, but only to 20.2 percent. Why? One theory casts the problem in an economic light: owing to the Depression, fewer families and friends in America were able to sponsor refugees by paying for their transportation and guaranteeing that they wouldn't become public charges. The historians who float this argument point to the quotas and say: you see, America couldn't even fill its quotas. David Wyman, on the other hand, takes a far more critical view. Wyman, a preeminent historian of the Holocaust, sees America's failure to fill its quotas as evidence of the intense pressure to keep the refugees out: you see, he writes, America *wouldn't* even fill its quotas. But whatever the subsequent interpretations of history, the practical result of American immigration policy during the rise of Nazi power was that Mexicali, Tijuana, and other border towns from California to Texas were overrun with would-be Americans forced by America to wait, firmly on the other side of its doorstep. Conceivably, Billie could have sat in Mexicali for years. Some refugees did.

Industriously, Billie managed to jump to the head of the line and get back into the States without having to do anything more than make pleasant conversation with a border guard. Naturally he tells a story about this: according to Wilder, world cinema owes a debt to an anonymous consulate official in Calexico. When he accepted the Thalberg Award at the Academy Awards in 1988, Wilder took the occasion to thank the anonymous bureaucrat who approved his reentry into the United States despite Wilder's lack of proper papers. When he learned that the young émigré was going to be writing movies in Hollywood, the functionary is said to have told him, "Write some good ones." He stamped Billie's new visa instantly, thus enabling Wilder to enter the States and stay indefinitely. There is clearly something missing here, but since the official never surfaced to take credit for his cultural prescience, Wilder's tale is the only explanation available. According to the tale, it took a matter of minutes for the United States to officially recognize Billie Wilder as exactly what he had been since the day his family moved from Kraków to Vienna: a resident alien.

Returning to Los Angeles with his papers but still without a job, Billie moved into the ladies' room at the Chateau Marmont Hotel. Maybe. It wasn't *precisely* the ladies' room; it was a sort of antechamber to the ladies' room, a glorified closet with a Murphy bed that the hotel, then five years old, rented to Wilder for $70 or $75 a month. Wilder tells a different story every time. He moved there after returning from Mexicali, he moved there in 1935, he lived there with Peter Lorre, Lorre's apartment was somewhere else and cost $5 a week, his room was in fact the ladies' room, his room was *next* to the ladies' room. . . . Whatever it was, it was cheap. Wilder once said that the Chateau rented the room to him only on the condition that he keep the door securely locked. He claimed later to have objected— he didn't want to inconvenience the poor women—but the spoilsport at the desk demanded that he keep himself as well as his room under lock and key. According to that account, Wilder made himself at home and even decorated the tiny room with more of those phantom paintings he was said to carry with him whenever he moved; this time they were contemporary French works he'd picked up in Paris.

One sees, beneath the requisite bathroom joke, the loneliness and subtle brutality of his life as a refugee who'd just been hit by the heartless glare of Southern California: "When I could not sleep, when women were coming in and peeing and looking at me funny, when I [. . .] knew that war was on the way for Europe, suddenly I wasn't sure if I fitted in around here in Hollywood. I had the feeling I was not in the right country and I didn't know if there was a right country for me. Right here was the low point of my life." Whether or not he actually saw women urinating in his room is quite beside the point. Billie's life at the Chateau Marmont wasn't much fun, if for no other reason than it marked the first extended time in his life when it wasn't easy for him to talk. He had little desire to hang around with Germans and kvetch in his native tongue. He wanted to become an American—fast.

He was game for almost anything. According to a desk clerk at the Chateau, Wilder was quite the young roué: "I doubt if he dated the same girl twice," the clerk reports. One imagines that the term *date* is something of a euphemism; Billie on the make must have been quite a spectacle. In a more public vein, for either fifteen or fifty dollars (depending on when he tells the story), he plunged fully clothed into a Hollywood swimming pool and swam from end to end at the behest of another transplanted Jew— Erich Pommer, who obviously knew he'd get a good little show for his money. Wilder had always been something of a show-off, but he'd never before been clownish.

Billie was living alone at this point. He didn't have Joe and Mia May to speak German with over homemade goulash. But Wilder was stalwart, not to mention desperate, and he knew that his future lay in yet another foreign language. "You know, when you are a writer, when you are deprived of your language, you know, more or less, you are dead. So I searched for very handsome young ladies who only spoke English—that is a great help—I went to night school, I listened to the radio. I kind of tried to make a living by writing stories in German which were translated, and I sold a couple here and made a few thousand dollars."

Wilder made a conscious decision not to situate himself in the ghetto of Europe's dispossessed. "I learned by not associating myself with the refugee colony, by going around with new American friends, by listening to the radio. Perhaps it helps you to learn the language if you go into it cold. It pours into you and it stays."

"If you think *I* have an accent," Wilder commented on another occasion, "you should have heard Ernst Lubitsch." For Wilder and the other Germans living in Hollywood in 1934, Lubitsch represented the pinnacle of achievement. He was funny and vulgar in person, funny and sophisticated as a director, and he managed to make films that appealed to Americans without ever giving up being a Berliner himself. A favorite joke among the Germans who'd fled to the United States was that a refugee is nothing but "an imported exporter, a man who has lost everything but his accent." Wilder's accent has always been pronounced; Lubitsch's was far worse. "But he had a wonderful ear for American idiom and slang," Wilder continued. "You either have an ear or you don't, as van Gogh said."

For the refugees, a harsh accent was the least of their troubles. The precise cases, endless portmanteaus, and complex syntactical structure of the German language made their transition to English a strain. It required a thorough rearrangement of thought. In German, the verb usually comes at the end of the sentence; in English, it appears everywhere but. In German, conversation as well as written discourse, like a well-ordered stream through a series of civilized farms, flows. In English, such constructions are stilted. We like to get to the point and get there fast. For a displaced screenwriter—an adaptable one, anyway—American English lent itself to the kind of direct, immediate, constantly unfolding expressivity that German tended to thwart. Linguistically at least, American emotions are more straightforward. The violinist Yehudi Menuhin puts it this way: "When you start a sentence in German, you have to know at the beginning what the end will be. In English, you live the sentence through to the end. Emotion and thought go together. In German, they're divorced. Everything is abstract."

For a flexible storyteller like Billie Wilder—or Joseph Conrad or Vladimir Nabokov, for that matter—the new mix of languages was wondrous, pregnant with sounds and bursting with meaning. Wilder's ear picked up our slang as well as our pragmatic syntax, and his inventive, hard-edged mind found twentieth-century poetry in them. Puns, jokes, verbal color, even the modern-sounding American tones and resonances one could make in the mouth—all were deeply engaging to the young writer-raconteur. It was exciting for him to get laughs in a new language. He was still speaking in song lyrics. If anyone asked him if he hoped to go back to Berlin someday, he had a ready-made punch line: "Gee but I'd give the world to see that old gang of mine."

It was the Fox Film Corporation, not Paramount, that gave Billie Wilder his second screenwriting job in Hollywood. The movie was *Music in the Air*, an aggressively Bavarian operetta featuring lots of singing birds and Bavarian music and men wearing lederhosen and a quaint brass band in town playing for peasants dancing around the maypole in the marketplace. Fox purchased the rights in June 1933, for $50,000 against 10 percent of the gross. It was a big investment, but then the authors were Hammerstein and Kern, kings of Broadway, where the musical had been a big hit.

Music in the Air is a merry, meaningless venture. Two young lovers from the countryside, Karl and Sieglinde, travel to Munich and meet a pair of sophisticated, squabbling theater people, Bruno and Frida. A tangle ensues but everybody ends up singing. Fox's original plan was to shoot the picture in either London or Paris. A deal had been struck in 1933 for Erich Pommer, then head of Fox-Europa, to produce the film, and Pommer arranged with a German director, Ludwig Berger, to shoot it for simultaneous release in English, French, and German. Fox also hired Billie's friend Walter Reisch to adapt the property for film. But by the end of 1933, Fox-Europa was in trouble. It wasn't just that the Continent was continuing to unravel politically and socially. More troublesome from the point of view of foreign film production was the fact that Roosevelt devalued the dollar, thereby rendering Fox-Europa's production plans unfeasible. *Music in the Air* was on its way to Hollywood.

Fox continued its efforts to maintain the project's beery flavor by hiring even more displaced Germans: Robert Liebmann, in Paris, signed on as a scriptwriter in January 1934, and Franz Wachsmann agreed to adapt Jerome Kern's score in February. By March, Liebmann had sent in two drafts—one in German, the other in English—but staff writer and story editor Howard Irving Young wasn't impressed. The Karl character, for example, had become a little too blustery in Liebmann's adaptation. Liebmann had turned Hammerstein and Kern's schoolteacher into a mountain climber who had the annoying habit of hoisting women up in the air with his bare arms to show off his strength, a display of Bayerische-Alpen prowess that Young found idiotic. In response, Young wrote some new scenes himself and submitted them.

By June 1934, Joe May had moved from Columbia to Fox, and he signed onto *Music in the Air* as a writer. Pommer, having moved to Los

Angeles with what seemed like the rest of Ufa, was still the film's producer, and May and Pommer generously brought their hungry young friend Billie Wilder along with them to complete the writing team. May ended up directing the film himself—it was the first of his ten American pictures—and the final screenwriting credit went to Liebmann, Young, and Wilder, in spite of the fact that two more writers, Joe Cunningham and William Counselman, contributed additional dialogue along the way. Eight writers had their hands in the beer.

Music in the Air flopped, but it's not all that clear why. The film's chic, magnetic star, Gloria Swanson, had been a top draw in the late 1920s and early 1930s, but her fortunes were sliding by the time she played Frida, the temperamental Bavarian diva. Maybe Swanson was too closely identified with the rollicking excesses of the Jazz Age; perhaps her glamorous persona made no sense in Bavaria; audiences may simply have grown bored with her. *Music in the Air* slipped quickly into the fog of forgotten movies, and Swanson didn't appear on-screen again for another seven years. After that, 1950.

With such a tortured trail of contributors, drafts, and revisions, it's impossible to attribute anything in the screenplay to anyone in particular, let alone Wilder. Swanson herself later claimed that Pommer convinced her to make the film on the strength of its screenplay, citing Billie Wilder's name in particular, but this is almost certainly hindsight's revision, since in 1934 Billie Wilder had no reputation at all in the United States. For a top producer to tell a top star that she should be in his film because it was cowritten by an unknown immigrant makes no sense.

Struggling young scripters hope for a hit as much as stars do, and Wilder was no exception. Disappointed, he was forced once again to start virtually from scratch, depending as usual on the kindness of people who spoke German. His next chance came with another Fox project, *Lottery Lover*. He had his work cut out for him. Firmly on the other side of insufferable, Fox's original treatment for *Lottery Lover* concerned a boisterous band of French military cadets, one of whom falls in love with a dancer at the Folies-Bergère and finds a rival in the form of a Balkan prince. Cadet and prince each court the luscious Gabrielle. When the prince buys the showgirl a lapdog, the contest appears to be over; cadet Pierre counterattacks with a superior dog. Somebody named Polette substitutes a mangy mutt for the prized canine, however, and, well, it all works out in the end because Gabrielle loves the new dog and she marries Pierre. *Lottery Lover* needed a great deal of work.

On April 12, 1934, Billie Wilder, Hanns Schwarz, and Franz Schulz signed a contract with Fox to write what the deal memo colorfully described as "a continuity entitled *Lottery Lover*, based on a continuity entitled *Lottery Lover*, by George Marion, Jr., and Dorothy Yost, and a story outline by Hanns Kräly, based on a continuity by Edward T. Lowe, Jr., based on an original story by the same name by Sig Herzig and Maurice Hanline." Like Billie, the Viennese Schwarz and the German Schulz were both eager to tap into the Hollywood pipeline. What Fox executives didn't know at the time, however, was that Wilder, Schwarz, and Schulz were confidently writing their screenplay in German with no intention of translating it into English themselves. That would be somebody else's problem.

The three screenwriters managed to turn in a polished draft—entirely in German—less than two weeks later. In total, Wilder worked for five weeks at $200 a week. Since the screenplay was now written in a foreign language, Fox had to hire somebody to translate it back into English. *Lottery Lover* dragged on through the summer, largely because the scheduled star of the film—Pommer's girlfriend, Lilian Harvey—walked out of another Fox production in a huff, forcing the studio to replace her in both projects. Compounding the mess, Hanns Schwarz, who had also been inked in to direct the film in addition to cowriting it, fell ill after an appendectomy. Two more screenwriters, Sam Hellman and William Thiele, joined the parade of typists in September, and the roster of writers on *Lottery Lover* finally reached its limit at twelve.

After *Lottery Lover*, Billie languished. He ghosted a number of scripts, including a late rewrite of Fox's *Under Pressure*, the story of a couple of roughnecking sandhogs named Shocker and Jumbo. The plot alone is enough to give anyone the bends: Shocker gets "the staggers"; Jumbo slugs him; there's a "blow" and Jumbo doesn't come up; Jumbo's leg becomes paralyzed and has to be amputated. . . . Another Fox production, *Thunder in the Night*, bore some of Billie's influence as well, though his name doesn't appear in the credits; at least seven other screenwriters worked on the film, a thriller set in Budapest. To the sound of thunder and flashes of lightning, the countess Madalaine's first husband reappears, seemingly back from the dead—everyone thought he'd committed suicide—and causes a lot of trouble for everybody. This is especially true when he dies for real, having been shot in the heart by a mystery killer, and so on.

Billie's more notable achievement during this period was that he changed the spelling of his name to Billy, having learned enough English to realize that in America the name his mother had given to him belonged to a girl. His last name no longer rhymed with *builder*, either. Like Thornton, he was now a Wilder.

In the summer of 1935, the possibility of remaking *Mauvaise Graine* in English surfaced, but it came to nothing. In July, the Gaumont British Picture Corporation contacted the Production Code Administration (PCA), headed by the reactionary Republican Will Hays. Since the previous year, the so-called Hays Office had been empowered to censor Hollywood films against explicit sex, raunchy dialogue, adultery, homosexuality of any sort, crimes that paid, on-screen drug use, and any mocking of religion and the law. In this regard, *Mauvaise Graine* was an unlikely prospect for approval, but Hays's assistant responded to Gaumont with the censoring office's stock answer to all inquiries: *Mauvaise Graine* would be acceptable with the proper treatment. However, the Hays Office continued, there was some concern about the essentially criminal nature of the story. Its protagonist, after all, was a car thief.

By September, the Hays Office had seen *Mauvaise Graine* itself and, not unexpectedly, pronounced it thoroughly unacceptable. The movie detailed the methods by which car thieves stole their cars; thus it might inspire copycat criminals in the mass audience; and furthermore, neither its male nor its female lead was brought to justice in the end. The office made it a point to note, however, that this judgment was based solely on the existing French film, so it might become acceptable if it were completely rethought, restructured, and rewritten.

This was a signal moment for Billy Wilder, who would be fighting American censors—not to mention run-of-the-mill, homegrown neopuritans—for the rest of his career. He lost the first round, but at least he saw what he was up against if he wanted to make films in the free world.

Despite his lack of artistic success, Billy was moving up in Hollywood circles. The more English he knew, the more he could make Americans laugh; the more he made them laugh, the more friends he made. They weren't close friends, necessarily—they were more like café pals, only without the cafés. The outdoorsy quality of Los Angeles meant that the athletic Billy could connect with people through the sports circuit. He became friendly with one of his tennis partners—a successful screenwriter named Oliver H. P. Garrett. Garrett was a thoroughbred easterner, an established member of the film community, a man who knew how to dress and generated a fine enough income to do so. He had cowritten *A Farewell to Arms* in 1932, *Manhattan Melodrama* in 1933, *The Story of Temple Drake* in 1934, and various other successful films. Garrett and Wilder enjoyed playing tennis together, and on this friendly basis they ended up cowriting two scripts in 1935: a musical called *Encore* and a spy story called *Gibraltar*. Thanks, no doubt, to Garrett's Hollywood-insider status, they quickly sold them both to Jock and Sonny Whitney's Pioneer Pictures. Billy earned a healthy $5,000 for the two scripts, but Pioneer soon folded and the films were never made.

In the fall of 1935, Wilder made a fascinating choice. As unsettled as he was in his little room at the Chateau Marmont, as intermittent as his screenwriting career was, and as much as he needed to just keep plugging and earn money, Wilder set sail for Europe—specifically, Vienna. He took his $5,000 and spent it on a round-trip ticket to Austria. Ever the news-hound, Wilder had been following international politics closely, and he was painfully aware of the month-by-month souring of both Germany and Austria. In July 1934, 154 Nazi storm troopers dressed in Austrian army uniforms strode into the Federal Chancellery in Vienna and shot the Austrian chancellor in the throat at a range of two feet. In March 1935, Hitler announced universal military conscription in Germany, thereby breaking the Versailles covenant. Anschluss, the German annexation of Austria, was looking more and more likely. Billy was getting jumpier in Los Angeles thinking about his mother. He wanted to convince her, in person, to get out of Austria once and for all and come to the States. The time, Wilder knew, was now. This was also precisely the first opportunity in Billy Wilder's life when he could return to his boyhood home in triumph as a big-shot Hollywood writer. No matter that he wasn't a big-shot writer in Hollywood. He *could* be one if he was in Austria. Billy seized the moment and went home.

He saw his mother and her new husband, but he didn't stay with them. Instead, he used up a little more money by checking into the Hotel Krantz-Ambassador, smack in the heart of the First District. He listed his nationality on the hotel registry as Polish.

Ensconced in a good hotel near the best cafés and nightclubs, Wilder spent the latter part of November visiting with old friends and plying them with Hollywood tales—people he'd met, movies he'd written, the sun, the swimming pools, the women. They were successful conversations, no doubt. But his attempts to talk his mother into getting out of Austria ended in failure. Genia, then in her mid-fifties, saw no need to panic over events transpiring across the border in Germany, and although there is no documentation to support it, her husband may well have resisted the notion of giving up his business and uprooting himself in order to follow his bragging and hyperactive stepson to the land of big dreams and wooden Indians.

One thing is clear, however: Billy's failure to get his mother out of Austria was one of the most painful experiences of his life, and it became even more so in the years to follow. Austrian independence was unlikely to continue much longer; that they all knew. But Billy had what his friends and family lacked. Not only could he afford a room in a First District hotel, but his instinct for survival had procured for him the residency permit that saved his life. Its existence was a matter of pride for Wilder, but the pride had a double edge: "I remember how embarrassing it was for Willi Forst to be seen walking down Kärntnerstrasse in Vienna with me, an emigrant."

Forst had been one of the ones who fled to Vienna; now he was stuck there while Billy was heading back to Hollywood. (On the other hand, Forst's embarrassment may have been a result of his being seen around town with a Jew who'd run away; Wilder's meaning isn't entirely clear.) In any event, Billy soon left Vienna. For the second time in his life, he bade farewell to his mother and left in order to pursue a better life in a foreign country.

Wilder returned to Los Angeles just before Christmas. It was at this point, he told yet another interviewer, that he moved into the ladies' room at the Chateau, and this time it was simply because he'd forgotten to reserve his regular room and the hotel was booked for the holidays. This explanation sounds likely enough, if for no other reason than the fact that in this version Wilder lived in the bathroom for only a few days. Peeing women or no, Billy needed to find work, as much to keep his mind off things as to earn a living. Influential new friends continued to help him.

Salka and Berthold Viertel lived at 165 Mabery Road in Santa Monica, a pleasant but unexceptional house that Salka turned into a most extraordinary nexus of art, intellect, and commerce. The salons she held there are legendary. Her guests were smart, sophisticated, and on the make, comfortably surrounded by other Germans with thick accents and awkward sentence structures, not to mention European-born movie stars. They included Ernst Lubitsch, William Dieterle, Fred Zinnemann (who had become Berthold's assistant), Erich Pommer, Greta Garbo, Charles Chaplin, Leopold Stokowski, Max Reinhardt, Artur Rubenstein, and many others. Wilder remembered meeting Thomas Mann at the Viertels': "I was so impressed—he'd won the Nobel Prize in the 1920s—that I don't remember what he said or if I said anything." The late Robert Parrish, who began his long Hollywood career as a child actor (he's one of the cruel paperboys who throw spitballs at Charlie Chaplin in *City Lights*), told of being a guest at Salka Viertel's house. Greta Garbo was asleep on the couch, Artur Rubenstein was tinkling on the piano, and an unkempt guy in the backyard was busily grilling something on the barbecue. The Viertels wouldn't tell young Bob Parrish who it was. Only years later did he realize it was Bertolt Brecht.

So many new émigrés needed employment, and so few of them knew anything about the way Hollywood worked. Salka, who had lived and worked there since the 1920s, put these all-but-desperate foreigners together with the more established Hollywood émigrés, especially those who were looking for new employees. As Gottfried Reinhardt recalled, "She was one of the few who knew and faced the fact that it was a ghetto. Hers was one of the few clearinghouses between the inmates and the guardians. It was neutral ground where, for a few hours, everything was allowed and many an opportunity was created." A house on Mabery Road in Santa Monica became the sieve through which the subtle filtration of refugee sensibilities through American popular culture took place.

Cultural historian Anthony Heilbut describes the effect of all this Austro-German talent on the new shores onto which the émigrés had washed: "Knowing so much already—no matter how partial or artificial the knowledge—they became in short order professional interpreters of the American temperament. Bertolt Brecht once observed the émigré filmmakers—although the demand was not limited to Hollywood—were expected to decipher the Americans' hidden needs and discover for them a means of fulfilling them: this was called delivering the goods."

Billy Wilder saw the goods and knew he could deliver them, but Hollywood, like Berlin, required contacts, mentors, protectors, and incessant back-scratching. This was not a problem for Billy. Through Salka Viertel, Oliver H. P. Garrett, the Mays, and Pommer—not to mention through the agency of his own sharp charm—he kept on making friends in Hollywood. One was the screenwriter Jacques Théry. In fact, Mrs. Théry fixed him up with his future wife; she knew it would work out for them. Judith Frances Coppicus was a tall, smart, good-looking woman who spoke French and knew about culture. Born in New York, she was five years younger than Billy and had the black hair and high cheekbones he tended to favor. She was funny, quick-witted. Well-versed in art, she was a painter herself. And she knew how to move. Judith was graceful and athletic, and it didn't hurt that she had some show business connections, too. Her father was George Coppicus, head of Columbia Artists agency. Judith's mother, after divorcing her father, had remarried the Basque caricaturist Paul Iribe, who had done some scenic design work for Cecil B. DeMille. Judith dressed elegantly, and she could navigate her way through Hollywood's competitive social world, though she also liked her privacy.

Their biggest stumbling block was politics—Judith was much more conservative than Billy, who in the mid-1930s still carried traces of his old leftist friend, Egon Erwin Kisch. But this was a couple who were on even ground when they disagreed. Judith could field Billy's wisecracks about the state of the world and throw them right back at him with perfect aplomb.

Billy and Judith eloped to Yuma, Arizona, on December 22, 1936, six months after he married Charles Brackett.

Until then, however, Billy was engaged with H. S. "Hy" Kraft, a former Broadway playwright, in the writing of a screenplay called *Vienna Hall* for Paramount Pictures. (A little later they changed the title to *Moon Over Vienna*.) It was the story of an American bandleader who travels to Austria and sets up shop next to a waltz hall. Wilder and Kraft turned in their first draft on May 11, 1936, after which the project was whisked away from them and handed over to two other writers, Don Hartman and Frank Butler. It was retitled again—this time as *Champagne Waltz.*

According to Zolotow, a Paramount producer named Lester Cowan offered Wilder and Kraft $10,000, jointly, for *Moon Over Vienna.* Cowan got as far as giving them each a $1,000 advance, the story goes, but then ran into some roadblocks. He couldn't seem to get the film through the production channels at Paramount, so he offered Billy a writing contract with the studio at $250 per week. Billy accepted the offer. The head of Paramount's writers' department, Manny Wolfe, interviewed Billy and gave him the position. This account makes little sense. Why would Wilder accept a job requiring sixteen weeks' work from him simply to earn what had been promised for work he'd already delivered? A more likely scenario is that Cowan gave Billy $750 toward an eventual $1,000, and when the film's production was postponed, Cowan compensated by offering Wilder a position on staff. In one week's time Billy earned what he was owed, and anything after that was steady employment.

Champagne Waltz still bears traces of Wilder and Kraft's original screenplay, not the least noteworthy aspect of which is the whirlwind arrival of a popular American swing bandleader in Vienna. A press agent, Happy Gallagher (Jack Oakie), brings Buzzy Bellew (Fred MacMurray) and his orchestra to Vienna. Happy sets the band up to perform at a dance hall owned by Max Snellinek (Herman Bing). No, an ambitious young reporter does not show up speaking in song lyrics. Instead, the complication is that Snellinek's dance hall is located next door to the Strauss waltz palace. The establishment not only plays Strauss waltzes, it's run by Franz Strauss (Fritz Leiber) and his daughter, Elsa Strauss (Gladys Swarthout). As in *Es war einmal ein Walzer* and *Scampolo,* Vienna is a city of misapprehended love, but now America (rather than Berlin or an airplane heading out of town) is the site of resolution.

Billy might have continued writing innocuous scripts like *Vienna Hall,* had he not found the right writing partner. But on July 17, 1936, Manny Wolfe appeared in Billy's office and led him away to meet his new collaborator. Wolfe was a snappy dresser and a shrewd executive. He had among his large staff of writers two literate, creative men who, separately, were working beneath their potential. He brought them together to work on a screenplay for Ernst Lubitsch, and they became one of the American cinema's greatest writing teams. Mrs. Jacques Théry dreamed up the perfect love match for Billy based on similarities; Billy and Judith soon married. Manny Wolfe put together a professional team based on essential differences; the team lasted longer than Billy's marriage. In temperament, background, political leanings, and personal style (not to mention amplitude and taste in women), Charles Brackett and Billy Wilder had practically nothing in common. What they shared was more vital: a love of language, a steely devotion to work, and a fine sense of humor. Wilder's marriage with Judith produced two children and a lot of acrimony. His marriage with Brackett produced a lot of acrimony and eleven of the best, most successful films Paramount Pictures ever made.

8. COUPLED

One discovers his intelligence at the end of five seconds, his cynicism at the end of five minutes, and his charm from one end of the year to the other.

—*Ghost Music*

A soft-spoken Republican gentleman from Saratoga Springs, New York, the gray haired, forty-three-year-old Charles Brackett stood at nearly six feet and could look Billy Wilder directly in the eye. He was Billy's senior by fourteen years. In 1914, when Billy was still a child pool shark in Kraków, Brackett graduated from Williams College. In 1920, while Billy was a semidelinquent Jewish teenager running loose on the depressed streets of postwar Vienna, the blue-blooded Brackett was finishing up at Harvard Law, having already served a short stint as vice-consul in St. Nazaire and as a liaison officer for a French general during World War I. Max Wilder failed at nearly everything; Charlie Brackett's father was a prosperous lawyer, a state senator, and the owner of a Saratoga Springs bank. Billy loved tennis and skiing; Brackett hated sports and sunshine. Other than a passion for cribbage, bridge, and words, Billy and Charlie had few affinities.

Wilder began writing because he thought newspaper writers were hot stuff. Brackett wrote because he was brought up to be a cultured man of the world and because he knew he was good at it. He wrote short stories during his time at Harvard, and when he graduated with his law degree, he returned home to Saratoga Springs and continued his nascent literary career while working in his father's law firm. At first he had to get the war out of his system. He'd composed a story called "War" while he was serving in Nantes and, once he was safely back in law school, sent it to an agent, who promptly turned it down. He·told Brackett that the story was censurable and therefore unpublishable. The young writer may have been discouraged, but the writer's mother was not, and she encouraged him to send "War" to the *Saturday Evening Post*. He did—anonymously—and they accepted it and asked for more. Brackett was ready for them. He immediately submitted his novella, *Counsel of the Ungodly*, which soon ran in the *Post* in three installments.

Breezy, knowing, and exquisitely fashioned, Brackett's literary works seem in retrospect to be the essence of their age, though their style is archaic. They read like a kind of talky, bland Fitzgerald—dry, lovely stories. The subtle ironies they may once have possessed were apparently so timely as to have disappeared almost entirely with the passage of the century. Their characters have names like de Missiac and Cousin Dorothea. Zolotow's description of Brackett's oeuvre is right on the mark: "bright, sardonic novels: crisp, lean books written in the manner of Aldous Huxley and Ronald Firbank, books about rich, decadent people." They aren't Fitzgerald; they're what Fitzgerald's characters would have read.

After spending six years toiling in the country-clubby sphere of Brackett and Eddy, his father's firm, Charlie took a big if impeccably financed chance. He moved to Manhattan and began writing full-time. His novel *Weekend* came to the attention of the *New Yorker*'s Harold Ross, who offered him a job as the magazine's drama critic. With his golden touch, Brackett wrote criticism and two more novels—*The Last Infirmity* (1926) and *American Colony* (1929)—and then, with the supreme confidence that old money can buy, he left his plum post and went off to write more books. Robert Benchley replaced him at the *New Yorker*.

RKO lured Brackett to Hollywood in the early 1930s. His agent in New York packed him onto an airplane, a Hollywood agent met him in Burbank, and together they sped directly to RKO's studios in Hollywood complete with Brackett's luggage. Brackett expected to be welcomed as the literary star he saw himself to be, but the RKO executive he was sent to Hollywood to meet, David O. Selznick, kept him waiting for an hour and then told him brusquely to talk to Adela Rogers-St. Johns about a *Liberty* magazine article that Selznick thought was kind of interesting. The story is said to have concerned Jack Dempsey's heart problems. Brackett did his best, but when it came time for the obligatory Hollywood story conference, the Brahmin lawyer/critic/novelist had no idea how to play it. As Brackett later recounted, "I simply got up and stammered out my story. When I got through there was a deadly silence. Then Adela said quietly, 'I don't see it that way at all. The boy loved that girl. That girl loved that boy. They loved each other.' And on that note I was wafted out of Hollywood."

Not for long. Brackett went on to write a number of successful scripts—successful enough, at any rate, to keep him employed at a fairly high salary. Three of his stories were adapted for the screen by others—*Pointed Heels*

(1930), *Secrets of a Secretary* (1931), and *Woman Trap* (1935)—but Brackett himself wrote or cowrote at least seven screenplays before teaming up with Wilder. First, for Paramount, was the atrociously named *Enter Madame* (1935), a romance starring Cary Grant. Also for Paramount were *College Scandal* (1935), one in a series of varsity-themed films at that studio; *Without Regret* (1935), a kidnapping melodrama; *The Last Outpost* (1935), a Cary Grant action-adventure film set in the desert; and *Rose of the Rancho* (1935). *Rose* marked the film debut of opera star Gladys Swarthout, who played an unlikely dual role: on the one hand, the fetching Rosita; on the other, a cross-dressed vigilante named Don Carlos. In one remarkable scene, Swarthout transforms herself from *bandido* to fiesta queen and nobody notices the similarities. With the possible exception of *The Last Outpost*, which survives in film history (however obscurely) thanks to Cary Grant, none of Brackett's early films lasted much beyond the year of their release. This isn't to say that Brackett was not thriving. By 1936, he was making $1,000 a week at Paramount—four times what Wilder earned. Brackett's talents were recognized by other studios as well. In April 1936, Brackett went out on loan to MGM to write *Piccadilly Jim*, a romance starring Robert Montgomery. In June, he was loaned to B. P. Schulberg to write the script for the screwball comedy *Wedding Present*.

However unconscious Manny Wolfe's perception may have been, he knew that Brackett needed somebody to toughen him up a little—someone who would make up for the edginess this sophisticated, quiet, erudite man lacked. In addition, by pairing Lubitsch with Wilder and Brackett for a new screwball comedy, *Bluebeard's Eighth Wife*, Paramount may have been trying to get the director into a snappier, more up-to-date mood than he took with *Angel*; that film, which Lubitsch was already preparing with Samson Raphaelson, turned out not to be a commercial hit.

In his 1993 profile of Billy Wilder for the *New Yorker*, David Freeman neatly sums up the dynamic between the two writers, who rapidly became the best known and, eventually, the highest-paid writing team in town: "Brackett's boozy Republican gentility was often at odds with Wilder's brash ambition. Wilder was the junior man but the more forceful personality. The partners were known for their screaming matches as well as for their scripts." Wilder himself is quoted: "We fought a lot. Brackett and I were like a box of matches. We kept striking till it lights up. He would sometimes throw a telephone book at me." Freeman goes on to say that the writers "walked out on each other several times, each vowing to go it alone. But, like a couple in a marriage that doesn't quite work but won't quite end, they kept at it, locked in productivity and combat, and came to be known as Brackettandwilder."

Individually, both men had spent their careers writing for hacks. Wilder's screenplays were directed by such functionaries as Hanns Schwarz, Paul Martin, Hans Steinhoff, and A. Edward Sutherland—Robert Siodmak was an exception—and Brackett was stuck with a similar roster of competent, now-forgotten men: Charles Barton, Louis Gasnier, Harold Young, Elliott Nugent, Marion Gering, and Robert Z. Leonard. For both Billy and Charlie, writing a screenplay for Ernst Lubitsch must have been like writing for God. "Lubitsch was one of the great ones," Wilder said many years later, "like Griffith, Eisenstein, and the early René Clair." Lubitsch's worst film, had he ever made one, would have been a damn sight better than anything either Brackett or Wilder had done before. They may have begun their long-lasting battle while composing *Bluebeard's Eighth Wife*, but each writer, separately, had an unimpeachably good reason not to screw up the relationship beyond repair.

Wilder had long admired Lubitsch's films, as many people did. But Billy, an acutely visual man, knew what he was *seeing*. Lubitsch's films were never merely clever words nicely filmed. They were cinematic, and exquisitely so. Billy understood that their art was on the screen, not the page—that their beauty lay not in mere art direction but rather the gradual unfolding of meaning and emotion. It was Lubitsch who taught Wilder how to think in film sequences—where the camera was, how long the shot held, where the cuts should be. Lubitsch's storytelling was the richest and most sophisticated Wilder had ever encounted. As he once said, "Lubitsch could do more with a closed door than most directors can with an open fly."

The taste and grace of Ernst Lubitsch's pictures stood in comical contrast to the man himself. He was surprisingly stubby in person. Both Wilder and Brackett dwarfed him, but only physically. Samson Raphaelson, with whom Lubitsch worked on nine films, once wrote that he "didn't notice, for months, that he was a short man—about five feet five or six. Only when an envious Berliner mockingly compared him to Napoleon did I think of Lubitsch in terms of height. Actually, not only was he short, but his hands and feet were small, and he walked with a faintly bowlegged, lilting step." Adept at depicting aristocratic foibles, Lubitsch himself came from a Galician petit bourgeois family that had moved to the drab eastern part of Berlin. And, strangely, the master of the discreet glance and the courtly doorway was always on the brink of losing his cigars and forgetting his own telephone number. He was a man who had more important things on his mind than where he last put his matches. Lubitsch ran around Hollywood wearing rumpled pants and shirts, and he waved his fork in the air while he ate. Wilder adored his films, and once they finally met long enough to have a conversation, he grew to adore the man as well. "If the truth were known," Wilder has said, "he was the best writer that ever lived."

Most writers respected Lubitsch, some loved him, but very few were ever truly chummy with him. Walter Reisch was one of Lubitsch's closest friends, maybe even his best friend according to Raphaelson, and still Reisch called him "Herr Lubitsch." There was a Promethean quality to him. *Bluebeard's Eighth Wife* was his thirty-fourth feature film, and despite the fact that his sound-film scripts had been penned by various sharp writers (Raphaelson, Kräly, Hecht), these movies not only looked but also sounded unmistakably as Lubitsch's own. As Raphaelson later wrote, "Lubitsch was not what a writer would call a writer, nor did he waste time trying to be. I doubt if he ever tried to create a story, a film, even a scene entirely on his own. He had no vanity or illusions about himself. He was shrewd enough to cherish writers, and he welcomed the best available, roused them to outdo themselves, and at the same time contributed on every level and in ways that I cannot measure or define."

Raphaelson, an eminently sweet-tempered man whose screenplays— *The Smiling Lieutenant, The Man I Killed, One Hour with You, Trouble in Paradise, The Merry Widow, Angel*—were even more so, was Lubitsch's chief writer in the 1930s; he was Jewish, but not foreign born. Lubitsch broke his association with Raphaelson only twice in the 1930s—first with Ben Hecht for *Design for Living,* and then with Brackett and Wilder for *Bluebeard.* (Hecht, too, was an American Jew.) Hecht's script for *Design for Living* is harsher and more brittle than anything Raphaelson wrote for Lubitsch, and the screenplay Wilder and Brackett composed took a similar turn. Based on a play by Alfred Savoir, the film Lubitsch proposed to make for Paramount, the last in his contract, was to be about a charming but impoverished French heiress, Nicole de Loiselle, and a surly, parsimonious, overmarried American multimillionaire named Michael Brandon. It would be Lubitsch's first screwball comedy; the others were romantic comedies, but Lubitsch announced to the press that this one would be different— "mental slapstick," he called it.

With screwball comedies, audiences laughed at the nagging hatred that develops between two people in love. Indeed, in screwball comedies fighting *was* loving—a way for two equals to express mutual respect and commonality of purpose. To set these ridiculous sparring matches in motion, screenwriters were in constant need of "meet-cutes"—funny setup scenes that bring two unlikely people into such close proximity that, following genre convention, they can do nothing but start some sort of emotional or physical brawl. Wilder even claimed to have had a little meet-cute notebook going, filling it with page after page of strained, funny introductions. For *Bluebeard's Eighth Wife,* he tried one out on Lubitsch and Brackett. Claudette Colbert would be Nicole, Gary Cooper would be Michael, and Billy suggested that they meet in the menswear section of a department store on the Riviera, each trying to buy only half of a pair of pajamas. Nicole wants the bottoms, Michael wants the tops. Wilder has said that the inspiration was personal—he himself slept only in pajama tops—but regardless of its origins, this particular pajama gag wasn't a question of the buyers' comfort but rather one of money: Nicole cannot afford more than half a pair of pajamas, and the immensely wealthy Michael is a bit of a miser. Thus Billy's meet-cute perfectly established the two key characters of this screwball comedy immediately: each has a problem, they both know how to argue, and they'll wind up in bed together at the end.

Billy's meet-cute was good, but not good enough—not on its own. It was too smooth, too neat for Lubitsch. One day the three of them were at the director's house batting around the problem of how to punch up the pajama bit when Lubitsch emerged from the bathroom with the solution: "What if when Gary Cooper comes into the store to buy the pajama top, the salesman gets the floor manager, and Cooper again explains he only wants to buy the top. The floor manager says, 'Absolutely not,' but when he sees Cooper will not be stopped, the floor manager says, 'Maybe I could talk to the store manager.' The store manager says, 'That's unheard of!' but ends up calling the department store's owner, whom he disturbs in bed. We see the owner in a close shot go to get the phone. He says, 'It's an outrage!' And as the owner goes back to his bed you see that he doesn't wear pajama pants either." (This is Billy's rendition of the event, not Lubitsch's.)

Bluebeard's Eighth Wife is an unusually irritating comedy—unusual for Lubitsch, not for Wilder, though even at the time it offered Billy greater latitude in exploring elegant romantic hostility than he'd enjoyed previously. Perhaps for this reason, critics haven't been very kind to the film. It seems to run against the Lubitsch grain, though in fact the grain it rubs is Raphaelson's, not Lubitsch's. Lubitsch's biographer, Scott Eyman, goes so far as to call it "the emptiest movie [Lubitsch] ever made." But screwball comedies of the mid-to late-1930s are not often charming, at least not in the blissful and airy manner of classic drawing room comedies, and their romances are anything but relaxed. One doesn't come away from the best of them feeling optimistic about love. Instead, these films are characterized by anger, rage, and frustration, and *Bluebeard's Eighth Wife* is no exception. When Nicole winds up getting Michael secured into a straitjacket toward the end of the film, she's simply developing screwball's conventionally frustrating, and bitterly funny late-'30s visions of love.

This zeitgeist of marital rancor was so widespread on American screens that one can only go so far with the parallel in Wilder's personal life: his own two marriages were full of rancor. Billy and Judith lived briefly in a suite at the Chateau Marmont, but for reasons that Wilder has never explored in interviews, they moved into Judith's mother's house at 8224 DeLongpre in West Hollywood. Money is a possible explanation, though Wilder was certainly making enough for them to have afforded their own place. But whatever the motive, Billy went home every day to his wife and mother-in-law.

At the same time, Brackett wasn't monogamous with Wilder. He strayed from his partner almost immediately by writing other films with other writers. Lubitsch was taking his time preparing *Bluebeard's Eighth Wife*, so in April 1937, Brackett went on loan to B. P. Schulberg to write a film called *Bonanza* (which seems never to have gotten made). After that, MGM borrowed him to work on the screwball comedies *Wedding Dress* and *Live, Love, and Learn* (the latter featuring Brackett's replacement at the *New Yorker*, Robert Benchley). Even at Paramount, Brackett worked with other screenwriters after meeting Wilder, contributing dialogue and story ideas to the gangster comedy-drama *Wild Money*.

Still, Brackett and Wilder were well on their way to becoming the squabbling Siamese twins of the film industry. In the summer of 1938, when Universal Pictures needed to put the finishing touches on a Deanna Durbin musical-comedy called *That Certain Age*, the studio borrowed Brackett and Wilder from Paramount as a team. The none-too-American Wilder was probably more of a draw than Brackett for this thin exercise about Boy Scouts, a phony haunted house, a teenage crush on an older man (Melvyn Douglas), and of course the sprightly Deanna. *That Certain Age*, after all, was a Joe Pasternak production (Pasternak having commissioned *Der Teufelsreporter*, not to mention Mr. and Mrs. Allan Dwan's ill-fated tour of Germany). Bruce Manning's screenplay needed some polish, and Pasternak knew that his old friend Billy, along with his new writing partner, could provide it—especially in regard to the scenario involving the older man and his response to Durbin's crush. Left unclear is the extent and nature of Wilder and Brackett's contribution to the script, however, since records of their work survive only in the form of production listings in Hollywood trade papers.

Durbin, who is much better than her material, is forced to set the tone of *That Certain Age* in her first song, which cheerfully but unequivocally extols the virtues of loyalty, bravery, and cleanliness. Given this spray of all-American fun, Melvyn Douglas's hard-bitten reporter is quite a relief. The best line of dialogue in *That Certain Age* is his. Extolling the virtues of urban life in contrast to dull Mt. Kisco, New York, where he faces exile for the duration of the film, Douglas growls, "What I need is a good steak every night—smothered in chorus girls."

Of Pasternak, Wilder said, many years later, "Pasternak didn't do anything memorable, but he was practical—commercial. We are an industry. There's nothing wrong with that, when you know you're commercial and aren't under any illusions of doing something else."

As Wilder moved up in Hollywood, he grew increasingly dissatisfied with the way his agency, H. E. Edington–F. W. Vincent, Inc., was managing his deals. He knew the business better than they did, or so he thought. In May 1938, he terminated his relationship with the agency and turned his career over, briefly, to Paul Kohner. Wilder was concise in his letter of termination; his current contract with Paramount hadn't been negotiated by Edington and Vincent, Wilder wrote, but rather by Wilder himself; hence he was no longer represented by Edington and Vincent, and that was the end of it.

Wilder found himself in familiar company with Kohner, who had opened his new agency the year before, and whose client list grew to include many if not all the top émigré talents in Hollywood: Edgar Ulmer, William Thiele, William Dieterle, William Wyler, Anatole Litvak, Max Ophuls, Joe May, Gottfried Reinhardt, and Robert Siodmak, as well as non-émigré John Huston. Kohner and Wilder's formal and financial relationship as agent and client didn't last very long, but as late as 1998 Billy continued to conduct informal business through the Paul Kohner Agency, which survived its founder by many years. And when, in 1938, Kohner cofounded the European Film Fund, with Ernst Lubitsch as its president, Billy was among the first to sign on. The Fund provided relief and support for the stream of refugees who managed to get out of Europe and the would-be refugees who were still trying to do so, with ever increasing urgency. The Fund operated entirely on the donations of its members; the theory was for everyone to give 1 percent of his income for the benefit of new refugees. According to the surviving records, Billy was generous.

Wilder's personal life in 1938 is almost entirely undocumented, but it was nonetheless a crucial year—a time when his lifelong bitterness proved to be absolutely justified. *Bluebeard's Eighth Wife* finished filming in January and was released on March 18, a week in which Billy had more pressing concerns than his own jokes and wardrobe. Only days before *Bluebeard*'s gala premiere—when audiences first saw Billy's marvelous meet-cute with the pajamas; the funny, ugly bathtub in which Gary Cooper is forced to sit; the straitjacket; the spanking scene in which Cooper turns Colbert over his knee—Hitler led his troops into Vienna, annexed Austria in a flash of military might, and immediately supervised the systematic torture of Vienna's Jews. With ghastly precision, the Anschluss occurred during the very week in which Billy ought to have been enjoying the release of his first major American film—a light if brutal comedy.

The Anschluss was not exactly a shock. Wilder's old friend Karl

Tschuppik, in what became his most famous bon mot, was among the many Austrians who predicted it. "The Anschluss will come," Tschuppik said in the mid-1930s, "and it will come in the form of a music festival." He was right: his Austrian compatriots greeted the Nazis with a sense of felicity and celebration—Aryan violence to the tune of a *biergarten* chorale. (Luckily for Tschuppik, by the time his prediction came true he was already gone, having died of natural causes in Vienna the year before.) Since late 1935, when Wilder returned from Vienna to the undying warmth of Southern California, newspapers, radio, and newsreels had been chronicling the Nazis' rise in great detail. When the Anschluss actually occurred, and the Jews were thrown into the streets and beaten, the news was widely reported in the world press. History has simply added more colorful details to stories that appeared in every major paper in the world. At the time, Billy Wilder knew what was going on and he understood keenly that he was powerless to do anything about it.

In the days following the Anschluss, the Jews of Vienna were hounded, kicked, beaten, and in many cases driven to suicide. Jewish stores were painted with scrawls reading "Jew" and "Jewish shop," and the gentiles who patronized them were forced by the SS to wear signs around their necks reading "I, Aryan swine, have bought in a Jewish shop." Jews were immediately deprived of their civil rights: the right to own property, the right to be employed and to give employment, the right to enter businesses and public parks. Jews were forced out of their homes and into the streets, where they were given hot water and little brushes and told to scrub the curbs and the pavement. The chief rabbi of Vienna, a man in his seventies, was hurled into the street in his prayer shawl and ordered to scrub the sidewalk to the general amusement of Viennese passersby. In late April, storm troopers forced as many Jews as they could find into trucks, drove them out to the Prater (Vienna's popular amusement park), and ordered them to get down on their hands and knees and eat grass like pigs. When the terrified Jews complied, the storm troopers jumped up and down on their heads. And Billy Wilder was spending his summer polishing up a Deanna Durbin Boy Scout comedy and going home to a little house in West Hollywood with his wife and her mother.

Judith Wilder and Charlie Brackett bore the brunt of Billy's anxieties. One can easily imagine Billy responding to the daily news reports out of Vienna by stepping up his already frenetic pacing and darkening his already troubled view of the way human beings treat one another. Even in the best of times, Brackett found that watching Billy work was like watching a tennis match—it gave him a stiff neck. Wilder was forced to contain himself as best he could in sunny California while his mother's life hung in the balance. It may be this—as much as love, lust, and social ambition—that explains his marriage to Judith. When he returned from Vienna in 1935, Wilder seized whatever stability marriage seemed to offer. Three years later he was still trying to settle down, and it wasn't working.

Wilder's two marriages provided stability and rancor in what appears to have been nearly equal degrees. Europe was about to blow up, but Billy Wilder was in Hollywood living with a beautiful and intelligent woman and working with a talented, literate cowriter. Each gave Billy enough of what he lacked to make up for what he held in contempt. They steadied him and helped make his life as tolerable as possible. With Charlie, he could keep getting top-drawer work. By this point, in fact, the genial and well-connected Charles Brackett had been elected president of the Screen Writers Guild. The Guild's war with the Academy was over by then; the Guild had won. Not only did the National Labor Relations Board recognize the Guild as the legitimate collective bargaining organization for Hollywood writers, but the Academy completely yielded its role in labor relations. By the time the conservative Brackett was elected as the Guild's president, there was no longer any need to put a radical in charge. Brackett's position certainly didn't hurt the team's chances for employment on pictures that mattered—pictures like *Midnight*, another screwball comedy about a mismatched couple.

Mitchell Leisen, who was scheduled to direct *Midnight* for the producer Arthur Hornblow Jr., was one of Paramount's most commercially successful directors. Indeed, in terms of box office clout, Leisen was second only to Cecil B. DeMille. In 1935, when Ernst Lubitsch assumed the position of head of production at Paramount, the first film he supervised from screenplay to screen was a project for Mitchell Leisen: *Hands Across the Table*, starring Fred MacMurray and Carole Lombard. Leisen also directed Jean Arthur in *Easy Living*, from a script by Preston Strurges; though not a commercial hit at the time, it ranks as one of the finest screwball comedies ever made. These and other Leisen films combine verbal wit and classy visual style. But Leisen wasn't Lubitsch, and Billy grew to hate him. Leisen hated Billy back.

Any comparisons between Mitchell Leisen and Ernst Lubitsch obviously favor Lubitsch, except for these: Brackett and Wilder wrote *Bluebeard's Eighth Wife* for a director they both loved; *Midnight*, much tougher on everyone's nerves, is the better film. Lubitsch, Wilder, and Brackett began *Bluebeard* from scratch—everything in it was theirs; *Midnight* began as a Marlene Dietrich project, it was to be directed by (of all people) Fritz Lang, a total of six writers worked on it, and it ended up being not only funnier but more whole artistically. (Edwin Justus Mayer and Frank Schulz, who had changed his name from Franz, won only story credit on *Midnight*, but as evidenced by their salaries, they wrote substantially more than just a story outline. In fact, even though the shooting script was written entirely by Brackett and Wilder, Mayer earned over $34,000 for his work on the film—more than twice what Wilder made.)

There's an old story, borne out by production records, about Arthur Hornblow Jr. deciding to exert his power by handing Wilder and Brackett's fully polished draft to a staff writer named Ken Englund. (Like many producers, then and now, Hornblow just wanted to put some more thumbprints on it.) Englund asked Hornblow what he was supposed to do with the script, since it looked good enough to him. "Rewrite it," said Hornblow. Englund did as he was told and returned to Hornblow's office with a new draft, whereupon the producer told him precisely what the trouble was: it didn't sound like Brackett and Wilder anymore. "You've lost the flavor of the original!" Hornblow declared. Englund then pointed out that Brackett and Wilder themselves were currently in their office doing nothing, so Hornblow turned the script back to them for further work. Charlie and Billy spent a few days playing cribbage and then handed in their original manuscript, retyped and doctored with a few minor changes. Hornblow loved it, and the film went into production.

We meet Eve Peabody (Claudette Colbert) in a train that has just arrived in Paris from Monte Carlo. She is lying on a bench in her compartment, asleep, and she is wearing a fabulous gold lamé evening gown. "So this, as they say, is Paris, huh?" she says. Though penniless, she hails a cab. This is a woman who remains in full control of her life despite her dire circumstances. She lands in Paris with $1,000 less than Wilder had when he first found himself in the City of Lights, but she surely has all of his gumption: "Here's how things stand," she tells the cabbie. "I could have you drive me all around town and then tell you I left my purse home on the grand piano. There's no grand piano, and no home. And the purse? Twenty-five centimes with a hole in it. That's what's left of the Peabody stake. . . . I need a taxi to find myself a job, and I need a job to pay for the taxi. No taxi, no job. No job, no soap."

The cabbie, Tibor Czerny (Don Ameche) is impressed. He asks if she always travels in an evening gown. "No," Eve replies, "I was wearing this in Monte Carlo when a nasty accident occurred." "What happened? Fire?" "No, the roulette system I was playing collapsed under me. I left the casino with what I had on my back." Like Carl Mayer's father and Billy himself, Eve has learned that system gambling doesn't pay very well. "What you went through!" Czerny says a little later, and Eve responds by alluding to worse events that remain otherwise unremarked: "How far do you think 'through' is for a woman these days?"

Midnight is a comedy of ruses and intrigues, adultery and great lines. The animosity between the principals is more vital than in *Bluebeard*, and their love is thus more real. Eve leaves Czerny alone in the rain, having concluded that she could never find happiness with a man with no money, and she crashes a party just to get out of the downpour. It's a dull affair. (In fact, it's a direct recycling of the hideously tiresome party in Wilder's *Der falsche Ehemann*, complete with a silly violinist.) In a terrific, irrelevant aside (a lost art), a guest remarks, "It always rains when Stephanie gives one of her dull parties—even nature weeps." Using a pawn ticket as her invitation, Eve enters Stephanie's beautiful home and promptly sits down on a dog. This woman is clearly in need of assistance, and she finds it in the form of a multimillionaire named Flammarion (John Barrymore), who hires her to help break up his wife's affair with a smooth-talking rotter named Jacques Picot (Francis Lederer). Eve, who has been passing herself off as the Baroness Czerny, quickly finds herself the beneficiary of cash, clothes, a chauffeur, and a suite at the Ritz.

They all proceed to the Flammarion estate at Versailles, where they're joined by a fey guest—the hilarious Marcel (Rex O'Malley). *Midnight*'s plot becomes increasingly twisted when Czerny shows up, since Eve has been finding herself increasingly attracted to Jacques—or, rather, to Jacques's money. ("Jacques's family makes a very superior income from a very inferior champagne," Flammarion tells her.) The Baron and Baroness Czerny, however, are clearly in love, though, a fact that becomes increasingly evident in the bitterness and rancor with which they treat each other. Mme. Flammarion's suspicions about Eve's real identity are allayed when Eve and Czerny get into a testy exchange about their fictitious daughter, Francie, and her equally fictitious case of the measles. Using one of Brackett and Wilder's best lines, Marcel treats the illness as a delightful fashion accessory: "That polka dot effect is very becoming!" This oblique, shorthand suggestion of Marcel's sexual orientation flew past the censors, of course, who couldn't very well object to a silly remark about fashion. But when Brackett and Wilder included a bit in which Marcel was seen removing women's clothes from his suitcase, the Hays Office vetoed it.

John Barrymore was of two minds about *Midnight*'s screenplay. On the one hand, Barrymore's wife, Elaine Barrie, asked Brackett and Wilder for a copy of the script. At this point in his downhill slide, Barrymore was so drunk and degenerate that he usually didn't bother to read the screenplays of the films in which he appeared. Instead, he just read his lines off slates held out of camera range. "I've never known John to be so amused by a picture," Barrie told Wilder and Brackett. "He's actually asked if he could read the script!" On the other hand, Barrymore still refused to learn his lines. For one scene, the set was so tight that there was no room for Barrymore's idiot cards. Leisen asked Barrymore to memorize his lines, and Barrymore refused, saying, "Why should I fill my mind up with this shit just to forget it in the morning?" They wedged the idiot cards in somewhere and filmed the scene. Not only that, but Barrymore was also known to piss in the plastic bushes used for the terrace of the Flammarion chateau.

Midnight ends with a wise judge (Monty Woolley) spelling out the law of screwball marriage: "There's a very healthy law—in Albania, I think it is—that a husband may bring his wife back to her senses by spanking her, not more than nine blows with any instrument not larger than a broomstick. What do you say to that?" Eve has no objection. She's evidently been watching 1930s romantic comedies: "I say it's a fine idea! A husband should have that privilege, and no wife would resent it. *If* she knew he loved her." (Punching, slapping, or spanking had already occurred in *Nothing Sacred* and *The Moon's Our Home* and would continue to occur in *The Mad Miss Manton*, *Mr. and Mrs. Smith*, *The Philadelphia Story*, and other comedies of the period. Billy Wilder eventually became notorious for his putative misogyny, but at this point in his career he had genre convention on his side.)

Midnight opened in March 1939 to a flood of laudatory reviews, the most revealing of which appeared in *Motion Picture Daily*. Wilder, Brackett, and Leisen had battled during the film's preparation, and on-screen the characters were all set to slug each other, but according to the *Daily*, the industry screening of *Midnight* was a love fest: "This is, in fact, just about the best light comedy ever caught by a camera, as of the glad evening of March 8, 1939, when a cross-industry turnout enjoyed its preview screening with that wholesome, whole-hearted enthusiasm which, about once a year, erases company boundaries, banishes professional prejudices, and makes of a top-flight Hollywood audience a mere theatreful of completely contented film fans for a night. It takes a pretty fine piece of entertainment to do that." In a snap, Billy Wilder and Charles Brackett became the hottest screenwriting team in town.

A measure of Billy Wilder, an intensely voluble but inordinately private man, emerges from the games he plays: Hollywood deal making, of course, but just as definingly, the game of bridge. He learned both more or less simultaneously in the mid- to late-1930s, about the time he began working with Brackett. Cards were seminal to the collaboration—bridge, cribbage, maybe some poker. Billy was particularly good at bridge. A contest of skill, intellect, chance, and risk, bridge requires several strengths—a crisp and complex logic, a sturdy memory, and a dextrous, adaptable strategy. The cards you hold are yours, but you get them by pure chance. Based on your hand, and your skill, and your degree of calculated avarice, you bid.

Your partner is crucial. Bridge, predicated on pairing, is profoundly psychological and dependent on subtle communication. To win, you have to understand and mesh with your partner's nature while sizing up and defying your antagonists. As one popular guide to the game points out, "bridge involves 'playing the people' as well as playing the cards," a task at which Billy always excelled. You must know who your partner is and who your opposition is, and you must imagine, based on highly educated guesses, how well your own hand fits your partner's and how the combination stacks up against your opponents'. A set of inviolable rules governs the information you can share with your partner. As phrased by the instructional guide, the game of bridge sounds a great deal like the screenwriting team of Brackett and Wilder: "Within these severe limitations, players must choose ways to exchange information in order to get the most out of the combined partnership assets."

For a restless mind like Billy's, bridge offers no chance of boredom. There are over fifty-three octillion possible deals. Moreover, bidding is a language—not only a means of communicating with someone else, but a way of connecting with him and moving forward toward a goal. Defense, of course, is all a matter of logic. And as the great bridge master Alfred Sheinwold once wrote, "One of the most important things to learn about bridge is how to tell your friends from the hyenas. Once you learn the difference, you act one way toward your friends and quite another way toward the other jokers."

Billy and Charlie played a lot of bridge together, but Charlie preferred cribbage. You could play it with two people rather than four, and it wasn't nearly as complicated.

9. HEIL DARLING!

This has the ugly sound of regeneration.
—Grand Duchess Swana (Ina Claire) in *Ninotchka*

On the night of November 9 and the early morning of November 10, 1938, groups of Austrians and Germans rampaged through the streets of the greater Reich and, with rocks, bats, and kerosene, tore as many synagogues as they could find into ruins. This was the so-called *Kristallnacht*, the night of broken glass. In all, 119 synagogues went up in flames, 76 of which were completely destroyed, along with 815 Jewish-owned stores and 171 houses. Twenty thousand Jews were arrested; thirty-six were murdered. In Vienna, the Nazis destroyed every synagogue in the city except the Stadttempel, and for good measure they looted Jewish shops all over town. It was the most concentrated and deliberate Nazi assault on Jews to date.

Anthony Heilbut describes the effect of the metastasizing European horror on Hollywood's refugees: "In a political age, the Hollywood émigrés found themselves in political situations. While few were more than salon gauchistes, most had no qualms about working again with Marxists to combat Fascism, as they had in Europe. But Red-baiting was abroad in the studios, and the refugees found themselves forced to choose between quietism and fellow-travelling. The problem was that if one chose the first, one might be able to live in America, but one couldn't live with oneself." As Heilbut notes, these were people who already knew enough to play it cool in the American democracy. The fact that they had been forced to emigrate in the first place meant that they were already "trained in the arts of concealment."

Billy Wilder, like the other Hollywood refugees, walked a thin line between politics and survival. Unlike some other screenwriters of his generation, he came down on the side of survival and therefore enjoyed a long and productive career in the United States. Wilder's political sympathies lay with the left, but as a refugee he knew he was vulnerable. He wanted to continue working. More to the point, he was compelled to work, if only for the sake of his sanity. This was his constitutional state, and it would have held firm even without emigration, an impending war, and the anxiety of knowing that his mother's and grandmother's lives were under direct threat. Motion had always been his way of surviving, and in order to keep going forward in Hollywood he knew he needed to keep his political sentiments in check.

Billy Wilder chose to work and play. He didn't join any leftist study groups and made a life and a career for himself instead; eventually he joined some refugee committees, but politics was never a primary focus. He lived in acceptable if somewhat cramped comfort in West Hollywood. He drove a new DeSoto convertible. He hung out after work at Oblath's, a homey, divey restaurant across from the Paramount lot; on better occasions he went to Lucey's. On the lot itself, Wilder spent a great deal of time at the precise spot where he could hear and share all the latest studio buzz while smoking cigarettes and telling off-color jokes. It wasn't the Writers Building, where walls had ears and rivals had mouths. It certainly wasn't the front office, where nobody went unless they had to. Billy's regular spot was Paramount's own Gossip Central: Oscar Smith's shoeshine stand, conveniently and pivotally located right inside the Bronson Avenue gate. Oscar Smith knew a lot and so did his customers. Eventually, then, so did Billy. (Wilder went on to cast Smith as the Pullman porter in *Double Indemnity*.)

Thanks to *Midnight*, Brackett and Wilder were now not only a respected team but a team that made money. They plucked the best secretary in the pool, Helen Hernandez, and installed her as their own assistant. In January of 1939, the president of the Screen Writers Guild and his slightly feverish young partner began to compose a new script. The film was not going to be a high-end comedy like *Midnight* or *Bluebeard*, and it wasn't being written for a top director like Liesen or Lubitsch. No, this was to be a Jackie Cooper high school picture called *What a Life*, and it was to be directed by someone named Jay Theodore Reed. The reason Brackett and Wilder wrote this movie can only be guessed: some executive assigned it to them. Maybe the Deanna Durbin movie had done well.

Then again, since *What a Life* began as a hit Broadway show, it may have been one of those Hollywood projects that seemed higher-class at the time. Whatever the case, *What a Life* hasn't survived as much more than a curious throwaway. Paramount bought the rights from the playwright, Clifford Goldsmith, but in characteristic fashion it was taken away from him and handed over to Brackett and Wilder for a rewrite so complete that Goldsmith's credit was ultimately reduced to "based on the play by Clifford Goldsmith." Jackie Cooper hadn't been the first young actor set for the role of clumsy Henry Aldrich, the sad-sack boy-hero; an unknown, William Holden, was announced for the lead. But Holden was soon replaced and ended up in Columbia's boxing melodrama, *Golden Boy*, and Jackie Cooper took over the role of Henry.

Like the Deanna Durbin movie, *What a Life* concerns the travails of an adolescent. This teen, however, is more or less a mess. Poor Henry can't do anything right. The other kids pick on him, and the teachers blame him for everything that goes wrong at school. In fact, the real troublemaker is sports star and all-around he-boy George Bigelow (James Corner), who makes Henry the fall guy. Nerdy Barbara Pearson (Betty Field) wants Henry to ask her to the dance, but he's too shy. The school secretary helps Barbara transform herself into a beauty; George makes his move; Henry gets depressed. (Yes, this was all being adapted for the screen by the men who went on to make *Five Graves to Cairo*, *The Lost Weekend*, and *Sunset Boulevard*.) Dumb Henry, under strong parental pressure to get into the Ivy League, cheats on a test and winds up expelled. Not only that, but he's accused of swiping the school's musical instruments and pawning them, a heist actually committed by George. Henry finally proves who the real thief is and, to top it all off, he asks Barbara to the dance. The end. (Ironically, this was the start of one of Paramount's most successful series. There were *eleven* Henry Aldrich movies—*Henry Aldrich for President* (1941), *Henry Aldrich Gets Glamour* (1942), *Henry Aldrich Haunts a House* (1943), *Henry Aldrich Plays Cupid* (1944). . . . The series' tag line became inescapable: "Henry? Henry Aldrich!" "Coming, Mother!")

By mid-March 1939, *What a Life* was in production and Brackett and Wilder could move on to something more engaging. Ernst Lubitsch was preparing a romantic comedy for MGM about a humorless Russian envoy and a suave, kept Frenchman. Lubitsch had recently brought Walter Reisch in to help him work out the bugs in this long-troubled script. Finally, to give it some more snap and polish, Lubitsch convinced MGM to borrow Brackett and Wilder from Paramount.

The idea that eventually became *Ninotchka* had been brought to MGM in 1937 by Gottfried Reinhardt, who proposed Greta Garbo for the lead. The story, by Melchior Lengyel, was based on a three-sentence note Lengyel had written with Garbo's approval: "Russian girl saturated with Bolshevist ideals goes to fearful, capitalistic, monopolistic Paris. She meets romance and has an uproarious good time. Capitalism not so bad after all." By January 1938, the leading man had been cast: Garbo would play opposite William Powell.

Lengyel's screenplay bears little resemblence to the script Lubitsch finally shot. Scott Eyman has traced its development and reports that originally the three Russian commissars who add such ridiculous luster to the film weren't at all comic. In addition, the central male character, Leon, "becomes a drunkard when a business deal falls through and, at the end, he accompanies Ninotchka to Moscow."

Late in 1938, Gottfried Reinhardt worked on two different screenplays for the film—one with Jacques Deval, the other with S. N. Behrman. *Ninotchka* wasn't even an Ernst Lubitsch project at this point. George Cukor was going to direct it. But Cukor soon left the project for another film with more prestige, *Gone with the Wind*. By that point Behrman and Reinhardt had worked out the Eiffel Tower scenes, some scenes in Leon's apartment, and the first draft of the working-class restaurant scene in which Ninotchka laughs. (In fact, *Ninotchka*'s advertising concept, "Garbo Laughs!" predated the writing of the laughter.)

Garbo gave MGM two choices for Cukor's replacement: Edmund Goulding, who'd directed her in *Love* and *Grand Hotel*, or Ernst Lubitsch. L. B. Mayer wasn't wild about the Lubitsch option—Lubitsch's *The Merry Widow* had been a money loser—but he decided on Lubitsch anyway, eventually acceding to the director's key demand. Lubitsch would have complete control over the screenplay.

He immediately began reworking the whole thing with Walter Reisch, though he told Samson Raphaelson that he was sorry Raphaelson was busy working on his own play because otherwise he would have hired him to write *Ninotchka*. MGM had originally hired Walter Reisch to be a director as well as a writer, but the Vienna-born Reisch realized he couldn't speak English well enough to direct, so he renounced that clause of his contract. Reisch and Wilder had become close friends in Berlin and stayed that way; they eventually spent fifty Christmases together. Lubitsch was very fond of him as well. (Not everyone liked Reisch. Kurt Weill once recorded his impressions of a Hollywood party by noting that "a movie and operetta writer, Walter Reisch, was leading the conversation. He ought to be shot right after Hitler.")

Ninotchka changed rapidly under Reisch's influence and began to acquire the comic panache for which it became famous. For example, Behrman's script for *Ninotchka* involved a nickel mine. Reisch turned it into diamonds. Lubitsch explained the shift from nickel to jewels to Behrman in one of two ways: either Lubitsch said, "The nice thing about jewels is that they are photogenic" or, more colorfully, "You can photograph them sparkling on the tits of a woman." But even after Reisch's rewrite, *Ninotchka* still needed something that Reisch alone apparently couldn't provide, so Brackett and Wilder joined him in March to finalize the film's structure, tone up the dialogue, and give the whole thing one last polish. At first, Lubitsch still wasn't satisfied with what Brackett, Wilder, and Reisch came up with. He didn't much like the first forty pages, so they converged at Lubitsch's house for a conference. And they were still stumped—until Lubitsch went to the bathroom and, once more, emerged with the solution. "Boys," he said, "I've got it. I've got the answer. It's the hat!"

For Wilder, the ridiculous hat that Ninotchka mocks, then covets, and ultimately wears defines Lubitsch's essential style:

> We worked weeks wondering how we could show that Garbo, in *Ninotchka*, was becoming bourgeois—that she was starting to become interested in capitalist things. We wrote a bunch of different things, then one day Lubitsch said, "We're going to do a scene with the hat." She would be seen arriving at the start, accompanied by three commissars; she then passes in front of a window in which she sees a rather extravagant hat. She says, "How can a civilization survive when women put such hats on their head! It's the end of capitalism!" [Her actual line is: "It won't be long now, comrades."] Then she passes in front of the window and laughs. Later, finally, she chases the three commissars out, closes the door, opens her package, takes the hat out, puts it on and looks in the mirror. That's pure Lubitsch—total simplicity.

Wilder's conclusion is emphatic: "That's not a screenwriter's idea. It's the idea of a plastic artist."

A month later the three writers and their director were nearly finished with *Ninotchka*'s script. Unlike *Midnight*, this film was a happy marriage between director and writers. Mitchell Leisen couldn't touch a single word without being met with a violent protest from Billy, but Lubitsch could scrap whatever he pleased without a whole lot of dissent. Originally, Ninotchka was supposed to comment on the discomfort of the hard benches offered to third-class train passengers by saying, "We communists, we will change this from the bottom up." Garbo thought it was crude and refused to utter it, but Billy caused no scenes to protect the script (though the line itself may actually have been Lubitsch's). In fact, Wilder rarely if ever caused real trouble with men who'd earned his respect. This particular collaboration was so successful that on April 8, Reisch, Brackett, and Wilder did what few screenwriters have ever done: they petitioned MGM to include the director's name along with their own in the screenplay credits, a request that was not met.

"He wasn't just a gag man," Billy has said of his mentor. Lubitsch was a *writer*: "He would look at our stuff and go 'Ho ho, very good,' and scratch out the next line. He'd read a bit more, go 'Ho-ho,' and scratch out another line. What he did was purify, and that was what made him a great writer."

On another occasion, Wilder expanded on the debt he owed to Lubitsch. Almost forty years after Lubitsch's death, Wilder still talked about his father figure in a mix of past and present tenses:

> I think that all the pictures that he made should have his name as a collaborator, at least on the script. You don't just sit down and write, "Lubitsch does this." You come up with twenty suggestions, and he picks the one that makes a Lubitsch touch. The way his mind works, everything is by indirection. He is not the kind of director who hits you over the head and says, "I have two and two. And two and two makes four. And also, three and one makes four." He just says, "Here is two, and here is two." And then he lets the audience add it up. The audience is the co-writer. And that's where the laugh comes in. . . . His technique is clear to the last village idiot, but he makes him feel that he is very smart.

Garbo, in contrast, was weird. Her contract with MGM granted her the right to cancel her participation in *Ninotchka*, an option she came close to exercising. She appeared on the MGM lot for a meeting with Lubitsch one day, but she refused to get out of her car, so Lubitsch proceeded to the parking lot, climbed into Garbo's passenger seat, and spent two hours talking the peculiar star into staying in the film. In particular, Garbo was worried about the champagne-drinking scene. Confusing *acting* with *being*, Garbo was not only worried about her screen image, but she was also terrified of acting like a foolish lush in front of other people on the set. It was episodes like this that led Lubitsch to call Garbo "the most inhibited person I have ever worked with." As Wilder points out, she just didn't fit in around the movie colony: Garbo was "as incongruous in Hollywood as Sibelius would have been if he had come to write incidental music for Warner Bros."

For her part, Garbo found Lubitsch crude, and she didn't particularly enjoy making the picture. "He was a vulgar little man," she once said, though she did tell other people over the years that Lubitsch was a "marvelous little man" who was to her "like a loving father."

As *Ninotchka* headed into production, the male lead, William Powell, became ill and had to bow out, so Lubitsch offered the part to Gary Cooper, who turned it down. According to Wilder, Lubitsch then offered it to Cary Grant. He, too, declined. Finally, Melvyn Douglas accepted the role.

For a film as widely admired and indelibly titled as *Ninotchka*, it comes as a shock to learn that MGM executives tried to change its name. Had Nicholas Schenck, the head of Loew's, Inc. (MGM's parent company), not insisted that the film retain its title, *Ninotchka* would have been released as one of the following: *A Kiss from Moscow* or *Intrigue in Paris* for the international flavor; *This Time for Keeps*, *The Love Axis*, *Time Out for Love*, *A Kiss in the Dark*, or *A Kiss for the Commissar* for the sake of romance; *We Want to Be Alone* for the sake of the reclusive star's already tired reputation for privacy; *Give Us This Day* for an entirely out-of-place bit of reverence; or, most cleverly, *A Foreign Affair*.

During the production, one of the screenwriters tried to watch Lubitsch actually film a scene with the great Garbo, but he didn't get very far. It was either Brackett or Wilder. No one can be sure, because each of them claimed the episode as his own. Brackett had a crush on Garbo, so Brackett's story went, and he hung around the set, trying to gaze upon her as she worked. But despite the fact that he kept a secure distance between himself and the neurotic star, Garbo saw him anyway and insisted that stagehands put up a black screen between her and the peeping eyes of Charles Brackett. Still, Brackett found a small hole near the bottom of the screen and got down on all fours to peep through. Billy arrived on the scene and remarked, "What would the directors of the Adirondack Trust Company say if they could see you now?" (On another occasion, Brackett claimed that Lubitsch himself carved the hole: "The only way I was able to watch her at work was to get Lubitsch to cut an eye-hole in the screen, and I peeked through that.") The other version is Billy's: "I remember going to the MGM studios one day and seeing Garbo on the set. I'd never seen her in the flesh before, and naturally I was very excited. But as soon as she knew I was around she insisted that a large screen be placed around her so that I couldn't see what was going on."

For all its charm, *Ninotchka* is nonetheless saturated with a looming sense of global catastrophe. There is a consistent thread of pessimism in Lubitsch's work; as critic Enno Patalas describes it, "Lubitsch's cinema is not a cinema of revolt. But making use of the movement inherent in things as they are, it pushes them a little further along toward their own self-destruction." But by the time he made this deceptively light comedy, current events had given Lubitsch an irrefutable reason to see the world in a dark, disturbing light. As the film critic William Paul writes, "In a universe of playful characters, Ninotchka must appear a fool, but the world itself has changed in this film: poised on the brink of chaos, it seems to certify her seriousness." "We did it with the best intentions," Comrade Kopalski explains to Ninotchka; "We can't feed the Russian people on your intentions," she replies, and she's right.

Three bumbling but appealing Soviet trade representatives arrive in Paris to sell off some crown jewels. They peer into a gorgeous Parisian hotel and decide to upgrade from their low-rent hotel, the Hotel Terminus. Comrade Buljanoff (lovingly played by Felix Bressart, who'd had such trouble with his dragon-landlady in the short film Wilder wrote for Robert Siodmak, *Der Kampf mit dem Drachen*) expresses his fear of reprisal from his Soviet superiors. "I don't want to go to Siberia!" he exclaims. "And I don't want to go to the Hotel Terminus!" is Comrade Iranoff's cosmopolitan reply. When they inquire about the price of a room, the concierge is blunt, but not blunt enough: "Well, gentlemen, I'm afraid our rates are rather high," to which Buljanoff responds, "Why should *you* be afraid?" The three Russians look at each other and laugh, enjoying their private joke.

Buljanoff, Iranoff (Sig Rumann), and Kopalski (Alexander Granach) soon make a mess of the sale. The Romanovs' surviving heir, the Grand Duchess Swana (Ina Claire), gets wind of the transaction and claims that the jewels are rightfully hers. Swana's gigolo-boyfriend, Count Leon D'Algout (Melvyn Douglas), helps her tie up the sale by bamboozling Buljanoff, Iranoff, and Kopalski with legalities, prompting the Soviets to send a stern, humorless official, Comrade Ninotchka Yakushova (Garbo), to get the job done. Ninotchka holds no truck with gentility of service in capitalistic Paris. When the porter at the train station tries to carry her bags, she fights him off with socialist logic: forcing someone to carry someone else's luggage is "social injustice," she tells him, to which he replies with equal moral certainty: "That depends on the tip."

Ninotchka is grim and unforgiving by nature; that's why she's funny for the whole first half of the film. The writers make this point with a line so cruel it takes one's breath away. Buljanoff asks, pleasantly, "How are things in Moscow?" and Ninotchka replies: "Very good. The last mass trials were a great success. There are going to be fewer but better Russians." This reference to countless murdered Soviets may be the first truly offensive line in Billy Wilder's screen career. He went on to write many more of them in the years ahead, of course; it was Wilder, not Lubitsch, who eventually earned a reputation for being the master of mass bad taste. Wilder learned from Lubitsch something even more long lasting than how to construct a scene and how never to talk down to an audience. With the inclusion of this single line of dialogue Lubitsch taught Wilder that bad taste is worth risking as long as you remain true to yourself and your art. If the audience didn't laugh at a good line, it might be the fault of the audience, not the writer.

Ninotchka bears some screwball traces, the most obvious of which is that Ninotchka insults D'Algout repeatedly, and, as a direct consequence of her contempt, he's charmed. "As basic material," she notes in characteristic utilitarian fashion, "you may not be bad. But you are the unfortunate product of a doomed culture. I feel very sorry for you." "Ah, but you must admit that this doomed old civilization sparkles. Look at it—it glitters!" "I do not deny its beauty. But it's a waste of electricity." Later, when she agrees to accompany him back to his apartment—she justifies it on the grounds of ethnographic study—Ninotchka reveals in a singularly dirty line that she had been injured while serving with the Soviet Army during the advance on Warsaw: "Would you like to see my wound?" Leon is dazzled by the prospect: "I'd love to!" he says excitedly. Unfortunately for him, it's behind her neck.

The restaurant scene, in which Ninotchka breaks her shell of Soviet functionalism, remains not only a beautifully built piece of writing, but more important, a finely constructed piece of cinema. When the script was published in 1941, the critic Otis Ferguson went so far as to declare that *Ninotchka* (which he'd reviewed quite favorably as a film) worked not because of either Lubitsch or Garbo, but because of its "absolutely stunning screenplay by Charles Brackett and Billy Wilder and Walter Reisch." Without taking away from the writers' achievement, however, one must note Lubitsch's exceptional graciousness and generosity toward his characters. The scene begins with Ninotchka sitting down at a table in a working-class bistro and ordering "raw beets and carrots." The proprietor is appalled, but he's not in the least bit rude or dismissive to his guest: "Madame, this is a restaurant, not a meadow," he replies. As written, the line seems sarcastic and curt. After all, he's comparing Ninotchka to a sheep or a pig. But Lubitsch directs his actor to inflect the line with a generous spirit—a sense of airy relaxation and friendship, precisely the kind of everyday camaraderie this comrade so sorely lacks. Later in the scene, when Leon shows up, their dialogue continues on the theme of felicity: "Oh, Ninotchka, don't take things so seriously. Nothing's worth it, really." She asks what she ought to be smiling at, and he responds: "At the whole ridiculous spectacle of life! At people being so serious—taking themselves pompously. Exaggerating their own importance," after which he tips his chair over, lands on his can, and sends a tableful of dishes cascading down upon him. He's not the least bit amused, but she finds it hysterical.

Ninotchka's laughter, on which the film's advertising campaign was based, is thus a mix of cruelty and empathy. She's the one who needs to be brought down a peg or two, but he's the one who lands on the floor. And yet it *is* her shell that cracks; Ninotchka's laughter, so sudden and unmediated by political restrictions, marks the beginning of her life as a complex woman. Through laughter, she *connects* with Leon; she laughs because she relates to him. Soon afterward, she buys the idiotic hat and wears it—not because it makes her look good, but because it's silly and irrelevant. When she shows up at Leon's door with the funnel perched on her head, she asks, "I don't look too foolish?" Garbo delivers the line with the slightest of smiles and just a touch of embarrassment. Still, Ninotchka knows she doesn't look foolish precisely because she transcends it; she's radiant enough, alive enough, to sport a dunce cap.

Later, drunk, she delivers the film's overarching message: "Comrades! People of the world! The revolution is on the march! I know, bombs will fall. Civilization will crumble. But not yet! Please—wait. What's the hurry? Give us our moment. Let's be happy! We're happy, aren't we, Leon? . . . So happy, and so tired." And at that she passes out in his arms. What's striking here is not the escapism of the words but the weariness of the woman who utters them—the tired despair that drives her to seek refuge from the truth.

Swana appears in the morning and points out some pertinent facts: "Yes, I know exactly how you feel, my dear. The morning after always does look grim if you happen to be wearing last night's dress." Swana has successfully gained possession of the jewels and offers to make a deal with Ninotchka: she offers to renounce her claim if Ninotchka leaves Leon and goes back to Moscow immediately.

When Leon declares that he's in love with Ninotchka, Swana isn't impressed: "But Leon! This has the ugly sound of regeneration!" For Lubitsch, his writers, and the worldwide audience in 1939, though, the possibility of regenerating must not have sounded quite as unpleasant as it does to Swana. In the spirit of renewal, Leon and Ninotchka end up together in the gloriously remote and exotic city of Constantinople. East as well as West, the ancient capital of Byzantium becomes new again—a place of regeneration at what must have seemed like the end of the earth.

Ninotchka's preview, held in Long Beach, was a success. Afterward, Brackett, Wilder, and Reisch accompanied Lubitsch back to Hollywood in the studio limousine. Wilder reports on Lubitsch's behavior as he read the preview cards filled out by the audience: "He had this very serious expression as he was reading, and you could tell that it was pretty positive. Well, he gets to this one card and he just stares at it for a while and then he breaks into this howl of laughter. He was rocking back and forth on the seat and pounding it with one hand. We were looking at each other and wondering what the hell was so funny. Finally, he hands me the card and this is what it said: 'Great picture. Funniest film I ever saw. I laughed so hard I peed in my girlfriend's hand.' "

Ninotchka premiered in early October 1939, to appreciative reviews, and it became a reasonably good-size hit. But L. B. Mayer wasn't impressed. Mayer compared *Ninotchka* unfavorably with any run-of-the-mill Andy Hardy movie: "A Hardy picture cost $25,000 less than Lubitsch was paid alone, but any good Hardy picture made $500,000 more than *Ninotchka* made." In fact, *Ninotchka* made $2.2 million worldwide. And, since Lubitsch was paid a total of $147,500 with his two-picture contract for *Ninotchka* and *The Shop Around the Corner*, Mayer was just being petty. (Andy Hardy pictures may have been cheap, but they certainly cost more than $48,750.) *Ninotchka* resonated with audiences more than Mayer expected. By then, bombs were falling, civilization was crumbling, and Ninotchka's plea—"Give us our moment"—was all the more poignant.

Despite his philistine misgivings, Mayer thought Lubitsch was worth another try. In November, MGM commissioned a new screenplay to be written by Lubitsch, Wilder, and Jacques Théry. It was called *Heil Darling!* The three émigrés were attempting to put romantic comedy to the service of propaganda: *Heil Darling!* was about a cynical, self-serving foreign correspondent for ABC radio in Vienna who falls in love with a Nazi doctor. Both are rehabilitated. Paul Kohner negotiated Billy's end of the deal. A rights question arose, since Wilder and Théry had come up with an earlier treatment of *Heil Darling!* while employed by Paramount. But Paramount told them the studio had no right or title to the property, and the authors were free to do with it what they wished. Around December 8, the three screenwriters delivered a draft of *Heil Darling!* to MGM. By the end of the month they'd been paid, after which their screenplay disappeared into the studio's files. No one else appears to have been interested in pulling laughs out of a brittle Nazi's love affair with a cocky, politically indifferent reporter.

Even at the time it was written, *Heil Darling!* was a morally precarious tale disguised by a stock romantic-comedy plot; history only renders it more appalling by degree. Set in Vienna and Berlin in March and April of 1938, Wilder and Théry's treatment of *Heil Darling!* lays out this most peculiar comedy in a cheery, ghastly arc. (What Lubitsch contributed is unclear, since the actual screenplay is lost.) "Listen, babe," Josh Crocker tells his journalist buddy on the evening of March 11, when he fails to see why he should ignore the imminent Anschluss in favor of a Viennese all-girl band. "The Germans are always massing on some border. You're talking like a fish. Nothing will happen, except that we'll lose the gals. You ought to see them! Oh, stop talking about Hitler." In the morning, with the gals having passed out in their dirndls, the boys—now a group of four—enjoy a roaring game of poker while airplanes and jackboots make distracting noises outside. "The cold facts didn't dawn on them until Josh shouted for fresh coffee. . . . Josh felt as if he had been hit by one of the tanks. Personally, he didn't give a hang, but he had talked his pals into muffing the biggest beat of the year."

When a rich Viennese widow named Wagner proposes that Josh marry her in order to secure her (and her money) hasty passage out of Austria, Josh accepts the offer as a pure business transaction. Since new Nazi regulations demand that anyone wishing to marry be certified as Aryan, Josh must undergo a medical examination at the Racial Bureau: "It was a doctor's office, all right, but the walls were plastered with a variety of rather strange looking charts. There was a chart comparing an Aryan gall-bladder with a non-Aryan gall-blader, another which bore a series of differently shaped skulls indicating the comparative value of the various races. No. 1 was the Germanic skull, naturally; No. 2 the Scandinavian skull; and so on down to No. 11, which was the skull of a monkey. No. 12, the last, was the skull of a Russian communist. There was also a map of the world, with brown spots showing which areas should go back to the Reich. Sudetenland, Danzig, half of France, and Milwaukee."

In the centerpiece of what is by far the most bizarre meet-cute Billy ever set down on paper, the beautiful but glacial Dr. Wilhelmine Mueller measures Josh's skull and finds that it corresponds to that of the monkey. When the ardent Nazi physician determines that Josh's upper lip is Aryan but his lower lip is not, she refuses to permit the marriage, at which point a further complication arises: Dr. Mueller is engaged to marry the head of the Austrian Gestapo.

At first, Josh simply tries to sweet-talk Wilhelmine into signing his racial certification, but when they get to know each other better in Josh's car on the way back from a pilgrimage to Hitler's birthplace, they begin to fall tentatively, awkwardly in love. She explains Nazi theory to him—the uses of the rubber blackjack, the virtues of lebensraum, the return of German colonies. "But she really warmed up when she started on the holy mission of the Nazi empire to save the world from the Russian plague. . . . The moon had risen nicely and Josh gave out with a swell impersonation of Chamberlain and Donald Duck. In return, she recited for him the second chorus of the Horst Wessel song. They had a good time." He asks if he could take her out some evening to enjoy the romantic beauty of Vienna. "She didn't say yes—but she didn't say no, either. Following that, he pointed out that the American equivalent for Wilhelmine was Billie. She found it strange but rather droll." When he tries to kiss her hand, she heils him instead. "And thus began the strange love story of an American mug, descent unkown, and the blondest fruit of a certified Nordic family tree."

Billie Mueller's ideological shell finally cracks along with her emotional reticence. Too bad Josh gets arrested by storm troopers. He's thrown into the back of a car and whisked away to Gestapo headquarters, where Billie's fiancé, the Gestapo chief Himmelreich, threatens to send Billie to a concentration camp unless Josh breaks up with her.

Heil Darling! winds toward a clumsy resolution when four members of the German-American Bund arrive in Vienna from Milwaukee. Josh fixes them up with the orchestra girls, and he and his reporter buddies usurp their identities. Pretending to be American spies for the Reich, the boys travel to Berlin to meet with Nazi leaders. Wilhelmine, flown to Berlin on special orders, is told that she must leave immediately for America on an important mission. She says she cannot—for personal reasons. (She believes Josh has been arrested by the Gestapo.) "At this moment, from behind her a voice floated softly. 'Baloney' said the voice. She didn't turn around. She knew." In *Heil Darling!*'s happy final scene, "Wilhelmine and Josh stood on the sun deck, as the *Normandie* steamed up New York harbor. There was a lady waiting for them, with her arm outstretched, but she didn't shout any Heils. There was a torch in her hand, you see."

That Nazi theories of racial supremacy might not serve especially well as the foundation of a Hollywood romantic comedy, even under the pretext of propaganda, seems obvious to the point of absurdity today. For the émigré comedy writers, the cost of alerting American audiences to the Nazi menace was that the genuine evil they'd fled had to be glossed, and given subsequent history, this central evasion is repulsive. It was one thing for refugee scripters to transform a humorless Communist and a selfish gigolo into a romantic ideal in *Ninotchka*. It was quite another to enlist a grim Nazi doctor as the new comedy's love interest, especially when the racial policies Dr. Mueller enforces (even after she falls in love) resulted in the beating, killing, and quotidian harassment of real Jews, Gypsies, Poles, and Communists. The world, moreover, was that much closer to war. Still, the very tastelessness of *Heil Darling!* testifies to the bitter despair of its writers. Wilder and his partners tried to make light of something vile, perhaps as much to relieve their own private terrors as to sell a new film project to their American employers. Calling the Nazi racist Billie, on the other hand, was simply (if sickly) clinical.

For Billy, *Ninotchka*'s success more than made up for the shelving of *Heil Darling!* The theme of regeneration and renewal, on which both comedies stood, found a parallel in his private life: he and Judith were awaiting the birth of a child sometime in late December. The immigrant was planting himself more and more firmly in his adoptive land. By that point Billy was an American citizen, having taken the oath earlier that year in the federal courthouse in Los Angeles (accompanied not by his wife but by Don Hartman, a screenwriting buddy at Paramount). The Wilders were living in Beverly Hills, though on the less desirable south end of town, in a rented apartment at 136 South Camden Drive. And they were making plans for their future as a family. In November 1939 they bought a piece of property on Tarcuto Way in Bel-Air with the idea of building a house. It was a charming piece of ground on a cul-de-sac; the back faced the Bel-Air Country Club. This was literally a most exclusive neighborhood; the Wilders' deed specified that blacks and Asians were not permitted to live there. In five years, Billy had come quite a long way from the ladies' room at the Chateau Marmont. He'd ventured even further from the little Berlin rooms he found thanks to his Communist friend Kisch.

Just before Christmas, Billy became a father. Early on the morning of December 21, at Cedars of Lebanon Hospital, Judith gave birth to twins. A baby boy, Vincent, arrived first at 6:00 A.M.; a girl, Victoria, followed at 6:08. Judith had carried them full-term, and they were both healthy and strong. In early January 1940, Judith and both of her babies left the hospital. The new family of four moved back in with Judith's mother. When they sent out birth announcements for the twins, the Wilders listed their address as 8224 De Longpre.

Billy immediately went back to work. His first project in 1940 was *Rhythm on the River*, a Bing Crosby musical. Wilder was quite familiar with the first few drafts of the screenplay he and Brackett were asked to spend a week revising. After all, he'd written them himself with Jacques Théry in the days before he'd teamed up with Brackett. He and Théry had called it *Ghost Music*. It was about a successful composer named Prescott who pays two ghostwriters to compose his songs for him—an attractive but naive young woman as lyricist, and a young man as composer. In the interim, *Ghost Music* had been going through the Paramount wringer, mostly remaining stuck. Théry himself began revising the script in mid-December 1939. Brackett and Wilder joined him in mid-January 1940. But it still wasn't right—at least not according to Paramount executives—so on January 15, Dwight Taylor took over and spent the next five months changing things around. Even these alterations weren't enough for the film's star, Bing Crosby, who brought two of his own writers, Barney Dean and Louis Kaye, in to do minor fiddling before the film went into production. Wilder ended up sharing only a story credit with Théry. *Rhythm on the River* is credited entirely to Dwight Taylor.

On February 12, 1940, Billy Wilder received his first Oscar nomination when he, Brackett, and Reisch were nominated for Best Screenplay for

Ninotchka. In the kind of Hollywood event that inspires broad satires, Melchior Lengyel's three-sentence idea was enough to earn him his own nomination for Best Original Story. But neither of *Ninotchka*'s nominations led to Oscars. When the awards were announced on February 29, the *Gone with the Wind* juggernaut proved too mighty, and Billy lost to Sidney Howard.

At home on De Longpre, things seemed fine in February and March. Victoria and Vincent were thriving. A doctor performed a routine exam toward the end of March and pronounced both babies in excellent health. Then, on March 31, at 10:15 P.M., Billy Wilder's son died. He was three months old. The cause of Vincent's death was listed as congenital atalectasis—the boy's lungs simply hadn't been able to develop and grow, though the condition appears to have been a shock to everyone. Vincent Wilder was cremated on April 2.

In June at the very latest, Billy was back on the Paramount lot preparing his next screenplay with Brackett. His state of mind can only be guessed, because he has never publicly discussed his son's death and what it meant to him.

The script Wilder cowrote was called *Arise, My Love,* the title having been drawn from the passionate, erotic love poetry of the Song of Solomon: "The fig tree putteth forth her green figs, and the vines with the tender grapes give forth fragrance. Arise, my love, my fair one, and come away." In Paramount's Writers Building, however, love was at a distinct premium. First of all, *Arise, My Love* was going to be a Mitchell Leisen film, and in Billy's mind, Leisen wasn't likely to have gained much sense since *Midnight.* In addition, war in Europe was no longer a threat. It had become a fact, and Billy was increasingly caught in the refugees' bind. What could he do in Hollywood other than sign his name to well-intentioned pieces of paper and hope he hadn't gone too far to offend any of the moguls? Hitler had invaded Poland in September 1939, so Billy's childhood home in Kraków was now under Nazi control. His past was threatened with full erasure—there was no way of knowing what had become of his mother and grandmother—and his son was dead.

Added to the typical turmoil of Billy's partnership with Brackett, these new tensions meant that life at the office was even more dangerous than usual. There was, needless to say, a lot of yelling. But once again, Brackett and Wilder pulled a fine piece of work out of their collaboration. In the years after its release, *Arise, My Love* was increasingly overshadowed by two other, more enduring early-wartime melodramas—*Casablanca* and *Foreign Correspondent*—but it remains a beautiful and emotionally rich work. The film's producer, Arthur Hornblow Jr., is said to have given Brackett and Wilder nothing but a short written treatment to develop. It was about an American flier, Hornblow explained, who was involved with the Loyalists in Spain. Then, according to the story, the producer told his writers not to distort their imaginations by bothering to read the treatment he had just handed them, so Wilder and Brackett ended up composing the story entirely on the basis of Hornblow's single-sentence synopsis.

The facts, of course, are quite different. If Hornblow was indeed feeling generous toward his writing team, it was because none of the treatments he'd bought or commissioned met his satisfaction. First there was a complete script, written by John Szekely and Benjamin Glazer, dated November 1939; next came a treatment by Jacques Théry and Ketti Frings in early March. This was followed later in March by another treatment, this time by Frings on her own. Szekely and Glazer turned in another draft of their script on the same day. Soon thereafter, Hornblow handed the project to Wilder and Brackett, who submitted their first draft on June 18 and continued to work on revisions through the first week of August. The script they wrote for *Arise, My Love* is assuredly their own—there are too many Billy-isms for it to be otherwise—but it's obvious that the writers read the earlier drafts they had at their disposal, since they transferred the two central characters and several key incidents more or less directly.

Still, *Arise, My Love* is thoroughly suffused with Billy Wilder's tough but romantic sensibility, not to mention Charles Brackett's literary rhythms. While playing casino with a priest in the hours before his death, Tom (Ray Milland) tells the padre of his choice of last words: "I sort of wavered between 'Death to Tyrants' or 'Long Live Liberty!' But I finally decided to say it with music. What do you think of this: (*singing*) 'Lookie lookie lookie, here's goes Cookie . . .' " "Isn't there anything I can do for you?" the priest inquires. "Yeah, gimme some better cards."

Pardoned after his wife begs the Fascist prison warden for clemency, Tom is mystified. He has no wife. When he arrives in the governor's office, he sees the woman who's saving him—it's Claudette Colbert, wearing a fabulous hat. His passport is produced. The governor reads: "It says here, 'Thomas Fuller Martin, born June 22, 1906.' (Later, the wiseacre card player modifies it further to "Thomas Fuller Mullarkey.") Colbert, who turns out to be a lady reporter, finally pulls him out of the Fascist's office, saying, "Oh come now, Tom—thank the governor for everything and tell him you've had a lovely time." They escape by hijacking a plane. Tom hates her name—Augusta. It's "like talking to a battleship" he remarks. "They call me 'Gusto,' " she explains. "For years I've had a column—'In Paris with Gusto.' " Colbert delivers this line with a certain irony, which it well deserves. (Of the many improvements Brackett and Wilder made in this screenplay, naming the central female character "Gusto" may have been the least astute.)

Brackett and Wilder spiced up the dialogue considerably, much to the consternation of the censors. Tom tells Gusto about his previous relationships: "Take Hazel, for instance. Hazel was the air hostess on a commercial liner I was flying from Fort Worth to New Orleans. One night in April, very bad flying weather, no passengers, just Hazel and I. That's how I lost my commercial license." The Hays Office flagged it as offensive, but it stayed in the film anyway. When Tom comes on to Gusto in the airplane, the writers had her express her skepticism about the depth of his feelings toward her by giving her the line, "After ten months in jail, anything would be your type—a St. Bernard." The Hays Office flagged this one as well, but it, too, remained in the film.

Wilder and Brackett also rewrote the scene in which the protagonist talks to his two friends so that Tom is seen taking a bath while conversing with his pals—two fresh-faced, all-American guys he's come to Europe with. Leisen filmed the scene precisely as written, and the Hays Office was especially offended. Joseph Breen, the earnest censor, wrote a memo to Hays himself expressing his outrage: "There is a scene in this picture which, in our judgement, is a new low in purported screen entertainment." First, according to Breen, came "shock number 1"—one of three men having this bathroom conversation appears to be seated on the toilet. (In fact, he's on a washstand.) "Shock number 2" came when Ray Milland was seen shaving in the tub, "and the camera angles are pitched in such a way as to come as near as possible to the exposure of Mr. Milland's sex organs." Breen's third shock occurred when Milland prepared to stand up in the bathtub a second or two before Leisen cut away from him. Breen minced no words in expressing his revulsion: "This whole sequence and, more especially, the scenes of Milland in the bathtub, constitute in our judgement the most shocking exhibition of consummate bad taste which we have ever seen on the motion picture screen."

Arise, My Love's editor, Doane Harrison, may have reedited this sequence very slightly—Milland makes no move to stand up naked in the release print—but all the other elements that horrified Joseph Breen remained on-screen. Tom's friends, Pink and Shep, spend a lot of time discussing Shep's mother's rabbit farm in New Jersey, and how she'll send him a return ticket to the States "if the rabbits'll only cooperate fast enough." The rabbit business stayed in the film. Left strangely unremarked upon by the Hays Office, however, was Pink's name. Calling a Spanish Republican mercenary "Pink" is one thing; making him the protagonist's likable best friend is something else again. Still, "Pink" sailed through the Hays Office without remark.

Brackett and Wilder kept Szekely and Glazer's idea of putting the two leading characters on a transatlantic liner and having the liner be blown up by a Nazi submarine. They were all aided by recent history, since the sinking of the British ship *Athenia* on September 3, 1939, was the first act of violence between Germany and Britain. But Brackett and Wilder didn't kill their characters, at least not literally. In a more complex character development, they have them commit a sort of symbolic suicide by tossing champagne glasses into the water moments before the torpedo hits. The two characters are leaving Europe and their professional lives, and, consequently, both Tom and Gusto lose sight of themselves. Tom is an energetic mercenary, Gusto is a driven journalist, but they have decided to return to America and settle down together as a sedate married couple. Facing four glasses of a strange champagne-and-crème-de-menthe cocktail, Tom proposes two toasts—the first to "those two dizzy fools with their outsized ideals," the second to Gusto, the career woman. They drink and throw the glasses overboard. Then Gusto bids herself good-bye. She proposes a toast to Tom; they drink and toss these glasses overboard as well: "Good-bye, Tom Martin, crusader." It's then that the torpedo hits. But Wilder and Brackett don't drown them; instead, they provide a more moral as well as morale-boosting conclusion. These independent spirits need to retrieve their own lost natures before they can ever hope to settle down with each other successfully as a couple.

Wilder and Brackett end their script at the French surrender in the forest at Compiègne. Hornblow, who was most interested in keeping the film current, encouraged his writers to work each day's war news into the script. The armistice occurred on June 22, 1940. *Arise, My Love* began filming on June 24. Gusto and the other war correspondents sit dejectedly after receiving their instructions from the Nazi officers. Faced with the humiliating calamity of France surrendering to Germany at the very spot where World War I had ended, one of the reporters proposes a Billy solution: "Well I don't suppose anyone feels like a rubber of bridge?" Gusto, in no mood for cards, goes for a walk in the woods by herself. She speaks to Tom in her thoughts, and he responds: he's found her, he's really there, alive. The film concludes with Gusto's rousing speech: "Remember your prayer. This time we have to say it to America: Arise, my love; arise, be strong! So you can stand up straight and say to anyone under God's heaven, 'All right—whose way of life shall it be? Yours or ours?' "

Claudette Colbert claimed, years later, that Gusto Nash was her favorite role. Less well known than the roles she played in *It Happened One Night*, *Midnight*, or *Cleopatra*, Gusto, however contrived her name may be, is nonetheless one of the most well-rounded female roles Wilder ever wrote. She's got all of the intelligence and wit of Eve Peabody in *Midnight*, but she also has an active, successful career. Moreover, both Tom and Gusto share Wilder's own difficulty balancing their personal and professional lives. Not only do they each need, constitutionally, to work in order to remain sane, but they're both troubled by a sense of incompleteness for which no amount of work can compensate. Only in the Compiègne woods, with Hitler arranging the subjugation of the French nation barely offscreen, can they find any kind of peace of mind with themselves and with each other.

Like almost everything Wilder and Brackett wrote, *Arise, My Love* took a distinctly ironic stance toward politics, careers, and romance. But the final irony of *Arise, My Love* occurred when the Academy Awards were announced. *Arise, My Love* won an Oscar for its fine writing—*not* the Best Screenplay award (Brackett and Wilder weren't even nominated), but the award for Best Original Story. Benjamin Glazer accepted. Szekely's name did not appear in the roster of winners and nominees, his place having been taken by the pseudonymous "John Toldy." As Glazer noted in his acceptance speech, his writing partner had returned to Europe—Szekely was Hungarian—and stood the risk of facing severe repercussions for having (supposedly) written this anti-Nazi story.

Billy, meanwhile, was putting his energies into two passions and a moral obligation. He continued writing throughout 1940—two other films were on the drawing boards at Paramount. And, with his ever increasing writing income, Wilder bought some important works of art: a Picasso drawing, for which he paid $900; Henry Moore's *Recumbent Figure*, a cast-lead sculpture Wilder purchased through the émigré art dealer Curt Valentin in New York; and, through Ludwig Charell's gallery (also in New York), Miró's *Le fermier et son épouse*, a gouache on board. Wilder also stepped up his involvement in the refugee crisis. According to Marlene Dietrich, Wilder, Lubitsch, and Dietrich formed the Hollywood Committee, the purpose of which was to gather money and send it to a contact in Switzerland, code-named "Engel," who used it to liberate people from Nazi detention camps and bring them to the United States. One of those helped by the Hollywood Committee's intervention was the composer Robert Katscher, whose song "Madonna" had so impressed Paul Whiteman. Unfortunately, Katscher was terribly ill at the time of his liberation and died shortly thereafter. Some of those who did manage to escape, thanks in part to the Hollywood Committee, were men deployed to load new prisoners onto train cars near the Swiss border. But as Dietrich notes, there were fewer and fewer escapees as the war in Europe progressed.

Those refugees who involved themselves in such efforts as the Hollywood Committee paid a price for their good deeds—surveillance, FBI files, and an end to their privacy. J. Edgar Hoover, who tended to see all foreigners as potential spies, had become especially interested in investigating anyone who had emigrated from Germany or Austria. According to Alexander Stephan, who has been researching the files Hoover kept on the refugees, FBI agents secretly found their way into the émigrés' houses and apartments, where they took pictures and made drawings of the mundane details of these people's lives. Secret mailboxes were installed, messages were sent in code, reports were written in invisible ink. . . . Hoover's agents went undercover to the meetings of American rescue committees, not to mention the Hollywood parties these committee members attended. There they recruited informants from among the crowd. Refugees thus reported on fellow refugees, providing not only information on their politics but details about their personal lives as well. (To date, Professor Stephan has found nothing in the FBI files pertaining specifically to Billy Wilder. It's hard to imagine, however, that Wilder was singularly excluded from the surveillance the United States brought to bear on prominent émigré film-makers at the time.)

The FBI was not the only government agency interested in the Hollywood émigrés. In the summer of 1939, Congressman Martin Dies launched his first salvo in what would eventually become a full-scale war on Hollywood leftists. Dies singled out three films that, to him, represented communism's infiltration of the American film industry: *Fury*, *Juarez*, and *Blockade*. The first was directed by Fritz Lang, the others by William Dieterle; both directors were refugees from the Nazis. The response from Hollywood's establishment was swift. Leland Hayward, for instance, convinced his client Greta Garbo to decline the starring role in a drama about the Resistance.

Liesl Frank, Charlotte Dieterle, and Wilder's own agent, Paul Kohner, were already intimately involved in the refugee efforts with their European Film Fund, through which Frank and Dieterle brought out the last batch of refugee writers to leave Marseilles and Lisbon in 1940 and 1941. Kohner used his studio connections on their behalf, approaching Jack Warner and L. B. Mayer, "playing on their Jewish loyalties." As a result, Heinrich Mann, Alfred Döblin, Leonhard Frank, and Walter Mehring among others found themselves whisked from the Pyrenees to Los Angeles in a matter of days with Hollywood jobs practically waiting for them.

For once, Tinseltown found itself distracted by something other than box office receipts and its own gossip. Each of the studios had a war picture or two in the works. Warner Bros. had *International Squadron* and a World War I combat film called *The Fighting 69th*; Columbia had *Escape to Glory*; Fox had *Four Sons* and *A Yank in the R.A.F.*; United Artists had *Foreign Correspondent*; even glossy MGM had *Thunder Afloat*. Paramount was developing a film about the Nazi takeover of Poland. It was called *Polonaise*, and it was going to be written by Brackett and Wilder, who were to start work on the script in the summer of 1940, after finishing

Arise, My Love. *Polonaise* would be the story of a young Notre Dame football star, to be played by William Holden, who attempts to rescue his Polish mother (or possibly his grandmother, since she was to be played by Maria Ouspenskaya) after the Nazi invasion and bring her to the United States. But *Polonaise* never got very far. The film was postponed when William Holden decided to do a western, *Arizona*, for Columbia instead. Brackett and Wilder became increasingly involved with *Arise, My Love*, and in early- to mid-July 1940, *Polonaise* was canceled completely.

In August 1940, Wilder talked with Paul Kohner about another idea—a Bob Hope comedy, something to do with diamonds. Kohner's client William Wyler was interested in the idea, Kohner told Billy—"even with Hope"—but only if Wilder and Brackett wrote the script. But Wilder, then vacationing in Crystal Bay, Nevada, wasn't interested. With no *Polonaise* and no Bob Hope comedy, Brackett and Wilder were free to write a film about a shifty, smooth-talking refugee forced to wait on the other side of the Mexican border for the United States to let him in.

In the writing of *Hold Back the Dawn*, Wilder obviously drew on his own experiences in Mexicali, but the original idea wasn't his. Paramount bought the story from Ketti Frings in 1939. In October 1940, a few weeks before Wilder and Brackett set to work developing and revising Frings's treatment, Louella Parsons reported on the film's genesis in her syndicated column:

> Just before Paulette Goddard caught the boat for New York, via the Panama Canal, she received word from her alma mater, Paramount, that should cheer the heart of any gal. None other than Monsignor [*sic*] Charles Boyer, the popular and romantic French actor, will be her co-star in *Hold Back the Dawn*. Interesting about the story *Hold Back the Dawn*, written by Katherine Hartley Frings, former fan magazine writer, that it tells the true experiences of her husband in a refugee camp in Mexico where aliens are detained waiting for a quota number to come into the United States.

Parsons was right. Ketti Frings was an ambitious young fanzine writer who fell in love with, and married, an Austrian lightweight boxing champ and ski instructor, Kurt Frings, in 1938. Since then, however, she had graduated into scriptwriting at Paramount. It was Ketti Frings, after all, who had written two treatments for *Arise, My Love* before the project was handed to Brackett and Wilder. Frings called her treatment "Memo to a Movie Producer." Brackett and Wilder later claimed they hadn't bothered to read Frings's novel when they wrote the screenplay, but then, of course, they didn't have to, since they worked closely from the treatment.

Kurt Frings, meanwhile, was attracting a lot of attention, some of which was not very flattering. In April 1940, still stuck in Tijuana after two years, Frings took his case to Congress. He was not alone. The Congressional Record is littered with similar cases, all of which attest to the tremendous difficulties and harsh bureaucratic obstacles refugees faced in their efforts to gain asylum in America. At first, Frings appeared to be headed for success. The Senate Committee on Immigration recommended that he be admitted to the States, and the House Committee on Immigration and Naturalization drew the same conclusion, but President Roosevelt vetoed the bill on June 19, 1940, citing evidence of Frings's moral turpitude.

An official from the narcotics division of the Treasury Department became alarmed at Louella Parsons's announcement of *Hold Back the Dawn* and wrote a terse letter to the Motion Picture Distributors and Producers' New York office: "The husband referred to is one Kurt Frings, who is a notorious international character. . . . In the best interest of the public, a picture on such a basis may do more harm than good. Will you please let me know if your people are in a position to cooperate in this matter?"

A small battle erupted between the Treasury Department and Paramount Pictures, and Paramount won. The film was made. Kurt Frings got into the United States and became a successful Hollywood agent. Ketti Frings went on to enjoy a productive career as a novelist, playwright, and producer; her 1958 Broadway adaptation of *Look Homeward, Angel* earned her a Pulitzer Prize. Brackett and Wilder's screenplay for *Hold Back the Dawn* turned out to be a significant improvement on the original material, and Leisen's direction was polished enough to make the film one of his best.

Wilder knew about Paramount's plans for *Hold Back the Dawn* as early as August 1939, when he tried to get Hornblow to hire an Austrian refugee actor named Hans Jaray for the lead. Hornblow got as far as looking at Jaray's picture before turning him down. It's probable that Hornblow had Wilder and Brackett in mind when he bought Frings's idea. After all, how many other top-flight screenwriters had spent time on the other side of the Mexican border trying to wangle himself a residency permit? Brackett and Wilder began working on the script in late 1939, but since they were involved in other screenplays, they only appear to have concentrated on *Hold Back the Dawn* in the last half of 1940, finishing it up in January 1941. (Another writer, Richard Maibaum, gave the script a polish after Wilder and Brackett turned in their final draft.)

Charles Boyer was Paramount's pick for the male lead. Boyer, whose screen persona hasn't aged particularly well, was nonetheless a great choice at the time. Other 1940s male stars of varying types—Cooper, Grant,

Bogart, Wayne, Stewart, Fonda—have survived much more fondly in the American imagination, probably because they were Americans. Boyer, of course, was French, and the romance associated with debonair French roués has dissipated in the intervening years. Otto Friedrich, describing *Hold Back the Dawn* in *City of Nets*, derides Boyer as "a onetime classical actor who now lived mainly by his toupee, his corset, and his heroic image of himself," but that's not fair—not to Boyer, certainly, but also not to the countless moviegoers on both sides of the Atlantic who continued to see him as an appealing movie star in films like *Gaslight*, *The Earrings of Madame de*, *Cluny Brown*, and *The Cobweb*, to name only a few. Billy himself grew to detest Boyer personally, but for a different reason.

For the leading woman, the refugee's naive American bride, Paramount chose Olivia de Havilland, with Paulette Goddard playing a prominent supporting role—the refugee's gold-digging girlfriend. Brackett and Wilder helped engineer de Havilland's casting themselves. They'd had her in mind for the role when they wrote it, even though she was under contract with Warner Bros. According to Tony Thomas, de Havilland's biographer, Paramount tricked Jack Warner into letting her go. When Warner read the list of available stars to the Paramount exec who'd called him to see about a loan, the executive feigned disinterest when de Havilland's name came up. He called Warner back a few days later and said that, well, he guessed she'd do. Brackett, meanwhile, had already slipped a copy of the script to de Havilland, who agreed to do the part. Since Warner wanted to borrow Fred MacMurray from Paramount for a war picture, *Dive Bomber*, the studios arranged a trade. Jack Warner reportedly thought he'd gotten the better deal.

"My papers give my profession as a dancer," Boyer's character announces in the beginning of *Hold Back the Dawn*, an annotation "which is correct in a general way. It was an easy life, if you had a deep voice and knew how to look at a woman." Georges Iscovescu is a Romanian gigolo, a man with few scruples. This was Brackett and Wilder's most significant revision from Ketti Frings's treatment. Frings's "Memo to a Movie Producer" wasn't just a good idea for a movie; it was a public relations effort on behalf of her husband, whom she sketched in wholesome, loving strokes. Brackett and Wilder turned him into a scoundrel—a lover-for-hire whose self-contempt isn't great enough to prevent him from looking for more work. At the beginning of the film, he shows up at the Paramount lot, desperate to see a film director named Saxon (played by Leisen himself). Iscovescu has a story to tell—*his* story, for which he asks $500. Except for a brief coda, *Hold Back the Dawn* is told entirely in flashback—a tale of deceit and remorse, with Iscovescu casting himself in a none-too-flattering light.

Informed by immigration officials that the quotas for Romanians are so tight that he'll have to wait five to eight years before he can enter the United States, Iscovescu tries to find a room in a hotel for the near-permanant transients who have crowded into town. He's lucky to get one; a Jewish refugee hangs himself in his room just in the nick of time: "There was an unexpected, shall I say, departure. A man by the name of Wechsler. . . . So the German moved out of Room 27 and I moved in." The maid hasn't even finished stripping Wechsler's bed before Georges Iscovescu has made himself at home.

He meets Anita, his former "dancing" partner. She's gained residency status thanks to the American who married her: "Shaughnessy was a jockey from Caliente," she tells a fascinated Iscovescu. "Five foot three. Once over the border I went to a judge. I said, 'A woman wants a man, not a radiator cap.' Divorce granted—$50." When Iscovescu meets Emmy (de Havilland), the harried American schoolteacher leading a station wagon full of ill-behaved American boys on a day-long tour of Mexico, he sees his pigeon. He borrows Anita's wedding ring and, before the night is through, he and Emmy are husband and wife.

De Havilland's performance as Emmy is one of her most restrained; her character is innocent but not to the point of stupidity. She's lonely, and she falls for him too quickly, but de Havilland keeps her from being as pathetic as she might have been. Brackett and Wilder provide her with a fine, depressing little scene in which Iscovescu and Emmy ride in the rain at night, and Emmy, with excruciating innocence, notices that the windshield wipers are beating out a message for the newlyweds. They sweep across the windshield in a terrible rhythm, meeting in the middle, over and over again: "Did you ever notice how things talk sometimes?" she says to a mortified Iscovescu. "Listen to those windshield wipers: Together. Together. Together. Together. . . . Can you hear it?"

Hold Back the Dawn is a study of a man's ascending self-loathing. Faced with someone who actually needs him, Georges learns just how worthless he is. Eventually, Anita takes Emmy aside and wakes her up to reality by advising her to read the engraved inscription on the inside of her wedding ring: "To Toots" it says—"for keeps." Emmy doesn't bother to take the ring off and check, but she knows it's true. Anita then delivers a line of breathtaking simplicity: "I know what you're thinking—'This woman's a tramp and she's in love with him.' Well I *am* a tramp, and I *am* in love with him!" She continues by explaining the attraction: "I'm his sort. I'm dirt, but so is he. We belong together."

Iscovescu eventually displays a modicum of honor, and he does succeed in gaining both Emmy and American residency (though Leisen shrewdly withholds the patriotic clinch from view, ending the film instead on a fade-out of Iscovescu walking through a crowd of people). But Iscovescu's role in the final third of the film is a bit truncated, and his reunion with Emmy is virtually nonexistent. This was Boyer's fault. Wilder and Brackett had no idea when they wrote "Scene B-8, Int, Iscovescu's Room" that it would be not only the pivotal scene of the film but also the turning point of their careers.

Absurdity, stupidity, and the gutlessness of Mitchell Leisen combined to make this one of Wilder's most treasured stories. The date is March 15, 1941: "Brackett and I are having lunch at the restaurant across the street from Paramount, and there is Boyer having lunch. And I said, 'Well, how's it going, Charlie?' He says, 'Beautiful. Love it.' And I say, 'What are you shooting today?' He says, 'Well, we are shooting that scene with the cockroach, but we changed it a little. I do not talk to the cockroach, because that's stupid. How can I talk to a cockroach if a cockroach cannot answer me?' I was really furious, and on the way out I said to Brackett, 'That sonofabitch. If he don't talk to a cockroach, he don't talk to nobody.' We went back and finished the third act, and we gave everything to Olivia de Havilland."

In one variation of the tale, Boyer adds a little insult: "I do not wish to have these discussions while I am at the table," Boyer is said to have told Billy. "Go away, Mr. Wilder, you disturb me." In this rendition, too, Wilder returns to his office, pounds on his desk, and shrieks, "I'll kill him! I'll kill him!" Whatever the precise dialogue happened to be at the time, Billy Wilder drew the correct conclusion from his lunchtime interchange with Charles Boyer. As always, Wilder phrases the moral lesson colorfully: "What we wrote was a bit of toilet paper that they either used or they didn't."

This was not the first time an actor had deleted some dialogue from a Brackett and Wilder script. *Midnight*'s script featured an even more elaborate version of the party sequence at the Flammarions' chateau, the centerpiece of which was to have been Eve, as the spurious Baroness Czerny, roasting hot dogs in the fireplace. On the day of shooting, however, Miss Colbert flatly refused to have anything to do with a weenie roast, and the scene had to be completely revised on the spot. The extended conga line in the finished film is Leisen's attempt to cover for the missing material. But there were several key developments between the hot dogs and the cockroach. Billy Wilder had written two more commercially successful films. His salary had risen commensurately, along with his prestige, though he was still being paid only a little more than half of what Brackett earned. (Brackett got $42,063 for writing *Hold Back the Dawn*, while Billy only got $23,025.) Still, Billy Wilder had been nominated for an Academy Award. People knew him. He had a bit of clout.

Even more important, Preston Sturges had become a director. Sturges was proving, right on the Paramount lot, that great writers could also become great filmmakers. Sturges blamed poor, much-maligned Mitchell Leisen for driving him into the directors' ranks as well; according to Sturges, Leisen totally ruined his script for *Easy Living* (a charge for which Leisen was once again quite innocent). Because Sturges was a Paramount writer-director, there was an excellent precedent to which Billy could point when he approached the front office. Moreover, although Sturges was the first Hollywood writer to attempt such a usurpation, he was no longer alone. Across town at Warner Bros., John Huston was making the same demand, and Huston was getting his wish as well. (He launched his directorial career with *The Maltese Falcon.*) For Billy Wilder, the cockroach episode may have been the final straw, but the salient point is that this straw hit Billy's back at a most opportune moment.

When Zolotow mentioned Leisen's name to Billy, Billy flew into a nasty tirade: "Leisen was too goddamn fey. I don't knock fairies. Let him be a fairy. Leisen's problem was that he was a stupid fairy." This exchange has been quoted as evidence of Wilder's homophobia, but Wilder never cared about anyone's sex life as long as the details were filthy enough to make a good story. Leisen was no exception. It was the director's putative idiocy, not his sexuality, that got Wilder's goat, though Leisen's penchant for fussing over the decor was always a thorn in Wilder's side. "He hated writers," Billy told David Freeman. "I would come on the set and stop him. 'What happened to that line?' I would say. He would say, 'I cut it. You're bothering me.' He came from set dressing."

As for Leisen, he was just as uncharitable, though in a different way. Leisen accused Wilder of writing scenes that made no emotional sense, and furthermore, "Billy would scream if you changed one line of his dialogue. I used to say, 'Listen, this isn't Racine, it's not Shakespeare. If the actors we have can't say it, we must give them something they can say.'" The reason Leisen ascribed to Billy's temperament is fascinating: "Wilder's the one with whom we had the most difficult discussions, because he comes from Central Europe and he was stubborn as a mule when anyone touched his words." Leisen claimed to have watched Billy directing one of his own scripts years after their professional collaboration had ended badly, and he was amused to see Billy facing the same problem from a different perspective: "It was very funny—he was having to rewrite the whole thing!"

Leisen claimed that Brackett "was sort of a leveling influence" on Wilder: "He would referee my quarrels with Billy. As a team they were the greatest." Wilder, when told of this remark, had none of it. "Charlie hated him as much as I did," Wilder exploded. "Charlie never was a peacemaker. That's bullshit. It was Arthur Hornblow who refereed our fights."

These ugly little snipes, of course, occurred decades after the fact. When they were actually working together, Wilder and Leisen managed somehow to get through it. After all, if fighting over a screenplay had been an insurmountable problem, Wilder's relationship with Brackett would have ended after *Bluebeard's Eighth Wife*. It was only after writing his *third* script for Leisen that Billy decided he'd had enough, and by that point Wilder's rage was fueled more by his own ambition than by anything else.

By March 1941, when the cockroach scene was aborted, Billy Wilder had had enough. He was through with actors who not only *thought* they could rewrite his dialogue but then brazenly went ahead and did it. He was absolutely and irrevocably finished with Mitchell Leisen. He'd also had enough of being confined—insofar as Billy Wilder could ever be confined— to an office suite in the Writers' Building. He had sworn after *Mauvaise Graine* that he'd never direct a film again. Now he changed his mind.

10. BALL OF FIRE

Make no mistake. I shall regret the absence of your keen mind. Unfortunately, it is inseparable from an extremely disturbing body.

—Professor Potts (Gary Cooper) to Sugarpuss O'Shea (Barbara Stanwyck) in *Ball of Fire*

Billy was sitting in the Paramount canteen enjoying his lunch one early afternoon in 1941 when an executive named Luigi Luraschi approached him with a favor to ask. One of Luraschi's jobs was to deal with the censors; another was to show important foreign visitors around the lot. That day, Luraschi was escorting some Austrian who wanted to see what a movie studio looked like. "I don't know what to do with the guy," Luraschi told Billy confidentially. Then he brought over his guest. "I want to introduce you to a fellow countryman," Luraschi said. "He is one of our scriptwriters—Billy Wilder from Austria. From your home, from Vienna. This, Mr. Wilder, is Otto von Hapsburg." Wilder was dumbfounded. This was the little boy he'd watched from the second floor of the Café Edison on that rainy day in 1916, when Franz Josef's funeral cortege paraded through Vienna. Now he was just an ordinary middle-aged man in a nondescript gray suit. "I considered how I should address him," Wilder reported. " 'Your Majesty!' or 'Mr. Crown Prince!' or simply 'How ya doin', Otto? Glad to see you again!' Ultimately I decided on 'What brings you here?' " The dream prince was on a lecture tour on the West Coast, trying, as Wilder put it, "to keep his head above water. And they weren't exactly the top universities he was visiting then—Long Beach College, Pomona, and Pepperdine." Since the deposed prince was in Hollywood, he thought he'd see how other people's dreams were made. "We talked for an hour in Viennese German," Wilder remembered. "I told him about the years of starvation during the war—how my brother and I, in the bitter winter, stood in line for sixteen hours for a handful of potatoes.

He wanted to know everything about Nelson Eddy and Jeanette MacDonald."

Obviously, some of Europe's mighty had already fallen by 1941. Others were still in midplunge, but Billy's fortunes continued to rise. He hadn't forgotten his old émigré friends, but he was good at making many new American ones. Of the old crew's fates, Joe May's was probably the most drastic. Wilder had been watching May's professional life decline since 1933, when the wildly successful director was forced to abandon his lucrative career in Germany and start almost from scratch in Hollywood. It hadn't worked out terribly well for him, and by 1941, May's depressing career as a Hollywood director was sputtering to a close. In 1940, the showman-director of *Das Indische Grabmal* was trafficking in *You're Not So Tough*, a Dead-End-Kids-Go-to-Los-Angeles picture for Universal. May also directed *The Invisible Man*'s less classy sequel. Both were far beneath him, but he had no choice in the matter. Joe May was an object lesson in the fate of immigrants who couldn't cut it in Hollywood.

Billy, meanwhile, was thriving—and seething with ambition. He craved the control directing would give him, but he was still a compulsive scriptwriter, and a well-known one at that, even outside the gates of Paramount Pictures. The scenes he'd caused with Mitchell Leisen were no secret around town, but neither were Billy's wit and charm, not to mention his talent, so when independent producer Sam Spiegel found himself in dire straits, unable to pull a project together, it was Wilder to whom he turned for assistance. He begged Billy for an idea—anything that would make a good, profitable picture. So Wilder offered him one of his old stories—the one he and Walter Reisch had used for their last Ufa film, *Der Frack mit der Chrysantheme*. Spiegel is said to have succeeded in getting the actual Ufa screenplay smuggled out of Nazi Germany thanks to a Hungarian aquaintance, and he remade the film as *Tales of Manhattan* with Charles Boyer, Henry Fonda, Charles Laughton, Ginger Rogers, Rita Hayworth, and Paul Robeson, among many others. The grateful Spiegel told Wilder and Reisch that he'd give them anything they wanted as payment. Wilder asked for two handsome chairs he'd been admiring in a Beverly Hills shop. For his part, Reisch requested two audio speakers. After fielding a cascade of complaints from Wilder and Reisch, Spiegel finally had the articles sent to the two writers—along with the bills.

Around this time, too, Wilder was approached by Leland Hayward to come up with a story idea for Sonja Henie, the Norwegian ice-skater-turned-movie-star. According to Billy, Billy was paid $2,500 for about a half hour's work—the dictation of a short treatment to Helen Hernandez, his own fingers snapping wildly while hers were occupied with the shorthand. (Wilder doesn't name the picture, and he was never credited; if this film was actually made, it would have been *Sun Valley Serenade, Iceland,* or *Wintertime.*)

Assignments like the Sonja Henie idea may have been lucrative, but they weren't enough. Neither was the never-simple act of writing a feature-length screenplay for a major Hollywood studio. It wasn't just that he wanted to keep his stories from being mangled. Billy Wilder wrote *for the screen,* not the page, and when someone else directed his work, it did not look or sound right to him *on the screen.* For Billy, Mitchell Leisen was a decorator, not a director, and was consequently unable to realize the full potential of Wilder's scripts. Wilder has always been unfair to Leisen, who was certainly competent. He never ruined Wilder's screenplays, but he didn't do much more than record them on celluloid and make sure the lighting was good.

Wilder, on the other hand—more than any other screenwriter with the exception of Preston Sturges—wrote scenes to be experienced richly, not merely recorded. His stories lived; his characters breathed and thought. To connect with these characters, Wilder knew, audiences needed to see every gesture in just the right way at just the right time. When Lubitsch directed them, they did. When Leisen directed them, they didn't—not in Wilder's eyes. At the same time, Billy was constitutionally disappointed; for all his worldly success, his wife and little daughter, his friends, his tennis, his bridge, and his art, the world still didn't measure up. Not by a long shot. Wilder couldn't live with himself knowing that Sturges and Huston were achieving something he could not achieve—or would not even try. He wanted to watch at close range as an expert director filmed his next screenplay.

The film was *Ball of Fire,* but since it was being made in Hollywood, neither the screenwriter nor the director drove the project. It was, instead, all up to the star. Gary Cooper, the great wooden Indian of the American cinema, was at the peak of his popularity in the spring of 1941. Cooper projected an appealing self-confidence in the face of his own lack of intellect. As one critic once described him, "His ineptitude was often his appeal. . . . Audiences ascribed more credence to his characters than he himself could actually inject." On-screen, Cooper's homegrown masculinity was conflicted enough to be recognizable and real. As a result, the characters he played were unable to appreciate how dumb they were and were thus able to survive. Gary Cooper was the perfect American man.

In 1941, Cooper was under contract with Samuel Goldwyn, an equally intuitive Hollywood success who was looking for the right picture for his star. He'd been looking for several years; Cooper's last three hits—*Northwest Mounted Police, Meet John Doe,* and *Sergeant York*—had all been made by other studios with Cooper out on loan from Goldwyn. Since his own story department was unable to come up with anything for Cooper since *The Westerner*, Goldwyn put in a call to William Dozier, the head of the story department at Paramount. "You know, Bill," Goldwyn told the young executive, "I'm thinking it's time you and I started doing each other favors. Let's start by you doing me one—I'd like to borrow Brackett and Wilder." Dozier wasn't keen on the idea until he and his fellow executives thought the deal through, at which point they realized they could exchange their two star writers for none other than Gary Cooper, whom Paramount coveted for the taciturn lead in *For Whom the Bell Tolls*. Goldwyn, always a shrewd Hollywood horse trader, convinced Paramount to add a little money and throw in Bob Hope as well, and soon they all had a deal.

At Goldwyn's studio on North Formosa (off Santa Monica Boulevard), the producer set his new writing team to work by handing them stacks and stacks of scripts and treatments that had been written with Cooper in mind. Nothing worked. Then Billy had an inspiration. They didn't need to start with somebody else's idea because Billy had already written the picture. "It was a story that I had written in Germany," Wilder reports, though on other occasions he said he'd come up with the idea in his early Hollywood days. It doesn't much matter. Whenever Billy thought it up, *A to Z* was one of his best ideas. "I found in my trunk this story of a conflict between brains and tommy guns": a gangster's moll meets a linguistics professor. Language on one side, muscle on the other. Gary Cooper as an intellect. It was intrinsically funny.

Of Goldwyn, Wilder has said, "He was a titan with an empty skull—not confused by anything he read, which he didn't." Still, Goldwyn retained a bit of Wilder's respect owing to his instinct for quality and his drive for work. He was, in Wilder's words, "an absolutely, totally dedicated man—like a passionate collector." After unearthing the story, Wilder handed it to a junior writer on the Paramount staff, Thomas Monroe, for a quick rewrite to update the idea. He and Brackett then gave it to Goldwyn, who did with it what Goldwyn usually did with scripts: he gave it to his wife to read for him. "Frances read the story," Goldwyn told Wilder the following day. "She likes it. How much?" "Ten thousand," said Billy. Goldwyn thought the price was on the high side, so he offered to strike a bargain: Goldwyn would pay $7,500 off the bat, and if the film was a hit, he'd pay the balance. Billy agreed, with one further condition: that he be permitted to be on the set while Howard Hawks was filming it, so he could see, firsthand, how a nonidiot directed a motion picture. Goldwyn agreed.

"I stayed constantly on the set, because I had a lot of esteem for Hawks, who knew his trade very well and made very good films. I wanted to know about everything. That lasted nine or ten weeks." Wilder's admiration for Hawks was pronounced, but it never came close to his adoration of Lubitsch. Still, Hawks was much more profoundly influential on Wilder's own cinematic style than Lubitsch had been. Lubitsch imprinted himself onto every frame; Hawks effaced himself. Lubitsch called visual attention to his own cleverness; he was exquisitely subtle about it, but movie reviewers all over the world could plainly see "the Lubitsch touch." So could audiences. Hawks, on the other hand, made films that unfold naturally and invisibly, apparently without any authorial intervention. When Hawks filmed a scene, he knew not only what each shot would look like but also how each of these pieces would fit together in a seamless flow of images. He was one of a handful of directors who edited in his mind as he filmed. The films of Howard Hawks were never assembled in the cutting room. They were made in Hawks's mind while his cameramen filmed them, and they were shot so that nobody else could monkey around with them during the editing process.

Hawks also had a graceful knack with actors. In fact, he'd already directed Cooper in *Sergeant York*, a smash hit. A man's man himself, Hawks hunted with Hemingway, fished with Faulkner, knew how to dress well without preening, and lost a lot of money gambling and playing the horses. He understood Cooper's sententious masculinity and used it to its best advantage. Hawks made his female stars look and sound good, too— Katharine Hepburn in *Bringing Up Baby*, Frances Farmer in *Come and Get It*, Rosalind Russell in *His Girl Friday*. . . . These were bright, sexy women who, under Hawks's direction, knew precisely how to irritate men to the point of abiding passion. *Ball of Fire* was to feature just such a woman—the charmingly named Sugarpuss O'Shea. The question was, who would play her?

So flawless is Barbara Stanwyck as Sugarpuss that *Ball of Fire* seems inconceivable without her. But Stanwyck wasn't even Goldwyn's *third* choice for the lead. At first, the producer wanted Ginger Rogers, but she turned him down. According to the legend, Rogers responded to Goldwyn's offer through her agent by saying that she didn't want to do a tough-talking comedy role—she only wanted to play "ladies"—to which Goldwyn replied by screaming, "You tell Ginger Rogers ladies stink up the place!" Goldwyn then approached Jean Arthur. She, too, wasn't interested in playing anyone named Sugarpuss, so he sent the script to Carole Lombard, who replied by saying that she liked neither the character nor the story. Only then did Goldwyn offer the role to Stanwyck, who quickly accepted it.

For his part, Gary Cooper didn't like Brackett and Wilder's screenplay at all. Coop detested the unusually articulate dialogue the writers proposed to give him. The star who was scheduled to play a brilliant grammarian called the script "gibberish that doesn't make sense." Cooper also faced a practical problem: "I can't memorize it if it doesn't mean anything!" the actor declared. So he burst into Goldwyn's office and demanded a story conference. This must have been a real meeting of minds. But the producer managed to work out this dispute with his star, and Cooper finally agreed to do the picture more or less the way Brackett and Wilder wrote it. "Two-dollar words, okay," Cooper muttered, "but not *ten-dollar* words."

Words—particularly low-price ones—are the backbone of Brackett and Wilder's script for *Ball of Fire*. Eight male professors live and work in a house in New York City. They are compiling an encyclopedia. Professor Bertram Potts (Cooper) has just finished his entry on *Slang* when a gar-bageman appears inquiring about the death of Cleopatra. He's trying to win first prize in a mail-in quiz: "I could use a bundle of scratch right now on account of I met me a mouse last week—whadda pair'a gams!" Then he mentions smackeroos. Professor Potts claims that no such word exists. "Oh, it don't, huh? A smackeroo is a dollar, pal." Potts is not willing to yield the point: "The accepted vulgarism for a dollar is a *buck*," he informs the man, to which the trash collector replies, "The accepted vulgarism for a smackeroo is a *dollar*. That goes for a banger, a fish, a buck, or a rock!"

Potts asks what is a mouse. "A mouse is a dish! That's what I need the moolah for—yeah, the dough! We'll be stubbin', me and the smooch, I mean the dish, I mean the mouse—you know, hit the jiggles for a little rum boogie? Brother, we're going to have some hoy toy toy!" The professors are most excited but still perplexed as to the precise meaning of *hoy toy toy*. "Yeah," says the garbageman, "and if you want that one explained, you go ask your papas."

Seven years before cowriting this dialogue, its rhythm as polished as its tone and definition, Samuel "Billie" Wilder from Kraków spoke next to no English. Now he was fluent—not only in American words and grammar but, even more important, in American thinking. The quickness and color of American slang gave Billy a voice for what was already inside him; fueled by the structure of the English language and the sheer beauty of American slang, he could live his sentences through to the end. For Wilder, language had never before been as immediate and expressive as it was in *Ball of Fire*.

The professors, whose stodginess might have been their only character trait had the writers and the director had less respect for them, are in fact eight of the most likable smart people in the American cinema. They're as sweet as their acknowledged antecedents, the Seven Dwarfs. There is some-thing infantile about them, but for Hawks, infantilism is underrated as a strategy for enduring a hostile world. The professors, isolated and cared for in the mansion provided them by the Daniel S. Totten Foundation, are essentially helpless as individuals. They function, insofar as they do, as a team: Potts, Gurkakoff (Oscar Homolka), Jerome (Henry Travers), Ma-genbruch (S. Z. Sakall), Robinson (Tully Marshall), Quintana (Leonid

Kinskey), Peagram (Aubrey Mather), and Oddly (Richard Haydn)—all fed, clothed, and reprimanded by a stern nanny, Miss Bragg (Kathleen Howard).

But as Potts discovers in his encounter with the garbageman, the life of the mind is severely limited. "That man talked a living language," he observes with evident self-contempt; "I embalmed some dead phrases." So, armed with a notebook and an acute mind, he sets out to hear his language come alive in the mouths of people who haven't yet calcified, as he has. He approaches a newsboy, who responds skeptically to Potts's taking notes: "Hey mister, what are ya checkin' up on me or somethin'? Blitz it, mister, blitz it, will ya? Ya gimme the mimis!" Thrilled, Potts invites the newsboy to an informational seminar at the Daniel S. Totten Foundation.

At the end of his day, Potts finds his way to a nightclub where, luckily, Gene Krupa and His Orchestra are playing. (Hawks was almost as much of a jazz and big band fan as Billy was.) Krupa's lead singer, Sugarpuss O'Shea (Stanwyck), is very hubba-hubba, especially when she sings "Drum Boogie," the title of which sends Potts into complete bafflement. "What does 'boogie' mean?" he asks the waiter. "Are you kiddin'?" the waiter replies. A little later, Potts asks him what the singer's name is, and the waiter tells him. "She jives by night!" the boy explains. (You can practically hear Wilder and Brackett enjoying their own Hollywood joke.) The waiter then provides his assessment of Miss O'Shea: "Root, zoot, and cute—and solid to boot!"

By that point, Sugarpuss has developed a problem backstage. She has been whisked into her dressing room by two thugs named Pastrami (Dan Duryea) and Asthma (Ralph Peters). "Hey sister," Pastrami informs her, "you gotta take it on the lam! You gotta get dressed and outa here before they slap a supeeny on ya!" "A *supeeny*?!" Sugar cries. The police have picked up someone named Benny the Creep on a traffic violation and, examining his car, have discovered a man named Kinnick. "In the accident?" asks Sugarpuss. "Yeah, that's what Benny was tryin'a tell 'em," Pastrami relates, "only they saw Kinnick's feet!" "They was in a cake o' cement," Asthma explains. Benny the Creep has an obscure but significant professional relationship with Sugar's gangster boyfriend, Joe Lilac (Dana Andrews), and although Sugar has no idea who Benny is, she nevertheless appreciates how precarious her own situation has suddenly become, thanks to the Creep's accident. When Potts knocks on Sugar's door, she naturally assumes he's a detective bearing forth a supeeny:

> POTTS: This inquiry is one of considerable importance.
> SUGAR: Stop beatin' up with the gums.
> POTTS: What was that?

SUGAR: Get this—I don't know from nothin'!

POTTS: Oh, but you do! Every word you say proves as much! Where's that paper?

SUGAR: Supeeny? Suppose you tell the D.A. to take a nice running jump for himself!

POTTS: Bewildering! And you want to tell me you're not the person I'm looking for!

(*Sugar figures out there's been some sort of mistake.*)

SUGAR: Say—are you a bull or aren't you?

POTTS: Well, if bull is a slang word for professor, then I'm a bull.

(*She throws him out.*)

SUGAR: Shove in your clutch!

POTTS: Exactly the kind of thing I want!

SUGAR: Okay, scrow! Scram! Scraw!

POTTS: The complete conjugation!

Back at the Foundation, Potts explains his research to his fascinated colleagues. "How do you account for the name?" asks Professor Peagram (Aubrey Mather). "You see," says Potts, "the word 'puss' means face—as for instance 'sourpuss.' 'Picklepuss.' 'Sugarpuss' implies a certain sweetness in her." Had there not been a Production Code to prevent him, Professor Potts might have gone on to describe the meaning of a term closely related to puss, but as it happens, he's merely interrupted by the other professors, who seem to know all about it already. "Never mind the etymology," says one pedagogue; "Was she . . . ?" "Was she blonde or brunette?" asks another, getting quickly to the point. "That I don't know," Potts answers; "I didn't notice."

Requiring a hideout, Sugar appears at the professors' door. Potts greets her. The other men scamper up the stairs, every bit as bashful and dopey as their forebears. "Say, who decorated this place?" Sugar asks as she looks around the house—"the mug that shot Lincoln?" And then: "How do we start, Professor? See, this is the first time anybody moved in on my brain." "Where do I sleep?" she asks; "I don't know—where do you live?" Potts answers. Feigning illness, she gets a few of the geniuses to examine her throat. Professor Magenbruch notes a certain rosiness of the laryngeal region. "Slight rosiness?!" Sugar cries. "It's as red as the *Daily Worker* and just as sore!" The other professors thus begin to fret about sending Sugarpuss out in the cold and rain. Sugarpuss herself concurs: "I'm a pushover for streptococcus."

Ball of Fire is the first Brackett and Wilder script since *Midnight* to have absolutely nothing to do with world events. No political problems trouble this sphere (if one excludes the matter-of-fact way in which the mob operates in the United States). While *Ball of Fire* was being filmed in Hollywood, the major cities of Allied Europe were burning from Luftwaffe bombs; by the time the film opened in December, the Japanese had attacked Pearl Harbor. But one gets no sense of nightmarish reality in this comedy. Freed from any obligation to be topical, Wilder and Brackett let their imaginations be governed only by the pure delights of language and story, character and setting. The ridiculous romance of Sugarpuss O'Shea, nightclub singer, and Bertram Potts, professor of linguistics, plays itself out against a backdrop of utter irrelevance.

The only problem here is to get Sugar together with Bertram, a task that becomes more difficult when Joe Lilac sends his henchman over to Sugar's hideout with an engagement ring, the theory being that a wife cannot be forced to testify against her husband. Sugar is less than impressed, so Pastrami tries to make her feel better: "He sends ya a love message! He says ta tell ya he gets more bang outa you than any dame he ever knew!" Pastrami then advises Sugar that he and Asthma will return to pick her up the following day, but "in the meantime," he tells her, she should "lie low and stick close to the Ameche!" Even Sugar is mystified by this reference. She stops in her tracks at the front door, does a small double take, and asks, "The what?" "The *telephone*," Asthma explains, evidently having just seen *The Story of Alexander Graham Bell*.

Bertram Potts, meanwhile, has concluded that Sugar must go. Not only is Miss Bragg offended by the presence of this flashy, sequined siren, but Bertram himself is unnerved by everything she represents. He clarifies his position: "Make no mistake. I shall regret the absence of your keen mind. Unfortunately, it is inseparable from an extremely disturbing body." For her part, Sugarpuss eventually comes to understand that this gawky guy loves her; "Pottsie" is the first man in her life who respects and covets her soul as well as her body. This revelation of mutual tenderness and affection between two deeply flawed, superficially ridiculous, and radically mismatched people is not unique in Wilder's career, but he would not achieve it on-screen again for another twenty-two years (when he made *Irma la Douce*). For whatever reason, Wilder was still receptive enough to this kind of heartbreakingly ideal love to write about it—and to write it so beautifully—in 1941. And he was lucky enough to be working with a director who knew precisely what he meant. *Ball of Fire* is as much a Billy Wilder romance as a Howard Hawks comedy.

Ball of Fire previewed in Sun Valley on October 29, 1941, to great success. The audience loved it, and Goldwyn was ecstatic. When the film was finally released in December, its box office receipts fulfilling and maybe even exceeding Goldwyn's expectations, Wilder made it a point to call the producer and demand the balance of his writer's fee. Goldwyn had no idea what Billy was talking about. "If I promise, I promise on paper," the producer insisted. Billy hung up on him. A few minutes later, Wilder's phone rang. "I just talked to Frances," said Goldwyn. "She don't remember it either." Enraged, Billy informed the producer that from that second on they simply wouldn't know each other anymore. "If you don't remember the deal and Frances doesn't remember the deal, the hell with both of you!" he yelled, at which point Billy hurled the phone down on the hook again. It rang again soon thereafter. "Look, Billy," said Goldwyn. "I don't want people going around Hollywood saying I'm not honest. Come on over, right now, and pick up the $1,500."

Wilder never got the last grand. But Goldwyn did tell Brackett and Wilder to order suits from the best tailor in town and to send him the bill. The suits cost the then-fabulous sum of $175 each. Brackett claimed later to have been mortified by Goldwyn's little tip: "Taking that suit was the most humiliating thing I ever did."

For his own gratuity, Billy had a whole lot more than a piece of menswear in mind. Since *Ball of Fire* was a hit, Wilder hoped that Goldwyn would reward him with what he really wanted—a film to direct. But he soon realized that Goldwyn wasn't about to take such a risk. After all, Wilder was not just a writer. He was a belligerent, abrasive writer—a loose cannon who fought with people and screamed at them and made trouble on the set when he didn't get his way. Entrusting an entire production to a novice as volatile as Billy Wilder must have seemed absurd to Samuel Goldwyn. But as Goldwyn's biographer A. Scott Berg reports, Billy retaliated, albeit in his own way: he made "an appointment with the producer just to tweak his nose." Billy pitched to the notoriously uncultured Goldwyn a fabulous story idea: "Why not do a picture about Nijinsky?" Goldwyn, of course, had no idea who Nijinsky was, so Billy explained to the former glove salesman that Nijinsky was the world's greatest ballet dancer. He was born a peasant, Billy said—he came from dirt, he was nothing, but he loved to dance, and his unquenchable drive led him to the great Diaghilev, head of the Bolshoi. They fell in love, Billy went on, and . . . "Homosexuals? Are you crazy!" Goldwyn shouted. Not to be deterred, Wilder insisted that the best was yet to come. Nijinsky went mad, Wilder explained to a stunned Goldwyn, and eventually the great ballet star landed in a Swiss nuthouse because he thought he was a horse. "A homosexual! A horse!" Goldwyn repeated in disbelief. Billy still wasn't finished with his little joke and, racing to the conclusion, related the story of Nijinsky's marriage, Diaghilev's envy, and the ensuing tragedy—Nijinsky spent the rest of his life whinnying.

Outraged, Goldwyn berated Billy for wasting his time and forced him out the door. "Mr. Goldwyn," said Billy, popping his head back into the office for the punch line, "you want a happy ending? Not only does Nijinsky think he's a horse, but in the end he wins the Kentucky Derby!" Goldwyn was not amused, but Billy certainly was. And rightfully so. He's been telling the story ever since.

PART THREE

1941–1950

11. MR. DIRECTOR

SUSAN APPLEGATE (Ginger Rogers): "Why not look around?" Well, I came and I looked around, from every angle. From the bargain basement to the Ritz Tower. I got myself stared at, glanced over, passed by, slapped around, brushed off, cuddled up against. But Mr. Osborne, in all that wrestling match there's one thing they didn't get out of me—not out of Sue Applegate!

OSBORNE (Robert Benchley): So you've got your self-respect. But self-respect isn't everything.

—*The Major and the Minor*

"Finally, I pissed them off enough that they got rid of me by making me a director." This is Billy describing how he came to make *The Major and the Minor* and twenty-four more films over the next four decades. He's probably right. The arguments Wilder floated in Paramount's front offices in 1941 aren't difficult to imagine in all their resonant amplitude. How inescapable was his lobbying? How incessant were his pledges of budgetary restraint? His proposals for stars and stories? His promises? He probably even begged, though not without dignity.

Charlie Brackett didn't think Billy had the temperament to direct. Helen Hernandez also had the benefit of experience, having grown used to listening to the would-be director screaming at his would-be producer inside their joint office suite, pitching objects at each other and slamming doors. At times, she was forced to act as their go-between because they stopped talking to each other. And these two were proposing not only to write another screenplay, a task they could barely achieve without maiming each other, but also to hand the script over to the more volcanic of the two to direct? The idea must have seemed lunatic.

But Wilder persevered. He made the executives so sick of him that they caved in just to shut him up. Wilder has also said that the men who greenlighted *The Major and the Minor* hoped he'd fail. It's a paranoid view, but given Hollywood's long-standing working methods, a sane one—particularly at the time.

Hollywood was a corporate system—from production and distribution to exhibition. To entrust the direction of a motion picture to a writer—

even one who had already directed a film—not only seemed inane, it violated the very premise of the division-of-labor basis on which Hollywood made its money. Wilder's experience in France counted for nothing in Hollywood. If it is indeed true that Paramount executives wanted Wilder's first film to fail, the failure would have been balanced by a profitable object lesson. As long as the budget of Billy's little experiment was tightly controlled, its failure at the box office couldn't do that much damage, and it would teach any other upstarts a valuable lesson.

Still, there was a precedent—Preston Sturges. In March 1941, when Billy was pressuring Paramount, Goldwyn, anyone, to let him take a crack at directing his own script, Sturges's screwball comedy *The Lady Eve* was the top-grossing film in the country. As a writer, Sturges was a firecracker; as a director, he was as brisk and efficient as anyone in town. The combination was dynamite. Sturges turned out to be as genial on the sets of his own pictures as he was in his off-hours. He invited his cast and crew to dinner at his house, he joked with his actors and made them feel important, and he often brought treats to the set, just to keep everyone happy and relaxed—another good lesson for a would-be writer-director. Sturges was on a winning streak, providing aid and comfort to aspiring writer-directors in what was still a company town.

In the fall of 1941, Billy got his wish. Paramount Pictures and Billy Wilder finally agreed that Wilder himself would direct the next Brackett and Wilder screenplay. His director's fee would be minuscule, but he would indeed direct. In November, at the behest of both Arthur Hornblow Jr. and a twenty-nine-year-old executive named Joe Sistrom, Paramount optioned an innocuous play that had been produced in New York in September 1923, eighteen years earlier. *Connie Goes Home* (based on a short story, "Sunny Goes Home," that had run in the *Saturday Evening Post* two years earlier) was about a grown woman who pretends to be a little girl. It was a piece of sweet-tempered fluff. Sistrom, a compulsive reader, must have found the tale by going through old story reports, since there is no other reason why such an obscure little comedy would have come to his attention. Sistrom knew Billy, and he knew Billy wanted to direct—they often played bridge together—so he proposed that Wilder and Brackett update the property as a screwball comedy. The writers found it appealing enough, and Paramount executives found it harmless enough; after all, Brackett and Wilder already had a good track record with kid movies (*What a Life* and *That Certain Age*). In December, Paramount took the next step and bought the rights to both *Connie Goes Home* and "Sunny Goes Home" for a combined total of $2,750. Since this was a trial, Hornblow himself would produce the film; Brackett had to wait until *Five Graves to Cairo* to become a full-fledged producer.

As Wilder and Brackett worked on the screenplay and gave the fluff some bite, Joe Sistrom, acting as both executive and spy, reported back to the writers that the project was the subject of great mockery in the front office, but this had been part of Wilder's calculated risk all along. Sturges was bold in choosing as his first film a political satire. At Warners, John Huston picked a thriller, *The Maltese Falcon*, and Orson Welles was in a different category altogether. Wilder's ambitions were long-term, so the insignificance of *The Major and the Minor* worked to his advantage. An adroit bridge player, Billy understood the concept of vulnerability: because he'd been scoring extremely well as a screenwriter, the penalties for losing the next round were much greater. By agreeing to direct something as apparently inconsequential as a light romantic comedy, Wilder reduced the chances of catastrophe enormously. The executives would still be watching his every move, but they would be doing so under lights that were much less glaring.

By the end of 1941, Billy and Charlie had the makings of a script, but they had no stars. For the role of Susan Applegate, formerly "Sunny" and "Connie," they needed someone who combined glamour and wholesomeness. They needed Ginger Rogers. For the military school commander who can't help but fall a slight bit in love with little "Su Su," they wanted Ray Milland. Both stars had eminently good reasons not to agree to perform in *The Major and the Minor*, chief among them being the fact that they were hot box office draws. Rogers, in fact, had recently won an Academy Award for the drama *Kitty Foyle*. But both agreed to star in Billy's movie—Rogers in large measure because her agent, Leland Hayward, was by that point also representing Billy. As for Milland, Wilder offered him the role by shouting through the window of his car at the intersection of Melrose and Doheny, Billy having followed the star all the way from Paramount after work one afternoon. "Would you work in a picture I'm going to direct?" Wilder yelled; "Sure," Milland replied. "I was too tired to go into it with him and thought he wasn't serious anyway." Moreover, as Milland put it, "Hell, in those days you finished one picture on Friday and started a new one on Monday." *The Major and the Minor* was not a big deal for anyone—except, of course, for Billy.

The script for *The Major and the Minor* was almost complete by mid-January 1942. Susan Applegate transforms herself into a twelve-year-old called Su-Su so she can get a half-fare ticket on a train. In the sleeper car she meets Major Kirby (Milland), an instructor at a military school; Kirby's obnoxious fiancée, Pamela (Rita Johnson) shows up and makes it clear who Kirby should *really* marry; Kirby doesn't realize that Su-Su is an adult until the final moments of the comedy; clinch. As usual with Brackett and Wilder's screenplays, there were matters of taste to be resolved. The Production

Code Administration was worried about several things, among them a line about glandular trouble running in Su-Su's family: "If it refers to her breasts," the PCA explained to Paramount, then the line must go. (Wilder solved the problem during filming by having Su-Su point to her throat.) There was also some concern over a line Wilder and Brackett proposed to give to Ray Milland: "Met your daughter on the train *and took care of her last night.*" *The Major and the Minor* may have seemed safe at first, but as the screenplay neared completion there was a dawning awareness on the part of both Paramount executives and the Production Code Administration that this little comedy was flirting with pedophilia.

In January 1941, Wilder learned another lesson about the value of bad taste from Ernst Lubitsch. After *To Be or Not to Be* previewed on January 21 in Westwood in the first of its less-than-triumphant screenings, Wilder, Brackett, and Walter Reisch took the unnerved director nightclubbing on Sunset Boulevard to help console him. Lubitsch's wife, Vivian, suggested over drinks that, given the carnage in Europe, the line "What he did to Shakespeare we are now doing to Poland" was not the brightest thing for a character to say, even (or perhaps especially) in a contemporary political satire. Everyone else agreed. According to Reisch, Lubitsch was stunned: "To be accused of lack of taste made his face waxen and the long cigar tremble in his mouth." Still, Lubitsch held his ground, just as Wilder would later hold his, because Lubitsch knew he was right. The line was funny. And, given Jack Benny's genuine hamminess and the Nazis' equally authentic destruction of Poland, it was true. If audiences didn't appreciate it, they could go to hell. The line stayed in.

In February, Paramount came up with a detailed budget for *The Major and the Minor*: the film would cost $928,000—an average price tag for an average A-grade picture. Of this total, a whopping $175,000 would go to Ginger Rogers. Ray Milland would be paid $46,667. Robert Benchley, cast in a small supporting role, would receive $10,000; this was more than Billy got for directing the picture. For writing the screenplay, Brackett's services were budgeted at $27,000, Wilder's at $17,233. Brackett eventually got an additional $4,500 for three weeks' worth of solo script polishing, which he performed while Billy was filming. For directing the film Billy received $9,800.

The whole premise of *The Major and the Minor* rested on Ginger Rogers's ability to transform herself *on-screen* from adult to child. Her makeup had to remain more or less uniform throughout the picture, leaving the burden of the transformation on costumes. This presented problems for Paramount's chief costume designer, Edith Head, as well as for Wally Westmore, the head of the makeup department. Westmore and Head conferred for weeks on how to accomplish the task, after which they presented their ideas to Wilder. But Billy had ideas of his own and kindly asked them to go back to the drawing boards and come up with something else. The fact that he wasn't Mitchell Leisen didn't mean that Billy would leave design issues to others.

One problem that both Wilder and Head faced was that Ginger Rogers was not built like a twelve-year-old girl. There is a dispute about how this obstacle was overcome. Wilder was blunt on the subject: "We had Ginger's marvelous tits strapped down." Ray Milland also claimed to have witnessed the flattening effect on Rogers' chest, which he attributed to the judicious use of tape. Miss Rogers, however, denied everything. In fact, she was outraged when presented with her colleagues' fond reminiscences: "Taped down, was it? Who the hell told you that, anyway? I can assure you that my tits were absolutely *not* taped down, *not* strapped down, not even a tight brassiere. . . . Don't give me this drivel about strapping down tits." However they accomplished the task, by the time the cameras were ready to roll in the second week in March, Head and Westmore had succeeded in making Ginger Rogers as presentably believable as a twelve-year-old girl as she was as an adult woman—at least to the extent of sufficing for a light comedy, where strains on credulity are part of the pleasure. And as Wilder points out, the issue was never whether or not audiences believed that Su-Su was twelve years old. The problem was to make sure that the other characters could believe her without themselves looking *too* moronic.

As he would remain for the rest of his career, Billy Wilder was flexible when he could be and recalcitrant the rest of the time. The Production Code Administration labeled the whole opening of the film distasteful, but Wilder stuck with it. He and Brackett planned to introduce Susan Applegate as an itinerant scalp masseuse who rubbed men's heads for money. In the opening scenes of the film, she arrives at the home of the leering Mr. Osborne (Robert Benchley), who obviously has more than a few healthy scalp strokes on his mind, and it's this tawdry encounter that convinces Susan to get out of New York City and head back to the Midwest as quickly and cheaply as possible. This, after all, is the moment at which Benchley utters the marvelous line, "You know what I always say—no matter what the weather is, I say, 'Why don't you get out of that wet coat and into a dry martini?!' Dry martini? Wet coat? Heh heh heh heh." He follows it up by noting that he'd offer her a whiskey sour, but it would mean thinking up a new joke.

When Wilder and Brackett gave the martini bit to Benchley they were under the impression that the line was already his, and the clever phrasemaker tacitly accepted credit for it; Wilder discovered later that Benchley had actually lifted it from his friend Charles Butterworth's 1938 picture *Every Day's a Holiday*, in which Butterworth delivers the line to Charles

Winninger. (*Every Day's a Holiday* was written by Mae West, who also starred.)

The week before filming was scheduled to begin, the PCA told Paramount that the Benchley scenes were unacceptable, based as they were on a "sex suggestive situation where Mr. Osborne actually seems to expect illicit relationships with girls that come from the massage offices." The PCA was also upset by one of the smirking elevator boy's lines: "Ain't it awful the way a fellow's scalp dries out this time of year?" Billy, not to be bullied by some humorless censors, kept Benchley's scenes almost entirely intact, and he retained the elevator boy's line as well. When faced with the finished film, the PCA raised no objections.

On the other hand, Billy did agree to dispense with four split-screen shots he'd planned for the film, deciding for reasons apparently both budgetary and artistic that these process shots were an expensive frill that he could do without. Although he and Brackett had wanted Paramount's ace cinematographer Ted Tetzlaff to shoot the film, they were tractable enough that when Tetzlaff's current film ran overschedule, they accepted the services of Leo Tover in his place. Tetzlaff was a technical genius with a taste for blazingly brilliant lighting and crisp, elegant cinematography; Tover was an accomplished journeyman—clearly a step down, but an unavoidable one. In addition, Wilder and Brackett wanted to use the George Military Academy in College Park, Georgia, for location shooting, while Arthur Hornblow favored the New Mexico Academy in Roswell; they all had to compromise. In order to get the right weather conditions they found that Wisconsin was a better bet for a May shoot, so they arranged with the St. Johns Academy in Delafield, Wisconsin.

Years later, Billy described his vocation: "A director must be a policeman, a midwife, a psychoanalyst, a sycophant, and a bastard." On March 11, 1941, he didn't know as much. In fact, he discovered on the evening before shooting started that he knew nothing at all. He ran into Ernst Lubitsch that night and said, expressively, "Don't tell anybody else, but I'm shitting in my pants." Zolotow actually claims that Wilder had uncontrollable diarrhea, but whatever balance Wilder struck between metaphor and diagnosis, Lubitsch knew exactly how his young friend felt. "Look," he told Billy, "I have made sixty pictures, and I still do the same thing every time I start a new one."

Billy's personal life was in flux as well. Only someone as peripatetic as Wilder would have launched his directing career and moved into a new house at the same time. On March 9, he and Judith bought themselves a large, isolated estate at 9590 Hidden Valley Road, near the top of Coldwater Canyon. The house, itself surrounded by a good deal of property, couldn't have been more removed from the high voltage of Hollywood.

Situated at the very end of a twisting lane, Billy and Judith's new residence was removed even from tiny Hidden Valley Road. It befitted Billy's new status. Now that he was a big man in town, he had a big house high in its outskirts. Judith could even keep horses up there. The place was a refuge—at least for Judith.

On March 12, 1942, a very large crowd of people met on Paramount's sound stages 16 and 17 to begin filming some of *The Major and the Minor*'s Grand Central Station sequences. There were electricians, props assistants, sound men, Leo Tover and his assistants, extras, script assistants, makeup artists, costumers, and every Austro-German émigré director Ernst Lubitsch could round up, the latter group hoping to give Billy moral support: William Wyler, Michael Curtiz, William Dieterle, Henry Koster, E. A. Dupont, and Lubitsch himself. Preston Sturges also showed up on the set that first morning. Billy was wearing a sweater, which Sturges promptly yanked up in order to examine what was underneath. "All wrong," he said. Sturges then explained to the puzzled Billy that since he was now engaged in what was essentially physical labor, he would end up with terrible back problems unless he wore a strong belt for support. "What size are you?" the seasoned pro asked the novice. "Thirty-two," Billy replied. Sturges promptly handed him a gift: a wide leather belt, which Billy gratefully accepted. He still ended up with severe and persistent backaches.

Ginger Rogers and her stand-in were called to the set on schedule at 9:00 A.M. The first shot was taken at 10:25 A.M. Billy Wilder was now a director.

"I would like to give the impression that the best mise-en-scène is the one you don't notice. You have to make the public forget that there's a screen. You have to lead them into the screen, until they forget the image has only two dimensions. If you try to be artistic or affected you miss everything." This is Wilder's aesthetic, a governing philosophy that holds true from the first shots he directed with Ginger Rogers in the Grand Central Station sets to sequences of war, romance, murder, heroism, sleaze, comedy, music, and drama. At no point does Wilder ever yank his audience's attention away from his characters toward self-aggrandizing, show-offy visual effects. Such ostentatious finger pointing simply isn't Wilder's style. From watching Howard Hawks, Wilder learned to shoot in ways both formally strict and relaxedly invisible. As he later said, "When somebody turns to his neighbor and says, 'My, that was beautifully directed,' we have proof it was not."

Wilder also quickly discovered that in order to make his films as self-effacing as he wished them to be, he had to depend on someone else. On the first day of shooting *The Major and the Minor*, Billy confronted the fact that if he wanted to keep his audience's mind on the characters and story he was creating, he needed an experienced editor to be close at hand *while he filmed.* Hawks, Ford, and Hitchcock could edit in their minds; Wilder knew he couldn't—at least not yet. So he summoned an editor named Doane Harrison to the set to tell him what angles worked and what angles didn't. A tall, slim, exceedingly low-key man with stooped shoulders, Harrison had been cutting film since the days of Mack Sennett. Most recently, he had edited *Arise, My Love* and *Hold Back the Dawn.* Wilder respected him greatly. He kept him by his side throughout the filming of *The Major and the Minor* and well beyond. The construction of each scene was Wilder's; the bridges between shots were also Wilder's, but with a lot of advice from Harrison.

Ray Milland was summoned for his first day of filming on March 18. Shooting proceeded on schedule until the second week of April, when over two hundred children stormed the set to film the scenes at the military school dance. All the kids had to be in wardrobe, there were welfare workers all over the place making sure the children weren't being overworked, the kids themselves had restricted working hours, and, since it was 1942, of course, all the girls had to have their hair done in the fashionable style of Veronica Lake. Filming of the school dance scenes took six days.

"Well, the bus is here. The zombies have arrived," says one of the cadets escorting Su-Su to the dance. "Who?" asks Su-Su. "The girls from Miss Shackleford's School," replies another boy. "We use 'em for women," a third chimes in. After a cut, the cherub-faced child continues: "May as well warn ya, there's an epidemic at Miss Shackleford's School." The cadets and Su-Su are now entering the ballroom, and Su-Su asks for clarification: "An epidemic?" "Yeah. They all think they're Veronica Lake. Look!" Wilder cuts to a shot of four girls seated and looking down at the floor. They look up and turn simultaneously to the camera, identical long hair falling alluringly over their right eyes. Ginger stifles a laugh.

Robert Benchley's scenes were shot at the end of April, and they required a great deal of rehearsal. It wasn't Benchley's fault; Wilder had quite a precise notion of how Susan's scalp massage should be performed and received. Wilder has said that Benchley was delightfully bookish, did everything perfectly on the first take, and then went back to his trailer and continued reading, but that's the generosity of hindsight speaking. In fact, Wilder and his actors spent most of Benchley's first day working out the mechanics of the extended scalp routine. The shot in which Rogers breaks an egg over Benchley's head took six tries before they got it right. As always, timing was essential. "Really, Miss Applegate, you shouldn't be so businesslike," says Mr. Osborne as the increasingly resistant Susan prepares to actually massage his scalp. "First we're going to have a little drinkey-poo, then a little bitey-poo, then a little rhumba-poo. . . ." When she forces him into a chair and breaks the egg methodically on his skull, he shuts his eyes and grimaces, caught in a prim, corn-fed American nightmare. She begins using an electrical contraption to mix the egg protein and create some foam, at which point he gets a smirk on his face, reaches around behind him with his eyes shut, and tries to grab her wrists. "I can't help it," he bleats—"it's the vibrator!"

Reading through the daily production logs of Wilder's first film, one is struck by how smoothly everything proceeded. Running against everyone's expectations, this volatile, often downright hostile man responded exceedingly well to the pressures of directing a million-dollar picture. With Doane Harrison's guidance, Billy knew what he wanted to shoot; with two exceptionally competent stars and a host of journeyman supporting players, he got what he wanted. Relations among Wilder, Rogers, and Milland were by all accounts fine. Even before shooting was finished, Rogers presented Billy with a tiny silver Oscar as a sign of her affection and respect. *The Major and the Minor* progressed so smoothly that Brackett went out on loan to RKO while *The Major and the Minor* was still shooting to write something called *Bundles for Freedom*.

By early May, *The Major and the Minor* was running six days behind schedule through the fault of no one in particular. Ginger Rogers's mother, Lela, was summoned from her ranch outside Medford, Oregon, to play the role of Mrs. Applegate. Her scenes required innumerable retakes, though this may not have been Mrs. Rogers's fault. On May 9, principal photography was completed. The St. Johns scenes and some backgrounds taken at Oconomowoc, Wisconsin, were filmed by the second unit, led by C. C. Coleman, with stand-ins for both Milland and Rogers as well as 350 actual military cadets from the school. Like Doane Harrison, Buddy Coleman was dependable and low-key, and he soon became a regular member of Wilder and Brackett's production team. He got along well with people—most crucially, with Billy.

Apart from the snickering Benchley sequence, *The Major and the Minor* is pretty saccharine stuff—until Lucy Hill (Diana Lynn) shows up. Ginger Rogers gets the job done in the train sequences, as does Milland, and she's more ironic as a fake twelve-year-old than one might imagine. Still, just when all the cuteness and light begins to grate on the nerves, in waltzes a character with a working brain. Pamela's little sister Lucy sees through Su-Su instantly. Lucy is a sardonic smart aleck—a wisenheimer who finds herself adrift in a sea of scrubbed, midwestern military school pabulum. Wilder introduces her at the top of the stairs, literally looking down on Su-Su with her arms folded knowingly across her chest, her eyes aiming at Su-Su like darts. Su-Su, sensing trouble, starts laying it on thick:

SU-SU: Oh, what a lovely room! Goldfishes! Look at the ones with the flopsy-wopsy tails! One's sticking his nose up—he wants his din-din!

LUCY: Oh, get up and stop that baby talk, will you? You're not twelve, just because you're acting like six. How old *are* you, anyway? Twenty? Twenty-five? Or what?

Lucy is a tough-talking adolescent intellectual. Not only has she pried open Su-Su's suitcase and investigated its contents, but she precisely observes that her experimental subject's "adolescent adiposity—*or baby fat*—has disappeared." (She spits out the "baby fat" remark as if speaking to a cretin; *she* knows what *adiposity* means, and so should everybody else.) "Hypotheses have to be checked and double-checked," she explains. Fearless, brilliant, scientific, and utterly bored with the constraints of the social world into which she was born, Lucy is a young Sherlock Holmes. She is the only character in *The Major and the Minor* Wilder fully respects.

"Well, at least I don't have to play Baby Snooks anymore," Susan sighs with notable relief. "Not with me you don't," says Lucy.

Lucy Hill is a minor character but a potent one, who embodies her creator's cynical, rip-through-everything intellect. In the insipid context of prep school Americana, Lucy is more than devilish; she's practically satanic. When Pamela closes a conversation with Lucy and little Su-Su in their room, looks around and notices all of Lucy's scientific paraphernalia, and remarks, "Does this room *always* have to smell like sulfuric acid?" one gets the sense she's sniffing traces of the devil himself. Lucy's sharp intelligence threatens to send Pamela and everything she represents straight to perdition. When Pamela leaves and the child whips out a stash of cigarettes and offers Ginger a smoke, 1942 audiences must have sensed that they were entering a new era of picture making, one that promised to cut through all the bland Hollywood crappola. The fact that Lucy goes on to decline a cigarette herself—she has found that "adolescents are nervous enough as it is"—only demonstrates the type of crappola Wilder felt the need to slice through.

The novice director brought *The Major and the Minor* in within spitting distance of the budget, a fact that vastly increased his chances to write and direct another film. Paramount executives were well pleased. If any of them were sorry the film turned out well, they never acknowledged it; faced with a moneymaker, the object lesson's value vanished. In fact, relations between Brackett and Wilder and the front office were so good that the writers were able to announce their next project as early as June: it would be a comedy about a traveling saleswoman, and it would be called *Women's Wear*.

Another film idea was kicking around Hollywood as well, though the facts are far from clear. This film is said to have concerned hypnotism, to have been set in San Francisco, and to have involved both Bertolt Brecht and Billy Wilder. These are the scattershot details that have survived; the rest is a matter of conjecture. Brecht's journal refers to the time the playwright spent developing a screenplay idea with the actress Elisabeth Bergner, another German émigré, and her husband, the producer Paul Czinner. Bergner suggested the story: a young woman pretends to be hypnotized at a party and then goes out and commits various radical political acts that she wouldn't have committed without the excuse of hypnosis. On April 11, 1942, Brecht wrote: "Czinner began to help Wilder (film writer, German) with some other production, and had no more time. Now Bergner tells me that my film has been bought by somebody else, a friend of Wilder's, with all the details of the story, only in another milieu—without the hypnosis introduction. $35,000."

Wilder denies any involvement in the dispute with Brecht: "I met him two or three times at parties during the war. That's all I can tell you." Paul Czinner was indeed on the payroll of *The Major and the Minor* as Wilder's assistant, though he may have received as little as $500 for whatever work he did. For his part, Brecht wrote a poem about the incident in which he is the sorry victim of a Hollywood refugee scam. He called it "Shame."

Reason is on Wilder's side. Wilder himself received less than $35,000 for writing and directing *The Major and the Minor*, and a payment of $35,000 for a story *idea* would have been so astronomically high as to merit comment in the trade papers. Moreover, Brecht himself tried to hit Billy up for a job several years later. The playwright may have held a grudge against Billy for helping to steal his great hypnosis story, but he found himself able to ignore the grudge when in need.

As *The Major and the Minor* neared its release, Louella Parsons announced a change in plans for the writing-directing team of Brackett and Wilder. The comedy *Women's Wear*, now called *Traveling Saleswoman*, was postponed indefinitely; Paramount was unable to put together the right cast. Instead, Brackett and Wilder would be doing a combat picture. By the time the Hollywood trade papers were pronouncing *The Major and the Minor* a surefire hit (the *Hollywood Reporter* called it "Wilder's brilliant debut"), Brackett and Wilder had already begun to write *Five Graves to Cairo*.

Billy's choice of material was again exceptionally shrewd. He was lucky not to have been able to cast *Women's Wear* to his satisfaction; two back-to-back light comedies would have typed him. A combat picture, on the other hand, gave Wilder a chance not only to direct a hard-edged drama, but also to try his hand at orchestrating action sequences. He'd proven his expertise at comedic timing. Now he could show Hollywood that he knew how to direct World War II.

Brackett and Wilder were officially assigned to *Five Graves to Cairo* on August 10. As usual with the writing team, they worked out the mechanics of plot and character jointly. Brackett was literally the *writer*, drafting everything in longhand on a yellow legal-size tablet, after which Helen Hernandez typed it. Billy, meanwhile, paced furiously around the office spitting out plot twists and waving a stick: "I just needed something to keep my hands busy and a pencil wasn't long enough."

The writers began sketching *Five Graves to Cairo* at a time when the outcome of the battle for North Africa was still in doubt. The Nazis and their Italian Fascist allies were storming across the Egyptian desert in the summer of 1942; the British were getting pounded. The shifting fortunes of the Allies were not the screenwriters' only concern. Paramount already owned the rights to the property they wished to adapt, but an internal Paramount memo noted that the title of the original source material was "very confidential"—and for good reason. Based on Lajos Biro's play *Hotel Imperial*, the property had already been filmed twice by Paramount, the second version only three years earlier. *Hotel Imperial*, after all, was one of the two pictures Erich Pommer had produced during his short tenure as a Hollywood producer in the mid-1920s. That version, starring Pola Negri, did well commercially, but Paramount's attempt to remake the silent picture in the mid- to late-1930s was an unmitigated disaster. The studio first tried to mount a production in 1936 under the direction of Ernst Lubitsch. The film was to star Marlene Dietrich, but Dietrich backed out. She was replaced by Margaret Sullavan, who proceeded to break her arm. Lubitsch departed as well. "The project was thrown into the drop-dead file," the film historian John Douglas Eames reports, but was resuscitated in 1939 with the signing of an Italian star named Isa Miranda. Paramount paired her with Ray Milland. The film flopped. Given this sad recent history, the studio was certainly not about to sabotage its latest attempt to remake *Hotel Imperial* by announcing that it was remaking *Hotel Imperial*.

Paramount executives were certain what they were *not* going to call the film, but they could not agree on a new title. Brackett and Wilder proposed *Five Graves to Cairo*; the executives fretted. At least one front-office lackey found the word *Graves* to be "objectionable" for use in a motion picture title and urged that it simply be deleted. What about *Five to Cairo*? he proposed. Wilder and Brackett ignored the suggestion. Even after the film was well into production, the executives were still fussing. In December, Brackett and Wilder responded to the studio's latest attempt to retitle their film: "We find on our desks an excerpt from the night letter to New York.

Rommel's Last Stand seems to us as poor a title as was ever suggested for anything and is completely inappropriate for this picture. Take our word for it: we would have nothing to do with any picture so baptized. Please communicate this to the source from which the suggestion came."

Brackett and Wilder had every reason to treat *Rommel's Last Stand* with contempt. The Desert Fox was not George Custer, North Africa was not the Little Bighorn, and the Nazis were not the American cavalry. *Five Graves to Cairo* was to be a World War II film—in other words, a film set in the present day. Indeed, the Nazis were still in control of North Africa when the two men began writing their script in August. In the spring of 1941, British forces in North Africa were overwhelmed by German and Italian troops led by Erwin Rommel, the brilliant strategist who sometimes took orders badly and thus stood in constant danger of proving his superiors wrong. Plowing across the Libyan desert in March 1941, Rommel had seized enough of North Africa that he began to seriously threaten British control of the whole eastern Mediterranean. Even the Allies couldn't help but marvel at the Desert Fox's skills, and he became a kind of dastardly folk-anti-hero in the American press.

But in June, Rommel's imminent triumph began to fade under the onslaught of American and British fighter planes. At the end of August, Rommel launched a last offensive against El Alamein, but his troops hadn't the strength they once did. He attempted a full retreat, but Hitler himself ordered the field marshal to hold fast. In the beginning of November, Rommel risked court-martial by disobeying the Führer's direct order: he withdrew his troops seven hundred miles to a position behind the Libyan port of Benghazi. This retreat marked the Allies' most decisive victory in the war to date.

Brackett and Wilder continued writing *Five Graves to Cairo* in September and October 1942 in an increasing state of confidence. The news was rosy. The war in North Africa was going their way, and so was the box office return on *The Major and the Minor*. On October 19, the *Hollywood Reporter* noted that *The Major and the Minor*, which had already been running for five successful weeks in New York, had cracked the opening-night box office records at the Paramount theaters in both Hollywood and downtown Los Angeles. The film's first-day receipts were also quite high, running at the same levels as the previous first-day record holder—*Wake Island*, Paramount's ripped-from-the-headlines combat film about American Marines' heroic but ultimately catastrophic attempt to hold a single island in the Pacific. *Wake Island*'s success clearly did not depend upon a happy ending; every American soldier dies in the end as the island is overrun by the murderous Japanese. Apparently, homefront audiences wanted to get a closer view of the battles they read about in the newspapers, even if they ended badly. A 1942 poll found that the two favorite movies in the country were *Mrs. Miniver*, William Wyler's melodrama about a British woman (Greer Garson) who holds down the homefront against the war's severity, and *Wake Island*. It was a most opportune time for a drama about the war in North Africa. *Five Graves to Cairo* was set to become another *Wake Island*, only this time the Allies would win.

On Tuesday, November 3, 1942, while Field Marshal Rommel was still in the act of retreating from his positions in the sands of North Africa, Billy Wilder took the 9:45 Sunset Limited from Los Angeles to Yuma, Arizona, the closest town to where the first location shooting for *Five Graves to Cairo* was scheduled to commence later that week. He'd gone to Yuma with Judith to get married; now he was going there to film a war. He was accompanied by Doane Harrison and Buddy Coleman. Billy's star, Franchot Tone, followed on Thursday. Brackett and Wilder had wanted Cary Grant, but Grant told them that Paramount Pictures simply didn't have enough money to make him spend a month in the desert, so Tone ended up with the role. He was an ingratiating, everyday sort of star— handsome, well spoken, a little bland perhaps, but not without a certain charm.

The location itself was eighteen miles out of Yuma on the Yuma–El Centro Highway. Paramount's advance men had already arranged for the cooperation of nearby Camp Young, and in fact Paramount succeeded in borrowing a tank from the army. In an attempt to be authentic, Brackett and Wilder had urged Paramount to get them a genuine English tank of exactly the type used in the battles of North Africa, but the cost of trans-porting such a behemoth out to the middle of nowhere proved to be ex-cessive. They would have to make do with an American General Grant M3 tank instead. In the planning of their own combat sequences, Brackett and Wilder did use photographs of the actual and very recent battles between the British Eighth Army and Rommel's Afrika Korps. The machinery of Hollywood studio filmmaking facilitated them greatly in this regard, since Paramount had an entire research department to find and check precisely that sort of detail.

The company was called to the dunes outside of Yuma at 6:30 A.M. on November 5 so that Billy could line up and rehearse his desert troops. Billy himself got up around 4:00 A.M. and went out to get an early look at the beautiful set of wavy, windswept sand dunes he'd picked. To his horror, he saw nothing but tire tracks. Evidently Camp Young had jeeps and the jeeps had drivers. This was not an insurmountable problem for Billy, who sent some gofers into Yuma to procure as many brooms as they could find once the stores opened. When they returned, Wilder put everyone to work sweeping the desert, and once the shifting sands were smooth enough to satisfy him, he began shooting the opening shots of *Five Graves to Cairo*.

John Seitz shot a mere ninety feet of celluloid when the borrowed General Grant M3 tank broke down, instantly pushing the film a whole day behind schedule. Even with this delay, though, the sand dunes sequences were in the can by the end of the day on November 8, and the company traveled back to Los Angeles.

Paramount, meanwhile, was already preparing a second location—one that was much more extensive than Yuma's sand dunes. Most of the action of *Five Graves to Cairo* takes place in the dusty Egyptian village of Sidi Halfaya, so Paramount built a replica near Indio, California, on the shores of the Salton Sea. Once again, a sense of authenticity prevailed. The set took several months to construct. Workers dug adobe from nearby hills and hauled it to the site, where it was mixed with water and straw to form bricks—forty thousand of them. The script required a working highway, so Paramount built one—by laying a solid foundation and then covering it with tons of raw clay. Major David P. J. Lloyd, MC, of the British Army Staff, A.F.V. Branch, was flown in to be a technical advisor; Lloyd had had firsthand experience of desert tank warfare in Libya. Brackett himself managed to locate a collector of enemy military uniforms and convinced him to loan one to Paramount's wardrobe department for reproduction. A total of 1,200 uniforms were made for the film. As for Franchot Tone, the star obligingly wore a specially built shoe with a four-inch-thick sole and a weight of five pounds (to force a drastic limp). Tone was only allowed to wear the shoe for fifteen minutes every hour because of the strain it caused. Clearly, Billy wanted to get every detail right.

Wilder's sense of authenticity included language, but perhaps needless to say, he was working under the constraints of mandated, institutional censorship, and thus found it necessary to write combat dialogue that would be equally acceptable in a particularly repressed kindergarten. One choice line stuck in the censors' communal craw: it had to do with a stick and a smell. The phrasing took various forms, but the censor Joseph Breen never found it funny and repeatedly objected to its inclusion. Wilder refused to back down. In the finished film, the line is uttered by the buffoonish Italian general, Sebastiano (Fortunio Bonanova): "As we say in Milano, we are getting the end of the stick that stinks!" When Brackett and Wilder proposed that a dead German officer be discovered in the chambermaid's bed, it was quite a bit too much for Breen, who forbade it. The writers solved the problem by keeping the corpse in her bedroom but hiding its precise disposition; as a line of dialogue puts it, the body is simply found "in a very particular spot."

The production of *Five Graves to Cairo* reopened the first week of January, alternating between the Salton Sea location and Paramount's own soundstages. Erich von Stroheim arrived to play Rommel. Stroheim had been appearing onstage in New York in *Arsenic and Old Lace*, but it was hardly difficult for him to assume a more military role. Stroheim was martial by nature. He was, after all, the supremely autocratic film director who, for his 1922 film *Foolish Wives*, demanded that Universal reconstruct the heart of Monte Carlo more or less to scale on the backlot, and when the studio's landlocked nature became a problem, Stroheim insisted that huge villas and palaces be constructed at a remote cliff near Monterey. When filming *The Merry Widow*, Stroheim halted production in a rage one day when he noticed that the blanket used by the protagonist's dog had been tied with strings instead of the requisite leather straps. It is thus of little surprise to learn that Stroheim's contract with Paramount included the right to supervise the design of every costume he would wear in *Five Graves to Cairo*. Stroheim also received $30,000 for his appearance.

The moment Stroheim and Wilder met must have been electric, at least for Billy, since it hadn't really been all that long ago that an impressionable if sardonic young Berlin journalist had written "*Stroheim, der Mann den man gern hasst*" ("Stroheim, the Man You Love to Hate") for *Der Querschnitt*. In the meantime, Stroheim's directing career had all but dried up, while the journalist had become a director swinging a riding crop of his own. "It's especially Stroheim who, in my youth, struck me," Wilder once said. "My ideal, if the mix is possible, would be Lubitsch plus Stroheim." In other words, it would combine elegant wit and hard, photographic realism in equal measure—with a beautiful, well-wrought screenplay and a camera that doesn't turn away from something ugly. Billy told Stroheim on the day they met that Stroheim was always ten years ahead of his time. Stroheim corrected him: "Twenty, Mr. Wilder, twenty."

According to Billy, he and Stroheim spent their time together talking about food, women, and Stroheim's sexual fetishes. Billy, of course, was Stroheim's ideal audience: "In regard to sex perversions, Mr. von Stroheim was not only twenty years ahead of his time—he was fifty years ahead of his time."

Wilder set up a number of purely formal problems to be solved while filming. In *Five Graves to Cairo*, as elsewhere, they always served the film at hand, but these cinematic puzzles also functioned like elements in a chess game or a round of bridge. They kept things interesting. Faced with a technical problem, Billy could never be bored. With *Five Graves to Cairo*, for instance, the set for the shabby seaside hotel was constructed with twelve four-walled rooms. The usual procedure would have been to build open, three-walled sets to make it easier to shoot, but to Billy, such convenience would also have conveyed, however subtly, a sense of built-in fakery. According to John Seitz, the cramped hotel set was one of the most shootable he ever worked with.

Knowing that Seitz wasn't afraid of taking chances, Billy trusted his cinematographer to come up with his own innovative ways of filming a given sequence, even (or perhaps particularly) if nobody else had ever done it before. Seitz was a master at his craft. He had been shooting films since 1917. His credits included *The Four Horsemen of the Apocalypse* (1921) for Rex Ingram and, more recently, Preston Sturges's *Sullivan's Travels*. *Five Graves to Cairo* is one of Seitz's finest achievements, but Seitz generously gave much of the credit for the inventiveness of his own cinematography to Wilder. In consultation with Seitz before production began, Wilder insisted that the film actually *look hot*, so for the outdoors sequences Seitz employed reflectors, black velvet, and natural lighting to achieve a shimmery, overheated effect. Seitz also captured a sense of the cumbersome mobility of tank warfare by lashing a camera to the turret of one tank and using it to follow another as it rolled across the sand.

For the indoor sequences, Seitz used the lowest key lighting possible. (The key light is the main lighting source for a scene; "high key lighting" describes a bright, wide area of intense illumination.) At their absolute brightest, these interior scenes are shadowy and dim, with much of the illumination shining obliquely through innumerable screens and grids. The result is gorgeous but understated, combining the bold visual play of Sternberg's *Morocco* with Hawks's self-effacing restraint. In one shot, the only thing visible on-screen is a round circle of light—a close-up of a flashlight's beam—while, in pitch darkness, one central character kills another. This is as close as Wilder ever comes to overtly aestheticizing the image, and he does so in this instance knowing that the audience will be too wrapped up in the tension of the fight to notice his art.

The title of the film was still in doubt late into January, when Paramount decided to run a spurious publicity contest to name Billy's movie for him. William Dozier and other executives picked the following semifinalists: *North Africa, Appointment in Africa, Hellfire Pass, Afrika Korps, Africa Aflame, Desert Fury, Beyond the Line of Duty, One Came Back,* and *Tunisia*, the last a particularly witless choice, since the five code letters that serve as the film's spy-movie subplot spell *E-G-Y-P-T*. Dozier wrote to Brackett and Wilder on January 20, asking for their views on the matter. They ignored him.

Tom Allen once described Wilder's hard-edged films lucidly in terms of power relationships: "Wilder's ability to wear the many masques of this planet's worldly overlords has been his most pungent contribution to nudging Hollywood away from the dreaming meek." Billy's Rommel is a case in point. Because of Stroheim's harsh magnetism, it's Rommel, not Franchot Tone's J. J. Bramble, who drives the film. Bramble is an unlikely war hero, and thus all the more intriguing as far as Wilder is concerned; he used to work as a clerk in the claims department of an insurance company in London, and he becomes a heroic figure only because he is unlucky enough not to have been slaughtered in his tank along with his fellows. But for Billy, perversely, Rommel is a figure of genuine authority and respect. Had Rommel been a successful American general, Billy would likely have found his military prowess dull. As a Nazi, though, he was riveting.

Wilder introduces him in a dramatically high-angle shot, taken from the interior balcony of the desert hotel he has seized as his temporary headquarters. One of the truisms of expressive film language is that high-angle shots, looking down on their subjects, tend to diminish characters (whereas low-angle shots are said to aggrandize them). Here, though, the elevated angle from which Wilder's camera records Rommel as he paces back and forth, riding crop in hand, only serves to reinforce the Nazi field marshal's complete control of the space. We see him from Bramble's perspective—Bramble is crossing the balcony looking down—and he is titanic, a hard, pragmatic force whose bearing and attitude leave no doubt as to his supreme authority. No matter that the real Rommel looked nothing like Erich von Stroheim. As conceived, written, and filmed by Billy, and as performed by Stroheim, the Rommel of *Five Graves to Cairo* is definitive: a shrewd, charming commander with ice in his veins; a restless man left unsatisfied and bored by others; a powerful man whose contempt for women is unmistakable.

According to Stroheim's biographer Richard Koszarski, the one-time director imposed his own personal stamp upon his character. Wilder assented. The irritable and demanding Stroheim possessed the sort of ineffable energy that film directors can use to their own advantage, as long as they don't fight it. With an eye toward the kind of veracity he had attempted to achieve as a filmmaker himself, Stroheim insisted on creating his own makeup design—a rich, weathered tan to the line of his cap and very pale the rest of the way, since Stroheim knew for a fact that Field Marshal Rommel never took his hat off out of doors. According to Koszarski, Stroheim then "ordered a special protective metal grid for the crystal of his wristwatch, something he claimed was always used by the German military. It was handmade for him. He ordered special German binoculars and Zeiss cameras. They were obtained. He ordered film to be put in the cameras, and Billy Wilder was incredulous. 'Who will know whether the cameras have film in them?' was Wilder's question. '*I* will know,' Stroheim replied."

Five Graves to Cairo was originally scheduled to be a seven-week shoot, but by the time it closed it was a week over schedule. Its final cost was in the neighborhood of $855,000, about $30,000 more than had been budgeted. (Billy earned $31,500 for cowriting the film and $21,000 for directing it.)

Wilder was especially concerned about the film's musical score. He wanted his old friend Franz Wachsmann—now Waxman—to write it, but Waxman was then under contract to Warner Bros. Favoring the sort of dark, richly orchestral scores that European émigré composers were known for by the early 1940s, Wilder interviewed another refugee, Miklós Rózsa. Indeed, one of the first blunt things Billy told Rózsa when they met was that he'd really wanted Waxman. But, Billy went on, if Rózsa did a good job with *Five Graves to Cairo*, he would be first in line to score Wilder's next movie. Wilder clearly took another lesson from Sturges—namely that a director's work was greatly facilitated when a team of trusted associates accompanied him from one project to the next. Rózsa's recollection of his first meeting with Wilder and Brackett echoes everyone else who knew them: "The volatile Wilder was all jokes and wit and couldn't sit still for a moment. They were like solid iron and quicksilver."

The score Rózsa composed was tense, textured, and dissonant; Billy loved it. But Paramount's executive musical director, Louis R. Lipstone, found it offensive, and he tried to get Rózsa to rewrite it—specifically, to remove the invidious discordance and make it sound nicer. A heated argument erupted. Wilder quickly came to Rózsa's aid and bluntly told Lipstone that he was a two-bit vulgarian. According to Rózsa, Wilder asked Lipstone to kindly remember that he was no longer in the *Kaffehaus* where he used to play his fiddle, he should leave the composing to the real composer, and he had better just go back to his office and stay there. Rózsa found the whole tirade most helpful and amusing. (Billy was wrong, however; Lipstone didn't begin his career in a *Kaffehaus* but rather a chop suey joint.)

If *Five Graves to Cairo* doesn't reach the heights of *Double Indemnity*, *Sunset Boulevard*, *The Apartment*, *Avanti!*, or Wilder's other masterpieces, it nonetheless remains a finely crafted film, one that deserves a higher rank than history has awarded it. The stark beauty of its opening sequence is especially impressive. Under the credits is a shot of mountainous sand dunes receding into infinity. A tank appears in the far distance on the right of the screen and slowly moves diagonally toward the camera. A dissolve after Billy's director credit brings us to a closer shot, one that sets a more precise tone: a dead body hangs out of the tank's turret, its head thrown grotesquely back, one of its arms hanging lifeless to the side. The camera stares for a moment before another dissolve leads to a still closer shot of the corpse, its eyes fixed and open and pointing to the sky in a death stare. At this point Wilder cuts to a shot of the dead man's feet swinging helplessly inside the tank. As the sequence continues, the tank's dead driver lurches back in his seat as the tank heads up the side of another dune. When it reaches the crest and tips down the other side, the cadaver falls forward again, slamming against the steering mechanisms. The morbid opening sequence of *Five Graves to Cairo* seems aimed to become even more demoralizing than the ending of *Wake Island*; only then does one of the bodies stir.

Wilder introduces his hero as an inadvertent survivor, a man who finds himself alive without reason. The sequence in which he is introduced is so breathtakingly beautiful that the art actually threatens to overwhelm the revelation of character, a rarity in Wilder's career. These are shots of extraordinary, luminous despair: a man staggers into consciousness, climbs halfway out the turret, passes out in the brilliant sun, is hurled from the tank when the vehicle tips over the crest of a dune, and snaps back into consciousness just in time to see the tank rolling away, leaving him alone in the scorching desert. Wilder presents this awful realization in a shot of the soldier lying on a bed of wavy, furrowed, burning sand. He cuts on action as the worn-out man gets up and starts desperately running, the intense sun rendering him simply as a silhouette racing along the deep black tracks of the tank, stumbling, and finally collapsing in the heat as the tank recedes into the distance. When the man stops moving, Wilder cuts to a medium shot of him lying faceup, exhausted, at which point he tracks forward to an intense close-up of the soldier's dog tag on his bare chest: "747289 J. J. Bramble." Only in this moment of utter futility does Wilder give his character an identity.

Wilder's three main supporting players—Akim Tamiroff as the hotel owner Farid, Anne Baxter as the chambermaid Mouche, and Peter Van Eyck as the Nazi Lieutenant Schwegler—each turn in performances as workmanlike as Tone's. Tamiroff's Farid begins as pure caricature but, through timing and nuance, grows into a somewhat more complex personality. Oily and obsequious, he plays the fool—specifically, the Arab fool. Schwegler, interrogating him when the Nazis storm into Sidi Halfaya, asks if he's Egyptian. Farid replies, grovelingly, "Oh yes, sir, only because my parents were Egyptian, sir." Schwegler then asks if he has a wife. "Oh yes, sir, yes, but she ran away." "With the British to Alexandria?" "No, sir— with a Greek to Casablanca."

As for Schwegler, he's a model of athletic Aryan splendor and is thus not to be trusted. The fact that he is a Nazi hardly stops Billy from giving him some plum lines, not the least of which is Schwegler's explanation of the Germans' standards as guests of Farid's hotel: "Our complaints are brief. We make them against the nearest wall."

Anne Baxter, as Mouche, is more problematic. A gracious, delicately featured actress, Baxter appears to better effect in Welles's *The Magnificent Ambersons*, made and released the year before *Five Graves*. In *Ambersons*, in which she plays an American nouvelle aristocrat, her lofty, rather brittle nature makes more sense than it does in a decrepit Egyptian hotel. (In the 1950 *All About Eve*, the role of Baxter's career, her built-in smugness speaks for itself.) In *Five Graves* she's also saddled with a French accent that limits her expressive range further than necessary. She executes the accent passably enough, but her *r*s are even worse than Marlene Dietrich's, a habit that leads to unintentional comedy when she has to pronounce such phrases as "when the Bwitish decided to evacuate theiw twoops." Since Mouche is defining and explaining the basis of her cynical, opportunistic character at that moment, the accent is particularly self-defeating.

More damagingly, Wilder asks Anne Baxter to play a role that requires a moral transformation, but as he and Brackett write it, the metamorphosis is a little too shallow and one-sided. Mouche's explanation for why she is in Sidi Halfaya to begin with rings false. What she says is true—there are many French chambermaids in France but only one in Sidi Halfaya—but that does not explain why the one in Sidi Halfaya chooses to stay there. Initially, Mouche has no trouble welcoming the Nazis into the hotel and her bedroom, serving them as she would any other guests from whom favors might be required. She is pragmatic, selfish, ambitious, hardened; these are traits many Wilder characters would bear in the years to come. To soften her, Brackett and Wilder give her moral indignation; righteously (but wrongly), she blames the British for abandoning French troops—including her own brothers—on the beach at Dunkirk. According to Mouche, they were left "wading out into the water, begging the British to come back for them. Did the British come back? *Did they?*" Bramble, angry but embarrassed, remains silent. Mouche continues: "I'm only a chambermaid. But if somebody rings for me I come—if it's only a towel they want, or an extra pillow. Not *life*."

In fact, however, the problem Wilder himself has with Mouche owes to her sex: when somebody rings for her, she comes, and she doesn't care who it is or what they want. For Wilder, when a man whores himself he gets contempt and empathy in equal measure—Fred MacMurray's character in *Double Indemnity*; John Lund's in *A Foreign Affair*; Kirk Douglas's in *Ace in the Hole*; William Holden's in *Sunset Boulevard* and *Stalag 17*. They may be callous opportunists, but *they're men*. When a woman takes the same course, she's more contemptible. "I don't like women in the morning," Rommel barks at her at one point. It's a sentiment with which Wilder commiserates.

And she pays for it. In one of the film's most unnerving moments, Rommel whips her across the face with his riding crop. Mouche has, by that point, redeemed herself as a moral character, but for Wilder, there is still a touch of pleasure in seeing her punished with a whack across the face. After all, she turns against the Nazis only because Schwegler fibs. At first, she is perfectly happy to sleep with him. (The only reason she doesn't is that Joseph Breen would never have approved it.) When Schwegler winds up dead and Mouche learns of his deception—he's lied to her about his ability to get her wounded brother out of a German concentration camp, and he does so just to get into her pants—Brackett and Wilder resolve her character's amorality promptly by setting her up to be killed. First Rommel lashes her; then he sends her before a firing squad. Wilder knows that Mouche is more emotionally resonant dead than alive. He is hardly alone in this practice. In Hollywood, sacrificial women have always been more tolerable than those whose heroism assumes a more dynamic nature.

At the end of the film, Bramble speaks to her grave: "Don't worry, Mouche. We're after them now. When you feel the earth shake, that'll be our tanks and our guns and our lorries. Thousands and thousands of them—British, French, and American. We're after them now, coming from all sides. We're going to blast the blazes out of them." It is a stirring enough speech, but nothing unusual. In 1942 and 1943, screenwriters from one end of Los Angeles to the other were outdoing themselves in patriotic rhetoric, and they were all encouraged and approved by the Office of War Information. The public liked it, too; like many war films, *Five Graves* sold well. But ultimately, what makes *Five Graves to Cairo* endure is not its effective wartime propaganda but its brutal lyricism—the hard reflections of light glaring on people's eyes, the latticed shadows of screens sending them into shades of gray and black, the absorbing tensions of an average guy caught behind the eight ball. These themes found even richer illustration in Wilder's next film, when he shifted his sights back home to Southern California.

12. DOUBLE INDEMNITY

PHYLLIS: *(describing her dull marriage to an older man)* So I just sit and knit.
WALTER: That what you married him for?
PHYLLIS: Maybe I like the way his thumbs hold up the wool.
WALTER: *(grinning)* Anytime his thumbs get tired. . . . *(leering)* Only with me around you wouldn't have to knit.
PHYLLIS: Wouldn't I?
WALTER: Bet your life you wouldn't.

—*Double Indemnity*

On October 16, 1944, a Mrs. Dreyfuss of 1235 N. Sweetzer Avenue, Los Angeles, California, placed a telephone call to Paramount Pictures. She was very upset. Paramount had used her telephone number in their recent film *Double Indemnity*, they'd done so without her permission, and what were they going to do about it? Mrs. Dreyfuss appeared to want to make some sort of financial settlement with the studio to soothe her jangled nerves. But one of Paramount's executives had a little man inside of him, an inner voice that alerted him to trouble, and he felt that something wasn't right about Mrs. Dreyfuss's claim. After checking the film's copious preproduction records and making inquiries with the telephone company, Paramount's investigators learned that the phone number had been given to Mrs. Dreyfuss on July 18, 1944; that she had personally requested that her old number be changed to the new number; and that she had requested this change four days after a preview screening of *Double Indemnity*.

Double Indemnity is a film about scams—financial scams, moral scams, erotic scams. It's about the lengths human beings will go to in trying to get what we want. It's about what we want and how we get it—the lies we tell, the murderous impulses we harbor, the sexual drives that compel us to act like the rutting beasts we wish we weren't. It's about desire and greed. It's also about guilt: the little voices inside us, the little men—for some of us, the little women—who try very hard to keep our own animal instincts in check, all the while remaining alert to the deceits and compulsions of others. *Double Indemnity* teaches us that we must listen to these little voices or else we'll slide into murder and ruin. But *Double Indemnity* also teaches us that if we *do* listen to these voices all the time, if we let them kill our instincts, then we'll end up bitter and alone. To the extent that *Double Indemnity* is a parable, its moral allows not only the price to be paid for crime but also the price extracted by civilized morality. This film is one of the most finely crafted in world cinema, a fact not lost on its director. Billy knew it was good when he made it. He began one day of shooting by announcing to his cast and crew, "Keep it quiet! After all, history is being made."

Wilder says offhandedly that he'd thought about doing a musical instead, but then he saw the popular *Cover Girl*: "I realized that no matter how good my musical would be, most people would say it was no *Cover Girl*. This *Double Indemnity* looked like a better chance to set Hollywood back on its heels." Indeed, among the first Hollywood heels rocked back by Billy's drive to film *Double Indemnity* were those belonging to Charlie Brackett, who refused to have anything to do with such seedy, inflammatory filth.

By 1943, *Double Indemnity* had sustained its reputation as an unfilmable property for eight years. The problem was simple: his name was Will Hays. In 1935, when James M. Cain wrote the novel, his agent sent a copy to MGM. Cain's agent began hearing from other producers who wanted to read it, and soon all five major studios were interested. Then, according to Cain, "the Hays Office knocked it in the head. I didn't see its letter, but was told it was an uncompromising ban of the story in toto, one of those things that begin 'under no circumstances' and wind up 'way shape or form.' The main objection was that the story in part was a 'blueprint' for murder, that it would show them how to kill for profit. That it would also show them how to wind up behind the eight ball was not mentioned. *Double Indemnity* was then sold to *Liberty*, getting an enthusiastic reception from the magazine's readers, with no reports of any murders having been committed as a result."

In 1943, when the story was about to be published in book form, Cain's agent sent advance copies of it to the studios again, and Paramount quickly became interested on Wilder's behalf. Cain read the Hays Office's report this time: "It was perhaps as stupid a document as I ever read—for it made not the slightest effort to ascertain whether the picture could be filmed with the changes commonly made in a novel when it is prepared for the screen. But Wilder, Dozier, and Sistrom (studio executives) are not easily frightened men, and they decided to make a try at it."

According to Cain, Wilder's interest in *Double Indemnity* had been long-standing, but in fact it didn't come to Billy's attention until 1943, when it was reprinted and published in the collection *Three of a Kind*. The story is that one of Brackett and Wilder's secretaries wasn't at her desk one morning, and when Billy asked where she was, another secretary told him, "I think she's still in the ladies' room reading that story." "What story?" said Billy. The first secretary then emerged from the bathroom with the bound galleys of *Double Indemnity*.

Brackett and Wilder's secretary may have been entertained by Cain's tale of lust and murder, but Brackett himself responded with pure disgust. If Billy wanted to make a movie out of such a distasteful book, Charlie announced, he would have to make it without Charlie. A film adaptation of *Double Indemnity* called for an unusual blend of finesse and vulgarity, narrative grace and sexual sewage. Some of Brackett's disdain for the property was likely due to the residual contempt he held for the low-class, thoroughly riveting journalism that accompanied the true-crime story on which Cain based *Double Indemnity*—the infamous Snyder/Gray murder, which occurred in New York in the late 1920s. At the time, Brackett was a mandarin scribe penning arts criticism for the *New Yorker* and high-toned novels about the upper class. New York's tabloids, meanwhile, were inflaming the mass audience with lurid details about a cheap, bungled murder in one of the outer boroughs. Albert and Ruth Snyder, of 222nd Street in Queens Village, had lived in their suburban-style, single-family house for four and a half years. Albert Snyder was a run-of-the-mill art editor for *Motorboating* magazine. Ruth Snyder was a housewife who was lately screwing a salesman for the Bien Joli Corset Company on the side. Ruth was a plain-faced woman with blonde hair, blue-green eyes, and a prominent square jaw. She'd tried to kill Albert earlier and failed, though her attempt completely escaped Albert's awareness. Then she met the corset salesman, whose name was Judd Gray.

A bespectacled, mealy sort of adulterer, Gray was thirty-five years old and lived with his wife and child in New Jersey. He called Ruth "Momsie" and had sex with her in her Queens Village bedroom, though sometimes they met in a hotel, where Ruth's nine-year-old daughter sat waiting patiently in the lobby while the couple screwed upstairs. This was clearly not territory with which Charles Brackett cared to become more familiar, even in retrospect. Damon Runyon, who covered the trial for the *New York American*, described the two killers: "A chilly-looking blonde with frosty eyes and one of those marble you-bet-you-will chins, and an inert, scare-drunk fellow that you couldn't miss among any hundred men as a dead set-up for a blonde, or the shell game, or maybe a gold brick—on trial for what might be called for want of a better name: the Dumb-bell Murder. It was so dumb!" Runyon was right. Ruth and Judd were very messy. They bashed Albert on the head with an iron window-sash weight, after which they chloroformed him. Then they strangled him with a length of picture wire just to make sure. The inept Gray bought the sash weight in front of witnesses who later identified him. He also made the mistake of involving a third party in the murder—a friend from Syracuse who was supposed to vouch for Gray's whereabouts and provide substantiation for his alibi. Gray went to Syracuse the day before the murder, came back to New York, whacked, poisoned, and choked Albert to death, and then returned to Syracuse, where he made his accomplice do the work of destroying the blood-stained clothes. As soon as the friend was questioned by the police he confessed his role in the crime.

The ugliness and stupidity of the Albert-Gray killing juiced up the public's morbid imagination. The murder weapons were put on display at the New York Police Academy, where they drew a large crowd of admirers. The trial itself was quite a sensation. Ruth tended to show up at court wearing mourning black and a crucifix, and so much of her testimony provoked such derisive laughter from the assembled onlookers that the judge repeatedly had to tell them to shut up. Albert was said at the trial to have been abusive, but the jury didn't much care; such testimony did not stop them from convicting the sad-sack couple in short order. New York was spellbound. But as appealing as the story of the bumbling murderers' conviction was, it paled next to their exciting executions. Photographer Thomas Howard of the *Daily News* even managed to snap a picture of Ruth Snyder in the electric chair at the precise moment that the jolt of electricity ripped through her body. Howard had strapped a small camera to his leg and concealed it under his pants. At the moment of electrocution he pulled his pant leg up and took the shot. It was, as the *Daily News* modestly described it, "the most remarkable exclusive picture in the history of criminology."

As a novelist, Cain was inspired not only by the sordid murder and trial but by the sustained frissons of delight with which the public greeted it. His book is a model of guilt and glory, horror and desire. His readers experience, however vicariously, the double thrill of snapping a man's neck and then gorging on all the fear and recrimination that follow. The killing Cain plotted is much tighter and smarter than anything Judd Gray and Ruth Snyder could ever have accomplished. For one thing, there is no third accomplice. This makes for a cleaner, less traceable crime. The adulterers crack the husband's neck simply and soundly and he goes without a struggle. More important, Cain's killers are motivated not only by lust but also by an even more popular American sin: greed. (As a younger Billie Wilder put it in his script for *Scampolo*, the most important words in the English language are *the money*.) Cain hangs the crime on insurance fraud, and he sweetens the scam by making one of the insurance company's own agents commit it. One of Cain's greatest lines is his protagonist's explanation of how his industry earns its profits. His theory is elegant and pure: "You bet that your house will burn down, they bet it won't, that's all." For Walter Neff, crooking the house might be fun.

Brackett found the whole business tawdry. Billy found it irresistible. Since each of them had separate long-term deals with Paramount, they were not contractually bound to work with each other. Given their stormy relationship, the writing team's breakup over *Double Indemnity* has been widely assumed to have been characteristic—which is to say nasty and violent. But it may just as easily have been nothing more than an awkward parting of the ways for the duration of a single film. They had each written scripts independently in the past; that was nothing new. The only difference was that Billy was now directing their films and Charlie was producing them, so perhaps the stakes seemed a bit greater when they decided to split up for this particular project. Years later, in an interview with Garson Kanin, Wilder characterized their temporary dissolution as just another kind of adultery, a sin he always treated casually: "1944 was 'The Year of Infidelities.' Charlie produced *The Uninvited*. I had nothing to do with it. Instead, I wrote *Double Indemnity* with Raymond Chandler. . . . I don't think he ever forgave me. He always thought I cheated on him with Raymond Chandler. He got very possessive after that." Brackett put a different spin on the episode. He told Kanin, separately, that "Billy got so despondent at being without me that we did *The Lost Weekend*," a depressing film about a writer who has trouble writing.

Whether they screamed and fought over it or simply parted for a few months knowing they'd get back together again in the end, the separation caused Billy an immediate headache. With Brackett bailing out he had to find a new collaborator. He was headstrong, but he knew he couldn't write this peculiarly American tale of loathing, killing, and sex all by himself, if for no other reason than to get the tough-talking language exactly right. "I wanted James Cain," said Wilder. "But Cain was working on a script with Fox—something called *Western Union* for Fritz Lang, believe it or not. And Joseph Stern said to me, 'There's a guy around town, an Englishman. He's never been inside the studio. And I think in order to support himself he was not too long ago stringing rackets for Spalding. But read a few stories in *Black Mask* and read a couple of his books.' I did. I was crazy about the guy."

By this Billy meant that he was crazy about the guy's *work*. The guy himself turned out to be more problematic. Raymond Chandler, a former businessman and oil company executive, had begun a new career as a writer ten years earlier at the age of forty-four. By the time he met Billy Wilder, Chandler had published about twenty short stories, mostly in the magazine *Black Mask*, and several novels—*The Big Sleep* in 1939, *Farewell, My Lovely* in 1940, and *The High Window* in 1942. He also had a new novel coming out—*The Lady in the Lake.* They were elegant but hard-boiled, gripping but mannered. Chandler's first problem as far as Billy was concerned was not that he had no idea how to write a screenplay, but rather that he thought he did: "When he came in, he did not understand that we were going to collaborate on the script. He said, 'All right, I'll write you a screenplay. Show me a screenplay—the way it's written.' I didn't show him a screenplay; he just wanted to see 'fade-in' and 'dissolve' and camera moves—crap that a writer should not even know about. And he said, 'This being Tuesday, I can't have it finished until a week from Thursday. Would that be all right?' Stern and I just looked at each other, it was so fast. 'And another thing,' he said. 'I want a thousand dollars for the script.' We just looked at each other. We said, 'Sure.' "

"By God," Wilder continued, "a week from Thursday, he came in with eighty pages. He said, 'I could not quite finish it, but that's all right. I'll still do it for a thousand dollars.' And we read it. It was full of technical things: fade-in, fade-out, dissolve. . . . And then we sat him down and said, 'Look, you're not going to write this thing yourself. You're going to write it with Mr. Wilder, and it's not going to be by next Thursday. It's going to take ten or twelve weeks, and you're getting two thousand dollars a week.' He almost fainted." Another version of Billy's response is saltier and simpler. After reading Chandler's first draft, Billy picked it up and threw it at him and said, "This is shit, Mr. Chandler."

For the next several months, the two men sat in Paramount's Writers Building pounding out a screenplay and driving each other to seething distraction. To their great credit, neither felt the need to get the job over with as quickly as possible and go their separate ways. Instead, they hammered methodically for months. Wilder and Chandler even went further in their adaptation than Cain did in his novel, and surprisingly Cain loved what they added: "It's the only picture I ever saw made from my books that had things in it I wish I had thought of. Wilder's ending was much better than my ending, and his device for letting the guy tell the story by taking out the office dictating machine—I would have done it if I had thought of it. There are situations in the movie that can make your hands get wet."

By the time Chandler came on board in May, Billy and Paramount were already battling the censors. Wilder himself once told an interviewer that "we had no problems whatsoever with the Hays Office," but that's nonsense. In mid-March, Joseph Breen informed Paramount that nothing had changed since the novel had originally been submitted for PCA approval, that the basic story line of *Double Indemnity* still stood in unequivocal violation of the Production Code. Breen could not help but notice that "the leading characters are murderers who cheat the law and die at their own hands." (Cain's novel ends with the promise of a double suicide.) Second, "the story deals improperly with an illicit and adulterous sex relationship," the representation of which was strictly forbidden. Finally, the novel helpfully provided details of the murder, and the PCA, ever vigilant, was firmly opposed to giving the American people instructions on how to kill others. This was clearly going to be a long battle, a test of wills, but Billy had made up his mind. He was going to make *Double Indemnity* and make it the way he wanted and nothing was going to stop him. The story was just too cruelly appealing.

Raymond Chandler went to work for Paramount Pictures on May 12, 1943, and he continued to work on salary until November. His collaboration with Billy was a productive hell. Chandler "didn't really like me—ever," Wilder avowed. "To begin with, there was my German accent. Secondly, I knew the craft better than he did. I also drank after four o'clock in the afternoon and I also, being young then, was fucking young girls. All those things just threw him for a loop. . . . He would just kind of stare at me. I was all that he hated about Hollywood."

It wasn't easy for Billy either. Chandler spent the whole day smoking his pipe but refusing *ever* to open the window, believing as he did that the fresh air of Los Angeles wasn't as fresh as it was cracked up to be. Between the stale smoke and the constant arguments, Billy kept having to take breaks. He was forever going to the bathroom, not to use the toilet but simply to calm down and ruminate over how much he detested Raymond Chandler. For his part, Chandler threatened to quit and kept on threatening, at least once a week, throughout the collaboration. "Marvelous writer," Billy once noted, "but he was a nut."

Some battles were actually won by Chandler. Wilder tried hard to convince the literate (though as yet largely unsung) master of tough talk to use Cain's own dialogue directly from the book. He thought it lent authenticity. So he brought in some actors to read aloud sections from the novel to his skeptical cowriter. It didn't work very well. Lines of dialogue that rang true on the page sounded forced and phony when spoken. Chandler explained the reason to Billy: "I could have told you that Cain's dialogue in his fiction is written to the eye. Now that we've gotten that out of the way, let's dialogue it in the same spirit as he has in the book, and not the identically same words." But Wilder, always stubborn, refused to budge. He brought Cain himself in for another reading, only to find to his chagrin that Cain agreed with Chandler. As Cain described it later, "Chandler, an older man a bit irked by Wilder's omniscience, had this odd little smile on his face as the talk went on."

Cain also reports on his own lesson from the meeting:

A thing was said at this story conference—and not by Chandler—that made even more of an impression on me. A young guy named Joe Sistrom was Paramount's producer on the picture. He was bothered that in the script and to some extent in the book this guy hit on the scheme for the perfect murder much too quick and easy. I said that it was implied that he had been subconsciously meditating on this for years. Well, this didn't satisfy Joe Sistrom. He sat there unhappily in a sulk and then suddenly said, "All characters in B pictures are too smart." I never forgot it. It was a curious observation, putting into words—vivid, remembered words—a principle that when a character is too smart, convenient to the author's purposes, everything begins getting awfully slack in the story, and slick. Slack is one fault and slick is another. Both are bad faults in a story.

For Billy, the tensions of collaboration were of an entirely different nature than what he was used to. Wilder and Brackett's cycle of working and shouting together had forged a tight bond between the two men, a kind of screwball love. The more they wrangled, the better they knew each other, the closer they became. But as Chandler and Wilder worked and fought, their hatred for each other only grew and festered. They didn't socialize, as Billy and Charlie did. They didn't play cards together, which alone should have told Billy that this collaboration would be personally disastrous. Wilder reported: "On the third or fourth week of writing, he didn't show up. I went to Stern and said, 'What happened?' And he said, 'Well, he was here at nine o'clock this morning, and he wanted to quit. He brought a long list of complaints about you.' 'Like what?' And Stern said, 'You told him, "Will you close the venetian blinds a little because the sun is shining in?" and there was no "please." ' "

Then there were the women: "And he says you have two, three, sometimes as many as six calls from females distracting you.' " Billy's hyperactive, many-partnered sex life seems to have been especially offensive to Chandler. Wilder enjoyed explaining Chandler's response to his own randiness: "Chandler was typical of a man who was an alcoholic and was on the wagon and was married to a very old lady, and so he had no sex and no booze. And the jealousy came out of him. . . . But the small revenge I had—because at the very end, he hated me—was that he started drinking, became an alcoholic again. It was tough, you know. Writing together is more intimate than being married."

When Wilder says that writing in collaboration is a lot like being married, he speaks as someone with a long history—a man who played around a bit in his youth, then settled down and wrote with only two partners for the rest of his life. Sure, there were a few dalliances here and there between these two marriages, and even during the marriages themselves there were sometimes third partners brought in to keep things interesting. But Billy Wilder was essentially monogamous as a writer. It may have taken his separation from Brackett to prove it to him, but he enjoyed a routine with Charlie, the reassuring flow of everyday life. With Brackett, Billy spent his days with someone he respected—a man who may have been enraged (often) by him and his quirky behavior but who, more fundamentally, knew him well and accepted him for the man he was. They created together. The suite they shared in the Writers Building was as much of a home as Billy had. It was certainly more congenial to him than the isolated estate he owned at the top of Coldwater Canyon, where he kept his wife and daughter. Billy's domestic life occurred at work. Mornings with Brackett were spent writing and schmoozing; then came lunch. Every working day after their meal they returned to the larger of the two offices in their suite, the room they called their "bedroom," and took a nap together. Wilder would no sooner have slept in the same room with Raymond Chandler than he would have wanted to catch a nap with Mitchell Leisen.

Wilder's actual marriage, meanwhile, was beginning to rot. Its deterioration was spurred by Billy's raging, insatiable energy. The degree of intimacy Billy enjoyed at work—even, apparently, with Raymond Chandler, who despised him—was less and less a feature of his relationship with Judith. She loved the distance that separated their house on Hidden Valley Road from the shrill buzz of Hollywood and the lunatic competition of Beverly Hills. She liked caring for Vicki, then age three, in the quiet and healthy environment of the upper canyon. She kept horses and loved to ride into the scruffy hills below Mulholland. She kept a garden and tended it in solitude. Billy hated horses, hated quiet, hated solitude. As far as he was concerned, a nurturing environment was one with jazz bands and fine cuisine. He spent less and less time on Hidden Valley Road.

The strain of a failing marriage, the continuing carnage in Europe—slaughter that was disturbingly complemented by his own rising fame and wealth in Hollywood—his absence from Brackett, and perhaps even lingering grief over the death of his son all combined to send Billy into an intense cycle of promiscuity at precisely the time that he made *Double Indemnity*. By Wilder's own admission, Chandler was not exaggerating: women were calling all the time, and Billy was answering. He was throwing his marriage away on a string of meaningless if satisfying lays while cowriting the tensest, most alluring, most convincingly rotten sexual relationship of his career. Only Kirk Douglas's muscular scorn for the whorish Jan Sterling in *Ace in the Hole* compares to the itchy, funky contempt Fred MacMurray displays toward Barbara Stanwyck in *Double Indemnity*. Wilder's explanation for his own state of mind at the time is brief but revealing: "Sex was rampant then, but I was just looking out for myself."

While he and Chandler conducted their waltz of loathing and brilliant dialoguing, Billy began the search for a leading man. Walter Neff, the anti-hero of *Double Indemnity*, is an intelligent, tough-talking dupe—a man smart enough to plan the perfect moneymaking murder, hard enough to actually commit it, and dumb enough to fall for the cheap charms of a much smarter, much harder blonde. For some reason Billy approached George Raft. The popular star of both crime and song-and-dance films had never been known for his mental agility nor his great range. Why Billy thought the beady-eyed gangster-hoofer could play the lead in a complex psychological drama is unclear. Perhaps Billy couldn't convince anyone else to take the role, owing to the project's disreputable nature. In any event, Wilder claims to have been surprised when Raft read the script and didn't get the point. He was amused and appalled at Raft's response. The actor inquired where was "the lapel bit?" Billy asked what he meant. "You know," Raft said, "when the guy flashes his lapel, you see his badge, and you know he's a detective." Wilder explained that there was no such scene, and Raft declined the role. (Raft's taste was impeccable; he also turned down *The Maltese Falcon*.) A grudge appears to have been held, at least in the short term. When *Double Indemnity* was released to great acclaim, Billy made a point of telling the press about Raft's refusal to accept the lead he'd offered him: "We knew then that we'd have a good picture."

Wilder then approached one of Hollywood's least likely actors. Fred MacMurray was among Paramount's chief song-and-dance men, a likable light comedian: *Hands Across the Table* (1935), *The Princess Comes Across* (1936), *The Bride Comes Home* (1936), *Sing You Sinners* (1938), *Star Spangled Rhythm* (1942). . . . What Wilder saw was MacMurray's grinning, guy-next-door affability. He wasn't glamorous and aristocratic. Or rugged. Or callow. What he was—purely, indistinguishably—was American. Fred MacMurray could play a glad-handing everyday salesman. In Billy's mind at least, he would be perfect as a scheming killer on the make.

MacMurray greeted Billy's offer with open disbelief. He thought the idea of playing a murderer was suicidal in terms of his career, and besides, he simply could not imagine that Paramount, with which he was under contract, would ever permit him to stray so far from the happy niche they had carefully tailored for him. Still, faced with the relentless, cajoling pressure of Billy Wilder, MacMurray agreed. According to MacMurray, Wilder pestered him about it every single day—at home, in the studio commissary, in his dressing room, on the sidewalk—until he simply wore him down. Then again, MacMurray thought he was safe. He figured he could afford to cave in to Billy's wheedling because the boys in the front office were certain to nix the idea anyway.

MacMurray tended to be pretty pliable as far as the executives were concerned. At least he *had* been, until his friend and costar Carole Lombard shrewdly and successfully taught him how to play hardball over contract negotiations a few years earlier. By 1943, MacMurray had wised up somewhat to his own authority as a star. His contract was up for renewal, and he was making noises about money again, so Paramount decided to let him hang himself by doing *Double Indemnity*. The disaster of *Double Indemnity* would teach him a lesson. And it did, though not the one Paramount's executives had had in mind.

For the murderous black widow who ensnares Walter in her trap, Wilder turned to Barbara Stanwyck. Never one to pull a pompous star trip and turn down a plum role for a respected director, Stanwyck hesitated nonetheless. She was frankly worried about the damage playing an evil killer might do to her image. Wilder responded simply but firmly— by taunting her. "Are you a mouse or an actress?" he asked. She took the role.

"I wanted her to look as sleazy as possible," Billy has said, lovingly, of his star. Barbara Stanwyck was naturally neither patrician (like, say, Katharine Hepburn) nor charmingly fresh-faced (like Jean Arthur or Ginger Rogers), but her unaffected, even common beauty wasn't quite common enough for Wilder. Since she would be playing a siren from Southern California—the kind who wears perfume from Ensenada—Stanwyck's hair needed to radiate on celluloid as intensely platinum-blonde as possible. So a wig was produced in a shade verging on pure white. This prompted Buddy De Sylva to take one look at the star and remark, "We hire Barbara Stanwyck and here we get George Washington."

As their screenplay neared completion in the beginning of September, Chandler and Wilder were still playing around with the central characters' names. Cain had called his protagonist Walter Huff, but the screenwriters changed it to Neff. Phyllis's surname, however, was still in flux. She's Nirdlinger in the novel, but that didn't quite work, so Chandler and Wilder tried "Derlinger." Since Paramount stood some risk of legal action if anyone by that name actually turned up, the research department ran a check and reported that "Derlinger" was fine, but only if it was pronounced "Derlinjer." No matter how it was pronounced, however, "Derlinger" didn't last. By the end of September when the film went into production, killer-blonde Phyllis had a new surname—the much more evocative "Dietrichson."

Wilder and Chandler were also kicking around the idea of changing the ending. Cain's novel concluded with a shipboard suicide for Walter and Phyllis, but Chandler and Wilder had something a little more graphic in mind. They wanted to gas Walter to death at San Quentin. This would certainly solve the PCA's problem with the story's glorification of crime, since Walter wouldn't be given the chance to end his life by his own hand. No, he would be caught, convicted, and punished—strapped to a chair and gassed on the twenty-five-foot-plus silver screen for all the world to see. Billy had a powerful urge to make sure that no one who saw *Double Indemnity* would ever be able to forget watching genial Fred MacMurray choke and die in a gas chamber. A generic prison set simply wouldn't do. So in the beginning of July, Wilder, Chandler, Sistrom, Buddy Coleman, and a few others traveled by train to the San Quentin penitentiary itself on a fact-finding mission. If Paramount was going to break new cinematic ground by executing the film's hero on-screen, the production team thought it had better look right.

The screenplay Wilder and Chandler developed from the basic story line of Cain's novel features an additional love relationship with a pivotal character, one that required precision casting. Cain's Walter falls in love twice—first with Phyllis, and then with Phyllis's stepdaughter, Lola. The first love affair is evil; the second, not being sexual, remains clean. For the screenwriters, neither of these relationships would be fully satisfying to an audience. Phyllis is increasingly repulsive, and Lola, who must remain uncorrupted, could not afford to get too close to an older killer, the man with whom her stepmother had already had an affair, the man who broke her own father's neck. There needed to be someone else—someone close. So Wilder and Chandler built up the role of Barton Keyes, Walter's boss at the insurance company. For Cain, Keyes serves as the force of rationality, a sort of master key that unlocks mysteries and sets them right. He's a character of justice and moral reckoning; he investigates people for a living. As Cain puts it (in a simile picked up by Wilder and Chandler), Barton Keyes "is a wolf on a phony claim."

Keyes is the conscience of the novel, but Wilder and Chandler make him much more *emotionally* central. He is not only a moral force in the film but also becomes instead a paternal, fraternal, and avuncular character, all in one. For Wilder, he's a figure of love—short, chubby, sweating love. Keyes smokes cigars compulsively. He is a man who has more important things on his mind than where he last put his matches, so in Wilder and Chandler's script, he constantly requires Walter's assistance, however little Keyes himself appears to be aware of it. Whenever the older man fumbles around his jacket pockets searching for the matches he never keeps, his younger friend pulls out one of his own, flicks it singlehandedly against his thumbnail, and provides the missing light. It's a gesture of affection, a poignant acknowledgment of one man's need for another. Billy picked Edward G. Robinson for the role.

The bond between Walter Neff and Barton Keyes would, in Wilder and

Chandler's adaptation, find its greatest expression in the final death house sequence. It would be the image of Keyes, standing alone, that ended the film. There would be a verbal setup scene, with Walter lying bleeding on the floor of the office. Then Billy killed him:

> Fade in: Witness Room in the Death Chamber—San Quentin—Day. . . .
> The Door to the Gas Chamber. It is open. The three GUARDS come out of the gas chamber and into the antechamber, where stand the WARDEN, EXECUTIONER, two DOCTORS, the MINISTER, and the ACID MAN, and possibly several GUARDS. . . . The WARDEN makes a motion to the ACID MAN [who] releases the mixed acid into a pipe connecting with a countersunk receptacle under NEFF's chair. . . .
> Int. Gas Chamber—Med. Shot.
> Camera is shooting above NEFF's head (just out of shot), toward spectators standing outside the gas chamber, KEYES in the center. Gas floats up into scene between camera and spectators. KEYES, unable to watch, looks away.

After momentarily gassing his audience, Wilder planned to cut away from the interior of the chamber to one of the doctors listening to Neff's heartbeat through a linked stethoscope. Once he pronounces Neff dead, and the guard escorts the witnesses out, Billy would cut to:

> Corridor Outside the Death Chamber. Camera shooting in through the open door at KEYES, who is just turning to leave. KEYES comes slowly out into the dark, narrow corridor. His hat is on his head now; his overcoat is pulled around him loosely. He walks like an old man. He takes eight or ten steps, then mechanically reaches a cigar out of his vest pocket and puts it in his mouth. His hands, in the now familiar gesture, begin to pat his pockets for matches. Suddenly he stops, with a look of horror on his face. He stands rigid, pressing a hand against his heart. He takes the cigar out of his mouth and goes slowly on toward the door, camera panning with him. When he has almost reached the door, the GUARD there throws it wide, and a blaze of sunlight comes in from the prison yard outside. KEYES slowly walks out into the sunshine, stiffly, his head bent, a forlorn and lonely man. Fade out. THE END.

Shooting began on September 27 after several days of testing the dreary, glaring opening sequence at Sixth and Olive Streets in Los Angeles, using doubles for MacMurray. The first scenes to go before the camera were those between Walter and Phyllis's maid, Nettie; they were soon followed by Walter's introduction to Phyllis as she stands at the top of a staircase wearing nothing but a towel—and an ankle bracelet. "I've just been taking a sun bath," she explains. "No pigeons around, I hope," he answers with a delightful smirk.

Even before Walter comments, "That's a honey of an anklet you're wearing, Mrs. Dietrichson," Wilder and John Seitz capture the cheap glamour of Phyllis's dazzling foot in a crane shot that follows her legs as they walk down the length of the stairway. Filmed through the iron grillwork of the railing, this L.A. housewife's shaved and beautifully lit calves take on an even more fetishized charge, thereby turning a single piece of costuming into one of the most memorable images in the American cinema. Encircled by a little band of metal, Phyllis's leg becomes lurid. The lust it sparks in Walter seems fresh every time—so fresh, in fact, that it's shocking to leaf through *Double Indemnity*'s itemized production budget and find that the whole bit was planned and detailed long in advance of its filming. There, under costuming expenses, is an entry for two ankle bracelets. They cost $25 a pair. (Paramount was nothing if not organized; the studio appears to have purchased a backup in case the first bracelet snapped.)

Walter and Phyllis wind their way into a scene that any self-respecting film buff knows by heart. Walter is on the make—so much so that he appears to have forgotten why he's even shown up at Phyllis's house to begin with. "He'll be in then," she tells him:

> "Who?"
> "My husband. You were anxious to talk to him, weren't you?"
> "Yeah, but I'm sort of getting over the idea, if you know what I mean."
> "There's a speed limit in this state, Mr. Neff. Forty-five miles an hour."
> "How fast was I going, officer?"
> "I'd say around ninety."
> "Suppose you get down off your motorcycle and give me a ticket."
> "Suppose I let you off with a warning this time."
> "Suppose it doesn't take."
> "Suppose I have to whack you over the knuckles."
> "Suppose I bust out crying and put my head on your shoulder."
> "Suppose you try putting it on my husband's shoulder."
> "That tears it."

The film had to look just as good. Wilder's admiration for John Seitz only grew during the filming of *Double Indemnity*. Of all the cinematographers Wilder worked with over his long career, he found Seitz to be (in his words) the most "realistic," a quality that for Wilder was supreme. As he had done with *Five Graves to Cairo*, Seitz was both technically adept and personally accommodating. "He was ready for anything," Wilder said. "Sometimes the rushes were so dark that you couldn't see anything. He went to the limits of what could be done." Seitz's gloomy, discreetly gorgeous photography paralleled the work of Paramount's set designer, Hal Pereira, who created a series of low-key but highly suggestive interiors that appear at once realistic and mythical. As Walter strolls through Phyllis's living room, for instance, Seitz's lighting carves up the space into subtle swaths of black-and-white stripes (thanks to the judiciously placed venetian blinds) while Pereira's set design reveals Phyllis's darker aspects without calling attention to anything in particular. (Legend has it that Pereira's design for Walter's drab apartment was based on the room Wilder occupied at the Chateau Marmont in 1934 and 1935, but since the very nature of that room remains doubtful, the story of Pereira's design is equally dubious. After all, Walter's apartment features no public toilets.)

For Neff's office at the hilariously named Pacific All-Risk Insurance Company (Cain called his, almost as amusingly, General Fidelity), Pereira and Wilder conspired to create a little in-house joke at Paramount. In the opening scenes of the film, Walter Neff stumbles into the office in the middle of the night to record a confessional memo to Barton Keyes. The vast two-tiered office is empty and dark. With the camera following him, Walter lurches toward a balcony railing overlooking rows and rows of hideously uniform corporate desks. He turns left, but the camera continues forward until it reaches the brink, whereupon it stares for an anxious moment into the abyss, a colorless American business purgatory. Pereira is said to have copied an existing office—the corporate headquarters of Paramount Pictures in New York.

The only set in *Double Indemnity* that looks like a set is the interior of the market in which Walter and Phyllis meet to arrange the final details of their crime. Pereira based the interior design on a real Hollywood grocery store—Jerry's Market on Melrose—but there's something hollow and unreal about the copy. Then again, the relative stiffness of these sequences may have been due in part to a certain tension on the soundstage on which the market set was built. The cans and boxes of food and supplies that line the store's shelves in perfect order were actually full of real food and supplies, and since *Double Indemnity* was made during a period of wartime rationing, Paramount found it necessary to hire cops to guard the set, even during the shoot, to keep the cast and crew from going shopping on the sly. Even with this surveillance, however, one can of peaches and four bars of laundry soap were pinched.

The actors in *Double Indemnity* are marvelous—MacMurray was never better—but *Double Indemnity* is essentially a director's movie. Wilder's precise sense of timing pulls the narrative inexorably forward—as Walter puts it, straight down the line—to its grim, fatal conclusion. Even in a scene as patently artificial as the one in which Phyllis's car won't start, Wilder mounts the tension so effortlessly but potently that you forget you are watching a time-honored Hollywood suspense device. At the time, Wilder's instructions during the shooting of that scene were excessive—at least as far as his leading man was concerned. According to MacMurray, he and Stanwyck sat in a dummy car busily faking the engine-failure scene and doing it just as they would have done it for any other director. MacMurray wanted to get it over with. "I was doing it fast, and Billy kept saying, 'Make it longer, make it longer,' and finally I yelled, 'For chrissake, Billy, it's not going to hold that long,' and he said, 'Make it longer,' and he was right. It held." As Billy explained to the *Los Angeles Times* when the film was released, "I have always felt that surprise is not as effective as suspense." He made it a point, he said, to identify the guilty parties right off the bat and then stand back and watch "the net closing, closing."

On November 24, the last day of production, the cast and crew headed out to do some final location shooting—first to the street in front of Phyllis's house (the corner of El Contento and Quebec in the Hollywood Hills), where they shot some footage of boys and girls playing baseball, and then to a bowling alley on La Cienega Boulevard to film the scene in which Walter kills some time on the lanes and tries to calm down after meeting Phyllis. Despite the fact that he'd been working hard for weeks on end, MacMurray still managed to bowl five straight strikes. Billy dared him to do it again, and his star ended up with a backache. "I just wanted to be sure you'd be through with the part before we crippled you," Billy told him. MacMurray and Wilder got along well, as did Billy and Stanwyck. The stars' initial misgivings gave way when they saw how beautifully *Double Indemnity* played during filming. According to Billy, MacMurray was "a notorious line-muffer," but "he got so interested he never missed one." This is a slight exaggeration on Billy's part. In fact, while filming his initial Dictaphone scene, MacMurray kept blowing his lines. It was a long speech in a single long take, and MacMurray couldn't manage to get it all out without flubbing something along the way: "You were pretty good in there for a while, Keyes. You said it wasn't an accident. Check. You said it wasn't suicide. Check. You said it was murder. Check. You thought you had it cold, didn't you? All wrapped up in tissue paper with pink ribbons around it. It was perfect. Except it wasn't, because you made one mistake. Just one little mistake. When it came to picking the killer you picked the wrong guy. You want to know who killed Dietrichson? Hold tight to that cheap cigar of yours, Keyes. I killed Dietrichson. Me. Walter Neff. Insurance salesman. Thirty-five years old, unmarried, no visible scars—till a while ago, that is. Yes, I killed him. I killed him for money. And for a woman. I didn't get the money. And I didn't get the woman. Pretty, isn't it?"

MacMurray tried hard, but he just couldn't do it. He took his line-reading misfires in stride. Without missing a beat, he continued, in character, speaking directly into the microphone: "Memo to Wilder—MacMurray blew his topper again."

At 5:55 on the afternoon of November 24, principal photography on *Double Indemnity* was completed with a shot of Walter in his car at a drive-in restaurant, a beer on a tray attached to the car door. Walter drinks it. It was a sort of culminating if inadvertent toast, a celebration of yet another smooth production under Billy's belt. The director was very pleased with the work his crew had done, and he respected most of his cast's performance as well. He told John Seitz later that he thought *Double Indemnity* was nearly perfect, the only two flaws being the relatively inexperienced performances of Jean Heather as Lola and Byron Barr as her boyfriend, Nino Sachetti.

Some retakes were shot in December and January owing to scratches on the original film, but these were minor, typical annoyances. Billy knew his gamble had paid off. The war with Chandler, the war with the PCA, the war with all the worried naysayers around the studio—they were worth it. *Double Indemnity* was a damn good movie. In January, high on his own success, Wilder breezed around the Paramount lot telling everyone that he was obviously the sole surviving genius at the studio now that Preston Sturges had left. (Sturges and Paramount parted ways at the end of December.) Wilder may have been a blowhard, but he had the talent to back it up. *Double Indemnity* works.

In Walter's final scene with Phyllis, just before they shoot each other, he explains something to her about the nature of their characters. "We're both rotten," says Stanwyck. "Only you're a little *more* rotten," says MacMurray. This is necessarily so. She's a woman. Pure, easygoing contempt, a man's self-awareness, and blame—particularly sexual blame. The line is a highlight of Billy Wilder's writing career, but the printed word falls completely short of conveying the moment's visceral intensity. Wilder's best lines were never meant to be *read*. Their resonance comes from their being as alive as art permits. Wilder's films are profoundly experiential. "We're both rotten," says Stanwyck; "Only you're a little *more* rotten," says MacMurray. It is not just the words, as clever as they are. It's the smirk on MacMurray's face as he utters them, the shadows that fall across the screen, the smutty energy of a man and a woman pointing guns at each other's guts—energy Wilder not only invites but compels us to share and enjoy. When MacMurray says "Good-bye, baby" and shoots her to death, it feels good.

Fred MacMurray's execution scene had been shot on November 17. One account claims that Paramount spent as much as $150,000 to re-create the gas chamber (said in this version to be Folsom, not San Quentin), but this was clearly not the case. The film's budget allocated $4,695 to that portion of the set. Still, the gas chamber ending was scrapped. More than fifty years later it is still not clear why.

Explanations have included disastrous previews and unbeatable demands from the Hays Office. But the fact is that Wilder and Chandler had written two possible endings for *Double Indemnity*, and they wrote them both before shooting even started.

A script dated September 25, 1943, features a romantic, male-bonding ending: Neff lies on the floor in the doorway and tells Keyes that the reason he couldn't figure out who killed Dietrichson is that the killer was sitting across the desk from him. "Closer than that, Walter," Keyes responds. "I love you, too," says Walter. The dying man tries to light his cigarette and fails. Keyes produces the flame and reaches out with it to Walter. They make eye contact. The end.

But the September 25 script continues: "See following pages for alternate ending." In the possible substitute, Walter, holding Keyes's handkerchief, says "At the end of that . . . trolley line . . . just as I get off . . . you be there to say good-bye . . . will you, Keyes?" at which point there would be a fade-out/fade-in to the gas chamber sequence. A script dated October 25 contains the gas chamber ending only. Wilder has claimed that the gas chamber sequence was one of the two best sequences he ever shot, but it's a claim he can afford to make, since the sequence disappeared without a trace into the vaults of Paramount Pictures and has never been screened since.

In any event, *Double Indemnity* was in the can. *Paramount News* announced—wrongly, as it turned out—that César Franck's lush but haunted Symphony in D Minor was to be the sole background score for the film; originally, it was to have been played only during the scene in which Walter and Lola sit in the hills above the Hollywood Bowl, but by May it was being considered for the opening titles as well. In fact, however, composer Miklós Rózsa ultimately provided the film with a full, pounding, orchestral background. Wilder gave Rózsa free reign to compose as disturbing a score as he wished. Wilder knew what he wanted in general, tonal terms; it was actually Billy's idea to use unsettled strings for the scenes between Walter and Phyllis. Rózsa's musical tastes—described by one critic as "stark and angular with bitter harmonic clashes"—blended well with Wilder's own visual and emotional style. In the opening credits sequence, Rózsa's characteristically stressful orchestrations set the tone for the rest of the film. He introduces the score's main theme immediately, as the silhouette of a man hobbles on crutches toward the camera; it reappears both for Walter and for the man he kills and impersonates. Later, Rózsa develops a different theme for Walter, a relatively neutral running figure for strings, but it sours whenever Phyllis appears; when Phyllis tells Walter that she has arranged the killing, "this theme is given so rancid a harmonization as to impress upon us the full force of her evil."

Once again, Louis Lipstone, Paramount's musical director, expressed his contempt for Rózsa's dissonant score, but Wilder turned to him and said, witheringly, "You may be surprised to hear that I *love* it. Okay?" Later, Lipstone was heard to complain that the *Double Indemnity* score sounded like something from *The Battle of Russia*.

Not only could the Hays Office find no good reason to reject the finished film, the whole thing came in under budget. Paramount had allotted $980,000; *Double Indemnity* ended up costing $927,262. Billy earned a little less than $44,000 for writing the film and $26,000 for directing it. MacMurray, Stanwyck, and Robinson each made about $100,000 for their performances.

This perverse film's marketing provided a few choice ironies. The exhibitors' journal *Boxoffice* suggested, for instance, that theater owners encourage insurance companies to arrange group screenings for their employees, blithely ignoring the fact that Pacific All-Risk is run by a nincompoop and that its star salesman has spent years figuring out a way to bilk his own company. The only reputable person at All-Risk is an embittered claims investigator who has nothing but contempt for everyone in the firm except Walter, who kills one of his clients. Paramount, meanwhile, was industriously arranging advertising tie-ins for the stars and planting fake stories in Los Angeles newspapers. Perhaps in an attempt to cover up the Dreyfuss affair, Paramount told the *Los Angeles Examiner* that some of the film's fans dialed the phone number quoted by MacMurray in the film and got none other than Judith Wilder. "How did you like the picture?" Judith is said to have asked. When the callers wondered who she was, Judith allegedly replied, "I'm Mrs. Billy Wilder. My husband used his own telephone number, and since so many people are calling, we just thought we would check up on how you like the movie."

More conventionally, though no less bizarrely, Paramount arranged for its leading lady, who played a coldhearted bitch in the film, to appear in ads for such things as Max Factor cosmetics, Bates bedspreads, and Deltah pearls. As the Deltah ad put it, pearls were essential "for that flattering finishing touch." In appreciation of Barton Keyes's stogies and the camaraderie expressed by their lighting, the Cigar Institute of America was thrilled with the film and happily distributed window cards to tobacco stores depicting MacMurray lighting Robinson's cigar. Never mind that the match was held by a double homicide. (One can only wonder what the

Cigar Institute's marketing department would do with the critic Frank Krutnik's psychoanalytic reading of *Double Indemnity*, in which Keyes's cigar is not just a cigar.)

Double Indemnity previewed in Glendale and Westwood in July 1944 to great success, though the latter screening provided a moment of panic when the film began and was almost immediately wolf-whistled. "There goes my picture," Billy muttered in despair, only to realize with relief that the whistles were for Stanwyck at the top of the stairs in her towel.

Knowing how good his new film was, and confident that he had become one of the best and most commercially successful directors in the business, Billy could afford to pull a few pranks in the trade papers to celebrate the release of *Double Indemnity*. Self-puffery, a staple of the industry, ran especially amok in the ads producers took out in the *Hollywood Reporter*, *Variety*, and *Motion Picture Herald* to promote their latest products. David O. Selznick, for instance, was constantly pumping up his pictures—and himself—in ostentatious trade ads designed to turn well-made feature films into paragons of cultural import. His latest opus, a homefront melodrama called *Since You Went Away*, made its entrance into the marketplace accompanied by a series of ads in which various dignitaries allowed themselves to shill for Hollywood. *Since You Went Away*, they claimed, was the finest drama they had ever seen, it served such noble purposes, it elevated humanity to unparalleled new levels, and so on, ad nauseum. *Since You Went Away* were, as Selznick himself said, the four most important words uttered in motion picture history since *Gone With the Wind*. These ads rankled Billy no end. So he placed an ad of his own: *Double Indemnity*, it claimed, were the two most important words uttered in motion picture history since *Broken Blossoms*, thus comparing Griffith's tender, self-consciously arty classic with his own dirty murder story. Enjoying the novelty of a parody ad in the trades, Wilder published a second one; it called *Double Indemnity* "the two most important words since Capital Gains." Selznick wasn't at all amused, but one of Selznick's ex-directors was. Alfred Hitchcock sent Billy a wire: "Since *Double Indemnity* the two most important words in motion pictures are Billy Wilder."

Selznick continued placing his self-aggrandizing ads, and so did Billy, though they took a rather different form. The idea that civic leaders were parading themselves around in the pages of the *Hollywood Reporter* was just too delectably annoying, so Wilder enlisted his own civic leader to help sell *Double Indemnity*: George Oblath, who ran the greasy spoon across the street from Paramount. "This is what a distinguished restaurateur thinks," Billy's ad trumpeted. It continued: "Dear Mr. Billy Wilder. I certainly do appreciate the opportunity you gave me to see your picture *Double Indemnity*. It held my attention, it held my wife's attention, it held my sister-in-law's attention. It certainly was a good picture, one of the best pictures we have seen in several days. Sincerely, George Oblath." Billy added the final kicker at the bottom of the ad: "Oblath's: The Best Foods for Less Money and Utmost Effort for Service." Wilder must have found that line particularly funny, given the cuisine at Oblath's. As he used to say, Oblath's was the only place in town where you could get a greasy Tom Collins.

David Selznick did not laugh. In fact, he went completely nuts and threatened to stop advertising in any trade paper that continued to run any more of Billy Wilder's little jokes. But Billy had no need to print any more of them, since the first three had so squarely hit their target.

Double Indemnity was an immediate hit, despite the fact that "this fat girl Kate Smith" was said by James M. Cain to have "carried on propaganda asking people to stay away from this picture." (The homespun singer implored the public to shun the film on moral grounds.) As for Raymond Chandler, his collaboration with a volatile, bullheaded foreigner who couldn't stop pacing was no happier at the end than it was at the beginning. In a widely quoted letter to his British publisher, Hamish Hamilton, Chandler complained that "working with Billy Wilder on *Double Indemnity* was an agonizing experience and has probably shortened my life." In 1946, Chandler published a scathing attack on Hollywood, and although he didn't name names, his target was certainly clear enough: "The pretentiousness, the bogus enthusiasm, the constant drinking and drabbing, the incessant squabbling over money, the all-pervasive agent, the strutting of the big shots (and their usually utter incompetence to achieve anything they start out to do), the constant fear of losing all this fairy gold and being the nothing they have never ceased to be, the snide tricks, the whole damn mess is out of this world." Chandler also griped bitterly in an article in *Atlantic Monthly* that he wasn't even invited to his own movie's preview. But as usual, Billy enjoyed the last laugh. "How could we?" Billy remarked. "He was under a table drunk at Lucey's."

13. REELING

It's like the doctor was just telling me—delirium is a disease of the night. Good night.
                    —Nurse Bim (Frank Faylen) in *The Lost Weekend*

I t is evident to me," Maurice Zolotow writes of *The Lost Weekend*, "that Brackett was writing himself in the characters of Don Birnam's brother and Jane Wyman, and that Wilder was writing Wilder in the opposing constellation of sardonic characters—Howard Da Silva's bartender, Doris Dowling's hooker, Frank Faylen's homosexual Bellevue Hospital nurse." As appealing as Zolotow's theory may be, *The Lost Weekend*'s appeal to the two screenwriters was much simpler and also more complicated. Both Brackett and Wilder were Don Birnam. They were writers, after all. And while neither Brackett nor Wilder was a terminal drunk, they each bore a familiar burden of self-contempt—familiar to writers, anyway. When Wilder read Charles Jackson's excruciating novel on a train bound for New York, he certainly found something he could relate to.

The Lost Weekend begins with an epigraph:

> And can you, by no drift of circumstance,
> Get from him why he puts on this confusion,
> Grating so harshly all his days of quiet
> With turbulent and dangerous lunacy?

This was Billy's kind of book—a psychologically sharp, miserably accurate page-turner about a man in awful trouble. Still, however much he responded personally to the central character's torments, given his own recent history with Raymond Chandler he must also have been quite entertained by the idea of writing and directing a detailed portrait of a lush novelist.

By the time he got to Penn Station he had an outline for the film he planned to make. He telephoned Brackett immediately upon his arrival. It was only 6:00 A.M. in Bel-Air, but Wilder knew his partner wouldn't mind the intrusion. He was certain that *The Lost Weekend* was a story to which Brackett would relate as well.

Charlie's wife, Elizabeth Fletcher Brackett, was generally reclusive, a severe alcoholic. Brackett had her institutionalized once, but the treatment failed and Elizabeth kept drinking. She was scarcely the only drunk in his life. Charlie Brackett had served as nurse and helpmate to a variety of other, more famous boozers over the years, including Robert Benchley, F. Scott Fitzgerald, and Dorothy Parker. One of Dashiell Hammett's biographers even credits Brackett with rescuing Hammett from a particularly unresponsive drunken stupor in the Beverly Wilshire Hotel in the late 1930s. Brackett and his wife paid Hammett's enormous bill out of their own pockets, so the story goes, after which they sobered him up enough to get on a plane back to Lillian Hellman in New York. (Then again, according to Diane Johnson's biography of Hammett, it was the Hacketts, not the Bracketts, who bailed out and dried out Dashiell Hammett.)

Brackett might have had another personal interest in *The Lost Weekend*—one that had nothing to do with drinking. If the story is true, Billy would have known about it, though he's never discussed the matter in public; if it's not true, it only serves as further evidence of how bogus Hollywood gossip can be. One of the most compelling and disturbing aspects of Charles Jackson's novel is its portrait of a deeply closeted gay man. Don Birnam drinks, in part, to deaden himself to his own identity. He knows it is true but he cannot come to terms with it:

> All the woeful errors of childhood and adolescence came to their crashing climax at seventeen. They gathered themselves for a real workout in the passionate hero-worship of an upperclassman during his very first month at college, a worship that led, like a fatal infatuation, to scandal and public disgrace. . . . It was a dread that he fully understood, but which carried so many other fears in its wake that he had never been able to free himself of anxieties since his seventeenth year.

Zolotow describes Brackett's failed attempts to get Wilder to cast his son-in-law, James Larmore, in a small role in *The Lost Weekend*. Larmore, according to Zolotow, was delightful when he was sober, but he was a mean drunk. A former chorus boy, Larmore was working as Brackett's assistant during the time Brackett and Wilder wrote *The Lost Weekend*, and Wilder grew to detest him. "Larmore was an actor," Zolotow writes, but "Wilder would not cast him in any picture he directed. Brackett pointed out that Billy put girlfriends into their pictures, so why shouldn't Larmore have a chance? Billy stopped going to the Bracketts' on Sundays because he did not want to run into Larmore." The missing element of Zolotow's pregnant description is this: the Hollywood rumor mill of the 1940s had it that Larmore had been Brackett's lover as well as his son-in-law.

Whatever the underlying personal dirt may have been with Brackett, *The Lost Weekend*'s appeal for Billy was its danger. This was a novel about a closet-case drunk. Its protagonist's mind is twisted, its authorial voice morbid in its self-deceits and overarching despair. Jackson painstakingly traces Don Birnam's obfuscations and denials, his clouded dreams and morose ramblings. Best of all, Jackson's is not a romanticized view of alcoholism. The hero of both the novel and the film of *The Lost Weekend* doesn't wallow and sink against a backdrop of neon and love. He's just a sad, ordinary drunk who wastes his life. He appealed to Billy's imagination.

Energized by the idea of writing something so wrenching—and evidently grateful to be back with each other again—Brackett and Wilder returned to their old routine in the spring of 1944: work, talk, cards, gossip, lunch, naps, work, talk, and work. They began writing *The Lost Weekend* at the end of May, having put another idea on hold—a picture for Joan Fontaine. Brackett and Wilder had been kicking around the idea of adapting a Ferenc Molnár play, *Olympia*, but for various reasons it hadn't gotten off the ground. A budget was drawn up, rights were purchased, preliminary casting decisions were made—Fontaine would play Olympia, Ray Milland would be her romantic interest, and Erich von Stroheim would play the chief of police—but then came some unpleasant news. Although Paramount had paid MGM $30,000 for what the studio believed were worldwide rights, the fact was that the purchase failed to include a crucial piece of the pie—the American rights. As a result, $29,999 had to be written off to overhead, and *Olympia* was postponed.

Brackett and Wilder threw themselves into *The Lost Weekend*. Billy's nose for publicity was sharp, and he had more than enough energy to tackle some new filmmaking challenges. He understood that it took guts to make a film about a drunk—the kind of guts that would get a lot of attention. He also set himself a difficult artistic task to keep his mind from wandering. He told the *New York Times* in mid-July that 70 percent of *The Lost Weekend* would be silent.

For the part of Helen, the concerned girlfriend, Wilder wanted Katharine Hepburn. In the novel, Birnam's girlfriend barely figures; Jackson's Birnam is barely interested in women. He makes some noises about Helen here and there, but there's no passion. Some nervous play with a prostitute named Gloria occurs, but it leads nowhere. At the same time, he finds himself thinking about his old boyhood chum Mel, and how they used to fool around in a shed behind the Presbyterian church, and how Mel fantasized about a girl while they were doing it while Don shocks himself by imagining Mel's father. And naggingly, his thoughts keep returning to his old fraternity brother and the story of why he'd been thrown out of the fraternity and how it was just a misunderstanding. He hadn't meant *that*, no. *That* wasn't what he meant at all.

That, of course, needed to be drastically downplayed for the film version, if not entirely eliminated. The Production Code permitted no treatment of homosexuality, let alone an emotionally sympathetic one. A ready method of covering over the central character's sexuality was to expand the role of his putative girlfriend and then give the part to a magnetic star. Hepburn was intrigued enough by what Billy told her initially, and she became even more so after he began reading whole stretches of the script to her over the telephone as soon as he and Brackett wrote them. But Hepburn had a problem: she was already committed to costarring with Spencer Tracy in *Without Love* at MGM in August, when *The Lost Weekend* was scheduled to roll. By the last week in July, the idea was history— Hepburn was officially out. Billy gave the script to Jean Arthur.

Throughout the summer of 1944, the Hays Office was reading those small portions of the script that Brackett and Wilder submitted to them and earnestly rejecting them on moral grounds. The start date of the film was pushed back to late September. Don Birnam was no longer gay, but he was still a drunk, and that fact alone was enough to rattle the PCA. Hollywood radio commentator Jimmie Fidler reported that Paramount had to "scrap the valuable property and rewrite the story," the Hays Office having "banned it because the plot concerns a man who spends a drunken weekend." Fidler's announcement wasn't just breathless. It was totally false; Wilder and Brackett did not have to scrap their work at all. Fidler's broadcast nevertheless illustrates some of the nervous buzz surrounding *The Lost Weekend* within the industry.

Billy thrived on precisely this kind of tension. It was scarcely the first time he had deliberately picked a troubled property, and it would hardly be the last. Remarkably, Paramount continued to green-light his ideas on the promise, or at least the hope, of their eventual approval by the PCA, in spite of the fact that *The Lost Weekend* was proving to be as difficult in this regard as *Double Indemnity* had been. Billy's chief goal was to make the film as brutally realistic as possible. There would be no soft-focus photography here, no back lot New York street scenes, no generic Hollywood sets. Once again, he wanted his film to be as hard as he was. He wanted to make a picture that was somehow both raw and polished—a work of art so involving that audiences, immersed in the harsh world he created for them, would never notice the artistry. *The Lost Weekend* was going to watch a man slide into a self-induced hell, and the trip would not be beautiful.

Wilder originally wanted to use a character actor for the lead. He specifically did not want the magnetism of any of Paramount's handsome stars to get in the way of his realism. "But the head of Paramount, Buddy De Sylva—a very wise man—said, 'No, take a leading man, because then the audience will feel with him. They will wish that he would reform.' " Wilder goes on to make clear that redemption was not his goal: "But of course I never went so far as to say, 'He will never drink again.' He just says at the end, 'I'll try,' and he takes that cigarette and throws it into that whiskey glass. That's as far as I would go. I cannot suddenly come out with a happy ending. It has to fit." Wilder expanded on the theme on another occasion: "Originally I wanted Jose Ferrer, who had just had a great success on Broadway as Iago in *Othello*. But I was told that no one would care whether he stayed an alcoholic or died of cirrhosis of the liver. Instead, if I took a seductive actor, people would have sympathy for him and wish he would stop drinking." He chose Ray Milland.

When Jean Arthur turned down the role of Helen, Billy offered it to Jane Wyman, who accepted it. (He's also said to have considered Barbara Stanwyck, but this is dubious.) She was under contract to Warner Bros., but her contractual obligations were of no concern; Jack Warner was happy to loan "little Janie" to Paramount for *The Lost Weekend*, or as he put it, "that drunk film."

For the role of Don's brother, Wick, Billy chose Philip Terry. Terry had been working as a stand-in for another actor when Billy was directing screen tests for *The Major and the Minor*. Impressed with the personable young man, Wilder told Terry that he wouldn't be a stand-in forever—that Wilder would actually cast him in a film when the right role came up. He was as good as his word. Finally, for the role of Helen's mother, Billy chose Lillian Fontaine (Joan's mother); it was her first film job.

In production meetings held on September 14 and 15, Billy spelled out his artistic goals for the benefit of the executives whose approval he required. They were typically skeptical, but Billy won most of the fights. He absolutely rejected the idea of using building miniatures for *The Lost Weekend*. He demanded that the set of Sam's Bar have four walls so he could shoot in all directions. He specified that the apartment set have a genuine Greenwich Village atmosphere, including the kind of minuscule kitchen that never seemed to enter into Hollywood art directors' imaginations. He insisted that John Seitz be able to film the skyline, the garden, the exterior of the apartment, and the bedroom window all in a single shot, so that he could achieve a slow but smooth revelation of Don Birnam's whiskey bottle hanging out the window. He spelled out the wardrobe for all the central characters and issued express commands regarding the songs to be sung in the bar.

As *The Lost Weekend* sped toward its start date, problems surfaced. In their script, Brackett and Wilder set a scene at a Metropolitan Opera performance of *La Traviata*—specifically, during "Libiamo," the drinking song. As written, the scene might have looked authentic, but it would also have cost money. The Met was demanding $1,000 for the use of the words "Metropolitan Opera" alone. The legal department, meanwhile, was increasingly nervous about Billy and Charlie's unwavering insistence on location shooting in New York City. Location work was always rife with tension; after all, this was why Paramount had built a whole New York City street scene on the lot, where everything could be carefully controlled. But for Wilder and Brackett, the canned quality of a Hollywood back lot was absolutely out of the question for *The Lost Weekend*. They would simply have to brave the onlookers and the traffic, the logistical headaches and the weather. There was no room for compromise on this point. Thus the mounting tension of the legal department. As an executive pleaded with them in a poignant mid-September memo, "Will you please see that we stay out of trouble?"

Staying out of trouble appears to have been a theme in Billy's domestic life as well. As much as Judith loved the house on Hidden Valley Road, the Wilders decided to get rid of it and move down the hill into the heart of residential Beverly Hills. They sold the house in May and bought a large, comfortable place at 705 North Beverly Drive. The Wilders abandoned their plans to build the house on Tarcuto Way; by November that property was sold.

Billy left for New York by train on September 21. Brackett joined him in Chicago after a side trip, and by the 24th they had taken up temporary residence at the Sherry Netherland Hotel in New York, along with the twenty other people on the production team. Ray Milland and his stand-in appeared on schedule on the 27th—they stayed at the Waldorf, apart from the others. Milland, who was quite troubled by both the novel and the screenplay, later described his mood as "increasingly snappish and morose." *The Lost Weekend* was ready to begin shooting.

For Paramount's front office, there was an additional worry: money was being spent on the picture, but Brackett and Wilder had not finished writing it yet. *The Lost Weekend* was not a blithe, interchangeable genre movie—a bobby-soxer romance with dialogue that could be filled in at the last minute if need be—but rather a difficult drama that had already sent a flurry of red flags flying at the censors' office. Brackett and Wilder had tended in the past to write and rewrite passages as they filmed, but never before had the gaps been so extensive. Whole stretches of *The Lost Weekend* were still incomplete when the film started rolling, and the executives were notably worried. On October 5, one of the men on location wrote to his colleague back in Hollywood, expressing both enthusiasm and mounting alarm over Billy and Charlie's idea of following Don Birnam the length of Third Avenue as he tries to pawn his typewriter for the price of a bottle of liquor: "The Third Avenue walking shot has really developed since we arrived here but we have no script as yet and it is difficult for me to know just how much or how little will be used in the final picture." The executive also reported another distressing fact: both Billy and Charlie had fallen violently sick with colds. Wilder's was the worse of the two. He was under a doctor's care, but, being Billy, he wasn't nearly "sick enough to stop him going out to shoot if we get light."

If they got light. *The Lost Weekend*'s exteriors were being filmed in New York, not Southern California. Shooting was well under way by that point, but as everyone knew, light could never be counted on in the Northeast. Filming had begun early in the morning of October 1 with exterior shots of Bellevue Hospital. In the days to follow, Billy, Charlie, and their actors and crew spent their time setting up locations on the streets of Manhattan, ignoring bystanders, shooting bits of film documentary style, and waiting, waiting. The corner of Third Avenue and Fifty-ninth Street; the exterior of the St. Agnes Church at Forty-third and Third; Gluck's Pawn Shop at Third and Fifty-seventh; Bloom's Pawn Shop at Third and 104th; Kelly's Pawn Shop at 124th and Third. . . . Light was an enormous problem. The dawn sequences really had to be shot at dawn, which meant that even under the best conditions only an hour or so of work could possibly be done.

In fact, no shots could be taken at all on the first day. Some footage was shot in the morning of October 2, but then they needed afternoon light and had to wait for it for several hours. Ray Milland was called for 8:00 A.M. on the 3rd, but once again everyone sat around waiting for the right light. They finally got some at three in the afternoon, but by that point they only had time for a single setup.

Even when they managed to get something recorded on celluloid, the results were often unusable. To catch Milland walking down the street as unobtrusively as possible, Seitz and his cameramen set up shop in a kind of box that was disguised on the back of a truck. Milland would walk, they would shoot from inside the box, and countless passersby had no idea they were being filmed. (Assistant cameraman Jack Etry may have come up with the idea for the television series *Candid Camera*, but apparently he demanded too much money for it and ended up with no credit at all.) They also hid a camera in an empty piano packing case on the sidewalk. The result of all this surreptitious filming was some serviceable material.

Much of it, though, was unusable footage showing passersby picking their noses and scratching areas forbidden by the Production Code.

Nothing at all was accomplished on October 4. The "company waited for light all day." The same thing happened on the 5th. And the 6th. They actually got something filmed on the 7th. A group of unruly New York street children caused a few headaches at the St. Agnes location, but they managed to work around them. A cop reportedly tried to pick up an especially haggard-looking Ray Milland in front of Bellevue, but an agitated Billy burst forward waving documents that demonstrated that they were filming a movie and that the derelict was really a movie star, and the cop went on his way. Later, when Bellevue's managing director saw the film, he was enraged at its depiction of his hospital and regretted ever having given Wilder permission to film there: "He showed me one script which I approved. Then he filmed a *different script.*"

The company's luck held out until the 13th, when another protracted burst of bad weather kept the whole crew waiting all day long and nothing was shot. The 14th was a washout as well. Some remaining Third Avenue shots were finally completed on the afternoon of the 15th. On the 16th the company traveled back to dependably sunny Los Angeles, where they would be shooting indoors. They left the New York transparency unit to finish filming the rest of the exteriors, including some of those that appear behind Milland as he makes his famous walk.

Now it was the star's turn to get sick. Milland developed a sore throat and, saying that he was worried about the air-conditioning on the train, refused to travel back to Los Angeles with the rest of the company. Perhaps he just found the level of nervous energy too high. Whatever his reasons, he left by train for Los Angeles the following day, by himself.

The script still wasn't finished. And the executives were really getting annoyed. The Hays Office wasn't pleased either. The censors were unable to approve or reject the screenplay simply because there was no screenplay for them to read. This, indeed, may have been Billy and Charlie's point in not finishing it.

Wilder and Brackett arrived in Los Angeles on the 19th and proceeded immediately to Paramount, where they inspected the film's sets, which had been constructed in their absence. They were thrilled with what they saw: the sets were cramped and drab, just as they had ordered. Production was scheduled to resume on the 23rd.

By this point, *The Lost Weekend* was attracting national attention, and not necessarily from friendly quarters. "I guess the distillers are watching nervously to see what we are doing with the picture," Brackett told the press. "They won't find it an argument for Prohibition because we're not dealing with the average drinker at all. . . . We are making the movies' first attempt to understand a drunkard, a chronic alcoholic, and interpret what goes on in his mind." At that point, the liquor industry did not plan to mount any sort of campaign against the film, but there was still great concern about the adverse effects *The Lost Weekend* would have on sales. Stanley Bear of the Allied Liquor Industries, a national trade organization, wrote to Paramount executive Y. Frank Freeman, pointing out that fully one-third of the counties in the United States were then legally dry and that twenty-five million people lived in those areas. The Allied Liquor Industries saw no need to increase these already extensive restrictions on alcohol sales, and the group was worried that an antialcoholism film would put them further on the defensive. He noted that Charles Jackson himself was certainly no temperance crusader. In March 1944, Jackson told the *New York World-Telegram* that he was "deathly afraid the drys may seize on his merciless, clinical portrait of a drunk as a weapon in their battle for the return of Prohibition."

Clearly, alcohol and alcoholism was still a touchy subject in wartime America. And the Hays Office did not like touchy subjects. The task of dealing with the censors fell, as usual, to Paramount's Luigi Luraschi. The studio had no choice but to submit the script "in piecemeal fashion," Luraschi told Joseph Breen at the end of October, because the film was already in production. In still another letter he blamed technical difficulties for the delays. For his part, Breen was already upset about what he had read so far. The character of Gloria, he told Luraschi, was definitely a prostitute—there was no question about that. As such she was unacceptable. Breen himself helpfully suggested "defining her as a buyer who entertains out-of-town visitors." Luraschi probably knew better than to forward that idea on to Brackett and Wilder.

Billy, meanwhile, plowed right ahead with Gloria the prostitute. After shooting scenes with Milland and Terry on the 23rd, he stayed around the set to film screen tests with the actress he had in mind to play her. Her name was Doris Dowling. She was twenty-one years old, a beautiful would-be starlet from New York, and she was currently enjoying an affair with Billy.

Dowling may have been one of the many eager young women who were calling Wilder on the telephone—and irritating Raymond Chandler—during the writing of *Double Indemnity*, but by October of 1944, she had become much more central to Billy's romantic life. Having arrived in Los Angeles in early 1943, Dowling soon found herself under contract to David Selznick. By the end of the year she was asking to be released from her contract. She speedily landed a new contract at another studio—Paramount. Billy's promiscuity appears to have wound down to some extent.

He began seeing Dowling as often as he could, and his friends assumed that when he got around to divorcing Judith he'd end up marrying Doris.

It was at this juncture that Billy met Audrey Young, the woman with whom he would spend the rest of his life. He soon started cheating on his twenty-one-year-old mistress, with whom he was cheating on his wife, so that he could have more time to see the swinging big-band singer he'd hired for a bit part in *The Lost Weekend*. The arrangements were complicated.

When *The Lost Weekend* was released, Dowling reported the circumstances of her casting in the *New York Sun*. She and Billy were having lunch at Lucey's along with Charles Jackson. She hadn't yet been cast in the film. Wilder and Jackson were talking about Gloria. Too bad Doris isn't more common, Jackson remarked—she could play Gloria. Billy, not bothering to look up from his plate, said, "She is." "I almost went crazy with excitement!" Dowling told the reporter, though it is entirely unclear from the phrasing whether Billy meant simply that she was going to be playing Gloria or that she was common enough to do so convincingly.

Whatever Billy's joke meant, Doris Dowling was hardly common. In fact, she was a knockout. In *The Lost Weekend*, Wilder introduces her immediately after Birnam settles into his first drink. Until that point, Milland plays his character as stiff and anxious, pressurized against a hostile world. Then he downs a shot of whiskey, at which point his body relaxes and he becomes an easygoing sweet-talker sitting on a bar stool, enjoying himself. At this precise moment Wilder cuts abruptly to a long shot of a slim, strong young woman getting up from a table. She's wearing a tight black lace top, tied closed at the top but open in the back, with a white bra underneath to keep it from being censorable; a tight black skirt that sets off the sharp angle of her hips; sheer black stockings; black high heels. She doesn't walk. She strides—slowly and confidently. The camera pans with her, as if unable to take its single glass eye off her. She strolls behind Birnam at the bar, runs her finger along the back of his neck, and with the cool authority of a dame who knows her business, says, low and smoky, "Hello, Mr. Birnam. Nice to have you back with the organization."

Then she points her index finger at him, cocks it, and clicks her tongue as she shoots, never missing a beat. The camera stares at her as she leaves the room. It is abundantly clear what Billy saw in Doris Dowling.

At the same time, Gloria is an object of mild, amused contempt. She's forever shortening words. She's too cool to say "naturally"; to Gloria, it's "natch!" After a couple of *natch*es and a "Don't be ridick!" Birnam can't take it anymore and whines: "Gloria, *please*, why imperil our friendship with these loathsome abbreviations?" A little later, he drunkenly invites her to see *Hamlet* at a theater on Forty-fourth Street. "Do you know *Hamlet*?"

he asks. "I know Forty-fourth Street," she answers. Taking his invitation seriously, Gloria blows off a rather wizened potential customer and arranges for Don to pick her up at eight that evening. "I live right on the corner house—you know, where the antique shop is, the one with the wooden Indian outside? They got the Indian sign on me, that's what I always say." Curious that Wilder picked up on his mother's favorite memory of New York in this manner.

Audrey Young, meanwhile, was every bit the looker Doris Dowling was, though perhaps without the starlet's exquisite features. A cool brunette with a hot voice, Audrey at twenty-two was a bit of a party girl. As Walter Reisch described her, she was "brilliant, beautiful, and as hard as he is." She was a jazz singer who knew her business. If you could make crystal as soft as velvet you'd have a way of describing Audrey Young's voice. She wasn't a belter. Her singing voice was strong but delicate and precise and effortless. Hearing her few recordings one can't help but fall a little bit in love with her on the basis of her sexy voice alone. She glides up and down the scale, casually nailing complicated vocal arrangements like a sharpshooter hitting a moving target. And she was nobody's fool. As one admirer once described her, "With her reed-slim figure and Louise Brooks bob of dark hair, [she] possesses a combination of earthiness and sophistication that Nora Charles would envy. Indeed, [the Wilders'] Thin Man–style banter is the stuff of Hollywood legends."

With Doris already on the payroll as Gloria, Billy proceeded to cast Audrey as a hat-check girl. Years later, a *Playboy* interviewer observed that "Wilder cut the scene so that only her forearm appeared, and both Wilders agreed that the forearm gave a superb performance."

The practical details of orchestrating two affairs at the same time were all part of Billy's quotidian frenetic pace. He was writing and directing a high-profile feature film while juggling three women. He was very busy. Audrey recalls their first date as having been conducted in secrecy—not because of Judith, but because of Doris. It was easier when Audrey took off for the East Coast on a tour with the Dorsey band, but when she found herself sitting in lonely hotel rooms at night, she started calling Billy in Hollywood—on his nickel. The fact that he took the calls proved to her that he wasn't disinterested.

It was a life of ordered chaos, and Billy managed it beautifully. He was never less than focused on his work. Wilder knew what he wanted with and from *The Lost Weekend*, and he got it. There was really only one man at Paramount who could shoot the film as grimly and grayly as Billy imagined it—John Seitz. Wilder, Brackett, and Seitz came up with ideas jointly for specific shots as well as for the overall look of the film. For *Five Graves to Cairo*, Seitz had gotten within ten inches of Franchot Tone's chest for the shot of his dog tag. That wasn't nearly close enough for *The Lost Weekend*. This was a film about the shadowy wretchedness of a man's interior life, a quality Wilder, Brackett, and Seitz wanted to express as vividly as possible with an intense close-up of a single haunted eye. Using a special effects lens and a camera mounted on a mobile boom, Seitz bore down on Milland's face—specifically, the dead-center of his pupil. At the beginning of the shot, Seitz's camera is only six inches away from Milland's eye. (The typical close-up in that era was taken from a distance of several feet.) Quietly but firmly urging the star not to breathe, Seitz orchestrated a complicated reverse tracking movement and simultaneous change of focus, all in the context of as little light as possible. It may well have been the single most extreme close-up ever achieved at that point; without doubt it was among the closest. The result is magnificent, but because the shot so neatly expresses the character's hungover agony, its formal beauty remains secondary.

For a less extreme but no less disturbing close-up of Birnam at the ugly moment that he threatens a shopkeeper for a bottle of booze after being discharged from Bellevue, Seitz made it a point to film the shot as harshly as he could. Milland's face was caked with chalky makeup, and Seitz compounded the effect by aiming the most severe light he could find at him. When they looked at the rushes, Milland actually trembled, much to his director's pleasure. Brackett loved it as well, saying that it was the most eloquent close-up he'd ever seen. Wilder then asked Seitz if he could duplicate precisely that look for the rest of the film. Seitz agreed. They continued using ghastly makeup, caustic lighting, and an orange-yellow filter over the lens. To everyone's credit, dapper Ray Milland looks truly dreadful for much of *The Lost Weekend*.

Other clever effects followed—some chancy, others simply inspired. One scene, for instance, features a shot of what Birnam sees as he falls down a flight of stairs. Seitz captured the effect by strapping a small camera to a stuntman's chest and having him do a tumble. For a sequence in which Birnam sits alone in his apartment, a gray rain falling outside the window, the film's musical arranger, Troy Sanders, supervised the filming such that the dripping raindrops would be in perfect synchronization with Milland snapping his fingers. (The moment ended up being cut from the film.) On a more ludicrous note, they had to film the smoky bar scenes with a tight lid on the cigarette stock. There was a severe wartime shortage. "Don't puff too hard," Billy instructed his actors. "And save the butts. We may have to do this scene over."

In the fall of 1944, when Wilder was filming *The Lost Weekend* in the insular surroundings of Hollywood, Europe was suffering through its fifth catastrophic year of war. The Allied invasion of Normandy in early June had been bloody but successful, and by November Allied troops had advanced well into Belgium and even as far as Aachen in Germany itself. On the Eastern Front, the Red Army was pushing toward Warsaw. The carnage would continue for months, but in the United States, at least, a mood of optimism was spreading. Across the country people began to think (unrealistically, as it turned out) that the war was all but over.

As encouraging as a lot of war news was, however, a series of shocking reports surfaced in the world press.

The Final Solution was known, or could have been known, as early as the summer of 1942, when Gerhard Riegner sent a cable from Switzerland and told the world about the Holocaust. But it was not until August 1944, when the Red Army overran Majdanek, a concentration camp near Lublin, that there was hard evidence. What the Soviets found at Majdanek was not just a concentration camp. It was a murder factory. Soviet authorities soon allowed American reporters on the scene to see for themselves the mechanics of the Nazis' continuing massacre of Jews: gas chambers, ovens to burn the bodies, piles of ashes, unmarked graves. By November, a detailed report of the mass murder at Auschwitz reached the Allied press. It was written by two young Slovak Jews named Rudolf Vrba and Alfred Wetzler, who had managed to escape the killing center in April. Vrba and Wetzler survived for two years at Auschwitz; once safe and free, they wrote a thirty-page report on what they saw and did. News of a death camp at Auschwitz surfaced in June 1944; the report itself was released in November.

"A bit like the old court Jews," Anthony Heilbut has written, the Hollywood refugees "exerted great authority in some areas, but in other places they remained vulnerable: their ultimate vision was composed of alarm and betrayal." These were men and women who escaped persecution, built lives for themselves, worked, made money, thrived. They wrote or sang or conducted business in a new language. They directed films or acted in them. They won awards; people knew who they were. In late 1944, these successful émigrés were made to understand, mercilessly, that had they not been free to exercise their paranoia in 1933 they would have ended up in a Nazi gas chamber along with millions of others.

The Lost Weekend worked its way toward completion in December. Jane Wyman's daughter, Maureen Reagan, visited the set for the filming of a scene with Wyman, Milland, and Philip Terry. It was a typically frustrating process, just another day on a Hollywood soundstage, and it took an hour to get one single usable take. Billy called for time out. Maureen was amazed. "Is that all you got to do to be an actress?" she asked her mother. "It's just make believe!"

It was make believe, but of a decidedly grim nature. When Birnam meets Helen, he couldn't be more rude and obnoxious. Their overcoats have been mixed up in the coatroom of the opera. They find each other when everyone else has gone. "My umbrella, if you don't mind?" she asks, coldly. "Catch," he says, and tosses it in her general direction, not even bothering to see if she can snare it. It falls on the floor in front of her feet. "Thanks very much," she says. He responds with a snarl: "I'm terribly sorry." It's Wyman's best moment in *The Lost Weekend*. After this initial burst of well-deserved contempt for the abusive and self-centered Don, she retreats into an ever-smiling, ever-gracious mode of forgiveness that lasts for the rest of the film. Hepburn would have played it harder.

Don Birnam's solo scenes are more brutal than any of the ones he shares with other characters. When he returns home from the bar to restart his novel, he gets as far as the title page and the dedication. After that it's every writer's nightmare. First, he lights a cigarette. Then he paces, rubbing his neck. Then he goes for the bottle, only it's missing, and that's all the writing he does. The film's producer and director must have recognized the feeling. They decided to enhance their own sense of realism by decorating the walls of Don's apartment with childhood pictures of themselves. A three-year-old Billy poses with his brother; Charlie, age two, stands in front of a Christmas tree with his mother. The photos were placed there for Billy and Charlie's own benefit; they are impossible to pick out when watching the film itself.

The Lost Weekend's representation of solitude reaches its most harrowing level when Don hallucinates two rodents in his apartment. The scene was meant to look demented, and it does, though probably more so now than it did at the time. In the 1990s, when elaborate special effects are often the entire point of a string of summer blockbusters, it may be difficult not to snicker at the artificial bat that flaps its way into Don Birnam's apartment courtesy of his alcoholic delirium. When the mechanical bat ends up chewing a mouse to death in front of Birnam's horrified eyes, the effect can seem more bizarre even than the filmmakers intended. It was less risible at the time. Contemporary accounts don't call attention to the sequence's fakery. Today, if one can get beyond anachronistic expectations about cinematic special effects, the hallucination sequence is still legitimately mad. The bat may look phony, but the mouse is all too real. The props crew pushed it through a crack in the wall of the set and held it by the tail as it frantically squirmed. This alone is terrifying. When the bat swoops down and devours it, leaving a trail of thick blood dripping down the wall, the sequence looks like a druggie fun house. As long as one doesn't expect unqualified mimesis, the sequence graphically and grotesquely expresses the horror of addiction and dementia.

Bim, the gay Bellevue nurse, sets the mood in an earlier scene. Milland had actually spent half a night in the Bellevue drunk tank to see firsthand what his character was up against; after hours of screaming, moaning, crying, and "a long ululating howl," all accompanied by the smell of piss and sweat, Milland decided he'd had enough and escaped in his bathrobe. "You're just a freshman," Bim tells a terrified Don. "Wait'll you're a sophomore. That's when you start seeing the little animals. You know that stuff about pink elephants? That's the bunk. It's *little* animals! Little tiny turkeys in straw hats. Midget monkeys coming through the keyholes. See that guy over there? With him it's beetles. Come the night he sees beetles crawling all over him. Has to be dark though." Bim concludes with a remark that is pure Billy Wilder: "It's like the doctor was just telling me—delirium is a disease of the night. Good night."

The vicious bat and the pathetic mouse became a central theme in Paramount's promotion of *The Lost Weekend*. In 1944 and 1945, Freudian psychoanalytic theory was finding wide support in the United States, and Don Birnam's rodent hallucination was one of its primary illustrations in the popular imagination. Paramount's own press people went beyond their usual puffery by announcing to the public that the hero's subconscious mind expresses his inferiority complex by way of the mouse, while the bat is the successful writer Birnam imagines himself to be while drunk. "The stronger ego kills the weaker and that is the tragedy's dramatic climax," Paramount's flacks explained. Wilder himself said that Jackson had spelled out the symbolism to him: "Birnam's hallucination is a result of his schizophrenia, or split personality. The mouse represents the everyday Birnam, the bat—or mouse with wings—the artist he dreams of being. The bat, of course, destroys the mouse. No, we don't explain it in the picture, either. It will give people a chance to use their heads, and besides, there isn't time."

The script still wasn't done in November, but already there was talk of the next Brackett and Wilder film. *Olympia* was still a good possibility. Joan Fontaine was now out; Greta Garbo had become interested. According to one contemporary report, Brackett and Wilder wanted Garbo but shelved the film again when Garbo decided instead to do some sort of Viking tale for another director. When she backed out of that project she was free to do *Olympia* with Brackett and Wilder. The film, of course, never got made. As for *The Lost Weekend*, Wilder and Brackett dealt with the PCA's objections over Gloria by ignoring them entirely. The PCA was irritated. Breen fired off a letter to Luraschi noting that the script Paramount had submitted only went up to page 46. He urged that the rest of the screenplay be turned over as soon as possible to avoid problems. The Gloria problem was still nagging at Joseph Breen. "It must be established," he insisted, "that Gloria is not a prostitute." The "present flavor," he observed, "seems to indicate that she is." Revisions were still being made in December, when, in addition to Gloria, the mouse and the bat were creating doubts in the minds of the censors. Breen was worried about "undue gruesomeness" as well as prostitution.

The final draft of the hospital sequences was completed on December 6 and went before the cameras on December 11. The company worked throughout the next two weeks, took a day off for Christmas, and resumed filming the following day. Scenes were still being written. On December 27, the final four pages of *The Lost Weekend* were received by Buddy Coleman and distributed to all the interested parties. The shooting schedule was pushed back through the 29th; the production was five days behind schedule. The need for retakes pushed it another day behind. On December 30, 1944, *The Lost Weekend* wrapped. Or so they thought.

At this point, the film was more or less on budget—$1,250,000, of which more than $90,000 went to Billy Wilder for writing and directing it. It was the first time he had earned more than his actors.

With *The Lost Weekend* in the can, at least for the time being, Brackett and Wilder announced their next project—a Danny Kaye musical. *The Count of Luxembourg*, from the Lehár operetta, would be light and pretty and fun—everything *The Lost Weekend* was not. Kaye hadn't committed to the film yet, but as Billy told the *Los Angeles Examiner*, the popular song-and-dance man could do one film per year "outside of what he does for Goldwyn, and he is very interested in our musical." In February Billy and Charlie began working on the script; Billy put in thirty-six days of work for $12,000. Soon, however, *The Count of Luxembourg* was put on hold owing to complications over musical rights, so Brackett and Wilder made another announcement. They told Louella Parsons, who told everyone else, that they were putting together a film adaptation of *Around the World in 80 Days*, with Ronald Colman as Phineas Fogg. They'd invited Paramount's leading exotic, Dorothy Lamour, to do one of the extended cameos. But that project didn't get off the ground either.

In February 1945, the Academy of Motion Picture Arts and Sciences announced the contenders for the 1944 Oscars. *Double Indemnity* was nominated as Best Picture, Billy as Best Director, and Wilder and Raymond Chandler as authors of the Best Screenplay. In addition, Barbara Stanwyck was nominated as Best Actress, John Seitz was named in the category of Best Black-and-White Cinematography (he had nine other competitors), and Miklós Rózsa was a candidate for the award for Best Score. Finally, the film's sound man, Loren Ryder, was a nominee in the Sound Recording category, bringing the total of *Double Indemnity*'s Oscar nominations to seven.

Wilder actually thought he might win. He was very disappointed when he didn't. His chances were never very good: apart from the fact that his film was much too nasty to win an Oscar, he had fierce competition from within his own studio. Paramount's *Going My Way*, directed by Leo McCarey, had several lovely things going for it, not the least of which were the five words that sum it up: Bing Crosby as a priest. *Going My Way* was heartwarming; *Double Indemnity* was not. *Going My Way* was reverential; *Double Indemnity* was not. In terms of drumming up Oscar votes, Paramount was throwing its weight behind *Going My Way*. It was not only a safer bet but a more moralistic one as well.

Even without this betrayal from Billy's own studio, *Double Indemnity* stood little chance of winning. The Oscars were essentially a public relations event for Hollywood, and the Academy inevitably picked Best Pictures that made Hollywood look good. Twentieth Century–Fox's *Wilson*, a now-all-but-forgotten biopic about America's twenty-eighth president, had just been honored by the American Nobel Committee as "a vital contribution to the cause of world peace." How could a movie about adulterous killers compete with that? The whole point of the Oscars was to elevate Hollywood's always questionable ethical standards in the eyes of the world to which they strenuously marketed. *Double Indemnity* did not serve that purpose.

The awards ceremony was held at Grauman's Chinese Theatre on March 15. Mervyn LeRoy announced the winner of the Best Director award: Leo McCarey. What happened next is a matter of some dispute. It has never been independently confirmed, but Billy claimed to have stuck his foot into the aisle and tripped McCarey as the jubilant winner made his way to the podium. McCarey fell flat on his face, said Billy. (Wilder later drew back a bit from this outrageous claim, saying simply that McCarey "stumbled perceptibly.") When the writing awards were announced, there, again, was Leo McCarey striding to the stage, grinning, and accepting the award for Best Original Story (though nobody, not even Billy, has ever said he tripped him twice). Most annoying of all was the fact that *Going My Way* also won in Wilder's own writing category; he and Chandler lost to somebody named Frank Butler and his collaborator, Frank Cavett. For Billy, the 1944 Oscar ceremony was a series of bitter moments.

Whether or not Billy actually did put his foot out and caused a less talented rival to fall, he was still fuming when the ceremony was over. On the way out to his limo, he's said to have shouted (to nobody in particular), "What the hell does the Academy Award mean, for God's sake? After all— Luise Rainer won it two times. *Luise Rainer!*"

Wilder's mood darkened further that spring at a Santa Barbara preview of *The Lost Weekend*. At first the audience laughed. When they finally stopped giggling they were repulsed by what they saw, and they said so, again and again, on the cards they filled out after the lights came up. They came expecting the usual light-comedy drunk routine, and when they didn't get it, they grew resentful and mean. Years later, Brackett reminisced about the film's initial failure: "The studio was against it right from the start. When it was finished we had numerous sneak showings and the reaction was unanimously poor. Henry Ginsburg [a Paramount executive] was wonderful about it. He told me, 'We all make a bad one now and then.' He was sympathetic." Wilder remembers a suspect detail: one of the preview cards for *The Lost Weekend* "told me it was a great movie but I should take out all the stuff about drinking and alcoholism."

One reason the preview audience laughed was that they were cued to do so by a terrible and inappropriate musical score that had been laid onto the print. The filmmakers knew it was only a temporary score; the audience did not. Accompanying the opening sequence, as Wilder's camera pans across the New York skyline and finds its way into the window of Don's apartment, was a jazzy theme with a lot of xylophone. This urbane faux-Gershwin jive set a decidedly false tone, one that reigned for the duration of the picture. *The Lost Weekend* was not *Another Thin Man*, in which a debonair New Yorker cracks jokes while getting looped on martinis, but given the music they heard the audience had no way of knowing that. The filmmakers, too close to their own film, were unable to see (or hear) what the problem was. All they knew was that the audience laughed when they weren't supposed to, then they got bored and confused, and the picture went straight down.

The audiences' hoots and jeers weren't the only problem. There were unconfirmed but no less unnerving reports that the gangster Frank Costello was offering to pay Paramount $5 million on behalf of the liquor industry for the negative of *The Lost Weekend*, which he planned to destroy.

Between the disastrous previews and the mob, Paramount's executives quickly lost what little enthusiasm they still had for *The Lost Weekend*. The head of production, Y. Frank Freeman, had truly hated the idea of making this movie to begin with. Buddy De Sylva had authorized the purchase of the novel while Freeman was out of town, and when Freeman returned, he'd declared that the film could only proceed "over my dead body." The single reason he could not carry out the threat was that his own boss, Barney Balaban, had okayed the film. They'd put up with the delays in the script, they'd acceded to Billy's demands about location shooting, and now they'd had enough. Freeman was adamant: audiences hated *The Lost Weekend*, too, and he was shelving it. They'd write the whole thing off as a total loss. Freeman's right-hand man, Russell Holman, backed him up. The film was dead.

When Hollywood talents discuss Hollywood executives, the talk often turns to stupidity. Even in this context, however, Y. Frank Freeman was considered unusually dumb, an assessment shared widely across the Paramount lot. "I wish I had the answer," Bob Hope once said to Bing Crosby. "To what?" Crosby asked. "Y. Frank Freeman," said Hope. The composer Jay Livingston once overheard Freeman talking to screenwriter Bob Hartman about Mitchell Leisen. Freeman said that he just couldn't understand Leisen, to which Hartman replied, "He's a homosexual." Freeman asked Hartman what *homosexual* meant. Hartman delicately replied that it involved "unnatural sexual practices." Freeman was stunned: "Does that mean he's unfaithful to his wife?"

This was the man who pulled the plug on Billy's movie. Billy descended into as morose a mood as he had ever been in his life.

14. PROOF

How about a kiss now, you Beast of Belsen?
　　—Johnny to Erika in an early treatment of *A Foreign Affair*

In the spring of 1945, with the fate of *The Lost Weekend* seeming quite dismal and his mood even worse, Billy Wilder left Beverly Hills and traveled back to defeated, ruined, starving Germany to work for the United States government. His mission: psychological warfare, a military imperative that remained vital long after physical combat drew at last to a close. Hollywood had been doing its share in the war effort all along, as Hollywood always made sure to point out. Clark Gable famously enlisted in the air force, became a major, and earned the Distinguished Flying Cross and Air Medal after leading bombing missions over Germany. Jimmy Stewart became an air force bomber as well. Colonel Stewart, in fact, remained in the reserves after the war, and by the time he retired in 1968 he'd risen to the rank of brigadier general. Frank Capra served as a colonel in the army and made war documentaries. Naval Lieutenant Commander John Ford led his own reserve intelligence unit and made countless informational films, some under the utmost secrecy.

Billy Wilder, on the other hand, did not join the army. He did what he could in Hollywood. He was a writer-director of motion pictures—an increasingly wealthy one at that—and his contributions to the war effort were financial and indirectly propagandistic. He gave generously to Paul Kohner's European Film Fund, and he and Paramount made *Five Graves to Cairo*. But as the war approached its merciless end, Wilder's adoptive country asked him to lend his expertise directly and in person, and he gave it gladly. As it turned out, he would have given the world much more, if only the United States Army had let him.

The Allies had discovered after the fall of Mussolini in late July 1943 that they were totally unprepared for victory. Allied troops controlled Italian territory, but Italian minds were left alone to wander unsupervised. So with the defeat of Germany seeming likely, British and American officials began to prepare a long-lasting assault on the German psyche. In September 1943, General Robert McClure proposed the establishment of the Publicity and Psychological Warfare Section for the Supreme Headquarters, Allied Expeditionary Forces (SHAEF). In early 1944, General Eisenhower voiced his preference for a single American head of the division, and he put McClure in charge. McClure's first task was to convince German soldiers that the Allies were reliably informed, completely united, and certain to win. Once the war ended, McClure would be in charge of turning German minds toward peacetime cooperation and rebuilding.

The Office of War Information (OWI) for the United States, meanwhile, was headed by Elmer Davis, a CBS radio commentator until his appointment to the OWI in 1942. Davis was a popular, genial on-air personality who radiated a sense of reassuring integrity both to his audience and to those who knew him. Never a great diplomat, Davis had a tough time administering the vast military/bureaucratic agency, which eventually employed ten thousand people worldwide. Still, Davis's respect for the American news and entertainment media led him to Billy Wilder. He read the *Life* profile of Brackett and Wilder when it appeared in mid-December 1944, and, impressed with Wilder's wit and intelligence, he contacted Billy and asked if the émigré writer-director would be willing to suspend his Hollywood career when the war ended to help the Allies recivilize his former home. There was certainly no one more qualified to supervise filmmaking activities in postwar Germany, and doubtless Davis knew that Wilder had personal reasons for wanting to be among the first refugees to return to the defeated Reich.

Wilder accepted Davis's invitation eagerly and was briefed on his upcoming tasks: his precise duties would be determined later, but in general terms he would oversee the reconstruction of the German film and theater industries, including the interrogation and de-Nazification of personnel. As the Allies moved slowly across the Western Front into Germany, SHAEF put a halt to all film and theater in the occupied territories. As the war neared its end, the Allies, having learned from their failure in Italy, began planning the defeated Germans' leisure activities. In addition to being able to provide technical expertise about filmmaking, Billy remembered (all too well, no doubt) many of the key players in the German film industry. He knew which ones were certified Nazis and which were merely careerist parasites who filled in the gaps when all the Jews were thrown out. More important to Billy personally was the fact that once the war was finally over he could try to find his mother.

Louella Parsons announced Wilder's appointment in early March. According to Louella, it was "one of the greatest honors ever paid a Hollywood director." She made sure to alert her readers to the fact that Billy Wilder already spoke German.

Billy's stint as a government employee was set to begin immediately after the end of the war. Paramount gave him a leave of absence to begin whenever necessary. He would depart for Europe on short notice, and since no one knew precisely when that would be, some of Billy's refugee friends in Hollywood threw him a farewell party on March 24. We know this because an FBI spy dutifully recorded the event for his superiors: "According to [informant] CNDI LA 2,718, Bert Brecht attended a farewell gathering given for Billy Wilder of Hollywood, California, who had been selected by OWI to handle American motion pictures in Germany after the war. Informant advised that in fact this gathering had been arranged principally so that Brecht might talk to Wilder, Brecht having previously expressed a desire to do so." Evidently Brecht wanted to participate in the anti-Nazi reeducation aspect of Wilder's official portfolio, but his hopes came to nothing. Wilder barely remembered even seeing Brecht at this party, let alone arranging any employment for him.

On April 30, 1945, with the Red Army advancing into the heart of Berlin, Adolf Hitler ended his life by shooting himself through the roof of his mouth in the concrete bunker he built fifty meters under the New Chancellery, the gargantuan seat of Nazi power on Vossstrasse near the Brandenburg Gate. One week later, when the Red Army finished pounding through what remained of the streets of Berlin, Germany finally surrendered. By that point Wilder had already left Los Angeles.

According to Billy, he was in New York on VE day (May 8), where he reported to an office in the Fisk Building. A paper-pushing functionary became annoyed at Wilder's appointment to the rank of colonel and demanded to know how much he was earning as a civilian. Wilder began to reply $2,500, whereupon the foul-tempered clerk berated him for taking a huge pay increase—all the way up to $6,500 per year, though of course he wouldn't be working that long—No, Billy broke in, he had been earning $2,500 *per week*. The idiocy of bureaucrats is always a pleasant topic of conversation and storytelling, but there is something wrong with this particular anecdote. Billy may have been paid and billeted at a colonel's rank, but army documents inevitably refer to him as Mr. Wilder, not Colonel Wilder. Rank is everything in the military.

He left for Europe on May 9 in a Dornier seaplane. He landed in

Limerick, took a bus to another airport in Ireland, and flew to England. "Everything was terribly clandestine," he recalled. Wilder was certainly no ostrich as far as war news was concerned—he'd followed it closely—and yet he was still shocked at the extent to which London lay ruined. Los Angeles had indeed been terribly remote from reality. A British newspaper tracked him down for an interview, but Billy's usual volubility was tempered by a sense of duty. He told the reporter only that he was on "a film mission to Germany for SHAEF," specifically as production chief for the Film, Theatre, and Music Control Section of the Psychological Warfare Division. "I can say very little now, as no final decisions have been taken," Billy allowed, leaving the job of clarification to the British Ministry of Information, which announced merely that Wilder would "advise on the kind of films to be produced in Britain for German consumption during the post-war years."

In England, Wilder is said to have met a man named Voss, who had apparently been in line for Wilder's job despite the fact that he spoke no German. True, Voss had once been a chauffeur for one of the Warner brothers, but according to Billy this was the extent of his knowledge of the world film industry. Wilder also spent some time with his old friend Emeric Pressburger. "All we did, I remember, was talk," Wilder said. "We talked about a thousand things. We wondered where we should go now that the war was over. None of us—I mean the émigrés—really knew where we stood. Should we go home? Where was home?" True to form, Wilder has a joke that clarifies his feelings (one that requires an explanatory setup— *glücklich* is German for happy/lucky): "Do you know the story about the two émigrés who meet in New York? One says, 'Walter! How are you!' And the other says, 'I'm fine. How are you, Leo?' He says, 'I'm happy— but I'm not *glücklich*.' "

The ban on all film and theater in Germany was lifted on May 12, only days after the war's end, while Wilder was still in London. Both arts, however, would remain strictly regulated for quite some time. (In the fall, for instance, *The Maltese Falcon* was released in Germany, but John Huston's diverting thriller was abruptly withdrawn a few days later when the authorities concluded that it made American police look stupid.)

At its best, the Americans' propaganda goal was four-pronged: the need to purge Nazis and Nazism and the desire to confront the German people with the extent of their atrocities were accompanied by the goal of providing the Germans with some relief from the wretched conditions under which they lived and to compete with the Soviets in doing so. For Billy, the first of these goals would occur only after he arrived in Bad Homburg, where the Psychological Warfare Division—known to its staff as PsyWar— was headquartered. But he began to accomplish the other three while he was still in London in May. There were, no doubt, innumerable staff meetings concerning strategies for rehabilitating the Germans and their culture, but these meetings probably didn't capture Billy's dark imagination as much as the film footage he began to see. It concerned concentration camps.

As early as the summer of 1942, American, British, French, and Russian intelligence officers knew that the Nazis were systematically killing the Jews of Europe. It was nevertheless a shock to most of the world to discover the fact in the spring of 1945. Once Allied cameramen began recording the barbaric physical realities of each of the death camps as they were liberated by Allied soldiers, it required no more proof. They filmed the crematoria and the ash piles. They filmed skeletal corpses, piles of shoes, lampshades made of human skin. They took motion pictures of mass burial pits, ovens made to burn vast numbers of people, dead babies, bones. Inhuman horror, unimaginable in scale, was photographed. They shipped some of this footage to London, where it was waiting for Wilder upon his arrival.

He began viewing this footage in London in May, and he continued viewing it during the weeks the army kept him waiting for his eventual posting in Germany. Whatever else he did in Europe, Billy wanted to use this footage as the basis of a documentary. He wanted to show Germany, and the world, what the Germans had done. In the late 1980s, the film director Volker Schlöndorff asked Wilder about the atrocity footage—in particular, scenes of the liberation of Bergen-Belsen. Wilder replied: "There was an entire field, a whole landscape of corpses. And next to one of the corpses sat a dying man. He is the only one still moving in this totality of death and he glances apathetically into the camera. Then he turns, tries to stand up, and falls over, dead. Hundreds of bodies, and the look of this dying man. Shattering." This was a particularly horrifying image for Billy Wilder because he knew that his mother's and grandmother's bodies might well have been in those acres of twisted, grimacing corpses. Every new frame of raw footage he saw thus held the potential of revealing his mother's fate. Every corpse might have been hers, but no corpse actually was. And when she did not appear in any image, each new frame of film led to an accumulating sense of failure and despair.

By the first week in June, Billy's coworkers in Bad Homburg were getting impatient for him to arrive. Wilder would be reporting to General McClure, but he would be working more closely with Colonel William Paley, the head of CBS who, as an army officer, had already moved from his wartime headquarters in London to Bad Homburg to supervise postwar information control. Paley's assistant, Davidson Taylor, wrote to the chief of the film section (in London) on June 4, noting that Wilder hadn't left London yet. Taylor understood that Wilder was working on the concentration camp footage while he was delayed in London, he wrote, and he acknowledged that Wilder should be put to work wherever it would do the most good. But, Taylor noted, they really could use him in Bad Homburg.

By mid-June, Wilder was on his way to Germany—via Paris, where he stayed at the Hotel d'Astorg across the street from the United Artists building. Characteristically, Wilder remembered the cuisine, a surprisingly marvelous set of meals produced by a trained French chef, who adeptly turned the only available supplies, Army K-rations, into excellent meals. (Billy described K-rations generously as "a kind of dog food.") While in Paris, too, Wilder met his old flame Hella Hartwig and spent a little time with her catching up on the last decade of their now-very-different lives.

Wilder then proceeded to Bad Homburg, where PsyWar had set up shop in a barbed-wire-enclosed compound that had been built as a training facility for German railroad workers. The compound included about twenty-five houses, a large auditorium, a dining hall, and a kitchen. True to character, Wilder managed to steer as clear of the army brass at Bad Homburg as he could. The front office had never been his favorite place on the Paramount lot, and the corresponding spot on an army base held no more appeal. General McClure's secretary, Sally Rice Taylor, recalls that Billy hardly ever came into McClure's office—even for the customary courtesy calls one is generally obliged to make to the commanding officer—but that Wilder and Paley became fast friends. The two got along immediately, owing to a shared love of food and gin rummy. They made a fine team, and not simply because of their energetic media expertise. As a high-ranking officer, Paley was able to obtain a pass to the generals' PX, where he could buy excellent chunks of beef. Wilder, meanwhile, could venture comfortably into the German countryside beyond the compound's barbed wire, where, owing to both his native language and his equally native talent for striking deals, the nightly dinner menu found completion. Local farmers wanted cigarettes, Billy wanted homemade bread, butter, and eggs, and everyone ended up happy.

Colonel Paley had a private house on the compound. Billy, billeted at the same level, had one of his own. They met often in Paley's kitchen, where the two men fashioned a workable barbecue out of a broken toaster. "Over and over we would fix up very festive and good-tasting dinners," Billy once said. "He did a lot of the cooking and he ate with tremendous enjoyment. The Germans have a word, *essen*, which means to eat. They also have *fressen*, which means to devour. That suited him much better, but the food had to be good."

One of Billy's favorite stories from the time concerns his single moment of combat. Civilians were not permitted out of the compound unless they were in uniform—an olive-colored, official-looking outfit designed to distinguish American personnel from Germans. Wilder wore one; McClure's civilian secretary wore one as well. According to Wilder, General McClure sent him and a few others out one day on a special mission—to get as much booze for the unit as they could find. As Wilder told it, he and his men commandeered a jeep and successfully liberated several cases of wine and champagne from enemy cellars. It was a dangerous mission. There was, after all, the possibility of meeting recalcitrant Nazi resistance fighters along the way. Uniformed and traveling openly in a U.S. Army jeep, Wilder and his men were an easy mark. They ventured as far as Salzburg. Finding himself in Austria for the first time since 1935, Billy grew edgy. He heard gunshots. Reacting as any military man would, Wilder instantly ordered his men to stop the jeep and hit the ground. When the Nazi barrage finally stopped, Billy retrieved enough presence of mind to understand that a few of the pilfered champagne bottles had blown open in the heat.

Because this is one of Billy's most treasured stories, it's even more dubious than usual, especially since the gunshot-that-turns-out-to-be-a-popping-champagne-bottle has been such a recurrent trope in his films. *Der Mann, der seinen Mörder sucht, Der falsche Ehemann*, and *The Apartment* aside, there's also the fact of postwar army life in Germany to consider. "We had an alcohol ration that would absolutely choke a horse," Sally Taylor declares. "Even in Bad Homburg—it was ten bottles a month per person. I used to think, 'Who can drink ten bottles a month?' We're talking hard stuff. General McClure never was without liquor in his life. He had a closet full of it. No way did he ever send Billy out to get any liquor. That house was loaded with it. So you can scratch that one."

The liberation of enemy booze was obviously the least of Billy's tasks. Because Wilder knew his way around the German film and theater communities, he was particularly qualified to oversee the army's de-Nazification program as it involved the entertainment industry. At Bad Homburg, Wilder and others supervised the interviewing of former Nazis to determine, in David Freeman's turn of phrase, "which ones were the least undesirable." Wilder knew or knew of many of these actors, directors, and other personnel. He remembered some personally and had heard about the exploits of others from fellow émigrés. One of the men Wilder interviewed was the actor Werner Krauss, known for his knack for doing horrible Jew impersonations in films like the notorious *Jud Suss*. Anton Lang was another. Before the war, Lang had played the role of Christ in the Oberammergau Passion Play. By the late 1930s he'd removed his stigmata and joined the SS. The Oberammergau's director asked Billy to recertify Lang, who hoped to be able to dust off his cross and return to Golgotha. Wilder told him yes, Lang could act again, but only on one condition: "that in the Crucifixion scene you use real nails." (A variation: "Six of the apostles were Gestapo men and the carpenter was a storm trooper. I said, 'Yes, as long as the nails are real.' ")

Apart from conducting de-Nazification interviews, the death camp documentary occupied much of Wilder's time while the search for his mother and grandmother took the rest. Neither came to anything.

The Red Cross simply had no information about Billy's family. And it was most uncertain whether any details would ever surface.

Concurrently, Wilder was trying as best he could to make a film that would prove—perhaps to himself—exactly what the Germans had done to the Jews, but thanks to the army, even that concrete task proved to be beyond his control. In the third week of June, Davidson Taylor urged that Billy take over the film from a Russian filmmaker, Sergei Nolbandov, who had also been trying to assemble the vast amount of footage into something usable. Nolbandov had had little success. The extent of the horror, combined with literally miles of raw footage, confounded his attempts to organize it into a coherent and effective documentary. So Taylor proposed a shift of personnel. It was Billy Wilder, he recommended, who really should "be in charge of the script, the material shot so far, the material shot in the future, and the cutting and recording of the film until its final approval for release." Together with some other writers, Taylor suggested, Wilder could "begin at once to prepare a script for the film at Bad Homburg." The documentary would later be "assembled at the Geiselgasteig studios using German cutters, film, materials, and technicians under Mr. Wilder's supervision." Once the film was completed, Taylor advised, Billy would bring it back to Bad Homburg for final approval.

One of Billy's most revealing stories about his time in Germany after the war concerns a test screening of the film in progress. The OWI, worried that German audiences would perceive an atrocity documentary merely as trumped-up Allied-Jewish myth making, decided to gauge audience response in a controlled screening. (Some accounts even claim that the idea for this test screening was Wilder's own, the result of his experience sneak-testing films in Hollywood, but PsyWar had been test-screening material even before Wilder arrived at Bad Homburg.) In any event, Wilder himself reports: "The preview occurred in the autumn of 1945 in Würzburg. First we showed an old film, a harmless operetta with Lilian Harvey. Afterward, we asked the audience to remain seated and watch the following film. We told them there were preview cards and pencils outside with which they could write their opinion of the picture they were about to see. There were 500 people in the audience; at the end, only about 75. Not one card was filled out, but every pencil was stolen." Wilder has even claimed that he convinced the OWI to work with the food-rationing office in Frankfurt to make it impossible for Germans to get bread or meat without seeing the film, which would eventually be titled *Todesmullen* (*Death Mills*).

In point of fact, the test screenings PsyWar arranged for *Todesmullen* and *KZ*, a preliminary, two-reel atrocity film, were as successful as these documentaries' nauseating, demoralizing subject matter allowed them to be. German audiences were generally receptive to these movies, a fact that Wilder himself reported at the time. The production history of *Todesmullen* is necessarily murky; there were too many people and too much footage involved—and too many governments and military officers. The Allies recorded and collected at least 600,000 feet of film taken by American, French, British, and Soviet correspondents, newsreel photographers, and cameramen. By December 1945, six separate versions of *Todesmullen* had been assembled in various locations. Wilder did work on at least one of these versions, but his was not the one that was finally released. At the end of June 1945, General McClure expressed his eagerness to see *Todesmullen* completed, but for reasons that only someone attuned to military logic could ever comprehend, McClure remained convinced that Wilder's time and expertise were better spent on other activities for the Film Section— managerial activities unrelated to filmmaking. The completion of *Todesmullen* was once again postponed. Handed one of the world's leading film directors, a man supremely capable of making a stinging anti-Nazi film specifically for a German audience, the United States Army put him to work doing something else.

PsyWar had been screening a variety of films for select German audiences in the occupied territories, after which individual audience members were interrogated and the crowd as a whole was polled. It was nothing out of the ordinary, then, when Wilder and Davidson Taylor attended a screening of *KZ* on June 25 in a four-hundred-person theater in Erlangen, just north of Nürnberg. They reported their experience of the screening in a memo to McClure. The film had been playing in Erlangen for a week, Wilder and Davidson noted, and the theater was filled to 90 percent of its capacity except for the final day of the run, when attendance dropped to 65 percent. The audience did resent seeing *nothing* but propaganda, they acknowledged, but that was scarcely surprising. When asked, the German moviegoers said they would prefer an additional entertainment feature as part of every program.

Still, Wilder and Davidson's report is clear: "There was standing room only at the performance we attended. The people are extremely anxious to fill out the questionnaires. Many volunteer their names, which are not required. No individual who has been asked to give an interview has declined." Wilder and Davidson continue:

The audience was respectful but scarcely enthusiastic. . . . The audience had expected that a picture called *Cowboy* would be the last film on the program. [*Cowboy* was an innocuous feature about the real function of American cowboys as seen through the eyes of a British child.] When the title *KZ* came on the screen there was a gasp throughout the audience. There were expressions of shock and horror audible throughout the picture. When the title "Buchenwald" came on the screen, the audience spoke the word almost as one man. The atmosphere was electric throughout the film, and a palpable feeling of incredulity ran through the audience when the narrator said that the wife of the commandant at Belsen had made lamp shades from tattooed human skin. We have footage showing this collection of tattoos and why it was not included I cannot say.

There is no mention of stolen pencils and fleeing Germans in Billy's memo. The only irony Wilder and Davidson reported to McClure is that after being presented with images of mass murder the grisly likes of which had never before been recorded on celluloid, the audience at Erlangen actually stayed in the theater waiting for *Cowboy* to start—"except three women who looked rather ill."

Encouraged by the test screening of *KZ*, Wilder kept pressing for the go-ahead to make the longer and more extensive *Todesmullen*, but army brass continued on its static and unproductive course. In fact, even the precise nature of Wilder's mission in Germany was still unresolved as late as June 26, a fact that Paley noted in a letter to McClure. One idea being floated at the time was to put him in charge of distribution and exhibition in occupied Germany, but Paley urged that given Billy's background as an internationally renowned writer-director, he should be *making* films, not trafficking them. "The atrocity film we now have in mind is much larger in scope than the one originally intended," Paley observed. "It now calls for someone of exceptional production experience, such as Mr. Wilder now has." One can see Billy's own hand clearly in this military paper trail, for two days later, Davidson Taylor fired off a letter of his own—this time to Paley—recommending that the colonel's frequent guest for cocktails and dinner "be made Chief of Film Production" in occupied Germany. Yet another letter from Taylor reported that Billy had no experience in distribution and exhibition but was most anxious to make the as-yet-untitled *Todesmullen*: "He is peculiarly equipped to make the atrocity film, and it is worthy of his talent in every way." Taylor also recommended that film production be split off from distribution and exhibition, with Wilder heading production. And still nothing came of it. Wilder reedited the ending of *KZ* after attending the Erlangen screening, but this fairly minor revision appears to be the only concrete film production work the army actually allowed him to complete in Germany in 1945.

He had come to Germany to find out what had happened to his mother, and after all of his inquiries, he found . . . nothing. Even the ghastliest of concrete details would have been preferable to the void of disappearance he encountered. Wilder traveled to Vienna at some point that summer and stayed in relative comfort in the Hotel Bristol, but he gained no new facts to anchor him. He learned only that Eugenia Wilder Siedlisker no longer existed. Her name, along with the names of his stepfather and grandmother, did not appear on any lists of the dead. Genia simply ceased.

What Wilder knows is only what history books can offer: after the Anschluss, the Nazis strongly encouraged the Jews of Vienna to depart, and when the beatings, burglaries, and everyday harassment weren't encouraging enough, they forcibly deported most of them to Kraków. Based on this scant information, Wilder came to believe that his mother and grandmother returned to Kraków and either died in the ghetto there or were crammed into cattle cars and shipped to Theresienstadt and then to Auschwitz. When he watched those miles of unedited atrocity footage in London and Bad Homburg, that is what he saw. He also found, none too surprisingly, a distinct lack of culpability among the Germans and Austrians to whom he spoke: "I never met a single Nazi. Everyone was a victim, everyone had been a resistance fighter." One reason he was not surprised was that he knew these people well, having spent the first twenty-seven years of his life with them. He knew, even as a child, that Christian Germans and Christian Austrians would never forget or ignore the fact that he was a Jew. He felt it in Kraków, he felt it in school at the Juranek, on the streets of Vienna and in the offices of Ufa. And he understood in a most visceral sense that if he hadn't run for his life they'd have murdered him, too.

He has described the German people—and humanity as a whole: "I know the decent ones, I know the indecent ones, I know the ones who stood outraged—but within them there was a little jubilation: one Jew less. But then, I don't think the world behaved very well after it became public knowledge that they had concentration camps. I think it could have done more. I could have maybe saved my mother—but I didn't dare because then there would have been one more." The last sentence is crucial. Billy Wilder was a survivor, but he paid a price for it in guilt.

Even then, these remarks were made after many years had passed. What he was feeling at the time is less clear. Sally Taylor recalls that Billy kept a Bible by his bed at Bad Homburg. She mentioned this detail to someone else at the compound and got a facetious reply: "Ha! He's getting gags out of it." Then again, this was somebody else's joke, not Billy's.

And yet Wilder didn't lose his sense of humor in the summer of 1945. If anything, World War II served as fodder for new jokes. For Billy, as for innumerable other Jews, the late Adolf Hitler soon began serving as a ready punchline for almost any occasion. For instance, Wilder claims that while he was traveling in Stuttgart he saw a nun who looked just like Hitler. It really *was* Hitler, Wilder convinced himself. The Führer had not committed suicide in his bunker after all and was making his way through Germany in a clever disguise, heading in a wimple toward points unknown. Billy imagined the triumphant headlines—"Film Director Apprehends Hitler on Stuttgart Street!"—but then found himself confronted with a more likely worldwide news flash: "Film Director Assaults Nun!" Billy prudently decided against making a citizen's arrest and let Sister Hitler go on her way.

Americans could not enter Berlin through most of the summer because it remained under Soviet control, but Wilder was able to fly over the city with a cameraman. "It looked like the end of the world," he said. His remark is not offhand. At the end of the twentieth century there are two categories of human beings on the planet: those who were born into a world inured to images of fire-bombed Dresden, decimated Berlin, the gas chambers and crematoria and burial pits of Bergen-Belsen and Auschwitz, and the ashes of Hiroshima and Nagasaki on the one hand, and, on the other, those to whom such images had once been unimaginable. Billy Wilder fell into the second category. Just as the footage of Bergen-Belsen's landscape of corpses was categorically unlike anything he had ever seen, so the unbroken miles of gutted, fire-bombed buildings and rubble he saw in Berlin had no meaningful point of comparison. The destructive technology of World War II had no parallel, and neither did its effects. When Wilder said that the city in which he had worked and played for seven years had come to resemble the end of the world, we can take him at his word.

There was also the smell. "The summer of '45 was very, very hot—it was the hottest summer in Berlin that anyone could remember," he said. "Thousands of corpses must have lain under the wreckage; the stink in the heat was intolerable. The dead swam in the *Landwehrkanal*; in the vegetable gardens lay putrefying corpses."

Billy Wilder never had a very high opinion of the human race. Its essential goodness tended to escape him. As Paul Kohner said, the dogs were chasing him by the time he was twenty-five, and no one could quite understand why. In the summer of 1945, Billy found visible proof.

In August, when Berlin was reopened to the Americans, French, and British, Wilder was reassigned there. When he and his young army driver were finally able to enter the city, or what was left of it, Wilder directed the driver to take him directly to the Soviet sector—to the cemetery where his father lay buried. Pummeled into ruin in the final days of the war as the Red Army advanced, building by crumbling building, into the center of Berlin, the Jewish burial ground was now littered with toppled and half-blasted headstones, burnt trees, tank tracks, and weeds. An old, emaciated rabbi and a one-legged gravedigger (who, according to the ever-ironic Billy, closely resembled Conrad Veidt) met them and told them that Max's grave would be difficult to find. Indeed, Wilder could not locate his father's tomb in the mud and debris. The rabbi then told Wilder the harrowing story of his recent life: he and his wife had actually survived the war in Berlin itself, living underground for four long years in the heart of the Third Reich. When the Soviet liberators appeared in April, they rushed outside to greet them, whereupon the rabbi watched in horror as their "liberators" raped and killed his wife.

Berlin in the hot late summer of 1945 was a bizarre landscape of rubble, Allied soldiers, starving Germans, and cocktail parties. In spite of the mass destruction and the stench of rotting bodies, the conquering Allied armies found a way to have a lot of fun. For the winners, Berlin was an ongoing cocktail party held in the surreal setting of an impromptu and overheated morgue. One of Wilder's assigned army drivers, Richard Deinler, remembers this string of celebrations well. Billy knew many of the German film and theater people, of course, and rather than make his young driver sit in his jeep and wait for him, Wilder generously took Deinler along with him to the parties. "They were always brown-nosing him," Deinler notes, none too surprisingly. After all, the Germans were eagerly trying to survive the rehabilitation program Wilder was helping to lead. They were angling for jobs. Thus the Jew from Kraków and Beverly Hills found himself with a lot of new German friends. But Wilder was not easily fooled. Deinler remembers his boss taking him aside at some point during these evening soirees, scanning the room, and quietly pointing out all the Nazis to his amazed young driver.

Deinler also remembers Billy taking him on tours of the city. The charred remnants of the Reichstag building, the Tiergarten, the bombed-out pile of bricks that had been the Romanisches Café as late as the final weeks of the war. . . . They went anywhere they could drive. They talked about what Germany had been, and what it had become. And they talked about the Germans. Deinler knew that Wilder was searching for his family, but it remained Wilder's private horror. "He may have been bitter," says Deinler, "but he never showed it."

Wilder and some army buddies were careening down the Kurfürsten-damm. (Where else would Billy have been careening, if not the heart of Berlin's entertainment district? Never mind that it was now a strip of rutted pavement running through mountainous piles of wreckage.) They were going so fast that they nearly ran over a pedestrian, who made the mistake of yelling "asshole" in German. The jeep stopped short, and Wilder jumped out and sternly informed the man—in German—that he should not simply assume that people in American uniforms wouldn't understand words like *asshole*. Wilder also noted, correctly, that the man would never have dared say anything like that to a Nazi. Billy then ordered the man to remain there while he summoned the authorities, a task he had no intention of performing. Hours later, Wilder and his friends passed by the spot and saw the terrified German still standing there, obediently awaiting his punishment.

One day, Wilder met with two Soviet colonels, one of whom looked—in Wilder's picturesque recollection—like a cross between Leon Trotsky and the cross-eyed silent comic Ben Turpin. Upon learning that Wilder was a Hollywood director, Trotsky/Turpin spun on his heels and left the room. Billy panicked, recalling in an absurd jolt of paranoia his own script for *Ninotchka*. He feared that he'd offended the Soviets. But Colonel Turpin returned a few minutes later with a big grin. *"Mrs. Miniver!* " he cried, pumping Billy's arm. "Mr. Wyler!" the other colonel beamed, whereupon he kissed Billy on the cheek. "We have seen all of your films, especially *Mrs. Miniver*! Your films are wonderful." Billy graciously accepted the praise.

In a more serious vein, Wilder was asked to report on the condition of Berlin's film facilities. He was able to visit Ufa's Tempelhof studios, which were in the American sector, and he reported that the soundstages were still in good condition. Wilder also visited Johannisthal, where the Tobis Studios had been located, in the Soviet sector—three soundstages there were totally unusable—and the Althoff Studios in Babelsberg, also in the Soviet sector. Two of those soundstages remained in working condition, while a third needed repair. Finally, at Ufa's Babelsberg studios, Billy found the situation complicated by the fact that the demarcation line between the Soviet and American sectors ran straight through the middle of the lot. The soundstages were in the American sector, while the workshops were squarely under Soviet control. Remarking on this senseless bifurcation, Wilder must have written one of the most literate military memoranda in the war: "The gentlemen who thought out this demarcation line certainly qualify for a new vaudeville act: sawing a live studio in half. However, I think I better reconsider the word 'live' because the heart and the lungs have been removed." The Russians, Billy went on to observe, had taken apart all the usable equipment and shipped it east.

By the time he left Bad Homburg Billy had given up on the atrocity documentary. But he arrived in Berlin with a fresh idea—he wanted to write and direct a fictional romance about postwar Germany. This movie would be produced not by the army but by Paramount Pictures, which could actually get the job done. As described in the letter of introduction Davidson Taylor wrote on Billy's behalf (to Lieutenant Colonel Ray Fried of Information Control in Berlin), Mr. Wilder's presence in Berlin had two objectives: to check out the condition of the city's once-extensive film studios, and more important, to gather background information for the feature film he wanted to make. Billy would need the army's permission, of course, since he proposed to film at least part of the movie in bombed-out Berlin, the visible symbol of the cataclysmic twentieth-century. No building remained unscarred. The city was divided into four sectors, each ruled by a conquering army's military police. The people, living in squalor, were all but hopeless. They were still digging rotten corpses out of the rubble and trying to salvage bricks. For Billy Wilder, Berlin was the perfect location for a new romantic comedy.

By the end of August, Billy had completed his preliminary research and laid the preproduction groundwork by lobbying the crucial military personnel for permission. Davidson Taylor was already promoting Billy's idea as "the film which we want him to make with Paramount" and urging his superiors that he "be dispatched to New York on military orders immediately to commence work on this film." Upon approval of Wilder's screenplay, Taylor concluded, PsyWar would wire the War Department agreeing to sponsor the film and would even make arrangements to take care of a Paramount filmmaking crew of eight to twelve people, including Billy, for the three to five weeks necessary to do exterior shooting in Germany.

While army personnel (Taylor, Paley, McClure, Douglas Schneider) debated the merits of supporting Wilder's Hollywood inspiration, Billy himself prepared to return to California. By the end of August there was little left for him to do but plan his next movie and keep the army brass from killing it. Some concern was beginning to be voiced in military quarters about the ethics of favoring one particular Hollywood studio over the others—Billy was nothing if not direct in proposing that Paramount produce and distribute the film—but Wilder's talent for sweet-talking proved to be as effective as ever (though the movie would end up taking far longer than he planned). Paley took Billy's lead on that score by insisting to McClure that there were precedents for this sort of favoritism (though Paley didn't bother to spell out precisely what these precedents were) and that film companies regularly received assistance from the military.

As for Billy himself, he contributed his own articulate rationale for the army's aid and support in the production of what would become *A Foreign Affair*. It took the form of a report on the vital propaganda value of mass entertainment. The Germans were receptive to the recent propaganda documentaries they had been shown, Wilder wrote to Davidson Taylor. But as he quickly went on to point out, this positive response would not last forever. "In Berlin it has worn off already," Wilder observed. The Allies, he predicted, would find it increasingly difficult to keep shoving the Germans' noses in their own misdeeds, as sickening as those misdeeds had been. "Will the Germans come in week after week to play the guilty pupil?" Wilder asked. Sure, they might show up at the theaters, but they'd probably end up sleeping through the dull propaganda so they would be "bright and ready for Rita Hayworth in *Cover Girl*."

Wilder had nothing against *Cover Girl*, he went on to say, but that kind of movie served no reeducational goals. "Now *if* there was an entertainment film with Rita Hayworth or Ingrid Bergman or Gary Cooper, in Technicolor if you wish, and with a love story—only with a very special love story, cleverly devised to help us sell a few ideological items—such a film would provide us with a superior piece of propaganda: they would stand in long lines to buy and once they bought it, it would stick. Unfortunately, no such film exists yet. It must be made. I want to make it."

Billy reminded the army of *Mrs. Miniver*'s political importance in 1940—a time when Americans still perceived the war in Europe to be remote from their own emotional lives. According to Wilder, Roosevelt himself had been so impressed with the film as a political tool that he had pushed MGM to release it as soon as possible. And Roosevelt was right: Wyler's melodrama served as more effective propaganda than fifty newsreels. Billy also presented his case for Paramount. He'd already talked it over with Barney Balaban and Russell Holman, Billy acknowledged, and they were all for it. In fact, Wilder insisted, "they would consider it unfair if I went out and made the film for another commercial company," especially "since I am on a long-term contract to them and only 'on a temporary loan to the U.S. Government.'" In fact, he reported, Paramount had already offered him "top stars, the best staff, and a budget of 1½ million to do the film." Each of the pieces was in place. All the army had to do was give Billy its approval.

The film would be a simple story, Wilder went on—the tale of an American GI and a German woman whose husband, an officer in the Luftwaffe, had been killed over Tunisia. In fact, Billy said, he'd already met such a woman: "She was working in a bucket brigade cleaning up the rubble on the Kurfürstendamm. I had thrown away a cigarette and she had picked up the butt. We started a conversation. Here it is: 'I am so glad you Americans have finally come because . . .' 'Because what?' 'Because now you will help us repair the gas.' 'Sure we will.' 'That's all we are waiting for, my mother and I . . .' 'I suppose it will be nice to get a warm meal again.' 'It is not to cook . . .' There was a long pause. I kind of felt what she meant, and I wished she would not say it. She did. 'We will turn it on, but we won't light it. Don't you see? It is just to breathe it in, deep . . .' I held out a brand new Lucky Strike to her. She did not take it. She just picked up the bucket and went back to the rubble."

Wilder plunged on. This would be the whole point of the picture—to give such a woman a reason to live. By the time *A Foreign Affair* was actually made, of course, the suicidally depressed German widow who stoically refuses the gift of a cigarette had become a supremely self-reliant ex-Nazi whore played by Marlene Dietrich—the kind of woman who would have accepted Billy's Lucky, lit it, taken a drag, and tossed the rest of it on the pavement next to Billy's shoes, all without a moment's hesitation.

"As for the GI," Billy wrote, "I shall not make him a flag-waving hero or a theorizing apostle of democracy. As a matter of fact, in the beginning of the picture I want him not to be too sure of what the hell this war was all about. I want to touch on fraternization, on homesickness, on the black market." Indeed, the scenes in *A Foreign Affair* in which Wilder introduces his GI involve him bartering a cake—specifically, a cake that has been brought to him from back home in the States—for a vile, stained, and obviously well-used mattress, which he presents as a gift to his whore (Marlene). Billy didn't spell out these choice details at the time, of course. His memo is a model of patriotism and discretion.

Wilder chronicled his research in Berlin: "I found the town mad, depraved, starving, fascinating as a background for a movie." One can only imagine the most lurid of Wilder's findings, since he limited himself to the most reportable: "I have lived with some of [the 82nd Airborne Division's] GIs and put down their lingo. I have talked to Russian WACs and British M.P.s. I have fraternized with Germans, from bombed-out university professors to three cigarette-chippies at the Femina. I have almost sold my wristwatch at the black market under the Reichstag. I have secured the copyrights to the famous song '*Berlin kommt wieder*.' I think I am quite ready now to sit down with my collaborator and start writing the script." He signed off his memo with a touch of well-deserved bravado: "I am conceited enough to say that you will find this 'entertainment' film the best propaganda yet."

Billy's confidence in his own talent was due at least in part to some surprising news from the States. Against all expectations, *The Lost Weekend* was getting good word of mouth from the small, select screenings that Paramount was nervously arranging. Given the right handling, together with its vastly improved musical score, the film might not be a colossal bomb after all. Eager to get back to America, both to shepherd *The Lost Weekend* (the wolves in the front office were still on the prowl) and to begin writing his new propaganda romance, Wilder needed only to get a release signature from his gin rummy buddy, Bill Paley. The problem was, Colonel Paley owed him about $2,000 and didn't want Billy to leave without evening the score. So (according to Billy) Billy systematically began to lose—"and with an opponent like Paley it wasn't easy." Finally, with his debt reduced to $700, Paley agreed to sign Billy's papers, and Wilder found himself on a plane bound for the States. He didn't return home empty-handed. The compulsive art collector managed to pick up a George Grosz painting during his summer in Germany, and for a very good price—a carton of cigarettes.

15. CHEERS

During the war he couldn't go fast enough for you. Get on that
beachhead, get through those tank traps, and *step on it, step on
it. Faster*—a hundred miles an hour, twenty-four hours a day,
through burning towns and down smashed *autobahnen.* Then
one day the war is over. And you expect him to jam on those
breaks and stop like that? Well, everybody can't stop like that.
Sometimes you skid quite a piece. Sometimes you go into a spin
and smash into a wall or a tree and bash your fenders.

        —Johnny (John Lund) in *A Foreign Affair*

On October 2, 1945, two weeks after Billy returned from Europe, Judith
Wilder filed for divorce. She cited "extreme cruelty," the current catch-
all explanation to describe to the court why a husband and a wife
didn't love each other anymore. Her petition was hardly a surprise.
Everyone at Bad Homburg knew that Billy and his wife were splitting up—
he and Paley sat around discussing it, along with everyone else—but Judith
waited until he was back in the States before actually filing the papers. The
couple officially separated on September 26. Their community property
included the house on North Beverly, a Studebaker, and a Buick convertible. Judith got the Studebaker; Billy got the Buick. Eventually, he'd get the
house, too, but in the meantime he moved in with Ernst Lubitsch.

Under the terms of their separation, Billy paid Judith $20,000 off the
bat plus an additional $15,000 in weekly payments of $96, plus $2,000
for alimony, and an additional $13,000 per year at $250 per week until
Judith remarried. Judith took custody of Victoria, then almost six. On
March 6, 1947, after a year-and-a-half legal separation, the divorce was
finalized, and Judith celebrated by announcing her engagement: as L.A.
newspapers reported it at the time, her groom was another writer, albeit a
less famous one. She became Judith Badner, moved to Brooklyn Heights
with her new husband, and took Vicki with her.

In the late 1940s and 1950s, when Billy had custody of Victoria for a
month in the summer, he would pick her up at Judith's place in Brooklyn
and spend a few days in New York taking her to see the top shows and
dining with her in the finest restaurants, after which the clumsily endearing

father and his adoring daughter would take the train together to Los Angeles. These trips on the Twentieth Century and the Super Chief were the only times they spent alone with each other, free from the entertaining distraction of Billy's many Hollywood acquaintances and, of course, his incessant work. Showering little Victoria with gifts throughout her childhood was Wilder's way of expressing affection. He even overcame his morbid fear of horses enough to take her horseback riding (though of course he never mounted a nag himself, but simply waited on the sidelines for Victoria to ride to her own heart's content). Victoria kept her childhood nickname after she grew up: her friends and family called her "Billi." The name once graced the vanity plates of her Mercedes. Billy's daughter remembered his cars with particular fondness: "I loved driving very fast with Daddy up the coast highway. I remember the Cadillacs when I was little, playing with the power windows." (Billy, having moved through Cadillac, Rolls, and Jaguar phases, eventually settled on Mercedeses as well.) She married twice—first a high school teacher named Fiorenzo Gordine, then the racecar driver Tony Settember. Eventually Victoria made Billy a grandfather by giving birth to a daughter, Julie (by Gordine). Julie in turn made Wilder a great-grandfather when she delivered her own little girl.

"My daddy is a hard person to get to know," Victoria Wilder Settember told Zolotow. "I worship him, but I cannot seem to get close to him. He is kind and generous, but he can't say 'I love you.' He never has to me, not once. It embarrasses him." A doting distant father, Billy was more enthusiastic about introducing his daughter to the things he loved—food and friends and the roar of Hollywood society. He once marched the eight-year-old Victoria into Romanoff's and ordered her a drink—Dubonnet with a twist. (Years later, in the 1970s, father and daughter took granddaughter Julie to The Bistro and sat her on a stack of telephone books because the deluxe restaurant possessed no child seats and she was too small to sit in a chair.) At sixteen, Victoria got her own sports car. At twenty-one, she got a two-and-a-half-month tour of Europe. Her parting words to Zolotow were, "I hope your book will explain my father to me. I never could understand him."

Billy and his family had been in the news even while Billy himself was still in Germany. Willie Wilder had grown tired of making women's purses, so he moved to Hollywood with his wife and son and began making movies. In August, with his brother still serving with the army, Willie announced that he was going to be directing *The Glass Alibi*, a dark thriller, for Republic Pictures. Willy told it to Louella: the film, Parsons announced, was about "a newspaperman who marries a $6,000,000 heiress believing that she is so ill she will die. But she fools him by recovering—so he kills her!" *The Glass Alibi* would be a low-rent *Double Indemnity*, an acidic film noir that had neither the need nor the money for any patina of respectability. It set the tone for the rest of Willie Wilder's film career.

Spurred by Billy's sensational success, Willie's own ambition to be a showman had been mounting for several years. Wm. Wilder Co., Inc., Original Handbags, was a successful Manhattan business, but it wasn't enough. Neither was Willie's house in Great Neck—especially not in comparison to what Billy had in Beverly Hills. Willie had made a few trips to Hollywood in 1943 and 1944—trips in which he'd talked to Paul Kohner about representing him as a producer-director. Kohner agreed. One idea was to do a Hollywood adaptation of *Emil und die Detektive*. Willie talked to Billy about the question of rights to the property, but nothing ever happened. Instead, Willie landed at Republic Pictures, the best and most successful of Hollywood's smaller, cheaper studios. His first task was to produce *The Great Flamarion* for director Anthony Mann. *The Glass Alibi* would be Willie's second film; this time he'd direct as well as produce. Under the professional name W. Lee Wilder, Willie kept working in the film industry for the next twenty-three years. Although his career remained decidedly on the low end of the industry, this worked to his benefit. As one admiring critic explained, Willie's artistic virtue lay in the fact that he was "one of the more extreme of the noir directors." On the other hand, Billy himself jokingly called his brother "a dull son of a bitch" and had nothing else to say about him in public.

What with Judith, Victoria, Doris, Audrey, Willie, Charlie, and Y. Frank Freeman, Billy Wilder certainly had his hands full in the autumn of 1945. But his mood actually improved. *The Lost Weekend* was reviving. In fact, its commercial prospects suddenly looked very good. The film now featured a revised ending and a moody, unnerving new score. And it was getting great word of mouth. In the turn-on-a-dime minds of Paramount's decision makers, *The Lost Weekend* transformed itself from bomb to blockbuster.

Before leaving for Europe, Billy had tinkered with the film's final sequences. Brackett spoke to Charles Jackson in the beginning of April, asking for suggestions for a new ending. Jackson submitted some ideas by mail from his farm in New Hampshire and was paid $500 for his work. The production reopened on April 10 to film a new final scene between Milland and Wyman; it closed again on the 11th, this time for good. More crucial was the film's score. According to Miklós Rózsa, Rózsa told Brackett after one of the disastrous early previews that the only real problem was the temporary jazz track that had been laid onto the print for the sole purpose of filling in the silence. Brackett told him to go ahead and write the music he thought would work, however disturbing that music might be. Rózsa had something eerie in mind for the central motif. He planned to write music for the theremin, the electronic box he had just employed to great acclaim to express Gregory Peck's strung-out mental state in Alfred Hitchcock's *Spellbound*. Rózsa's theremin would produce no light xylophone sounds, no upbeat Gershwinesque syncopation. Constructed out of vacuum tubes and antennae, the theremin emitted oscillating, otherworldly pitches, all the better to express Don Birnam's own distortions. (The theremin was eventually used to produce the trippy background tones of the Beach Boys' "Good Vibrations," not to mention countless sci-fi soundtracks in the 1950s.)

With the full support of Brackett and Wilder, Rózsa composed a dark-tempered score he thought was even better than *Spellbound*'s. Indeed, when *Spellbound*'s producer, David Selznick, discovered that Rózsa had also used a theremin for the score of *The Lost Weekend*, he fell into a rage. Rózsa responded that not only had he used a theremin in his new composition, he'd also used a trumpet, a piccolo, a triangle, and a violin.

All this tinkering cost money. By June, *The Lost Weekend* was nearly $90,000 over budget. But by August, it looked as though the expense was worth it. Paramount screened a print of the revised, fully scored *The Lost Weekend* for industry people on August 9, and it was very well received. The film was also making its way through the Hollywood "projection circuit," the select showings in private screening rooms, where it was earning great acclaim. "As things finally developed," Brackett later recalled, "we found we had a hit on our hands."

Y. Frank Freeman and his idiotic opinions faded quickly into the background. Freeman's boss, Barney Balaban, said after one of the wretched early previews, "Once we make a picture, we don't just flush it down the toilet," and he kept to his word. The liquor industry, meanwhile, decided to maintain a dignified silence and urged its own trade press not to run editorials against the picture. The individual members of both the Allied Liquor Industries and the Alcoholic Beverage Industries were asked to "take no steps that would in any way stir up a controversy about the picture."

The censors, however, weren't quite as easily dispatched. As a matter of fact, they threatened to proliferate. The Production Code Administration was only the beginning. The PCA ultimately approved the film, once its objections had been met, but some states and cities had their own censor boards, each with a different set of requirements and objections. New York, Pennsylvania, Kansas, Maryland, Massachusetts, and Virginia each had its own board; Atlanta, Chicago, Memphis, Kansas City (Missouri), Detroit, Portland, and Milwaukee censored films on a local basis. Canadian censorship occurred province by province. And as if that weren't enough, the Legion of Decency ruled—or tried to rule—every practicing Roman Catholic in the United States.

Given the disturbing nature of this film, Paramount was bracing itself to deal with the other states' and cities' censors as well as with that of the Legion of Decency. The studio's sales representatives were the censors' contacts in each locale, and these reps referred all questions and requests for cuts to Paramount's home office in New York. "We of course battle all rejections," the home office told Brackett and Wilder. But, the home office immediately went on to say that, if a request was small and seemed reasonable to the New York executives, they would grant it without a battle. There were exceptions: "In instances where the eliminations requested are substantial or unjustified, and particularly where they would seem to affect revenue, we go to bat."

To everyone's surprise, *The Lost Weekend* passed almost everywhere without any deletions at all. In some cases the film even won special commendation from the censor boards. Only two boards objected. Pennsylvania demanded several cuts before *The Lost Weekend* could be screened in the state, including all views of the bat killing the mouse and the blood dripping down the wall. The most graphic of the hospital scenes had to be excised as well—this owing entirely to the opinion of the state's three-member board, only two of whom had seen the picture. For its part, Ohio insisted that Bim's critical view of Prohibition be removed from the film: "Good old Prohibition days. Say, you should have seen the joint then! This is nothing. Back then we really had a turnover, standing room only. Prohibition—that is what started most of these guys off." Known for its popular support of temperance, Ohio also found one of Helen's lines to Don objectionable: "I am just ashamed of the way I talked to you—like a narrow-minded insensitive small-town teetotaler."

Shrewdly, Paramount opened the film in England before trying it out at home. "London is on a praise binge for *The Lost Weekend*," the *Hollywood Reporter* announced. "Even with the paper shortage it's gotten more comment than any picture since *Gone With the Wind*."

Back in the States, the very people who had threatened to pull the plug on *The Lost Weekend* were now proclaiming themselves the film's heroic champions. The studio released its ad campaign featuring a huge close-up of an eye, set on the diagonal, with the tag line "Paramount found the courage and daring to film this strange, powerful, and terrifying novel." When the film was released in New York in November, the nation's critics took over where Paramount's writers of ad copy left off: "A milestone in moviemaking. . . . It is adult, off the beaten track, terrifyingly real, and every inch a cinematic masterpiece. The Brackett and Wilder script is a model of consummate screenwriting; the Wilder direction is infallibly imaginative, and the principals play way over their heads in interpreting the work." "This is undoubtedly the best horror picture of the year." "One of the best films of the past decade." "One of the best motion pictures ever made in Hollywood . . ."

The *New York Times*'s Bosley Crowther weighed in as well: *The Lost Weekend*, he wrote, had been brought to the screen "with great fidelity in every respect but one: the reason for the 'dipso's' gnawing mania is not fully and convincingly explained. In the novel, the basic frustration which drove the pitiable 'hero' to drink was an unconscious indecision in his own masculine libido. In the film . . . the only cause given for his 'illness' is the fact that he has writer's cramp." Crowther evidently meant writer's *block*.

Paramount was now advertising the film they had nearly canned as "The Most Widely Acclaimed Motion Picture in the History of the Industry." Suddenly even the House of Seagram's was plugging *The Lost Weekend*: "Paramount has succeeded in burning into the hearts and minds of all who see this vivid screen story our own long-held and oft-published belief that . . . *some men should not drink!*, which might well have been the name of this great picture instead of *The Lost Weekend*." For his part, Billy promoted the movie by making a cirrhosis joke: If *To Have and Have Not* established Lauren Bacall as "The Look," he told the *New York Times*, then *The Lost Weekend* should certainly earn Mr. Milland fame as "The Kidney." The Paramount publicist accompanying Billy on the *Times* interview blanched, and only then did Billy agree to play the role of the typical director promoting his latest film. He didn't keep up the charade for long though. When it came time to discuss his new movie idea, he told the *Times* that he wanted Paramount to let him make a story about life in Berlin, which he promptly described as Sodom and Gomorrah.

Once again Wilder made a point of sticking it to David O. Selznick. *Spellbound*'s producer, capitalizing on Hitchcock's reputation, was busily placing ads in the trades featuring a photo of Gregory Peck and Ingrid Bergman embracing, with Peck holding a straight razor behind Bergman's back. Warner Bros., meanwhile, was pushing its pictures on the grounds of civic responsibility, using the line, "Good Citizenship with Fine Motion Picture Making." So Billy and Charlie placed a little ad of their own. It showed the two famously squabbling collaborators hugging and holding knives behind each other's backs. The caption read "Combining Good Citizenship with Good Cutlery."

By mid-December, Billy was getting used to life as a bachelor again, not that it took much readjustment. He was tooling around town in his new jeep—one of the first army vehicles to find civilian use in Southern California. He was seeing Doris, he was seeing Audrey, and he was buying art, including Picasso's 1926 pencil-on-paper drawing *"le récit."* He won the New York Film Critics' Best Director award for *The Lost Weekend*. (The film also won for Best Picture, and Ray Milland won as Best Actor.) *The Lost Weekend* was poised to be a strong Oscar contender, though once again Paramount executives were nervous. They were worried about whether the Academy's voters would go for such a depressing movie, so they considered rushing Ray Milland's next film, a costume drama called *Kitty*, into the theaters at the very end of the year so it would be eligible for the Oscars. As a Hollywood columnist reported: "Paramount can't decide whether *Lost Weekend* or *Kitty* will be their entry for picture of the year. Are they kidding?" After much hand wringing, *Kitty* was held back until 1946, and Billy, Charlie, and *The Lost Weekend* were in the clear.

Still, trouble loomed again in the form of Leo McCarey. After the enormous commercial success of *Going My Way*, McCarey decided to stick with piety. His next film was *The Bells of St. Mary's*. Not only did Der Bingle reprise his role as Father Chuck "Dial O For" O'Malley, but Ingrid Bergman now joined him as a lovable nun. Luckily, McCarey made *The Bells of St. Mary's* for RKO, not Paramount, so there was no in-house competition between God and Bacchus. When the Oscar nominations were announced, *The Lost Weekend* earned seven. *The Bells of St. Mary's* earned eight.

Wilder and McCarey were the favorites for Best Director, *The Lost Weekend* and *The Bells of St. Mary's* for Best Picture; Milland and Crosby for Best Actor. Billy told friends he planned in his acceptance speech to thank W. C. Fields.

Double Indemnity was most decidedly not the kind of movie Academy voters favored, but *The Lost Weekend*, though equally dark tempered, didn't have quite the same burden. For one thing, it had earnestness on its side. This was a social-problem drama, and in early 1946, with thousands of GIs returning home from the war with emotional as well as physical scars, the time was right for Wilder's brand of realism. *The Lost Weekend* was also a good marketing tool for the industry. Sold by Paramount as daring and courageous, the film would also work as good public relations for Hollywood in general, since it proved—or tried to prove—that Tinseltown had some inkling of real people's problems.

The ceremony was held, as usual, at Grauman's Chinese. William Wyler announced the winner of the Best Director award—Billy, who strode to the podium and said, "Thank you, Mrs. Miniver." Wilder was immediately followed by Hollywood's newly appointed chief censor, Eric Johnston, who had taken over from Will Hays. It was the censor who revealed the winner of the Best Picture award with what the Oscar historians Mason Wiley and Damien Bona call "little-boy enthusiasm": "Oooooh! It's *The Lost Weekend!*" Billy and Charlie then won the Best Screenplay award. And when

Ingrid Bergman opened the envelope for Best Actor, she announced from the podium, "Mr. Milland, are you nervous? It's yours!" It was a *Lost Weekend* sweep. Take that, Leo McCarey.

Billy and the other winners sang "The Star-Spangled Banner" onstage at the close of the show, after which he, Charlie, and Ray Milland headed to Romanoff's for drinks. The following morning when Brackett and Wilder returned to work, they were greeted by the sight of whiskey bottles hanging from every window in the Writers Building.

Then it was back to the routine. Only now Brackett and Wilder were Oscar winners. Their price was going up, as was their ability to get what they wanted from the front office, but the team's volatility hadn't changed. The odd-couple nature of their relationship, the bickering, the constant threat of divorce—all of it had turned into a publicity device. *Life* reported that Billy was a "fervid New Dealer with leftish leanings," while Brackett, of course, was a conservative Republican. "Brackett is an agoraphobe who jitters if the office door is left open. Wilder is a claustrophobe who can't stand closed doors. . . . Wilder is galvanic, facile, prolific with ideas, endowed with visual imagination. Brackett is critical, contemplative, gifted with a graceful literary style and cultivated taste." Both men, however, knew their joint health needed as much help as it could get, so each took a weekly injection of B-1. Cribbage in the morning, some writing, a good lunch (or maybe just lunch at Oblath's), a nap, writing, drinks in the late afternoon, and a reclusive, alcoholic wife or either Doris or Audrey in the evenings—a fine routine.

"So now we're together again," Billy said, referring to Charlie, "and we're the happiest couple in Hollywood."

16. HOMESICK

JOANNA (Joan Fontaine): His majesty is in no mood for a ball.
EMPEROR (Richard Haydn): You're quite right. I'm in the mood for
   a cemetery. Let us proceed to the ball.

—*The Emperor Waltz*

On February 17, 1946, Brackett and Wilder went on the radio as guests of Louella Parsons. They hadn't yet won their Oscars, but they were still Hollywood's best-known writing team. People called them the Gold Dust Twins. Or the Katzenjammer Kids. Even Hansel and Gretel. Usually, though, there was just one word used to describe them: "Brackettandwilder." "I'm scared of columnists," Billy admitted on the air, "and please don't involve me in long explanations—I have an accent." Charlie played the patriot he actually was: "Now stop that complex about your accent, Billy. We've all got accents! That's what makes it a great country!" "Right you are, Charlie!" said Louella.

Billy may actually have been worried about his intractable but sweet Viennese accent, an inflection more mellifluous than guttural-Germanic, but for whatever reason the loquacious director remained silent for much of the interview. He did manage to work in a few choice lines, though. First was his excuse for not having won an Oscar before. He blamed Charlie: "People know Brackett's a Republican." Then Louella asked what the team had in mind to follow *The Lost Weekend*. Charlie answered first. "This time we're just having fun," Brackett said. "It's an operetta called *The Emperor Waltz*."

"And instead of the bat and mouse," Billy chimed in, "we're having Bing Crosby and Joan Fontaine."

Berlin was still such a dangerous wreckage in the spring of 1946, and its residents sufficiently unruly, that Wilder was forced to postpone his propaganda film. He'd told the army the previous summer that he could

turn over a finished movie by the spring of 1946. It was now the spring of
1946, the script hadn't been written, and since Berlin was still essentially
off-limits and would remain so at least for the next year, there was no rush.
As it turned out, the suicidal *Fräulein* whom Wilder met on the Kurfürstendamm would have to wait a long time to be cheered up by a Hollywood
movie about postwar reconciliation.

With *A Foreign Affair* on hold, Billy's thoughts still turned to his own
Austro-German heritage. Or better, they turned to a heritage that existed
only in the imagination of someone who hadn't been alive at the time. *The
Emperor Waltz* was to be a lavish costume comedy-romance set in Vienna
just after the turn of the century. Palaces, waltzes, courtiers, costumes,
Technicolor, and the Emperor Franz Josef himself—Billy's bright new comedy was going to cost a fortune.

On the opening page of their new screenplay, which they completed at
the very end of May, Billy and Charlie made clear their aesthetic goals:

TO ALL CONCERNED IN THE PRODUCTION:

1. This is not a fantasy, it is not an operetta. It is a comedy with a
scattering of songs.

2. Our action is not set in Graustark, Flausenthurm, or any other
mythical kingdom. It is set in Vienna, 1901. It should be anchored to
that time and place with good strong chains of reality.

3. In casting, set-designing or costuming, let no one open his mouth
too wide. No exaggerations, no conscious comicalities, please.

4. Just because it plays in Vienna, don't let's have everyone talk like
Herman Bing. And just because it's in Technicolor, don't let's have the
Emperor wear canary-yellow jaegers and a purple jock strap.

And now, soldiers of Paramount: on to new glory,

By order of the High Command,

BRACKETT AND WILDER

Brackett and Wilder had a valid concern—if not over Edith Head's ideas
of what costume spectacle should look like, then certainly over the front
office's philistinism. For Brackett and Wilder, a certain realistic, understated taste had to prevail, even if their new film was a baroque imperial
fantasy.

The Emperor Waltz was a weird film for Wilder to make, even—or
perhaps especially—at the time. For one thing, he hated operettas. He has
always claimed, for good reason, to have been sick of writing them in Berlin
in the early 1930s. Now, as an Oscar-winning writer-director who could
have chosen to make practically any film he wanted to make in 1946, here
he was returning to royalty, romance, and song. *The Emperor Waltz* was

part of Billy's ongoing attempt to keep directing films against his own type. From *The Major and the Minor* Wilder moved on to a combat picture; from *Five Graves to Cairo* he took on and helped to invent film noir; from *Double Indemnity* he moved to social-problem drama with a horror twist. What was left after *The Lost Weekend* except a gaudy musical starring the Hapsburgs?

His imagination drawn back to Vienna and Berlin, Wilder made two films in the mid- to late-1940s that attempt to reclaim his own wounded history. His urge to document the harsh ironies of postwar Berlin in *A Foreign Affair* parallels the desire to re-create, in *The Emperor Waltz*, the stately, mannered Vienna that predated his own birth. Wilder's cultural heritage, the artistic patrimony of a displaced Viennese-Berliner, had not been obliterated by Nazism and the war, but his family had been. Where did this leave him? *The Emperor Waltz*, just as much as *A Foreign Affair*, is a lavish, high-budget effort to come to terms with himself and his double-edged identity.

The conflict was not unique to Billy Wilder. Who and where he was, the languages he spoke, his childhood and how differently his life was turning out, the continuing doubt about whether he fit in anywhere—these were questions of the mind and soul, and the whole refugee community was asking them. The end of the war only brought the matter into the realm of practicalities. When the Allies defeated the Germans a new set of decisions surfaced: Should they remain as increasingly assimilated refugees in a foreign land that accepted them, or to return home to people that had tried to slaughter them? To reclaim their rightful place as humanistic, enlightened Austro-German culture makers, or to abandon it altogether in favor of the great wash of Americanism?

Erich Pommer, after years in exile, returned to Germany in 1946 to work with the Americans to rebuild the German film industry. Indeed, by that point Pommer was an American himself, having earned United States citizenship in 1944. Hans Albers repatriated as well. Eventually so did Max Horkheimer, Theodor Adorno, and Bertolt Brecht. Douglas Sirk went back and soon left again, as did Fritz Lang. Marlene Dietrich maintained a harshly ambivalent attitude about Germany for the rest of her life; to many Germans she was a traitor. "This was the most poignant of endings," Anthony Heilbut writes. It went "beyond the loss of language or a reading public, for it called into question an entire cultural inheritance: What could one possibly retain from this 'shitty people'? Writers of dissimilar persuasions shared a sense of fatal estrangement. Perhaps the most famous statement about this was Adorno's postwar remark that to write poetry after Auschwitz was barbaric." Stefan Zweig described Rilke as an exotic bird who would never be able to fly again, thanks to the violent heritage be-

stowed upon Germany by the Nazis: "Will such lyricism again be a possibility in this era of turbulence and universal destruction? Is it not a lost
tribe that I am bemoaning?" Zweig resolved his own conundrum fatally;
he committed suicide in 1942 in South America. For his part, of course,
Adorno didn't have to face the question of whether or not to write poetry
after Auschwitz because he had never written poems to begin with.

Billy Wilder made movies—specifically, world-class Hollywood movies—and there was no question about his continuing to do so after Auschwitz. What's bizarre is that after scrutinizing countless thousands of feet of
celluloid that chronicled the horrors of the death camps, Wilder turned to
a Viennese-Tyrolean reverie in glorious Technicolor. *The Emperor Waltz*
would be his first film that wasn't toned in various shades of gray. Still,
this supersaturated extravaganza was going to tell Billy Wilder's kind of
story. It is the tale of two dogs and how they rut.

Brackett and Wilder opened their script at Schönbrunn Palace, where
an American, Virgil Smith (Crosby), climbs an exterior wall. He makes his
way onto a balcony, opens the shutters, smashes the window, and enters
the palace still wearing his earmuffs. He meets the countess Johanna Franziska von Stoltzenberg-Stoltzenberg (Fontaine). They argue. She calls him
"Swine!" He waltzes away with her. Nobles, including a gossipy monsignor, sit on the sidelines discussing the relationship, at which point a flashback takes the audience to the beginning of the scandalous affair, with
Virgil arriving at the palace with a mysterious black box and a dog.

The dog, an American impure-bred, is named Buttons. He soon meets
a chic black poodle named Scheherazade, whose mistress is Johanna. The
canines fall instantly in love with each other, though in their initial encounter they express their passion in screwball style by snapping at each
other viciously. Buttons takes the worse bruising; Scheherazade bites him
clear to the bone. (This is a pleasure Brackett and Wilder deny Johanna in
her dealings with Virgil.) Virgil's box turns out to be a gramophone, an
invention he tries to sell to the emperor. Buttons, one then realizes, is a
dead ringer for the RCA Victor dog. Complications, insults, love, emotional
turmoil. . . . By the end of the movie, Scheherazade and Buttons have exercised their concupiscence. Three mongrel puppies result. On the set they
nicknamed them Hart, Shaffner, and Marx.

In a stroke of commercial if not artistic aptitude, Brackett and Wilder
cast Paramount's most popular star, Bing Crosby, in the lead. In 1946, the
two-time "Father O'Malley" was both America's top box office draw and
the nation's most successful radio crooner. As one musical director described it, Bing's voice was "phonogenic"—smooth and melodic in person,
exquisite and resonantly velvety when recorded. One 1946 estimate claimed
that more than half of the eighty thousand weekly hours of recorded radio

music were filled by Bing Crosby alone. Twenty-five million people listened to his radio show every week. Each of his films was seen by 250 million people worldwide. In 1948, when *The Emperor Waltz* was released, Crosby was named by the *Motion Picture Herald* as the year's male box office champ, but the award startled no one because it was the fifth year in a row that Bing had nabbed the title. "Mr. Crosby is entitled to the all-time box office championship," the *Herald* concluded. Crosby got $125,000 for his appearance in *The Emperor Waltz*.

Joan Fontaine's deal was more complicated, since she was under contract to David O. Selznick, who then proceeded to loan her to RKO. For Selznick, she did *Rebecca*; for RKO Fontaine starred in *Suspicion*; both were directed by Alfred Hitchcock. For her appearance in *The Emperor Waltz*, Paramount was obliged to pay RKO $249,000 for Fontaine's services, with RKO paying a portion back to Selznick. Fontaine herself earned a signing bonus of $50,000 for doing the film as well as $3,000 per week, with $36,000 guaranteed.

The Emperor Waltz featured two stars—one very big, the other gargantuan. Their billing order was resolved diplomatically. Fontaine's contract reads: "Joan Fontaine shall receive first star billing, except however that Bing Crosby may be accorded first star billing, providing the Artist is co-starred with Bing Crosby on the same line, in the same size of type, and with equal prominence." It might go without saying that both Crosby's and Fontaine's names were placed over the film's title, an honor the film's Oscar-winning director wouldn't be granted for fifteen more years.

For the pivotal role of the emperor, Wilder chose Oscar Karlweis, a fellow refugee. Karlweis had recently starred on Broadway in a musical, but he was an unknown in Hollywood. And yet he didn't come particularly cheap. Karlweis's deal with Paramount was set for $3,500 per week for a period of almost twelve weeks. This was higher than Billy's $2,500 weekly rate for writing the screenplay. (Brackett was now up to $3,000 per week as a writer—the same as Billy's rate for directing.)

Brackett and Wilder turned a first draft of *The Emperor Waltz* in to the PCA in late March or April. Joseph Breen got back to them in early May. As usual, there was trouble. The PCA rejected the whole thing outright. The censors, Breen wrote, "regret to have to report that in our opinion this material is unacceptable from the standpoint of the Production Code. This basic unacceptability arises from the offensive sex-suggestiveness inherent in a parallel between the mating of two dogs and the love affair of their respective owners. Such a story idea would, we believe, be enormously offensive to mixed audiences everywhere." A meeting was arranged. Billy, Charlie, and Luraschi sat down with Joseph Breen and Geoffrey Shurlock from the PCA and went over the first draft of *The*

Emperor Waltz in detail. Together, they removed the dogs' sexuality from the movie as well as all references to excretions.

After caving in to the censors' demands on some obvious points, including the excision of the word *bitch*, Brackett and Wilder were now free to make *The Emperor Waltz* more or less the way they wanted. With Breen's own fingerprints on the revised script he could scarcely fail to pass the picture. Minor annoyances continued in the months to come, though. "The expression 'poop' is unacceptable," the writers were later told, "because of its vulgar connotation." Actually, Brackett and Wilder's use of *poop* didn't even have to do with the dogs but was, instead, a reference to a tiresome human character. Even as late as the end of August, Brackett and Wilder, having not fully learned their lesson, were still writing new scenes in which the canines were doing things they shouldn't: "The dog wetting business is unacceptable," at least as far as the PCA was concerned. Through all of this, clearly, it was Brackett and Wilder who were really being the bad little doggies. The thankless task of training them fell to Joseph Breen.

Much of the film was to be shot on location in Alberta's Jasper National Park, a place of sumptuous natural beauty. Drastic mountains, lush green forests, a glacial lake, the intense blue of a Canadian Rockies sky—Jasper would photograph extremely well. It also meant that Paramount's expansive entourage would have to be housed and fed in Alberta for a full month. The elaborate palace interiors and exteriors, meanwhile, would be meticulously constructed on the Paramount lot. First of all, there was Schönbrunn Palace to re-create. An enormous ballroom, the emperor's throne room, a lengthy gallery, and the emperor's private closet needed to be built, all in eighteenth-century rococo style. Then there was the emperor's hunting lodge, with various living rooms done up in a more rustic baroque. The Countess von Stoltzenberg-Stoltzenberg needed a palace of her own. It was no Schönbrunn, of course, but it did require at least a vast marble parlor in which to insult Virgil. There was also an inn in the mountain village, both interior and exterior. *The Emperor Waltz* was going to be shot in Technicolor, which itself didn't come cheap. Paramount's "quick figure" cost estimate in April was $2,742,000—more than twice the price of *The Lost Weekend*. By May, when a more detailed budget had been prepared, Paramount was looking forward to spending $2,879,000 on Billy's new movie.

Billy, Charlie, and Doane Harrison left Los Angeles for Jasper on May 19. They were followed by the rest of the cast and crew over the next two weeks. About three hundred Paramount people showed up in all—a record-breaking number for location shooting. Helen Hernandez was able to accompany the producer and director this time, and she was amazed at how beautiful Jasper was: "This is the dream spot of the world. No scenic photos do it justice." Then again, mere scenic justice had never been Brackett and Wilder's goal. Their point was to do Jasper National Park in Technicolor, which was far more dazzling than any natural scenery would be on its own. For once, John Seitz was not the man for the job. Brackett and Wilder needed a cinematographer who had experience with the elaborate three-strip Technicolor process. George Barnes was summoned from RKO. (Technicolor also supplied its own team of personnel as well as all the equipment, and charged Paramount accordingly.) Paramount already had confidence in Barnes, since he had shot the richly colored *Frenchman's Creek* for Mitchell Leisen two years earlier. Since *Frenchman's Creek* had also starred Joan Fontaine, the match was doubly good.

The production opened on June 1. As with the location shooting of *The Lost Weekend*, bad weather was a continuing problem. Rain or sometimes just gray cloudiness delayed or completely prevented filming on eighteen of the thirty days the company spent at Jasper. Even more exasperating was Crosby. "It wasn't a very happy picture for me," Joan Fontaine says. The costars' relationship started off badly. Fontaine was introduced to Crosby in his dressing room. Crosby was in his makeup chair and didn't find it necessary to get up and say hello. "I think Crosby was more used to the *Road* pictures, with Hope, and he treated *The Emperor Waltz* a bit like that. And me also. I mean, I wasn't even Dorothy Lamour to him."

Crosby pulled rank on Wilder as well. Fontaine has described Crosby as "pretty much the king of Paramount," and from what she saw, she didn't think Wilder was used to dealing with such a royal personage. For example, the king arrived at Jasper with his own team of speechwriters, except that in Crosby's case they were there to rewrite Billy and Charlie's dialogue. These revisions were made whenever der Bingle thought Wilder and Brackett's words weren't good enough. "He had his writers with him—*his own writers*," Fontaine remembers. "They came en masse on the set in the morning. We all felt peripheral." One member of Crosby's writing team was an old vaudevillian gag writer named Barney Dean. He'd worked on Hope and Crosby's *Road* pictures. Now he was improving upon Brackett and Wilder. It was one thing to bring on a for-hire collaborator to polish the script while Charlie and Billy were busy producing and directing. Jacques Théry, in fact, performed that service on *The Emperor Waltz*. Théry worked on the screenplay for two months, though he received no screen credit. But Barney Dean?

Fontaine was also put off by two other issues: the company's late-night carousing and the complete lack of rehearsals. "We were on location, and the first day I was in makeup and dressed, and there I was with Bing Crosby, and they said, 'Here are the lines, say them.' There was no introduction or getting together or team work or any of that feeling at all. Billy Wilder didn't do that. Mr. Brackett, of course, was a gentlemen of the old school—a charming and delightful man. I don't think he was used to the autonomous thing that Crosby was doing." Then there was the partying. "I had my own cabin on the other side of the lake, but at night I could hear a great deal of, uh, 'happiness' going on."

Billy filmed *The Emperor Waltz* in one of the most spectacular spots in the Western Hemisphere, but Jasper National Park was still incapable of measuring up to Wilder's image of the Austrian Tyrol. The park's failure became increasingly expensive for Paramount. The script demanded an island in the middle of the lake. No island existed, so on Billy's insistence the studio built one for him. Earth, rock, and trees were placed onto a wooden platform and floated out onto the park's Leach Lake on hidden oil drums. The cost was said to be about $90,000.

The roadway turned out to be the wrong color. Paramount's crew painted it ochre.

Then four thousand daisies were all wrong, completely wrong. They looked fine to the naked eye, but Technicolor bleached them out. So Paramount's crew painted them all blue.

According to Billy there weren't enough pine trees in the pine forest. Paramount hauled more trees into the park at a cost of $20,000.

By the time the company left Jasper on June 30, the budget was out of control and the studio publicists had a lot of material.

Crosby kept insisting that Barney Dean and his team rewrite his lines when the company returned to Hollywood. According to Fontaine, "One morning on the set when we were back in Hollywood I remember well that Mr. Crosby handed Billy some new lines and said, 'This is what we're going to do.' " On another occasion, Crosby handed Billy the day's rewrites and simply said, "I'll be playing golf. Let me know." As Fontaine said, "It must have been very demeaning for Billy."

The production continued apace. For one of the elaborate court scenes, Wilder wanted a sense of nobility and decorum to prevail. In both scope and detail he was trying to out-Stroheim von Stroheim. Unhappily, all too many extras simply were not able to execute the lengthy curtsey Billy ordered. Camp chairs had to be fitted under the gowned rumps of about 250 women so that they could maintain their curtsey in front of the emperor for the full seventy seconds Wilder required. Wilder got sick toward the end of July, causing further delays. And all the while they were working with a pair of canine costars who sometimes didn't take direction very well. The company manager filed a personal injury report on July 9: "Dog jumped into Crosby's arms during scene—dog's teeth broke the skin near nose, causing bleeding." The script was not yet complete.

When Oscar Karlweis showed up on July 22 to film some of his scenes, he was met by a surprise. It was his last day of work on the film. For undocumented reasons, Karlweis simply wasn't working out, so Billy replaced him midpicture. All the scenes involving the emperor had to be reshot, but first, a new emperor had to be cast. Wilder and Brackett settled on Richard Haydn, the brilliant character actor who'd played the nasal Professor Oddly in *Ball of Fire*. To age Haydn properly for the role of Franz Josef required him to be in makeup for three hours every day.

The dogs, Crosby, and illness were constant plagues in August as well. Fontaine was under medical care to pull excess fluid from her tissues; the treatment involved mercury dissolved in a large volume of water and infused into her system. It took about an hour every morning. The dogs, meanwhile, were never quite able to do their parts right on the first take. At one point, Crosby got so worked up over Buttons's inability to jump in a bag on cue that he shouted, "Get your damn ass right in here!" It worked. On the very next take, the dog was so cowed that all Bing had to do was shoot him an angry look and the dog jumped.

Like everyone else on the production team, Edith Head and her costumers were vaulting over their original budget, but Wilder and Brackett weren't at all concerned. It was Billy, in fact, who insisted that Head be as extravagant as possible. The gowns she designed for Joan Fontaine are gorgeous, though Fontaine later told a reporter that the low neckline on her dresses "was the only way I could steal a scene from those dratted dogs."

On September 3 the script was finally finished. The production closed on September 20, a full twenty-eight days behind schedule and so far over budget than an entire feature film could have been made from the difference. By the time of its release, *The Emperor Waltz* sported the astronomical price tag of $4,070,248—nearly $1,200,000 more than Paramount had originally approved.

Many years later, long after his breakup with Wilder, Brackett called *The Emperor Waltz* one of the "stinkers." "I don't suppose I ever understood it very well," he said. "I was sure Billy would know. After all, Vienna. And we did have Bing Crosby. I can't imagine *what* went wrong. The final result was quite boring, wasn't it?" *The Emperor Waltz* also created some acrimony in Billy's relationship with Lubitsch. Billy's friend and former mentor had been mulling over a film idea in which a dog acted as intermediary between a squabbling couple. Then Wilder invited him to a rough cut of *The Emperor Waltz*. Lubitsch appeared to be amused and entertained by the film—until the dogs took over. Then he was quietly enraged. He kept whispering to his wife throughout the screening, "That's my story! That's my story! The son of a bitch has taken my story!" Father figures sometimes require mutinies.

The Emperor Waltz is one of Wilder's weakest films. It must have made great sense in 1946 to feature Bing Crosby yodeling in lederhosen, but the device hasn't aged well. Willy Fritsch or Willi Forst would have been much more winning in the role, had either of them been from Newark. Crosby's essentially solitary persona, on the other hand, doesn't work very well in a romance. It is not coincidental that Crosby's most popular film roles were those of a celibate priest and Bob Hope's sidekick. In *The Emperor Waltz* he's simply too self-absorbed to connect with Fontaine. To top it off, Brackett and Wilder insist on giving him the annoyingly folksy habit of calling Johanna "honey countess."

The film still features its share of clever lines, not to mention dazzling set design and brilliant cinematography. (Wilder himself hated the way *The Emperor Waltz* looks. "Everything looked like it was in an ice cream parlor. . . . Even the dialogue sounded wrong in color." It would be nine years before he tried color again, and he hated that film, too.)

The film's punch comes from a few revealing characterizations, not the least of which is Johanna's ne'er-do-well father (Roland Culver)—a mustachioed gambler, philanderer, dilettante, and failure. He is an oily embarrassment, a piece of necessary baggage. Family matters plague the family dog as well. At one point, Scheherazade suffers a nervous breakdown. Dr. Semmelgries (Sig Ruman, now Americanized with one *n* instead of two), the royal veterinarian, performs a familiar Viennese treatment. The dog lies on her back on a couch and fields the following question: "Now I must ask you for your earliest recollections—your father and mother. Was your home life congenial?" Scheherazade responds by squealing and writhing in distress.

The emperor, meanwhile, is just a sad old man whose only pleasure lies in the possibility of breeding his elderly poodle. ("His majesty's dog is asking for the paw of Scheherazade!") Franz Josef lives under the constant threat of death. The script merely alludes in passing to the assassination of his wife, the Empress Sisi, and the double suicide at Mayerling of his son, the Crown Prince Rudolf, and his seventeen-year-old lover, Maria Vetsera. (As Billy later explained, "It's always better to go to a hunting lodge and die with a prince than go to the Riviera with some schmuck.") But one hardly needs a history book to see that his recent life has been joyless. When the emperor's courtiers overhear Virgil proudly declare in American slang that his gramophone "is going to kill him," they naturally assume that Virgil is yet another of the many assassins who wish to see him dead. "Oh dear," Franz Josef sighs, "this gets to be such a bore."

Curiously, only one character in *The Emperor Waltz* speaks with a German accent—the vet. At first, his thick, harsh inflection seems designed only to reinforce the Freud joke, but when he takes the newborn mongrel puppies, puts them in a wire basket, hangs the basket methodically on the side of a sink, and proceeds to run water into the tub to drown them, one gets the sense that something deeper is being played out with this character. Wilder handles the moment in a single shot, with Dr. Semmelgries actually pulling the pups off of their mother, at which point the camera pans with him, tracks slowly forward to the sink, and then stares in for an attenuated moment as the water runs. When Virgil saves the infants, he races into the ballroom with them just as the emperor arrives to the tune of "Deutschland Über Alles." "They're not pure enough for you, huh?," he shouts angrily. "Not quite your sort. Freaks! Little mongrels you wouldn't have around. So what are you going to do? You're going to shake them off that great big noble family tree of yours. And let them rot, as if nothing had happened." Wilder doesn't relate much to Crosby, but he clearly sees himself in the puppies. If Crosby's acting was as rich as his voice, there would be no doubt that *The Emperor Waltz* is really a film about genocide.

Unlike history, though, *The Emperor Waltz* has a happy ending. The emperor insists on keeping the puppies, and the low-bred American man and the high-bred Viennese woman win the right to mate. More convincing, though, is an earlier scene of emotional brutality between the principals. "No hard feelings?" Virgil asks Johanna. "No feelings at all," she answers.

The mopping up of Berlin had progressed by the spring of 1947 to the point that *A Foreign Affair* could proceed. Billy's ideas for his propaganda comedy had shifted a bit. It still bore the same general story line—struggling German woman meets American GI—but now it featured an additional character: a congresswoman on a fact-finding mission. This accessory was the brainchild of screenwriters Irwin and David Shaw, who'd sold an original story of airborne congressional romance called *Love in the Air* to Paramount for $11,000. (Irwin Shaw went on to write best-selling novels, including *The Young Lions, Two Weeks in Another Town*, and the epic melodrama *Rich Man, Poor Man.*) The Shaws' treatment begins: "The Second World War was not only witness to the most enormous movement of material goods in the history of the world. It also saw the greatest mass movement of lust in recorded time. Six million young and vigorous Americans leave the memories of the most gigantic pass in history. . . ." The Shaws' tale concerned a randy GI named Jasper who has left a girl in every ruined port. He wants to see them all again and gets the chance to do so when he is assigned to accompany Congresswoman Kinnicutt to London, Paris, Moscow, Rome, and Sydney. He ends up proposing to the legislator as they fly into Washington, D.C.

Since Paramount owned the rights to *Love in the Air*, Brackett and

Wilder were free to incorporate a few of the Shaws' ideas into their own proposed comedy about postwar Germany. With the help of another screenwriter, Robert Harari, they submitted their first full treatment on May 31, 1947. It begins with this memorable description of Berlin: "The city looked like a great hunk of burned Gorgonzola cheese on which rats had been gnawing. The rats were gone, and ants had taken over, putting some neatness into the ruins, piling the crumbs of destruction into tidy piles." The GI, now called Johnny, has received the gift of a chocolate cake from back home. He promptly trades it on the black market for the decidedly used mattress. Johnny's thoughts on the exchange are concise: "Some hungry Kraut had a mattress and two pillows to spare—let him eat cake." The mattress is for a loose German woman named Erika. The treatment describes two GIs' response to Erika at a nightclub: "As far as Mike and Joe were concerned, only one thing remained to be settled: whose pig was she?" Best of all, when Johnny gives Erika the mattress, here is how he demands his payment: "How about a kiss now, you Beast of Belsen?"

Charlie and Billy were now very much accustomed to going into production without having finished writing the screenplay. Their method allowed not only for a certain organic development as far as dialogue and action were concerned, but it also kept both the censors and the front office in the dark. A complete script for *A Foreign Affair* would not appear until November; by that point Richard L. Breen, a former journalist had replaced Harari as Billy and Charlie's collaborator.

Typically, there was fuss over the title. Owing to its untoward mingling of sex and American foreign policy, *A Foreign Affair* made the executives nervous. They offered some suggestions: *Operation Candybar, The Feeling Is Mutual, Out of Bounds, No Limit, Irresistible, The Honorable Phoebe Frost*, and, most grating of all, *Two Loves Have I*. Brackett and Wilder considered *Operation Candybar* but ended up sticking with *A Foreign Affair*.

In July, during an intense heat wave, Billy and *tout*-Hollywood attended the premiere of Brecht's *Galileo* at the Coronet Theater on La Cienega Boulevard. The star of the play was Charles Laughton. The crowd was an assemblage of the sort that could only make sense in Hollywood in the 1940s: Charles Chaplin was in the audience along with Ingrid Bergman, Frank Lloyd Wright, Charles Boyer, Olivia de Havilland, Igor Stravinsky, Gene Kelly, John Garfield, and of course Brecht himself. Wilder may or may not have been impressed with the highbrow playwright, but there is no question that he was fascinated and amazed by Laughton, a man of extraordinary talent and intelligence playing a man of even greater talent and intelligence. Laughton would eventually become one of Billy's closest friends.

Soon after seeing *Galileo*, Billy left for Europe to supervise the location shooting of *A Foreign Affair*. He stopped over in London and arrived in Berlin on August 12, along with Buddy Coleman. He found the city somewhat neater than he left it, but only to the extent that the industrious German ants had swept the rottenest bits of their Gorgonzola into orderly heaps. The corpses had all been cleared away, but the results of the 363 bombing raids the Allies flew over Berlin during the war were still very much in evidence. About 500,000 of the city's buildings had been destroyed by those raids, and that figure doesn't even include the damage the Russians inflicted when they shelled the place in the weeks before the Nazis' final collapse. But Berliners were resilient, tough. They were already buying and selling and bartering, rebuilding what they could, leveling the rest, and above all, surviving.

Erich Pommer had become chief of the film section at the Information Control Division in Berlin, and he greatly facilitated the production of *A Foreign Affair* by arranging for the reconstituted Ufa to advance all of Paramount's expenses in German marks. Paramount did have to bring all of its own raw film stock because there wasn't any in Berlin. Food was still scarce; the black market was thriving; there were military police everywhere. Despite the calm imposed by foreign occupation, Wilder and his crew were literally filming in a war zone. But they weren't the first to do so. Even with all his advance planning, his schmoozing of army personnel, and his connection to Pommer, Wilder was still beaten to the punch by the crew of RKO's *Berlin Express*. They'd shown up at the end of July and had already begun filming by the time he arrived.

Location shooting for *A Foreign Affair* in Berlin began on August 17 and lasted through September 6. Billy and his crew, including cameramen Dewey Wrigley and Kurt Schulz, made their way through the desolate city streets filming the ghastly but typical scenes of devastation they encountered. They set up their cameras at the blackened Brandenburg Gate as planned. They filmed moving camera shots following a jeep as it sped down empty, rubble-lined boulevards. Twisted girders, concrete chips, and freestanding facades were all that remained. They shot footage in the rutted Tiergarten and along the now-desolate Kurfürstendamm. In the finished film, some of this footage can be seen in rear projection behind the congressional delegation as the commanding officer gives them a tour. "That pile of stone over there was the Adlon Hotel," he tells his fascinated guests. They pass Hitler's New Chancellery, now in ruins: "There's the balcony where he bet his Reich would last a thousand years. That's the one that broke the bookies' hearts."

The location footage Billy and his crew shot in August also provides the film with its most sardonic joke. After Captain Johnny Pringle (John

Lund) piles the ratty mattress into his jeep's backseat and takes off to visit his glorified hooker in her hovel, Wilder's camera follows along as he rides around Berlin's decrepit, ghostly streets to the sweet tune of "Isn't It Romantic?"

Billy was clearly of two minds about all of this. John Woodcock recalls a moment when Billy's irony broke. They were in the editing room: "After viewing aerial shots of block after block of Berlin levelled to the ground, I remarked that I couldn't help feel sorry for the Germans. With that Billy jumped to his feet and yelled, 'To hell with those bastards! They burned most of my family in their damned ovens! I hope they burn in hell!' "

Even with periodic bouts of bad weather, the shoot ran only three days over schedule. By September 4, Wilder had left for Paris, where Brackett met him for conferences and fun, after which they joined the vacationing Mr. and Mrs. Ray Milland on the *Queen Elizabeth* for passage back to the States. The chief purpose of Billy's stopover in Paris was to convince Marlene Dietrich to take the role of Erika, the cabaret star who has a habit of sleeping with influential men of various political persuasions. Simply put, Erika is a Nazi. ("She was Goebbels's girl, or Goering's—one of 'em, anyway," says one GI to another in the film.) Dietrich herself was adamantly and vocally anti-Fascist, and in fact she was the first woman to be awarded the Medal of Freedom for her passionate and tireless efforts on behalf of the Allies. Marlene's initial response to the idea of playing a Nazi was quick and negative. Dietrich, who was living at the Hotel Georges V at the time, was willing to talk to Billy, though, and, as usual, Billy cajoled and wheedled and charmed his potential star until she caved in.

Part of the draw as far as Marlene was concerned was that Wilder had already commissioned some new songs by their mutual old friend Friedrich Holländer, now Frederick Hollander. Hollander was then under contract to RKO and had to be borrowed, but that was no problem. Even with Hollander's songs written expressly for her, Marlene only agreed after Billy shrewdly showed her the screen tests of two American actresses he claimed to have had in mind for the role, should Marlene turn him down. It was an obvious ploy, but it worked perfectly on Dietrich. Her compensation must have proven enticing, too. She earned an initial $110,000, plus $66,000 more for additional time.

For the role of Phoebe Frost, Wilder and Brackett convinced Jean Arthur to come out of her self-imposed retirement. Arthur had grown weary of acting in high-pressure films and all the ensuing publicity demands. Her last film had been in 1944 (*The Impatient Years* for Columbia). So in 1947 she enrolled at Stephens College, a women's school in Columbia, Missouri, where she took courses in philosophy, biology, and geology. As she told the press at the time, "I've had to work all my life, and now I want to learn." But when *A Foreign Affair* came along, the forty-two-year-old actress dropped out of school with only two weeks remaining before her final exams. She, too, must have responded to the money: $175,000 with an additional $10,000 for four extra weeks.

A Foreign Affair is a political film, albeit an unconventional one. But its effectiveness as propaganda in Germany diminished as the script evolved. Erika is entirely unrepentant about her Nazi past. As written, let alone as embodied by Dietrich, Erika von Shlütow is a far cry from Billy's initial character sketch. While Brackett and Wilder give Johnny a respectable reason for cuddling up to Erika (we learn, eventually, that he's trying to smoke out her lover, a former Gestapo leader, now a wanted war criminal), it's perfectly clear that his most urgent undercover mission occurs every night in her bed. Johnny's lust for Erika is enflamed not despite the fact that she is a Nazi but *because* she is a Nazi. In their first scene together, he pulls her close to him, and roughly so. He nuzzles her hair; she asks what he's doing. "I'm wiping my face," he explains. Dialogue follows:

JOHNNY: What you Germans need is a better conscience.
ERIKA: I have a good conscience. I have a new Führer now. *You. (She raises her left arm in a Nazi salute.)* Heil Johnny
JOHNNY: You heil me once more and I'll knock your teeth in.

(They draw together in a sticky embrace.)

ERIKA: You'd bruise your lips.
JOHNNY: I ought to choke you a little. *(He places his hands around her neck.)* Break you in two. Build a fire under you, you blonde witch.

(They kiss deeply and passionately.)

Beyond the creation of a beautiful, remorseless enemy lust object, Wilder gave full voice to whatever camaraderie remained between the Americans and the Soviets at the dawn of the Cold War. The lowlife Lorelei cabaret in which Erika performs is a haven of postwar cooperation, with American GIs and Russian soldiers constantly carousing, singing, and dancing the *gazatsky* together in harmony. (At the Lorelei, both Reds and Yanks buy drinks with packs of cigarettes. "Five packs for champagne, four packs for wine, one pack for beer," says the waiter; "*Eine kleine* clip joint," one of the GIs mutters.) Moreover, one of the visiting congressmen describes, in a comico-serious manner, his definition of a healthy leftist foreign policy. Explaining his desire to send food to the German people without engaging in what he derisively calls "dollar diplomacy," the liberal representative says, "If you give a hungry man a loaf of bread, that's democracy. If you leave the wrapper on, it's imperialism!"

On the face of it, this bit of dialogue may not seem terribly dangerous. On the other hand, when the House Committee on Un-American Activities (HUAC) held its first round of hearings earlier that spring, one of the lines Dalton Trumbo had written for Ginger Rogers for the 1943 wartime melodrama *Tender Comrade* was cited as evidence not only of Trumbo's own treasonous activities but of the Communist infiltration of Hollywood in general: "Share and share alike—that's democracy." Charles Brackett's impeccable Republican credentials and his well-known conservative politics, not to mention his new position as vice president of the Academy, protected him from ever having to explain what he meant by "democracy" and "imperialism," and they also appear to have been enough to prevent any shadow of suspicion from falling upon his liberal writing partner.

It was the *Hollywood Reporter* that coined the term "unfriendly witnesses" to describe those directors and screenwriters who refused to testify before HUAC. The second round of hearings, the round in which the Unfriendly Ten refused to testify and were cited for contempt of Congress, occurred while Brackett and Wilder were making *A Foreign Affair*. Wilder was mildly involved in liberal Hollywood's response. In September, the Committee for the First Amendment was founded by Philip Dunne, William Wyler, and John Huston while sitting around a table at Lucey's. The Committee's first regular meeting was held at Ira Gershwin's house. Supporters of the Committee included Billy and his former producers Arthur Hornblow Jr., Joe Pasternak, and Joe Sistrom, as well as Judy Garland, Edward G. Robinson, and others. These were not rabble-rousers. Mostly, they wrote petitions, signed their names, and simply let the right wing know they weren't going to remain silent. The Committee itself was specifically and expressly Communist-free. Real Reds were asked overtly to keep their distance so as not to ruin their relatively few friends' careers along with their own. Wilder's politics had always leaned to the left, but he was becoming even less actively so by 1947. He supported the Committee, but on principle. It certainly wasn't because he had any particular respect for the Unfriendly Ten. "Only two of them have any talent," Billy said in a widely quoted remark. "The rest are just unfriendly." "Blacklist, schmacklist," he also said—"as long as they're all working."

Billy Wilder was getting rich. For *A Foreign Affair* his director's fee alone had escalated to $111,000, and that didn't include his salary as a writer. But as Billy's own fortunes continued to rise in Hollywood, so his old friend Joe May's declined, ever more precipitously. Now that May's directing career was over, he was nearly destitute. His last picture was a 1944 B movie comedy for Monogram called *Johnny Doesn't Live Here Any More*. The Mays were in such dire straits in the fall of 1947 that they stood in real danger of losing their house. So Paul Kohner, always a gentleman and a friend, took matters into his own hands and frankly asked Billy, Wyler, and Lubitsch each to give May and his wife, Mia, $100 a month for six months. Kohner discreetly called it an "advance," though it's likely that nobody ever thought they'd be repaid.

In late November, with *A Foreign Affair* ready to begin filming, Billy accepted an invitation to attend a screening of a French film, *Le Diable au Corps*, at the home of William Wyler. Marlene Dietrich was trying to introduce her new discovery, the actor Gérard Philipe, to those members of the Hollywood community she continued to respect. Dietrich had set up the screening particularly for Lubitsch's benefit, since he was considering making *Der Rosenkavalier*; she thought Philipe would be great in the picture. Wilder arrived for the screening on Sunday, November 29, along with Dietrich, Walter Reisch, Otto Preminger, Edmund Goulding, and the restaurateur Mike Romanoff. But no Lubitsch.

Billy's friend and mentor suffered a fatal heart attack in the shower that afternoon. When they received word of Lubitsch's death, everyone at Wyler's house moved over to Reisch's, along with about fifty others, to mourn their friend and tell Lubitsch stories. The turnout for the funeral was grander still. The great director's honorary pallbearers included Paul Kohner, Arthur Hornblow Jr., Frederick Hollander, Louis B. Mayer, Franz Waxman, William Wyler, Walter Wanger, and Darryl Zanuck. Charlie Brackett delivered the eulogy. Billy himself was one of the actual pallbearers, along with Reisch, Henry Blanke, Mervyn LeRoy, Gene Raymond, Gottfried Reinhardt, and Richard Sale. They came very close to dropping Lubitsch on the pavement. Only Sale's quick reflexes prevented catastrophe; he managed to wedge his knee under the coffin and kept it from crashing down. The seven shaken pallbearers were rescued by the funeral home attendants. It was after this harrowing moment and the burial that followed that Wilder said to Wyler, "No more Lubitsch." "Worse than that," Wyler famously replied. "No more Lubitsch movies."

Years later, Billy flatly denied a story that had flown around town at the time regarding the circumstances of Lubitsch's death. As the tale had it, Billy arrived at Lubitsch's house moments after Lubitsch died. He saw a weeping blonde sitting in the living room and, in an effort to comfort her, encouraged her to cheer up. After all, Billy told her, Lubitsch had been like a father to him, and he wasn't crying, so neither should she. "Easy for you to say," the blonde replied. "He didn't fuck you and then stiff you for the money." Billy is said to have handed her $50; this was enough to make her stop crying. "Absolutely not true," Billy declared when asked for verification. "It was Otto the chauffeur who paid her off."

The week after Lubitsch died, Louella Parsons announced one of the most bizarre mismatches between writer-director and property in Hollywood history. Billy Wilder, Louella reported, had been approached to direct *The Robe*. ("This picture will do much to bring a message of religion into a world that needs it," said Louella.) There was just one problem: Brackett and Wilder were under contract to Paramount, and *The Robe* was then scheduled to be an RKO picture unless, of course, Paramount bought the rights from the other studio. Louella's zany news flash is almost certainly the result of wish fulfillment on the part of the producer Frank Ross, who owned the rights to *The Robe* and was eagerly trying to drum up support for the expensive religious spectacle he hoped to create. Ross may well have approached Brackett and Wilder; whether they expressed any interest at all is questionable. (*The Robe* was ultimately made by Henry Koster in CinemaScope for Twentieth Century–Fox in 1953, and Brackett and Wilder had nothing to do with it.)

They did, however, do some rewriting for Samuel Goldwyn on another religious picture, a comedy called *The Bishop's Wife*. David Niven plays an Episcopal bishop who wants to build a new church, and Loretta Young is his wife. Cary Grant is the angel who comes down and helps them. This wasn't exactly Brackett and Wilder's emotional terrain; they did the quick polish for Goldwyn as a friendly gesture, nothing more. Initially, Goldwyn offered them $25,000 for the job, but after completing their minor revisions the two writers decided that since most of the money would end up going to taxes anyway, they'd take no fee at all. When they announced their generous decision to Goldwyn, the tight-fisted studio boss responded, "That's funny—I've come to the same conclusion."

A Foreign Affair remained Brackett and Wilder's chief concern, especially when the PCA registered its latest set of objections on the brink of the film's going back into production. The United States government, the United States Army, and members of Congress were not to be ridiculed, the PCA advised. "We further believe that the portrayal of the Congresswoman, Phoebe Frost, getting drunk in a public nightclub of poor reputation, hanging from the ceiling, and being arrested and carted off to jail in the police van is in violation of that portion of the Production Code which states that 'the history, institutions, prominent people, and citizenry of all nations shall be represented fairly.' " There was an "overemphasis on illicit sex [that] seems to run through most of the script." Brackett and Wilder agreed to some revisions, first and foremost the disposition of the mattress. As the PCA's Stephen S. Jackson noted, "The following basic changes will be made: It will be clearly indicated that John brings the mattress to Erika's apartment for some reason other than making the bed more comfortable." Dialogue changes were ordered as well: "Page 33: We suggest you change the expression 'pig' as applied to the girls." When Phoebe is on the bed with another congressman, the PCA insisted, she should not be asking, "Anything I can do for you?" Another line, too, was completely unacceptable: "Yes, sir, there's the kind of dish makes you wish you had two spoons."

Marlene moved into Billy's house while filming *A Foreign Affair* in December, January, and February, and she proved to be a great companion. They told filthy jokes and stories to each other in German, both on the set and off. Billy liked to get her going on the subject of her torrid affairs with both sexes, and Marlene was all too happy to oblige. Her costar Jean Arthur, meanwhile, became increasingly flustered by Dietrich's worldly charm. The more Dietrich swept around the soundstage amusing the cast and crew and looking fabulous, the more Arthur kept to herself in her dressing room. Dietrich's fascination with her own glamour found its obverse in Arthur's escalating paranoia about hers. *A Foreign Affair* features a cruel observation about Arthur herself. Erika describes Phoebe Frost as "that funny little woman with a face like a scrubbed kitchen floor," whereupon she throws her head back and laughs derisively. Arthur took such things personally; she found herself on the set of this film trying to compete on-screen with one of the world's great sirens. As the filming went on she was less and less happy about doing so. Dietrich's omnisexuality probably unnerved Arthur as well. Here was Marlene, openly enjoying her body and lending it to anyone she pleased; there was Jean, frightened of revealing her own desires and trying her best to avoid the subject entirely. One night she showed up at Billy's door with her husband, Frank Ross, in tow. She was, in Wilder's words, "absolutely frenzied, with eyes bulging." "What did you do with my close-up?" she demanded. "You burned it! Marlene told you to burn that close up! She does not want me to look good!"

Billy grew frustrated. "What a picture," he said to John Lund in exasperation. "One dame who's afraid to look in a mirror, and one who won't stop." He stayed very friendly with the dame who wouldn't stop, but by the time the production closed he'd had enough of Jean Arthur, whom he later called "a doozie."

Arthur fell ill for a few days in January, but the shoot was otherwise fairly smooth. *A Foreign Affair* wrapped on February 12.

A Foreign Affair is a most brutal comedy. Wilder sticks Jean Arthur with the bluntly descriptive name "Phoebe Frost." He makes her wear her hair in a constricting, repressive style ("What a curious way to do your hair—or not to do it," says Erika). And he compares her, inevitably and unfavorably, to Erika's continental sophistication. For Billy, Phoebe Frost embodies everything wrong with American women. She can't help but extol the virtues of her native Iowa. Johnny is from Iowa, too, but it's perfectly clear that he prefers his life in depraved Berlin to anything in the American heartland, and he adamantly resists her attempts to get him to return home. "We won a lot of honors last year," she sighs, dreamily. "All the 4-H prizes!" Billy then sets up a mean little joke. Phoebe continues: "We had the lowest juvenile delinquency rate in the country till two months ago." "What happened?" Johnny asks, and she answers: "A little boy in Des Moines took a blowtorch to his grandmother. We fell clear down to six-teenth place. It was humiliating."

As far as Johnny's character is concerned, Brackett and Wilder were forced to tread a thin line. Johnny has to enjoy the pesthole of Berlin, but he also has to fall in love with a repressed puritan from Iowa. They end the film with the latter, but they give much more emotional weight to the former. Billy still hadn't gotten the erotic allure of a blonde Nazi bitch out of his system. And since John Lund is by far the weakest of the three stars, the film's resolution is even more unsatisfying. Ultimately, Johnny seems to end up with Phoebe simply because they are both Americans.

Soaring above them is Erika, the hot Nazi. "That's the kind of pastry makes you drool on your bib!" says one GI admiringly. In Wilder's view of the world, she is the moral center of the film; her dazzling amorality makes her so.

When the film was released, Billy found himself denounced on the floor of Congress for treating Germans and Americans with equal irreverence, but it was only hot air. Similarly, and equally uselessly, the Defense Department stated that there was absolutely no similarity between the GIs depicted by Wilder and the real American soldiers who were serving in Berlin. Most ironic of all, *A Foreign Affair*, which began its life as a propaganda film, was banned in Germany. "Crude, superficial, and insensible to certain responsibilities which the world situation, like it or not, has thrust on" Hollywood was the way an American in charge of approving films put it; "Berlin's trials and tribulations are not the stuff of cheap comedy, and rubble makes lousy custard pies."

After a long delay, *The Emperor Waltz* enjoyed its world premiere at the Paramount Hollywood Theatre on May 26, 1948. *The Hollywood Reporter* loved it: "Here's a picture that'll bring lots of joy to the box-office and even more to those who go in to see it. . . . Bing has never been cast better, nor has he given a better performance and in wonderful voice, too. . . . Charlie Brackett and Billy Wilder get better with every picture." *Variety* applauded as well: "It's Crosby all the way down the line. As a result, there's a long, long line of greenbacks indeed in store for *The Emperor Waltz*." The *Motion Picture Herald* agreed: "Bing was never better than in *The Emperor Waltz* and not as good since *Going My Way*."

Wilder did not attend the premiere of *The Emperor Waltz*, having left for a vacation in Europe. He told the press before departing that he was thinking about making a film in Palestine and was trying to win permission to film some preparatory footage there, but the day after the *Examiner* printed this detail, the state of Israel was created and the Middle East fell into deeper turmoil. The film project was scuttled.

Wilder's private life was settling down somewhat. He ended his affair with Doris Dowling, who appears to have felt the need to make an unusually clean break: she moved to Rome and stayed there for three years. According to Billy, he never considered marrying Doris because of their constant arguments. The end of the affair might have given Billy more time to spend with Audrey, but to the extent that one believes Hollywood gossip, he filled the gaps in his schedule by dating Hedy Lamarr on the side. Hedy and Billy were "seeing each other all the time," Louella gasped in April 1949, adding that "most of the girls who fall in love with him really fall."

Whatever happened between Billy Wilder and Hedy Lamarr, on June 30 Billy married Audrey in Linden, Nevada. Billy's new but close friends, the designers Charles and Ray Eames, were the Wilders' attendants. (The graphic designer Alvin Lustig, who was using Billy's garage as a design studio, introduced Billy to Charles; Billy promptly ordered one of the prototypes of Eames's 1946 plywood chairs.) Said Billy, "We asked them one day whether he would like to be the best man and she the maid of honor, and they said okay. And then the four of us took off to Nevada, where you can get married for two dollars in three minutes." It was hasty but not without a touch of romance: "I bought her some bouquet of flowers," Billy noted.

Audrey supplied another detail or two: "The morning we were leaving to get married, Charles and Ray Eames showed up at the house. And Billy had a convertible Cadillac. And we all got in, and we start for Linden, Nevada. I said, 'Okay, I want to change.' I had on jeans (or the version of that in those days) and a sweatshirt. And he said, 'No. You either get married like this or you don't get married at all.' " She continued: "We stopped in the San Fernando Valley at a jewelry shop on the road, and he bought me my wedding ring. $17.95."

The spirit of camaraderie prevailed throughout the trip. The Eameses also accompanied Billy and Audrey on their honeymoon.

Louella broke the news to the world. Audrey, she reported, called her father, Stratton Young, and told him over the phone that she had gotten married. Parsons also declared that nobody in Hollywood was surprised by Billy's marriage to Audrey, "for they have been keeping steady company for two years," thus ignoring completely her own chronicling of his affair with Lamarr. Marlene, meanwhile, wasn't pleased. "She was the worst,"

Audrey reported, referring to the general dismay of Billy's friends when she and Billy married. "What sign are you?" Marlene demanded of Audrey. "Cancer." In ominous tones, Marlene informed the new Mrs. Wilder that a Cancer-Gemini relationship would never work out. Marlene also made a point to bring over some homemade mushroom soup one night because she knew how much Billy liked it. Later, when Audrey and Billy opened the Thermos container in preparation for dinner, they found precisely one portion of soup.

On June 8, 1948, Elizabeth Brackett died at her home on Bellagio Road in Bel-Air. The obituaries cited her long illness and left it at that. Charlie headed east for the funeral in Saratoga Springs. The following month, he was back in Hollywood delivering a eulogy for another sad alcoholic when D. W. Griffith died, virtually alone and thoroughly ruined. Wilder recalled a disturbing incident that occurred a few months earlier in which Griffith drunkenly accosted Samuel Goldwyn at Romanoff's. The Goldwyns and Wilder were enjoying dinner in one of the booths near the bar when a stately but dissipated old man appeared at their table waving his index finger in Goldwyn's face. "Here you are, you son of a bitch," he slurred. "I ought to be making pictures . . ." Frances Goldwyn, having no idea who the old man was, shooed him away. Once he was safely gone, Goldwyn, shaken, told her that the old drunk was Griffith.

At the end of July, Griffith was dead and Charlie was delivering his eulogy: "Many of us who didn't know David Wark Griffith personally have in the last years lost our awareness of what he meant in our industry. Perhaps it would be more accurate to say that our view of him has been obscured by a disturbing shadow, the shadow of an elderly man living in our midst, but outside the industry."

Brackett spoke movingly of Griffith's achievements, but he had to ac-knowledge—twice, in fact—that he'd never met the man. Griffith had be-come one more disturbing shadow in a town full of shadows—just another old-timer who used to be big.

With blacklisting now in full force, the Committee for the First Amend-ment found itself unable to do much beyond tying itself to a sinking ship. So it dissolved. Billy's political interests turned back to Europe. By 1948, Paul Kohner's European Film Fund had evolved into the European Relief Fund, the purpose of which was now to provide assistance to the war's survivors. Billy was named to the board of directors, along with Walter Reisch, Henry Blanke, Robert Siodmak, Robert Thoeron, and Gottfried Reinhardt, who served as the organization's president. Wilder contributed to the Fund at least as generously as other directors of his stature, if not more so, but it appears that most of his spending that year was directed toward his burgeoning art collection. Through the Galerie Pétridès in Paris, he bought Picasso's *Tête de femme,* a pastel on paper. As his signature makes clear, Picasso drew the work in Fontainebleau in September 1921. The 25½-by-19⅞-inch drawing depicts a sculptural, contemplative woman's head and shoulders set against a roughly sketched blue background. It proved to be one of the best investments Billy Wilder ever made.

Through Curt Valentin and the Buchholz Gallery in New York, Billy bought two Henry Moore bronze sculptures: *Family Group* and *Stringed Figure.* He told a puzzled friend, who was unaware of a certain Dada collagist, that he'd begun collecting "cashmere Schwitters." He also purchased Rouault's 1930 work *Critique* through the Stendahl Gallery in Los Angeles. The gouache, pastel, brush, and India ink on paper represents in very stylized form a dour, gray-headed and gray-mustachioed gentleman seated in a posture of judgment. Billy soon began calling it "Judge Brackett."

The real Judge Brackett, meanwhile, remained a staunch defender of the film industry he loved and the American system that enabled it to thrive economically. He and his conservative Hollywood friends—the very crowd against which Billy and the Committee for the First Amendment had rebelled—were eagerly looking forward to Truman's defeat in the presidential election and a return to respectable, proindustrial Republican rule. On election night they all met at Samuel Goldwyn's house on Laurel Lane. It was a merry scene, and it became even more so as each radio report suggested, ever more enthusiastically, that the next president of the United States would be named Dewey. Billy left around midnight to pick up Audrey. He returned to a funereal mood. "Sitting in the living room on the carpet, with their backs to the wall, were Charlie Brackett, Mary Pickford, and Louella Parsons, all dissolved in tears." " 'We're leaving the country. Truman won. The Reds are taking over,' " he recalled them moaning. "Goldwyn was just staring into space, completely pale. Now believe me, I lived through Hitler being appointed Chancellor, and we took it better than that."

As acting president of the Academy, Brackett might have chosen to downplay the more acerbic aspects of his and Billy's joint view of the world in favor of the bland respectability the industry promoted in its public relations campaigns. Instead, he and Wilder began planning a new film about an old silent screen star who had a few problems. Curiously, it was also around this time that Billy invited Greta Garbo to his house on North Beverly for a drink. He and Walter Reisch wanted to talk to her about returning to films. According to Wilder, Audrey was upstairs in the bedroom. Billy yelled up to her, "Come on down, we've got a visitor!" "Who?" Audrey asked. "Greta Garbo," said Billy. "Oh, fuck off," said Audrey.

Wilder and Reisch went on to describe a few story ideas to Garbo.

Billy's involved a death mask he supposedly saw at the Louvre—*la inconnue de la Seine*. The tragic story he wove concerned an unknown girl who drowns in the river and goes on to narrate the story of her life in flashback. She was the wife of a banker, Wilder said, and . . . Garbo dismissed the idea by saying that she didn't want to play the wife of a banker. At that point Audrey offered drinks. Reisch took over. He pitched an idea about the Empress Elizabeth of Austria, whose only dream is to run away from her life as an empress, and . . . Garbo reminded Reisch that she'd already done *Queen Christina*. Reisch drove her home. On the way, she told him that the only role she would be at all interested in playing was that of a male clown—actually a woman *playing* a male clown. "And all the admiring girls in the audience who write him letters are wondering why he does not respond. They do not understand." Wilder explained many years later that all Garbo really wanted to do was "to hide behind greasepaint. She could play the clown in white makeup so no one would be able to see her face."

A much more extreme career collapse was on Billy's mind when he and Brackett were writing *Sunset Boulevard*. In an effort to earn some kind of living in Hollywood, Joe May decided to open a restaurant. His wife, Mia, once one of Germany's leading stars, was the cook. The restaurant had a Hungarian theme; it was called the Blue Danube. Some of the Mays' old friends, including Billy and Joe Mankiewicz, invested in the fledgling operation and did what they could to bring in the crowds. Billy himself contributed $3,000 to the effort. The Blue Danube opened during the first week of April 1949. It closed two weeks later, an utter failure. The Mays became so despondent that they rarely left their house.

17. SUNSET BOULEVARD

JOE GILLIS (William Holden): Wait a minute—haven't I seen you before? I know your face.

NORMA DESMOND (Gloria Swanson): Get out! Or shall I call my servant?

JOE GILLIS: You're Norma Desmond. You used to be in silent pictures—you used to be big.

NORMA DESMOND: I *am* big. It's the pictures that got small.

JOE GILLIS: Uh-huh—I knew there was something wrong with them.

—*Sunset Boulevard*

On December 21, 1948, Brackett and Wilder turned in the first sixty-one pages of their new screenplay. It began with a curt notation: "This is the first act of *Sunset Boulevard*. Due to the peculiar nature of the project, we ask all our co-workers to regard it as top secret." What was peculiar about the film was its central female character, a batty silent screen star who'd passed her prime. Its narrative structure was also strange. *Sunset Boulevard* began in a morgue. Its leading man, the film's narrator, was a cadaver:

An attendant wheels the dead Gillis into the huge, bare, windowless room. Along the walls are twenty or so sheet-covered corpses lying in an orderly row of wheeled slabs with large numbers painted on the walls above each slab. The attendant pushes Gillis into a vacant space. Beyond him, the feet of other corpses stretch from under their sheets: men's feet, women's feet, childrens', two or three Negroes—with a linen tag dangling from each left big toe. The attendant exits, switching off the light. For a moment the room is semi-dark, then as the music takes on a more astral phase, a curious glow emanates from the sheeted corpses.

A MAN'S VOICE: Don't be scared. There's a lot of us here. It's all right.
GILLIS: I'm not scared.

> (*His head doesn't move, but his eyes slowly wander to the slab next to him. There, under a partially transparent sheet, lies a fat man aged 60 or so. His eyes are open, too, and directed at Gillis.*)

FAT MAN: How did you happen to die?

GILLIS: What difference does it make?[. . .] It'll be a good joke, lying here like a jigsaw puzzle all scrambled up, with the cops and the Hollywood columnists trying to fit in the wrong pieces.

FAT MAN: Hollywood? You in the movies?

GILLIS: Yeah. Came out in forty-five, to catch me a swimming pool. And, by gosh, in the end I got myself one. Only there turned out to be blood in it.

FAT MAN: Were you an actor?

GILLIS: No. A writer. Never had my name on anything big, though. Just a couple of B pictures. One stinker, and the other one—well, that wasn't so hot either. I was having a tough time making a living.

FAT MAN: It's your dying I was asking about.

(*Gillis chuckles.*)

GILLIS: Well, I drove down Sunset Boulevard one afternoon. That was my mistake. Maybe I'd better start off with the morning of that day. I'd been out of work for six months. I had a couple of stories out that wouldn't sell, and an apartment right above Hollywood and Vine that wasn't paid for. . . .

Brackett and Wilder listed their cast of characters along with "the actors we hope to get" to play the roles. For Dan Gillis they wanted a bright young star—Montgomery Clift. Gloria Swanson, herself a silent star who hadn't made any movies in a while, would be the demented Norma Desmond. Erich von Stroheim would appear as her butler, Max. The character of Betty, a Paramount script reader, would be played by "a new face," and Brackett and Wilder hoped that the role of Kaufman, a Paramount producer, would be taken by Joseph Calleia. There would also be a number of smaller roles—"movie people, cops, and corpses."

Magnificently handsome and charismatic, Montgomery Clift had appeared in only two films—Howard Hawks's *Red River* and Fred Zinnemann's *The Search*—when Wilder approached him for the lead in *Sunset Boulevard*. His third picture, Paramount's *The Heiress* (costarring Olivia de Havilland) hadn't finished filming yet, but the buzz surrounding him was extraordinary. He was a studied, upper-crust twenty-eight-year-old who assiduously played the role of a relaxed bohemian in his public life. The combination was dazzling. Billy gave him the first section of the screenplay, Clift loved what he read, and he agreed to play the role. Paramount's contract with Clift for *The Heiress* included options on future films, so all Paramount had to do was exercise the first of these options for *Sunset Boulevard* and Monty was ready to go. He'd get $5,000 per week for a guaranteed twelve weeks on the film. Clift agreed to report for work in early April—about six weeks after he officially signed on. In the meantime, Billy and Charlie wanted him to stay in Hollywood for story conferences, as did Clift's protective agent, Herman Citron. But Clift, having finished work on *The Heiress*, was in the mood for a nice vacation, so he flew to Switzerland and went skiing.

Clift was a fine match for Gloria Swanson. Hollywood's hottest young man would play beautifully opposite the Jazz Age's flashiest, most glamorous woman. Swanson had been a genuine sensation in the 1920s. "You must remember," said Wilder, "that this was a star who at one time was carried in a sedan chair from her dressing room to the soundstage. When she married the Marquis de la Falaise and came by boat from Europe to New York and by train from there to Hollywood, people were strewing rose petals on the railroad tracks in her direction. She'd been one of the all-time stars, but when she returned to the screen in *Sunset* she worked like a dog." In the film, Wilder gives Norma's butler a punchline that plays on Swanson's own erotic allure: "She was the greatest of them all. You wouldn't know, you're too young. In one week she received seventeen thousand fan letters. Men bribed her hairdresser to get a lock of her hair. There was a maharaja who came all the way from India to beg one of her silk stockings. Later he strangled himself with it."

When he described Swanson's dedication to her performance, Wilder makes an important point: she was not the crazy diva she played on-screen but a tough and hard-working actress. But then nobody had ever called Gloria Swanson either lazy or dizzy. Swanson's movie career appeared to be over, but she never stopped working. By the late 1940s, Swanson was acting in summer stock productions, doing radio shows, and trying to keep her company, Multiprises, from going bankrupt. Still, Swanson continued to consider herself one of the greatest film stars in the world; she'd earned the title in the 1920s, and in the late 1940s she saw no need to give it up. As one contemporary account explained, Gloria was "keeping up appearances by spending $7,000 a year on clothes, which, in her special instance, she regarded as more of a professional expense than an extravagance."

In June 1948, Swanson began earning $350 a week on WPIX radio in New York City. When Paramount called her in September to see if she was interested in returning to motion pictures, Swanson naturally assumed it was a bit part and said that she might be able to leave her radio show for two weeks. No, the studio told her, it was for the lead in the picture, and she'd get somewhere in the neighborhood of $50,000 for a ten- to twelve-week shoot. Swanson said she could be in Hollywood by the first of the year (though *Sunset Boulevard* didn't start to roll until April). She promptly divorced her fifth husband, to whom she had been married less than twelve months, and—according to Swanson, anyway—flew to Hollywood and arrived on the set having no idea of the plot of the picture or the role she was to play.

On the day Swanson returned to Paramount Pictures, the studio she had indeed helped to build, she found a huge likeness of herself on a bill-board near the gate. Paramount's publicity department was working on a self-promotional campaign to tie the studio in, decidedly obscurely, with the centennial celebration of the 1849 gold rush. The billboard featured a huge comet blazing through the sky leaving pictures of past and present Paramount stars behind it. The size of the picture and its position relative to the comet's tail was determined by the star's perceived importance to the studio. At the head of the tail was Gloria Swanson. According to her, the chief casting director, Bill Meiklejohn, explained why: "Baby, am I glad to see you. You took me off a helluva spot! If I'd put Crosby's picture on the front end of that comet, Hope would have blown his top, and Crosby would have had a fit if Hope was up there. Stanwyck or Hutton would've scratched my eyes out if one got top billing over the other. You turned out to be a real lifesaver." "That's when I knew I was home," Miss Swanson told the press. "Right back in the jungle, up to my ears in the rat race." A more likely rationale is that the studio had already begun its publicity campaign for *Sunset Boulevard*. They also wanted Swanson to feel the way Norma Desmond feels when *she* returns to Paramount in the film, except of course that Norma Desmond is delusional.

Brackett reported that he and Billy had never considered anybody else for the part: "We knew no time would be wasted getting into the story as soon as Swanson appeared on the screen. Youngsters who never saw her would immediately accept her as an old-time movie queen. Older fans would identify her with the characterization and get a bigger emotional wallop from the story." To the degree that the extended comedy routine that served as Billy's memory can be trusted, however, Brackett and Wilder originally wanted another old-time star. "For a long time I wanted to do a comedy about Hollywood," Wilder claimed. "God forgive me, I wanted to have Mae West and Marlon Brando." He also said they tried Pola Negri: "We called her on the phone, and there was too much Polish accent." Then they went up to Pickfair, Mary Pickford's immense estate high in the hills. "Brackett began to tell her the story, because he was the more serious one. I stopped him. 'No, don't do it.' I waved him off. She was going to be insulted if we told her she was to play a woman who begins a love affair with a man half her age. I said to her, 'We're sorry, but it's no use. The story gets very vulgar.'"

Frustrated at his lack of success in casting this most particular, most peculiar role, Wilder turned to his colleague and friend George Cukor for help. They were sitting in Cukor's expansive garden drinking tea when

Cukor mentioned Swanson. Wilder probably hadn't thought very much about her since *Music in the Air*. He'd predicted in the pages of *Der Querschnitt* that *Queen Kelly*, the film Swanson made for Erich von Stroheim, would be a huge hit. Little did he know at the time that Swanson, on the other side of the world, was becoming increasingly horrified at such Stroheimian touches as her costar (Tully Marshall) drooling brown tobacco juice on her delicate hand while slipping a wedding ring on her finger. *Queen Kelly* died before completion; Swanson's producer/lover, Joseph Kennedy, pulled the plug, and Swanson's fame began a protracted collapse as well. *Music in the Air* all but finished her off. In Cukor's garden, Billy saw several reasons why Gloria Swanson was the ideal Norma Desmond.

One of these reasons served doubly as the solution to another problem—the casting of Max, the servile butler who used to be a famous film director. Erich von Stroheim came naturally to mind. Von Stroheim did not become a butler; he became an actor and, at times at least, a good one. Before playing Rommel in *Five Graves to Cairo*, von Stroheim played the gentleman soldier von Rauffenstein in Jean Renoir's *La Grande Illusion*. After *Five Graves*, though, von Stroheim descended into drastic self-parody. The only two film roles he landed in the mid-1940s were in cheapies, and, humiliatingly, each required him to play a ruined artiste—a mad Hun on the skids. In Anthony Mann's *The Great Flamarion* (the first of Willie Wilder's film productions for Republic), von Stroheim played a pathetic vaudevillian sharpshooter who comes to a depressing end, thanks to a woman. In *The Mask of Dijon* (1946) von Stroheim was a third-rate hypnotist whose end was even worse. He trips over a guillotine and beheads himself. But even in decline, Erich von Stroheim had no equal as an arrogant Teutonic grotesque. "There was something great in him," Billy said. "When he made an error, it was grandiose, and when it was good, it had class." He would be perfect as Max von Mayerling.

Von Stroheim was living in France at the time. Wilder approached him through Paul Kohner, von Stroheim's agent. Von Stroheim responded in a letter to Kohner: "I don't have to tell you that I would not mind at all working again with 'witty-Billy.' His last endeavor with me had a tremendous success here in France, or was it my extraordinary popularity here that made his picture go over big? Ask him."

Von Stroheim already knew the nature of the role Wilder wanted him to play in *Sunset Boulevard*: "I read in the old bitch Parsons' column that Billy wants me to play the role of a crazy motion-picture director. . . . He likes his actors true to type, does not he? Tell him for me that if he were as smart as he likes to be considered he would play the part himself! But even in craziness I prefer to be the first and therefore I would accept his proposition."

With the three major roles cast, Brackett and Wilder continued to pull *Sunset Boulevard* together in preproduction. As was their practice by this point, they had already brought a third cowriter onto the project—a former Time-Life reporter named D. M. Marshman Jr., whom they'd gotten to know as an affable card-playing partner. After an early screening of *The Emperor Waltz*, Marshman critiqued the film so extensively and so intelligently that Brackett and Wilder told him they'd ask him to collaborate on something in the future. When they found themselves stumped on how to proceed with *Sunset Boulevard*, they made good on their promise. Jacques Théry, Robert Harari, Richard Breen, and now Marshman—in the mid- and late 1940s, Brackett and Wilder did their best work together when there was someone else there with them.

Montgomery Clift, meanwhile, had had time to think. Abruptly, he decided he didn't want to do the picture after all. He called Herman Citron and told him what the problem was. He'd just gotten through with *The Heiress* and didn't want to play any more love scenes with yet another older woman. What Clift specifically said was that he didn't think he could be convincing. So he quit. Citron tried to talk him out of it, but Monty was adamant. Wilder was enraged. "Bullshit!" Billy yelled. "If he's any kind of an actor, he could be convincing making love to *any* woman."

Sunset Boulevard was getting ready to roll, and Clift's sudden departure caused a crisis. Under great pressure, Wilder and Brackett were forced to debate the merits of various available Paramount stars, someone who could step into a difficult, high-profile part very quickly. The most promising was William Holden, who had been kicking around the studio for years. Holden was a solid professional who took the roles they gave him but had never quite connected with audiences. He was tall, handsome, muscular—a classic all-American guy with a bright smile and the slightest suggestion of trouble underneath. There was a problem, however. Holden had been great in *Golden Boy*, but that film was already ten years old. *Sunset Boulevard* wouldn't make much sense if one has-been simply hooked up with another. On the other hand, the fact that he'd never really delivered on his *Golden Boy* promise actually worked to his advantage for *Sunset Boulevard*. Even though he'd been in pictures for over a decade, audiences still didn't know William Holden.

Wilder invited him for drinks. They talked about the film for a while, and Billy began to see some of the depth and intelligence that hadn't come across to him before. He decided that Holden's lack of stardom wasn't Holden's fault at all—it was the lackluster films he'd starred in, and the men who made them. Wilder gave Holden the portion of the screenplay that had been written, and Holden took it back home to read. He phoned back quickly and enthusiastically, beginning what would be a long friendship with Billy—one of Wilder's most intimate—with a typically gung ho and efficient message: "I like it, I'll do it, let's go." But at home, with his wife, Holden was a lot shakier. "Jesus, I'm scared," he told her. "I'm not sure I can deliver."

Brackett and Wilder were happy with Holden, and so was the front office. Replacing Clift saved Paramount $39,000.

By the middle of February, Brackett, Wilder, and Marshman had made various changes to the still-incomplete script. Dan Gillis's name became Dick Gillis. Kaufman's name became Millman. Norma Desmond's mansion, once described as being an enormous hovel with tattered wall hangings and a lot of litter, was no longer quite so dilapidated. Her car, once a Rolls, turned into a Hispano-Suiza, if only for the sound of the name. (*"Parlez-vous français? Do you speak English? Hispano Suiza?"*) And Norma herself was no longer engaged in the endless writing and rewriting of her own pompous, semiliterate memoirs. Early on, Gillis had said, in voice-over, "I was feeling a little sick at my stomach. It wasn't just that sweet champagne. It was that Sunday supplement trash of hers. The memoirs of an egomaniac, not even spelled correctly." But now Norma would be writing an endless screenplay—a mess of a Salome epic that would serve, for lack of a better word, as her comeback.

The original idea for *Sunset Boulevard* has been credited variously to Brackett and to Wilder. Brackett, according to one popular account, had wanted to make a comedy about a silent-screen star for a number of years, but neither Brackett nor Wilder knew what to do with the idea until they met Marshman, who offered the idea of having the star get involved with a young man. Wilder then came up with the idea of killing him: "Suppose the old dame shoots the boy." Brackett is said to have favored a lighter-humored comedy, while Wilder pushed for the film's bleaker, more sardonic tone. On the other hand, Wilder's friend Armand Deutsch claims that the whole idea had been Billy's all along: "Billy once showed [George] Axelrod a scrap of paper which he had saved on which he had scribbled the words, 'Silent picture star commits murder. When they arrest her she sees the newsreel cameras and thinks she is back in the movies.' This note had been made almost ten years before *Sunset Boulevard*." Whatever its genesis, though, the three screenwriters produced a script that twists comedy into something quite disturbing but never stops being bitterly funny, as long as one doesn't take their jokes personally.

If Paramount's accounting figures bear any relation to the work performed, the actual composition of the screenplay for *Sunset Boulevard* was done almost entirely by Marshman and Wilder. By the time they made *Sunset Boulevard*, Brackett and Wilder had been describing themselves as "executive writers" for years, and the string of collaborators with whom they produced scripts testifies to their working methods after 1945. The authorship of *Sunset Boulevard* is not in doubt; the film was written by Charles Brackett, Billy Wilder, and D. M. Marshman Jr. Whether or not Charlie and Billy were still sitting, pacing, napping, and squabbling in their office suite while laying down precise dialogue is another matter entirely. Curiously, Paramount paid Brackett handsomely for producing *Sunset Boulevard*—about $130,000—but *only* for producing it; Wilder and Marshman earned all the money for writing the film. Marshman was officially assigned to the project on August 9, 1948. By February 1949, he'd worked on the screenplay for 182 days and received $11,600. Billy, meanwhile, was paid for 306 days of screenwriting and earned $211,416; this was in addition to his directing fee of about $90,000.

In March and early April, the writer-producer, the writer-director, and their for-hire script writer jointly worked out more of the details of their "peculiar" Hollywood project. Since this was a film about an industry they knew and loved, they wanted to suffuse it with familiar people and places. In this spirit Brackett and Wilder hired the nudgy Hollywood gossip columnist Sidney Skolsky to appear in a sequence set at Schwab's Drugstore in the heart of downtown Hollywood. Enticing Skolsky to play himself wasn't difficult; as Brackett told him, "It won't be Schwab's without Skolsky. And the whole picture won't be typically Hollywood without you and the Schwabadero." This is the scene: Skolsky is seated at a stool at the counter. He asks Gillis, who has failed to land any scriptwriting work and is now completely broke, whether he has anything juicy for Skolsky's column. Gillis responds, "Sure. Just sold an original for a hundred grand—to the King Brothers. The Life of the Warner Brothers. Starring the Ritz Brothers. Playing opposite the Andrews Sisters. But don't get me wrong—I love Hollywood."

Sunset Boulevard's script also contained lots of references to real people, each of whom had to agree to the use of their names. Some didn't. Darryl Zanuck's refusal might have precluded references to himself and Twentieth Century–Fox. Tyrone Power declined as well, as did Olivia de Havilland and Samuel Goldwyn, but Brackett and Wilder decided to use Zanuck's and Power's names anyway. For the scene in which Norma Desmond returns to the Paramount lot in the deluded belief that she is being hired to make another movie, the writers wanted her to recognize one of the juicers (industry slang for an electrician) and greet him like long-lost friend. "Hog-Eye!" Norma cries. In fact, "Hog-Eye" was real—it was the nickname of a former Paramount electrician named John Hetman, who didn't mind the reference. Oddly enough, the reclusive Greta Garbo also granted permission, though when she saw the film itself she was sorry she had done so. She felt that Wilder used her name in a past-tense context, and she was offended. "I thought Billy Wilder was a friend of mine," Garbo told a friend.

Billy and Charlie also tried to get *two* town criers for the film's operatic final scenes, not just one: "I wanted two gossip columnists—Hedda Hopper and Louella Parsons—each on the phone, one upstairs, one down, neither of them giving up the phone and saying 'Get off the line, you bitch! I was here first!' Hedda I got easily, but Louella knew quite well she would lose that duel because Hedda was a former actress and she would wipe the floor with her."

The starting date grew closer, and the usual tensions and egos of Hollywood filmmaking continued to surface. Swanson was miffed at having to do a screen test, but she was reassured that it wasn't really to test *her* but rather her makeup. Told by Brackett that she might need to be artificially aged for the role, Swanson countered by asking, "Can't you put the makeup on Mr. Holden instead, to make him look younger?" They did, though they also added subtle touches of gray to Swanson's hair and a few extra wrinkles on her fifty-two-year-old face. For his part, Holden's worries escalated. He told Wilder nervously that he didn't know who Gillis (now Joe, not Dick) really was—he couldn't get a fix on the character. "Do you know Bill Holden?" Billy asked. "Of course," said Holden. "Then you know Joe Gillis."

Paramount's location scouts were busily finding excellent examples of the way Hollywood's citizens variously lived. The Alto-Nido Apartments, at 1851 North Ivar at the top of the hill at Franklin, would work well for the drab barracks of an unemployed screenwriter. For Norma Desmond's mansion, they had to look farther afield than the 10,000 block of Sunset Boulevard, on which the fictitious house is situated in the script. They found it, about six miles away, at the northwest corner of Wilshire and Irving Boulevards. The immense heap of a house, built in 1924 for the then-astronomical figure of $250,000, currently belonged to J. Paul Getty's ex-wife, who hadn't lived there for several years. More ghostly than derelict, the building itself fit the filmmakers' description superbly, as did the vaguely seedy-looking yard and garage:

I had landed myself in the driveway of some big mansion that looked rundown and deserted. At the end of the drive was a lovely sight indeed—a great big empty garage, just standing there going to waste. . . . It was a great big white elephant of a place. The kind crazy movie people built in the crazy twenties. A neglected house gets an unhappy look. This one had it in spades. It was like that old woman in *Great Expectations*—that Miss Havisham in her rotting wedding dress and her torn veil, taking it out on the world because she'd been given the go-by.

There was no pool, so Paramount built one. (The ex-Mrs. Getty was said to be thrilled to get a free swimming pool, but the pool the studio built had next to no plumbing and was never used for swimming once filming was completed.) Paramount also sweetened the mansion's interior by adding stained glass windows to the front hall, heavy draperies and a pipe organ in the living room, and palm trees in the conservatory.

The script was undergoing modifications as well. For the morgue scene they gave a drowned boy's corpse a grim little joke: "I drowned. Right off the pier at Ocean Park. I bet Pinky Evans I could stay under water longer than two minutes, and I did, too." Gillis was now skirting obscenity in a line to Kaufman, the producer: "You trying to be funny? Because I'm all out of laughs. I'm up that creek and I need a job." Max was given a limp. Gillis comments on it in his room over the garage: "I figured he was a little crazy. Maybe it was that stroke—he'd had a stroke a while back—part of his brain was limping too. Come to think of it, the whole place was like that—half paralyzed—withering away in slow motion." Finally, the producer Kaufman became Sheldrake, and he was given a new clincher at the end of his speech about his many debts and financial obligations: "Now if Dewey had been elected," Sheldrake begins, whereupon Gillis leaves the office in disgust.

The PCA was unusually restrained in its response to the script drafts Paramount submitted. The "up that creek" line had to be cut—that was one of Breen's few specific demands. A larger issue remained, but it was one over which the PCA had little direct control, namely the "sex affair" between Gillis and Norma. "It seems to us at this point that there is no indication of a voice for morality by which the sex affair would be condemned, nor does there appear to be compensating moral values for the sin." The protagonist's grim end made no difference to the PCA: "We are quite aware that the story is told in flashback and the leading man is shown to be dead when the story opens."

Costuming Gloria Swanson for the role of Norma Desmond presented designer Edith Head with a tricky set of problems. Here was a woman who was a throwback to a bygone era, but she was a very rich, very stylish throwback who could buy whatever she wanted in the best stores in Beverly Hills. Moreover, Norma had to remain blissfully unaware that she *was* a throwback. Thus her clothes had to be both in style and out-of-date, all at once. Head's ingenious solution was to combine Jazz Age materials with so-called New Look styling. (Dior brought out the New Look in 1947, and it dominated women's fashions through much of the 1950s: an hourglass form and tightly cinched waists that created a kind of rigid femininity that postwar culture found attractive.) She employed current fashion trends but added the odd element here and there—for instance, a 1949 hat trimmed in peacock feathers. For the film's final scene, though, Head abandoned the New Look entirely in favor of a barely defined waistline; when Norma is ready for her last close-up she looks just that much more out of time. Ironically, Head was already familiar with Gloria Swanson from her earliest days at Paramount. As a young costumer's assistant she used to wash Swanson's hosiery.

On March 26, 1949, shooting began at dawn with preproduction shots of the L.A. County morgue and its exterior courtyard; they were filmed at the Hall of Justice itself. Preproduction shooting continued through April 16, with shots of the Sunset Strip, the Alto-Nido exteriors, and various other locations around Hollywood and Beverly Hills. The script was still incomplete when the production of *Sunset Boulevard* officially opened on April 18. Wilder began that morning by shooting scenes of Gillis in the apartment, which had been constructed on the lot. Von Stroheim was called to Soundstage 9 in the afternoon to film the scene in which Max welcomes Gillis into the Desmond mansion, and Swanson appeared the following day to film various shots of Norma in her bedroom.

"Johnny," Billy told cinematographer John Seitz, "keep it out of focus—I want to win the foreign picture award." For the scene in which Swanson lies in bed with her wrists slashed, Seitz asked Billy how he wanted to film it. "Johnny, it's the usual slashed-wrist shot." For the monkey scene, Seitz was told, "Johnny, it's the usual dead chimpanzee setup." For the New Year's Eve tango sequence, Seitz employed a dance dolly—a platform on wheels hooked onto the camera, which itself was mounted on a movable platform, thereby enabling Seitz to take a shot of Swanson and Holden making a smooth, vertiginous sweep of the room. It wasn't an innovation; Seitz first used the technique to shoot Rudolph Valentino and Alice Terry tangoing in *The Four Horsemen of the Apocalypse* (1921).

On April 21, the company was called to the mansion location at Wilshire and Irving for exterior shooting, but the quality of light deteriorated and Billy had to call off shooting early. Holden, Billy, and the crew spent the next day rushing from location to location: from Stone Canyon Road to the Bel-Air golf course, from North Vine Street (for Rudy's shoeshine parlor: "Rudy never asked any questions about your finances—he'd just look at your heels and know the score") to Paramount's ornate entrance gate—not the imposing main gate on Melrose, but the smaller, more beautiful one set back from the corner of Melrose and Bronson.

It is through the Bronson gate that Gillis walks on his way to see Sheldrake, the "smart producer." The scene is one to which Billy related, if not because of his recent past, then certainly because of his earliest days at Ufa and at Columbia, Fox, and Paramount itself. "All right, Gillis, you've got five minutes, what's your story about?" Sheldrake snaps. Wilder's camera

tracks back from Sheldrake distractedly lighting a cigar to Gillis hunched
forward in his chair, his hands waving around in a gesture that seems more
Billy than Holden:

> GILLIS: It's about a baseball player, a rookie shortstop that's batting
> .347. Poor kid was once mixed up in a holdup but he's tryin'a go
> straight, except that there are a bunch'a gamblers that won't let him!
> SHELDRAKE: *(bored)* So they tell the poor kid he's got to throw the
> World Series or else, huh?
> GILLIS: More or less, except for the end. I've got a gimmick that's *real*
> good.
> SHELDRAKE: You got a title?
> GILLIS: *Bases Loaded.* There's a forty-page outline. . . . They're pretty
> hot about it over at Twentieth, except I think Zanuck's all wet. Can
> you see Ty Power as a shortstop? You got the best man for it right
> here on this lot—Alan Ladd! Be a good change of pace for Ladd.
> And another thing—it's pretty simple to shoot. Lots'a outdoor stuff.
> You could make the whole thing for under a million.

Sheldrake burps loudly from the bicarbonate he has been belting back
while Gillis goes on and on about Ladd and the outdoor stuff. Gillis pretends not to notice.

At this, Betty Schaefer enters and rips *Bases Loaded* to shreds. She
describes it with throwaway cruelty: "It's from hunger." Sheldrake then
comes up with a possibility:

> SHELDRAKE: Of course, we're always looking for a Betty Hutton. Do
> you see it as a Betty Hutton?
> GILLIS: Frankly, no.
> SHELDRAKE: Now wait a minute—if we made it a girls' softball team,
> put in a few numbers. . . . Might make a cute musical. "*It Happened
> in the Bull-Pen*—the story of a woman."
> GILLIS: Are you trying to be funny? Because I'm all out of laughs. I'm
> over a barrel. I need a job!

Gillis heads desperately to the pay phone at Schwab's. First he puts the
bite on his friend Artie Green, but Green can only offer $20. "Then I talked
to a couple of yes men at Metro. To me they said no. Finally I located that
agent of mine. The big faker. Was he out digging up a job for poor Joe
Gillis? Huh-uh. He was hard at work in Bel-Air, making with the golf
sticks." This is where the Bel-Air golf course location came in. On the
green, Gillis's agent does him a big favor:

AGENT: So you need three hundred dollars. Of course I could give you three hundred dollars. Only I'm not going to!

GILLIS: *(apprehensively)* No?

AGENT: Gillis, get this through your head. I'm not just your agent. It's not the ten percent! I'm your *friend*!

GILLIS: You are?

AGENT: Don't you know the finest things in the world are written on an empty stomach? Once a talent like yours gets in that Mocambo-Romanoff rut, you're through!

Gillis responds to this helpful suggestion by glaring at him and snarling "*I need three hundred dollars.*" He does so with much the same vocal tone and facial expression Don Birnam has when he holds up the liquor store for a bottle.

Location shooting continued for the next two weeks, all of which were taken up with filming sequences at the Desmond mansion, including, on May 3, the scene in which Norma invites a few old friends to her house to play a rubber or two of bridge. Gillis nicknames them "the waxworks," and they look and act accordingly. In one of the film's crueler touches, the waxworks are played by three old, washed-up movie stars: H. B. Warner, Anna Q. Nilsson, and the greatest silent comedian of all, Buster Keaton. According to Billy, Keaton was actually an excellent bridge player, no small compliment coming from Billy. He was also a severe alcoholic whose once-handsome face had turned puffy and sagging. Brackett and Wilder had approached another former star, William Haines, but Haines turned them down; he was content with his second career as one of Hollywood's most successful interior designers. "It's clean," he told Brackett and Wilder— "no mascara on the face."

The three silent screen stars who did agree to caricature themselves in *Sunset Boulevard* worked for precisely one day. Nilsson was called at 7:00 A.M., the others at 9:00 A.M. They performed diligently like the professionals they had once been, needing only two or three takes per setup. By 5:15 P.M. Wilder was done with them and they were has-beens again.

For his part, von Stroheim was happy to be back on a top-notch production after his forays into B-picture purgatory, and he came up with several of his own ideas about the relationship between Max von Mayerling and the woman he serves. It was von Stroheim's idea to have Max write all of Norma's fan letters. According to Wilder, von Stroheim also suggested a scene in which Max washed Norma's underwear, but Wilder nixed that one. One von Stroheim element Wilder did add was a piece of the ruined *Queen Kelly* itself. For $1,000 Paramount purchased 122 feet of its footage for Norma Desmond to project in her own living room as evidence of her greatness. She is luminous indeed, her face, in close-up, surrounded by bright candles that still fail to draw attention away from her. When Wilder reveals that Max von Mayerling is himself a ruined film director reduced to servitude, the joke that is Norma Desmond becomes all the more bitter. Wilder acknowledged that the idea to use the *Queen Kelly* footage was von Stroheim's.

The shooting of *Sunset Boulevard* continued smoothly through May. The important chase sequence—in which Gillis escapes from the repo men, blows a tire, and ends up by pure chance at Norma Desmond's house— was delayed by some bad weather and complicated traffic problems, but the production stayed more or less on schedule. Sidney Skolsky appeared at Schwab's according to plan on May 16. An even more recognizable Hollywood figure, hired for the sake of his name and reputation, showed up on May 23, when the scenes of Norma's return to the Paramount lot went before the cameras. Paramount's most famous director, Cecil B. DeMille, was going to play himself. "He was shooting *Samson and Delilah*," Billy remembered. "We used his sets when Norma visits. We had him for one day. Ten thousand dollars." The gossip around town was that DeMille had trouble doing his scene and required seven takes before he got it right. DeMille also demanded and received the right to change one of his lines. Originally, he was to have said to Norma, "I haven't seen you since Lindbergh landed in Paris and we danced on the nightclub table." DeMille refused to say it. "I never go to nightclubs," he declared. "And if I did, I wouldn't dance on a table, even if Lindbergh flew to Paris twice. And if I did dance, it would be with Mrs. DeMille." If Wilder had a problem with C.B., he didn't broadcast it; he told the press, "Mr. DeMille was too courteous to make suggestions, and I was too afraid."

Originally, Wilder wanted DeMille to ask Delilah (Hedy Lamarr) to get out of her chair so that he could give it to Norma Desmond. Lamarr, with whom Billy either had or hadn't had an affair (depending on whether one trusts Louella Parsons), agreed to do it—"for twenty-five thousand dollars," according to Billy. "I said that it would be enough for Norma to sit in a chair with Hedy Lamarr's name on it. That was ten thousand dollars. So I put her in DeMille's chair." It cost nothing to do so, since DeMille had already been well paid for his efforts. After filming DeMille's scenes, Wilder is said to have patted C.B. on the back and said, "Very good, my boy. Leave your name with my secretary. I may have a small part for you in my next picture."

As it turned out, Wilder hadn't finished dealing with DeMille about his appearance in *Sunset Boulevard*—and would not until the studio anted up a new black Cadillac limousine and a billing order revised in DeMille's favor. DeMille demanded and received not only higher listing in the credits, but also a crediting order in which his illustrious name did not appear immediately (and, to DeMille, insultingly) next to Franklyn Farnum's; Farnum played the monkey mortician.

In *Sunset Boulevard*, Joe Gillis learns to make a good living by endlessly rewriting Norma's ghastly *Salome*. He's a kept man who survives by smoothly humoring his patron, first by writing a part for her in a movie that will never be made, and then by making love to her. In each case he has to hold his nose a little to be able to go through with it.

But Gillis doesn't give up his own writing career. He meets Betty Schaefer (Nancy Olson), an attractive story editor, and launches a new script with her. They work together in the evenings and at night, once their day jobs have been put to bed. Billy worked a personal reference into the scene: "The night shot where Holden and Nancy Olson walk on the lot, she tells how she grew up there, at Paramount. How she wanted to be in movies. That's my wife's background we used. Audrey's mother worked in wardrobe. Aud grew up like that." (Audrey, meanwhile, was getting used to being married to Billy. One night during the production of *Sunset Boulevard* Billy woke up and told her, "Darling, it's late, and I have a hard day at the studio tomorrow. Would you be so kind as to take a cab home?" "You idiot," Audrey informed him—"we're married already.")

In an effort to get his actors to live their roles as fully as possible, Wilder actually scheduled the filming of Gillis's scenes with Betty in the late evening and well into the night. Holden, Olson, Billy, and the crew worked from 7:30 P.M. to 12:10 A.M., and after a break for supper, they continued filming the readers' office scenes until 4:30 in the morning. For the shot of Gillis and Betty kissing on the balcony of the Writers Building, Billy knew that Olson was feeling some discomfort at performing the scene in such a semipublic place, so he arranged only a brief rehearsal for them, after which they performed the kiss very well on the first take. "Cut! Print!" Billy yelled. But just to be on the safe side, he asked them to do it a second time. This time he didn't call cut. After an extended period of time, the crew began snickering. Finally, someone else yelled "Cut!" It was Mrs. Holden, who had appeared in the meantime and didn't find the joke very funny.

By the end of the first week of June, the need for retakes as well as generally slow progress brought the production five days behind schedule, a manageable delay. One problem was the weather; Los Angeles was plagued by unusually foggy days, so whenever a little sun came out they would drop what they were doing and film outdoor scenes. They weren't looking for the characteristically brilliant sun of Los Angeles, however—not for *Sunset Boulevard*. The film may have been set under the cruel sun of Hollywood, but both Wilder and Seitz preferred more gray than Southern California's sky tended to provide.

The grimly amusing morgue interiors were shot on June 10. The lead cadavers and all the extras were laid out on their metal slabs and covered with sheets from head to ankle; their feet stuck out. Filming went smoothly until a strange rumbling disturbed a take. Amid snickering from the crew, Wilder's assistant rushed down the rows of covered corpses until he found the one who was snoring.

Norma's descent down the staircase—equally funny, though in a more Grand-Guignol manner—was shot six days later. Finally, at 3:00 A.M. on June 19, *Sunset Boulevard* wrapped after Holden and von Stroheim completed their work at the Desmond mansion location.

Nobody believed the film was actually finished. The need for retakes, special-effects photography, pickups, and the filming of added scenes meant that the production would simply reopen the following week. Some of these scenes involved Max serving as Norma's chauffeur. The car had become an Isotta Fraschini, not a Hispano-Suiza. Von Stroheim was helpless. "Erich didn't know how to drive," Swanson later reported, "which humiliated him, but he acted the scene, and the action of driving, so completely that he was exhausted after each take, even though the car was being towed by ropes the whole while." Wilder was blunter, and probably more inventive as well: "He still crashed it into the Bronson gate." According to Swanson, she and von Stroheim suffered no tensions left over from their disastrous past. They were no longer close, of course, but they'd reconciled long before being cast in *Sunset Boulevard*.

Wilder had also come up with an idea for a spectacularly unnerving low-angle shot of Joe Gillis's dead body floating in the swimming pool, taken from underwater. The shot proved to be so central to Wilder's vision of the film, and so difficult to achieve, that several whole days in late June were spent solving the problem of how to do it. The script was quite clear: "we see blood flowing from chest wound," and in addition, the shot had to include a group of policemen and a photographer staring down at the body from the side of the pool. The photographer would be snapping pictures, so flashbulbs had to be popping behind Gillis's floating corpse.

Billy was insistent. "Baby," he said to John Meehan, the film's associate art director, "the shot I want is a fish's viewpoint." This rang a bell with Meehan. While waiting at the barbershop earlier that week, he had read a magazine article on the subject of the way fishermen look to the fish they are trying to catch. He returned to the barber's the following morning and frantically searched for the article, but he couldn't find it. He proceeded to the studio in defeat, but the germ of an idea had been planted. He got an aquarium, a mirror, and a few plastic dolls from the props department and performed some trial setups. At a certain angle, the objects in the water were as clear as the objects above the water.

There was a water tank on Soundstage 9. Holden was summoned, along with the men playing the police. With Holden in the pool and the other actors surrounding him looking down, the shot was actually taken from above the water, the camera pointing down toward a mirror on the floor of the tank. Behind the policemen was a large piece of sky-colored muslin. Holden was quite chilly by the time the shot was successfully filmed; the water couldn't be warmed for his comfort. The effect is spectacularly macabre. A dimly recognizable body floats slowly across the screen as the cops look down and flashbulbs fire. The audience is unnerved not only by the ghastliness of the corpse but also by the position we are asked to assume. At least Joe Gillis floats. We, on the other hand, have sunk to the bottom. There is no inconsistency between Wilder's refusal to film a shot looking down from a catwalk and his demand for "a fish's viewpoint." Wilder chooses his shots to express emotions—his own as well as his characters'. Looking down on his characters from an isolated perch isn't his style. Sinking to the bottom and staring up at them in disbelief is.

One more crucial scene needed to be reshot. On June 23, the cast and crew gathered at the stairway of the Desmond mansion, where Norma would prepare for the close-up of a lifetime. Wilder filmed the scene as he planned it; Norma came down the stairs not toward an actual close-up but toward a final fade-out. The production reopened one more time on the 25th for shots of rain and fog at the mansion location, after which *Sunset Boulevard*'s production closed again. The film's budget of $1,572,000 was still essentially on target.

Billy and Charlie weren't satisfied with some of the rushes. The tone was off; something was missing. More retakes were necessary. The scene in Norma's bedroom, in which Gillis assures the suicidal star that he loves her, was reshot on July 7. On July 9, Holden and Swanson reworked their first scene together—the one in which Norma leads Gillis toward a small dead body draped with a satin coverlet and set upon a kind of altar. Norma announces: "I put him on the massage table in front of the fire. He always liked fires—and poking at them with a stick. . . . I want the coffin to be white, and I want it specially lined with satin—white, or a deep pink . . . !" (at this moment Norma draws the coverlet back partway and a tiny, very hairy dead arm falls down.) ". . . maybe red! Bright flaming red—let's make it gay!" Wilder then tracks forward to the monkey's face.

Sunset Boulevard wrapped once more. August, September, and October were taken up by editing. By October 10, Sidney Skolsky was on the cutting room floor. Looking at the footage again and again, especially with a preview audience or two, Wilder concluded that other scenes weren't quite right either, and the production was forced to reopen yet again on October 20 for location shooting—in particular, the beginning of the film and the chase sequence. The corner of Sunset and Rexford, Billy's own block of North Beverly Drive, and a driveway on the actual 10,000 block of Sunset Boulevard—all were shot that day just after dawn with two identical sets of cops and reporters—one set proceeding on Rexford, the other turning into the driveway on Sunset.

More retakes of Gillis's body in the pool followed, along with interiors of the Desmond mansion and a revised scene with DeMille. "We required one more close-up," Wilder reports. "I asked him to come back and do it. He understood. It was the shot outside the stage where he says good-bye. He came back. For another ten thousand dollars." (Wilder is slightly mistaken on this point. Instead of $10,000, DeMille got his $6,600 Cadillac limo and an extra bonus of $3,000.) *Sunset Boulevard* wrapped once more.

Reviewing footage in November and December, Billy and Charlie decided that a certain scene *still* wasn't right. The tone was *still* off; the mood was wrong; it just didn't play well enough. They had to redo it. So on January 5, 1950, more than six months after it was supposed to have closed for good, the production of *Sunset Boulevard* reopened again. It would be the last time. The scene was Norma's. Gillis was dead, Norma having shot him in the back. (She explains her action by noting, "No one ever leaves a star. That's what makes one a star. The stars are ageless, aren't they?") The homicide squad has arrived at her mansion, along with Hedda Hopper. The butler, Max, Norma's former director, must convince her to come down the stairs, and he does so by telling the madwoman that she is filming her new movie's climactic scene. She descends the staircase.

Holden was long gone from the production; so were von Stroheim and Hedda Hopper. This would indeed be Norma Desmond's final scene, and she wouldn't have to share it with any of her costars. To start the day, Wilder ordered a total of nine different takes of the dialogue between the two homicide detectives, with slight changes from take to take. He then called for ten different takes of Norma's descent down the staircase, all accompanied by music, just as filmmakers used to do in the days of silent pictures. The music: the "Dance of the Seven Veils" from *Salome*, Richard Strauss's opera. ("Strauss for the rehearsal," Wilder said; "Then we got better than Strauss. Waxman!")

They tried various effects with Swanson. Take two, for instance, featured a wild, demented look on her face as she descended, after which she raised her arms at the foot of the steps. For take four she was asked to effect a relaxed, pleasant look and to raise her arms at the end. A pleasant look without the raised arms was the point of take six. The first six takes were in medium long shot, after which Wilder moved the camera farther away for the following four. The pleasant look and the wild look were each filmed again with alternating arm postures. Finally, on the last take of the day, Gloria Swanson as Norma Desmond descended the stairway from a long distance with a deranged look in her eyes and her arms raised in a bizarre, inimitable gesture—a mad, contorted dance, her hands waving invisible veils. She walked toward the camera, her image went briefly out of focus, Wilder yelled "Cut!" and the filming of *Sunset Boulevard* was truly completed.

With all of this reshooting, *Sunset Boulevard* was now about $180,000 over budget. But Paramount was not terribly concerned. *The Emperor Waltz* had been the exception, not the rule; Billy and Charlie had a good, solid financial track record. Their stars, too, were happy. Holden sent Wilder a special walking stick from Japan with a collapsible fishing rod tucked inside. Swanson gave no gift; she got one, though—a plaque with this inscription: "To proclaim that Gloria Swanson is the greatest star of them all and the idol of cast, staff, and crew of *Sunset Boulevard*."

In consultation with the front office, Brackett and Wilder had decided to preview the film somewhere other than Los Angeles. It was a matter of self-protection. "We didn't want Hollywood people to see the picture because it was about Hollywood," Wilder explained. So they took it to Evanston, Illinois, just north of Chicago. The lights went down and the film began. The camera rolled down Sunset Boulevard and into the morgue, the corpses started talking, and the audience erupted into peals of laughter. Wilder was shocked: "I just sat there for a few minutes, and then I left the theater. There were some steps leading down to the toilet. I sat there on the third step—that was one of the black moments of my life. And a lady came down the steps who had also left the theater. As she passed me, she said, 'Have you ever seen shit like this in your life?' And I said, 'Never.'"

They tried another preview—this time in Poughkeepsie: "Same goddamn reaction." The Great Neck, Long Island, preview began badly as well. "The public wasn't interested in the other cadavers," said Billy. "They wanted to hear Holden, and they found the atmosphere of the morgue depressing." Preview audiences weren't alone in their response. According to John Seitz, Barney Balaban, the head of the studio, also took a particular dislike to the opening morgue scene. Balaban, who had so steadfastly defended *The Lost Weekend* against the naysayers, was now asking that the scene be cut and that *Sunset Boulevard* be given a new opening.

Wilder was forced to agree. He cut the whole morgue scene out of the picture and filmed a new traveling camera shot of the Sunset Boulevard pavement (and a tilt up to the police cars) and a shot of the cops arriving at the Sunset driveway. Finally, he added a new voice-over narration by Joe Gillis. The last element, at least, preserved the film's crucial talking corpse setup, though the revision disguised the fact from the audience until the end, at which point they could appreciate the sour humor of it. Even if they didn't, at that point in the film it was too late for them to rebel.

The final element to be added to *Sunset Boulevard* was its musical score. The songwriting team of Jay Livingston and Ray Evans, fresh from receiving an Oscar for the song "Buttons and Bows" (from Paramount's *The Paleface*) had been hired to appear as themselves for Artie Green's New Year's Eve party; they led the guests in a good-natured sing-along rendition of none other than "Buttons and Bows." Wilder and Brackett also commissioned Livingston and Evans to write a new song especially for *Sunset Boulevard*—"The Paramount-Don't-Want-Me Blues." The song was cut.

For the film's score, Wilder turned to his old friend Franz Waxman. Since moving to Hollywood, Waxman had become one of the industry's most dependable and original composers. After writing the moody, eminently apt score for James Whale's *Bride of Frankenstein*, Waxman took over as the head of Universal's music department. In the late 1930s he moved over to MGM. He scored *Rebecca* for Hitchcock and Selznick, *Suspicion* for Hitchcock and RKO, and moved to Warner Bros. in 1943. In each case, Waxman's rich German Romanticism enhanced the dark psychology and unsettling emotional tension of the films. Inspired by Wagner, Strauss, and Korngold, Waxman's compositions were elegant, full, and slightly tortured. Even more than Miklós Rózsa, Franz Waxman was quite the man for the job of scoring *Sunset Boulevard*.

Even in the opening moments, as the movie-music historian Christopher Palmer points out, Waxman's nervous, percussive music suggests the tenor of the film in microcosm; one key note, "trilled, jabbed, and pecked out, heavily accented, syncopated, or merely repeated in fast notes" foretells Norma's obsessive lunacy. And Palmer notes, her own theme begins here as well, "as if incidentally, beneath the racket of roaring, screeching brass and motoric rhythms." For Gillis's theme, Waxman composed what Palmer calls "an aimless, nonchalantly syncopated melody—deliberately flat in tone, gray in color (it is usually given to the piano)," it reflects his "ingrained hopelessness." As a musical joke, Waxman took the familiar, ridiculously jumpy theme from old Paramount newsreels and slowed it down drastically to accompany Gillis and Betty Schaefer as they walk on the Paramount lot at night. For the climactic murder, a tango theme reappears (Waxman introduces it during Norma's distressed New Year's Eve celebration), but now it's "twisted and tortured." And for Norma's ghastly descent down the staircase, "a bevy of unseen trumpeters, as if in the far distance, sound a muted fanfare, always over the sustained trills." The tango reappears, along with a vague echo of Strauss's own *Tanz der sieben Schleier*," to sweep her "in an ecstasy of madness down the stairs. . . ."

No stars' names appear over the title of *Sunset Boulevard*, nor does Billy Wilder's, though such high billing for a director wasn't unheard of at Paramount. Cecil B. DeMille, William Wyler, and Frank Capra all demanded and received above-the-title billing, with their names printed at fully 75 percent of the size of the title itself. Brackett and Wilder were important enough to merit inclusion in the film's ad campaign, however. The studio's ads for *Song of Surrender* omitted the name of Mitchell Leisen, and the ads for *Copper Canyon* didn't mention John Farrow, but Paramount sold *Sunset Boulevard* specifically as a film "from Brackett and Wilder." This, Paramount reminded audiences, was the same team who had made the Oscar-winning *The Lost Weekend*.

Paramount launched *Sunset Boulevard* with a series of twenty-one private screenings for various taste-making leaders of the Hollywood community. Publicity chief Norman Siegel played the movie colony expertly by setting up a waiting list; only when the list reached seventy-five to a hundred names was a screening arranged. Almost everyone loved the film. At one of the particularly large screenings, most of the three hundred honchos in the audience burst into applause at the final fade-out. Barbara Stanwyck was so impressed that she reportedly knelt down and kissed the hem of Gloria Swanson's silver lamé gown.

But one member of the audience was not very happy with the film. Louis B. Mayer left the screening room in a rage. The other movie people may have loved watching Hollywood shoot itself in the back on-screen, but MGM's in-house emperor apparently took it personally. Storming out of the theater, Mayer is said to have shrieked at Wilder, "You bastard! You have disgraced the industry that made and fed you! You should be tarred and feathered and run out of Hollywood!" Mayer may also have employed phrases having to do with coming over to this country, biting hands that feed you, and horsewhipping, but there were no tape recorders present.

"Fuck you," said Billy.

Or: "Go shit in your hat."

Onlookers are said to have gasped. But however the crowd may have responded, Billy wasn't playing to them. He was speaking to L. B. Mayer. And he had a point. When Mayer attacked the creators of *Sunset Boulevard*, he did appear to be taking his ire out on the immigrant, not the native-born Republican. Charlie Brackett, still president of the Academy, appears to have escaped the incident unscathed.

As *Sunset Boulevard* neared its release, the trade papers issued their appraisals. *Variety* liked the movie well enough but found it disturbing. The *Motion Picture Herald* applauded as well. The *Hollywood Reporter*, on the other hand, was ecstatic: "That this completely original work is so marvelous, satisfying, dramatically perfect, and technically brilliant is no haphazard Hollywood miracle but the inevitable consequence of the collaboration of Charles Brackett and Billy Wilder. . . . You want to applaud *Sunset Boulevard* frame by frame." The *Reporter* mentioned admiringly that Paramount's publicity department had already been pushing Swanson and her performance "for months" before the film's opening. "Parts like this come once in a lifetime," the *Reporter* declared; "personalities like Gloria Swanson come once in a generation." This was an observation Paramount hoped the public would make as well. The studio sent Swanson on a national promotional tour. Swanson, only too glad to be back in the public eye after an almost unbroken sixteen-year absence, seized on the chance to shill for an industry that had once tossed her aside. For her efforts, Paramount paid her $1,000 per week as she gamely trooped around the nation on the dual mission of convincing the public that Hollywood was a healthy, thriving, trustworthy place and simultaneously promoting *Sunset Boulevard*, which still ranks as one of the nastiest and most derisive films about Hollywood ever made.

Sunset Boulevard's world premiere occurred in August at Radio City Music Hall, where the critic Andrew Sarris claims to have seen it at least twenty-five times during its run. The film was a hit, and Paramount was already banking on Academy Award nominations. The film's pressbook, written and printed before the film even opened, heralded it as a major Oscar contender. Indeed, when the nominations were announced in February 1951, *Sunset Boulevard* was named in eleven separate categories, including Best Picture and Best Director. Erich von Stroheim was nominated as Best Supporting Actor and responded angrily. He was too big for that category, he told the press, and he even threatened a lawsuit.

For Wilder and Brackett, the problem was much more clearly defined. Its name was *All About Eve*. Joseph Mankiewicz's highly polished backstage drama, starring Bette Davis, had featured more than its share of bitterness about show business, but it still wasn't as nasty as *Sunset Boulevard*. The two films seemed to have equal support among Academy members in the weeks between nominations and the ceremony itself, but when the Oscar for Best Picture was announced it was Mankiewicz who accepted it, not Billy. According to Billy, Mankiewicz, with his Oscar in his hand, then told Wilder that Wilder would certainly win the directing award, at which point Mankiewicz's name was called for that award and he scurried away from Billy's side to accept his second statuette. (Mankiewicz himself denied the incident, saying that it was just another one of Billy's fabrications.)

After the ceremony, the disappointed *Sunset Boulevard* partisans moved to the party Paramount arranged at the Mocambo on Sunset Strip. Holden, having lost the Best Actor award, was morose. Trying to cheer him up, Wilder told him, "It was a miscarriage of justice, Bill. You should have won tonight." At that point Holden's wife, Ardis, responded, "Oh, I don't think so. Jose Ferrer was much better than Bill." [Ferrer won for *Cyrano de Bergerac.*] The grim mood didn't stop Billy from providing an unprintably salty story to some reporters who happened to be hanging around looking for quotes. Billy greeted Barbara Stanwyck warmly at the party and proceeded to tell the reporters what Stanwyck said to an aging star who'd complained that her youthful lover was spending a hundred thousand dollars of her money on fast cars and slick outfits, all for himself. Billy claimed Stanwyck had said, "Tell me, darling, is the screwing you're getting worth the screwing you're getting?"

Billy and Audrey, meanwhile, were planning for the future. In late 1949, while *Sunset Boulevard* was still in production, they commissioned their friends Charles and Ray Eames to design a house for them for a hilltop property in Beverly Hills—on Sunset Boulevard, in fact. The design the Eameses produced was classically industrial—a 4,600-square-foot rectangle constructed in prefabricated steel and glass panels and surrounded by concrete. Filled with the sharp light of Southern California, the interior was to include a two-story living room, several dining areas, three bedrooms and bathrooms, a study, dressing areas, and a functional, easy-upkeep utility room. Boldly colored panels separated these areas from one another— sky blue upper walls in the living room, a bold red panel here, a sunny yellow one there. From the Sächsischen Palais in Berlin to the new house he planned to build in Beverly Hills, Billy never lost his taste for Bauhaus simplicity; the Eames commission was a natural step. The Wilders' house would have been as sleek, contemporary, and hard as its owners, providing great freedom of movement and a kind of steely grace. It was never built. Audrey talked Billy out of it on the grounds that it would require too much maintenance. "Are you crazy?" she said to Billy finally. "It's completely idiotic."

Billy and Audrey's marriage was thriving, but Billy and Charlie's was not. In the summer of 1949, before *Sunset Boulevard* had even finished shooting, Brackett and Wilder made a stunning announcement. They were splitting up.

The men themselves had actually decided to split up the previous autumn. They signed new contracts during the writing of *Sunset Boulevard*, and this time their contracts specified independence from each other, though their deals only became effective after the completion of *Sunset Boulevard.*

Wilder and Brackett each ascribed to an old-fashioned code of honor— the honor of gentlemen. They fought often while working together, but when they decided to split up they didn't air their old grievances. They parted responsibly if not entirely amicably and finished *Sunset Boulevard* in peace. This sense of courteous integrity remained in force for the rest of their lives. Neither ever stole credit from the other. Neither bit the other's back in public. When it became necessary for one to put himself on the line in defense of the other, he did. Brackett and Wilder had enjoyed a relatively acrimonious marriage, but their separation and divorce were as quiet and honorable as Hollywood could possibly have allowed.

In 1960, Brackett told *Time* simply that "Billy had outgrown his divided fame." But a few years later, when he was ailing, Brackett spoke in a little more detail about the breakup. He told the screenwriter-director-raconteur Garson Kanin that he didn't see it coming: "I never knew what happened, never understood it. We were doing so well. I always thought we brought out the best in each other, didn't you? But we met one morning, as we always did, and Billy smiled that sweet smile of his at me and said, 'You know, Charlie, after this I don't think we should work together anymore. I think it would be better for both of us if we just split up.' I could say nothing. It was shattering. And Billy—you know how he is, bright and volatile—got right into the business of the day, and we said no more about it. But it was such a blow, such an unexpected blow. I thought I'd never recover from it. And in fact I don't think I ever have."

For four years Brackett and Wilder had been bringing other writers in to keep their own joint creativity fresh; theirs was a monogamy that allowed other partners. Brackett thought the civilized way they'd worked out their relationship meant everything was fine, but he was mistaken. "It was just that I loved working with him," Brackett continued. "If he wanted to write alone and direct, I'd have been pleased to be his producer. Or even work together now and again. Maybe not every picture. But he was firm and didn't want to work with me again ever at all. I suppose it was foolish of me to think it was going to go on forever. After all, it wasn't a marriage."

Billy, who does appear to have engineered the split entirely on his own, has always been much more reticent on the subject. "It's like a box of matches," he once said. "You pick up the match and strike it against the box, and there's always fire, but then one day there is just one small corner of that abrasive paper left for you to strike the match on. It was not there anymore. The match wasn't striking." A more confessional moment occurred when Maurice Zolotow asked him to respond to what Brackett told Kanin. Billy turned, stared out the window, and said nothing at all.

PART FOUR

1951–1956

18. ACE IN THE HOLE

How'd you like to make yourself a thousand dollars a day, Mr. Boot? I'm a thousand-dollar-a-day newspaperman. You can have me for nothing.
      —Chuck Tatum (Kirk Douglas), immediately before
      dropping dead in *Ace in the Hole*

The breakup of Hollywood's best-known, highest-earning screenwriting team was hot, uncomfortable news, and Paramount's flacks were under pressure to explain it nicely. Generally, couples divorce when times are tough, but Brackett and Wilder broke up during a smooth production. The team's very success was in fact the seed of the explanation Paramount devised. Brackett and Wilder were so successful, the PR department announced, that the studio could no longer afford to keep them together: "Paramount feels their combined salaries of $400,000 a year are too exorbitant to check up against one super film annually. That's why they're on their own in the future." It was true enough as far as it went. It just didn't go very far.

At first, being "on their own" meant that they would each be working separately for Paramount, but by the end of October 1950, Brackett was even more on his own than Billy. He quit the studio angrily after an absurd, last-straw encounter with the head of production, Sam Briskin. Trouble had been brewing for months beforehand. Briskin insisted that Brackett produce at least two films every year, and Brackett, accustomed to producing only one film and producing it well, steadfastly declined. When Briskin berated Charlie for taking a two-day trip to New York to speak at a meeting of the Motion Picture Advertisers' Association, Brackett decided he'd had enough. He asked to be released from his contract, and Paramount was happy to oblige. "I am not in the habit of giving anyone an accounting of my comings and goings," Brackett sniffed, after which he swiftly signed a lucrative new deal with Darryl Zanuck at Twentieth Century–Fox.

The solidity of Brackett and Wilder's long-standing bond heightened the tension of their separation; Billy was now a free-firing cannonball without the weight of the cannon to guide him, while Brackett was left with his affable dependability without Billy's insatiable energy to spark him. And yet both succeeded very well on their own. In 1951, along with Richard Breen and Walter Reisch, Brackett went on to write *The Model and the Marriage Broker* for George Cukor and *The Mating Season* for none other than Billy's old scourge Mitchell Leisen. His script for Fox's 1953 *Titanic*—also with Breen and Reisch—won him an Oscar from the Academy over which he continued to preside, and the threesome followed up their triumph with *Niagara* (1953), a tight thriller starring Marilyn Monroe. After *Niagara* Brackett produced a string of films written by others: *Woman's World, Garden of Evil, The Virgin Queen, The King and I*. . . . And he kept writing with Reisch, apparently needing the ongoing verbal exchange with another loudmouthed Jew from Vienna; together they wrote *Journey to the Center of the Earth* (1959). He married his deceased wife's sister in 1953 and stayed at the top of the Bel-Air social scene until his death in 1969.

Brackett and Wilder found themselves back together again in October 1951, though not by choice. They were sued—jointly—for plagiarizing *Sunset Boulevard*. Stephanie Joan Carlson, a former member of the accounting department at Paramount, alleged that between 1943 and 1947 she had written a series of stories about the studio—stories, she claimed, that bore too close a resemblance to *Sunset Boulevard*. Some of these tales were fictional, while others were based on a mix of known fact and studio lore. In 1947, Carlson charged, she submitted some of these stories in manuscript form to two of the studio's writers—Brackett and Wilder. One story was called "Past Performance." *Sunset Boulevard*, she insisted, was the result of this material.

According to Carlson, Brackett and Wilder specifically asked her to give them a copy of her manuscript, and—again according to Carlson—they kept it for several weeks before returning it to her. There seems to have been no more contact between Carlson, Brackett, and Wilder. But after seeing *Sunset Boulevard*—or more pointedly, after seeing that *Sunset Boulevard* was a hit—Carlson came to believe that she had a right to some of the proceeds. She asked the court for $100,000 in general damages, $250,000 in exemplary damages, and an additional $700,000 based on the box office returns; $350,000 was thrown in for good measure, bringing the total of Carlson's claims against Brackett, Wilder, and Paramount to $1,400,000.

Hollywood plagiarism suits became commonplace in the 1970s and have remained so. In the 1950s, however, they were relatively rare, and they received little press attention. Carlson's suit, which went unreported at the time, was eventually dismissed, though in the characteristically supine fashion of American justice it took another two and a half years before the matter was officially settled. (A second, completely nonsensical suit over *Sunset Boulevard* was filed in 1954 by a frustrated playwright, Edra Buckler, who claimed that Paramount had actually swiped *her* material; Miss Buckler's suit was thrown out the following year.) Carlson's allegations seem outlandish in retrospect. While there is no doubt that Billy and Charlie needed a third writer to pull their script together, they scarcely required the additional assistance of an accountant in the writing of *Sunset Boulevard*.

Billy began preparing his first solo film in October 1949, before *Sunset Boulevard* even finished shooting. This meant, of course, that he was breaking in a new screenwriting partner before the old one was out the door. There must have been a certain awkwardness in the office. Then again, the new collaboration was of a rather different nature. Wilder was now the sole executive writer; his new partner—if one can even call him a partner—was more like a draftsman. Twenty-year-old Walter Newman, a radio writer, suggested a script idea to Billy, and Billy took it. It was about a cave, an accident, and a cynical newspaper reporter. The more Wilder thought about it, the more he liked the premise. He'd met Newman after hearing one of his dramas on the car radio. (Newman, shocked that the famous director wanted to meet him, remembered two things about their first meeting: Billy's incessant pacing and the black velour Tyrolean hat he wore and never took off.) First they kicked around a few of Billy's wackier ideas: a gangster who can't stop crying sees a shrink, then plots to kill him because he knows too much; and a comedy for Charles Laughton—an impoverished British nobleman keeps up appearances thanks to his secret identity as a TV studio wrestler. Laughton is said to have loved the idea of playing the "Masked Marvel" to the point of being reduced to helpless hysterics, but Wilder and Newman couldn't flesh out the idea. Then Newman suggested the cave accident story.

It was an idea close to Billy's heart: a fiercely ambitious newspaper reporter stuck in the middle of nowhere pulls a scam and ends up stewing, then dying, in his own self-contempt. *Ace in the Hole* would not be relieved by light comedy. It would, instead, reveal American culture as the shithole Wilder saw it to be. And thanks to his own authority as the nation's most successful writer-director, Billy would finally be able to shove Americans' faces right into it. Newman was soon charged with laying out a basic story line and developing characters under Billy's supervision while Billy himself finished up with *Sunset Boulevard*. Gone were the days of cribbage and flying telephone books. In their place was a less intimate, more corporate kind of composition. Newman began punching the clock on *Ace in the Hole* at the end of November.

Free from the burden of writing and producing films with the cultivated president of the Academy, Wilder jumped at the chance to make a truly mean movie. The first story he told entirely on his own would be an unrelievedly sour immorality play about two men who are buried alive—one physically, when an Indian cliff dwelling falls in on him as he attempts to steal artifacts from a burial site, the other morally, when his insatiable ambition and self-contempt close in and crush him. The naive victim lies trapped in a dank pit that threatens to engulf him completely; the cynical reporter, aided by the victim's sleazy wife, parlays the disaster to his own advantage and winds up dead himself. *Ace in the Hole* would be Billy's most closely conceived and personally expressive film to date. He drew the title of the film (as yet unannounced) from a poker hand. "I don't like the looks of it, Chuck," the reporter's young assistant remarks soon after discovering a life-threatening catastrophe. "I don't either, fan," Chuck says with a grin, "but I like the odds."

Loosely based on both a 1920s cave-in accident and an even more heart-tugging, paper-selling tragedy in 1949, *Ace in the Hole* bears a passing resemblance to history, but its merciless slant is Wilder's own. In 1925, Floyd Collins, the owner of the Crystal Cave in central Kentucky, was trapped inside after a landslide. Due to the *Louisville Courier-Journal* reporter who helped command the rescue operation, covering the story all the while, Floyd's misfortune was America's entertainment. The story gripped the nation for several weeks before (and immediately after) Collins died in the cave. Roaring Twenties readers never tired of the ghastly details, especially when certain oddities began to sweeten the story. One of the supposed rescuers lied about having reached Collins with food; items meant for Collins were found tucked into niches in the cave wall. A man claiming to be Floyd Collins turned up in Kansas one week into the rescue operation. (He was not Collins.) Finally, Floyd's brother Homer, who doggedly and heroically attempted to aid his brother during the crisis, announced upon Floyd's death that he was putting a road show together to tell his own version of the tragedy for anyone willing to buy a ticket.

The tragedy of Kathy Fiscus, both sadder and more farcical, was more influential on *Ace in the Hole*. In April 1949, in the Los Angeles suburb of San Marino (just south of Pasadena), a three-year-old girl fell into an abandoned well and launched a media sensation. Her mother, summoned by the girl's frightened friends, rushed to the well and spoke with her terrified daughter. An hour later a rescue operation was well under way, and before too long several thousand people showed up to watch the excitement unfold. Rescue efforts continued for the next few days as workers attempted to dig a parallel shaft to reach the child. Cave-ins and seeping water delayed the operation, which included klieg lights donated by Hollywood studios, power drills, earth movers, and a host of engineers, miners, and cesspool experts. Jockeys from the Santa Anita racetrack showed up and volunteered to be lowered into the well. Johnny, the Philip Morris cigarette midget, appeared, too, as did an earnest contingent of dwarf clowns from the Cole Bros. Circus. When the rescuers finally reached her, Kathy Fiscus was dead, and the disappointed crowds dispersed.

As hard-hitting as Wilder's realism may be, *Ace in the Hole* is not a docudrama. The carnival that sprouts around Wilder's cave-in disaster certainly found its inspiration in Johnny and the other volunteer midgets who crowded around Kathy Fiscus's well, but they, at least, had an authentic purpose in rushing to the scene, however bizarre and useless their presence may have been. In Wilder's vision, the true grotesques are neither the selfish reporter who covers the story nor even the victim's trashy wife but the thousands of heartless dopes who turn a man's suffering into a tourist curiosity, not to mention the millions of faceless readers who derive the same degree of safe, vicarious fun from their living rooms—and movie theaters. Wilder's future collaborator I. A. L. Diamond, asked in 1960 about whether or not *Ace in the Hole* was a cynical film, stated the case simply: "Sure, they called it cynical. And then you see thousands and thousands of people turning up at Idlewild airport in New York to watch a plane coming down with bad landing gear. People clog the runway waiting for it to crash—and you ask yourself how cynical *Ace in the Hole* really was."

In the beginning of March 1950, Newman submitted a treatment called "The Human Interest Story." In the opening sequence, on-the-skids reporter Charlie Tatum drives from his dreary, dull newspaper office in Albuquerque to a remote gas station near a cliff dwelling in the desert. Tatum, once a successful journalist back East until "a libel suit tossed him out of his job," has been a small-time failure ever since—all the way to Albuquerque. He stops at a filling station but is told that there's no gas available on account of an accident. Tatum thinks nothing of it and drives away, then smells a whiff of a story, wheels the car around, and heads back to investigate and exploit.

"The Human Interest Story" is credited to Newman alone, but a second assistant writer had already signed on to the project the week before he turned in his treatment. Lesser Samuels, a chubby, cigar-smoking former playwright, began working with Newman at the end of February. Samuels offered the following observation immediately after finishing work on *Ace in the Hole*: "The dramatist who sets out to write on a social theme should not get angry. He should keep his own temper while driving his audience to anger. . . . In *Ace in the Hole* we indict morbidity and lust for others, but we try to do it so subtly that the onlooker will both laugh at and deride some of our characters before slowly realizing he is, perhaps, pointing the finger of scorn at himself." Samuels may have thought he was indicting morbidity and lust. Wilder himself balances the indictment by reveling in them.

As with *Sunset Boulevard*, Wilder imposed a code of strict confidentiality on his *Ace in the Hole* team. "Do not give out under any circumstances—to anyone!!" reads a handwritten notation stapled to the partial first draft, dated May 3 1, 1950. Secrecy was not the only similarity between *Ace in the Hole* and *Sunset Boulevard*. Billy saw fit to begin yet another film with a talking cadaver.

In a busy western train station, "we see a baggage truck being wheeled down the platform, on it a pine box containing a coffin. Behind it walk two men"—Mr. Boot, a newspaper publisher, and Herbie, a young photographer. "The coffin reaches the baggage car. A couple of baggage men deftly and unceremoniously lift it onto the train." Chuck Tatum, whose body is now cargo, speaks in voice-over: "Good-bye, Mr. Boot. So long, Herbie. Thanks for seeing me off. I always wanted to go back. Only I never figured on the baggage car. There's one more thing I want you to do for me. When you write the obituary—lay it on the line! All you got on me! What I wanted and how bad I wanted it—put that in! What I did to get it—that goes in too! Friendship—pity—conscience—don't let any of those things stop you! I never let them stop me! Not me! Not Chuck Tatum! Not since the very first day I hit this God-forsaken town of yours, remember. . . ." A dissolve flashes back to Tatum's arrival in Albuquerque in a convertible with a New York license plate.

With the catastrophic previews of *Sunset Boulevard* still ringing in recent memory, Billy Wilder's insistence on repeating the talking corpse conceit in his very next film seems all the more compulsive. The fact that audiences and executives detested the device made no difference. Billy had to repeat it. He may not even have believed he would film the sequence, but the lavish, macabre irony of a man describing the circumstances of his own death was something he had to get out of his system, if only in a first draft. A voice inside him demanded to speak—a dead voice. Tatum's postmortem narration is, if anything, even more bitter and self-incriminating than *Sunset Boulevard*'s. Joe Gillis regards his death with bemused distance; Chuck Tatum not only despises himself but sees the need to proclaim it to the world.

By this point, Billy had already cast his surrogate. Chuck Tatum, the fiercely self-centered, ambitious, wisecracking writer, would be played by a muscular heartthrob—a Jewish one at that. By 1950, Issur Danielovitch had changed his name twice—first to Isidore Demsky, then to Kirk Douglas. A wrestler turned actor, Douglas appeared on Broadway in the early- and mid-1940s, then moved to Hollywood and, with his dynamic on-screen physicality (not to mention his notorious offscreen ballsiness), Douglas soon made a name for himself in the movies. *Champion* (1949), Stanley Kramer's tough boxing drama, turned him into a star. By 1951, Douglas was a very hot property in Hollywood, and Warner Bros., to which Douglas was contracted, did not make it especially easy for him to appear in *Ace in the Hole*. Only after a protracted series of angry, threatening letters between Warner's lawyers and the star's own was Douglas officially free to take the role. He earned $150,000 for his appearance.

Douglas was set to play opposite Jan Sterling, a well-educated, talented New Yorker with a face she could turn cheap-looking with a well-timed sneer. Trained in dramatic arts in London, Sterling tended to play scum; one of her recent roles was that of the jailbird "Smoochie" in the women's prison spectacle *Caged* (1950). *Ace in the Hole* "was the first really good part I'd had," Sterling says. "It was really just a question of meeting him. I didn't even read for it. He said he only had fifty pages of the script, so we might as well all go down to Arizona and get it together." She was paid $11,750.

By mid-June, Newman, Samuels, and Wilder had developed their screenplay to the point at which Tatum, having turned Leo Minosa's burial into the hottest story in the country, gets his old New York job back at $1,000 a week. (*Ace in the Hole* no longer began with a voice from beyond the grave.) A so-called final script was ready in early July, but an important new scene turned up two weeks later—a crucial scene between Tatum and Leo's wife, Lorraine (Sterling). With Leo safely trapped under a fallen beam in the deserted cave, Tatum and Lorraine plot to keep him there as long as possible, but the contemptible Lorraine is so miserably cheap that she continually needs to have the scheme spelled out for her:

"Look," says Tatum, after motioning her away from a crowd of people outside the trading post. "They're having a rosary at that little church this evening. I want you to be there." "I don't go to church," she explains. "Kneeling bags my nylons."

Under the force of Chuck's persuasion (which includes a slap in the face) as well as her own greed, Lorraine agrees to become religious—"But only because you wrote me up so pretty in today's paper. You can sure make with the words—'a figure of fair-haired loveliness in the lengthening shadows of the cursed mountain.'" "Don't kid yourself," Tatum responds. "Tomorrow this'll be yesterday's paper and they'll wrap a fish in it."

As Tatum turns to leave, Lorraine looks at him and adds a sweet kicker to the scene: "And another thing, Mister. Don't ever slap me again. I may get to like it."

As Wilder, Newman, and Samuels polished the script, the star offered the writer-director some advice—just a few things he'd like to see changed. Douglas wrote to Billy on June 19, expressing his enthusiasm for the project and saying how much he loved what he'd read so far, but, he added, he did think the whole scene from the bottom of page 7 to page 10 wasn't up to par. Tatum, Douglas wrote, shouldn't be so hard-edged. He had, after all, been working in Albuquerque for a full year at that point, and he really should have a better relationship with his coworkers—especially Herbie (Robert Arthur), the baby-faced young photographer who idolizes him. Douglas had no way of knowing it, but Herbie, the direct descendant of Eddie Polo's apprentice in *Der Teufelsreporter*, was another of Billy's alter egos—the boyish, impressionable lamb Wilder would never allow himself to be. Douglas, unaware of his director's unconscious quirks, complained that Herbie's relationship with Tatum was too one-sided, and he suggested that Billy add at least a new line to the effect that Tatum planned to take Herbie with him when he returned to the limelight in New York.

There was one more thing: "What the hell is Yogi Berra?" Douglas demanded to know. "I asked several people who don't know, and now I must admit that my secretary, who is taking this down, is amused that I don't know. She says that he's a catcher." Douglas closed his letter with a heartfelt plea: "For God's sake, Billy, please understand that I am not becoming one of those typical actors who is trying to write a screenplay."

Wilder did end up suggesting more of a bond between Tatum and Herbie, but it may well have evolved on its own without Douglas's input. In Wilder's films even the prickliest, most ruthless men tend to forge links with other men. For the most part, though, Billy insisted on keeping Chuck Tatum as hard as possible. Kirk Douglas may have been tough, but Billy Wilder was tougher. "Give it both knees," Billy told the former wrestler— "right from the beginning."

Makeup and wardrobe tests commenced on June 28 in preparation for a July 10 start date on location in Albuquerque, the sleepy southwestern city to which Tatum has been exiled. (Regarding the town's newspaper with dismissive contempt, Tatum tells its publisher, "Even for Albuquerque this is pretty Albuquerque.") The script, of course, wasn't truly finished as late as July 6. It still required Code approval, but by 1951 the censoring office was starting to lose its clout, a fact evidenced by Joseph Breen's unusually mealymouthed response: he thought there should be "a proper voice for morality" at the end. He also didn't like the word "lousy" on page 3.

Ace in the Hole went into production with a budget of $1,538,000, of which Billy's fee alone was $250,000. This figure covered Wilder's services not only as a writer and director but also as a producer: it was his first real one-man show. As the film's executive writer, Wilder paid Samuels out of his own pocket, whereas Newman's fee appears to have been covered at least in part by Paramount. The film required several vast crowd scenes, and the preliminary budget reflected the need for as many as 550 extras in the desert. So $150,000 was budgeted for location shooting, including the replication of Escadero, New Mexico—an ancient cliff dwelling, a dusty trading post, and eventually an enormous carnival.

Production of *Ace in the Hole* began on July 10 with the filming of Albuquerque street scenes. The opening sequence of the film nails Chuck Tatum's personality—Billy's, too. In the film's first shot the camera stares morosely at the ground. But after the credits finish rolling, Wilder cuts away from his dejection to a visual joke told in a single tracking shot—an auto repair truck heads left across the screen, the camera moving alongside the truck and then panning to the right to reveal a jacked-up car on the rear of the truck and a man in the car with his hat thrown back on his head reading a newspaper from the driver's seat. Chuck Tatum is a man who turns adversity to his advantage. He may have broken down, but he's shrewd enough—and opportunistic enough—to turn a repair truck into his own personal chauffeur.

On the 11th, the company moved to a location outside Gallup, New Mexico, where Paramount's advance team had prepared the enormous cliff dwelling, parking lot, and trading post, with room to spare for a traveling circus. Working around cloudiness on the following days, Billy and his crew began shooting crowd scenes. The more they filmed the larger the crowd became. On the 14th, there were about a hundred adults and twenty children. On the 16th, over six hundred extras appeared. Billy knew what he was talking about when he wrote the film: he correctly argued that Paramount didn't need to recruit all the extras they needed because gawkers would turn up on their own. Wilder and his cinematographer, Charles Lang, managed to organize this transient army and shoot some footage before a cloudburst ended the day's work early.

The term "media circus" was not yet in use when Billy presciently devised and shot the carnival that springs up around Leo Minosa's living hell. An entire day was set aside purely for rehearsal; the circus was filmed on Saturday the 22nd on what Paramount's public relations team claimed was the largest noncombat set ever constructed. The set—235 feet high, 1,200 feet across, and 1,600 feet deep—included the cliff, roadside stands, a parking lot for 500 cars, and kiddie rides and booths and concession stands and musicians. Over a thousand extras showed up that day along with 417 rented cars.

Wilder scheduled a helicopter shot for the following day, when only seven hundred or so extras turned up; they stood by patiently watching as the shot was lined up just in time for clouds to roll in. Clouds and rain prevented shooting for several more days; at some point the company is said to have discovered that meteorologists were conducting high-altitude rain-making experiments directly over the location. The aerial shot was finally filmed on the 25th, just before a real storm hit.

The company moved back and forth between the cliff dwelling location and a church at Old Laguna, finishing up midmorning on August 2, after which everyone returned to the safe, dry, controllable comfort of Soundstages 1, 2, and 5 on the Paramount lot in Hollywood. The production was five days behind schedule.

Wilder complements his attack on journalism in *Ace in the Hole* with a healthy stab at politicians: the manipulative Tatum is in cahoots with the corrupt local sheriff. As this subplot developed, the Code's Joseph Breen was decreasingly pleased with the wider social implications of presenting a corrupt law enforcement officer on American movie screens. In early August, he wrote to Paramount to express his concern over Sheriff Kretzer (Ray Teal), "who, we believe, breezes out of the story a little too easily, considering the malice of his misdeeds throughout the body of the story. It is our understanding that some slight additional dialogue will be developed which will make it clear that Kretzer will be answerable for his evil in the near future." In the release print, Tatum makes a sarcastic remark about helping to reelect the sheriff, suggesting that he and Herbie are going to write some sort of redemptive exposé, but fortunately for the amoral thrust of the film he manages to die before making good on his promise.

Having been shooting *Ace in the Hole* for two months, Billy was finally ready to complete the script on September 5. The production wrapped on the 11th, after Billy made sure to consult a physician for advice about the exact way in which a man lying immobile and partly crushed in a clammy, filthy cave would die. It was a morbid shoot in other ways as well. When filming Tatum's cruelest scene with Lorraine, Douglas got a little carried away. Toward the end of the film, Leo, slipping into the mild delirium of dying, tells Chuck that he has bought Lorraine an anniversary gift—a ratty furpiece that he has secreted away in a duffel bag in the closet—and he asks Chuck to make sure that she gets it. Tatum complies. Lorraine is not impressed. "Gorgeous, isn't it?" she comments, holding the shabby thing firmly away from her so as not to get too close to it. "He must'a skinned a couple a' hungry rats."

Turning to Chuck, she purrs, "You wouldn't want me to wear a thing like this," then throws the unpleasant string of pelts on the floor. Tatum picks it up and forces her to wear it. Then he chokes her with it.

With the camera looming over Tatum's shoulder as he tightens the fur around Lorraine's neck, Wilder bears down on her as she gasps for breath, then he cuts on action as she stabs Tatum with a pair of scissors. He wants us not only to see her look of terrified helplessness turn to vengeful rage but also to experience as fully as possible Tatum's look of shock as she shoves the scissors into him. For the over-the-shoulder shot, Douglas fell a little too deeply into his role as he yanked the mangy fur around Sterling's windpipe. When the take was completed the actress fell backward, desperately gasping for breath. Douglas was horrified. "Good God, Jan! If I was squeezing you too hard, why didn't you tell me?!" "I couldn't," she rasped. "You were choking me."

Ace in the Hole is one of Billy Wilder's two most personal films. He wrote, produced, and directed it with less interference than he had ever been cursed to receive before. It is about a fast-talking smart-ass who despises the world he lives in and plies all the seediness and corruption he encounters to his own advantage, knowing that the millions of idiots whose attention he craves will follow his entertaining stories wherever he leads them. Chuck Tatum is a sexual man who aches for and loathes women in equal measure. Indeed, those aspects of women he most detests are those to which he finds himself most attracted. Like Billy himself, Tatum delights in his own offensiveness, playing it for entertaining kicks even if the only person being entertained is Tatum (or Billy, or Billy's many fans). When he arrives in Albuquerque, he gets out of his towed car and walks toward the front door of the *Albuquerque Sun-Bulletin*. The sidewalks are full of Indians—women in traditional tribal dresses, men in jeans and tall felt hats. As he enters the office, the first word out of his mouth is supremely insulting. It's also funny, in a mean, smart-alecky sort of way: "How," he says to the Native American clipping newspaper articles at a desk. ("Good afternoon sir," the man answers.) Later, after Wilder dissolves from a shot of Tatum walking directly into the camera to a shot of him walking away, thereby advancing time a full year without shifting the camera an inch, Tatum is still pacing the office, bored and contemptuous of his circumstances and everyone else around him. The Indian assistant brings him his lunch. "Thanks, Geronimo," says Tatum, not having changed a bit over the course of the intervening year in the heart of the American Southwest.

In his first scene in the office, Tatum spies a middle-aged woman sitting at a desk under a needlepoint wall-hanging. TELL THE TRUTH it reads. He moves toward it, and Wilder pulls his camera in a little closer. "Who said it?" asks Chuck, smartly. "Mr. Boot said it," she says, "but I did the needlework." Tatum gives her a nasty reply delivered in such an unctuous tone that she can't tell whether he's flattering her or ripping her heart out: "I wish I could coin 'em like that. If I ever do, will you embroider it for me?"

Herbie gets a very different treatment. In his first scene with the youth, Tatum tries to get in to see Mr. Boot, Herbie's boss. The seasoned pro and the callow apprentice engage in what is really a type of desexualized meet-cute dialogue, sizing each other up verbally as well as visually. Tatum is tough and aggressive, but the handsome kid doesn't blink. In fact, the two men look each other directly in the eye until Herbie ends the scene by saying to Tatum with an imperceptible nod of approval, "Cagey, huh?" Then he leaves, giving Tatum the chance to whip out a cigarette and strike his match by letting the carriage of Herbie's typewriter slide across it, making the classic "ding" at the end of the stroke for punctuation. It's a gimmick Chuck Tatum performs for nobody's entertainment but his own.

His insults are masterpieces. "Apparently you're not familiar with my name," he says to the man he's desperate to work for. "That's because you don't get the eastern papers out here. I thought maybe once in a while somebody would toss one out of the Super Chief and you might have seen my byline." His self-deprecation is equally well stated: "You'll be glad to know that I've been fired from eleven papers with a total circulation of seven million, for reasons which I don't want to bore you." ("Go ahead, bore me," says Boot.) Boot asks him if he drinks a lot. "Not a lot," he answers—"just frequently."

"Mr. Boot," Tatum announces, "I'm a $250 a week newspaperman. I can be had for fifty. I know newspapers backward forward and sideways. I can write 'em, edit 'em, print 'em, wrap 'em, and sell 'em. I can handle big news and little news. And if there's no news, I'll go out and bite a dog. Make it forty-five."

A year later, he is still unhumbled. "When the history of this sunbaked Siberia is written," he declares in the office to nobody in particular, "these shameful words will live in infamy—No Chopped Chicken Livers. No garlic pickles. No Lindy's. No Madison Square Garden. No Yogi Berra!" He spins around and faces the prim "Tell the Truth" woman accusingly: "*What do you know about Yogi Berra?*" "I beg your pardon?" she answers. "YOGI BERRA!" Tatum roars in her face. She pauses: "Yogi? Well, it's a sort of religion, isn't it?" "You bet it is," he says. This tossaway is Billy Wilder speaking directly from his heart about one of the few things he believes in.

Tatum ends up pulling into Leo Minosa's trading post by pure chance, much the way Marion Crane drives up to the Bates Motel in *Psycho*, and with similar consequences. He and Herbie have been sent out on assignment—to a rattlesnake hunt. Tatum is scarcely enthusiastic over what he sees as a hayseed ritual, but Herbie, already in Tatum's thrall, sees ghoulish potential: "You know, this could be a pretty good story, Chuck. Don't sell it short. That's quite a sight—a thousand rattlers in the underbrush, and a lot of men smoking them out, bashing in their heads. . . ." "Big deal," Chuck gripes. "A thousand rattlers in the underbrush. Give me just fifty of them loose in Albuquerque." Warming to the notion of mass hysteria, he continues in a kind of reverie. Billy must have had a particularly good time writing this dialogue:

> TATUM: The whole town in a panic. Deserted streets. Barricaded houses. They're evacuating the children! *Every man's armed!* Fifty rattlers on the prowl—*fifty*! One by one they start hunting them down. They get ten. Twenty. It's building—they get forty, forty-five, they get *forty-nine!* Where's the last rattler? In the kindergarten? In a church? A crowded elevator—*where*?
> HERBIE: I give up. Where?
> TATUM: In my desk drawer, fan. [Then he clicks his tongue in triumph, just like Doris Dowling does with Ray Milland.]

Tatum's first scene with the trapped, hurt Leo culminates in a moment of hilariously understated viciousness. The camera is set beside Leo on the floor of the cave so that it peers up in low-angle at Tatum, who sticks his head through an opening in the upper center of the screen as Leo lies helplessly at the bottom. Tatum picks up Herbie's camera and tells Leo to hold up the fine specimen of ancient Indian pottery he came into the cliff dwelling to loot. When Leo asks what he's doing, Tatum explains that he's taking Leo's picture so he can put it in the newspaper in Albuquerque. Leo—instantly forgetting his own wretched condition—thrills to the prospect of gaining publicity. He doesn't even notice that Tatum discards the used flashbulb by popping it out smack in Leo's direction and hitting him with it. Characteristically subtle and restrained, Wilder films it all in a single shot and doesn't call any extra attention to the used flashbulb as it hits the victim.

Tatum's ruthless opportunism leads to gratifying mass entertainment as the crowds roll in to share the catastrophe. The Federbers, Mr. and Mrs. Middle America, and their two boys eagerly pull up to the trading post in a camper, having read about Leo's terrible ordeal in the *Albuquerque Sun-Bulletin*. Mr. Federber (Frank Cady) phrases his morbid excitement with perfect duplicity: it's a good educational opportunity for his sons, he says, though the boys are fast asleep in the backseat and he has to wake them up to share the thrill. The Federbers are not even the first bystanders. A family is already standing near the opening of the cave when Chuck and Herbie arrive. Soon there are hundreds. Before too long a snarling teenager mans the gate and extracts payment even from Herbie, who tries to beg off as a member of the press. "Two bits," the boy insists, and just in case

Herbie still doesn't get it, he spells it out: "*Twenty-five cents. Everybody* pays. Mrs. Minosa says so. Now *keep moving*."

Herbie himself is increasingly pleased with the way the story is unfolding. Earlier he was concerned about Leo; now he's talking about getting a four-page spread in *Life* or *Look*. "You *like* it now, don't you?" Chuck declares, beaming in approval as he hits Herbie playfully on the side of the head. The knock brings back a bit of Herbie's compassion, though he continues to deny his own culpability: "I like the *break*," he clarifies. "We didn't make it happen."

Lorraine plays the worried wife at times, but mostly she's too busy slinging burgers for the crowds, who reach across the counter waving their hands and empty plates in an image worthy of Nathanael West. Itchy and greedy, she comes into old Mr. and Mrs. Minosa's bedroom (which Mr. Minosa has gratefully given to Chuck), but she doesn't say anything right away. Tatum gets impatient. "Come on, come on, what is it?" he says, snapping his fingers restlessly in a gesture familiar to anyone who ever met this film's director. Lorraine talks of the day's proceeds and begins to calculate. "By tonight it ought to be a hundred and fifty. Seven times a hundred and fifty—that's over a grand!"

She goes on: "That's the first grand I ever had. Thanks." She snuggles in a little closer and with a certain gleam in her eye says, "Thanks *a lot*." Chuck advises her to keep on playing the anxious little lady. Lorraine keeps smiling. He tells her to wipe the smile off her face. She doesn't. She grins even more broadly, steps closer, and says, playfully, "Make me." He slaps her twice, hard, backhanding her the first time and then whacking her with the flat palm of his hand as a kickback. Lorraine grabs her cheek and stares, shocked and hurt. "That's more like it," he says.

"He didn't 'direct,' " Jan Sterling has observed. "He never said, 'A little more this,' or 'A little more that.' He used the camera as his instrument of direction. He knew what he wanted to show and what he wanted to see. He never stopped and said, 'No, that's not right, let's do it again.' He just uses your own personality—and the camera." Asked about Wilder's misogyny as reflected in the part of Lorraine Minosa, Sterling was adamant: "No, no, absolutely not. She may have been hateful to the observer, but when you were playing her, you understood absolutely why she did what she did. She wasn't happy. People do very odd things when they're not happy. She felt she had a right to be mean to Tatum. She wasn't on the make or anything—she just wanted out."

The masses, meanwhile, immerse themselves thoroughly in the ongoing festivities. The Federber children soon sport Indian headdresses purchased, no doubt, from Lorraine. Mr. Federber even gets the chance to be interviewed on the radio. "Mr. Federber," the announcer cries, "what is your reaction to this wonderful job being done here?" "Well," says Federber, "I think it's—wonderful! I run up against accidents all the time. I know what I'm talking about. I'm in the insurance game myself—you never can tell when an accident is going to happen! I sure hope Leo had the good sense to provide for an emergency like this! Now you take my outfit—the Pacific All-Risk. We have a little policy. . . ."

Leo looks progressively worse, but Wilder doesn't much care about him either, using him merely as a foil for his own bilious observations on human nature. From a high-angle shot of Leo lying in his dark grave talking about Lorraine, the precious love of his life, Wilder cuts to an eye-level shot taken in broad daylight of Lorraine watching approvingly as the circus rolls into Escadero. On the side of each truck is painted (without any further comment from Billy) "The Great S&M Amusement Corp." Minosa's trading post is crammed full of customers. A waitress struggles through the crowd holding a platter of food. Parents are buying headdresses. Tourists wave trinkets. Everybody is happy. It is Billy's most corrosive vision of postwar America.

Wilder then launches into one of the most disturbing sequences of his career. It's really two sequences, but the transition between them is as much a link as a division. Herbie and Chuck are alone in "Chuck's" room after Chuck receives the news that he's gotten his old job back at a huge salary. He has promised to take Herbie along with him, and they grin at each other, pleased at the prospect of heading east together. Chuck reaches around and grabs Herbie playfully by the neck just as Mrs. Minosa enters with her votive candles. Wilder's camera turns away from the two men, panning with Mrs. Minosa as she walks to a little shrine, replaces the old candles, and lights the new ones. Wilder then cuts back to a two-shot of Chuck and Herbie as Chuck removes his hand guiltily from Herbie's neck.

Fade to black. Fade-in to a shot of crowds of people and cars marching to a nasty little anthem Billy commissioned from Paramount's Oscar-winning songwriting team, Livingston and Evans. The rotten circus is in full swing. Wilder cuts to a country-western singer crooning the song, then pans to reveal a woman in a black cowgirl outfit selling copies of the tune for twenty-five cents apiece. Pulling his camera back over the heads of eager buyers waving money and grabbing sheet music, he pans to the right and cranes up higher over the crowd as the "Leo" song fades out on the sound-track; it is replaced by the garish thud of a circus oom-pah-pah band. After a cut, Wilder cranes down to Sheriff Kretzer giving a self-serving speech to a crowd of lemminglike onlookers. A montage follows, in which we see, among other things, the Federber family happily enjoying a ride on the Ferris wheel. Mr. Minosa is shown handing out sandwiches to the workers. Wilder pans with him, following him to the ledge overlooking the carnival parking lot as cars pour into the site in long distance. Mr. Minosa stares out in dumbstruck wonder as a train arrives on the track in the extreme background. Wilder cuts to a closer shot of the train as it pulls into Escadero; a huge sign on the train itself reads LEO MINOSA SPECIAL. Tourists jump off even before the train stops, and they run at full speed across the highway and the parking lot in a race to get closer to the tragedy. Wilder pans with these stampeding morons, staring both horrified and gloating at the country that adopted him.

The carnival sequence derives at least some of its malignant force from the intimate scene that precedes it. As in *Double Indemnity*, the sole redemptive relationship Wilder creates for his protagonist is with another man, only this time he takes the form of a good-looking, impressionable youth rather than a surly-lovable father figure. The transition from Tatum's affectionate horseplay with Herbie to Mrs. Minosa and her votive candles is crucial. It's guilt-inducing for Tatum—one of two such moments in the film. His guilt has nothing to do with the circus he created; he registers it *before* the carnival montage. And his guilty expression is sharp and affecting *despite* the fact that Mrs. Minosa's reverence is so unconvincing. (Billy resorts to bathing her face with the conventional key light Hollywood tends to employ as visual shorthand for piety. On the other hand, maybe that's his point. *Ace in the Hole* is so bitter that even the victim's mother's grief looks phony.)

The second revelation of Tatum's guilty self-awareness occurs in a similar all-male context. Leo cries out for a priest to administer the last rites, and Tatum, disregarding his own fatal stab wound, brings one to him. "Bless me, Father, for I have sinned," says Leo in close-up, at which point Billy cuts to an even tighter close-up of Tatum. With the camera in his face, it's Tatum himself who receives absolution. Leo says "I'm sorry" in voice-over, but given the placement of the camera, it's Tatum who feels the greater remorse.

Wilder has better taste than to show the actual moment of Leo's death. Not only would it detract from the more powerful revelation of Tatum's self-recrimination, but Wilder also knows that his audience cares as little for Leo as the crowds who flock to the circus at Escadero. Leo Minosa leaves the film just as he entered it—as a means to Tatum's end. Chuck emerges from the cave, hitches a ride on an ascending crane, reaches the top of the cliff, grabs a microphone, and shouts for silence: "Leo Minosa is dead. He died a quarter of an hour ago, with the drill just ten feet away. There's nothing we can do anymore. There's nothing anybody can do. He's dead, do you hear me? Now go on home, all of you. The circus is over."

The crowds disperse. The Federbers put away their camping gear. Mrs. Federber weeps, and the big-top tent comes down. Billy films Tatum in a low-angle tracking shot as he walks the distance of parking lot, and though he keeps cutting away to show other aspects of the circus's end, he keeps returning to the shot of self-loathing Tatum. Lorraine, meanwhile, merely walks down the steps of the trading post with her suitcase, misses her bus, and heads down the road on her own. She faces no retribution or punishment for stabbing a man to death. Tatum dies, slowly, from the wound, but Lorraine just disappears.

Tatum returns to the offices of the *Albuquerque Sun-Bulletin* so he can exit the film in style. In one of the few attention-calling setups of Wilder's life, the camera is on the office floor looking up at Tatum in extreme low-angle. "How'd you like to make yourself a thousand dollars a day, Mr. Boot?" Tatum asks. "I'm a thousand dollars a day newspaperman. You can have me for nothing." He staggers toward the camera and drops dead, pitching headfirst onto the floor, his face inches away from the lens. If Billy couldn't begin his film with a talking corpse, he ended it by forcing his audience to stare a silent one in the face at the closest possible range.

For the score, Wilder approached Hugo Friedhofer, a Hollywood composer who was always more respected by those he worked with than by the public at large. (He wrote the scores for *The Best Years of Our Lives* and *The Bishop's Wife*, among others.) Originally, Billy wanted Friedhofer to create a more melodic score than the dissonant one Friedhofer gave him. According to Friedhofer, Billy "was upset by the fact that I hadn't written a schmaltzy score, or at least something Wagnerian, since that's his favorite composer. When we were recording, he said, 'It's a good score, but there isn't a note of melody in it.' I replied, 'Billy, you've had the courage to put on the screen a bunch of really reprehensible people. Did you want me to soften them?' He got the point."

As though his film wasn't mean enough, Billy added one last touch. He altered the well-known Paramount logo at the beginning of the film to fit his own personal vision. Walter Newman described the result: "Well, you had the circle of stars but there was no mountain, and you didn't know quite what you were seeing within that circle. Actually it was an oblique shot from a height of about three feet down at a bit of desert sand. And then a rattlesnake slithered in and suddenly went into coil, its rattles vibrating and buzzing, its jaws wide, fangs exposed and forked tongue flickering, and it was so unexpected women screamed. *I* even stiffened in my chair. . . . But the studio was afraid that pregnant women would give birth prematurely right in the theatres if they used that shot and so it was cut."

Billy brought *Ace in the Hole* in for $1,821,052—a reasonable cost had the film done reasonable business. But it bombed.

When it was released in May 1951, *Ace in the Hole* was a disaster at the box office. For the first time in Wilder's writing-directing life, American audiences either hated what he gave them or simply didn't care enough to show up and face it. His inaugural one-man show proved to be one of the two most bitter disappointments of his professional life. Billy Wilder was stung—badly. And he was scared. Tellingly, his next three films were adaptations of already successful Broadway plays, he based the fourth on an already best-selling biography, the fifth was another adaptation, and so were the sixth and seventh. Not until 1960, eight pictures later, would he dare to make another film from his own original story.

The *Hollywood Reporter*'s reviewer set the tone for the American public's response: "Ruthless and cynical, *Ace in the Hole* is a distorted study of corruption and mob psychology that, in this reviewer's opinion, is nothing more than a brazen, uncalled-for slap in the face of two respected and frequently effective American institutions—democratic government and the free press." The film, the *Reporter* continued, "proceeds on the premise that Americans are a bunch of dopes, easily duped, victims of mass hysteria and emotionally placated by vicarious experience." According to the *Reporter*, this was unfair.

By the 1980s, when it had become impossible to argue Wilder's basic contentions about American media and culture, *Ace in the Hole* finally found its audience in the United States. But in the early 1950s, with faith in the nation's ideological institutions assuming fanatical religious proportions, Wilder was offering a vision of Americans and their news media that few Americans themselves wished to confront, let alone applaud. Jan Sterling is blunt on the subject: "You know why it was a failure? Columnists came out and said it could have been made by Art Kino [the Soviet company]. They seemed to feel it was anti-American." *Ace in the Hole* found greater favor in Europe. British critics heartily approved of Wilder's attack on American values, and the film ended up winning one of three "International Awards" at the Venice Film Festival. But Paramount Pictures wasn't especially impressed with the award. What the studio wanted was a healthy box office return on its investment, and Wilder, for once, didn't give it to them.

Like Chuck Tatum, Wilder was prone to bragging. He'd always enjoyed rubbing the noses of others in his own success, but now the tables had turned. "Cut it out, Chuck," one of Tatum's reporter-colleagues tells him while Tatum is still flying high; "We're old buddies! We're all in the same boat!" "*I'm* in the boat," Tatum snaps; "*You're* in the water." Until the disastrous release of *Ace in the Hole*, this was true for Billy as well. But thanks to *Ace in the Hole*, Billy's boat had just sprung a severe leak. Paramount's Y. Frank Freeman autocratically changed the title at the very last minute to *The Big Carnival*, and he did so without Billy's consent. "Fuck them all," Billy was heard to shout years later. "It is the best picture I ever made."

Wilder's sinking sensation only intensified when he was slapped with yet another lawsuit over plagiarism. Stephanie Joan Carlson never had much of a case with her allegations about *Sunset Boulevard*. This plaintiff was different. On October 1, 1951, the screenwriter Victor Desny filed suit in Los Angeles County alleging that in November 1949, just around the time that Wilder was beginning to work on *Ace in the Hole*, he, Desny, had submitted the story of Floyd Collins to Paramount Pictures—specifically to Billy Wilder. Now Desny thought he should be paid.

Desny's case was of a fundamentally different order than, say, the suit launched by Mrs. Florence Peschel of Denver, Colorado, whose fox terrier, Tippy, played the role of Buttons in *The Emperor Waltz*. (In January of 1951, Mrs. Peschel asked the court for $125,000 in damages for the alienation of Tippy's affections at the hands of Paramount Pictures.) Desny's suit was scarcely frivolous. It was most disturbing, because it called into question not only Billy Wilder's integrity as a writer-producer-director but also the whole system by which Hollywood studios acquired material. According to Desny, in November 1949, Desny told the Floyd Collins tale to Wilder's secretary, Rosella Stewart, several times over the telephone. (Helen Hernandez had departed with Brackett.) Although he claimed to have told her the story in some detail, he had submitted nothing in written form. He asked for $150,000 in damages.

Wilder's lawyers responded quickly, arguing first that submitting an idea over the phone was insufficient to prove plagiarism. In addition, they claimed that the material Desny submitted was not legally protected, given the highly publicized and factual nature of the Floyd Collins case. So in June 1952, Desny filed an amended complaint, this time submitting a written treatment of the life of Floyd Collins together with a chunk of Billy's script as a point of comparison. Later that summer Billy filed papers, denying everything.

Desny argued that his conversations with Rosella Stewart constituted a formal story submission. At first, he described the Collins story only in brief, to which Stewart responded that it would have to go to Paramount's story department first, and that the story department would condense the material to three or four pages before showing it to Wilder. "I don't like my story to be hacked," Desny replied, and he said he'd rather do it himself. "Why don't you do that," Stewart answered. The persistent screenwriter called back again a few days later and read Stewart his synopsis, which she claimed at the time to be writing down in shorthand as he told it to her. Stewart's only comment was that the idea seemed interesting and she would talk it over with Billy. Desny never spoke with Wilder directly.

Judge Stanley Mosk returned a summary judgment in favor of Wilder and Paramount on December 18, 1953, based on the fact that the Collins story was a historical incident. Moreover, the judge was compelled to find for the defendants because no manuscript had been submitted, and an "oral recitation of a synopsis over the telephone cannot be construed to be submission of a written manuscript."

Desny appealed, of course. The District Court of Appeal reversed Judge Mosk's ruling in the summer of 1955 and ordered the matter returned to Superior Court for trial. The case went to the California Supreme Court, which eliminated one of Wilder's and Paramount's key contentions— namely, that an oral submission was insufficient to prove plagiarism. Thus the defendants found themselves heading to trial without their central line of defense. The case was settled privately in August 1956. Desny won $14,350 and, no doubt, a certain satisfaction.

19. CALCULATIONS

MANFREDI (Michael Moore) *(preparing to escape an Austrian prison camp)*: We stick to the forest west until we hit the Danube.

JOHNSON (Peter Baldwin): Then we follow the Danube up to Linz. In Linz we have a barge and go all the way to Ulm. Once in Ulm, we lie low until night. Then we take a train to Friedrichshafen.

MANFREDI: Once in Friedrichshafen we steal a rowboat, get some fishing tackle, and start drifting across the lake. Always south, 'til we hit the other side—*Switzerland.*

SEFTON (William Holden): Once in Switzerland just give out with a big yodel, boys, so they'll know you're there. It's a breeze! Just one question: Did you calculate the risk?

—Stalag 17

Hollywood filmmaking was always a big crapshoot, with accent on the crap. Before Billy unexpectedly threw snake eyes in May of 1951 with the release of his latest movie, he had stayed on top of the game for too many years. He was getting bored with so much winning, and he needed some extra risk to keep the game fresh. "Talk is that Billy Wilder may also leave Paramount," Louella Parsons reported in November 1950; "This, however, I have been unable to check." No one who knew Billy could have been surprised at the rumor. *Ace in the Hole* had finished shooting but hadn't yet been released. There was no reason for anyone, least of all Billy, to think it wouldn't be another hit. For the moment, he was able to call his own shots, and if that meant leaving the studio that nurtured and sustained his talent for fourteen years, so be it. Billy's loyalties were above all to himself, and given his constitutional distrust of the human race even that allegiance was questionable.

It was an opportune time to make waves. By the end of 1950, the economic system under which Hollywood had reaped its profits for decades was in full collapse. A year earlier, the government had ordered the studios to deconstruct themselves. Grudgingly, they began to do so. One tends to think of the old Hollywood studios as filmmaking enterprises, but they were really distribution and exhibition companies that supplied themselves with a steady stream of their own product. Paramount, MGM, RKO, Fox, and Universal owned large and profitable theater chains, and to ensure that these theaters would have a near-constant stock of films to screen, these companies kept the system well oiled by making the films themselves. With the settlement of *United States v. Paramount Pictures Corporation et al.*, the protracted antitrust suit aimed at cracking the Big Five's monopoly, the so-called studios were forced to divest themselves of their theaters, and Hollywood's tidy, vertically integrated system fell apart. Independent producers suddenly had a much better crack at providing product, and as power shifted from the old front offices on the big lots in Hollywood to smaller offices located anywhere one chose, an iron-willed, one-man-show director saw the chance to become independent.

Decentralizing also meant destabilizing the chain of command, and in the free-for-all, directors might as well become independent producers, too. With *United States v. Paramount*, the government handed Billy a brand-new pair of dice. They may not have been loaded, exactly, but they would tend to roll in his favor. His films for Paramount almost always made money, and in the months following *Sunset Boulevard*'s release the studio had great incentive to keep him. But if he chose to leave Paramount, he could quickly find either another studio to keep him happy at a fine salary or an independent financier to set him up on his own. When Billy and Audrey set sail for Europe on the SS *Liberte* in early December 1950, he had every reason to be confident. Paramount ended up meeting his terms, and he signed a new three-picture contract immediately before embarking for a three-month tour of the Continent, including stops in London, Paris, Berlin, Munich, Vienna, Italy, and Switzerland.

He was mulling over the idea of making a movie about the dead. *The Loved One* was a prime candidate for a Hollywood film adaptation, and Wilder was on its trail. What could be more delightful than Evelyn Waugh's brittle satire on mid-twentieth-century Hollywood funeral rites? Forest Lawn Cemetery, where the corpses of the rich and famous and low and bourgeois earned passage to eternity at the Wee Kirk o' the Heather, the cemetery chapel located on the Burbank border? Forest Lawn, where, for a price, you could get yourself and your kids buried in Whispering Pines, Everlasting Love, Kindly Light, and Babyland? By the time he left for Europe, Billy had already discussed with John Seitz the idea of directing *The Loved One*, and Seitz agreed to shoot it. Billy would be vacationing on the Continent, but part of the time would be spent in London meeting with Evelyn Waugh.

The Loved One was not Billy's only idea. He'd been interested in adapting Jules Romains's *Dr. Knock* for some time. The play concerns a doctor duped into buying a small-town practice only to discover that everyone in town is unusually healthy; he proceeds to convince them that they're all desperately ill and thus spurs the local economy as well as his own career. In January, Paul Kohner wired Billy in Paris to alert him to the fact that a French company had just released its own adaptation of *Dr. Knock*, and this may have put an end to Billy's idea. As for *The Loved One*, whether Waugh himself didn't go for Billy's ideas for an adaptation, or Paramount nixed them, or Wilder simply lost interest, *The Loved One* went into hibernation. Instead, Billy turned his sights to a Maurice Chevalier film.

A New Kind of Love was to be a romantic comedy based loosely on some incidents from Chevalier's own life. Wilder reportedly considered writing in a role for Marlene Dietrich as well. Returning from Europe in early 1951, Billy planned to turn around and go back to Paris in March for talks with Chevalier. But *A New Kind of Love*, too, ended up scuttled. American red-baiting was to blame.

Billy himself managed to steer clear of HUAC, Senator McCarthy, and Hollywood's own homegrown celebrity right wing and thereby stay afloat as a filmmaker. Unfortunate others, including the French citizen Chevalier, found themselves drowning in a swamp of radical conservatism in the States. Among Hollywood directors, it was Cecil B. DeMille who saw himself as the right's great suzerain, and his milquetoast minions agreed. DeMille chose as his battlefield the Screen Directors Guild and its membership lists. First, he set up the DeMille Foundation for Americanism, the chief task of which was to collect dossiers on liberal-left directors. Then, in October of 1950, DeMille tried to take over the Guild itself. Billy's friend and colleague Joseph Mankiewicz, the director of *All About Eve*, was in the midst of his term as the Guild's president. He was generally well liked, but his administration suddenly became tenuous when DeMille insisted that all Guild members be required to sign a loyalty oath. Mankiewicz refused. DeMille and his attendants threatened to throw him out of office and force all the directors in town to pledge allegiance to the flag.

On October 13, 1950, the day *All About Eve* premiered in New York, Mankiewicz summoned those Guild members he trusted most to a meeting in the back room of Chasen's, the elegant Beverly Hills restaurant. Billy was one of the chosen, along with William Wyler, Elia Kazan, John Huston, George Seaton, Don Hartman, King Vidor, Richard Brooks, John Farrow, and H. C. Potter. The stage was set for a clash between the two factions. The ugly battle was fought on Sunday, October 22, in an unlikely setting for a war: the Crystal Room of the Beverly Hills Hotel.

Mankiewicz's biographer Kenneth Geist has recorded every delicious detail of this meeting, the essential elements of which included DeMille's linking his own struggle with that of the GIs fighting the Korean War ("You all read this morning about the American boys who were prisoners, who were taken out, promised food, and then were machine-gunned with their hands tied behind their backs . . ."). It is the kind of story that rings funnier in retrospect than it did at the time. In the early 1970s, when Geist asked Wilder about the meeting, Billy didn't even remember that Mankiewicz was central to the affair. What he recalled was DeMille's having attacked him for being an immigrant. According to Wilder, part of DeMille's performance at the meeting was the reeling off of a list of foreign-sounding names, all with a pointedly thick foreign accent. Billy's was among them. When Geist asked Billy if he responded to DeMille's scurrilous attack himself, Wilder replied that he didn't have to, because John Huston said it all for him: "Huston applied a samurai sword to Mr. DeMille's withered neck." ("Mr. DeMille," "Mr. von Hindenburg," "Mr. Hitler . . ." Billy never lost his proper Viennese manners.) When all was shouted and done, Cecil B. DeMille was vanquished.

DeMille's demise was a triumph for Mankiewicz and his friends, but it did nothing to alter the steady flow of paranoid anticommunism in the United States. Mankiewicz survived and thrived. So did Billy. But *A New Kind of Love* fell victim to the State Department. Maurice Chevalier had made the mistake of signing the so-called Stockholm Appeal, which urged a ban on atomic weapons. He'd also erred by appearing at a benefit for the French Resistance some years earlier. Promoting world peace, deploring weapons of mass annihilation, and fighting the Nazis—in 1951, these activities were enough for the State Department to bar the man from entering the United States.

A New Kind of Love was listed on Paramount's production schedule for the summer of 1951, but as Chevalier's visa problem dragged on, Paramount's corporate feet grew colder. In March, the studio's lobbyists in Washington tried to convince the State Department to change its mind, but before too long the studio caved in, and Billy's next project was on indefinite hold.

By May, when *Ace in the Hole* opened to scant box office returns and a flood of mixed to negative reviews, Wilder was in no position to argue the point. Having just directed his first big dud, Billy was no longer able to dictate terms to Paramount; having calculated the risks, as always, he knew that to get the independence he wanted he needed at least one more big hit.

He also required a new collaborator. Lesser Samuels and Walter Newman were decent enough writers, but there was none of the buddy-based camaraderie he needed to ensure an ongoing relationship. Even if the three of them had all been bound together as tightly as Brackett and Wilder at their most marital, rehiring the two writers who helped him write his first fiasco was out of the question. He needed someone fresh.

Wilder's friend and former agent Paul Kohner pushed one of his clients,

Robert Rossen. Tough-minded, athletic, Jewish, and conflicted, Rossen might have been an ideal match for Billy, except for three things: he was too much like Billy, he'd already directed films himself, and he was an ex-Communist. Wilder worked best with lower-key men who offered no competition, at least in terms of grabbing public attention, and having steered clear of Communist affiliations *before* McCarthyism, he had little reason to embrace anyone who had been subpoenaed to appear before HUAC, as Rossen was that year. Rossen invoked a modified Fifth Amendment. Declaring that he was not currently a member of the Communist Party, Rossen then refused to answer any other questions.

Billy met with Rossen, and Rossen came away from the meeting thinking he had the makings of a deal. He reported back to Kohner that Billy seemed to welcome him onto the team, but more tellingly, Wilder himself doesn't appear to have responded to Kohner about it, and no deal was ever struck. Rossen went on to testify more fully before the Committee in 1953, but he never worked in Hollywood again.

Norman Krasna was next up. An accomplished screenwriter, Krasna had worked in Hollywood a little longer than Billy, mostly on comedies. Krasna had a real knack for writing screwballs. Hitchcock's *Mr. and Mrs. Smith* (1941) was the best of them. Others include Mitchell Leisen's *Hands Across the Table* (1935) and Garson Kanin's *Bachelor Mother* (1939). Wilder, after getting at least some of the bile out of his system with *Ace in the Hole*, was in the mood to make a screwball comedy himself—one with a contemporary slant: the screwball couple would consist of two men. Laurel and Hardy's joint career was creaking to a close, but Billy saw possibilities. Transplanting the premise of *Ein blonder Traum* to Los Angeles in the days of Mack Sennett, Wilder wanted to introduce the two comedians with a shot of the famous Hollywood sign, and as the camera tracked forward, the audience would find Laurel asleep in one of the Os and Hardy asleep in the next. They'd live in a cemetery. A woman would come between them.

Krasna was surprised but pleased when Billy asked him to lunch at Romanoff's. They worked together for less than a month, then Krasna quit. He simply couldn't take the barrage of verbal indignities to which Billy subjected him as part of his daily routine. He hit Krasna where he knew it would hurt the most, and he did it consistently. As Krasna described them, "They were sharp wisecracks. . . . I wouldn't repeat them to you. They could still be used against me. I just couldn't take the abuse."

When Billy hired one more new partner to help him write his next movie, he chose another journeyman. Edwin Blum wrote two good films before Billy hired him—*The Canterville Ghost* (1944) and, perhaps more crucially as far as Billy was concerned, *The Adventures of Sherlock Holmes* (1938). Conan Doyle's brilliant, misogynistic, drug-addicted detective had long appealed to Billy's imagination, and many of the world's Holmes fans considered Blum's script (not to mention Basil Rathbone's performance) to be suitably Holmesian, even definitive, though without the cocaine. Mostly, though, Blum penned sequels and toss-offs—everything from *Tarzan and the Green Goddess* (1938) and *Henry Aldrich Gets Glamour* (1942, yet another in the series engendered by Brackett and Wilder's *What a Life*) to the Peter Lorre–Boris Karloff spooker *The Boogie Man Will Get You* (1942). Blum was scarcely an artist, but he knew how to map out a screenplay and follow Billy's instructions. Not coincidentally, he also played tennis and bridge.

They started working on the Laurel and Hardy comedy, but Ollie soon fell ill and the project was scrapped. Billy, flying madly from idea to idea, landed briefly on the notion of a jazzy black *Camille*. "Unless she's a whore, she's a bore," Billy once instructed Walter Newman; his Camille would be anything but dull. Lena Horne would be an elegant Harlem hooker, Paul Robeson would be her father. A navy lieutenant, Tyrone Power, would fall for her. Duke Ellington, one of Billy's favorite musicians, would write a jazz score. As a final kicker, the drama was to be complicated by the fact that Ty Power would turn out to be part black himself. Paramount had no interest at all in the idea.

Then Billy took a trip to New York, saw that season's big Broadway hit, and returned to Los Angeles with a new idea. Blum couldn't quite see the appeal and asked Wilder what he saw in *Stalag 17*. "Guys in underwear," said Billy. Blum was put on the payroll in September 1951, at $1,000 a week.

"Along with *Sunset Boulevard*," Wilder once declaimed, "*Stalag 17* is one of my favorites, perhaps because there are eight minutes that are any good." Those eight minutes, left unspecified by the ever-hyperbolic Billy, were conceived and executed, like the rest of the film, under unusually great pressure. The *Ace in the Hole* flop meant not only that Paramount's executives could no longer give Wilder carte blanche, but also that they expected his next film to perform doubly well. In fact, Paramount told him directly that the next movie he made had to earn enough profits to cover both itself and *Ace in the Hole*.

Stung by the failure of his own original story, and forced to deliver double the goods on his next project, Wilder wisely retreated to the safety of a Broadway hit—that is, if the writing, producing, and directing of a Hollywood feature film can ever be said to occur in a zone of safety. *Stalag 17* was a known quantity with a proven track record, at least among New York theatergoers. But Billy did not abandon his sensibilities in his greed for another hit. *Stalag 17* was a comedy about American GIs held captive in a squalorous Nazi prison camp—a Nazi prison camp in Austria, to be precise. The real Stalag 17 was located near Krems, about forty miles west of Vienna. Wilder didn't make a point of it when he adapted *Stalag 17* for the screen, but when he wrote, cast, blocked, and filmed it Billy knew that all his Nazi camp guards, and all his guard dogs, were really Austrians, and that when the heroes escaped from Stalag 17 they were getting the hell out of Billy's own country.

Paramount's script-reading department earnestly rejected *Stalag 17* five times before an executive decided to pay over $100,000 to acquire the rights. By then, of course, it was a huge success on Broadway. In late 1948, a theatrical promoter had submitted an early script to Paramount on behalf of the playwrights, Donald Bevan and Edmund Trzcinski, but to no avail. A year later, another script was submitted, this time by a New York theatrical manager. *Stalag 17* bore a new ending, but Paramount's on-staff reader was still unimpressed: "The play is too sprawling and monotonous, and too lacking in plot progression, action, suspense, to stand a chance with any ending." Yet another script found its way to Paramount in late 1949 or early 1950, and Paramount assigned the same reader to cover it. She was getting annoyed: "All they did this time was type it over. . . . It was a very poor POW play the first, second, third, and fourth times I read it, and it hasn't changed a bit." Bevan and Trzcinski were themselves survivors of a Nazi prison camp, but as far as Paramount's reader was concerned, they still didn't know how to write a play.

By the spring of 1951, *Stalag 17* was selling out on Broadway in a production directed by Jose Ferrer. Covering the play was no longer the province of the script reader, but rather a theater specialist; he loved it. Louella Parsons announced Wilder's interest in directing the movie version at the end of May. When Bevan and Trzcinski submitted their play to Paramount yet again later that summer, a new reader gave it an enthusiastic report, and by the end of August Paramount had purchased the rights and officially announced Wilder as the director. Billy revealed his choice of star: the part of Sefton, the manipulative cynic-turned-hero, would be played by Charlton Heston.

In order to take the role, Heston would have to be borrowed from Hal Wallis, with whom he was under contract, but Wilder saw no difficulty in that transaction. For the role of Lieutenant Dunbar, the war hero who must be smuggled out of the prison camp, Wilder chose one of Paramount's most promising young leading men, the affable and unpretentious Don Taylor, who surprised the director by mulling over whether or not to take the part. ("I had the feeling he was a little pissed off at me for debating," Taylor says.) Wilder also announced to the press that he'd hired Robert Strauss to repeat the role Strauss inaugurated on stage—the loud, vulgar, hilarious Stosh—while Cy Howard, a radio and television writer-producer (*My*

Friend Irma was his big hit), would take over the part of Stosh's friend Harry Shapiro from Broadway's Harvey Lembeck.

Smart, practical, and sublimely exploitive, Sergeant Sefton was precisely Billy's kind of character, and he became even more so in Wilder's rewrite. Described by Bevan and Trzcinski as "a handsome but sullen young man dominated by an animosity toward the world in general," Sefton could have been played well enough by Heston, but as Wilder and Blum finessed Sefton even further away from heroism toward hard-bitten cynicism, it began to dawn on Billy that handsome Chuck Heston wasn't his man. Kirk Douglas claims that Billy asked *him* to be Sefton before asking William Holden and that he turned it down, but what is certain is that Wilder did ask Holden and Holden was smart enough to accept the role even though he didn't like the play. In fact, Holden walked out after the first act.

Since *Sunset Boulevard*, Bill Holden and Billy Wilder had become extraordinarily close. On the surface they were so different. Holden was a laconic descendant of George Washington who hid his deep insecurities with an easygoing demeanor, a killer grin, and liquor. But Holden admired Billy's intellect, experience, and taste, and Wilder was enthralled by Holden's rugged good looks and low-key friendliness. To Wilder, Bill Holden was the all-American guy Billy himself could never be. According to Holden's biographer Bob Thomas, the two men eventually spent so much time together and became so well acquainted with each other's habits and tastes that when Holden asked Billy for his opinion on a painting he was thinking of buying, Wilder replied, "If I were you—*and I am . . .*"

Holden was, Billy said, "the kind of leading man who not only wears well but he does not rub men the wrong way. Just because women like a man on the screen is not necessarily it—men should approve of their wives and daughters carrying a torch for the guy. The refreshing thing about Holden is that coming from Pasadena he has never been exposed to the deep-dish acting seminars. If a scene requires him to ask a girl if she wants two lumps of sugar in her coffee, he does not ask me if his grandmother on his father's side is supposed to be a screaming nymphomaniac. And he uses underarm deodorant."

Still, Holden was an actor, and, like many actors, he seemed to want his audience to like his character as much as he wanted them to like *him*. Concerned that in *Stalag 17* he was playing the very essence of a mercenary louse, Holden asked Billy to add a line—something, *anything*—to show that Sefton really did hate the Nazis after all. Billy refused.

In preparation for a February start date, Paramount built Wilder his own prison camp on a ranch in Calabassas. The production was well timed; it was Southern California's version of a rainy season, so the ersatz camp would have the benefit of gray skies and acres of mud. *Stalag 17* would be a moderately inexpensive film, with minimal sets and costumes. It went into production with a projected cost of $1,315,000, a smaller budget than *Ace in the Hole*, which wasn't especially costly either. Holden got about $48,000, Taylor $25,000. In a masterstroke of stunt casting, Wilder snared the services of yet another in a series of famously fierce Teutonic movie directors—the tyrannical, brilliant Otto Preminger, who was paid $45,000 for three weeks' work as the Nazi commandant, Oberst (or Colonel) von Scherbach.

A production meeting held only days before *Stalag 17* went before the cameras spelled out some remaining details: Billy insisted that Preminger should be given a special wardrobe (à la Stroheim); that the commandant's office should not contain even so much as a single picture of Adolf Hitler; and that there should be nine hundred extras for the biggest day of the shoot. The dependable and conservative Buddy Coleman thought they could make do with five hundred; the crowd scenes, after all, would have to be shot on location, not at the studio, and everyone needed to be fed. Notes taken at this meeting reveal, once again, Billy's characteristic approach to music: "Wilder: Main title, end music and in certain sections a drum only. Will not change mind this time." This was true: he didn't.

After a week of rehearsal, *Stalag 17* began shooting on February 4, 1952. The production proceeded efficiently. Only there was a problem: Cy Howard, the actor Billy hired to play Harry Shapiro, was awful. Apparently Wilder wanted someone who could be broadly, identifiably Jewish, but the blustering and abrasive Howard gave him more than he bargained for. So he got rid of him in the middle of the shoot and went back to Harvey Lembeck, who could take over the role quickly, since he'd originated it on Broadway. When Don Taylor asked Billy why he axed Howard, Wilder's response was direct: "He's making me anti-Semitic."

The Calabassas ranch was a muddy mess—that was the point—and the company only worked there a few days at a time, returning regularly to the comfort of the lot for interior shooting. The relative ease of a soundstage was the practical result, but the back-and-forth schedule also had an emotional consequence for the performers: even when they filmed indoors in the heart of Hollywood, they had recent (and future) experience of working in a mucky mess to remind them that this comedy was rooted in real despair.

A few days were lost for rain, a few more for delays in shooting interiors. By March 18 *Stalag 17* was a week behind schedule. This time, Wilder's failure to complete the script before shooting was partly to blame, as the actors found themselves unable to rehearse as well as they wanted or needed simply because Wilder had given them nothing to practice. They took it in stride, mostly. Wilder was known for the relative happiness of his productions, and *Stalag 17* was no exception. Billy's cast and crew could joke around with one another and get boisterous without their director stepping in to squelch the fun, but one day Bill Holden finally snapped. "Goddamn it!" he shouted to a lot of startled bystanders. "Can't you guys shut up for a minute? Some of us are trying to get some work done!" If this is the worst thing that can be said about a film's production, everybody should have considered themselves blessed.

Finally, on March 19, a complete script appeared, but every extra day of filming meant that the cost would escalate (about $100,000 per day), and the front office began to register its dismay. The pressure on Billy increased. Wilder and his cast and crew returned to Calabassas on the 20th. The company shot at night on the 22nd, 23rd, and 25th, Taylor and Holden working as late as 4:20 A.M. The production closed on March 29th.

Having taken a few chances with the censors on *Ace in the Hole* and finding that the Production Code was more easily bent than ever, Wilder was emboldened to include ever more graphic puns, double entendres, and dirty bathroom references. This was a war picture, and soldiers aren't prudes. "Why don't you take that whistle and shove it?" said one character in a draft submitted to Joseph Breen in February; another employed the word *bitchin'*; a third, referring enthusiastically to a group of Russian women prisoners, let fly with "Just get us a couple with big glockenspiels!" Sheets from a roll of toilet paper were to have been used as napkins. And there was to have been terrible violence, crime, and no punishment: guard dogs would be set upon a dead prisoner's body, and the men in the barracks would kill one of their own and go unpunished. Billy took more liberties than usual with *Stalag 17*, and it was too much for Joseph Breen, who threatened to reject the film entirely unless Wilder cleaned it up.

Promises were made; some were kept. *Stalag 17* was Billy's most vulgar script to date, the fact of which he was quite evidently proud, and he saw no need to make anything other than the barest of revisions. He changed the "shove it" line in a minor way and substituted a pack of what could be seen (by Pollyanna herself) as single-sheet paper napkins for the roll of toilet paper. *Bitchin'* was cut.

There was a limit to Billy's accommodation. He was not about to make any changes at all to one scene he and Blum added to Bevan and Trzcinski's original script. The film departs from the play in two key ways: Manfredi and Johnson die graphically on-screen in the film, whereas they are already dead when the play opens, and Harry Shapiro and his best friend ("Stosh" in the play, "Animal" in the film) have a lot more fun together than Joseph Breen thought they should. From a single line in the play, Wilder expanded their relationship into a whimsical kind of romance, complete with court-ship, cross-dressing, and even a hint of sexual pleasure as Harry turns him-self into Betty Grable for Animal's benefit. Breen forbade it—or tried to. "We are concerned," he wrote to Luigi Luraschi, "about the scene in which Harry and Stosh dance together. If there is any inference in the finished scene of a flavor of sex perversion, we will not be able to approve it under the Code. We are particularly concerned about the action on page 106 with the particular reference to the following stage directions: 'A peculiar ex-pression comes over Harry's face. . . .' "

Breen continued: "We think the two men should not be snuggling to-gether, nor should Stosh be singing 'I Love You.' Also, we suggest omitting the word 'darling.' "

It wasn't just the extended gay joke Breen found troubling. He was upset by everything Stosh/Animal represented: "Unless Stosh's originally unacceptable characterization as a man obsessed with sex to the point of mania has been completely changed, this whole sequence will be unac-ceptable no matter how it is shot. . . ." Breen claimed that Luraschi and Wilder agreed to alter Stosh's character—essentially that of a walking, grunting libido—into something more tolerably middle-American. All was not unsuitable about *Stalag 17*, however; Breen did approve the use of the lyrics of "O Come All Ye Faithful."

Billy may have found some protection in adapting a Broadway play rather than composing his own original story, but that hardly meant that he wouldn't rewrite the play drastically to suit his own style. Apart from Bevan and Trzcinski's backbone plot and central character sketches, Wilder retained very little of the play. Hardly any of Bevan and Trzcinski's dia-logue survives; the movie's dialogue is Billy's, with help from Edwin Blum. And almost all the best gags are Billy's as well—the "horse race" Sefton operates, using rats as the nags; the peep show Sefton runs, using a tele-scope aimed at the Russian women's bathhouse; Sefton's own foray into the Russian women's barracks ("Those dames, they really know how to throw a party! I've known some women in my time, but between you and me, there's nothing like the hot breath of the Cossacks!"). Virtually the only comedy bit Wilder kept from the play is the character—and loony nasal voice—of Marko, the camp mailman and town crier (played by Wil-liam Pierson both onstage and on-screen). Wilder and Blum also added one important new character: they gave Sefton his only friend—the callow young Cookie (Gil Stratton Jr.), who serves not only as Sefton's personal factotum but also narrates the film. Cookie idolizes Sefton in precisely the same way Herbie loves Chuck Tatum in *Ace in the Hole*. He's not corrupt, like Sefton, but he still gets to enjoy Sefton's depravity vicariously.

At the same time, Wilder demoralizes his men—and his audience—in ways that Bevan and Trzcinski couldn't bear to do. In the play, when the guys listen to the shortwave radio they hear optimistic war news: six hundred Allied bombers and B-24s are pounding cities in Austria, and Winston Churchill says the turning point in the war has been reached. The men cheer, heartened by the news. Billy's prisoners, on the other hand, hear reports of the Allied disaster at Malmédy. For a 1953 audience, this radio broadcast would have been particularly chilling; the men on-screen are necessarily unaware that when the real battle at Malmédy was over, the Nazi SS dealt with its American prisoners by lining them up in a field and murdering them in cold blood. Few adults watching *Stalag 17* in the 1950s would have forgotten the Malmédy Massacre.

Wilder also made a minor but potent change in the character of the shell-shocked soldier—"Horney" in the play, "Joey" in the film. Wilder does indulge in a bit of sentimentality here, but the mawkishness of this soulful mute had a personal foundation for Billy. Bevan and Trzcinski cite as the reason for the GI's derangement the fact that he was forced to spend six months in solitary confinement after punching a guard. This was too mild for Billy, and too detached from his own experience. Wilder's Joey loses his mind after seeing those closest to him get slaughtered by the Nazis.

Finally, Bevan and Trzcinski's conclusion was entirely unsatisfying for Wilder. Sefton's final line was just too weak, let alone too nice: "Only in a democracy can a poor guy get his ass shot off with a rich guy," he says as he leads Lieutenant Dunbar offstage to freedom. Given the bitterness of the kiss-off line Wilder eventually gave to Sefton at the end of the film, it's striking that he and Blum originally considered ending *Stalag 17* with a rousing patriotic montage: a shot of Dunbar with his arm thrown fraternally over Sefton's shoulder as they make their escape was to be followed by shots of all the other POWs in superimposition, "their spirits marching with them through the forest."

This was exhilarating, but not in the right way—not for Wilder. Even though he was making a war picture for the Eisenhower era, his *Stalag 17* needed to end on a bracingly sour note, so the POW parade gave way to something more personal. As in the play, Sefton offers to lead Dunbar out of the camp not for patriotic reasons but for the money; Dunbar's rich mother is certain to pay a handsome reward. But Wilder's Sefton is hardbitten to the end, a caustic son of a bitch. He tells Animal, who has asked about how to get into the Russian women's compound (a task Sefton has already achieved), "Tell you what to do—get yourself a hundred cigarettes for the kraut guards. Then get yourself another face." Sefton's last, nasty words to his mates became infamous—exemplary of Billy Wilder's cruel selfishness and cynicism: "Just one more word—if I ever run into you bums on the street corner, just let's pretend we never met before." He disappears

JAZZ COMES TO VIENNA: The conductor Paul Whiteman (with mustache and black hat) with some bandmembers, having just arrived in Vienna in June, 1926. Note the rakish young reporter standing slightly behind Whiteman. [Courtesy of Günther Schifter]

ALTER EGO: A poster for *Der Teufelsreporter (The Daredevil Reporter)*, Billy Wilder's first film. [Courtesy of the Bundesarchiv-Filmarchiv, Berlin]

THE FIRST AUDREY HEPBURN?: Dolly Haas stars in *Scampolo*, written by Wilder. [Courtesy of the Bundesarchiv-Filmarchiv, Berlin]

FATHERLY LOVE:
Wilder and his
daughter, Victoria,
on the set of *Five
Graves to Cairo*.
[Courtesy of the Academy
of Motion Picture Arts
and Sciences]

THE GLAMOUR AND
MAGIC OF SCREEN-
WRITING: Brackett
and Wilder huddle
over a typewriter in
the mid-1940s.
[Courtesy of the Academy
of Motion Picture Arts
and Sciences]

THE TEAM: Charles Brackett, Wilder, and Doane Harrison on the set of
Five Graves to Cairo. [Courtesy of the Academy of Motion Picture Arts and Sciences]

THOU SHALT NOT STEAL: Wilder directs Barbara Stanwyck and Fred MacMurray on
the set of *Double Indemnity*, as uniformed guards make sure nobody pinches anything during wartime rationing. [Courtesy of the Academy of Motion Picture Arts and Sciences]

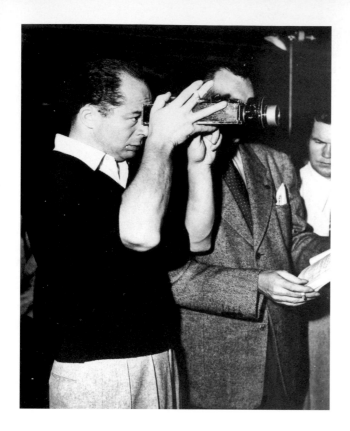

THROUGH THE
VIEWFINDER:
Wilder sets up a
shot on the set of
The Lost Weekend.
[Courtesy of the
Academy of Motion
Picture Arts and
Sciences]

"NATCH!": Doris
Dowling as Gloria in
The Lost Weekend.
[Courtesy of the Academy
of Motion Picture Arts
and Sciences]

HOMECOMING, 1945: Wilder, wearing the uniform issued to civilian employees of the Army, in Berlin.

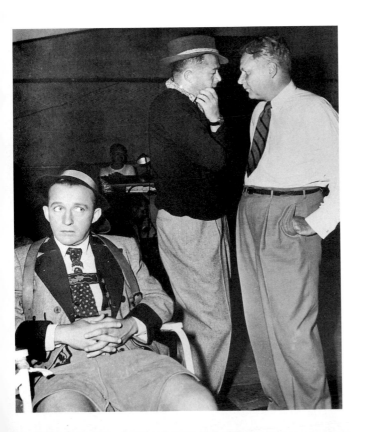

SCRIPT CONFERENCE: Wilder and Brackett try to have a private conversation on the set of *The Emperor Waltz* as Bing Crosby waits for his call.
[Courtesy of the Academy of Motion Picture Arts and Sciences]

DID THEY OR DIDN'T THEY?: Wilder and Hedy Lamarr in the late 1940s. [Courtesy of the Academy of Motion Picture Arts and Sciences]

FOREIGN AFFAIRS: Wilder plants one on Marlene Dietrich's cheek on the set of *A Foreign Affair.* [Courtesy of the Academy of Motion Picture Arts and Sciences]

MODEL HOME: Billy and Audrey Wilder take a look at a scale model of the house Charles Eames designed for them in 1949-1950; Eames himself took the picture. [Courtesy of the Library of Congress. Eames Office © 1989, 1998 www.eamesoffice.com]

MAKEOVER: Norma Desmond (Gloria Swanson) gets a beauty treatment in *Sunset Boulevard*. [Courtesy of the Academy of Motion Picture Arts and Sciences]

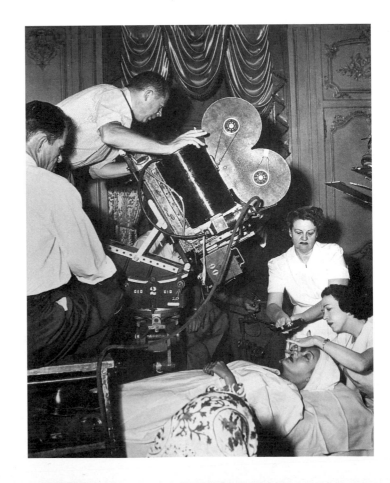

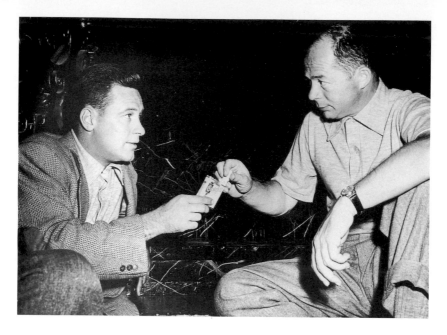

TO YOUR HEALTH: William Holden offers Wilder a cigarette, circa *Sunset Boulevard*. [Courtesy of the Academy of Motion Picture Arts and Sciences]

POSTMORTEM CELEBRATION: Gloria Swanson accompanies Billy and Audrey Wilder to a *Sunset Boulevard* party. [Courtesy of the Academy of Motion Picture Arts and Sciences]

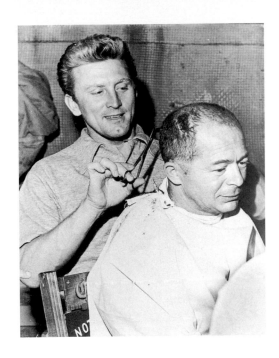

MORE OFF THE TOP:
Kirk Douglas tries
his hand at barber-
ing on the set of
Ace in the Hole,
using his director as
his guinea pig.
[Courtesy of the
Academy of Motion
Picture Arts and
Sciences]

IF YOU WANT TO
MAKE AN OMELETTE:
Wilder and Audrey
Hepburn on the
Parisian cooking
school set of *Sabrina.*
[Courtesy of the Academy
of Motion Picture Arts
and Sciences]

COOLING OFF:
Wilder and Marilyn
Monroe enjoy them-
selves on location in
New York City dur-
ing the filming of
The Seven Year Itch.

A HOLLYWOOD
MOMENT: Wilder and
Monroe make nice
for the benefit of the
gossip columnist
Sidney Skolsky on
the set of *The Seven
Year Itch*. [Courtesy of
the Academy of Motion
Picture Arts and Sciences]

FLYING HIGH:
Maurice Chevalier
visits Wilder and
Jimmy Stewart on
the set of *The Spirit
of St. Louis*.
[Courtesy of Photofest]

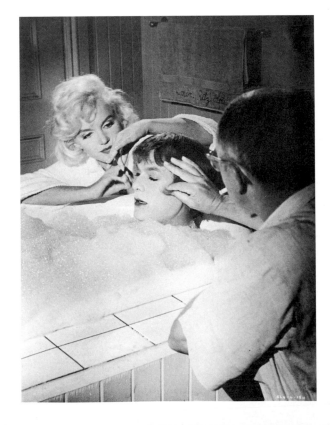

FINAL TOUCH:
Marilyn Monroe
and Wilder adjust
Tony Curtis's make-
up on the set of
Some Like It Hot.
[Courtesy of Photofest]

THE BUSINESS WORLD: Jack Lemmon works out some comedy bits, much to his director's amusement, on the set of *The Apartment*.
[Courtesy of Photofest]

AN ARMLOAD: Backstage after the ceremony, Wilder balances the three Oscars he won for *The Apartment*, accompanied by his fellow winner Elizabeth Taylor.
[© Copyright Academy of Motion Picture Arts and Sciences]

COQUETTE: Jack Lemmon, Shirley MacLaine, and Irma's dog receive some technical instructions from their director on the set of *Irma la Douce*. [Courtesy of Photofest]

TAKING THE CAKE: Wilder's birthday party on the set of *Kiss Me, Stupid*: (l. to r.) Cliff Osmond, Ray Walston, Tony Curtis, Jack Lemmon, Felicia Farr, Wilder, Kim Novak, and Dean Martin. [Courtesy of the Academy of Motion Picture Arts and Sciences]

HOW TO DO IT: Wilder shows Jack Lemmon and Walter Matthau the precise way to kick Judi West on the set of *The Fortune Cookie*. [Courtesy of the Academy of Motion Picture Arts and Sciences]

OLD FRIENDS: Walter Matthau listens to Wilder on the set of *The Front Page*. [Courtesy of Photofest]

ANOTHER ALTER EGO: Wilder directs Robert Stephens on the set of *The Private Life of Sherlock Holmes.* [Courtesy of Photofest]

THE GLAMOUR AND MAGIC OF DIRECTING: Wilder and I. A. L. Diamond take a break from filming *The Private Life of Sherlock Holmes.* [Courtesy of the Academy of Motion Picture Arts and Sciences]

A FUNEREAL MOOD: Wilder wheels Hildegarde Knef through the set of *Fedora*, with Hans Jaray (left) and Jose Ferrer (right). [Courtesy of Photofest]

TRIBUTE: Billy Wilder accepts the 1987 Irving G. Thalberg Award from the Academy of Motion Picture Arts and Sciences. [© Copyright Academy of Motion Picture Arts and Sciences]

down the tunnel, pops his head back out and gives a sarcastic little salute, a final *screw you*, and leaves. Cookie, notably, gets the last line: "Maybe he just wanted to steal our wire cutters. Did you ever think of that?"

Edwin Blum, like Norman Krasna, must have seen quite a bit of Billy Wilder in the character of Sefton. Blum reported later that during the writing of *Stalag 17* he found himself being treated by Billy as "little more than his butler." Blum was philosophical: "I know he is a man that the more he likes you, the more sarcastic he gets, but I couldn't take it." Asked whether the writing of a smash hit with a verbal firecracker was worth it in the end, Blum was blunt. No, Blum said, it wasn't. The reason: "I just couldn't take his insults."

David Denby has written of *Stalag 17* that Wilder's interest lies in "proving the essential rightness of the realist who sees through everything. The movie is more of a self-portrait than anything else Wilder made." Wilder buffs may argue the point, but Denby's basic contention is right on the mark. "What's the beef, boys?" Sefton declares early in the film when he explains his close commercial relationship with the Nazis. "So I'm trading. Everybody here is trading. So maybe I trade a little sharper. That make me a collaborator?" He goes on: "You can be the heroes—the guys with fruit salad on your chests. Me? I'm staying put. I'm going to make myself as comfortable as I can. And if it takes a little trading with the enemy to get me some food or a better mattress? That's okay by Sefton," at which point he strikes his match on Duke's sleeve, just for the sake of dramatics.

In the action-sequence escape, Wilder films Johnson and Manfredi as they crawl under the pilings of the barracks, steal across the dark courtyard avoiding searchlights, run into the latrine, and enter the escape tunnel, all to the ominous sound of a drumroll. Ernest Laszlo's grimy cinematography exacerbates the mood's tension; this is heroism on a decidedly dirty and hard-headed scale. The two escapees crawl through the tunnel, firing up a cigarette lighter in order to see. Wilder cuts back to the barracks. "They've got a good chance—the longest night of the year," says Price (Peter Graves). "I bet they make it to Friedrichshafen," says Duke. "I bet they make it all the way to Switzerland!" says Animal.

"And I bet they don't get out of the forest," says Sefton. He isn't speaking figuratively: Billy's hero wagers the others two packs of cigarettes that his own compatriots will be shot to death. "He'd make book on his own mother getting hit by a truck," Shapiro remarks. Wilder cuts back to Manfredi and Johnson, who emerge from the tunnel and crawl forward, straight into a line of machine gunners. The camera is too far away to distinguish one from the other, but it scarcely matters. One dies quickly in a burst of gunfire, and Billy makes the other watch his buddy take the hit and fall dead next to him. He reaches out reflexively and touches the body, then uses it as a shield. Wilder cuts to the machine gunners letting another round flare, then back to the American soldier, who takes the gunfire in the back as he tries to crawl away. He's hit, goes rigid, slumps, and dies.

Wilder cuts back to Sefton, who looks disturbed by the sounds he has just heard, but not enough to make him hesitate before piling his winnings into a box and taking them back to his side of the room and locking them safely away in his treasure chest.

Extracting comedy from this material might have been difficult, but not for Billy Wilder. *Stalag 17* is as funny as it is depressing. In fact, Wilder's characters are ennobled by their sense of humor under pressure. When Animal spies the Russian women, he blurts, "Get a load o' that blonde, she's built like a brick Kremlin!" Harry Shapiro tells Sergeant Schultz (Sig Ruman), "*Sprechen sie Deutsch*? Then *droppen sie dead*!" The fact that the movie's comedy is often fairly low makes no difference; if anything, its lowliness only makes it more refreshing. ("I'm tellin' ya, Animal, these Nazis ain't kosher!" says Harry. "Yeah, you can say that again," Animal replies. "I'm tellin' ya, Animal, these Nazis ain't kosher!" says Harry.) These guys tell jokes to survive, and it doesn't matter if nobody else finds them funny. "Look at them, Lieutenant—everybody is a clown!" Schultz declares. "How do you expect to win the war *mit* an army of clowns?" "We sorta hope you laugh yourselves to death," says Harry. For Wilder, comedy is one of the only saving graces of a world that would otherwise be intolerable.

Even the camp commandant, von Scherbach, is comical, albeit in a ghastly way. (The character is Wilder and Blum's invention; he does not appear in the play.) Here is Otto Preminger's first line, delivered in consummate, harsh Germanic tones: "*Guten Morgen*, sergeants. Nasty weather we are having, eh? And I *so* much hoped we could give you a white Christmas, just like the ones you used to know." Later in that scene, von Scherbach makes another little joke, this one for his own amusement: "All right, then, gentlemen, we are all friends again. And with Christmas coming on I have a special treat for you. I'll have you all deloused for the holidays." Still later, he makes this amusing quip: "Curtains would do wonders for this barracks. You will not get them."

The intelligence and discretion of Wilder's camerawork reaches its highest level in a single shot of violence and perfect timing. Marko brings a copy of *Mein Kampf* to the men by orders of von Scherbach. He discards it contemptuously by tossing it to the rear of the image, and Wilder cuts on action to Duke catching the heavy volume in the next shot. "That's the wrong direction," Duke says in medium distance, whereupon he swings around and hurls the book—hard—toward the back of the room. Wilder pans to reveal Duke's target—Sefton. The book hurtles toward him—all in the same shot—and misses his head by a fraction of an inch. It slams against the wall. Duke's perfect shot would be marvelous on its own, but one then realizes that at the moment that the book shoots just over Sefton's head and slams against the wall behind him, Sefton is having his face shaved, by Cookie—with a straight razor. Sefton doesn't flinch. It's a remarkable moment for Holden, who could easily have been smacked square in the face by a hardbound book. "Give that man a Kewpie doll!" Sefton says mildly, and only then does Wilder cut to the next shot.

When *Stalag 17* opened in May 1953, Wilder got all the applause, approval, and financial return he lacked with *Ace in the Hole*. The film is said to have made about $10 million in the United States alone, which more than compensated for *Ace in the Hole*'s losses. This was due in part to better marketing. Despite its violent opening scenes, in which two good-looking American boys get machine-gunned to death, Paramount's publicity department sold *Stalag 17* as a comedy—a "star-spangled, laugh-loaded salute to our POW heroes!" The studio shrewdly previewed it at the annual convention of the American Ex-Prisoners of War in Oklahoma City, and American Legion groups, the VFW, and the Military Order of the Purple Heart were treated to advance screenings as well. The press material made sure to note that Wilder had written to a number of former prisoners of war offering them parts in the film, and that a few of the on-screen POWs had really been prisoners of the Nazis. Paramount invited fourteen former POWs to the premiere at the Warners Beverly Hills Theater and a post-premiere supper party. The Hollywood trade papers loved it, and so did most of America's movie reviewers. Billy Wilder was back on top. He was probably even more relieved that he'd gotten rid of Cy Howard, too. Howard managed to get picked up in a whorehouse raid right before *Stalag 17* premiered.

When the Oscar nominations were announced the following February, Wilder found himself named in the Best Director category. *Stalag 17* failed to earn a Best Picture nomination, nor was it mentioned in any of the three writing categories, but Bill Holden was one of the five Best Actor nominees (the others being Marlon Brando, Richard Burton, Montgomery Clift, and Burt Lancaster). The awards themselves were personally disappointing for Billy; it was a sweep for his old *Menschen am Sonntag* gofer, Fred Zinnemann, whose *From Here to Eternity* won eight awards, including Best Director and Best Screenplay. (*From Here to Eternity* is a World War II picture as well, but a much more romantic one.) All was not lost, though. When Shirley Booth announced the Best Actor award via a live television hookup from her backstage dressing room in a Philadelphia theater, it was Bill Holden's name she announced, and Holden ran happily to the podium. Emcee Donald O'Connor whispered to him that the show was running overtime and he'd better make it quick, so Holden simply said, "Thank you, thank you," and left the stage. Billy was pleased for his friend and told him so, but later that night when Holden headed home, his wife, Ardis, set him straight about the quality of his performance in *Stalag 17*: "Well, you know, Bill, you really didn't get the award for *Stalag*. They gave it to you for *Sunset Boulevard*."

Relieved by the commercial success of *Stalag 17*, Billy turned his sights to his next projects, invested in some more art, took some trips with Audrey, and rose even higher on the Hollywood social scale. Through a New York gallery he bought a Joseph Cornell box, *Untitled (Grand Hotel Pharmacy)*, made in the 1940s; given Cornell's reputation at the end of the century it was a most prescient purchase. In Paris, he bought Rouault's *Passion*, a gouache and black wax crayon work on paper—another astute buy, though not as remarkably foresighted. Always a clotheshorse, Billy continued buying himself the finest menswear the world's best stores had to offer, and by this point he was so rich that it didn't matter how much he spent. With Billy's full encouragement, Audrey became a well-known fashion plate as well. Her shopping trips to the Parisian couture houses were becoming legendary. Slim, beautiful, and exquisitely poised, Audrey Wilder looked fabulous in the elegant high-style clothes she bought with an abandon to rival her husband's, and by 1953, she was one of the few Hollywood women to whom other Hollywood women turned when they wanted a living definition of the word *chic*.

After shooting *Stalag 17* Wilder remained undecided about his next film through the remainder of the year. He told Don Taylor that he wanted to adapt a then-best-selling novel about a depressive teenager, but like a number of Billy's overflowing ideas, it went no further than talk; Billy Wilder did not end up directing *Catcher in the Rye*. In May 1952, before leaving for a trip to Europe, he told Louella Parsons that he wanted to make an independent German-language film—in Germany—with Marlene Dietrich. Billy reported that he would still be in Europe in mid-June, when he was scheduled to attend the Berlin Film Festival; he and Audrey would be joined there, he said, by Bill and Ardis Holden. He also told Parsons that he would be stopping off in New York on his way to the Continent so that he could meet with Yul Brynner about yet another film idea. As Louella put it, "all [Wilder] knows about the Brynner story is that Yul will play a Soviet ballet dancer who comes with a troupe from Russia to appear at the Venice Art Festival."

Brynner was enthusiastic about Billy's idea, and by the end of the year Wilder had fleshed out his plans with yet another in a string of new collaborators—Julius Epstein. Best known for writing *Casablanca* (1942), Epstein had also written such successful films as *The Man Who Came to*

Dinner (1942), *Mr. Skeffington* (1944), and *Arsenic and Old Lace* (1944). On December 10, Wilder and Epstein met with the censors to discuss their ideas. A memo describes the meeting: "Messrs. Vizzard and Shurlock had a conference with Messrs. Luraschi, Billy Wilder, and Julius Epstein. It is their intention to do a modern story very much along the lines of *Anna Karenina*. The lead, Jule [*sic*] Brynner will be a member of the Soviet embassy in Washington. He will fall in love with the wife of some other foreign diplomat. The situation will develop to the point where they will have to flee the country to Mexico. The Soviets will be after him throughout the story. After a very unhappy and tragic time in Mexico, our lead will realize the impossibility of the situation and will let the Soviets catch up with him and kill him, somewhat as in the case of Trotsky. The wife will then be free to endeavor to rehabilitate herself." The censors found little to object to, as long as "the proper compensating moral values are injected."

Wilder and Epstein planned to call their film *A New Kind of Love*; the fact that Chevalier was out didn't mean that they couldn't still use the title. But the name turned out to be as jinxed as Chevalier, and *A New Kind of Love* fell apart. Brynner was paid $15,000 on his acceptance of the role, but casting complications prevented the project from getting any further off the ground. A comely young all-but-unknown, Audrey Hepburn, is said to have been cast in the film, but she soon backed out because of prior commitments. Billy announced that Katharine Hepburn would take the role, but she, too, withdrew. The only other details of *A New Kind of Love* that appear to have survived come thirdhand from Billy's friend Armand Deutsch, who recalls George Axelrod telling him about some of Billy's meet-cute ideas, including this one: "We find Audrey Hepburn in her bed, late at night, perhaps with glasses on, working a crossword puzzle. She is the wife of England's Ambassador to the United States. She picks up the telephone, calls the Russian Embassy, and asks for someone who can give her assistance. It is Yul Brynner who answers the phone. Hepburn politely asks Stalin's middle name. Brynner angrily replies, 'We are not here for such nonsense!' He hears Hepburn's distinctive tinkling laugh and bangs down the phone. The next night at a large ball Brynner hears that laugh. Looking up, he sees Hepburn, walks over to her and says, 'Ilyich.' They meet and fall in love."

A New Kind of Love got no further than the earliest drawing-board stage, but Wilder's association with Audrey Hepburn had just begun. He wrote his next film especially for her, and—thanks to Audrey Wilder's taste and Hepburn's own extraordinary figure—she immediately became a world-renowned exemplar of fashionable good taste, not to mention a first-rate actress and glamorous movie star. Billy himself was well on the way to setting the tone for some of the best-known taste-making elements of 1950s culture: Givenchy originals in *Sabrina*; Tom Ewell's emblematic sexual frustration—and Marilyn Monroe's comic timing—in *The Seven Year Itch*; the wistful romance between Hepburn and Gary Cooper in *Love in the Afternoon*; and eventually, of course, *Some Like It Hot*.

How different it might have turned out. Had his gambler's luck and persistence not been so sharp, the desperate immigrant of 1934 might have remained so twenty years later, his talent notwithstanding. The shadow of what might have been was never far from his thoughts. Hollywood was too full of *memento mori* for him to forget. Where was Franz Schultz in 1952? Where was Wilhelm Thiele or Hanns Schwarz? Lubitsch was dead. Lang was surviving well enough. Reisch was working, but his scripts were never that great. Robert Siodmak was on his way down, Curt was already deep into *Tarzan's Magic Mountain*–land. And oy, Edgar Ulmer (*The Man from Planet X*; *Babes in Bagdad* . . .). Even Willie was cranking them out—*Phantoms from Space, Killers from Space*. . . . What could he possibly think of next—an abominable snowman movie? If Billy Wilder hadn't been as smart as he was—and as tough as he was—his artistic life might have been equally pathetic. Billy was a big shot, and he planned to stay that way.

20. AUDREY

FAIRCHILD (John Williams, playing Sabrina's father): May I ask, sir, what exactly are your intentions?
LINUS LARRABEE (Humphrey Bogart): My intentions? Unethical, reprehensible, but very practical.

—Sabrina

Wispy, delicate Audrey Hepburn had two notorious pit bulls running interference for her—her mother, a fat baroness, and Lew Wasserman, a thin agent. The Baroness Ella van Heemstra bossed Audrey's personal life, Wasserman orchestrated her deals. When the *Sabrina* deal was struck, Audrey was twenty-two years old—a fresh Hollywood meteor who had just set the screen ablaze in *Roman Holiday* as a disenchanted princess who ends up with Gregory Peck. In *Sabrina* she's even more luminous. According to some accounts, *Sabrina* may have been Audrey's idea all along—not Paramount's or Wilder's. She's said to have read the script of Samuel Taylor's play *Sabrina Fair* before it even opened on Broadway (with the sprightly but rather long-of-tooth Margaret Sullavan already cast in the title role) and knew it was a perfect role for her: the chauffeur's daughter who wins the hearts of two wealthy brothers, her father's bosses. Whether Hepburn asked Wasserman to convince Paramount to buy the film rights and cast her in the title role, or whether Wilder asked Paramount to buy it for her without her input (as Billy himself claims), by March 1953, *Sabrina* was Audrey's vehicle. (The film's title remained *Sabrina Fair* until just before its release, when it was shortened.) In early May 1953, just as the brutally comic *Stalag 17* was about to be released, Louella Parsons announced to the world that this slight romantic fairy tale would be directed by Billy Wilder.

Billy was dazzled by Audrey's beauty, as were many men. But he was just as impressed with her graceful intelligence. "She looks as if she could spell *schizophrenia*," he noted. Better still, unlike many movie stars, she could spell it without being it. Billy waxed enthusiastic: "After so many drive-in waitresses in movies (it has been a real drought) here is class— somebody who went to school, can spell, and possibly play the piano. The other class girl is Katharine Hepburn. There is nobody else—just a lot of drive-in waitresses off to the races, wriggling their behinds at the 3-D camera." Audrey, Billy said, was "like a salmon swimming upstream. She can do it with very small bosoms. Tit-ism has taken over this country."

The critic Walter Kerr once described her as "every man's dream of the nymph he once planned to meet," a true enough claim as far as Billy was concerned. (Billy was forty-seven when he made *Sabrina*.) But Hepburn's nymph-hood was always counterbalanced by the fortitude of Hercules. On-screen and off-, she had a core of iron that sustained her through difficult times. Audrey was as fearless as she was industrious. When the Nazis rounded up the citizens of her town for transport, she found herself guarded at gunpoint by a young soldier who eventually made the mistake of putting down his rifle to roll a cigarette. So Audrey made a run for it. Luckily, the girl was small and fast, and her escape was successful. Still, she ended up spending the next month slipping in and out of consciousness while hiding in a rat-filled cellar. This tenacity is an essential part of her appeal, and Billy saw it quickly and clearly. In both *Sabrina* and *Love in the Afternoon*, Hepburn projects a tough inner core disguised by a fragile exterior. With most other stars it's the other way around—the surface may be pure vigor, but the inside is a mess.

It was this reversal that captured the attention of the French writer Colette, who in 1951 was scouting actresses for the title role in the theatrical adaptation of her novel *Gigi*. By then, Audrey had already broken into films, but mostly in minor roles: a hotel clerk in *One Wild Oat*; a cigarette girl in *Laughter in Paradise*. In *The Lavender Hill Mob*, the character she played actually had a name, and a most un-Audrey one at that— Chiquita, the girl to whom Alec Guinness gives some cash in the opening sequence. After *The Lavender Hill Mob*, Audrey landed a bigger role in *Secret People*, a political assassination drama, but the director, Thorold Dickinson, wasn't much impressed. Still, she kept working. She was busy filming a glossy farce called *Monte Carlo Baby* when a heavyset woman with hair the color of shredded carrots showed up on the French set and relentlessly disrupted the day's filming with an intrusive running commentary on the action. The clownish grande dame took an immediate shine to Audrey. This young thing, Colette declared, simply had to be Gigi. When the old woman met with her shy star-to-be, Audrey was self-deprecating to the point of refusing even to consider the role on the grounds that she was utterly talentless. To every one of Colette's protests to the contrary, Hepburn presented a solid argument, but the pure stubbornness of her modesty only served to charm Colette further. With a novelist's eye for clarity, Colette saw that underneath this young woman's superficial insecurities was an unbendable core of will.

Billy Wilder shared Colette's eye for talent. He knew that tiny Audrey could stand up to both of the costars he had in mind for *Sabrina*—William Holden and Cary Grant. Holden was most amenable to doing another film with Wilder, and when Grant agreed as well, Wilder and Samuel Taylor began to rewrite the part of Linus, the elder Larrabee brother, especially for him. Then, suddenly, Grant pulled out for reasons he never explained, and Billy was left in the lurch. The role of Linus Larrabee demanded the stature, weight, and scope that only Grant and a handful of other stars possessed. Not only did Linus have to be of a certain age and import, but he had to provide a convincing alternative to devilish, athletic-looking Bill Holden.

There was Jimmy Stewart, who hadn't yet been cast in Paramount's *Rear Window*. There was Gregory Peck. Tyrone Power or James Mason might have worked, too. Joseph Cotten was by all accounts terrific in the role on Broadway; if only he'd been a bona fide movie star on the level of Grant or Stewart or Peck. Whether these dapper actors weren't available or Wilder just didn't like them, when the dust settled after Grant's departure Humphrey Bogart was Linus Larrabee—to the thundering tune of $200,000. One measure of his stature was that Bogart also won the right to approve Billy's script before setting foot in front of a camera (though he never got the chance, because the script was written concurrently with shooting). Holden got $80,000, Hepburn $35,000; Billy's fee stayed firm at a hefty $250,000.

It boded well, the teaming of Billy and Bogie. By the early 1950s Wilder was one of the few directors Bogart eagerly consented to work with. (A contract Bogart signed with Warner Bros. specified that the only directors he approved in advance were Wyler, Dmytryk, Huston, Ford, and Wilder.) Bogart and his wife, Lauren Bacall, were leaders of Hollywood's liberal wing. Bogart himself joined Wilder in the formation of the Committee for the First Amendment back in 1947. Since then, the Bogarts and the Wilders had become friendly, the Bogarts having hosted Billy and Audrey at their own home. They liked each other. Their personal styles were in synch—a love of dirty jokes, a flat refusal to suffer fools, and a surfeit of talent. The two men looked forward to working together.

Bogart initially agreed to take the role based on pure trust of Billy; only after agreeing in principle did he demand script approval. He heard not a single word about the nature of the part. His agent, Phil Gersh, later said that he had been the one who'd suggested Bogart to Wilder, and that Billy had called two weeks later requesting a meeting with Bogie himself. They met at five in the afternoon and spoke relaxedly for two hours. *Sabrina* was never mentioned. Bogart, who had another appointment that evening, finally said, "Look, let's just shake hands on it, and you take care of me." There was only one problem: as Wilder said at the time, "Audrey is a tall girl. She's five foot seven, I think. She'll need tall leading men. Maybe she'll have to wear flat heels in *Sabrina* and Bogart will have to wear high heels."

Wilder and Taylor turned in a preliminary draft in early July, but by that point their collaboration was in deep trouble. Taylor found it impossible to stomach Billy's insistent revisions. With his play running on Broadway to great acclaim and a healthy box office, Taylor was shocked that Wilder saw the need to scrap so much of it. One day Taylor decided he'd had enough, and suddenly Billy found himself writing alone—never one of his favorite pastimes. He needed a new writing partner, as Walter Neff would say, *but quick*. He found him in Ernest Lehman. One morning, Lehman later reported, he was in his office at MGM working on his own original script (that would eventually be made as *Sweet Smell of Success*, a dazzlingly vicious movie). That afternoon he was at Paramount, having been summoned by a frantic call from Billy.

Sabrina was scheduled to begin shooting at the end of September on location at an estate on Long Island Sound. Paramount's location scouts probably didn't have much trouble gaining access to the perfect place they found in Mamaroneck; it belonged to Barney Balaban, the head of the studio. When the scouts went looking for a good swimming pool, they found one with almost the same degree of access in Billy's old friend William Paley's yard. Billy left Los Angeles for New York on September 22, taking the Super Chief to Chicago and the Century the rest of the way. He moved into a suite at the St. Regis, as did Lehman, the Bogarts, the Holdens, and Hepburn. It may have been the only time during the production that everyone got along.

Sabrina's troubles began right away. High winds coming off the Sound disrupted the shooting, though cinematographer Charles Lang took a magnificent shot of Bogart and Hepburn, in silhouette, as they stand by the water at dusk. Problems continued as location shooting progressed. Transparencies (to be used as backgrounds for process shots) taken at the Glen Cove railway station for the pivotal scene in which Sabrina returns from Paris and David Larrabee doesn't recognize her, proved insufficient and unconvincing, and Billy was irritated. "It was my original intention to shoot it at the Fox lot where they have a perfect small station standing. I was talked out of it." He urged Paramount to approve reshooting the scene. "We simply must sell the girl's transition. She must look delicious reappearing on Long Island. We must also play Holden's approach gayer and more spirited." Later, in Los Angeles, the scene was reshot.

Workmanlike but tense, the company soon returned to Los Angeles, where the production of *Sabrina* resumed on October 6. Billy shot scenes every day and wrote new ones with Lehman every night. Often they found themselves composing in a frenzy. Gofers picked up new pages from a bleary Lehman early in the morning after these all-night sessions and rushed them over to Hepburn, who studied the new dialogue in her car on the way to the studio. Billy didn't sleep much. Lehman was stressed. Wilder himself began to suffer health problems, primarily backaches. At times, he found that he had nothing to shoot because the missing scene hadn't been written yet. "We'll do retakes," Billy would snap.

Paramount's Don Hartman was nervous about Hepburn's bony neck and told Charles Lang to be especially aware of it. Bogart didn't much like Hepburn. Holden drank. So did Bogart. Then there was the issue of Audrey's wardrobe. As Hepburn's biographer Alexander Walker notes, Sabrina returns from a two-year course at a Parisian cooking school with a trunk full of Givenchy originals, which have clearly not come with her chef's diploma: "More likely [they] come by courtesy of a fellow pupil, an elderly baron who is taking a refresher course in getting soufflés to rise." In any case, some accounts say that it was Hepburn's idea to dress Sabrina in Givenchy. Others say it was actually Audrey Wilder who'd discovered Givenchy during one of her Paris shopping sprees and called his glorious designs to her husband's attention. (Billy has often remarked proudly of his wife's extravagance and taste.) Whether Hepburn was really concerned about offending Edith Head, with whom she had worked well on *Roman Holiday*, is unclear. What is certain is that Head was told—by Billy himself, it's said—that the Oscar winner's contribution to *Sabrina* would consist only of what *Vanity Fair*'s Amy Fine Collins calls "a pre-Paris ragamuffin frock and two insignificant sportswear ensembles."

The costuming crisis began in June. *Sabrina*'s production memos reveal that it was indeed Billy's idea to have Hepburn buy herself some fashionable clothes in Paris—particularly what one memo colorfully describes as "a particularly Frenchy-looking suit." Some "extreme French hats" were also on the shopping list. Paramount's front office had one key concern. It was not which haute couture designer Audrey selected, nor was it a matter of soothing the feelings of Edith Head. Paramount executives were adamant: these gowns would have to be purchased by Audrey Hepburn for her own private wardrobe because the studio did not want to pay any customs fees. In addition, Paramount was concerned about the credits. If Hepburn wore her own clothes Paramount needn't worry about citing the dressmaker.

Givenchy was not the first choice either of Audrey Hepburn or Paramount Pictures. Cristóbal Balenciaga had the bigger name, and it was to him that they first turned. Moreover, at this point the studio frankly assumed that Edith Head would perform significant alterations on anything Hepburn chose. Balenciaga, however, quickly gave way to Givenchy. One tale is that Balenciaga simply didn't know who Audrey Hepburn was. The maestro had been delighted when his staff told him that Miss Hepburn was requesting his services, but when he discovered that it wasn't Katharine but some other Hepburn—a far lesser Hepburn in those days—he turned her down flat. Dismissed by the king, Audrey settled on the crown prince in the form of the younger and less-established Givenchy. On the other hand, Givenchy himself tells the same story about thinking that Katharine Hepburn was paying a call, so perhaps Balenciaga's refusal is fiction. However the relationship transpired, Hepburn and Givenchy together developed an inimitably elegant look for Sabrina, one that served Hepburn herself extraordinarily well for the rest of her life.

A memo records the fact that Audrey insisted on one particular Givenchy gown. Wilder and Edith Head approved it, and Hepburn bought it for the royal sum of $560. It was a black cocktail dress with a high neck, and when the movie hit the screens the following year it rocked the fashion world by ushering in what was to become known as "the Sabrina neckline." Edith Head won her Oscar for it, even though it was pure Givenchy. Like Paramount's front office, the designer noticed Hepburn's anorexic collarbones; the "Sabrina neckline" covers the collar but reveals the throat. Audrey also picked out a strapless gown in white organdy, with black silk embroidery and an immense train that flowed out from the sides. When she wears it in the film, Audrey looks like a finely crafted butterfly on its way to an elfin ball. She also chose a tailored gray wool suit, which she herself topped with a turban.

Clad in Givenchy, Audrey Hepburn was even more breathtakingly lovely than she had been in *Roman Holiday*. When David Larrabee (Holden) screeches his car to a halt in front of the Long Island train station, having seen a splendidly chic fawn as if in a mirage, you not only know exactly what he's stopping for—you *feel* it.

Hepburn knew only half-consciously what she was doing when she starved herself. Billy, on the other hand, gave his full approval for Givenchy's designs on Hepburn's tiny body knowing exactly what they meant: Sabrina would be the perfect understatement in a world of 1950s excess. With her skinny-boy's body, Audrey Hepburn was appearing on the scene in the midst of the most breast-obsessed period in modern history. Billy knew that world already had its Marilyn Monroes and Jane Russells; what it didn't have was a waif. In *Sabrina*, her pencillike legs would be highlighted with stretch pants. Her Modigliani neck wouldn't be covered up with turtles and cowls. And her tiny breasts were left well enough alone.

During the production of *Roman Holiday* Edith Head came right out and told Audrey to face facts: "You should wear falsies." Billy saw things differently.

If the production of *Sabrina* had been as airy and delightful as Hepburn's wardrobe, the film itself might play better. But the shoot was an extended nightmare, the first truly disastrous production Billy directed. Almost everyone blames Bogart.

First he started doing malicious imitations of Audrey's precious accent—British kissed by someone who first spoke French. When Wilder tried to intervene, Bogart cleverly began mimicking Billy. At least once he asked somebody to translate Billy's remarks into English.

Bogart was surprised and then infuriated by all the close-ups of Hepburn—shots taken over Bogart's own aging shoulder, his back to the camera. Bogie was a fine actor, but Billy knew that most people would prefer to see Audrey's sweet face than Bogart's craggy one. Bogie was a tough guy, but he was still a movie star, and the young beauty threatened him. He turned sullen.

The lack of a completed script did not work to Billy's favor this time. It continued to keep the front office off guard, and it still lent a certain immediacy to the production, but this immediacy was a little *too* immediate. Even Billy was thrown off by his own spontaneity. One day well into production, Wilder told Doane Harrison to get some electricians to think up some sort of complicated lighting effect for the next scene. "Get them to do something that will take some time," he said. Harrison was baffled. "What for?" he asked. "We haven't got the dialogue written yet," Billy said.

Bogart, meanwhile, was requesting—and receiving—a glass of scotch every day at five or five-thirty, whereupon he grew even meaner and more surly. When Billy began inviting Hepburn, Holden, and Lehman back to his own office for a drink after work, he pointedly excluded Bogart, who became resentful. "Bogart gave me some bad times," Billy later said, "but he was a needler anyway, and somehow he got the idea that Bill Holden, Audrey Hepburn, and I were in cahoots against him. Bill at one point was ready to kill him. Eventually we smoothed it out and everything worked out well."

No, it didn't. One day Bogart was offended that only Holden and Hepburn got revised script pages and he walked off the set in a rage. On another day, Bogart did receive new dialogue and promptly asked Billy if he had any kids. Yes, Billy said, a thirteen-year-old daughter. "Did *she* write this?" Bogie asked.

Holden and Hepburn, meanwhile, were falling in love. Their offscreen romance might have given *Sabrina* the kind of ineffable, unscriptable charge of *To Have and Have Not*, or *Woman of the Year*; you can actually *see* Bogart fall for Bacall, Tracy for Hepburn. When Ernest Lehman walked into Holden's dressing room one day and found Hepburn and Holden looking deep into each other's eyes, he knew that "something profound was happening between them." Unfortunately, the "something" defied the plot of the film they were making. It also served to fuel Bogart's alienation. Hepburn was supposed to stop loving Holden and fall for Bogart, but Audrey and Bill's love for each other—and their growing disgust with Bogart—got in the way.

Anyway, as far as Bogie was concerned, Hepburn wasn't worth his trouble. Clifton Webb ran into Bogart on the Paramount lot one day and asked him, "How do you like working with that dream girl?" "She's okay," Bogie replied, "if you like to do thirty-six takes."

Then Bogart called Holden "a dumb prick." Holden is said to have gotten so angry that he lunged at his costar and had to be physically restrained by Billy. Bogart called Billy a "kraut bastard Nazi son of a bitch." Billy finally snapped and said either: "I look at you, Bogey, and beneath the surface of an apparent shit I see the face of a real shit." (Or, more elaborately: "I examine your face, Bogie; I look at the valleys, the crevices, and the pits of your ugly face, and I know that somewhere underneath the sickening face of a shit is a *real* shit.") Even in a rage Wilder knew how to compose a good line.

In the press, Bogart called Billy "the kind of Prussian German with a riding crop." He complained that while he was making the movie he didn't even know who got the girl at the end. This was an exaggeration, but only slightly. Holden needed to be freed up quickly so he could do *The Bridges at Toko-Ri*, so Wilder wrote and shot the concluding board meeting scene between Holden and Bogart to enable Holden to depart the production. This meant, however, that Wilder and Lehman wrote Holden out of the story before they resolved the love relationship between Hepburn and Bogart. The least convincing aspect of *Sabrina* is Linus's attraction to Sabrina and her full return of his all-but-nonexistent love. Then again, that the film works on any level is a small miracle.

Then Bogart told a reporter that *Sabrina* was "a crock of shit."

Toward the end of the production, Lehman collapsed in exhaustion, crying uncontrollably. For the first time in his life (but not the last), Billy Wilder successfully hurled a man into a nervous breakdown. Having achieved this degree of intimacy with his writing partner, Wilder was horrified. He instantly dropped the raging torrent of put-downs and all the driving pressure, put his arm around his friend and cowriter, and told him not to worry about a thing; Ernie should just go home and take a well-deserved rest. Lehman's doctor ordered him to bed for two weeks. A few days later, the physician paid a house call. He pronounced his patient in good health, then said, "You can tell Mr. Wilder to come out now," at which point Billy burst out of the closet looking very pleased with himself. He'd stopped by to go over some script details and jumped into hiding when he heard the doctor at the front door.

The production of *Sabrina* closed on December 5, 1953, eleven days behind schedule, Wilder and Lehman having rewritten scenes until the very end of the shoot. Its final price tag: $2,238,813.19. After the final take, Billy looked up in the sky and screamed "*Fuck you*" at God.

His nervous breakdown notwithstanding, Lehman appears to have stood up better than most of Wilder's other writing partners to the ongoing barrage of slurs. What got Lehman's goat was Wilder's insistence on dominating Lehman's tastes as well as his prose: "Billy has to take over your whole life. You don't just collaborate on a script with him. He has to change what you wear and what you eat." Still, the slurs stung. Lehman told of an extended fight Billy picked when Lehman refused to go along with one of Billy's ideas. Wilder suggested, insisted, *demanded*, that Sabrina have sex with Linus at the end of the scene in Linus's office in which she fixes the omelette. They'd have to do it in a covert way, of course, but Lehman couldn't countenance it in any form. Hepburn seemed too pure to him, and he was convinced that audiences would be outraged at any suggestion of sex. Billy went wild. He flew into a violent fury and ripped into Lehman with a torrent of invectives. As usual, he hit his friend where he thought it would hurt the most. As Lehman described it, Wilder spewed "all kinds of names—eunuch, fag, didn't know women, hated sex, was afraid of women, in this vile and vicious manner he has when he's insulting you." Lehman, who was securely married to a charming woman named Jacqueline, wasn't thrown by Billy's abuse. He still wouldn't budge, and Billy gave it up.

Sabrina didn't open until the following August. The trades loved it, as did most critics and, more crucially, most audiences; *Sabrina* was a commercial hit. Paramount shrewdly capitalized on the fact that the film boasted a total of four Oscar winners—Bogart for *The African Queen*, Hepburn for *Roman Holiday*, Holden for *Stalag 17*, and even Billy himself for *The Lost Weekend*. The director, finally, was getting to be a kind of star. The studio was hedging its bets in one regard, however. One of the posters Paramount designed for *Sabrina* features a picture of Audrey Hepburn looking over her shoulder. Her head is anatomically correct, but the rest of her body has been drastically retouched to provide her with the huge Monroe-esque rear end the marketing department apparently thought she needed to sell the film.

Sabrina is minor Wilder—gracious and elegant at times, pleasingly vulgar at others, but never entirely satisfying. After *Stalag 17*, Billy clearly wanted to do a Lubitsch-like romance set in a rarefied world of New York money, and to a limited extent he succeeded. The script is both sharper and funnier than Taylor's dull, talky play. Just as he did with *Stalag 17*, Billy tightened the structure, beefed up the central characterizations, and scrapped almost all the dialogue, writing more rhythmically and colorfully than the playwright. The film's musical score, adapted and composed by Billy's old friend Frederick Hollander, is delightful, and Charles Lang's cinematography is cheerfully elegant, as finely buffed as his *Ace in the Hole* photography is gritty. Hepburn is enchanting, Holden unusually cocky and buoyant, and Bogart ranges from serviceable to awful. When he utters a line like "Oh, you look lovely, Sabrina," Hollywood's greatest tough guy sounds ridiculous.

Despite its failures, *Sabrina* contains a few unforgettable moments nonetheless, chief among them the spectacular first shot of Sabrina as she sits in a tree peering through the branches, a full moon shining behind her in extravagant size, light glancing off the leaves as she poignantly watches the love of her life dancing with some silly, giggling debutante. When David hurries through the woods to meet the girl for a tryst in the indoor tennis court, Sabrina jumps out of the tree and surprises him. "Sabrina! I thought I heard somebody," he says. "No, it's nobody," she says, though she waits until after he leaves before saying it, at which point Hollander shifts smoothly into "Isn't It Romantic?" as David swaggers into the indoor tennis court to enjoy yet another in a string of meaningless lays.

An essentially wordless sequence follows. David and the giggler do have a few lines, but they're immaterial compared to the silent seduction of gesture and symbol Wilder orchestrates on their behalf. They stand on opposite sides of the tennis net. With a practiced gait, David strolls toward the post holding up the net, just as he's evidently done hundreds of times before, then bats the net-tightening lever with a loud, ugly jolt. It spins, the net slackens, and he steps over it. Sabrina, watching him from the window and understanding completely what she sees, turns away and cries, the camera staying on her as she walks away, miserable and alone. This is practically the first time Billy Wilder wrote and directed a seduction scene from a woman's point of view— or, more precisely, a girl's—and, for once, it's neither smirking nor grotesque but, instead, disappointing, plain, and sad.

With "Isn't It Romantic?" still playing in the distance, Sabrina, in her room over the garage, continues to mull over David and his latest conquest. She walks to a desk and with a look of self-assurance writes a suicide note to her father: "I don't want to go to Paris. I want to die." Wilder makes it subtly clear that there's no chance that this frail fawn will kill herself— this is just schoolgirl melodrama. All the more disconcerting then when

Sabrina proceeds to the garage, closes the door, and starts running all the engines of the eight cars parked there, so as to methodically gas herself to death. (There is no suicide attempt in the play.) As noxious air fills the room, Wilder adds a bizarre joke—the last car blows smoke rings out of its tailpipe. Sabrina's morbid self-annihilation goes on for longer than one expects until Linus saves her—dour, haggard Linus.

Billy consciously evokes Lubitsch in the scene when her father, Fairchild (John Williams), reads one of Sabrina's letters from Paris to a group of servants. As William Paul points out, Lubitsch's films sound like Lubitsch no matter who wrote them. They are so rhythmic that the lines practically scan:

FAIRCHILD *(reading)*: "I don't think of David very much any more."
THE MAID: That's good.
FAIRCHILD: "Except at night."
THE BUTLER: That's bad.
FAIRCHILD: "I decided to be sensible the other day and tore up David's picture."
THE DISHWASHER: That's good.
FAIRCHILD: "Could you please airmail me some Scotch tape?"
THE COOK: That's bad.

Lubitsch's influence continues in the scenes set in Paris, especially when Sabrina meets the Baron (Marcel Dalio), her fellow soufflé student, who explains why he knows that Sabrina's soufflé has failed to rise at all: "A woman happily in love? She burns the soufflé! A woman unhappily in love? She forgets to turn on the oven." The Baron concludes the scene with the promise of a complete makeover for Sabrina. Regarding her hair, which is gathered in the back and hanging down her neck, he comments, "To begin with, you must stop looking like a horse."

One of Billy's most subtly filthy jokes explains their relationship. Wilder needs to suggest—but only in the vaguest, least censorable way—that Sabrina and the Baron have enjoyed each other's company. After all, Sabrina does return home with all those Paris originals, and she certainly cannot be assumed to have paid for them herself. The Baron must be given a rationale for buying them for the pretty little maiden. So when Fairchild reads a later letter from Sabrina, these are the words Billy Wilder makes him speak: referring to the Baron, Sabrina writes, " 'He came to the cooking school to take a refresher course in soufflés and liked me so much he decided to stay on for the fish.' "

Sabrina returns to the States mature and self-assured. She is now a woman of some experience. David, speeding by the train station in his convertible (wearing a suspiciously Billy-like hat tossed back on his head) and whistling "Isn't It Romantic?" squeals to a halt after seeing the gorgeous wisp of a woman in a turban and a slinky black dress standing at the curb. She greets him warmly: "Well hello! How *are* you!" "Well I'm fine!" he says with a grin. "How are you, and, I might add, *who* are you?" "We must be neighbors," he decides, "and if there's one thing I believe in, it's 'Love Thy Neighbor!' "

Later, they arrange one of David's patented rendezvous in the indoor tennis court, Sabrina looking utterly poised, so relaxed as she waltzes with David at the ball, so delicate and radiant. . . . It's shocking to realize that Sabrina looks forward to her meeting with this flippant stud, with his champagne and the band playing "Isn't It Romantic?," knowing full well how the scene will end. (Or *should* end; events transpire to prevent the consummation from occurring.)

Sabrina marks Billy's return to the terrain of *Ein blonder Traum*—two men in love with the same woman. Linus and David may not boast the same degree of friendship as the two Willies do in the old German film, and they don't bear any trace of Laurel and Hardy's screwball romance, but there's still a palpable bond-rivalry between them, and they, too, end up coming to blows. Low comedy is likewise employed. Gone are the sausage jokes; in their place is an extended butt routine. David has put two champagne glasses in his back pockets in preparation for his tennis-court date, and Linus forces him to sit down, thereby cutting his ass to ribbons.

Cue "Isn't It Romantic?" as Linus takes David's place on the courts. Sabrina and Linus embrace and twirl, dancing with champagne glasses in their hands. Wilder cuts to a deadeye shot of Holden lying with his head facing the camera and groaning, shards of glass being extracted from his rear end by a doctor wielding forceps. His father stands with the doctor as David moans in agony. "How are we going to make sure that all the fragments have been removed?" old man Larrabee asks. "Very simple," the doctor replies. "We will reconstruct the two champagne glasses." Holden lets out a particularly loud wail. "Now I cannot possibly be hurting you!" the doctor snaps. "The area has been completely anaesthetized!" "It's not you," Holden whines—"*it's that song*."

Always the entrepreneur, Linus has both the means and the creativity to invent a plastic hammock with a hole cut out for David's hindquarters. Indeed, David's rear remains the nagging joke of the subsequent hammock scene. Not only do his buttocks poke through the hole in a manner verging on obscene, but the two brothers begin the scene by pointedly attempting to find, for David's poem, a word that rhymes with *glass*. "Alas!" Linus cries, snapping his finger. "Of course!" says David with another snap. "So long, Scarface," are Linus's parting words at the scene's end.

Even with all the vulgarity Wilder inserted into Taylor's bland romance, the nastiest moment in Billy's *Sabrina* occurs when a son takes vengeance on his father. Old man Larrabee, who runs scared from his wife throughout the film and appears to have nothing to do but drink, smoke cigars, and attempt vainly to extract the last olive out of a jar for his martini, nevertheless begins stupidly second-guessing the deal Linus proposes to give Sabrina for leaving David alone. Linus snaps. "How would *you* do it?" he roars. "You can't even get a little olive out of a jar!" Then he grabs the jar out of his father's hands, smashes it to bits, picks the olive out of the shards, and jams it violently into his startled father's mouth. "Eat it!" he snarls.

Audiences seem not to have minded the edge Billy gave to *Sabrina*; the film was a big hit. There was cause for celebration. After Holden was through with *The Bridges of Toko-Ri*, he and his wife joined Billy and Audrey on a trip to Europe. Wilder delighted in introducing Holden to European culture. Restaurants, galleries, museums—and they all ended up at Billy's favorite mountain retreat, the spa at Badgastein, where one could take the waters in style.

Back home, Billy's influence on Holden began to show itself clearly when Holden bought a new painting—Paul Clemens's graphic nude of a model named Maddy Comfort. It was precisely the sort of shocking art Billy loved—the full-frontal exposure of a woman who seemed easy and available. Holden had to hang the work in his office because his wife wouldn't have it in the house. Unlike most of his art purchases, Holden picked this one entirely on his own without Billy's input. So when Wilder showed up at Holden's office one day and said nothing about the obscene new painting, Holden was first confused, then amused and fascinated by Billy's nonchalance. Billy simply refused to acknowledge it. But at the end of the conversation, Wilder got up from his chair, kissed the painting squarely on the pussy, and exited.

Sabrina fulfilled Billy Wilder's obligation to Paramount under the three-picture deal he signed after *Sunset Boulevard*, and given the economics of Hollywood in the mid-1950s, Wilder had little reason to sign another. The studio era was over, and in a way, Billy had made his last three films under already archaic conditions. Moreover, he was not just a writer-director. He'd produced his last three films, too, albeit under Paramount's aegis. Why did he need Paramount Pictures anymore?

The camel's back broke when a second-tier functionary called Billy one day and told him that the studio was planning to make some changes in the German release print of *Stalag 17*. The spy, Price, wouldn't be German anymore, he'd be Polish instead, and would that be okay? Wilder flew into an unusually severe rage: "I wrote them a letter that I was absolutely outraged, that I didn't understand anything like this," he says. "Asking me to permit anything like this—*me*, whose family died at Auschwitz." He demanded an apology and said that if he did not receive one he would leave the studio. "I never heard anything from Paramount—no excuse, no nothing."

He decided that Paramount Pictures could screw off. He would not help promote *Sabrina*—he would never work for those bastards again. After eighteen years and seventeen pictures, Billy Wilder left Paramount and went out on his own, and he never forgot or forgave the studio's ungrateful slap.

Billy Wilder was not on his own for very long. He had a few ideas. He'd already snapped up a deal to write and direct a long-running Broadway comedy, he was trying to get the rights to a play by Ferenc Molnár so he could use it as the basis of a film he planned to call *One, Two, Three*, he was still thinking about *A New Kind of Love*, there was a biography of Charles Lindbergh in the works at Warners, there was that old *Count of Luxembourg* musical he still wanted to put together, and he was hoping to remake a 1931 romance called *Ariane*. In May 1954, with a handsome deal already in place at Warners (for the Lindbergh picture) and a distribution deal in the making at Fox (for the Broadway comedy), Billy signed yet another deal with yet another company. Originally called Monogram, one of the Poverty Row studios, Allied Artists had been transformed by the new economics of Hollywood moviemaking; studio chief Steve Broidy was forging it into a much more prominent company with far loftier goals. Almost overnight it boasted three of the biggest directors in Hollywood; John Huston had already agreed to direct for Allied, and William Wyler was set to sign as well. Allied's vice president, Harold Mirisch, was largely responsible for attracting the talent. Mirisch, a former theater owner and popcorn concessionaire, gave these three headstrong men exactly what they wanted: money, clout, and independence.

21. TROUBLES

Oh, you better get her up higher, much higher. Play it safe. If
anything happened you could cling to the sky a little longer.
—Charles Lindbergh (James Stewart)
in *The Spirit of St. Louis*

H ere's the itinerary for tonight," Linus Larrabee tells his secretary in
preparation for his evening's date with Sabrina. "I want two tickets
to *The Seven Year Itch*, a table for two at the Colony before the show,
a table for two at the Persian Room after the show. Make it a corner
table—a dark corner." The couple ends up staying in Linus's office for
Sabrina's homemade omelette, so Linus's secretary (Ellen Corby) takes the
tickets. She arrives late to work the next day. With sleeplessness and tension
written all over her face, she apologizes to her boss: "I'm sorry. I had a
very bad night last night. I used your theater tickets *and took my mother*."
Linus cuts her off before she can explain any further.

George Axelrod's adultery comedy *The Seven Year Itch* was a smash
hit when it opened in November 1952. Defying the era's prescribed domestic values—cheery marriages, persuasive monogamy, kids, devotion to
work—the play was daring to the point of being shrill. Tom Ewell played
Richard Sherman, a Manhattan book editor and all-around American dad
whose wife and child depart for the country in the summer, leaving him
alone to face his personal demons. For Sherman, the devil is his new upstairs neighbor, a beautiful young woman who is built, as *Stalag 17*'s
Animal might say, like a brick Pentagon. She's so generic a dumb 1950s
blonde that Axelrod doesn't give her a name. She's just "the Girl." Guilt
and craving ensue, but only for Sherman. "The Girl" is oblivious to everything. Audiences adored it.

Billy couldn't have helped noticing the roar of acclaim for *The Seven
Year Itch*, especially when the *Hollywood Reporter* dubbed it the "lust

weekend." Various movie deals were in the works even before the play opened. MGM was interested, and so was the millionaire gadfly Hunting-ton Hartford. By December, Warner Bros. was making noises about buying the film rights as well. Jack Warner, planning to see the play while on a Christmastime trip to New York, asked his staff to look into possible cen-sorship problems. The Code office replied bluntly. They would never ap-prove a play about adultery, the censors stated, and even if the play's hanky-panky were eliminated completely, *The Seven Year Itch* would re-main unacceptable because "the subject material of adultery would still be the springboard of all the comedy." Screenwriter Nunnally Johnson, then at Twentieth Century–Fox, also queried the censors about the acceptability of the play under the Code, but when the Code's Geoffrey Shurlock replied that it was impossible, Johnson gave up.

Having battled the censorship office for almost two decades, and having won nearly all the big fights, Billy Wilder was scarcely intimidated by any-thing as trivial as the Production Code. He proved to be correct. By the time the film was released, the Production Code Administration concluded, astoundingly, that *The Seven Year Itch* was not about adultery. (Since no adulterous sexual acts were committed in the film, there was therefore no adultery in the film.) So with an eye toward the end of his three-picture deal with Paramount, Wilder began negotiating for the rights in January 1953. Haggling on his own behalf—but fully backed by his current agent, MCA Artists' Lew Wasserman, and his lawyer, Larry Beilenson—Billy pro-posed a deal not for one film but for three. First, there would be an English-language *Seven Year Itch* in which Wilder proposed to star Tom Ewell and Marilyn Monroe. For a French version, Fernandel would take Ewell's part. Cantinflas would get the Spanish-language lead.

Charles Feldman, a successful Hollywood agent who listed Monroe among his clients, was also considering making an offer, but he was not yet in discussion with Axelrod or his agent. Since Feldman had Wilder in mind to direct the film anyway, Feldman proposed a deal directly to Billy: they would buy the property together, with Feldman putting up the money and taking title in exchange for Wilder's agreeing to write and direct the film in at least three languages—English, French, and (instead of Spanish) German. An Italian version was also mentioned. Billy, of course, would withdraw from negotiations himself, so there would be no self-defeating bidding war. Billy agreed to Feldman's terms. When the deal was done, the Feldman Group paid George Axelrod $255,000, and Billy got both a nice fee and a hefty share of whatever gross proceeds the film generated.

The original idea—at least for Feldman—was that Wilder would write the screenplay himself. But, characteristically, Billy insisted that he needed a partner. His newest choice: George Axelrod. By April 1954, the playwright was on board. (There was no great rush to make the film, since Axelrod was adamant that the film not be released until the play's run on Broadway wound down.) Axelrod found Wilder to be rather mean; "He sees the worst in everybody, and he sees it funny," the playwright declared. When Axelrod showed up for his first meeting with Wilder, he brought along a copy of the script of the original play. "I thought we might use this as a guide," he said mildly. "Fine," said Billy, who took the script and dropped it on the floor. "We'll use it as a doorstop."

Even before *Sabrina* opened to great acclaim, Billy was running around telling everyone that Audrey Hepburn "singlehandedly may make bosoms a thing of the past." Like most phrasemakers, Wilder knew that a good line bore repeating. But now that he was writing for Marilyn Monroe, he tempered his enthusiasm for the new flat-chested look and heartily embraced the breast obsession of his era.

Wilder and Feldman quickly got into a bit of a battle over both the casting and the distribution of *The Seven Year Itch*. They argued their cases for months; it was Hollywood gamesmanship. While the dispute dragged on in the spring and early summer of 1954, Feldman consulted Wilder on practically everything, and the production developed smoothly. Feldman never thought Axelrod's collaboration on the screenplay was necessary. Billy did, so Axelrod was hired. Feldman—who had an earlier deal with Warner Bros. that fell through—wanted to strike a distribution deal with United Artists or else go ahead and make the film without a distributor in place. Billy liked a deal proposed by Fox; the Fox deal was struck. Both Feldman and Wilder agreed completely on the casting of Marilyn Monroe, which was convenient, since she was not only Feldman's client but was also under contract to Fox and was provided by the studio as part of the distribution deal. When the dust cleared, Wilder's only major concession was to give up his plans for the simultaneous production of foreign-language versions of *The Seven Year Itch*. He fought for them, but he lost.

Under the Fox deal, $500,000 went to the Feldman Group and Billy Wilder, plus money to make the film, plus Monroe, plus distribution prints and advertising. Fox got the gross distributor's proceeds up to $3,200,000; above that, money went first to pay the costs of foreign dubbing, after which 60 percent went to Fox and 40 percent to the Feldman Group. Of that 40 percent, Feldman was allowed to reimburse itself for the cost of the property (the $255,000) as well as all payments to Wilder and Axelrod that weren't reimbursed by Fox. Wilder got 50 percent of the balance. If there did happen to be a French version later, Billy would get an additional $50,000. The studio system was dead, and this is what took its place.

Wilder and Feldman traveled to New York in May 1954 to scout locations and interview actors. Billy also spent time working with Axelrod on the script. When they returned to Los Angeles, Axelrod accompanied them and stayed until early August. Axelrod later recalled driving with Billy back and forth between Wilder's offices—one at Fox, the other at Warners—stopping habitually at little boutiques and antique stores and galleries and bookstores between Beverly Hills and Burbank. According to Axelrod, Billy was particularly obsessive about buying skinny neckties, which Axelrod thought was strange, since he never saw Billy wearing any ties at all.

Casting was still up in the air—particularly the male lead. Wilder, having second thoughts about Ewell's ability to stand up to Monroe on-screen, now wanted a better-known actor. On August 3, the trades reported that Jack Lemmon was being tagged for *The Seven Year Itch*, but it was a false rumor. Walter Matthau, on the other hand, actually auditioned for the role. In July, Wilder set up a screen test for the jowly comedian, after which he and Feldman had to decide between the three top contenders: Matthau, Ewell, or Gary Cooper.

Forty years later, Billy claimed to have been bowled over by Matthau: "He was so funny I just screamed with laughter. I thought I must have this guy because he's so interesting." But by July 19, 1954, Billy was in fact no longer interested in Matthau. Given the two men's long and (reasonably) happy collaboration, blame for Matthau's having been turned down for *The Seven Year Itch* has tended to fall on Darryl Zanuck and Twentieth Century–Fox. "I was not powerful enough to get Matthau," says Billy, but in fact it was Billy who didn't think Matthau was right for the role. He simply wasn't a big-enough star, and Wilder thought that the role of Richard Sherman required a major screen presence to match Monroe, who had become a top-ranked star in such box office winners as *Niagara*, *Gentlemen Prefer Blondes*, and *How to Marry a Millionaire*. Gary Cooper was precisely the star Wilder wanted, but Cooper was nixed as well—this time by Zanuck, who earnestly pushed William Holden. Apparently Wilder didn't think his good friend was right either. Jimmy Stewart expressed interest—on a cash basis only—but Stewart had another commitment, a western for director Anthony Mann. When it was determined that *The Man from Laramie* (1955) couldn't be postponed, Stewart had to bail out, and Wilder and Feldman finally decided to go with Ewell.

A budget of $1,721,500 was drawn up by the end of August, by which time Marilyn had read the script and called Feldman to tell him how very happy she was with it. She'd get $100,000 for her appearance; Ewell would be paid $25,000. In addition to exercising her talents as a comedienne, Monroe would also be singing the film's title song, which Darryl Zanuck insisted on commissioning from Jule Styne and Sammy Cahn. Billy didn't much like it, but the song was a problem he could put off for a while.

He had other things on his mind. In addition to preparing both *The Seven Year Itch* on the Fox lot and the Lindbergh picture, *The Spirit of St. Louis*, at Warners, he and Paul Kohner were working together to get *Ariane* off the ground. Kohner specialized in foreign rights and deals involving foreign actors, and in late August, Wilder told Kohner that because the Lindbergh picture was scheduled to go into production the following spring, he wouldn't be able to do *Ariane* until the fall. *Ariane* would be his first Allied Artists project, Wilder noted, and it would star Audrey Hepburn. As if his plate wasn't full enough already, Wilder also mentioned to Kohner the possibility of making *A New Kind of Love*, saying that the property was now his, not Paramount's, though he'd need to buy some songs from Paramount if he wanted to do the film. He closed by saying that he was off to New York on Monday, August 30, to start filming *The Seven Year Itch*; he'd be there until September 12.

Shooting began September 1 at Yankee Stadium in the Bronx for a scene that ended up being cut. Wilder, who hadn't done location shooting in New York City since *The Lost Weekend*, found it exhilarating but exasperating. "Personally I prefer to shoot in the studio because I can control it," he later said. "And then there's the bother of working with strangers." He delegated some of the latter responsibility to his art director, George W. Davis.

The number of people who participated in the production of *The Seven Year Itch* expanded greatly when the crass but industrious Harry Brand, head of Fox publicity, alerted the New York metropolitan area to Monroe's arrival on September 9. It was great publicity—as far as publicity was concerned. But when hundreds of people showed up at the first location, the film itself was thrown into jeopardy. This was not a question of a stray bystander or two recognizing a made-up, transformed movie star, as had been the case with *The Lost Weekend*. This was pandemonium on the scale of *Ace in the Hole*, except that the disaster the crowds came to witness was Marilyn Monroe and her personal life, though nobody knew it was a disaster. Billy began shooting her scenes with Ewell in a leased apartment on East Sixty-first Street, with a barricade set up on both ends of the block to keep the crowds away. Still, the noise level was so high that he had to shoot the film without sound, to be looped later in the studio. Wilder knew Monroe was drinking to soothe her nerves, but he wasn't terribly concerned; he knew she photographed beautifully.

Marilyn's husband, the baseball star Joe DiMaggio, hadn't accompanied her when she flew from Los Angeles, but he joined her on the 11th. The marriage was already unsettled, and the shakes were about to get worse. DiMaggio stayed out of the way of the filming as best he could, but when Marilyn arrived for a night shoot at a subway grating near the corner of Lexington Avenue and Fifty-first Street, DiMaggio made the mistake of tagging along. Harry Brand, with his flawless touch for generating publicity and his equally perfect disregard for everything else associated with making movies, had seen to it that the cast, crew, and director of *The Seven Year Itch* were not left alone. A crowd of reporters and (according to those reporters) from 1,500 to 2,000 sight-seers greeted Marilyn with a roar.

"There were a good 5,000 people there waiting to see Marilyn's legs," Billy later declared, "and under the grating the electricians who were working the ventilator were accepting jugs of wine from gawkers who wanted to see Marilyn from below. We reshot the scene several times. It wasn't working. The crowd was becoming agitated, asking for autographs. It was becoming very embarrassing, and DiMaggio didn't like his wife putting herself up for display."

The shot Billy wanted was one of Marilyn standing on the subway grating letting the air rush up under her skirt. It took about fifteen takes before they got it right, the crowd chanting "Higher! Higher!" all the while. The scene was set in the summertime—that was the point (well, *half* the point) of Marilyn's wanting to cool herself off—but the night air was chilly. "I'm freezing," Marilyn complained. DiMaggio, watching from the sidelines as the crowds tried to catch a glimpse of his wife's crotch, was mortified. He left for Los Angeles the following morning, the marriage essentially over.

Wilder had other problems on his mind. The chaos at the location meant that at least some of the scene had to be reshot. He returned to the Fox lot, where, he remembered, "we reconstructed a corner of the street and it was perfect." Another issue was, for Wilder, much more unusual: instead of the script remaining unfinished during production, this one was polished—and too short. The *Sabrina* fiasco had made an impression on Billy. This time, the front office did get the script beforehand and responded with alarm at its brevity. Wilder kept insisting that the film would play longer with all the comic business he planned to add as he shot, but Feldman fretted. If a single scene didn't work, he pointed out, the film would simply not be long enough. He urged Billy to put back some of the scenes he and Axelrod had cut from the play, especially those involving Dr. Brubaker, the psychiatrist.

The filming of *The Seven Year Itch* continued in Hollywood through the rest of September and October. Apart from the fact that Monroe was chronically late, the production progressed smoothly. As always, Wilder had surrounded himself with dependable technicians, true team players who knew their business and performed it without fuss. Doane Harrison once again provided advice on how each shot Wilder planned would fit with those on either side, this time with the added technical problem of editing in CinemaScope. George Davis recalls Harrison as "a tall, lanky fellow who didn't look very healthy." But, Davis goes on, "he was a gentle guy and as nice as could be. He was at Billy's elbow all the time." Cinematographer Milton Krasner, who had just shot *Three Coins in the Fountain* (1954) in both CinemaScope and Technicolor, proved to be equally low key. Davis found his own work with Wilder to be remarkably free of intervention: "I made some sketches and showed them to him and he okayed them right away and I just went ahead and built them. When we were building them I'd show him a sketch and he'd say, 'Oh, hell, go ahead and build it.' And that's all there was to it."

Both Feldman and Zanuck left Billy and his team alone. Once Zanuck read the script in mid-September, he knew his instincts weren't as good as Billy's as far as the casting was concerned. He told Billy that he thought the screenplay was an improvement on Axelrod's play, and now that he'd read it he couldn't imagine anyone but Tom Ewell in the role. William Holden, he realized, would have been as much of a mistake as Gary Cooper. Zanuck was also pleased with the rushes he saw, except for one thing: don't get too close to Ewell in CinemaScope, Zanuck warned Billy: "In medium shots he is very likable and attractive, in a strange sort of way. When we get too close to him he sort of loses something."

By October 21, the film was nine days behind schedule, partly because of bad weather in New York; the rest was largely Marilyn's fault. One of Zanuck's assistants reported back to the front office at Fox that "although Wilder tries to break up scenes due to [her] inability to memorize dialogue, he still has to make from fifteen to eighteen takes on almost every setup." He suggested, both to Billy and to Zanuck, that a second unit do some of the shooting to pick up lost time, but Wilder detested the idea and refused. Billy did remain calm, though, even when Monroe kept showing up late to the tune of about $80,000 per day. As Davis remembers, "Billy was a great baseball fan. He had a baseball, and he used to say to me, 'Come on, let's play catch.' So we'd go outside the stage and we'd play catch until she arrived."

"I had no problems with Monroe," Billy later claimed:

It was Monroe who had problems with Monroe. She had trouble concentrating—there was always something bothering her. Directing her was like pulling teeth. But when you finished with her, when you had made it through forty or fifty takes and put up with her delays, you found yourself with something unique and inimitable. When the film was finished, you forgot your troubles with her. It's not that she was mean. It's just that she had no sense of time, nor conscience that three hundred people had been waiting hours for her. However, she had a great sense of timing for herself. At times she could do three pages of text without making a mistake. At other times she had real mental blocks. She needed the best psychoanalyst or a team of psychoanalysts to figure out what was going on in her head.

On another occasion, he reported that he "didn't realize what a disorganized person this was until I looked in the back of her car. It was like she threw everything in helter-skelter because there was a foreign invasion and the enemy armies were already in Pasadena. There were blouses lying there, and slacks, and dresses, girdles, old shoes, old plane tickets, old lovers for all I know."

Axelrod traveled to Los Angeles to see a rough cut in early November and liked what he saw. Zanuck liked it, too, except for the escalating cost. The film was already running almost two full working weeks over schedule, there were many retakes still to be done, and the head of the studio was getting irritated. "Wilder did a sensational job from the standpoint of quality," he told Charlie Feldman, but "he certainly did not do a sensational job from the standpoint of shooting time and schedule." Zanuck decided that it was Billy's fault, not Marilyn's. After all, Zanuck pointed out, she'd gone from her last Fox picture, *There's No Business Like Show Business*, into *The Seven Year Itch* with no rehearsal, not to mention time off. In fact, she'd left for New York the very day she finished *Show Business*, and she gave up her planned vacation in order to do *The Seven Year Itch*. By mid-November, Zanuck had been pestering Feldman for some time over the escalating price tag, and Feldman knew that the film would have to gross well over $4 million for there to be any profit at all. The announcement of Monroe's divorce from DiMaggio and the flood of publicity caused her to miss an entire week of shooting, but when she returned she worked for fifteen days straight.

Zanuck, Feldman, and Wilder watched another rough cut just before Christmas and immediately began planning more retakes. To Zanuck and Feldman's dismay, the title song was still not in the picture, and Feldman cajoled Billy to put it in, in part because Jule Styne and Sammy Cahn were telephoning Feldman every day about it.

Monroe finished her retakes on January 11, 1955, after which Billy and Audrey threw a celebratory party. The cast and crew of the film were there, of course, as were Mr. and Mrs. Gary Cooper, the Holdens, Mr. and Mrs. Jimmy Stewart, Doris Day, Claudette Colbert, and, amazingly, Lauren Bacall and Humphrey Bogart; apparently any grudges had dissipated. The party was a happy event. Near the end of the evening Marilyn joined Audrey Wilder in a duet of "Let's Do It." Her first experience with Wilder having been so successful, Marilyn looked forward to working with him on another picture. "Billy's a wonderful director," Marilyn told George Axelrod. "I want him to direct me again. But he's doing the Lindbergh story next. And he won't let me play Lindbergh."

At this point, the film was running long; Billy was right about the comedy business. Zanuck begged him to cut it down, a demand Billy initially ignored. Zanuck became furious. He liked the film, but Billy wasn't listening to him. Only 150 feet had been deleted since he'd seen the film. "Apparently I wasted the evening and none of my recommendations were followed," Zanuck told Feldman tersely.

The Seven Year Itch was trimmed a bit in the months to come, though Billy was quite stubborn about the process. Feldman had to nag him repeatedly about cutting some of Ewell's monologues down, and several cuts had to be made in order to get Code approval, including one of three shots of Marilyn with her skirt blown up over the subway grating. In addition, all references to glands were deleted from an early scene between Richard and his wife (Evelyn Keyes) on the terrace.

Wilder hired a rising young graphic designer, Saul Bass, to design the credits sequence for *The Seven Year Itch*. There are two versions of the way Bass first met Billy: either they were introduced by the Eameses, or else Bass was hired by Fox first and then met Billy through the Eameses. In either case, it was the beginning of a long and successful collaboration and friendship.

Fox was increasingly anxious to release the film ahead of schedule. In May 1955, Axelrod agreed to modify his original agreement with the studio not to release the film before February 1, 1956, for which he received a bonus of $175,000. *The Seven Year Itch* was set to open in June.

The New York premiere was arranged for June 1 at the Loews State theater in New York, where a racy, fifty-two-feet-tall billboard of Monroe was erected over the theater during the last week of May. In fact, the billboard was so revealing—and Fox was flooded with so many complaints—that the studio was forced to take it down and replace it with a more modest version. The premiere itself was pandemonium, especially when Marilyn showed up (ten minutes after the picture began) with her escort—her ex-husband Joe DiMaggio. It was, by pure coincidence, Marilyn's twenty-ninth birthday, so Fox had a huge cake delivered to the theater. The cake was cut just before the film began, so Marilyn missed her own birthday party.

Fox received one particularly vocal complaint from the Legion of Decency. The studio arranged a meeting with one of the Legion's chief moral arbiters to try and work something out. Billy was outraged, both personally and professionally. "I do not have the reputation of having ever been connected with pictures of lascivious character," Billy snapped. In fact, he thought *The Seven Year Itch* was too soft. He really wanted Sherman and The Girl to sleep together. "I could have done it very easily," he said many years later. "I went to Zanuck and Feldman and I said, 'Look, unless they do it, we have no picture. I would just like to have one tiny little scene where the maid of the Tom Ewell apartment is making the bed and finds a hairpin. That's all I want, nothing more.' The whole aspect of the picture would have changed." He was forbidden.

Audiences seemed not to miss it, though. *The Seven Year Itch* was an enormous success. A little over a year later, the worldwide gross was $5,734,471. Even with its cost overruns, the film turned a healthy profit.

Popular, funny, and very thin, *The Seven Year Itch* is one of Wilder's weakest films. Sherman's mind is "disoriented by temporary celibacy" as François Truffaut described it, but it's a one-note theme. Truffaut applauded the "deliberate, measured, finally very effective vulgarity" of the comedy; Wilder, he wrote, "the libidinous old fox, moves along with such incessant suggestiveness that ten minutes into the film we aren't sure what are the original or literal meanings of faucet, Frigidaire, under, above, soap, perfume, panties, breeze, and Rachmaninoff." Movie parodies abound, as Sherman draws his overheated fantasies from the silver screen—*From Here to Eternity*, *Picnic*, each more ridiculous than the last. But as Truffaut observes, "the film Wilder constantly refers to, so that each scene becomes a vengeful slap, is David Lean's *Brief Encounter* . . . , the least sensual and most sentimental film ever wept over." From *Brief Encounter* Wilder draws the pounding, high-drama theme from Rachmaninoff's Second Piano Concerto, which (in Sherman's fantasy) sends The Girl over the edge: "It shakes me. It quakes me! It makes me feel goosepimply all over! I don't know where I am, or who I am, or what I'm doing! Don't stop! Don't stop! Don't ever stop!"

The film is too faithful to the play to be anything other than dated. Wilder and Axelrod don't click as cowriters; their words are slack and charmless. "My theory about collaborators," Wilder once wrote, "is that if there are two guys that think the same way, that have the same background, that have the same political convictions and all the rest, it's terrible. It's not collaboration, it's like pulling on one end of the rope. You need an opponent there, and then you'll have it stretched and tense." There is no tug-of-war in *The Seven Year Itch*, and the rope is just a piece of string.

With *The Seven Year Itch* in release, Billy might have turned his sights fully toward *The Spirit of St. Louis*—he had been traipsing back and forth between Fox and Warners all the while—but he still had *A New Kind of Love* on his mind. Paramount was trying to lure him back to do it. A studio executive told the *New York Times* in mid-June that the film would be "a Hollywood story with and about Chevalier" to be written and directed by

Billy Wilder. Billy also bought a two-year option on the rights to an Arthur Schnitzler play, *Fräulein Else*, a deal negotiated by Kohner. Told by Schnitzler as an interior monologue, *Fräulein Else* is a satirical melodrama about a young woman who is forced by her mother to extract money from a rich man in order to pay off her father's debts. The rich man agrees, on one condition—that she strip for him. Else, a moralist but a sensual one, is torn. Eventually she breaks down and takes off her clothes—in a public place before a crowd of gasping onlookers. Else's tale does not end well. She faints, comes to, repairs to a bedroom, and commits suicide by overdosing on sleeping pills.

All the while, of course, Billy was preparing *Ariane*.

He was also forced to give up yet another set of plans: Billy wanted to direct the film version of a Broadway show about an evil, murderous little girl. *The Bad Seed*, Maxwell Anderson's play (based on the novel by William Marsh), opened on Broadway on December 8, 1954, to a cascade of great reviews. It starred the gleefully hateful Patty McCormack as a little pigtailed child who slaughters people brutally and without any trace of remorse. Billy thought it was a great idea and immediately tried to buy the movie rights. Wisely, his first stop was the Production Code office. On December 30, he told the PCA that he was interested in purchasing the rights to *The Bad Seed* himself with an eye toward producing and directing the film independently, and he asked for a copy of the censorship report on the play. Wilder wasn't the first to be interested, the PCA's Geoffrey Shurlock advised him; Warner Bros. had already asked, and the PCA had made it clear that it could not approve the material under any circumstances.

On January 11, 1955—the day he finished shooting Marilyn Monroe's retakes for *The Seven Year Itch*—Wilder met with a group of censors and Swifty Lazar (representing Maxwell Anderson) to discuss whether *The Bad Seed* could ever be acceptable on American movie screens. By the following day, the censors had met privately and concluded that they would be compelled to reject *any* treatment of any story dealing with any elementary-school killer. Shurlock got Billy on the phone, told him of the decision, and asked if he needed a letter to confirm it. Billy replied that he understood the decision and required no additional confirmation.

As it turned out, of course, Warner Bros. had more success with the censorship office, perhaps because it was a studio and not a lone individual. Warners made and released *The Bad Seed* the following year under the direction of Mervyn LeRoy.

Billy was also approached by Jerry Wald, a Columbia Pictures producer, to direct the film adaptation of *Pal Joey*, the Rodgers and Hart musical. It might have been a good project for Wilder, given that the protagonist is an unredeemed crud, but it never came to fruition. Billy proposed casting Marlon Brando and Mae West in the leading roles, and he got as far as floating the idea to Harry Cohn over lunch at the studio commissary. Cohn despised the notion and rejected it instantly, and then, supposedly, turned around and billed Wilder five dollars for the lunch.

Wilder's first official day on the Warners lot was January 3, 1955, by which time he'd taken up with yet another new writing partner. Charles Lederer, who had been writing screenplays in Hollywood since 1931, was a whimsical choice for *The Spirit of St. Louis*, having written neither action-adventure films nor biographies. Lederer's métier was witty, abrasive comedy: the battling-buddy movie *The Front Page* (1931), a hilarious screwball farce called *Love Crazy* (1941), and three fairly brutal comedies for Howard Hawks—*I Was a Male War Bride* (1949), *Monkey Business* (1952, cocredited to Ben Hecht and I. A. L. Diamond), and the deceptively glossy *Gentlemen Prefer Blondes* (1953). Now he was mapping out a lone aviator's odyssey, a story of technology and stamina. Lederer was hired to do fourteen weeks' worth of writing on *The Spirit of St. Louis*, for which he received $30,000.

The Spirit of St. Louis was troubled from the start. Lederer, like others before him, made a valiant effort to work with his volatile, high-strung writing partner (who was still zipping between studios, spitting out ideas, and dreaming up future projects, snapping his fingers all the while), but the daily barrage of insults was more than he could take. "For surgery that takes off three-quarters of a person's hide, I can't compete with Billy," Lederer later declared. So he quit. (To be fair to both Lederer and Wilder, Lederer went on to say that "Billy doesn't have malice. I don't think he's aware of other people's constant fear that they are the target of malice. I don't believe Billy would open his mouth—and believe me, that would be a deprivation to him—if he thought he would hurt somebody's feelings.")

Billy, reading the morning paper soon thereafter, noticed a review of a teleplay written by Wendell Mayes. Hire him, Billy told *Spirit*'s producer Leland Hayward. Mayes, living in New York, had never written a film, never been in Hollywood, never heard of Billy Wilder. Soon he was on a plane to Los Angeles with a plum new assignment. As it turned out, Mayes loved working with Billy, largely because he treated the slurs Billy threw at him as nothing more than an ongoing joke between good friends—a kind of love. (Funny that Lederer was great at writing screwball comedies but found living one unbearable, while Wendell Mayes fell into the constant joke routine with all the self-assurance of Myrna Loy standing up to William Powell.)

The next problem was casting the lead. Charles Lindbergh was twenty-five at the time of his flight, so Billy needed someone young, unassumingly handsome, and Nordic for the role. His first choice was the engaging John Kerr, fresh from his appearance as a psychiatric patient in Vincente Minnelli's *The Cobweb* (not to mention his stellar performance in the hit Broadway show *Tea and Sympathy*). But Kerr turned down the role on moral grounds. Lindbergh was a Nazi sympathizer, and Kerr refused to play him.

Kerr's objection is striking, not only because of what it reveals about the limitations of Lindbergh's popular appeal in the 1950s, but also because Lindbergh's morality was not a problem for Billy Wilder. Ernest Lehman once theorized that Wilder wanted to make the film because Lindbergh was so purely American, but Wilder's interest in Lindbergh is much more perverse. Lindbergh made several trips to Germany in the late 1930s as a guest of the German government, and he made no secret of his admiration of what the Nazis were achieving in terms of air power. Much of what the Nazis told Lindbergh about the Luftwaffe's superiority was false, but the aviator's gullibility pointed not only toward his own naive character but also toward the genuine sympathy he felt for the Nazis and their Fascist cause. As war with Germany seemed more and more likely, Lindbergh went out of his way to lobby the British and American governments to forge an alliance with Hitler. He was one of the leading isolationists in the United States and Britain.

In October 1938, while Billy Wilder found an outlet for his fears by helping to fund other refugees' passage out of hell, Charles Lindbergh was being decorated with the Service Cross of the German Eagle, an honor presented by Hermann Goering on Hitler's direct order. Lindbergh and his wife even went to look at a house in Wannsee with the idea of moving there to raise their children. After Kristallnacht, when storm troopers beat and killed Jews, burned Jewish businesses, and desecrated synagogues, Lindbergh's reaction was to say that, yes, the Nazis "have undoubtedly had a difficult Jewish problem, but why is it necessary to handle it so unreasonably?" Even as late as 1955, Lindbergh felt absolutely no remorse for having accepted Hitler's medal: "I always regarded the fuss about it as a sort of teapot tempest." He never understood why his reputation had been so tarnished.

John Kerr had a problem with Lindbergh, but Wilder did not. Neither did Jack Warner, who was also Jewish. The filmmakers were delighted to have the chance to make *The Spirit of St. Louis*. Justifiably impressed by Lindbergh's daring, they ignored whatever qualms they may have had about further mythologizing the flying ace, and they were unable to resist the lure of making what they were certain would be a commercial blockbuster. *The Spirit of St. Louis*, Lindbergh's own book about the historic flight, had been a Pulitzer Prize–winning best-seller in 1953, and despite

Kerr's demurral on moral grounds, neither Wilder nor Warner could see any reason why the rest of America would reject a laudatory biopic about Charles Lindbergh. And anyway, Billy had his own ideas about transforming Lindbergh's story. He would make it his own. Wilder's *The Spirit of St. Louis* would be about a man's effort to convince the money boys to finance his preposterous idea, his sweating blood to achieve it, his near-paralyzing fear of failure midflight, and the confusion and letdown of his enormous success.

With Kerr out, Billy and Leland Hayward picked a familiar face. Jimmy Stewart, a twenty-year, fifty-picture veteran of American moviemaking, saw himself as the perfect Charles Lindbergh. Having just appeared opposite twenty-six-year-old Grace Kelly in *Rear Window*, the forty-six-year-old Stewart somehow believed that he could be equally convincing as a twenty-five-year-old aviator—that there was nothing about his middle-aged face, body, and voice that a little makeup and a diet couldn't hide. He lobbied hard for the role, even after Jack Warner flatly said no. "I need a star," Warner declared, "but not one that's pushing fifty." Stewart's father took up where Stewart himself left off. Having recently remarried, the eighty-four-year-old and his new bride visited Los Angeles on their honeymoon. They dined with the younger Stewarts and Mr. and Mrs. Leland Hayward, and much of the dinner was taken up with the old man hectoring Hayward about casting his son as Lindy. Hayward took the idea to Billy, and against all reason, Billy agreed. Warner knuckled under as well. A deal was signed. Hayward, Wilder, Lindbergh, and Stewart would each have a share of the film's profits in addition to their individual fees.

Lindbergh wouldn't be participating directly in the production of *The Spirit of St. Louis*, but Hayward and Wilder invited him out to the coast for an informal meeting over dinner at Billy's house on North Beverly. Lindbergh ended up taking the bus all the way from Pasadena. (Hayward, assuming that Lindbergh had his own chauffeur-driven car, ignored his wife's suggestion that they pick their guest up on their way.) Lindbergh arrived a few minutes late and explained to his startled hosts that it was because he'd underestimated the walk from the bus stop to Billy's house in Beverly Hills. "You took the *bus*?" Billy asked, incredulous. Lindy explained that he liked to travel by public transportation so that he could get a feel for how ordinary people lived, and since he hadn't permitted any photos to be taken of himself for twenty years, nobody knew it was him.

Wilder found Lindbergh to be impenetrable. "I couldn't get into his private life," he recalled. "He had become a Scandinavian Viking hero, without flesh and blood." Billy did, however, slip a little jibe into their conversation. At one point they flew together (on a commercial airline) to Washington on a research trip; Lindy was going to personally show Billy the original *Spirit* at the Smithsonian. Their plane hit some rough weather and began to bounce, at which point Wilder leaned over to his seat mate and said, "Mr. Lindbergh, would it not be embarrassing if we crashed and the headlines said, 'Lone Eagle and Jewish Friend in Plane Crash'? He just smiled. He knew exactly what I had in mind."

Wilder and Mayes worked together through the summer with an eye toward a late-autumn shoot. Billy found in his new collaborator a kindred spirit. They could work together, but more important, they could bullshit together. They filled their days with laying out scenes, pitching and fielding insults, composing dialogue, and hurling requests for minutiae at Warner's research department. Le Bourget was to be reconstructed based on photographs from 1927, but that was the least of the researchers' tasks. Wilder and Mayes asked for details concerning 1926 license plates and whether women wore nail polish in those days and, if so, what kind. Billy wanted to know how much a gallon of gasoline weighed. (Answer: It depends on the grade.) Mayes wished to know the complete line of Egyptian dynasties, and it was duly provided for him, beginning with Lagus, the Macedonian nobleman of Eordaea, through various Ptolemys all the way through to Cleopatra and her brother and husband, Ptolemy XIV. Billy, meanwhile, inquired as to the date on which Gene Tunney won the heavyweight title from Jack Dempsey. (Answer: September 23, 1926, in a ten-round decision.) This was their daily routine.

In August, Billy, Mayes, Charles Eames (who had been hired as a photographic consultant), and aerial cameraman Tom Tutwiler flew east with the goal of shooting footage of the first leg of Lindbergh's flight—from Long Island to the skies over St. John's, Newfoundland. Accompanied by Hayward, Doane Harrison, and cameraman Ted McCord, they made their way from New York to Boston, to Halifax, to St. John's, and finally to Gander, shooting aerial footage all the while. In Nova Scotia, Billy decided he needed to take a nap, so he found a wooden plank just wide enough to accommodate his body. Eames was fascinated as Billy explained the design: you lie down on it, he said, and since there is no place for your arms, when you go into a dead sleep your arms drop to the floor and you wake up. Moreover, Billy allowed, a man of his stature simply couldn't have anything as obvious as a real casting couch in his office; the gesture would be too blunt. So Wilder asked Eames to design a real piece of furniture based on this dual principle, and Eames agreed. Then it was off to Paris, where the *Spirit* team set up headquarters at the Ritz.

At Guyancourt Airport, Wilder worked out some preproduction details for the film's climax—Lindbergh's arrival at Le Bourget. Actually, he had two arrivals in mind: before the tumultuous greeting Lindbergh described in his book, Billy wanted to show Lindbergh, in his imagination, greeted by a lone gendarme. Before shooting either scene, however, Billy and his crew flew first to Shannon to get some of the Irish coast footage out of the way. By the time they returned to Paris, their star had arrived.

In late August and early September, the Le Bourget scenes were filmed at Guyancourt. ("Since it was night, who could tell?" said Billy.) First they did it with the single gendarme. Then came 3,500 Frenchmen, 1,500 Frenchwomen, 30 gendarmes, 150 French soldiers, and a 30-piece French band. As Wilder reported, "There were three thousand extras that we were trying desperately to transform into an hysterical crowd that had to break down the barricades and run on to the airfield. Then they had to take the half-conscious Lindbergh out of the cabin and carry him triumphantly while others broke the plane into pieces to take home souvenirs." About seventy vintage cars and taxis, along with forty bikes and motorcycles were also pressed into service, along with a total of twenty-one assistant directors. The film's production records make special note of one salient fact: "Note: no children."

Vast amounts of footage had already been shot by this point, and filming had only just begun. Strangely, Billy saw the need to extend the most famous transatlantic flight in history all the way to Cairo. The production schedule of *The Spirit of St. Louis* allotted time and expenses for shooting point-of-view shots, from what Billy later called Lindbergh's "half-dazed" perspective, all the way from Ronda, Spain (for a bullfight seen from the air) and the Rock of Gibraltar to Algiers (the Casbah), Libya, and Egypt (the Sphinx). These shots were ultimately taken by the second unit team, led by Eames, specifically to save money. None of them made it into the final cut.

Jimmy Stewart, meanwhile, was every inch the obnoxious superstar in Paris, and by September 19, the rest of the company was sick of him. In fairness to Stewart, he was late getting started with *The Spirit of St. Louis* because of delays in shooting *The Man Who Knew Too Much*, and he'd had no time to rest. Stewart arrived in Paris grumpy and his mood deteriorated from there. Hayward and Wilder met him personally at the airport and took him out to dinner, and Hayward, of course, had seen to it that his star was put up in style at the Ritz, the finest hotel in Paris. Stewart also had his own car and driver, and yet by mid-September Stewart was bitterly complaining that nobody was paying enough attention to him. He threatened to leave, even though Wilder was trying to get shots of Stewart in the replica *Spirit* in actual fact as well as in the process shots to be effected later at the studio. Stewart's response was to tell Wilder it would look better in process shots anyway and he was wasting his time.

The star's central concern, though, was that (as Hayward put it) "this is the most important picture in his whole life and it's essential to him to look as physically well as possible for the part." Hayward pointed out that the beds in the Ritz were very comfortable, to which Stewart grumbled that he couldn't rest there, he hated Paris, the food made him sick, his wife had the trots, and he had to get back to Beverly Hills immediately.

Hayward, who knew Stewart for at least twenty-five years and considered him one of his oldest friends, was perplexed about why the usually agreeable star was being so difficult. Then Billy tried to help. He got together for a private chat with Stewart and left convinced that he'd calmed him down enough to agree to stay until they got all the shots they needed. But a few days later, Stewart started whining all over again, and he picked the worst time to do it: during Billy's meal. Billy lost his temper. "For God's sake," he snapped, "let's don't talk about it now. *We're having dinner!*"

Stewart called his agent, Lew Wasserman, and declared that he wanted to go home. Wasserman called Hayward and said that he thought that if Wilder and Hayward just took Stewart out to lunch and explained the situation to him he'd be fine. Wilder and Hayward issued the invitation and, unbeknownst to Stewart, held a long meeting with the key members of the production team to forge a plan to make Stewart happy and keep him that way. Then they had lunch, which Hayward described as "a very unpleasant experience." The producer and director patiently explained why they needed their leading man, but the leading man insisted on going back to California. At one point, an exasperated Billy told him, "Jimmy, you've got us in a very bad position. If you go home we'll be sore and if you don't go home you'll be sore and I've got a long picture to make with you of about four months' shooting and I want it to be pleasant for all of us because that's the only way you get good work and for God's sake trust me and believe in me and let me get these shots."

Stewart responded by becoming, in Hayward's words, "semi-hysterical." He repeated his intention to leave in ever shriller tones. Wilder continued to explain all the planning they'd done, but suddenly Stewart bolted from the table, saying "I've got to go." Wilder and Hayward were stunned. By the time Warner Bros. personnel told Mrs. Stewart that the studio had procured plane reservations for them, the Stewarts had already bought their own tickets, and they were on the eight o'clock flight for Los Angeles that very evening.

While production assistants and the Stewarts were busily making airline reservations, Wilder and Hayward spent the afternoon discussing the possibility of replacing their star. After hours of pacing and debating, they decided that too much publicity had already gone into the film for them to recast Lindbergh. Besides, as Hayward noted at the time, "We haven't got anybody to change to." As for Stewart himself, he was just walking out on Paris, not the whole project.

The production of *The Spirit of St. Louis* sunk further the following week when Jack Warner took a look at the first set of bills. He was enraged by what he saw. Hayward couldn't explain it, he told Warner. He and Billy were just as shocked as Warner was, he said, and they couldn't figure out what they should have done differently. The only excuse Hayward offered was that neither he nor Billy had had anything to do with the accounting.

By the end of September, the distressed company was back in Los Angeles, having stopped in New York to do some shooting at the Woolworth Building along the way. The production proper had not yet begun. The script proper was not yet complete. Warner, Hayward, and Wilder met in early October and agreed not to start shooting *The Spirit of St. Louis* again until the script was finished and there was a final budget and schedule. This was wishful thinking. When the production reopened on November 14, the script was unfinished and several parts were still uncast.

Warners prepared a huge location, or set of locations, up the California coast at Santa Maria. The Curtis, Georgia, and Roosevelt Field scenes were shot there, along with some hangar scenes and a Minnesota landscape. Shooting the film's many airplane stunts was a terribly elaborate and time-consuming process. Planes were sent down the runway for takeoff, stopped, reset, and sent again and again. In fact, there were often *two* planes—one to be shot, the other to do the shooting. At one point, Billy himself boarded the *Spirit*—*on top of the plane, in a harness*—and flew, standing on the top wing with his arms outstretched. Jimmy Stewart had bet him $100 he wouldn't have the nerve. That cinched the deal.

There were up to 386 cast and crew members on these days in November; by December 6 it was up to 448 and the pricetag was rising all the time. The original estimate of $2 million had become an old joke. "God, it was horrendous," Billy declared. "The weather would change from one minute to the next. I never should have made this picture."

The script for *The Spirit of St. Louis* was still not complete as 1955 turned to 1956. Because of the turmoil and pressure, Billy was finally forced to give up on *A New Kind of Love*.

By February 6, the production was running ten days behind schedule. The aerial unit flew up to Massachusetts, but even the North Atlantic didn't look like the North Atlantic—there weren't enough waves—so they couldn't shoot. The process shots Jimmy Stewart depended upon when he bolted from Paris were unusually slow and painstaking to film. Often they worked all day for a minute of usable film just to get Lindy to look like he was really flying when Stewart was in fact on the ground. During a night shoot at the Platt Ranch in Canoga Park, Stewart's parachute caught the wind and dragged the star fifty feet along the ground. (He was shaken but not badly hurt.) Billy himself was losing his usual grip on what he wanted. He rehearsed the air circus scene all week long but waited until Friday to decide he didn't like it and had to rethink the whole thing. Stewart, meanwhile, was unnerved by a visit paid by Lindbergh himself. Stewart asked him at what point he got tired. "I never got tired," Lindy replied. "This was rather disconcerting," Stewart later said, "as I had based the whole performance on the fact that he did."

Still, there were some gratifying moments. Now that Billy had the authority earned by years of success, he could finally film the kind of interchange between man and insect that had been denied him with *Hold Back the Dawn*. Unlike Charles Boyer, Billy later observed, "Mr. Stewart did not object to talking to insects. After all, he had to deal all of his life with agents and producers." Wilder's script for *The Spirit of St. Louis* devoted not only one scene to Lindbergh and his friend—a fly rather than a roach— but thirty separate scenes (numbers fifty-nine through eighty-nine). Billy admired the insect's skills: "Who ever saw a fly crash?" he once pointed out. A prop master named Limey Plews was put in charge. First he tried an artificial fly tied onto a strand of human hair and manipulated by way of a stick. Wilder hated it, saying "Do you know what it looks like? It looks like an artificial fly attached to human hair and being handled from the end of a stick." Then they caught real flies with a trap, retaining only those that were photogenic. The trouble was to find a way to stun them long enough to get them to walk on Stewart's face and across the control panel without flying away. They tried spraying them with various substances, but the stuff either killed them or revved them up into a kind of mania. Icing them worked better, but not well enough, and they ended up using animation to fill in what strands of hair, chemicals, and refrigeration failed to accomplish. Billy rewrote some bits of business—the script originally described a "massacre of fly"—and ended up sending it out the window over St. John's.

Spirit closed on March 2 only to reopen again on the 27th. The production had a 64-day shoot scheduled; ultimately it took 115. Wilder shot footage through April and most of May. On May 21 at eleven-thirty at night, after shooting Lindbergh in the cockpit at Le Bourget, the production of *The Spirit of St. Louis* closed. Or so they thought.

On May 27, clips of *The Spirit of St. Louis* were showcased on one of American television's most popular programs, *The Ed Sullivan Show*. Jack Warner instigated this publicity ploy—over Hayward's and Wilder's objections—because he wanted to capitalize on the anniversary of Lindbergh's flight on May 20th. As far as Billy and Leland Hayward were concerned, it was a total disaster. For one thing, there was no mention at all of Wilder's name, despite Hayward's insistence that Billy should always be connected with the film. In addition, Wilder was enraged that the format was wrong: the clips were shown not in CinemaScope and Warnercolor but cropped for television and in black-and-white.

The Spirit of St. Louis now required a lot of editing. The lone-gendarme arrival was cut. Much of the relationship between Lindbergh and his closest friend, Bud Gurney (Murray Hamilton)—a friendship Wilder and Mayes explored at some length in order to develop Lindy's character and make him less of a loner—had been deleted even before it was shot; now it was cut back even further. New fog shots were taken in July. But by that point, Billy himself was no longer working on *The Spirit of St. Louis*.

He'd gotten bored with it, it was out of control, and anyway he had more important items on his mind, things to do, deals to make. For one thing, *Ariane* was well into preproduction. For another, he still wanted to get moving on the Molnár farce *Egy-kettö-három*. This was turning out to be an expensive proposition, so the matter was put off for another day. Next: Billy and Mirisch revised their agreement on *Ariane*, and Billy ordered a print of German film called *Spionage* with an eye toward making a film about the same subject: the Colonel Redl Austro-Hungarian drag-queen-spy scandal of 1914. Next: Billy and Audrey set sail for France on the SS *Liberte* in July and arrived in Paris on the 25th. They checked into the Hotel Raphael. *Ariane* was scheduled to go before the cameras around September 1.

So Hayward and Jack Warner took over *The Spirit of St. Louis* and immediately handed it over to the director John Sturges, who had already been lined up to begin work on Hayward's next film, *The Old Man and the Sea*. Sturges filmed retakes of some of the process shots and inserts and even a number of retakes of Stewart himself, though he got no screen credit. This second round of filming continued as late as January 7, 1957, when Sturges reshot some scenes of Stewart in the Garden City hotel lobby and bedroom as well as some of the Le Bourget sequence.

Warner, after seeing the assembled film in early November, demanded all kinds of revisions: "Add comedy music when Lindbergh as boy is sleeping on railroad tracks. Music too somber; also, get to gag faster." Billy had filmed the young Lindy lying with his head on the tracks holding a fishing pole as a train speeds toward him from the rear of the image. Because of the angle, it looks as if the child is about to be beheaded; only when the train reaches the foreground can one see that it's on the adjacent track. It's a "gag," but a grim one. (Billy, by the way, had always held Warner's sense of humor in contempt: "Warner would have given everything he owned to be a stand-up comedian. He tried it all the time, and the results were pathetic.")

Warner and Sturges could only go so far in tampering with Wilder's film, one of the most remarkable features of which is its Godlessness. This is the exchange between Lindbergh and Frank Mahoney, who is in charge of designing the plane:

MAHONEY: How are you going to navigate?
LINDBERGH: Dead reckoning. I take up a compass heading of sixty-five degrees out of New York, keep correcting the heading every hundred miles. Over the water I keep watching the waves, see which direction the wind's blowing, allow for the drift. . . .
MAHONEY: And hope the Lord'll do the rest!
LINDBERGH: I never bother the Lord. *I'll* do the rest.
MAHONEY: Might need a little help up there, dontcha think?
LINDBERGH: Only get in the way.

Who else but Billy Wilder would, at the height of the 1950s, describe God as a piece of jetsam? (Wilder has a characteristic ambivalence about his spiritual life. When Chris Columbus asked him why each Wilder script has "Cum Dio" written on the first page, Billy answered, "I got that from a writer whom I worked with in Germany. He said, 'It can't hurt.' Look, this is the cheapest way of bribing that thing in the clouds there.")

For all of Jack Warner's "good, Americana kind of feeling," *The Spirit of St. Louis* is a surprisingly dark-tempered film. Wilder's Lindy descends into morose musings to a far greater degree than Lindbergh himself does in his book, and Stewart's itchy anxiety reaches practically the same pitch as it does in *Rear Window*. At one point, Lindbergh's backers, fearing for his life, try to talk him out of the flight. "Nungesser and Coli would understand," Lindbergh explains, Nungesser and Coli having just drowned in the icy drink of the North Atlantic.

Neither Wilder's morbidity nor Stewart's neurotic performance were to blame for the film's failure. Warner Bros. was shocked to learn after a sneak preview of the film that hardly anybody under the age of forty knew who Lindbergh was. Their solution was to send teen heartthrob Tab Hunter out on a twelve-city tour. As Tab explained to the press, "I had an overwhelming feeling that every American who belongs to this generation—my generation—should see the picture. I know what *The Spirit of St. Louis* did to me, and *for* me. Because I'm one of them, I can get the word to young Americans, and I'll be doing them a favor." Jimmy Stewart, meanwhile, fled to South America with his family.

The Spirit of St. Louis received its West Coast premiere at the Egyptian Theater in early April. Warner personally invited Lindbergh to the star-studded gala at the Egyptian, but Lindbergh sent his regrets, having already seen the picture at Radio City. Warner planned a real blowout for the Hollywood opening, inviting such luminaries as Clark Gable, Gary Cooper, George Murphy, Burt Lancaster, Donald Crisp, Walter Brennan, Jayne Mansfield, and Zsa Zsa Gabor. Warner also got Frank Sinatra to perform a special show at the postpremiere party at the Mocambo. Hollywood Boulevard itself was covered in a red carpet for the festivities, which included televised spots on everything from *The Tonight Show* to *Truth or Consequences*. There was, however, one celebrity Jack Warner couldn't convince to show up. As he wrote in a note to Hayward, "I asked Billy Wilder several times, but he alibied that he was leaving town. Have you any people you would like to invite to the premiere and party? Do not include Wilder. You will just have to forget this fellow as he belongs in another world—you know which one."

Reviews of the film were good, but it bombed. Most people didn't get the chance to dislike it. They just stayed home. Warners' poll proved accurate: Americans didn't know who Lindbergh was, and they didn't care to learn. Lindy's obscurity, and the film's failure, were the subjects of a *New Yorker* cartoon: a father and his little boy are seen exiting from a movie theater showing *The Spirit of St. Louis*. With a puzzled expression on his face, the boy asks, "If everyone thought what he did was so marvellous, how come he never got famous?"

Having cost the astronomical sum of $6,000,000, the end-of-year gross of $2.6 million was more than just a disappointment. It pushed Warner Bros. into the red for the first time in twenty years. Leland Hayward's other big picture for Warners, *The Old Man and the Sea*, turned out to be a big bomb as well. If it hadn't been for the studio's top-grossing film—*The Bad Seed*—Warners' balance sheet would have looked even worse. "I felt sorry for Jack Warner," Billy claimed. "I thought of offering him his money back, but then I thought he might take it."

Wendell Mayes blamed the title: "The picture should have been called *The Lindbergh Story* or something like that, because when they put it out as *The Spirit of St. Louis* everyone thought it was an old musical. They didn't know what *The Spirit of St. Louis* was. They had no idea it was the name of a plane."

Curiously, Wilder's assessment of the film's failure had nothing to do with the enormous technical difficulties he and his staff faced, nor Stewart's performance, nor Stewart's age. Billy blamed himself: "I succeeded with some good moments, but I wasn't able to depict the character. That's what was lacking—the exploration of a character." He thought it was his worst movie. "I should confine myself to bedrooms maybe," he said. That the General Federation of Women's Clubs gave *The Spirit of St. Louis* an award for being "the most typical American story" and the Airline Stewardesses and Stewards Association bestowed a "Miss Spirit of St. Louis" medal to the "world's ideal airline stewardess" were of no consolation.

PART FIVE

1957–1961

22. IN THE AFTERNOON

ARIANE (Audrey Hepburn): If people loved each other more, they'd shoot each other less.

FLANNAGAN (Gary Cooper): Are you a religious fanatic or something?

—*Love in the Afternoon*

A few days after Billie Wilder turned fourteen, the man who was to become his closest friend was born in Romania. Itek Dommnici, from the mountain town of Unglieni, made it to America before Billie did. In 1929 he moved to New York with his mother. There, they rejoined the father and husband who left them to find enough work to finance their reunion in a more promising country. Itek, now of Brooklyn, now named Isadore, enrolled at Boys High School, learned English, and became a math whiz, and by the mid-1930s the young ex-Romanian was an Ivy League engineering student. He changed his name to Diamond and adopted the initials I. A. L., which stood for Interscholastic Algebra League, of which he had been tri-state champion (the 1936 and 1937 seasons). His friends called him Iz.

At Columbia University he teamed up with a fellow student, Lee Wainer, and wrote the Varsity Show for each of the four years he was a student. Every summer, the duo continued their writing in the Catskills, where they came up with Borscht Belt skits and revues aimed strictly at the Jews who could appreciate them. Back at the patrician university, Iz edited the *Columbia Daily Spectator*, abandoned math and engineering, and graduated with a degree in journalism and a professional need to spin words. For the rest of his life he never earned a dollar doing anything other than writing.

"I wanted a *goyische* handle," I. A. L. Diamond once said of his made-up initials, "in case I should ever try to join the Los Angeles Country Club or work at Disney." He never worked at Disney, and his country club memberships haven't been quantified, but Diamond did land many Hollywood screenwriting jobs after his Columbia graduation—first at Paramount, then at Universal, and still later at Warners and Twentieth Century–Fox. Diamond's original deal at Paramount was for ten weeks, but the junior scripter ended up staying for seventy-eight, even though all he did was write unproduced sequels and earn a living. Billy Wilder, the biggest of all the big shots in the Writers Building at Paramount, had no reason to know Iz Diamond.

Diamond's first screen credit was for Universal's *Murder in the Blue Room* (1944), a haunted-house mystery-comedy with music. While Billy was winning his Oscars for *The Lost Weekend*, Diamond was at Warner Bros. for *Two Guys from Milwaukee* (1946). He landed at Fox in the early 1950s, where, after a few more anonymous fliers, he had the good fortune to be assigned to rewrite a script called *The Fountain of Youth*. Darryl Zanuck liked Diamond's revisions, but when Howard Hawks signed on as the film's director with Cary Grant as his star, the journeyman Diamond was tossed off the project in favor of the eminently more bankable Ben Hecht and Charles Lederer. The film was rewritten and retitled *Monkey Business* (1952). Diamond's career was not clicking. He was successful enough at making a living, but his most characteristic work may have been the humor column he published in the Writers Guild newsletter and the skits he wrote for Guild dinners and testimonials.

In April 1955, Billy and Audrey Wilder attended one of those dinners. The evening's entertainment took the form of two sketches Billy found funny. Both were written by Diamond. In one, two screenwriting collaborators struggle to think up precisely the right word for the parenthetical description of the tonal inflection of a certain line of immaterial dialogue. One writer sits at a typewriter, stumped, while the other paces furiously around the room. *Quizzically,* suggests the one, to which the other doesn't bother to reply. The first one tries again with *truculently.* This gets a response: "That's close." Suggestions begin to flow back and forth and eventually build to a crescendo. "With mixed emotions!" the first writer shouts. "With wild surprise!" the second one cries in triumph, to which the first one responds, "How about *quizzically*?"

The other skit parodied the "Fugue for Tinhorns" number in *Guys and Dolls,* except that instead of lowlifes discussing horses, three agents try to sell their screenwriting clients to Samuel Goldwyn. These sketches made Billy Wilder laugh, so Billy, who was getting used to hiring screenwriting collaborators with less deliberation than he employed when buying a new pair of shoes, quickly handed *Ariane* to their author. This left him more time to concentrate on *The Spirit of St. Louis.*

In their long career together, Wilder and Diamond may have done battle over words and lines, stories and characters, congressional elections, and the rules of card games, but their partnership was far less heated than the one Billy forged with Brackett. Each was happily married, Diamond to a charming woman named Barbara, herself a novelist and screenwriter. Each was a father—Diamond had two children, a son and a daughter. Theirs was a partnership of security. Telephone books were rarely, if ever, thrown. If there were violent shouting matches, they were not of the magnitude that plagued Charles Brackett. Diamond was even more low-key than Brackett—pathologically so. He was too restrained even to engage in a fight, let alone pick one. ("I was married to him for ten years before I noticed that when I was talking no one was answering," Barbara Diamond once observed.) Wilder and Diamond were two Jews from middle Europe, so of course they argued and told jokes at each other's expense. The more salient point is that when he met Iz Diamond, Wilder was a more perspicacious, one might even say *kinder*, man than he was when he first knew Brackett. He could afford to be. In the second and final long-term writing relationship of his life, it was Wilder who had the age, the experience, the wealth, and the prestige. With Brackett he'd been all too junior. More important, Diamond knew, as Brackett didn't (not to mention most of the others who came in between) that—under the crust—Billy was a softie.

"The highest compliment you could get from him would be, 'Why not?'" Billy once said of his friend and partner. He and Diamond understood each other. They were harmonic.

Diamond once claimed that "in the top 10 percent of directors you'll find mostly men who came up from writers' ranks. The other 90 percent of directors I consider nothing but traffic cops." Diamond was wrong, needless to say. John Ford didn't start out as a screenwriter, nor did Alfred Hitchcock, Howard Hawks, Charles Chaplin, Otto Preminger, Buster Keaton, F. W. Murnau, Josef von Sternberg, George Cukor, Douglas Sirk, or Erich von Stroheim. Ernst Lubitsch was an actor first, and Orson Welles was so young when he directed *Citizen Kane* that he can't be said to have come from any ranks at all. However fallacious Diamond's point may have been, Billy agreed totally: directors who did not start out as screenwriters did not understand what good directing was. In these men's joint mind, great filmmaking stands upon a finely wrought screenplay, a detailed verbal blueprint. It was Diamond, after all, who suggested that they do a final polish on their script for *The Apartment*, an idea he proposed three months after the film was released.

In a perceptive essay called "The Private Films of Billy Wilder," the critic George Morris wrote of Diamond and Wilder that "the two men complement each other beautifully. Diamond's ready wit leaves Wilder free to tap his emotional resources more fully." After meeting Diamond and working with him on *Ariane*—or *Love in the Afternoon* as it was soon retitled—Billy Wilder turned inward, allowing himself far greater latitude in exploring the heart as well as the mind. *Love in the Afternoon* is *Sabrina* with a more finely wrought script, more Paris, no Bogart, and a wiser feel for love. Wilder's movies continued to have a sour streak, sometimes violently so. But in the scripts he composed with Diamond, Billy found himself able to develop themes of affection, even joy. Of course, when he met his newest partner Billy Wilder was himself in the afternoon of his glorious life. The sun was warm, the day was long, and it wasn't even close to dinner.

Love in the Afternoon was Billy's first film for Allied Artists under the deal orchestrated by Harold Mirisch. There were two other Mirisches, Walter and Marvin, and before too long people in Hollywood started calling Billy the fourth Mirisch, so closely was he associated with the wheeling-dealing brothers. Wilder's deal with Allied allowed him to do pretty much whatever he wanted, provided that he and the Mirisches ran Billy's ideas past Steve Broidy, the head of the company. When *Love in the Afternoon* was taking off, they met in Broidy's office, and Billy started to tell Broidy the story of the film he wanted to make. It's about an older man, Billy began, and a younger woman, and they're in Europe—Paris—and—"Just tell me the highlights," Broidy demanded. "What's the title? Just give me the title." "*Love in the Afternoon*," said Billy. "That's a terrible title!" Broidy exclaimed. There was silence for a moment or two. "So what do you think is a good title?" Billy inquired. Broidy thought for a second and said, "*Omaha*."

They all sat there pondering *Omaha* for a while, and then they left. Out in the hall, one of the Mirisches made the mistake of remarking, "That's not a bad title, *Omaha*," and Billy went nuts.

According to Wilder, the idea for *Love in the Afternoon* came from one of the increasing number of artworks he was purchasing. "I bought a painting by Pierre Roy in New York," he says. "There was a black derby and a soft hat, and the sun was shining on the parquet floor. I thought of *Love in the Afternoon* there." The inspiration was actually planted much earlier—in 1931, when Wilder's morose café friend Carl Mayer wrote the script for Paul Czinner's *Ariane*, starring Czinner's wife, Elisabeth Bergner. In particular, Billy fondly recalled a scene from *Ariane* in which the two lovers bid farewell at a train station while the train hissed and steamed behind them.

In 1954, when Billy began seriously to plan his own remake, it was all about Audrey Hepburn. He cabled Hepburn in late December 1954, telling her that he was very interested in signing a deal for the rights, but he wouldn't commit himself without Hepburn's own promise: "*Ariane* without you unthinkable," he wrote. He was right—the part seemed tailor-made for her. Still, despite his enchantment with Hepburn, whom he clearly respected more than most of the actresses he worked with, Wilder only gave her roles originally created by others. He rewrote Hepburn's characters beautifully, but he was apparently incapable of imagining them entirely on his own.

Billy made sure to sign Hepburn a year before the film was ready to roll—even before she filmed the megaproduction *War and Peace*. (Hepburn was now represented by a new agent—Kurt Frings, the original subject of *Hold Back the Dawn* who had threatened to sue Paramount for defaming his character under Billy's and Brackett's mean-spirited hands. Now he was Billy's poker buddy. It was Wilder who introduced Frings to Hepburn.)

Originally, Billy's idea was to pair Hepburn with Cary Grant, but Grant once again found himself unavailable for a Wilder film. In the spring of 1956, Billy and his new collaborator, Diamond, considered writing the part for Yul Brynner, with Brynner's character modeled on the glamorous international playboy Aly Kahn. Diamond was dispatched to the home of the socialite Doris Vidor, who was known to be friendly with Khan, to pick up some details and flesh out the character with true-life observations. Mrs. Vidor described her friend simply as "charming." Diamond, sensing a certain reticence, pressed her for more details. Well, Doris Vidor noted, Aly knew all about the most fascinating things. Like what? Well, like Paris fashions. And horse racing. After thinking for another moment, she confessed: "To tell you the truth," she said, "Aly Khan is a fucking bore."

Wilder and Diamond are then said to have considered using Howard Hughes as their model; that's supposedly when they thought of Gary Cooper. There may be a trace of Hughes in the character Wilder and Diamond ended up creating, but just barely. By the time Wilder and Diamond were writing *Love in the Afternoon*, Hughes was no longer the playboy he'd once been. Increasingly eccentric, Hughes drove the studio he'd bought, RKO, straight into the ground by the mid-1950s, and despite his having sold the tattered company for a $10 million personal profit, most Hollywood sharpies considered Hughes an idiot and a crank.

Cooper was fifty-five years old when he was tapped for the role of Frank Flannagan in *Love in the Afternoon*. Wilder, himself nearly fifty, was plainly drawn to the idea of matching a decidedly middle-aged man of the world with a wispy girl-woman half his age. *The Spirit of St. Louis* was still in postproduction; critics were not yet remarking on Jimmy Stewart's maturity, so Wilder proceeded with Cooper unperturbed. He used gauze to disguise the wrinkles, a lot of shadow on the face, and many of the same type of over-the-shoulder shots of Hepburn that so bothered Humphrey

Bogart. Wilder was also forced to contend with Cooper's gracelessness. The lumbering Coop, fresh from *High Noon*, simply could not dance. "Old Hopalong Nijinsky" is what Billy called him. (That and "Coopsy.")

Love in the Afternoon, a paean to the romantic comedies of Ernst Lubitsch—in particular, *The Merry Widow* and *Bluebeard's Eighth Wife*—concerns an ingenue's love for an aging playboy. Like the dashing Danilo in *The Merry Widow*, Frank Flannagan lives a life of splendid, unfettered promiscuity, and the girl's father is a private detective who specializes in tailing the graying lothario and chronicling his many affairs for a string of outraged husbands. The ingenue, at first glance a proper young lady, understands with steely determination that the way to win the playboy's heart is to convince him that she herself has been well used. Lubitsch's merry widow pretends to be a whore at Maxim's and drives Danilo to drink; Ariane, a woman of the 1950s, torments Flannagan by leaving a lengthy account of her lovers on his Dictaphone machine. *Bluebeard's Eighth Wife* starred Gary Cooper. *The Merry Widow* starred Maurice Chevalier.

Billy saw the popular song-and-dance man perform at the Empire Room of New York's Waldorf-Astoria and decided to offer him the role of Ariane's father. He'd been wanting to do a film with Chevalier for years, and now that the red-baiting era was on the wane, he could afford to take the chance. Wilder recalls that Chevalier had been considered for a big star buildup at Ufa in the early 1930s, but that the studio bosses decided against it because of the conspicuous mole that graced Chevalier's left cheek. Wilder didn't care about the mole, but he was dissatisfied by something else: by 1956, Chevalier's English was far too good for the role of a Parisian detective, and Billy had to keep begging Chevalier to be "a little more French." Chevalier, meanwhile, was irritated and insulted by Wilder's refusal to allow him to sing in the film.

The shooting of *Love in the Afternoon* at the Studios de Boulogne and on location in Paris remained free of turmoil until the vicissitudes of international relations got in the way. The Soviets chose October 1956 to invade Hungary. This caused street rioting in Paris. The Soviet embassy was firebombed and stoned, and one of the French crew working on *Love in the Afternoon* is said to have been struck by a rock. There was no immediate danger to the film's stars or director; the rioting didn't take place anywhere near the filming. Still, Wilder sped rapidly through the rest of the shoot in order to get everybody out of Paris as soon as possible. The news struck a chord in Wilder. A refugee himself, he was personally upset by it, and between setups he huddled over the most recent editions of Paris newspapers to try and make sense of the world he lived in.

On top of the Soviet-Hungary turmoil, the Suez Canal crisis reached a head when Israeli troops plunged into the Sinai Desert and Britain and France moved to occupy the Canal Zone. Panicky Allied Artists underlings were ordered to make block bookings on airlines every day in the event of a sudden evacuation. There was a lot of tension but no catastrophe, though, and *Love in the Afternoon*'s cast and crew made it safely out of France in December.

"How proud I would be, and full of love I would be, if I really had a daughter like you," Maurice Chevalier told Audrey Hepburn via telegram on the first day of shooting. Chevalier was being courtly, and Audrey appreciated it, but there was no particular warmth in their offscreen relationship. The film's French crew was known for its Friday-night get-togethers. Described by Hepburn's and Chevalier's biographers as wild blowouts, they were really just sociable, relaxed affairs with aperitifs and conversation. The Wilders were there, of course, as well as Cooper and Hepburn. Once or twice Billy asked the gypsy band to stick around and provide background music, and they graciously obliged. (In the film, the band absurdly follows Cooper around town, accompanying him even in a steam room.) But Chevalier didn't like these affairs, particularly the bills that served as their finale, so he stayed away. Chevalier did, however, introduce Wilder to his old friend and former collaborator Henri Betti, from whom Chevalier had been estranged for years over a loan. The two reconciled at the time of *Love in the Afternoon*, and Wilder ended up hiring Betti to write a song for the movie. The result was "C'est Si Bon," and it became a huge hit.

Apart from the threat of rioting and Cooper's lead feet, the biggest complications that occurred during the shooting of *Love in the Afternoon* were the bad weather and mosquitoes that hung over the Château de Vitry, the location Wilder chose for the picnic scene. When the bugs weren't biting, the microphones started picking up noise from the many airplanes heading in and out of Orly Airport. All of this resulted in many retakes. Mostly, though, filming was tranquil. Audrey Wilder got into the act in a literal way when Billy cast her in the wordless role of the brunette whose tryst with Flannagan is interrupted by the arrival of her husband and Ariane. It has been reported that Audrey never worked again after her arm appeared in *The Lost Weekend*, but in fact she appears in small roles in at least nine subsequent films, including *Letter from an Unknown Woman* (1948), *Easy Living* (1949), and the Doris Day–Jimmy Cagney musical *Love Me or Leave Me* (1955), in which she sings an introductory jingle for a vaudeville act. With *Love in the Afternoon*, Billy must have enjoyed directing his wife in assorted clinches with Gary Cooper, though he does keep her face mostly in shadow.

Newsweek flatteringly chronicled the day Cooper and Hepburn rehearsed and finally shot the sequence in which Ariane, having spent the afternoon in Flannagan's room at the Ritz, crawls around the floor looking for a lost slipper. Cooper kept falling asleep. "Somebody wake up Coop," Billy requested time and again. (The magazine described Billy as "a near-sighted man of fifty with a face rather like a Kewpie's and a comedy German accent.") It took hours before Wilder was ready to shoot, and when the take was completed, "Wilder began to smile gently. his eyes brimmed with a kind of loving tenderness. His head tipped from side to side as if to sentimental music. His expression became that of a proud father setting eyes on his newborn child for the first time. At the end of the scene, he lay back in his chair, threw up his hands, and laughed wildly, as if he had never watched the scene before."

In addition to marking his first script with Diamond, *Love in the Afternoon* sparked a second long-term collaboration for Billy. Alexander Trauner, a Hungarian Jew who fled his country's endemic anti-Semitism, wound up in Paris. He arrived there more or less in tandem with sound film, which created special conditions for scenic design and, consequently, more jobs for designers. Trauner, who began as a painter, now found work in the cinema. Beginning as an assistant to René Clair's designer, Trauner quickly developed such technical skill and taste that he became one of the chief visual architects of poetic realism, the dominant French film style of the period. Perfected by Marcel Carné and Jacques Prévert, with whom Trauner was closely associated, poetic realism was also influenced by the westward expansion of Expressionism, with which Trauner had grown up in Hungary. (Trauner designed both *Le Jour Se Lève* and *Les Enfants du Paradis*, leading François Truffaut to dismiss Marcel Carné simply as the fellow who directed Prévert's words and Trauner's sets.)

"It was exactly thirty years ago that I met Alex and Lina Trauner," Wilder wrote in his introduction to Trauner's lavish, 1980s *catalogue raisonné*. Lina Trauner was not the art director's wife. She was his dog. Wilder was shooting the colossal Le Bourget crowd scene of *The Spirit of St. Louis*, and "Trau, who had been taken there by my friend Noel Howard, looked at this frenetic agitation with a skeptical eye. He held Lina, his beloved dachshund, in his arms, clutching her to keep her from being trampled. After the seventh take, he turned to me and said: 'Why are you shooting that?' 'What do you mean? It's an important scene in the film.' " Trauner replied: " 'That's second unit work. You should be at Maxim's eating a superb supper.' " Wilder had found a kindred spirit. So impressed with Trauner's sensibility was Wilder that he decided to begin *Love in the Afternoon* with a shot of Trauner himself. A painter is seen tacking his work up on a board; Trauner is the artist.

For *Love in the Afternoon*, Wilder insisted on re-creating the Paris Opéra after the Opéra refused to allow him to film on location. Trauner calmly told Billy that they would just build a set. *What?* Billy exclaimed. The shot Wilder wanted began on the huge central chandelier. The camera was supposed to pull back as the lights dimmed and then tilt down, past the Opéra's tiered balconies, all full of people, and wind up onstage as the conductor mounted the podium and the music began. The largest set available at the Studios de Boulogne wouldn't have accommodated this grand vision, so Trauner built a tiny chandelier ("the size of a pear"), took some pictures of extras wearing evening clothes, cut them up and pasted them on a painted background. "His theory was that as long as the camera moves, the characters don't need to."

Trauner had guts, a trait Billy always respected: "It's this sort of illusionism, essentially simple but totally convincing on the screen, that makes him so unique. After having worked years in small studios with small budgets, nothing scared him. And in all the years I worked with him, I never heard him say 'impossible.' "

Love in the Afternoon finished shooting in December and was released the following July, but only after an additional voice-over was added to the final scene. Originally, Flannagan swoops Ariane into his arms and onto the train and kisses her; her father (Chevalier) remains on the platform watching the train pull out and, finally, smiling. There was no marriage, no promise thereof, or even any indication that the lovers *ever* planned to make their relationship more licit than the many afternoon trysts they enjoy throughout the film. The Legion of Decency threatened to issue *Love in the Afternoon* a C rating—"Condemned." So Billy had Chevalier record a line or two: "They are now married, serving a life sentence in New York." The Legion was only mildly placated. *Love in the Afternoon*, the Catholic watchdogs reported, "tends to ridicule the virtue of purity by reason of an undue emphasis on illicit love." The Legion ultimately gave the film a B: "morally objectionable in part for all."

Still, this was no *Seven Year Itch*. With *Love in the Afternoon*, Wilder deliberately fought the 1950s. "There isn't a sweatshirt in this picture," he told the press at the time. The romance between Ariane and Flannagan is suggestive but not raunchy, delicate not lurid. Asked why he hadn't tried to make a Lubitsch-like romance before, Wilder was blunt: "Because it's too——hard to do." More to the point, as an American director Wilder hadn't had the chance to be as fully European as he was—or wanted to be once more. *The Seven Year Itch* appealed to him because it was loud and glaring and coarse, but that kind of vulgarity was fun only because Americans were such prudes. *Love in the Afternoon* wasn't just set in Paris, it was filmed there, with Wilder specifically encouraging the entire company to enjoy the moods and rhythms of the city before and after every day of shooting.

"This is the city—Paris, France," says M. Chavasse in the opening scene of the film. "It is just like every other big city—London, New York—except for two little things. In Paris, people eat better. And in Paris, people make love—well, perhaps not better, but certainly more often."

A street-washing machine approaches, spraying a gush of water from its sides. It sweeps past a couple locked in a passionate embrace and drenches them; they don't notice. "They do it anytime, anyplace," Chevalier's voice-over continues against a montage of kissing couples. "The butcher, the baker, and the friendly undertaker," who whips off the widow's veil and kisses her. "Poodles do it," Chavasse continues. "Tourists do it. Generals do it" (a shot of two officers smooching). Wilder cuts to a shot of a mustachioed man sitting at a table next to a head of hair. "Once in a while, even Existentialists do it," Chavasse explains as the man parts the hair in the middle and kisses the morose young woman hiding underneath.

Love in the Afternoon is one of Billy's most sweet-tempered films and surely the most leisurely paced. It pales next to *Some Like It Hot* or *Stalag 17* or even *The Seven Year Itch*, but perhaps the disappointment lies in the fact that the bite one expects gives way to a graceful bemusement. Lubitsch's soul suffuses it; one can hear his voice throughout. Here is Chavasse describing Flannagan: "He's very objectionable, and quite immoral, and utterly no good."

Thus, while America was reveling deliriously in the Jerry Lewis era, Wilder was turning fondly to the past—to the Continental grace he had been keeping more or less under wraps as a big-budget Hollywood director of the 1940s and 1950s. Ironically, though, Wilder's most dismissive critics were French. Enthralled by American culture and jealous of its energy, the brash Young Turk critics at *Cahiers du Cinéma*—François Truffaut, Jean-Luc Godard, Jacques Rivette, Claude Chabrol—were drawn to the bold-face, cartoon comedy of Lewis and Frank Tashlin as well as the deadpan cruelty of Howard Hawks. Wilder, meanwhile, was too restrained. Truffaut, speaking for the group, ejected Wilder from the *panthéon des auteurs* on the grounds that he was merely a "lecherous old chansonnier out of touch with the world." Stylistically, Wilder seemed to be leaning toward the French *cinéma de qualité*—exactly the kind of filmmaking against which the French New Wave so rudely rebelled.

Love in the Afternoon was beautifully old-fashioned. In addition to Trauner's restrained design for the apartment Ariane shares with her father—shabby but nice, full of arches and doorways to frame and anchor those who live there (and in that regard it's like Jack Lemmon's place in *The Apartment*, only French)—there is Franz Waxman's sweet-tempered adaptation of the old chestnut "Fascination." As a grace note to the aura of reminiscence that pervades *Love in the Afternoon*, Billy reached back even further into his own past than Lubitsch and Waxman: three songs ("Love in the Afternoon," "Ariane," and "Hot Paprika") were written by Matty Malneck, one of the jazz musicians he'd met in Vienna when Paul Whiteman and his band showed up in 1926.

Produced at a cost of $2.1 million, *Love in the Afternoon* was a money loser for Allied Artists, but not because it bombed particularly badly. The company was chronically underfinanced, and in order to raise the money to make the film, Allied sold the rights to foreign distribution. The film did well enough at the box office, but Allied's own balance sheet didn't reflect it. "It was a flop," Billy said several years later, exaggerating the case a bit for the sake of a punchline: "Why? Because I got Coop the week he suddenly got old."

The Mirisch brothers were hardly unhappy with Wilder or his ability to pull films together. When they left Allied shortly afterward to forge a new federation with Arthur Krim's United Artists, Wilder was one of the first directors they signed. Their goal: high quality, low overhead.

Schlepping around Paris in a chauffeur-driven, chocolate brown Rolls-Royce, Billy Wilder was riding high when he filmed *Love in the Afternoon*, and he intended to fly much higher in the years to come. As always, other less prudent men provided an ongoing warning about the transient nature of Hollywood success. Hawks's biographer Todd McCarthy reports that Billy met Hawks for drinks at the Hotel Raphael at the time of *Love in the Afternoon*. As soon as Hawks left the table for a moment, a member of the hotel staff approached Billy and asked if he knew his companion very well; the hotel was concerned because Hawks had been staying there for a full month without paying his bill. Fortunately, Hawks still had some films left in him. Preston Sturges, also broke, was on the skids artistically as well, and he had been for some time. Sturges's biographer Diane Jacobs describes how Wilder invited Sturges to one of the *Love in the Afternoon* parties, "replete with caviar and champagne on the set of the Ritz Hotel. That may have been Preston's only meal of the day."

The following May, Erich von Stroheim died. Paul Kohner had to take up a collection to finance the headstone. Billy promised $100. Kohner had to remind him twice to pay it.

In December 1956, Billy and Audrey sold the house on North Beverly. They could well have afforded a palatial estate on the order of, say, George Cukor's, but they chose instead to buy a penthouse apartment on Wilshire Boulevard. They paid $55,000 and put another $50,000 into renovations. Their neighborhood, full of tall residential buildings with doormen and no lawns, is unusual in that it suggests New York or Paris more than it does Los Angeles. The flat, dull plain of lower Beverly Hills gives way to rolling hills again. The tedious grid of wide, untraveled streets is defied by Wilshire's busy, sweeping curves. The Wilders' is an elegant address. Their biggest problem in the compact aerie was always the lack of wall space for Billy's art.

In January 1957, while editing *Love in the Afternoon*, Wilder kept his mind occupied by preparing an adaptation of Agatha Christie's mystery *Witness for the Prosecution* with still another new collaborator, Harry Kurnitz (he'd already tried and failed with Larry Marcus); by mulling over another Chevalier film as well as *Egy-kettö-három*; and by trying to buy the rights to Carl Haensel's *Kennwort Opernball 13*, a German novel about the Colonel Redl affair. By March, he added Stefan Zweig's *Amok* to the list of scandals he might like to film someday: a European doctor, exiled to the tropics because of a crime he has committed, performs an abortion and demands sex from the patient as his payment; she runs away in terror; he goes berserk (hence the title), tracks her down, and extravagantly propositions her in a public place before a crowd of gasping onlookers. Billy's desire to shock the middle class was growing fiercer.

There were two more ideas on the table by May. First was a $2 million Audrey Hepburn–William Holden picture for United Artists. Wilder and Lew Wasserman both confidently assured UA's Seymour Peyser that the Hepburn-Holden romance, called *My Sister and I* (from the comedy by Louis Verneuil) would be Billy's next film after he made *The Catbird Seat* for Hecht-Hill-Lancaster. Neither, of course, ever got made. In July of 1957 Billy talked to Rex Harrison about playing Sherlock Holmes. "This should be quite a combination of two temperamental people working together," Louella Parsons wrote with a distinctly icy edge. "Billy never used to be temperamental," Parsons continued in an absurd fib, "but all of a sudden he is taking himself big." Parsons kept her own temper long enough to report the latest buzz: "Wilder is planning to stage a musical about the gaslight era in London in the manner of *My Fair Lady*, with sexy Rexy as the star. It's said Wilder tied up the Sherlock Holmes stories both for his stage show and for a motion picture to be made later." Louella was right on the money with this one, and early, too: Wilder actually signed the deal with Arthur Conan Doyle's estate later that summer.

At the end of 1957, the fourth Mirisch was ready to sign a two-picture contract with Harold, Walter, and Marvin at their new independent production company. The Mirisch Company was formed earlier that year, the idea being that a small and efficient organization could negotiate contracts, arrange financing, sign stars, coordinate pre- and postproduction, and supervise distribution and merchandising through United Artists, all without the unwieldy fat of a large studio. (No real estate, no array of on-site crafts and technical departments, no huge payroll, no bureaucracy.) Harold was president, Marvin vice president and secretary-treasurer, Walter the executive in charge of production.

According to Harold, Billy hadn't yet decided whether to do the Hepburn-Holden film next or still another idea, an update of a German farce called *Fanfaren das Liebe* (*Fanfares of Love*), to which he had acquired the rights. That one was about two musicians who have to wear disguises in order to find work. The Colonel Redl idea had evolved a little further by this point. Now it starred Charles Laughton. A *New York Times* reporter asked Billy when the Sherlock Holmes musical would be ready. "I wish I knew," replied Billy.

All of these plans were being made while Billy was writing, shooting, and editing *Witness for the Prosecution*, which Agatha Christie herself would come to find (according to Billy, anyway) the best film adaptation of her work. If she said it, she was right. The reason was simple: Wilder rewrote Christie's play substantially, beefed up all of her characterizations, and didn't tamper with her clever plot. The play had opened in London in October 1953. By December 1954, it was on Broadway. By June 1955, Hollywood was waving big money around. L. B. Mayer was interested; he wanted Clarence Brown to direct the film, and he thought somewhere in the neighborhood of $300,000 was fair for the rights. Mayer was soon outbid by the producer of the Broadway show, Gilbert Miller, who snared the movie rights for $325,000. The independent film producer Edward Small then bought the rights from Miller for a whopping $435,000.

A certain productive chaos prevailed at this point in Hollywood's economic life. The studio era was well over, and the deck had been reshuffled so many times in the intervening years that even the old careerists were growing accustomed to being on their own, free from the studios that once anchored them. One such stalwart, Arthur Hornblow Jr., had become an independent producer. At Paramount in the early 1940s, Hornblow produced *Hold Back the Dawn, Arise, My Love*, and *The Major and the Minor*; in 1955, after spending over a decade at MGM (*Gaslight*, 1944; *The Asphalt Jungle*, 1950), he produced the gargantuan *Oklahoma!* as an independent production. By early 1956 he was in league with Edward Small on the production of *Witness for the Prosecution*. Their first choice as director was Sheldon Reynolds. This was peculiar, since Reynolds hadn't directed a single motion picture. Having forked over close to half a million dollars simply for the rights to *Witness for the Prosecution*, Small and Hornblow soon came to their senses; by April they were talking to Billy, who agreed to write and direct *Witness* for $100,000 and 5 percent of the gross.

Central to Small and Hornblow's plans for the film was Tyrone Power. Lucky for them, Power was very much interested in being directed by Wil-

der. But Billy had other ideas for the part of Leonard Vole, the handsome
but irresponsible fellow who stands accused of the murder of a lonely spinster. Billy liked Power well enough, but he really wanted Kirk Douglas. For
the role of Vole's German-born wife, Romaine, Billy thought of his old
friend Marlene.

The Kirk Douglas plan went nowhere; there was a problem with Power,
too. The glamour boy and box office knockout of the late 1930s was neither a boy nor a knockout by the mid-1950s, and he had grown increasingly depressed, not only about his career's decline but also about his
troubled personal life. He did not want to do another picture.

Regardless of who starred in the film, Billy still needed to write it. He
began working, first with Marcus, then with Kurnitz, to develop what he
clearly found to be merely a skeletal stage play. The reason Wilder didn't
hire I. A. L. Diamond to cowrite *Witness for the Prosecution*, the story
goes, was that Kurnitz had already been hired, but this seems dubious; Billy
himself doesn't seem to have been involved in *Witness for the Prosecution*
until after he met Diamond. Maybe he didn't fully appreciate Iz until after
Iz was gone. Or perhaps Diamond was unavailable; around this time he
was writing *Merry Andrew* (1958) for Danny Kaye. Whatever the reason,
Diamond failed to get the job, and Billy specifically picked Harry Kurnitz
to write this murder mystery because Kurnitz was not only an Anglophile
but also an experienced author of mysteries—he wrote detective stories
under the name Marco Page.

Wilder started filming *Witness for the Prosecution* before any of the
leading roles were cast. In the summer of 1956, while in Paris preparing
to film *Love in the Afternoon*, Billy and Audrey hopped the Channel to
London, where Billy did some exterior shooting from August 9 through
11, whereupon he returned to Paris on the 12th and continued preproduction work on *Love in the Afternoon*.

In September, Hornblow met with someone who was interested in the
role of Romaine, soon to be rechristened Christine; Ava Gardner told
Hornblow that it was Wilder, not the role, that attracted her. Billy still
preferred Dietrich, though he told Hornblow that he'd go for Gardner if
she was paired with Jack Lemmon. Billy was adamantly against another
of Hornblow's ideas: he did not want Rita Hayworth. In October, Hornblow traveled to Paris, where he and Billy met with Dietrich and offered
her the role at a fee of $100,000. Since Power was out, they told her, she
might be playing opposite Gene Kelly. This was most wishful thinking on
their part. "We must face the fact," Hornblow wrote to Small around
this time, "that with Power's final refusal, even with the bait of Wilder's
direction we can't continue to hope for a name for this Vole part." Hornblow and Wilder then met director Joshua Logan for dinner, and Logan

came up with a good idea—a young, romantic British actor named Roger Moore.

Power was eventually wooed, partly because the producers gave him a percentage of the gross in addition to his magnificent salary of $300,000. Power and Dietrich gave *Witness* some star clout even though by the mid-1950s both actors were past their commercial prime, but the film really belongs to the third name on the bill—Charles Laughton. It's unclear when Laughton agreed to take the part of Sir Wilfrid, the lawyer who defends Leonard Vole against the charge of murder, but he remains the central figure of Wilder's adaptation. He was paid far less than Power—$75,000—but as Wilder explained at the time, "In our film it is Laughton who pulls the whole thing together. He is much more important than he was in the play. The puzzle is good, but it is still a gimmick. Laughton is a person, a man." Laughton modeled Sir Wilfrid on a British lawyer named Florance Guedella, who'd been his own lawyer as well as Dietrich's. Guedella had a nervous tic—he would twirl his monocle relentlessly while questioning a witness. The device serves as the bedrock of Laughton's courtroom technique; as his biographer Simon Callow remarks, Laughton's monocle reaches an apotheosis.

Witness for the Prosecution began filming on June 10, 1957, at the Goldwyn Studios in Hollywood. In the play, Sir Wilfrid is a solid figure of authority and diligence; a responsible, brilliant advocate; a dull character. In Wilder's adaptation, he's a man of advancing age whose driving fixation on work has given him a severe heart attack, from which he is quite obviously still recovering in the opening shots of the film. In the play, the drama revolves entirely around Leonard Vole and his trial; in the film, the courtroom drama is heightened by the possibility that Sir Wilfrid will drop dead, having labored himself to an early grave. Wilder and Kurnitz wrote a bit of a gimmick into their script as well. In place of Sir Wilfrid's innocuous servant in the play, Wilder and Kurnitz give Wilfrid a chirping dominatrix of a nurse. Billy handed the part to Laughton's wife, Elsa Lanchester. Beloved as the monster's hideous newlywed in James Whale's *Bride of Frankenstein* (1935), Lanchester was an accomplished actress who was adept at excess, but she's restrained under Wilder's direction; in Callow's phrase, she's "less busily kooky than usual." As a final touch, Wilder brought in seventy-six-year-old Una O'Connor to repeat the role she played onstage—that of the murder victim's housekeeper, a fierce old Scotch woman with the personality of dried salted cod. (Coincidently, O'Connor also appeared in *Bride of Frankenstein*.)

Shooting began on Soundstage 5 with Laughton and Lanchester doing scenes in Wilfrid's private office and anteroom. Power appeared two days later, Marlene the following week. They filmed through July and August.

Before shooting began, of course, Alex and Lina Trauner arrived from Paris to supervise the construction of Trauner's elaborate set designs. London's Old Bailey and Wilfrid's quarters at the Inns of Court were meticulously re-created on various Goldwyn soundstages. Shooting at the actual Old Bailey was out of the question, and according to Trauner he couldn't even take pictures of it, so his research task was substantial. Trauner's sets are so accurately realized, so rich in plausible detail, that most audiences probably don't notice them. Trauner rebuilt the Old Bailey in actual mahogany, or perhaps it was Austrian oak. (The film's publicity contradicts itself.) In either case, it was an exceedingly heavy set, not to mention a cumbersome one, so Trauner designed it in sixty sections, each of which was set on wheels. Within each section there were hinged panels, too, so that the camera could poke through if the setup called for it. Working from blueprints, Trauner designed the set to be exactly the same size as the original—forty-three feet by fifty-six feet with a twenty-seven-foot ceiling. Even the floor was moveable; it contained nineteen detachable panels.

In the first shots of the film, the ailing Sir Wilfrid is a tired old toad being carted away from the hospital, but by the time he gets home—which is to say back to the office—he's already in full recovery. He's outraged by his infirmity. They've put his barrister's wig in mothballs. "Might as well get a bigger box, more mothballs, and put me away too," he gripes. The aggressive Miss Plimsoll, a sadistic Mary Poppins, confiscates his beloved cigars. She is infuriated when two visitors show up—Mayhew (another lawyer) and Leonard Vole. Their arrival offers Billy the chance to rewrite the play. Christie's Sir Wilfrid takes Vole's case because he is interested in it; Wilder's takes it because Mayhew has two cigars in his pocket and Vole has a lighter.

Wilfrid's servant appears: "Sorry, Sir Wilfrid, but Miss Plimsoll has issued an ultimatum. If you are not in bed in one minute, she will resign." "Splendid," Sir Wilfrid replies. "Give her a month's pay and kick her down the stairs."

After Vole is arrested and departs, Wilfrid, seated on the personal lift that has been installed on his staircase, goes on elaborately about how his associate (John Williams) should treat Vole's wife, Christine, with the utmost delicacy. Being a foreigner, she'll probably become hysterical. She may faint. She'll need smelling salts, handkerchiefs. . . . From offscreen a deep, authoritative voice is heard: "I do not think that will be necessary." Wilder cuts to a smartly if inexpensively dressed woman in a tailored gray suit and hat. The camera tracks forward: "I never faint because I am not sure that I will fall gracefully, and I never use smelling salts because they puff up the eyes. I am Christine Vole."

In tandem with Miss Plimsoll, the exquisitely brittle Christine drives Sir Wilfrid back into the fray. Like Billy himself, he would rather keel over from a massive coronary than submit to a life without cigars, and the two women's abject malignancy rouses his sense of honor. The tired old toad rises like a stalwart lion to defend an innocent man, especially one who is held at the mercy of a bitch. As Wilfrid tells his nurse, "If you were a woman, Miss Plimsoll, I would strike you."

Shooting was peaceful. Wilder and Hornblow got along very well—Billy filmed, Hornblow ran interference. "He took the dark load off my shoulders," Billy admitted. "I didn't have to go to the front office and say, hey, you can't cut this budget here because I need the set as it is. Hornblow did it." All the Old Bailey sequences were completed by the end of July, and Wilder and his cast and crew moved on to the scenes set at Euston station involving Dietrich with her fake nose and accent. Orson Welles stopped by to help Dietrich build the nose out of putty while Laughton dealt with the accent. Laughton demonstrated to Marlene the technical points of Cockney dialogue at his house while lounging around the pool with Elsa, and he stayed at the studio with Marlene after his own scenes had been shot, just to help her out a little more. Even Noël Coward got into the act. He was visiting Laughton, and as Coward put it in his diary, it was "not easy to teach Cockney to a German glamour-puss who can't pronounce her r's." Still, the acidic playwright thought she did a pretty good job in the end.

Wilder brought Matty Malneck in once more, not only to compose the score but also to work with Marlene on her cabaret song. By mid-August, the company was finishing up with the exteriors of the bombed-out German street and the interiors of the nightclub, all of which were built on Soundstages 8 and 5. The final day of filming was August 20, with Power and Dietrich finishing up with scenes set in Christine's room as well as the nightclub. In those scenes, Leonard Vole, a soldier in postwar Berlin, meets and gets to know Christine. She leads him into the dank back room of the cellar bar. The hovel is her bedroom. He responds in a way Agatha Christie could not have dreamed: "This is pretty horrible, in a *gemütlich* sort of way."

Billy was struck by Dietrich's extraordinary commitment to the role. As he described it later, she acted "as if she thought her career depended on it." "You'll never win an Oscar for this," Billy told her; "People don't like to be made fools of." Indeed she was "desperately disappointed" at not even earning a nomination. In the spring of 1958 when the nominations were announced, Dietrich was performing a one-woman show in Las Vegas, and she was so certain of being named in the Best Actress category that she began her act with a recorded voice trumpeting, "Ladies and gentlemen, we are proud to present the Academy Award nominee for *Witness for the Prosecution*, Miss Marlene Dietrich!" They had to rerecord the introduction.

Wilder earned a nomination for Best Director, but he ridiculed it, at least in retrospect. As he said some years later, "To give an Academy Award to a man who directs a play is like giving the removalists who took Michelangelo's *Pietà* from the Vatican to the New York World's Fair a first award in sculpture."

Marlene may not have impressed the Academy voters, but she sure knew how to keep the town talking. Billy and Audrey invited her to dinner, and as always she made herself the center of attention. Billy, knowing the many answers in advance, began asking her to recall some of the men in her life. Marlene responded in intimate detail. The guests were riveted, amazed, enthralled. Wilder then asked her to talk about the women in her life. She was only too glad to do so. "Well, of course there was Claire Waldoff," and on and on and on. A silence fell over the room. "Oh," Billy said, turning to his guests. "Are we boring you?"

Laughton, meanwhile, told the press that Marlene often cooked him lunch in the small working kitchen that was set up for him in his dressing room. When Dietrich was busy, Elsa took over as chef for the corpulent actor. According to Laughton, Dietrich made such specialties as goulash, strawberries in red wine, beef Stroganoff, Wiener schnitzel, and *palaczinki*. Billy added his own remark: the men in Marlene's life tolerated her legs, he said, just for the sake of her cooking.

As was often the case, Billy went into production on *Witness* without a complete script, but this time it was for an unusual reason. The screenplay was finished, revised, and polished at the start of filming, but because of the surprise ending, Wilder left out the last ten pages when he distributed it to the company. Even the scripts received by Dietrich, Power, and Laughton ended with the immediate aftermath of the verdict, with Sir Wilfrid voicing his nagging doubts about the way it all worked out so neatly. Much of this was just a publicity ploy; Power could tell the many interviewers who sought the inside story that even *he* didn't know what was going to happen until the end, though of course Wilder filmed the courtroom ending well before the last day of the shoot. *Variety* reporter Leonard Lyons insisted that Wilder stationed armed guards at the doors of the set to keep people from knowing the secret plot twist. When *Witness for the Prosecution* was shown at a command performance in London, Hornblow was even said to have succeeded in getting the British Royal Family to "sign pledges that they would not divulge the film's surprise ending to the Commonwealth."

During their work together on *Witness for the Prosecution*, Marlene developed quite a crush on Tyrone Power, but then so did everyone else. As Billy said, "Everybody had a crush on Ty. Laughton had a crush on him. I did, too. As heterosexual as you might be, it was impossible to be impervious to that kind of charm." Wilder found Power to be a real gentleman—very shy, very honorable. If anything he liked Laughton more, so the three men planned a lengthy trip to Europe together—in part to promote their film, in greater measure to have a good time in one another's company. Wilder seemed to have worked himself into a state of exhaustion over the past several years, and as *Witness* neared completion he announced that he was taking a four-month vacation—"for health reasons."

Laughton was a most entertaining companion. The fact that a man was gay was certainly no reason for Billy not to enjoy his companionship. If the man had the confidence to divulge some of his own dirty details, so much the better. Wilder claims never to have seen any indication of homosexuality in Tyrone Power. But, he quickly added, "I'm fully aware that if someone doesn't make a pass at me, that doesn't prove he's a heterosexual. He may happen to be a homosexual with excellent taste."

So with Elsa Lanchester heading to New York to star in a Broadway show, and with Audrey Wilder apparently at home, Wilder, Laughton, and Power flew off together to Paris and Vienna, after which they drove to Badgastein, where Billy once again shared the pleasures of the fabled, naturally irradiated waters with his two movie-star friends. As Wilder explained to the press, the trip to Badgastein "was supposed to be a men's cure"—thus they left Marlene and the wives behind. (Badgastein's waters were world renowned. Pumped fresh from thermal springs, they contained lithium, manganese, phosphoric acid, fluorine, cesium, a touch of arsenic, and up to three hundred Mache units of radium per liter.) From Badgastein they went to Berlin. Although they did work a bit of publicity in along the way, the whole trip was essentially a holiday.

For Wilder, Badgastein was pleasant as always. Vienna was not. Wilder's visit to his boyhood home was dreadful. What should have been a triumphant homecoming turned into a sour disappointment.

He went shopping, of course: a crocodile handbag for Audrey, a Schiele print to add to his growing collection of works by the modern Viennese master, and a Fritz Wortuba sculpture. Egon Schiele was, and would remain, a central inspiration for Wilder—in sexual attitude if not in formal style. During Wilder's youth, Schiele was Vienna's most successful avant-garde artist, a position Wortuba assumed in the 1950s. Billy knew precisely what he was doing when he bought both artists' work: they were shocking. He also tried to buy a watercolor by a very young artist named Friedensreich Hundertwasser, who later became an extraordinarily successful painter and architect, but unfortunately the work had already been sold.

The attention Billy got from the Viennese took several forms. According to one account, Wilder received about four hundred manuscripts from Austrian writers in addition to self-introductions by any number of would-be Austrian starlets. Somebody even offered to sell him an Austrian castle for only $300,000—not to live there, but to use for some kind of arts festival. Billy declined these various propositions.

Amid all the festivities and the shopping and the crowds of people wanting him to give them jobs, Billy couldn't help but notice that the Viennese were still quietly, methodically, and guiltlessly relegating the city's Jewish history to a position somewhat lower than a footnote. Having slaughtered or exiled virtually all of the city's Jews less than twenty years before, the Viennese of the late 1950s were making no effort to atone for the murders and destruction they committed in the name of racial supremacy. For one thing, Wilder noticed, the residence and psychoanalytic office of the twentieth century's most famous Viennese Jew remained entirely uncelebrated. "I counted sixty-three statues for Johann Strauss," Billy said, "but at Berggasse 19 there wasn't even a marble plaque."

His own treatment was scarcely better. In 1957, Billy Wilder was one of the most successful film directors in the world, and although he knew he'd never be Vienna's favorite son, he was still shocked by the lack of warmth accorded him upon his return. The Viennese newspaper *Kleine Blatt* devoted only fifteen lines to his homecoming. The *Volksstimme* ignored him completely. (Tyrone Power's appearance, in contrast, was celebrated under the headline "Holidays in Vienna and Salzkammergut.") *Der Kurier* managed to report on the heartwarming relationship between Billy and a sausage seller on the street, but that was the sole aspect of Wilder's trip the paper reported.

Only one newspaper covered Billy Wilder's return to Vienna in any detail. *Die Wochen-Presse* devoted a good deal of space to the press conference held by Wilder, Power, Laughton, and (mysteriously) Oskar Werner. In keeping with Viennese good taste, the paper was discreet about Wilder's family background. According to *Die Wochen-Presse*'s capsule history of Billy's life, Wilder's father accompanied him when he moved to Berlin back in the 1920s, his mother having already passed away. The paper devoted just five words to Genia Wilder, and they were dead wrong.

But Wilder was upset about the Viennese even before he saw the way they obliterated his mother a second time. He remembered his father's failed attempt to become an Austrian citizen; the names he'd been called; the way Viennese doors tended to close on the low-born Jew. As he observed in *The Emperor Waltz*, when the low-born has the impertinence to come distastefully close to the high-born, what can he expect but to be bitten? He was already testy at the news conference, particularly when the subject of Vienna came up. "That's the way it is when you have a little success," he snarled at the assembled journalists. "When I came as a little boy to Vienna, they called me 'the Polak.' After that, they called me 'the bootlicker.' Now suddenly they call me 'the Viennese.' " Billy Wilder had come home. He couldn't wait to leave.

23. SOME LIKE IT HOT

DAPHNE (Jack Lemmon): Oh, you invest in shows?

OSGOOD (Joe E. Brown): Show*girls*. I've been married seven or eight times.

DAPHNE: You're not sure?

OSGOOD: Ma-ma's keeping score. Frankly she's getting rather annoyed with me.

DAPHNE: Wouldn't wonder.

OSGOOD: So this year when the George White Scandals opened she packed me off to Florida. Right now she thinks I'm out there on my yacht—heh-heh—*deep sea fishing*. Ahem.

DAPHNE: Well pull in your reel, Mr. Fielding, you're barking up the wrong fish.

—Some Like It Hot

I n jazz, we must distinguish between two ways of interpreting: 'straight' and 'hot,' " the French jazz historian and impresario Hugues Panassié wrote in the 1930s. Panassié is describing what makes *le jazz hot* hot: "In general, you could say that 'straight' playing is playing the piece just as it is written without modifying it. To play 'straight' is to follow a direct line." Other jazz writers use the word *sweet* instead of *straight*, but their point is the same: sweet and straight is dull and flat. But as Panassié put it, the term "hot" was coined "to describe the style of certain jazz musicians who played their solos with warm, eloquent intonations of a very special kind." It was *real* jazz—dirty, sweaty, sexy, spontaneous.

In the spring of 1958, Billy ran into Jack Lemmon at Dominick's, a restaurant in Hollywood. "I have an idea for a picture I would like you to play in," said Billy. "Sit down," said Lemmon. "I haven't got time now," said Billy, "but I will tell you what it is about. It is about two men on the lam from gangsters, running for their lives, and they dress up in girls' clothes and join an all-girl orchestra."

"If anybody else had said that," Lemmon said after the picture was released to tepid reviews but great box office, "I would have run like a jackrabbit. Go in *drag*? Since it was Billy Wilder, I said, 'Fine, I'll do it if I'm free to do it, and if I'm not free I'll get free.' "

Wilder and Diamond had been meeting every day at Billy's office on the Goldwyn lot since at least the beginning of the year, trying to work out the plot of the farce they wanted to make for the Mirisches. It would be based on *Fanfaren das Liebe*, they knew, though neither was especially fond of that film. They liked its basic premise but not the execution, and even then their interest focused on only one of the film's three central incidents. In *Fanfaren das Liebe*, two hungry musicians resort to a series of disguises in order to find work: first they dress as gypsies and join a gypsy band, then they put on blackface for a jazz ensemble, and finally they don dresses, wigs, and makeup and join an all-female orchestra. As Diamond later recalled, *Fanfaren das Liebe* was "heavy-handed and Germanic. There was a lot of shaving of chests and trying on of wigs. When one of the musicians is seen sneaking into his room in men's clothes, the other girls beat up his roommate because 'she' has disgraced the honor of the band. It was all rather *Mädchen in Uniform*."

After ditching two of the three incidents in *Fanfaren das Liebe*, Wilder and Diamond had to decide what kind of tone their comedy would take. It wouldn't be a Teutonic *Mädchen in Drag*, but rather a lighthearted farce with sexual tension and a lot of dirty jokes—in short, sublime but filthy. They were concerned about motivation. In *Fanfaren das Liebe*, the two musicians were spurred by hunger, but Wilder and Diamond realized that if poverty was their own characters' sole incentive, they could just take off the dresses once they had enough to eat and move on in men's clothes to another gig. Diamond and Wilder understood precisely what it would take to force an American man even to play at being a woman in the 1950s— the threat of death. Iz killed the second bird with the same stone by suggesting that they make the comedy a period piece, his theory being that "when everybody's dress looks eccentric, somebody in drag looks no more peculiar than anyone else." Thus Americans of the repressed 1950s were disguised in roaring, Jazz Age clothing.

"The next morning," Diamond recalled, "Billy came into the office and said, 'Driving home last night I was thinking about what you said, and I think I have the solution: 1929, Chicago, St. Valentine's Day Massacre.' That was the breakthrough, and suddenly we had a wealth of material to work with—speakeasies, bootleggers, Florida millionaires. We started writing."

Some Like It Hot's casting is the *Rashomon* of drag comedy. Everybody has a slightly different tale to tell about who'd be wearing skirts for Billy Wilder. According to Tony Curtis, United Artists (which distributed the film for the Mirisch Company) originally pushed the idea of casting Bob Hope and Danny Kaye as the two musicians, with Mitzi Gaynor in the role of Sugar Kane. Billy is said to have rejected all three suggestions, choosing instead to sign Curtis right off the bat, believing that the dazzlingly handsome actor could play either male role. Wilder first knew Curtis when Curtis was starring in *Houdini* for Paramount in 1953.

Tony Curtis was fine as far as UA and the Mirisches were concerned, but they still felt strongly that there had to be at least one very big star in this film. Their suggestion: Frank Sinatra. As I. A. L. Diamond recalled it, Billy made a lunch date with Sinatra, but Sinatra didn't bother to show up, and that was the end of the matter. According to Diamond, too, there was no need for a big star on the order of Frank Sinatra once Marilyn Monroe signed on and filled the bill herself.

Sinatra was more central at the time. And Monroe's appearance didn't obviate the need for Ol' Blue Eyes—at least not in the beadier eyes of either the Mirisches or United Artists. In late March, UA's Arthur Krim was told that the film (still referred to as *Fanfares of Love*) would start shooting in July and would probably star Sinatra, Curtis, and Monroe. The Mirisches were budgeting Sinatra and Monroe at $200,000 each, plus a quarter of the film's profits. (Monroe ultimately got 10 percent of the gross over $4 million.) Curtis would get $100,000 against 5 percent of the gross over $2 million. As for Billy, he'd be getting $200,000 plus 17.5 percent of the gross above two times the cost of the negative. If the film grossed $1 million after the break-even point, Billy's take went up to 20 percent. It was a very sweet deal.

Another young actor was approached, too, and he remembered Sinatra's importance as well. According to Anthony Perkins, "Billy Wilder stopped by my dressing room [in New York, where Perkins was appearing in *Look Homeward, Angel*] and asked if I'd star in a movie with Frank Sinatra. I told Billy I'd committed myself to Mel [Ferrer, for *Green Mansions*] and couldn't go back on my word." Sinatra was apparently going to play Joe, while Perkins would have been given the Jerry role. Tony Curtis has similar memories: "It's you, Marilyn, Sinatra, and Edward G. Robinson and George Raft as the gangsters," Curtis remembers Billy telling him.

Wilder and Sinatra were buddies, though the friendship was periodically strained. For instance, Frank supposedly screamed at Billy over *Love in the Afternoon*. "He was quite vehement about it," Wilder rememberd—"so vehement that he made my wife cry. He said he didn't like the picture because he thought it was immoral for an elderly man to make love in the afternoon to a young girl." This must have struck Billy as peculiar, given Sinatra's own notorious womanizing. (It probably seemed even more peculiar at the 1966 party Billy and Audrey threw when the fifty-one-year-old star married twenty-one-year-old Mia Farrow.) Wilder also reported, years after Sinatra stood him up for lunch, that he never cast Sinatra precisely because of the performer's unreliability: "I'm afraid he would run after the first take—'Bye-bye kid, that's it. I'm going. I've got to see a chick!' That would drive me crazy."

Still, Billy loved the way Sinatra looked and acted on-screen: "I think this: instead of involving himself in all those enterprises, nineteen television shows and records by the ton and four movies all at once and producing things and political things and all those broads—this talent on film would be stupendous. That would be the only word—stupendous. He could make us all—all the actors that is—look like faggots."

In any event, Jack Lemmon landed what started out as the Tony Curtis role, and Curtis took over Sinatra's. As for Monroe, Diamond remembered that while he and Billy were still writing their first draft, Billy got a letter from Monroe telling him how fondly she recalled their work together on *The Seven Year Itch* and hoping that they'd be able to work together again. This was amusing, given the *tsouris* he'd endured with her. But as trying as *The Seven Year Itch* had been for Billy, he'd always loved her performance. Besides, as Wilder himself put it in 1959, Sugar was "the weakest part, so the trick was to give it the strongest casting." When he read her a few passages of the script, she agreed to appear in *Some Like It Hot*. She liked Billy well enough, and she liked Curtis, too, having been friendly with him when they were both aspiring stars. Curtis even claims to have spent the night with Monroe in a Malibu beach house in the early 1950s.

The relaxed bonhomie between stars and director dissipated all too quickly. At the 7:00 P.M. dinner party Harold Mirisch threw to welcome Marilyn back to Hollywood, Marilyn showed up at 11:20. Then Arthur Miller put his arms around both Wilder's and Diamond's shoulders and patronizingly began to lecture the two literate screenwriters on the essential differences between comedy and tragedy. They rolled their eyes in irritation. Marilyn, watching the interaction, became tense.

Lemmon, who claims to have literally fallen off a couch laughing when he first read the script, didn't yet realize that he'd been cast in the role of a lifetime by a director who would become one of his closest friends and most devoted employers. Wilder knew what Lemmon didn't: "Within three to four weeks after the start of production," Billy reported, "Diamond and I had decided that this was not to be a one shot thing with Jack. We wanted to work with him again." Lemmon himself didn't quite see it. As he noted it later, his girlfriend, Felicia Farr (whom he'd just begun dating and later married), "kept asking me what I thought of Wilder and I told her, 'I guess he's okay.' She's never let me forget that one." Wilder described his friend with genuine affection—which is to say with a put-down: "Lemmon had to be an actor. I doubt he could have done anything else, except play piano in a whorehouse."

Wilder understood quickly, and Lemmon eventually, that the two men could forge a rare kind of bond between director and actor. Even more than Bill Holden, Lemmon's average-Joe Americanism gave Everyman's voice and gesture to Wilder's quirky, immigrant-Jewish imagination. On-screen, Lemmon was a nebbish, but a goyish one—small and fidgety but white-bread. As spoken by Lemmon, Billy's lines could never seem alien to the Americans he so wanted to please (and appall).

Tony Curtis, meanwhile, was able to lend glamour to the character Wilder and Diamond wrote for him, but his persona was essentially foreign to Billy. He was a prettyboy. Curtis was known for wearing exceptionally tight clothes, some of which he designed himself, all the better to show off his pinup, classic 1950s vealcake physique. As Billy once said, "Tony's pants look as though someone dipped him in India ink up to his waist." One day on the set of *Some Like It Hot*, Curtis raised a fuss over whether or not his name would or would not appear in the large-size type his contract specified. He approached his director and launched into a lengthy remonstration. Billy listened patiently and then slid the knife in: "The trouble with you, Tony, is that you're only interested in little pants and big billing."

With his pants off and his flapper skirts and wig on, Curtis was ill at ease when filming began. He walked onto the set markedly discomposed. Lemmon, however, clomped onto the set waving happily to the crew and introducing himself with "Hi, I'm Daphne!" "You create a shell and you crawl into it" is the way he later described it. (This was a switch; Lemmon generally thinks of himself as a Method-oriented actor who finds his character in precisely the opposite way.)

The shells he and Curtis created in *Some Like It Hot* were designed in part by one of the twentieth-century's preeminent drag artists. Barbette, whom Billy fondly recalled from his own days in Berlin and Paris, was lured out of semiretirement (at Billy's behest) to teach Lemmon and Curtis how to effectively transform themselves—not into women, but into drag queens.

Billy flew Barbette in from Texas to train Lemmon and Curtis in the art of female impersonation. It wasn't just a matter of seeing to it that their chests were properly shaved, their eyebrows plucked to the correct degree, their hips padded just so, and their penises strapped down. Barbette's lessons were those of a performance artist, not a costumer. She taught them, *tried* to teach them, how to walk: you cross your legs in front of each other slightly, which forces your hips to swing out, subtly but noticeably, with each step. Thus you draw attention to the leg and buttocks. Then there was the art of sitting still: you make it a point to hold your hands with the palms down, so the muscles in your arms won't flex and give your masculinity away. Tony Curtis was a perfect student as far as Barbette was concerned. Under her tutelage, Curtis's Josephine was a model of classic, discreet femininity. Lemmon, however, couldn't be taught. Daphne was a disaster.

Lemmon simply wouldn't follow Barbette's rules. It was the walking that Lemmon particularly refused to learn. He claims to have found it not only awkward but, more important for his performance, uncharacteristic: "The goof I was playing wouldn't be very proficient at walking in heels. I needed to be barely good enough to look like a clumsy woman." There is a more fundamental point, though: Lemmon's Daphne is utterly irrepressible. She's not especially feminine, but the funnier fact is that Lemmon's male character, the whining and pushed-around Jerry, gives way to an androgyne of startling gumption. This creature does precisely what she pleases. As men, Joe (Curtis) and Jerry (Lemmon) plan their names—Joe will be Josephine, Jerry Geraldine. But when, in drag, they introduce themselves to the bandleader Sweet Sue, *"I'm Daphne!"* is what pops out of Jerry's mouth. The amazed look on Joe's face at that moment is second only to the look of shock Jerry himself registers upon Daphne's self-proclamation. *Nobody* tells Daphne how to behave—certainly not Barbette, who stormed off in a queeny huff after three days. As Lemmon recalled, "He told Wilder that Curtis was fine but Lemmon was totally impossible." Billy found the whole thing hysterically funny. He knew he was onto something.

Men who love drag love it because it gives them access to an otherwise hidden part of themselves. It isn't just their feminine side. Both Lemmon and Curtis report that when they put on dresses for *Some Like It Hot* they became their own mothers. On one occasion Curtis claimed that he modeled Josephine after Grace Kelly (for glamour) and ZaSu Pitts (for comedy), with a bit of his mother thrown in (for soul). Another time he said, "I looked like a combination of my mother, Dolores Costello, and Eve Arden." For Lemmon, the family resemblance came as a shock. After describing his own mother as "Tallulah Bankhead's road company," Lemmon claims to have been stunned when he saw a photograph of Daphne standing next to Mrs. Lemmon on the set, the resemblance was so unnerving.

Does one require a background in clinical psychology to appreciate that another aspect of men's attraction to drag is the temporary disavowal of their own penises? Maybe. But the fact remains that with the Production Code all but dead, *Some Like It Hot* pays a great deal of attention to penises—their presence as well as their threatening absence. This is in keeping with the sexual thrust of hot jazz. (Louis Armstrong's Hot Seven? Jelly Roll Morton and His Red Hot Peppers?) The comedy of *Some Like It Hot* is literally phallocentric. Wilder's dick jokes begin in the office of Sid Poliakoff (Billy Gray), the music booking agent, and they continue to the very end of the film:

JOE: What kind of a band is it, anyway?
POLIAKOFF: You gotta be under twenty-five.
JERRY: We could pass for that!
POLIAKOFF: You gotta be blonde.
JERRY: We could dye our hair!
POLIAKOFF: And ya gotta be girls!
JERRY: We could . . .
JOE: No we couldn't.

Then there's the scene in which Daphne and Sugar snuggle together in the upper berth on the train:

DAPHNE: No lights! We don't want them to know we're having a party!
SUGAR: But I might spill something.
DAPHNE: So spill it! Spills, thrills, laughs, and games—this might even turn out to be a surprise party!
SUGAR: What's the surprise?
DAPHNE: Heh-heh—not yet!
SUGAR: *When?*
DAPHNE: Better have a drink first.

Daphne and Sugar's get-together soon expands to include the rest of the band. It gets raucous. One of the girls suddenly blurts "Anyone for salami?" and waves one center-screen.

Earlier, Dolores (Beverly Wills) tries to tell a joke, but the brassy, big-boned Sweet Sue (Joan Shawlee) finds it in such bad taste that she cuts Dolores off before the punchline. "Say kids!" Dolores announces. "Have you heard the one about the girl tuba player who was stranded on a desert island with a one-legged jockey?" Luckily, Dolores finally gets to finish her joke in the upper berth:

DOLORES *(drunk)*: And so the one-legged jockey says. . . .
DAPHNE *(drunk)*: Well, wha'did'e say?"
DOLORES: And so the one-legged jockey says, "Don't worry about me, baby, I ride sidesaddle!"

It was fun for Lemmon and Curtis to pretend not to have one for a change, and their performances have delighted countless millions over the years, but on the practical side it was plain uncomfortable because they had to wear steel jockstraps. While Lemmon suffered through hours without a convenient bathroom break, Curtis had the good sense to rig up a funnel and hose contraption so he could urinate without having to get all the way out of his costume. He could do it anytime, standing up. Unaware of his invention, everyone else marveled at his stamina.

Drag comedy is all about gender anxiety and sexual panic. It forces people to worry about presence and absence, but the worry is part of the pleasure; the laughter is literally hysterical. Jack Lemmon reports that after putting the finishing touches on their outfits, the two stars approached their director for final approval. With clinical precision, Billy's first thought was of the ladies' room: "We had our dresses on and the whole goddamn thing. And [Billy] says, 'Follow me.' And we did. We go into the commissary and he brings us into the ladies' room in the commissary. Well, I thought, 'Oh, Jesus.' We just sat in the outside part, you know—where the girls are making up and everything? They paraded in and out. Nobody batted an eyeball. I'd say, 'Hello, girls!' and girls would come in and out saying, 'Hello, girls!' And they just thought we were doing a period piece or something. We went back to Billy, and he said, 'That's it, lock it, keep it, boom.' " Wilder knew it was a riot: "Audiences will be laughing so hard they won't hear half the dialogue," he told the press midway through production. "I may be the first to put English subtitles on an English-speaking movie so people will know what's being said."

Wisely, Wilder avoids explaining the mechanics of his characters' transformation from men to women. He just cuts from the men arranging for their employment with Sweet Sue's Society Syncopators to Josephine and Daphne at the train station, thus leaving out entirely the question of how they accomplish the transition. They simply *are* women at that point. Or better: they are not themselves anymore. And audiences accept them.

Throughout the first half of 1958, Wilder and Diamond wrote together on their usual schedule—from 9:00 in the morning to 6:00 in the evening, Billy having been up for three hours already at the start of his workday. When filming began in early September, they continued the same schedule and added evening rewriting sessions as well, from 8:30 to 11:00 P.M. More than any other film to date, this was a Wilder movie that demanded to be written concurrently with its filming. Drag comedy was dicey, he knew, so he and Diamond saw what worked and what didn't and developed the screenplay organically on that basis. David Selznick told Billy it was impossible from the start: "You want machine guns and dead bodies and gags in the same picture? Forget about it, Billy. You'll never make it work." But by growing it slowly and essentially, by constructing each piece on its own, he did precisely that.

Along with the sexual drive of this comedy, a certain Judaism emerges in Wilder's second script with Diamond; the writers are having fun being themselves. Listen to the booking agent Sid Poliakoff on the phone trying to round up some "girl musicians": "Gladys! Are ya there? *Gladys!*" (He hangs up.) "Meshuggeneh! Played a hundred and twelve hours in a marathon dance, now she's in bed with a nervous collapse!" When Poliakoff tells Joe and Jerry about a gig, he inflects his declarative statement with the eastern European lilt of a question: "At the University of Illinois they're having (you should pardon the expression) a St. Valentine's dance?" Even Geraldine's line "We spent three years at the Sheboygan Conservatory of Music" sounds like a Catskills routine (or a Columbia Varsity Show written by a Jewish boy from Brooklyn).

The final preliminary budget called for a total cost of $2,373,490. When filming began, Monroe was up to $300,000; Curtis and Lemmon each got $100,000. Diamond got $60,000, Billy $200,000. Filming began in September 1958 at the Goldwyn Studios in Hollywood (off the corner of Formosa and Melrose, where the Mirisches rented space) and on location at the Hotel del Coronado near San Diego. Arthur Krim of UA gave the go-ahead, but he was a little worried. This was going to be an expensive picture, and he wanted to protect his company against the big loss he thought *Some Like It Hot* might incur simply because of its high salaries. Marvin Mirisch wrote to UA's lawyer in early August noting that if they wanted to call the film *Some Like It Hot*, as Wilder demanded, they'd need to get a waiver from MCA, which owned the rights to the 1939 Paramount film of the same title. This, however, would not be much of a struggle, since Billy was represented by MCA's own Lew Wasserman (who also represented Curtis and Monroe).

The script called for a Miami resort hotel, the Seminole-Ritz, but by the late 1950s very little was left of the Roaring Twenties Florida, the magnificent old resorts having been pulled down to make room for the gaudy, streamline-rococo gloss of postwar beach development. The Coronado, however, was perfect—a grand 1887 heap with turrets, a big veranda, and a wide white beach in front. Given Monroe's participation, the *Some Like It Hot* location shoot was scarcely a secret. Hundreds of onlookers crowded behind ropes in mid-September "as Miss Wiggle-Hips put her all into an ill-fitting 1929-vintage bathing suit." Billy was quoted as calling the film "a combination of *Scarface* and *Charley's Aunt*."

Back at the studio, shooting continued in fits and starts. Wilder and Diamond were piecing the film together as they went along, Monroe was characteristically late to arrive in the morning, and when she did show up she had a tendency to miff even the simplest of lines. Then a minor catastrophe occurred. In the St. Valentine's Day Massacre scene, in which Spats Columbo rubs out the diminutive Toothpick Charlie and his gang before Joe's and Jerry's horrified eyes, Wilder insisted that George Raft (as Spats) perform a final indignity upon the bullet-riddled corpse of Toothpick Charlie—namely, to kick the toothpick out of Charlie's mouth. (Raft seems either to have forgotten or forgiven Billy's jibe about him after *Double Indemnity*.) The actor playing Charlie, George E. Stone, was an old friend of Raft's, and Raft couldn't bring himself to kick him so close to his jaw. Two takes, three takes, five, ten . . . Billy was getting frustrated. It was bad enough that Marilyn was constantly requiring multiple takes to speak the simplest of lines. Now George Raft was using up film stock as well, and Billy couldn't take it anymore. "Please, *please*, George—kick the tooth-pick!" he begged. Then he marched over and demonstrated it himself, missed, and kicked Stone right in the head. The actor had to be rushed to the nearest hospital.

Monroe was, of course, a bigger problem than any character actor's broken jaw could possibly have been. She cost more. Things didn't start off badly. "I want the world to know that Marilyn's not only on time, she is three hours early," Billy told the press when *Some Like It Hot* when into production in August. By September, some tension surfaced when Marilyn declared that Billy wanted her to lose weight—eight pounds, to be exact—but she refused. "Don't you want your audience to be able to distinguish me from Tony and Jack?" she claimed to have asked Billy. "Besides," Marilyn added, "my husband likes me plump." In October, Wilder was still putting a happy face on things: "There are very few leading ladies in the business today. Of the few, there is just one Marilyn Monroe," he told a reporter. But by that point, he had to confess that his earlier declaration about her punctuality was false: she was frequently late or absent altogether, Billy admitted, "but she does beautifully once she gets under way. She warms up to her scenes and will work untiringly. If I demand sixty takes Marilyn accepts the additional work without question."

The reason Billy demanded sixty takes was, of course, that it often took Marilyn that many before she got it right. The tales are legendary:

Diamond (in retrospect): "One morning a couple of hundred extras waited on the set while reports kept filtering in on Marilyn's progress—she was in makeup now, now she was in hairdressing. Finally, at eleven o'clock, Marilyn walked on the stage carrying a copy of Thomas Paine's *The Rights of Man* under her arm. Without a word of greeting or apology, she crossed to her dressing room and locked herself in. Billy waited another fifteen minutes, then sent the assistant director to fetch her. The A.D. knocked on her door and called, 'We're ready for you, Miss Monroe.' From inside came the answer: 'Drop dead.' "

Lemmon (at the time): "The whole idea is a laugh. We were called for the first shot this morning, so we arrived at 7:00 A.M. Here it is, noon, and we still haven't been in front of the cameras. They've been retaking Marilyn's scenes."

Diamond (in retrospect): "After each scene, Marilyn would call out to her secretary, 'May! Coffee!' And May Reis would bring her a Thermos bottle." It contained not coffee but vermouth.

Lemmon (in retrospect): "One day she walked onto the damned set and it's the train scene, and she crawls up into my upper bunk and snuggles in next to me, and it goes *on*—really, it's a pretty long scene—and Billy shot it in *one*. And that was it. And I damn near shit. It was five minutes after eight and we're done."

Curtis (at the time): "I don't know why they go into these huddles. Maybe Paula [Strasberg, Marilyn's personal acting trainer] helps her read her lines. I never saw anybody else with a coach like that on the set."

Wilder (in retrospect): "I knew we were in mid-flight and there was a nut on the plane."

Paula Strasberg earned $1,500 a week to flutter around her neurotic boss whispering suggestions in her ear and holding a big black umbrella over her head, always urging Marilyn to "relax! relax!" Strasberg herself offered the press her views on Billy's work: "Everything is in such good taste. It's naive purity." She'd learned to keep her mouth shut on Wilder's set. On the first day of shooting, which covered some of the sequence with Sugar at the train station, Monroe looked not at her director but at Strasberg for approval. "How was that for you, Paula?" Wilder barked, after which no more was heard from Strasberg.

With all of Monroe's *mishegoss*, however, Billy still loved the work she did: "We were filming the scene in which she appears for the first time on the train platform: Lemmon and Curtis dressed as women, and Marilyn with her ukulele. She came up to me and immediately said, 'Billy, you have to come up with something for this. The scene doesn't work. If I'm just walking here, that's no entrance.' She was totally right, and I couldn't sleep that night, but the next morning I found the solution. She walks alongside the train, and then I let out the hot steam at the exact right moment—pffft, right on her fanny. She was very happy with that, and I was, too, because it was the right lead-in for the star of the film."

At least some of Monroe's legendary dispute with Tony Curtis ("It's like kissing Hitler," Curtis said at the time) appears to have been rooted in mutual jealousy. The costume designer Orry-Kelly had the pique to point out to Monroe that "you know, Tony's ass is better-looking than yours." "Oh yeah?" Monroe replied. "Well he doesn't have tits like these," whereupon she opened her blouse and proved it.

"It's me, Sugar." That was the line, and Marilyn couldn't say it. Over and over, she flubbed it. "It's Sugar, me." Cut. "It's Sugar, me." Cut. "It's Sugar, me . . ."

Finally she said it. Billy, trying to soothe her, told her (after yelling "Print!"), "Don't worry." "Worry about what?" said Marilyn.

"Where is that bourbon? Oh, there it is." With Curtis and Lemmon standing by through take after take, Monroe was utterly unable to complete the line. They tried taping a tiny cue card in the dresser drawer she opens in her search for the bottle, but it didn't help. It seemed only to confuse her more. "Where's the . . ." "Where's . . ." "Bourbon is . . ." After the forty-second take in a row, a bleary Billy offered a suggestion: "Marilyn, possibly—" "Don't talk to me now!" Marilyn snapped. "I'll forget how I want to play it!" As Lemmon recalls, "I have never seen a director stopped so cold—Billy Wilder, the fastest mind on earth. He was absolutely stunned." According to Diamond it took forty-seven takes over a period of two days. Even then, one can't help but notice that her back is to the camera when she says the line; the voice track may well have been dubbed in later.

By late October, Marilyn missed twelve days "because of so-called illness" and was late for a total of thirty-five hours, which translated to a five-day lag. As one jittery Mirisch noted, only a small part of this was covered by insurance. The cost was escalating, and UA, never particularly gung-ho about *Some Like It Hot*, was growing alarmed. Marilyn's absences had cost the company $200,000, bringing the total negative cost up to $2,600,000, and the film wasn't finished yet.

Monroe was a constant problem, but Lemmon and Curtis were consummate, responsible actors. Curtis may have come away from the film a bit rankled—not only by Monroe, but by Billy himself ("I never felt he really cared that much for me")—but he got the job done. Lemmon was more enthusiastic. As the filming proceeded, his admiration for Wilder grew exponentially. "I walked in all excited, early in the morning," Lemmon remembers. "Billy was just pacing up and down, as usual, waiting. And I said, 'Billy, I was thinking. . . . ' And he stopped right there and said, 'No you weren't.' I said, 'I wasn't?' I thought—oh God, he's not going to let me try. He said, 'No. You may have been thinking, but now you're going to be showing. Don't tell me, because I may misinterpret what you're talking about. Do it. Do anything you want, always, at any time. I don't care what it is or how long, whether I think you're crazy or not, do it—always do it. Don't hold back, but *do* it—don't talk about it.' "

Lemmon also noticed that his inventions were strictly circumscribed by Wilder and Diamond's screenplay. He claims that the only time he ever changed a line of dialogue in a Wilder script was in the music agent's scene in *Some Like It Hot*, in which he wanted to repeat the line "Now you're talkin'!" "It was twenty minutes before he said yes. He and Iz talked that thing over, I swear to God, *a half an hour*, and then finally he came back and said, 'Okay, you can repeat it.' "

Curtis, for his part, was impressed by Billy's willingness to accommodate an actor's creativity—as long as it had nothing to do with changing the words. It was Curtis's idea to play Shell Oil, the phony millionaire Jerry invents to impress Sugar, as an extended Cary Grant routine. Originally, Wilder simply wanted him to be Bostonian or at least some sort of American aristocrat. Curtis not only did what Billy wanted, he topped him. Grant himself found the idea amusing when Wilder told him about it, but behind the goof was a rather more biting observation about Cary's image. Not only was Grant's manliness something of a hoax, but the hoax was the key to his charm.

Jack Lemmon describes a scene that occurs midway through *Some Like It Hot* as probably "the best scene I've ever been in." It's about men:

> JERRY: I'm engaged!
> JOE: Congratulations! Who's the lucky girl?
> JERRY: I am. *(He sings and shakes his maracas.)*
> JOE: What?!
> JERRY: Osgood proposed to me. We're planning a June wedding. *(Sings, dances, shakes.)*
> JOE: What are you talking about? You can't marry Osgood!
> JERRY: *(Getting up from bed and entering two-shot)* You mean he's too old for me?
> JOE: Jerry, you can't be serious!
> JERRY: Why not? He keeps marrying girls all the time.
> JOE: But, but, you're not a girl! You're a guy! And why would a guy want to marry a guy?
> JERRY: Security! *(Sings, dances, shakes.)*
> JOE: Jerry, you better lie down. You're not well.
> JERRY: Will you stop treating me like a child? I'm not stupid. I know there's a problem.
> JOE: I'll say there is.
> JERRY: His mother. We need her approval. But I'm not worried, because I don't smoke. Ha ha ha ha! *(Sings, dances, shakes.)*
> JOE: Jerry, there's another problem. Like *what are you going to do on your honeymoon?*
> JERRY: We've been discussing that. He wants to go to the Riviera, but I kinda lean toward Niagara Falls.

Joe presses further in his quest to end Jerry's joy, and Jerry finally admits that his goal is a quick annulment and a handsome settlement. But even this ultimate recouping of the character's heterosexuality is not quite so ultimate, for it is here that Jerry mourns: "I'm a boy, I'm a boy, I wish I were dead. I'm a boy. Oh boy am I a boy." Daphne, one might add, does not depart without a struggle. She reappears in spirit if not in form very soon afterward when Jerry feels hurt and insulted that Joe could note with surprise, "These are real diamonds!" "Of course they're real," Jerry snaps. "What do you think—my fiancé is a bum?"

Lemmon remembers the dynamic business of the scene: "Billy handed me a set of maracas and I thought he was crazy. If Billy hadn't had me dancing around with those things in my 'joy,' most of the dialogue would've been lost. Every time I'd read a line I'd follow it by waltzing around with those maracas while Tony was looking at me like I'm out of my mind." Apart from their value as comic punctuation, Wilder gave the maracas to Lemmon as a way of prolonging the enormous laughs he knew the sequence would provoke. After the film's previews, he tinkered with the editing to allow even more time for laughs. After all, Billy wanted to please his audience: "Movies should be like amusement parks," he said at the time. "People should go to them to have fun."

Critics have rarely taken issue with the fact that *Some Like It Hot* is fun. They just can't bring themselves to figure out why. Neither did Diamond and Wilder, who claimed that the reason he didn't shoot his comedy in color is that it would have turned into a "flaming faggot" film. Their defensiveness is striking, Diamond's in particular:

Diamond: "The whole trick in the picture is that while the two were dressed in women's clothes, their thinking processes were at all times a hundred percent male. When there was a slight aberration, like Lemmon getting engaged, it became twice as funny. But they were not camping it up. They never thought of themselves as women. Just for one moment Lemmon forgot himself—that was all. The rest of the time, Curtis was out to seduce Monroe no matter what clothes he was wearing."

Wilder: "But when he forgot himself it was not a homosexual relationship. It was just the idea of being engaged to a millionaire. It's very appealing. You don't have to be a homosexual. It's security." Wilder was just as defensive on other occasions; to listen to him talk, you would think *Some Like It Hot* had no gay content at all: "Those thin-magazine people I mentioned before said *Some Like It Hot* had homosexual overtones as well as transvestite undertones. Well, I know that transvestites are cases for Krafft-Ebing, but to me they are terribly funny."

Those thin-magazine types (whoever they were) probably didn't dispute the fact that drag comedy is funny, but the question remains: why? As Wilder and Diamond themselves prove in the final moments of their film, the reason is perfectly clear. Because no one is 100 percent male or 100 percent female, it's funny to realize we're all somewhere in the middle. In hot jazz, it's the pleasure of veering off the tune purely on impulse: "One can hardly play hot while following the tune literally, for there is something about any tune, however beautiful, that is rigid, symmetrical, and unfriendly to that spontaneity necessary for hot interpretation." In *Some Like It Hot*, it's a form of comic relief. The ending of *Some Like It Hot* is hilarious, but it's also true. As everybody knows, nobody's perfect.

For the pivotal role of Osgood Fielding, the randy millionaire coot with whom Daphne finds enduring joy, Billy chose the biggest mouth in show business. It wasn't that Joe E. Brown talked a lot. It was that his mouth was abnormally large. Brown and his gaping grin, staples of late 1920s and early 1930s screen comedies, appeared in a range of later films—from the 1951 remake of *Show Boat* (as the riverboat captain) all the way down to Judy Canova's hillbilly caper *Joan of Ozark* and his own tailor-made vehicle, *Shut My Big Mouth* (both 1942). Brown's trademark gesture, a nearly silent laugh effected by stretching his huge orifice as wide as possible, is infectious—Daphne does it, too. These two are clearly made for each other.

Brown's personal history was, if anything, even more appealing to Billy than his mouth was. The comedian was a baseball fanatic of equal or greater proportions than Wilder; his son was the general manager of the Pittsburgh Pirates. Nineteen fifty-eight was not only the year in which *Some Like It Hot* was filmed; perhaps more gratifying to Billy, it was the Dodgers' first season in Los Angeles. Much to his hostesses' annoyance, Wilder made it a point to tote a transistor radio to dinner parties all season long. Radios didn't yet have earphones, so Billy just held the radio up to his head until the game was over, punctuating the drinks, meals, and after-dinner conversation with shouts of "Oh my God!" and "I don't believe it!" whenever anything notable occurred in the game. Sometimes an insensitive hostess would scold him for what she considered his rudeness, but for Billy it was not a question of manners. Baseball was more important than sociability. As long as Joe E. Brown was on the set, Billy conveniently had the inside track on all the players, managers, and umpires in the National League.

The production of *Some Like It Hot* appears to have been amusing and miserable in nearly equal measure. George Raft was a genial presence, offering to teach Brown and Lemmon how to tango when it became clear that the young dance instructor Wilder hired couldn't manage the task. Jack Lemmon, meanwhile, was constantly muttering "Magic time!" before every take, a habit he'd developed early in his career to give his performance that extra sparkle. "It's a habit of his on the set," Wilder explained. "Each time he starts to act, he acts as if it were a magic moment: 'Magic time!' That means—we're going to enter into this character, we are going to make the public enter his make-believe world." Jack Lemmon is verbally reminding himself that the camera is on and he must do reality one better. "Magic time!" Monroe is flubbing her lines; it's take thirty-eight. "Magic time!" Lemmon is in a dress and wig and ghastly greenish makeup, and

Monroe is still blowing her cues. Take forty-one. "Magic time!" Tony Curtis says the whole thing drove him slightly mad.

With Monroe running late, being ill, and finally getting pregnant, Wilder and Diamond found themselves having to write and film around Monroe's unreliability. With uncanny foresight, they'd written Sweet Sue's first complaint before the trouble began: "*Idiot broads!* Here we are, already packed, ready to leave for Miami, *and what happens?*! The saxophone runs off with a Bible salesman and the base fiddle gets herself pregnant!" Faced with a pregnant broad of their own, Wilder and Diamond decided to get rid of Sugar quickly by writing a short scene in which she and Joe drop out of the shot in the boat at the end, presumably to keep kissing. This leaves Jerry alone in the image with Osgood. Curtis may also have been aware that Wilder thought his girl-voice wasn't right and decided to loop it all later in a recording studio. Sensing the ongoing tension on the set and hoping to dispel it, Curtis hired a real stripper to pop out of the cake during the filming of Spats's birthday party. With the cast and crew laughing all around him, Billy was mortified. A *Playboy* photographer covering the shoot tried to get him to kiss the stripper. He simply shook his head and refused.

The precise ending to this farce was most unresolved when *Some Like It Hot* went into production, and it remained so for much of the filming. According to George Raft, Monroe suggested ending the film with Sugar and Spats tangoing together. Wilder is said to have liked the idea at first, but he and Diamond decided to end the movie with Brown and Lemmon— in part because Marilyn wasn't available. Raft's story has an unreliable air, given that Spats is otherwise occupied at the end of the film, having been rubbed out by the machine-gun-wielding thug in the birthday cake. More important, the whole thrust of the narrative points toward the two central male characters each finding a mate. Spats Columbo dancing with Sugar would scarcely have served that end.

"Diamond and I were in our room working together," Billy recalled, "waiting for the next line—Joe E. Brown's response, the final line, the curtain line of the film—to come to us. Then I heard Diamond say, 'Nobody's perfect.' I thought about it and I said, 'Well, let's put in "Nobody's perfect" for now. But only for the time being. We have a whole week to think about it.' We thought about it all week. Neither of us could come up with anything better, so we shot that line, still not entirely satisfied. When we screened the movie, that line got one of the biggest laughs I've ever heard in the theater. But we just hadn't trusted it when we wrote it; we just didn't see it. The line had come too easily, just popped out." Originally, Diamond wanted to stick the line into the security scene, but he was afraid it would kill both jokes.

The last moments of *Some Like It Hot* are probably the best known in Wilder's career. Osgood's line is openly gay, there's no question about that. The line is meaningless otherwise. The scene also includes one last off-color joke, as Daphne insists upon retaining her penis:

OSGOOD: I called Ma-ma. She was so happy she cried. She wants you to have her wedding gown. It's white lace.

DAPHNE: Uh, Osgood, I can't get married in your mother's dress. She and I—we are not built in the same way.

OSGOOD: We can have it altered.

DAPHNE: *Oh no you don't.* Osgood, I'm going to level with you. We can't get married at all.

OSGOOD: Why not?

DAPHNE: Well, in the first place, I'm not a natural blonde.

OSGOOD: Doesn't matter.

DAPHNE: I smoke. I smoke all the time!

OSGOOD: I don't care.

DAPHNE: I have a terrible past! For three years now I've been living with a saxophone player.

OSGOOD: I forgive you.

DAPHNE: I can never have children.

OSGOOD: We can adopt some.

DAPHNE: You don't understand, Osgood. *(He whips off the wig.)* I'm *a man.*

OSGOOD: Well, nobody's perfect.

Indeed, perfection is impossible to attain—especially for the writer-director, who was so anxious, enraged, and queasy during the filming of *Some Like It Hot* that his chronic backaches grew worse and he even threw up from all the fear and tension. Once shooting was completed and he could step briefly off the field of eggshells with which Monroe surrounded herself, Wilder told the press that since he was the only director ever to make two films with her, the Directors Guild should give him a Purple Heart. Somebody asked him if he'd ever make another picture with her. "In the United States, I'd hate it," Billy said. "In Paris, it might not be so bad. While we were waiting we could all take painting lessons on the side." Monroe didn't think any of this was very nice.

Shooting was over, but certain details still needed attention, among them the score. Matty Malneck, who was out of his element with the *Witness* score, was back to his metier with hot jazz and swing. (In fact, Sugar sings one of Malneck's most popular compositions—"Stairway to the Stars.") Malneck flew to New York to work with Monroe, who was also to sing the title song (tune by Malneck, lyrics by Diamond). He tried to forge a working détente between the two inflamed egomaniacs. He said he'd call Billy at home, right then and there, and he'd help them work it out. The call was placed. Malneck put Marilyn on. The conversation ran as follows:

"Audrey?"

"Hi, Marilyn."

"Is Billy there?"

"No, he's not home yet."

"Well, when you see him, will you give him a message for me? Tell him to go fuck himself. And my warmest personal regards to you."

The Monroe partisans (Marilyn, Arthur Miller, his mother, and hundreds of thousands of her fans) blamed Billy for the miscarriage she suffered only twelve hours after filming her last take on *Some Like It Hot*. Gossipmeister Earl Wilson got the scoop from the family: "She had to run upstairs about fourteen times in the picture and the temperature was about 104," Mrs. [Isadore] Miller said. "All the time she was expecting and not feeling well."

Arthur Miller seconded the notion, in public. Wilder fired off a telegram to the playwright: "Had you, dear Arthur, been not her husband but her writer and director, and been subjected to all the indignities I was, you would have thrown her out on her can, Thermos bottle and all, to avoid a nervous breakdown. I did the braver thing. I had a nervous breakdown."

To the press, Billy was even more succinct. His work with Monroe was over, he declared, and therefore "I am able for the first time to look at my wife again without wanting to hit her because she's a woman."

Earl Wilson, fanning the flames, got Marilyn on the phone. "Who says stars are temperamental? Now it's directors who get that way!" Wilson quoted Monroe as saying. He went on to say that "she wishes that Billy'd remember that *Some Like It Hot* cost her the baby." But as Diamond pointed out, of course, it was a fallopian pregnancy, doomed from the start.

Everything was kissy-kissy again when the movie was released. Wilder and Monroe each had a percentage of the gross. "I would make a picture any time with Billy Wilder," Marilyn told Louella. "I liked making a comedy, and I would like to do another comedy with Mr. Wilder." "She is a very great actress," said Billy. "Better Marilyn late than most of the others on time." He still had a few zingers left in him, though. "The question is whether Marilyn is a person at all or one of the greatest Du Pont products ever invented," he said. "She has breasts like granite and a brain like swiss cheese." For the sake of her talent, Billy declared, he wished that her endless therapies and acting training wouldn't work: "It is better for Monroe *not* to be straightened out. The charm of her is two left feet. Otherwise she may become a slightly inferior Eva Marie Saint."

Some Like It Hot came in half a million dollars over budget for a total negative cost of $2,883,848. The first preview of *Some Like It Hot* occurred in December 1958, at the Bay Theatre in Pacific Palisades before an audience of 800. According to Billy, 799 of them didn't like it. Wilder ran down the aisle at the end to shake the hand of the film's only fan—comedian Steve Allen. *Some Like It Hot* also previewed in New York, where it was sneaked at the Fiftieth Street Loews. Monroe herself showed up. She was so mobbed by fans that her friend Montgomery Clift, who accompanied her to the screening, couldn't even get into their limousine after the show and had to pound his fist on the roof to be let in.

After the previews, Wilder made one minor change to *Some Like It Hot*: the train station sequence was extended to allow for more laughs. Billy claims to have put in every take of the scene he'd filmed; according to him, Lemmon and Curtis walk past the same three train cars five times. (In fact, they don't.)

Able to shill for the film more reliably than she could work in it, Marilyn delighted the boys of the press with comments on underwear ("I have no prejudice against it") and her role as a sex symbol ("How do I know about a man's needs for a sex symbol? I'm a girl"). Her luminous face graced the cover of *Life*, and everyone was happy—except for the Legion of Decency. The Very Reverend Monsignor Thomas F. Little, S.T.L., the Legion's executive secretary, wrote a testy letter to Geoffrey Shurlock explaining why the Legion issued *Some Like It Hot* a B rating ("morally objectionable in part for all"). The reason: "gross suggestiveness in costuming, dialogue, and situations. . . . Since the initiation of the triple-A method of classifying films in December 1957, this film has given the Legion the greatest cause for concern in its evaluation of Code Seal pictures. The subject matter of 'transvestism' naturally leads to complications; in this film there seemed to us to be clear inferences of homosexuality and lesbianism. The dialogue was not only 'double entendre' but outright smut."

The critics weren't particularly impressed with Wilder's taste either. As one sniffed, "I suppose Billy Wilder is entitled to a farce now and then but I personally wish he'd stick to ironical and satiric comedy. He's not at home in a burlesque show, which is all *Some Like It Hot* is." Diamond recalled the fact that the picture didn't do especially well in its first week of release, but word of mouth made it grow. He recalled the *Los Angeles Times* review having been headed "*Some Like It Hot* Not As Hot As Expected." But if the Mirisches and UA were worried at first, they were certainly happy by the end of 1959, by which point the film was the year's third biggest blockbuster (behind *Auntie Mame* and *The Shaggy Dog*). By the end of 1963

Some Like It Hot had earned more than $7.5 million in the United States alone and another $5.25 million abroad. Billy himself pulled in $1.2 million.

He celebrated by buying a Paul Klee drawing; a Paul Klee painting; Egon Schiele's *Akt mit grünem Turban*; Braque's *Nature morte* and another Braque, too—"*La théière grise.*" He wasn't finished. In 1959 alone he also purchased Nicolas de Staël's *Nature morte* and Balthus's 1957 painting *La toilette*. These he added to the works he bought the previous year, including a Matisse, a Klee, a Nicholson, a Schwitters, and a de Staël, in addition to a captivating nude by Suzanne Valadon—*Femme nue devant un miroir*.

Wilder also took the occasion of *Some Like It Hot*'s release to issue his opinion of television: "We should all thank God for TV. It is the most wonderful thing that could have happened to us. We have always been the lowest of the low, but now they have invented something which we can look down on." He evidently changed his mind by 1960, when a television series based on *Some Like It Hot* was briefly in the works and he voiced his intention to direct the first episode.

Some Like It Hot didn't get quite the attention from the Academy of Motion Picture Arts and Sciences that one might expect. True, the film garnered six nominations—Lemmon for Best Actor, Wilder for Best Director, Wilder and Diamond for Best Adapted Screenplay, Lang for Best Cinematography, Ted Haworth and Edward G. Goyle for Best Art Direction, and Orry-Kelly for Best Costume Design. But Orry-Kelly was the only winner. Fortunately for Billy, the Writers Guild gave its award for Best Comedy to Wilder and Diamond.

After the film opened, the Wilders, the Diamonds, the Harold Mirisches, and Jack Lemmon headed for Europe on the luxury liner *United States*. Their fellow passengers included the duke and duchess of Windsor. *Some Like It Hot* was screened in the ship's theater, but the duke and duchess, trying to beat the crowd, got up from their seats before it was over. A steward (obviously an American) blocked the royals' path. "You don't want to miss this," he advised them, and according to Diamond, the duke and duchess meekly took their seats again. At dinner, the Wilders and their extended party were seated at the table next to the Windsors, whose dinner partner leaned over to them and whispered, "I think one of the actors from that picture is at the next table." "The one I liked?" asked the duke audibly. "No, dear," said the duchess—"the other one."

24. THE APARTMENT

From what I hear through the walls you got something going for
you every night. Sometimes there's a twi-night doubleheader! A
nebbish like you.

—Dr. Dreyfuss (Jack Kruschen) to Baxter
(Jack Lemmon) in *The Apartment*

He was up to four packs of cigarettes a day. He'd give it up, Billy said,
except that he might get hit by a car and he'd hate to lie bleeding to
death in the gutter thinking about all the pleasure he missed by not
smoking. He also favored icy martinis—not a lot, just frequently. He
thrived on his vices.

And why not? In 1959, Billy Wilder was a fifty-three-year-old firebrand
with a huge hit on his hands and thirty years of filmmaking experience
under his belt. He had the added virtues of wealth, cunning, and a healthy
contract with the Mirisches. He was eager to make another blockbuster
with complete artistic control.

As Billy and Iz moved on to write their next film, they found themselves
the objects of an increasing number of profiles and interviews. Always good
for the insulting remark, Wilder had become every journalist's dream; in
addition to his highly quotable wit, he was making an extraordinary
amount of money even by Hollywood standards, and his vast wealth gave
him extra color. Wilder possessed forty or fifty walking sticks by that point,
Hollywood Close-Up reported in a characteristic profile. The journalist
found him working with Diamond in their joint office and chain-smoking
(alternating between cigarettes and cigars). On the wall were the Japanese
woodcuts Bill Holden presented Billy after returning from shooting *The
Bridge on the River Kwai*. There were tiger skins on the floor—a gift from
John Huston. In Wilder's pocket, the reporter noted, were a money clip—a
present from his friend Joan ("Sweet Sue") Shawlee—and a little gold me-
dallion from Marlene Dietrich. The reporter found Wilder and Diamond

struggling over the title of their next picture. Neither of them especially liked *The Apartment*, so they were mulling over alternatives—*Someone's Been Sleeping in My Bed* or *Who's Been Sleeping in My Bed?*

It should not be surprising to learn that Billy had other projects on his mind during the composition of *The Apartment*. He changed his mind once again about *A New Kind of Love*, deciding in early January 1959 not to part with the rights in case he found the time and money to make the film someday. (Fox's Jerry Wald had been interested in buying them.) Louella, obviously prematurely, announced at the end of May that Billy and his friend William Wyler would codirect and coproduce something called *The Human Strong Box*, from a story by Wyler's brother Robert, but nothing ever came of it.

There was still the Colonel Redl thing with Laughton. In June, Paul Kohner pointed out to Billy that a new biography of Redl had just been released, and to keep others away he advised Wilder to announce his interest. Billy seems to have let it slide. And later that year, Louella revealed that the late Charles Vidor (who died in early June) felt that if anything should happen to him, he wanted Wilder to take over his pet project—*The Nijinsky Story*. Parsons asked Billy about it. He replied, "Naturally I would like to carry out the wishes of my good friend, but I don't want to go to work on the story until all the rights have been cleared." Vidor, it seems, had been battling a Broadway producer for the rights, and although he won every suit, there was still one more round to go. Louella herself continued: "Billy says if he makes the movie it will be another *Red Shoes*." The talking horse bit he told Goldwyn would have been pretty good, too.

For fun, Billy did what he'd been doing since childhood: laying bets. When Douglas Sirk's latest film, *Imitation of Life*, approached its release, Billy bet Kohner $100 that the film's domestic gross would be closer to $4 million than to the $8 million Kohner predicted. Harold Mirisch then joined Billy in the bet, whereupon Billy promptly laid a separate bet with Mirisch, also for $100 but this time at 3:1 odds. *Imitation of Life*, Billy declared, wouldn't even hit $4 million. He lost.

When he ran into Satyajit Ray around this time, Wilder was blunt: "You won a prize at Cannes? Well, I guess you're an artist. But, I'm not. I'm just a commercial man and I like it that way." Having gotten away with all the dirty jokes in *Some Like It Hot*, he turned back to an idea he had been carrying around since the 1940s: "I remembered having seen a long time ago a very good film by David Lean—*Brief Encounter*, the story of a married woman and a man who use the bedroom of a friend for their rendezvous. I always thought there was an interesting character there—the one who loans the apartment, a touching and funny character, and I kept this idea with me. After finishing *Some Like It Hot*, I wanted to make another film with Lemmon and I found that such a role would fit him well." He offered the role to Lemmon in the car on the way to a private screening of *Some Like It Hot* (according to Lemmon, the *first* screening) at the Long Island home of Billy's old army buddy William Paley.

Wilder says he actually made a note to himself after seeing *Brief Encounter*: "What I had written was, 'What about the friend who has to crawl back into that warm bed?' " For Billy, there was something appealing about this premise—emotionally, sexually, thematically, commercially. Before meeting Jack Lemmon and seeing the sweet intimacy with which he expressed Wilder's harsh imagination, Billy was prone to lavishing his attentions on the exploiters of the world—the evil manipulators (Phyllis Dietrichson in *Double Indemnity*, Chuck Tatum in *Ace in the Hole*), the hustlers (Sefton in *Stalag 17*), the self-pimps (Gillis in *Sunset Boulevard*). Even his Oscar-winning victim (Don Birnam in *The Lost Weekend*) was a diseased liar and a compulsive cheat. But in Jack Lemmon Billy saw new potential—the endearing comedy of an American loser. Tom Ewell was good at it, but Jack Lemmon was brilliant. Overwhelmed with possibilities, Billy found he had far too much to say about such a dud: "I started with this character and this theme: a man who lets himself be exploited, a solitary bachelor who comes home at night and gets in the bed still warm from the lovers. I called my friend Diamond and we started working. Once you have an idea like that, millions of others follow. The problem then is to eliminate, to simplify. In other words, what's important is the elimination of what has been invented."

To Shirley MacLaine, whom he wanted for the film's leading lady, he was more succinct: "This is about a young fellow who gets ahead in a big company by lending his apartment to executives for that grand old American folk ritual, the afternoon shack-up." She agreed to do *The Apartment* based on this one-line précis and some early script pages. The time was right, the Production Code ineffectual, the Legion of Decency exercising its waning authority only over the nation's Catholics, and even then many of them simply ignored the peril to their souls and went to whatever movies they wanted. "I would have done it in 1948 or 1949 but for the censorship," Wilder had said. But, by the end of the 1950s, thanks to much of that decade's innovations—Elvis, Monroe, Little Richard, Jayne Mansfield, *Some Like It Hot*—any attempts to erase overt sexuality from American mass entertainment had become laughably out-of-date.

The heartlessness of American corporate culture, meanwhile, had become a standard theme in American film drama. *Executive Suite* and *The Man in the Grey Flannel Suit* struck a chord with the public—glacially impersonal architecture, callous bosses, and professional lives devoid of hope, let alone soul. Fifties' audiences related to it. So into this conventional world Wilder dropped his own creation: C. C. Baxter, the perfect WASP *schmeggege.*

Tony Curtis offers another account of the film's genesis, defying everyone else's. Curtis claims credit for inspiring *The Apartment*: "The reason it came about was because there were a lot of beautiful girls who were extras and bit players that I wanted to fuck, and I did. . . . Most of the time the problem wasn't the girl, it was the place." So Tony used his friend Nicky Blair's bachelor pad somewhere off Laurel Canyon. According to Curtis, the hose-nosed Hollywood columnist Sidney Skolsky ran into Blair one day when Blair was killing time by sitting in his own parked car. Why can't you go home? Skolsky inquired; "Tony's up there with a girl," Blair answered. According to Curtis, "Skolsky wrote it up as a treatment and sold it and it became *The Apartment*." Curtis also claims Wilder didn't cast him in the Nicky Blair role because he was too good-looking.

If Hollywood backdoor romances lie at the heart of *The Apartment*, another dazzlingly tawdry real-life incident was probably more influential. In 1951, producer Walter Wanger discovered that his wife, Joan Bennett, was having an affair with the agent Jennings Lang. Their encounters were brief and frequent. When Lang and Bennett weren't meeting clandestinely at vacation spots like New Orleans and the West Indies, they were back in L.A. enjoying weekday quickies at a Beverly Hills apartment otherwise occupied by one of Lang's underlings at the agency. When Wanger found proof of the affair, he did what any crazed cuckold would do: he shot Lang in the balls. Given the prominence of all three principals and the lurid, just-deserts vengeance extracted by Wanger, Hollywood was delighted by the story. Given its timing, *Life* couldn't help but observe that his passage from cell to police desk, a walk punctuated by flashbulbs and the hum of newsreel cameras, looked and sounded uncomfortably like the end of *Sunset Boulevard.*

From whatever source Wilder developed *The Apartment*, had he found the means he might have staged it as a theatrical production, but according to Diamond, it proved to be too unwieldy: "Originally Billy wanted to do *The Apartment* as a play, but since there had to be such a visual contrast between the apartment and the three-hundred-desk office, it was not feasible."

This was going to be a film about a clerk and an elevator operator, but none of the filmmakers who created *The Apartment* were themselves anonymous little people anymore. Lemmon and MacLaine were each paid straight salaries of $175,000 for their appearances. (This was an ample sum, certainly. Still, because neither of them got a percentage of the profits, let alone the gross, their combined salaries didn't even equal what Tony Curtis alone made on *Some Like It Hot*.) Billy's own deal with the Mirisches remained the same: $200,000 and 17.5 percent of the gross above two times the cost of the negative, 20 percent if the film pulled in $1 million over the break-even point. As long as Billy didn't blow it, and there was little chance that he would, more art was likely to be purchased after *The Apartment* hit the marketplace.

For Shirley MacLaine, *The Apartment* confirmed her status as a top-ranking star. She'd done some good comedies in the mid-1950s (*Artists and Models*, 1955; *The Trouble with Harry*, 1955; *Around the World in 80 Days*, 1956), but her most recent role was a major dramatic one—Frank Sinatra's trashy girlfriend in Vincente Minnelli's *Some Came Running* (1959). Wilder nevertheless credits himself for MacLaine's later success as an accomplished dramatic actress. "Take Shirley MacLaine," Billy boasted. "She was infected with that one-take, Rat Pack, all-play-and-no-work non-sense, but when she came to work for Iz and me in *The Apartment* she got serious and worked as hard as anybody. Now she's playing drama." Wilder is being overly generous to his friend Iz here. In no sense did MacLaine or anyone else work for Wilder and Diamond. They all worked—Diamond as well—for Wilder and the Mirisches. As Diamond himself explained at the time, "I am listed as a coproducer on the film. In essence this means no more than my being allowed to stay on the lot after the shooting has started." Billy, on the other hand, explained Diamond's recurrent role as associate producer by saying that he was "the only one willing to associate with the producer."

In any event, MacLaine did a little on-the-job training for her role as the working-class Fran Kubelik. She spent a day preparing for her part by operating one of the elevators in the Los Angeles Times building. As usual for MacLaine in this period, this wasn't a glamour role. Her entire ward-robe for the film is said to have cost $178.50.

According to MacLaine, "There were only twenty-nine pages of script, maybe thirty-nine—that was all we had when we started. And then Billy and Izzie observed Jack and me together, and as they observed us they wrote the screenplay—as we were shooting." According to Diamond, he and Billy went into production with a complete screenplay, though they'd only just finished "in the last four days and nights before shooting." Filming began in November 1959 on location in New York. Ignoring his own account of the film's genesis, Wilder once declared that "*The Apartment* occurred to me while I was in New York, where I go twice a year. On the other hand, maybe that theme would have occurred to me in Oklahoma." The theme, perhaps; the look, impossible. This was a purely New York story—harsh, funny, and fast, full of tiny people in tall buildings. Ironically, Billy would be filming this most vertical of cities in CinemaScope.

A picturesque, spindly tree–lined block of West Sixty-ninth Street was chosen for the exteriors of C. C. Baxter's run-of-the-mill apartment (the interiors of which Alex Trauner designed as anything but ordinary). Other sites included the exterior of the Majestic Theater, a Columbus Avenue bar, and a Chinese restaurant, which was actually a below-street-level barbershop dressed with a neon COCKTAILS sign. Wilder and his crew also filmed in the gleaming lobby of a brand-new $38 million Wall Street office tower, which Billy knew would superbly reflect the polished stoniness of the world he wished to depict.

It was a cold New York November. On the day the scene involving Buddy-Boy Baxter sitting drenched on a park bench was shot, the temperature dropped to sixteen degrees. No matter. Jack Lemmon still had to be sprayed and soaked—with a mixture of water and antifreeze.

Originally, the script called for Baxter to wait for the woman he tries pathetically to date, the perky and suicidal elevator operator Fran Kubelik, outside the theater in which *The Sound of Music* was playing. This was because Billy is said to have invested some money in the show and thought he'd work a plug into his own film. Then Billy went to see *The Sound of Music* himself. No surprise here, he hated it—so much so that he switched Baxter's tickets to *The Music Man*.

Location shooting in New York was arduous—reminiscent of *The Lost Weekend*, only worse. "We weren't making progress," Trauner recalled, "and besides it was so cold that we were always running to the bar to warm ourselves. Billy even claimed that my little dog was becoming an alcoholic because she would run ahead of us to the bar. Finally he had enough, and we decided to reshoot the exteriors of New York on a set at the Goldwyn Studio, where we also had the advantage of controlling the bad weather that was important to the film. I think the only part of the real New York that made it into the film were a few shots of streets and two shots in Central Park."

At least one casting decision was made in New York as well. Ray Walston, who plays the leering Mr. Dobisch, remembers the audition: "I met him at the Warwick Hotel in New York, while he was there doing exteriors. I was sent over there by my agent, and I went over about eight-thirty one night and went into this living room, where he was sitting at a French table that served as a desk. He said to me, 'Josh Logan tells me that you are a good actor.' I nodded, and he said, 'Do you have an overcoat.' I said, 'Yes.' He said, 'Is it an expensive overcoat?' I said, 'Yes.' He said, 'Good. Then you got the job.' How can you resist a man like that?"

Billy and his crew returned to Los Angeles just before Thanksgiving, and shooting resumed on November 30 at Goldwyn. The block of brownstones was completely rebuilt (facades only, of course), as was the office building lobby. The restaurant and bar interiors were constructed anew.

Most important of all, Trauner designed and built the vast office in which Baxter and hundreds of his coworkers drudged. Trauner's skill at using perspective reached its epitome in *The Apartment*. The idea was Billy's, who took his inspiration from King Vidor. As Vidor himself said, "Wilder copied the scene in *The Crowd* for his picture *The Apartment* and asked how many desks I had had." *The Crowd* is one of the jewels of the American silent cinema—a poignant look at the drab disaster that comprises an average working man's life in New York. Both heartbreakingly realistic and poetically stylized, *The Crowd* is *The Apartment*'s antecedent in tone as well as set design. Since American corporate anonymity had become even more grotesque by 1959, Wilder took Vidor's vision to a heart-of-chrome-and-glass extreme. Vidor makes "John" (James Murray) seem small in his office in *The Crowd*; Wilder practically atomizes Buddy-Boy Baxter in *The Apartment*, an effect Trauner achieves by way of forced perspective.

Billy later insisted that midgets played an integral part of Trauner's design: "Take the big office set of *The Apartment*—the one that looks as big as a football field covered with five thousand individual desks. We shot it in a Goldwyn sound stage on a medium-sized set. How? By using perspective. Some tall extras seated behind normal desks, others shorter, behind smaller desks, some dwarves at miniature desks, then some cut-outs and toy desks." Trauner himself said, less colorfully, that they used children.

To dress this frighteningly modern set, Trauner and his staff borrowed $2.5 million worth of office equipment (calculators, punch card machines, and sorters) from the corporate behemoth IBM. Whether or not there were midget people behind midget desks, there still had to be a vast floor; it took half an acre of linoleum. For Trauner, though, the real gem was the aluminum ceiling: "Most of the points of view took advantage of the ceiling, which offered another advantage—the spectator simply fills in the background for himself and concentrates on the action in the foreground." Thus a 120-foot-by-200-foot set took on the demoralizing force of a 650-foot-by-800-foot corporate hell.

Despite the noticeable presence of Eastern Europeans (Dobisch, Eichelberger, Kubelik), Consolidated Life is essentially heartless. But home offers a kind of architectural love. However solitary and depressing it may seem at first glance, Baxter's apartment is warm—worn and shabby, perhaps, but in a *gemütlich* sort of way. Wood and plaster make it solid, carved archways soften the edges and offer a kind of shelter. Like the apartment Maurice Chevalier and Audrey Hepburn share in *Love in the Afternoon*, Trauner's design combines with Wilder's sensibility to create a snug refuge against an ugly world, but in both cases the ugliness seeps in anyway and is not entirely unwelcome. Just as Ariane is thrilled by the sleaze she finds in her father's filing cabinets, Baxter finds a certain vicarious thrill in what other men do in his bed. He's put upon, but he likes it. Even the apartment is world-weary.

And so are the neighbors. In *The Apartment*, home is where the Jews are. The Dreyfusses live next door, while Mrs. Lieberman, the landlady, runs the house. As a character type, Dr. Dreyfuss (Jack Kruschen) became extinct in the decades following the film's release; he's a middle-class physician. More to the point, he is the film's benevolent paternal figure to counterpose Sheldrake's malignant one. Dr. Dreyfuss is the man to whom Wilder entrusts the film's only moral: be a mensch, Dreyfuss advises the less-than-fully-human Baxter, who eventually takes him up on the suggestion. (Be a mensch doesn't just mean *be a real person*. It means *be a good and decent person*.) Wilder doesn't fully come to public terms with being a Jew in this film, but he nods in that direction. The Poliakoff scene in *Some Like It Hot*, as funny as it is, is really just a prelude to the surprisingly redemptive Jewishness of *The Apartment*.

Billy had scarcely been running away from his heritage, but before the late 1950s he didn't embrace it on-screen. (Harry Shapiro in *Stalag 17* is the big exception.) Then again, he couldn't. Jews may have controlled Hollywood behind the scenes, but on-screen they were virtually nonexistent, and the Jewish producers and studio bosses wanted to keep it that way. (It was the profoundly goyish Darryl Zanuck who had the nerve to make the ground-breaking anti-Semitism drama *Gentleman's Agreement* in 1947.) But now, in middle-age and with the Borscht Belt veteran Diamond as his sidekick, Wilder was relaxed enough about who he was to let some of his Jewishness come out in front of an international audience, and Hollywood conventions no longer stood in his way. Still, one measure of the novelty of Jewish characters in American films in 1959 is the actor UA executives suggested to play the role of Dr. Dreyfuss. If Billy wanted a Jew, UA was ready to give him one—Groucho Marx. Fortunately, Billy had someone less extreme in mind. Confident, unpretentious, professional, and a real mensch, Jack Kruschen's Dr. Dreyfuss embodies everything that Wilder sees as being right about the world.

It's too bad that Wilder's mellow enjoyment of his own heritage is marred by Naomi Stevens's hammy performance as Mrs. Dreyfuss (for which Wilder is equally to blame). What with the chicken soup and the apron and the napkins and the fussing, Wilder gives Stevens maybe one *nu* too many. "*Mit* the drinking, *mit* the cha-cha!" she clucks at Baxter, and although it's rather funny, one wishes Wilder could have exercised a little more control over the actress's delivery. Frances Lax's Mrs. Lieberman is more appealing, less of a caricature. Her offhand remark about "that *mish-egoss* at Cape Canaveral" sounds like something somebody's Aunt Dora might actually say. Mrs. Dreyfuss does have one of the better lines, though:

appalled at Baxter's apparently raging promiscuity, she turns on him and, with a withering stare, accuses him of being "Max the knife."

With its grim, black-and-white-and-gray cinematography, its low-key lighting, and its moodiness and morally compromised tone, *The Apartment* echoes 1940s film noir. Watching Baxter huddle in the shadows of his brownstone, clutching his unprotective overcoat around him and shivering while some other guy usurps his apartment, is as oppressive and bitter as the scene in *Laura* (1944) in which Clifton Webb lurks, freezing and snow-battered, outside the apartment of the woman he loves while she makes love to another man. Wilder chose Joseph LaShelle to shoot *The Apartment*, LaShelle having had some experience with film noir—he shot *Laura*.

LaShelle and Wilder went on to make a number of other films together, despite Billy's having threatened to scuttle LaShelle's career during a run-in during filming. Wilder had his heart set on a very low-angle shot, and LaShelle said no. "He kind of peered at me over his glasses like an owl," LaShelle recalled. " 'What did you say?' So I said, 'No, I don't think so.' And he said, 'Joseph, you must be a very wealthy man.' I said, 'I have some savings.' And he said, 'But you do have to work, don't you?' I said, 'Oh, I don't have to work—not all the time.' And he said, 'But Joseph, you're *never* going to work. . . . Nobody ever says no to me. So what do you think about my low setup?' And I said, very loud, '*No.*' "

This was bold. But Billy wasn't angry at his defiance. He was impressed. Grinning broadly, Wilder relented: "Oh, shit, then do it the way you want." LaShelle never specified which shot he and Billy argued about. Maybe it was the one in which Baxter and Dr. Dreyfuss drag Fran back and forth across the apartment trying to return her to consciousness after her suicide attempt—a very low-angle shot taken almost from the floor.

LaShelle, like other pros, was amazed at Wilder's shooting style. Billy didn't shoot what are called protection shots—the extra close-ups and master shots that can be inserted during editing if the original intention isn't achieved, or, just as likely, if the producer simply decides there should be more close-ups and master shots. On other people's films, LaShelle noted, "the director only had the right of first cut. Zanuck was like that. Cohn was like that. Jack Warner. All of them. With Billy they couldn't do it. He wouldn't give them these protection shots. There was nothing left on the cutting room floor when he was finished." Wilder was one of a handful of Hollywood directors who shot in this manner.

Shooting progressed methodically, though with a certain awkward stress involving star and director. Jack Lemmon remembers the tension between Wilder and MacLaine: "She hated rehearsals and had a bad habit of ad-libbing, which didn't set well with Billy Wilder." To say the least. MacLaine herself is markedly cool on the subject of Wilder. She's appreciative but reservedly so. At a 1982 tribute to Billy, she spoke of him fondly: "In a Wilder film, nobody is spared that Wilder X-ray cynical wit. As a matter of fact, there is no institution so sacrosanct that it can't be punctured by Billy's sense of humor. I'm rather glad he hasn't put his talents to the life story of Mother Teresa yet." In one of her books, on the other hand, she writes: "I wished Billy Wilder would pay as much attention to my talents as he did to Jack's." The attention Billy lavished on Lemmon, MacLaine writes, "had its downside, too. Billy was so enamored of Jack that he pressed him to do take after take just to see what would happen. Jack, being the cooperative professional, complied, often to his own detriment. The later takes were forced, and often those were the ones Billy printed. I, on the other hand, only had to do it three or four times because frankly I don't think Billy thought I was capable of much more, but at least I stayed fresh."

How strange that Wilder's confidence in MacLaine's ability was taken by MacLaine herself as a form of disinterest, while his insistence on Lemmon's retakes she recalls as evidence of infatuation. Still, MacLaine echoes Joan Fontaine describing her experiences on *The Emperor Waltz*. To particularly self-assured, strong-willed actresses, Wilder's sets probably did seem like boys' clubs. Girls were tolerated only as long as they didn't get in the way too much and never talked back. The atmosphere is easy to imagine. To keep Jack Lemmon happy and occupied, for example, Billy had a pinball machine installed on the set. Lemmon's personality was something Billy could appreciate. Men played games like pinball and poker. Women played mind games. Billy preferred men's games. He always liked spending his days with his buddies, and they were hardly ever female. That was for later.

Wilder found Shirley MacLaine's mouthiness exasperating in person, but he made it seem admirable on celluloid. Notice the brisk way Fran turns and walks away from the sniveling Baxter in the middle of their conversation in the office lobby. Watch the crisp confidence in MacLaine's eyes. She knows what Fran knows: many men want her, but she's the one who does the choosing. One can hardly say she's nobody's fool—*The Apartment* is about people willing to kill themselves for scum—but Fran Kubelik has the kind of raw vitality that makes her attempt at self-annihilation seem all the more a pity. Wilder wrote her that way, but MacLaine embodied her. On-screen, her resistance to Billy's bossiness pays off.

MacLaine's performances for Wilder, like much of the best filmmaking, are a set of fortuitous accidents strung together with an unbreakable cord of talent. So are Fred MacMurray's. In 1943, Wilder cast him in *Double Indemnity* because George Raft turned the role down and nobody else would take it. In 1959, he cast him in *The Apartment* because Wilder's original choice, Paul Douglas, died two weeks before shooting began, felled at the age of fifty-two by a heart attack. Burly and formidable, Douglas would have made a more conventional romantic heavy, especially in a businessman's drama. His character's extramarital affair in *Executive Suite* is a pivotal plot device. Douglas's widow, Jan Sterling (who costarred in *Ace in the Hole*), remembered the circumstances of his casting in *The Apartment*: "We came out of a restaurant one night, and Billy said, 'I want to do a movie about' (a word that starts with *f* and ends with *g*). 'You're the one to play the lead.'"

Fred MacMurray, on the other hand, was fresh from Disney's *The Shaggy Dog* and was therefore a downright appalling choice for J. D. Sheldrake—insurance executive, Westchester dad, philanderer, swine. Brought to life by MacMurray, Sheldrake is the very essence of magnetic, everyday rottenness, the kind of man who could drive a woman like Fran Kubelik to suicide.

Having radically shifted MacMurray's persona in the early 1940s from that of the happy-go-lucky hoofer to a guilt-ridden, sex-sniffing killer, Wilder was in an excellent position to effect a similar change in the late 1950s. MacMurray recovered his good-natured image soon after *The Apartment*'s release when his TV sitcom *My Three Sons* began its long run. But according to MacMurray, there was still a price to pay for playing such an evil lout. On a visit to Disney's Magic Kingdom in 1960, shortly after *The Apartment* opened, MacMurray found himself accosted by a former fan— someone who'd loved *The Shaggy Dog*: "I saw *The Apartment* last night," the woman snapped. *"How could you?* You spoiled the Disney image!" At which point she slammed him over the head with her purse.

To his credit as a judge of human nature, Wilder understands why people hit other people, or shoot them, or strangle them with ratty furs, and why, when violence isn't directed outward, it turns in on the self. Fran's suicide attempt is entirely motivated. She loves Sheldrake precisely because he doesn't care about her; she feels a passion for him she'll never feel for Baxter. Even at the end of the film there's no ardor. "I love you, Miss Kubelik," Buddy-Boy tells her in the final moments. "Shut up and deal," she replies. This is not *Tristan and Isolde*. Not only is the romance muted, there's little in the way of closure. Wilder likes to throw his characters off into a void—that is, if he doesn't kill them. In *Mauvaise Graine* the two lovers sail toward nowhere. At the end of *Five Graves to Cairo* Billy sends Bramble running off to keep fighting World War II. In *Stalag 17*, Sefton and Dunbar walk into the dark. In *Some Like It Hot* the four principals, also left in the dark, are running away. *Where are they going?* Even in *Sabrina* we don't see the final clinch. It's no different in *The Apartment*.

Fran Kubelik and Bud Baxter have given up their past to begin some kind of life together, but its nature is cloudy, tentative, and, for Wilder, practically unimaginable.

David Denby describes Billy's mewling protagonist well: "Baxter is a study in spinelessness—prissy, sexless, and passive." His first great moment of joy in the film occurs when Fran's brother-in-law beats him up. Karl (Johnny Seven) throws but a single punch to lay Buddy-Boy to waste; Baxter, having never been treated like a man before, is thrilled. Wilder films him lying against the wall with blood trickling out of his mouth, grinning in ecstasy. (Lemmon had to fake this look of joy. According to the pressbook the punch actually knocked him cold.)

The other moment of physical violence in *The Apartment* has proven to be more controversial because it is directed at a woman. Wilder responded to one of his critics on this score:

> I read Axel Madsen's book about me. It's composed for the most part of interviews already published elsewhere. But I have to address this idea that he has that he develops assiduously in all the passages of his work that he wrote himself—an idea moreover false. It's about my alleged misogyny. According to him, the best example is the sadistic satisfaction I took in having Shirley MacLaine slapped in the face in *The Apartment*. But I had three doctors on the set whom I'd asked what you would do to a patient who'd taken twenty-five sleeping pills. They told me that it would be absolutely necessary to keep her awake, then to slap her, make her drink coffee and walk without stopping. We did a take and I asked the doctors if it was correct. They said, "You have to slap her harder." And I refused to do a second take.

There is, without doubt, a pronounced streak of misogyny in Wilder's career, but *The Apartment* is not a key work in this regard. Here, it's the human race that Wilder finds vaguely contemptible, not merely half of it. Just as he accurately describes Walter Neff's company in *Double Indemnity* by calling it Pacific All-Risk, Wilder characterizes the world he represents in *The Aparment*: Consolidated Life. It's men and women together. They just reveal their near worthlessness in different ways, that's all. Baxter's bosses (later, his colleagues; still later, his underlings) at Consolidated Life—Dobisch (Ray Walston), Eichelberger (David White), Vanderhof (Willard Waterman), and Kirkeby (David Lewis)—are crass, heartless users, midlevel sharks in a brackish corporate pool. What Fran says of Sheldrake applies to them all—"He's a taker. Some people take, others get took." In *The Apartment*, women and Baxter are part of the ranks of the took.

And for once, Billy's on *their* side. A romantic at heart even when the romance is sour, Wilder puts the world's baseness to the service of a higher good in this film, his most genuinely sweet-tempered and generous work to date. "In my opinion it is a highly moral picture," he once told an interviewer. "I had to show two people who were being emancipated, and in order to do that I had to show what they were emancipated by." ("*From,*" said the interviewer. "*With,*" Billy replied.) Wilder's colleague, the filmmaker Volker Schlöndorff, echoes the point when he describes the way *The Apartment* ends: "For me, there is nothing more liberating than this cut from a long, frustrating, static, hypocritical dialogue sequence [Sheldrake wishing Fran a happy New Year] to a wonderful tracking shot of MacLaine running to rescue Lemmon from despair." (Woody Allen picks up the same graceful, vigorous formal figure to end *Manhattan*, but he adds his own characteristic style: his tracking shot is longer and showier, the camera is at a greater distance from the subject, and the subject is himself.)

Wilder and Buddy-Boy are scarcely one and the same. One suspects that Billy wrote himself more into the smirking Dobisch than anyone else. Still, Billy felt the need to add a personal touch: he donated his and Audrey's own beautiful bentwood bed for Fran to try to kill herself in. Billy had used the bed on-screen before. With remarkably similar logic it graces Audrey Hepburn's room in *Sabrina*.

The words in Wilder and Diamond's screenplay were sacrosanct, but as far as bits of business were concerned they were only a blueprint. For the scene in which Baxter, plagued with an extravagant cold, is summoned to Sheldrake's office for the dual purpose of promotion and humiliation, Jack Lemmon had an idea: "I went to props and I had him cut the top off, empty it, and put milk in it. Well, MacMurray is about ten feet away from me. I say, 'Oh, it won't,' and this thing shot right under MacMurray's nose, and all MacMurray did was just keep on going. Oh, man, I—I blessed him for that. Then Billy said 'Cut,' and the whole place fell apart." The fact that Lemmon's milk squirts in an arc all the way across the width of the CinemaScope screen makes the bit all the funnier.

Lemmon's description of the filming of that scene is incorrect: Wilder doesn't cut the shot for quite some time after the squirt. Instead, he lets his actors continue to play the scene. The squirt isn't sledgehammered by way of an abrupt cut. Wilder favors long takes throughout *The Apartment*. Often they occur as two-shots, which grant characters equal emotional weight. One of the best of these occurs when Baxter, disheartened by his discovery that Fran is sleeping with Sheldrake, picks up a drunken blonde in a bar. To the tune of "Oh Come All Ye Faithful," Buddy-Boy and Margie MacDougall (Hope Holiday) sit in a widescreen two-shot, each staring straight ahead, musing drunkenly on Christmas Eve:

MRS. MacDOUGALL: 'Twas the night before Christmas and all through the house, not a creature was stirrin'. Nothin'. No action. Dullsville. You married?

BAXTER: No.

MRS. MacDOUGALL: Family?

BAXTER: No.

MRS. MacDOUGALL: Night like this it sort of spooks you to walk into an empty apartment.

BAXTER: I said I had no family. I didn't say I had an empty apartment.

In apparent contrast, Wilder cuts an earlier scene between Baxter and Fran more dynamically, but here, too, the editing remains expressive, character-based, and categorically unself-conscious. Alone in Baxter's office as the wild office Christmas party rages just a few feet away, Fran and Baxter have a moment of quiet near intimacy. Wilder films them in a two-shot over Fran's shoulder as Baxter fusses with his ridiculous new bowler. Fran hands him her compact so he can adjust it to its best advantage (a contradiction in terms, given the hat and Lemmon's head). At the moment of revelation, Wilder cuts to a close-up of the mirror in Lemmon's hands. Because the mirror is broken, his reflection is split in two with a crack down the middle at the precise moment that his image of Fran fragments along with his own. We watch his expression change from grin to devastation, at which point Billy cuts to a reverse two-shot as Lemmon hands the mirror back to Fran. He comments on the fact that the mirror is broken. "Yes I know," says Fran, still in two-shot. "I like it that way. Makes me look the way I feel." Where another director might cut to a close-up of Fran on that line, Wilder keeps his distance. His restraint serves a purpose: he keeps the emotional emphasis not just on Fran but on Baxter as well. Both characters get to suffer equally.

As *The Apartment* rumbled toward its release, Wilder and Diamond found themselves growing uneasy. They wondered if this blend of comedy and drama would find an audience. Diamond in particular worried about the suicide scene and its aftermath. After all, there was Fran dying from an intentional drug overdose in the background while Baxter comically yanks tacky Mrs. MacDougall out the door. (Margie, taken aback at what she thinks is Baxter's sexual enthusiasm, cries "Not so rough, honey!") Nonetheless, Diamond's wife, Barbara, remembers that UA and the Mirisches planned a huge party at Romanoff's after the film's first preview.

"You don't usually do that," Mrs. Diamond points out, "so somebody must have thought they had something very good there."

Billy, always one to pull a good prank in the trades, decided to run a parody of the ads Columbia used to promote its cannibal melodrama: "*Suddenly, Last Summer*—She knew she was being used for something evil," they boded. Wilder's ads trumpeted, "Suddenly, Last Winter—He knew his Apartment was being used for something evil!"

The Apartment premiered at Grauman's Chinese on Tuesday, June 21, 1960, having already been screened for select members of the Academy. For the national release, UA spent almost $560,000 promoting the film, including $10,000 for the director's personal appearance tour, the first of Billy's career. He held forth on any number of subjects to a fascinated press corps. "Better the *nouvelle vague* than Albert Zugsmith," he declared. He was impressed with the quality of their questions, he told them; time was, he noted, that all they cared about was whether or not Dorothy Lamour wore a bra. If only the reporters had been able to print more of what Billy told them. Practically every account of Wilder's conversations mentions the profanity of his language, but owing to what is sometimes known as journalistic standards, none of them offers much proof.

UA was very pleased with *The Apartment*'s initial performance, and it would only get better as the year progressed: "10 regional premieres rack up over a quarter of a million dollars in the first week," a full-page ad in *Variety* proclaimed. Billy brought *The Apartment* in on (or near) budget at $2,825,965. By the end of 1963, the film had taken in a domestic gross of $6.5 million, with an additional $2.7 million coming in from abroad.

A "tasteless gimmick," a "dirty fairy tale," "immoral," "dishonest," "without style or taste"—this is how some of the nation's leading film critics described *The Apartment*. Stanley Kauffmann in the *New Republic* didn't think Wilder had the talent to mix comedy and melodrama: "the script wanders from near slapstick to the near tragic," Kauffmann opined, and while he was at it he ripped into Shirley MacLaine: "She can 'do' small-scale, snub-nosed humor appeallingly enough," Kauffmann wrote, "but see how flat she falls when she is called on for anything else—compassion, for instance." Dwight Macdonald didn't like the comedy-melodrama blend either—*The Apartment* shifted "gears between pathos and slapstick without any transition"—and he found the whole thing phony, "fuzzed up with a queasy combination of slick cynicism and prurient sentimentality." Wilder, who was finally showing some genuine warmth for his characters, wasn't nasty enough for Macdonald: "He uses bitter chocolate for his icing, but underneath is the stale old cake."

Time was more enthusiastic: "The funniest movie made in Hollywood since *Some Like It Hot*." The *New York Times* liked it, too. MacLaine and

Lemmon were widely applauded, and nobody was surprised when they each landed an Oscar nomination.

Money was cascading in. By the end of the year, two new Schieles graced the Wilders' crammed penthouse walls—*Stehender Akt* and *Zwei Freundinen*. Jawlensky's 1917 painting *Blauer Mund* and Léger's 1948 gouache-and-ink drawing *Etude pour le Cirque* were added to the collection as well.

Wilder was in the finest of forms in an interview he granted to *Playboy* in 1960. He said:

> "I wouldn't drink the water in television."

> "Somebody asked me once if I thought any of the television stories would be good on the big screen. I said I didn't think most of them were worth even the small screen."

> "France is a place where the money falls apart in your hand and you can't tear the toilet paper."

> "When I am finished there is nothing left on the cutting-room floor but cigarette butts, chewing gum wrappers, and tears."

> "I could clean up in the film festivals if I took $25,000 and made a picture about the sex life of fishermen in Sardinia—as long as it had a certain morbid message and was slightly out of focus."

> "What seems to make the European pictures more adult than ours is that we don't understand the dialogue."

This highly flattering interview did not come about by luck. UA arranged for *Playboy* to get a plug in *The Apartment* so they could strike a deal with Hugh Hefner for what UA's publicity department artfully called "editorial cooperation." Still, *Playboy* gave Billy precisely the right kind of extensive national exposure to an audience he coveted. It also offered him the chance to retell some of his favorite stories, and his friends got to put their two cents in as well. Mike Romanoff ("ex-prince, ex-imposter, den father to Those Who Count in the Industry") called Billy "the most unusual and amusing man in Hollywood." Walter Reisch reported, "He's always been the way he is today. He was never sentimental; he was always fearless, even when he had nothing. He was sassy and aggressive—he would rather have lost a job than compromise or say yes."

Two of Wilder's best Otto Preminger jokes finally found a wider audience than the Hollywood mavens who'd been telling them for some time:

the story of Preminger screaming at Sam Goldwyn and Wilder saying, "Calm down, Otto, I'm not going to fight with you—I've still got relatives in Germany"; and the line Billy used when somebody asked him where Otto had gone: "His summer home—in Belsen."

Several of Wilder's old chestnuts about his wife appeared, along with a new one. When the couple met, the writer Richard Gehman noted, Audrey was living in the decidedly downscale Pico–La Brea district, though she told Billy it was East Beverly Hills. When he found out where she really lived, he told her, "I'd worship the ground you walk on if you lived in a better neighborhood." On their first wedding anniversary, Billy was reading the *Hollywood Reporter* at breakfast when Audrey got up. "Do you know what day this is, dear?" she asked. He informed her of the day of the week. "It's our first anniversary," said Audrey. "Please, not while I'm eating," answered Billy. The previous year, Billy made a trip to Paris. Audrey asked him to bring back some Charvet ties and, while he was at it, to ship home a bidet as well. After a few days she received a cable: "Charvet ties on way. But bidet impossible obtain. Suggest handstand in shower."

The Wilders had recently been paid a visit by Vladimir Nabokov. "Which of my paintings do you think Nabokov liked best?" Billy asked Gehman. "*That* is the one he liked," he said, pointing to a Balthus painting of a preteenage girl wearing a camisole. Billy was quite evidently pleased to share an appreciation of nymphets with the world's preeminent authority. Wilder's chronic backaches were brought up, obviously by Billy. As Audrey explained, "It used to be headaches, then it was stomach trouble—now it's the back." Things hadn't changed much over the years. In 1944, Judith Wilder claimed that Billy was such a hypochondriac that he was planning a case of meningitis.

In a shorter, less detailed profile in *Time* earlier that year, Wilder claimed to be working on several script ideas with current-events themes. One began in West Berlin with a meet-cute opener in which Soviets kidnap an American bombshell ("who might be Marilyn Monroe"). "They take her away to brainwash her, but she beats them because she has no brain to wash." Another idea centered on a high-ranking Communist official who defects to the West. He leaves his wife and three small children behind in Russia. They are summarily liquidated. The Communist quickly returns to Russia. He didn't really defect, he says—he just wanted to get rid of his family.

The Academy announced its Oscar contenders in February 1961, a few weeks after the Directors Guild bestowed its own Best Director award to Billy in ceremonies at the Beverly Hilton. Despite all the charges of smut leveled against it, *The Apartment* racked up nine nominations. United Artists' press agents began stumping.

On Oscar night—April 17, 1961—the crowd at the Santa Monica Civic Auditorium was treated to a Bob Hope monologue: "And how about those movies this year? *Exodus*, the story of the Republican Party; *Sons and Lovers*, the Bing Crosby family; *The Apartment*, the story of Frank Sinatra. . . ." The gorgeous Italian bombshell Gina Lollobrigida mounted the stage three-quarters of the way through the ceremony to announce the year's Best Director award. *The Apartment* had picked up only two Oscars thus far. Alex Trauner won one of the Art Direction awards, and Daniel Mandell won for his editing. Jack Kruschen lost to Peter Ustinov for *Spartacus*. Joseph LaShelle lost to Freddie Francis for *Sons and Lovers*. The sound award went to *The Alamo*. It was not a foregone conclusion when Lollobrigida opened the Best Director envelope and announced, "The winner is Billy Wilder for *The Apartment*!" A triumphant Billy ran to the stage, accepted his first Oscar in fifteen years, and said, none too humbly, "Thank you so much, you lovely discerning people."

When Kitty Carlisle and Moss Hart presented Billy and Iz with the award for Best Original Screenplay, Hart whispered something in Billy's ear that made him chuckle: "This is the moment to stop, Billy." At the microphone, Wilder said, "Thank you, I. A. L. Diamond," and Diamond said, "Thank you, Billy Wilder." William Wyler then arrived to present an honorary award to Gary Cooper (in absentia) and expressed his gratitude to the Academy for Wilder's trophies, knowing he'd be congratulated for them himself.

Jack Lemmon swiftly lost to Burt Lancaster (for *Elmer Gantry*). Shirley MacLaine then lost to Elizabeth Taylor—a sympathy award for Taylor's illnesses and past performances (Malta fever, *Suddenly, Last Summer*, meningitis, *A Place in the Sun*, a car wreck, *Cat on a Hot Tin Roof*, a tracheotomy) rather than for her current film, *Butterfield 8*. Finally Audrey Hepburn announced the Best Picture award and Billy bounded up to collect his third Oscar of the night. Graciously, he said that "it would only be proper to cut it in half and give it to the two most valuable players—Jack Lemmon and Shirley MacLaine." MacLaine herself was in Japan at the time filming *My Geisha* for her husband, Steve Parker. Billy sent her a telegram: "Dear Shirley, You may not have a hole in your windpipe but we love you anyway."

In June of 1960, the Mirisches (in association with producer Edward Alperson) bought the rights to a 1956 French musical comedy about a whore. Wilder not only signed on as director but took part ownership of the property. The transaction was rather complex: United Artists agreed to finance the film at a projected budget of $5 million, with ownership of the negative and all profits to be split between UA, the Mirisches, Wilder, and Alperson. According to *Variety*, the purchase price for *Irma la Douce* was as astronomical as *Witness for the Prosecution*'s—$330,000. Jack Lemmon was mentioned as the likely choice to play the prostitute's jealous lover, but the whore herself was still uncast.

Billy might have been intrigued by *Irma la Douce* even if the crowd-pleasing show hadn't featured a well-worn prostitute. The play's self-description sounds a lot like something Wilder himself could have written: *Irma la Douce*, the narrator declares, is "a story about passion, bloodshed, desire, and death—everything that makes life worth living."

Billy soon announced that Charles Laughton had agreed to star in the film. Laughton would not be playing Nestor, the young leading man (a law student in the play, a failed policeman in Wilder's adaptation); he would be the narrator/host, Bob-le-Hotu.

As soon as July 1960, Billy was in Paris doing preproduction work. He'd settled on Laughton's costar—none other than Marilyn Monroe. "I'm possibly mad, but that's who I want," he told British journalist Roderick Mann. "All right, I know that after *Some Like It Hot* I swore I'd never use her again. She's like my smoking. I keep swearing off cigarettes but I still get through sixty a day." Mann pressed for a serious explanation of why Wilder would work again with a woman he was still calling "a nightmare." Wilder answered: "Marilyn is very talented and a huge box office star. And that's what matters. After all, if her picture is running in Manchester and a man tells his wife, 'There's a Monroe picture showing,' the wife doesn't turn around and say, 'We don't want to see *her*—she's always rowing with her directors.' They go to see her, and that's why I want her."

"I'd settle for Elizabeth Taylor," Billy added.

Billy told the *Herald Tribune*'s Art Buchwald the same thing, only with even more wisecracks about Marilyn and a few new ones about himself. "We made up at the Khrushchev luncheon at Twentieth Century–Fox," Wilder declared. (The Soviet premier toured the United States in September 1961.) "The FBI asked all of us to be there at noon for security reasons, and Marilyn, who flew in from New York, not only showed up on time but was twenty minutes early. This was the first time I had ever seen her early for anything, and I was so thrown by it I threw my arms around her and we made up on the spot. I vowed then that if I did another picture with her I'd hire Khrushchev to hang around the set so she'd show up on time."

But, asked Buchwald, didn't you have to wait for her for hours? "Exactly," said Billy. "But we didn't waste those hours. We played poker. I managed to read *War and Peace*, *Les Misérables*, and *Hawaii*, and we all got wonderful suntans. The extras made twice as much money as they expected, and while it might have taken slightly longer to make the film, we did get to know each other so much better."

But, asked Buchwald, didn't you say she couldn't remember her lines? "That's the beauty of working with Monroe," Billy declared. "She's not a parrot. Anyone can remember lines, but it takes a real artist to come on the set and not know her lines and give the kind of performance she did." Buchwald then had the bad taste to point out some of the nasty things Billy had said about her in the past. "I was speaking under duress and the influence of barbiturates," Billy confessed, "and I was suffering from high blood pressure and I had been brainwashed."

"You know how it is," Billy told still another reporter. "You hate your dentist while he's pulling your teeth out, but the next week you're playing golf with him." Just to be on the safe side, Billy also mentioned that he might decide to cast Taylor. Brigitte Bardot would work, too, he said, and so would Shirley MacLaine.

In September, Elizabeth Taylor signed a deal to play the lead in *Irma la Douce*. Iz Diamond also had a contract by the end of September. As far as writing and schmoozing were concerned, Diamond handled Billy himself, but when it came to negotiating his deals he had Swifty Lazar do the talking. Diamond agreed to start working on *Irma la Douce* the following week at rate of $2,000 per week for fifty-two weeks guaranteed. Publicly, Billy and the Mirisches were saying that the film was scheduled to roll the following spring, but if Diamond's year-long contract was any indication, they all knew the schedule was hopeful at best.

By late October, it was official—*Irma la Douce* was postponed. According to the terms of the movie-rights sale, the film could not be released until the play's road show engagements ended. *Irma* had been on Broadway for two years, London for three. Both productions recently closed, but the tour had just begun. The estimated start date was now August 1962.

A controversy erupted; the Hollywood buzz had it that Liz quit the picture. Taylor's agent, Kurt Frings, denied the rumors—Taylor was still going to star in *Irma la Douce*, he said—but Frings soon announced that she'd withdrawn from the film, though not by her own choice.

Deals sometimes move fast in Hollywood. *Variety* reported in the same article that Shirley MacLaine had already agreed to replace Taylor.

MacLaine certainly had incentive to take the role. Her deal called for sixteen weeks of work for $350,000 against 5 percent of the gross, with an escalator clause (should the film become an enormous success) bringing her share up to 7.5 percent. The billing order was left up to Billy to decide, though if Jack Lemmon did end up in the picture, his standard contract at that point specified top billing and Billy would have to try to convince him to make an exception.

With *Irma* postponed, Billy had a year's time on his hands. He had several ideas to fill the gap; world politics helped him make his choice. At the time Nikita Khrushchev facilitated Billy's rapprochement with Marilyn, the Cold War appeared to be winding down. Despite the presence of some unruly demonstrators at the airports, the Soviet delegation's tour of the United States in 1959 was an outstanding public relations success. But whatever goodwill such cultural exchanges engendered suddenly vanished in May 1960 when the Soviets shot down an American U-2 spy plane. Everybody found a reason to be hostile. Americans were furious that the Russians shot down one of their planes, and the Russians were outraged that the Americans were spying on them, a charge American officials vehemently denied for the few weeks it took to accustom themselves to the fact they'd been caught. The superpowers' imminent summit conference in Paris was canceled.

Thus in November 1960, Billy announced his next project: a Marx Brothers comedy set at the United Nations. "We want to make a satire on the conditions of the world today," Wilder declared, "a satire on the deterioration of diplomatic behavior, on brinksmanship, wild jokes about the H-bomb—that type of stuff. It's all so dramatic that a few jokes put over by the Marx Brothers should alleviate the tension." He estimated that the number of jokes would be somewhere in the neighborhood of three thousand. "That's quite an order, isn't it?" Billy said. "We might have the Marx Brothers mixing up all the flags with, say, Nasser coming in under the Star of David. Mad fun like that. We will keep the same Marx Brothers technique of playing against a very serious background. We'll try to keep it all—the dignity of the locale, the procedure, the enormity of the problem—with Groucho, Harpo, and Chico in the middle of it."

Billy was convinced his idea had vast international appeal: "It's fun and it involves the world as a whole. It will be understood universally—therefore it's worth a film. Making a film is like gambling with the chips getting more expensive every day. That way you can't afford too big a gamble. So we've got the UN and we've got the Marx Brothers. Put them together, and—*boom!*"

Having finally acquired the rights to Molnár's *Egy-kettö-három*, the 1929 one-act comedy about a raging capitalist, his dippy houseguest, and her surprise husband, a Socialist cabdriver, Billy Wilder was in an excellent position to capitalize on current events. With the world edgily watching the two superpowers focus much of their hostility on the still-divided city of Berlin, Billy Wilder knew from experience that he could get some pretty good laughs out of Berliners' misery. He was itching to characterize the German people as greedy, money-grubbing ex-Nazi liars on one side of Checkpoint Charlie and dull, fascist, out-of-time dummkopfs on the other. He thought it would be funny.

For Billy, the ongoing crisis in Berlin wasn't the only incentive to adapt Molnár for the modern age. At least as much of a goading spur was the fact that Michelangelo Antonioni's ponderous *L'Avventura* had been a huge art house hit on both sides of the Atlantic the previous year, and American art house critics were still falling all over themselves spreading the gospel of serious cinema. For Wilder, Bergman was bad enough. Now there was Antonioni, whose films were even more nose picking. In response, Billy wanted not only to make yet another enormously successful and crowd-pleasing comedy, but to make the most raucous farce he could think up. He was compelled to make the absolute antithesis of *L'Avventura*, if only to prove a point to himself. So 1961 was the perfect time to make *One, Two, Three*.

PART SIX

1961–1970

25. SELLING IT

PIFFL (Horst Buchholz, in despair): Is *everybody* in this world corrupt?
BORODENKO (Ralf Wolter, with a shrug): I don't know everybody.
—*One, Two, Three*

n 1929, a feverish young reporter with too much wit on his hands declared in the Berlin newspaper *Tempo* that Coca-Cola "tastes like burnt pneumatic tires." Thirty-one years later, Berlin was segmented and half ruined, Germany torn in two. *Tempo*, the frenetic Jewish daily with multiple editions and sharp opinions, was out of business for years, many of its readers gassed. The journalist had become a wealthy film director living in a Beverly Hills penthouse. The Americans and the Russians, formerly allies against the Germans, were now suspicious foes. The Germans were schizophrenic but pragmatic, their ideology running along geographical lines. The entire Free World was drinking Coca-Cola, and everyone on one side of the Iron Curtain believed that everyone on the other side thirsted for it in vain. But despite the shifting winds of politics, trade, art, and personal fortune, one thing hadn't changed: Billy Wilder still thought Coke tasted like burnt tires with fizz.

The same year Billy slammed Coca-Cola in *Tempo*, Ferenc Molnár's play *Egy-kettö-három* opened in Berlin as *Ein, Zwei, Drei*. It was a wild farce about a frenzied capitalist, Norrison—played by and, in fact, written for the great comedian Max Pallenberg—whose young female houseguest, the daughter of an important banking client, throws his life and career into jeopardy by marrying a Socialist taxi driver. Pallenberg spat his lines in "a sharp, penetrating, crystal-clear, amazingly fast staccato, like the rapid clatter of a machine gun." In other words, he was like a gangster on Benzedrine. Wilder saw the play and loved it.

One, Two, Three played itself out furiously in a single act, all of which takes place in Norrison's office. Young Lydia waltzes in, announces that she has married the cabbie and is pregnant with his child, so the manipulative Norrison uses all the power at his disposal to turn the cabbie, Anton, into an ersatz nobleman before the day is through. With tailors, haberdashers, barbers, and shoe salesmen rushing madly in and out (the stage design calls for curtains to separate the rooms, since the opening and closing of so many doors would prove to be impossibly loud), and with Anton reduced nearly to tears not only by Norrison but by the surprisingly fierce Lydia as well, the banker triumphs. Molnár offers a moral at the end. "It must be very wonderful, sir, to be as you are and have almost all mankind at your disposal," Norrison's aged servant tells him. "You're quite right, Pynnigan," Norrison says. "But as regards mankind, after what was just done here, I think mankind—or as you so carefully put it, almost all mankind—should damn well be ashamed of itself."

Wilder and Diamond weren't constrained by Molnár's preachy conclusion, nor by any of his lines. By the time Wilder got through adapting the farce, practically none of the dialogue remained intact, and the moral ending turned absurd. At one point during the shooting of *One, Two, Three*, Scarlett (formerly Lydia) whines to MacNamara (formerly Norrison), "Why didn't you take better care of me?" Pamela Tiffin, playing Scarlett, had some trouble delivering the line with great enough amplitiude. "Pamela, dear," Billy began. "A little louder, please. We want to hear this line very clearly. It's the only line we've kept from the original play, and it's a very expensive one."

For the role of the manic capitalist, Wilder chose one of the most recognizable faces and voices in the world. *The Public Enemy* (1931), *G-Men* (1935), *Angels with Dirty Faces* (1938), *The Roaring Twenties* (1939) *Yankee Doodle Dandy* (1941), *Blood on the Sun* (1945), *White Heat* (1949), *What Price Glory?* (1952), *Mister Roberts* (1955), *Love Me or Leave Me* (1955), *The Gallant Hours* (1960)—James Cagney was a Hollywood titan. Like George Raft, Cagney could sport a machine gun and tap shoes with equal grace and credibility, and by 1961 he had been doing so for thirty years. A three-time Oscar nominee (he won once, for *Yankee Doodle Dandy*), Cagney knew his business well. This was an ominous sign.

For the role of Cagney's wife, essentially a wisecracking human caboose, Wilder and his team were initially stumped. At a casting meeting, Billy said something on the order of "I'm tired of clichéd typecasting—the same people in every film. Let's get someone whose face isn't familiar to moviegoers—a type like Arlene Francis." (Pause.) "In fact," said Billy, "why don't we get Arlene Francis?" Best known for her good-natured appearances on the TV game show *What's My Line?*, Francis's only film-acting roles had been in Robert Florey's *Murders in the Rue Morgue* in

1932 and small roles in *Stage Door Canteen* (1943) and *All My Sons* (1948). (Her appearance in *Murders in the Rue Morgue* is brief but lurid: she plays a prostitute whose corpse gets dumped in the Seine after Bela Lugosi bleeds her to death on a torture rack.) With her easygoing personality and television domesticity, Arlene Francis's casting in *One, Two, Three* is inspired. Was it a pure coincidence that the mystery guest on *What's My Line?* on Sunday, May 15, 1960, was none other than James Cagney, or was Billy watching something other than *Roller Derby* that day?

The familiarity of the leading actors is essential to *One, Two, Three*. Cagney and Francis were recognizable figures in 1960 to 1961, though perhaps not to everyone. Wilder used to tell a suspect but funny story about this. According to Billy, he and Audrey were dining at the home of Mr. and Mrs. William Goetz, Mrs. Goetz being the daughter of Louis B. Mayer. She asked Wilder what his new picture was and who would be playing the lead. Jimmy Cagney. *"Who?"* "Jimmy Cagney! You know, the little gangster who for years was in all those Warner Bros.—" Edith Mayer Goetz cut Billy off: "Oh, Daddy didn't allow us to watch Warner Bros. pictures."

One, Two, Three was scheduled to shoot on location in Berlin in June 1961, after which the company would move to Munich's Bavaria Studios for all the interiors. Wilder assembled twenty-five key people for his production team, all of whom had worked with him before: Doane Harrison, of course; editor Danny Mandell; special effects expert Milt Rice; script supervisor May Wale; cameraman Danny Fapp, who had just gotten through filming the Mirisch Company's *West Side Story*; and others. These were brisk, efficient men and women, and Billy trusted them—more than he let on. Alexander Trauner would be designing the film—a crisp, bland Coca-Cola Company office in West Berlin; the ballroom of a crummy East Berlin hotel; the interior of Cagney's and Francis's residence. . . . *One, Two, Three* seemed as if it would be a relatively easy and straightforward project.

When June rolled around, East Germany's Walter Ulbricht emphatically told a Western newspaper that, no, his government had no intention of building a barrier between the eastern and western sectors of Berlin. The flood of immigrants from East to West grew into a raging torrent, and Wilder's timing seemed all the better. *One, Two, Three* had always been conceived as topical political humor. Now it was more topical than Wilder ever dreamed.

Wilder and Diamond's script begins with this description (or warning, or threat): "THIS PIECE MUST BE PLAYED *MOLTO FURIOSO*—AT A RAPID-FIRE, BREAKNECK TEMPO. SUGGESTED SPEED: 100 MILES AN HOUR ON THE CURVES— 140 MILES AN HOUR ON THE STRAIGHTAWAY" Originally, a voice-over narrator opened the film by explaining: "In February 1945, with Hitler's legions crumbling under the relentless onslaught of the Allied Armies, the Big Three, meeting at Yalta, agreed on the partition of Germany and the joint occupation of Berlin. Subsequent events have proved that this decision was—to put it diplomatically—a boo-boo."

After a few days of filming *One, Two, Three*, Billy asked Cagney if he had ever played anything so fast before. Cagney immediately replied that he had—*Boy Meets Girl* (1938), with Pat O'Brien. This was another bad sign. Cagney had despised playing everything at such rapid-fire, screwball speed and considered *Boy Meets Girl* one of the low points of his career. Cagney claimed that when he saw the film even he couldn't understand what he was saying. Faced with Billy's more extreme pacing, Cagney was already annoyed. Only two days into his work on *One, Two, Three* he was telling people that he wanted to go home.

Following the skeleton of Molnár's play, *One, Two, Three* concerns a command-spitting Coca-Cola executive in West Berlin who is forced to play host to his boss's hot-blooded, seventeen-year-old daughter, who sneaks out of his house behind his back, crosses into East Berlin, and marries a Communist student named Otto Piffl. Adding to the capitalist MacNamara's hyperactive agony is the fact that his wife discovers the mercenary affair he has been conducting with his secretary, the gum-chewing Ingeborg (Lilo Pulver), and leaves him. MacNamara is trying all the while to crack the Iron Curtain market with the incompetent assistance of three Russian trade commissars. ("Napoleon blew it, Hitler blew it, but Coca-Cola's going to pull it off," he predicts.) To top it all off, Scarlett's parents announce their arrival from Atlanta, she announces she's pregnant with Otto's baby, and a reporter shows up having sniffed out the story of an American teenager having married an East German. MacNamara turns Otto into a suitable husband for Scarlett by paying off a destitute German nobleman—now the men's room attendant at the Kempinski Hotel—and turning Piffl into the junior Count von Droste-Schattenburg. He outfits the Communist-turned-aristocrat with a full wardrobe of men's formal wear and hires him as a Coke executive in the car on the way to the airport, where Scarlett's parents fly in on schedule. All of this occurs to the naggingly antsy tune of the Lenin Prize–winning Soviet composer Aram Khachaturian's "Sabre Dance."

The Brandenburg Gate is Berlin's best-known monument. Its portals, through which vehicular traffic must squeeze on its way onto or away from the boulevard Unter den Linden, consist of a dozen weathered Doric columns, atop which the Goddess of Victory roosts along with her chariot and four stone horses. It's an elaborate heap with historical overtones. When Berlin was divided into sectors immediately after World War II, the

Brandenburg Gate served as an easy point of bifurcation; the line was drawn a few yards to the west.

A symbol of Germany's old imperial grandeur, its relatively recent ruin, its tenacious survival, and the conflict of Wilder and Diamond's precarious farce, the Brandenburg Gate was to serve as the focal point of several sequences in *One, Two, Three*—most notably the crash site of a chase sequence involving MacNamara's sleek American limousine and the three Russians' decrepit Moskowitch, which was supposed to slam itself against one of the mighty Doric columns. In an earlier scene, too, Otto Piffl rides a motorbike through the Gate from West to East. For these two sequences, Billy arranged to shoot on location at the Gate itself. This, of course, required the permission of (at least) two governments. The West Germans were happy to oblige. The East Germans needed a little finessing, but they, too, agreed.

Wilder's MO with the Communist authorities was reminiscent of his treatment of Bellevue Hospital's director for *The Lost Weekend*. He told them the basic facts of the shots he wanted but left out a few choice details, in particular the fact that Piffl's cycle has a RUSSKI GO HOME balloon inflating on its tailpipe. On a cloudy but shootable day in mid-July, the cast and crew departed from their headquarters at the Berlin Hilton for the location on the Strasse des 17 Juni, the broad boulevard in West Berlin that leads through the Brandenburg Gate onto Unter den Linden. Billy rallied his troops: "Okay, get your steel helmets, everybody—we're going back to the Gate!" A little later, with the camera rolling and the bright yellow balloon firmly attached to the bike, Horst Buchholz sped off toward the Gate, a camera truck following him. A few shots were successfully taken, but the weather turned for the worse and the sequence couldn't be completed that day. "It was Hitler's last revenge," said Billy, because by the following morning a regiment of uniformed East German police forbade him to shoot anything on their side of the border. They stood their ground at the Gate, quite visibly, and monitored Wilder and his crew through powerful binoculars.

Lesser men would have been bullied. Not Billy, who rehearsed the scene on his side of the frontier and sent a message to the East Germans on the other: since he was shooting toward the Gate, he said, the East German officers were visible in the shot. This was fine with him, he added, but he was just afraid that international audiences would get the false impression that East Germany was a police state.

The officers scattered, and Wilder reopened negotiations to film the sequence the way he wanted from the angles he wanted, including those in East Berlin. The East Germans were willing to talk again, but now they insisted on reading the script. "I wouldn't even show my script to President

Kennedy," Wilder replied, and that ended the matter. The price of *One, Two, Three* soared instantly higher, as Trauner and his crew were asked to build a replica of the Brandenburg Gate on the lot in Munich. The cost of the new Gate was either $100,000 or $200,000, depending on who reported it.

"We got to Berlin the day they sealed off the eastern sector and wouldn't let people come across the border," Billy said a few years after the fact, bending history slightly to make a snappier tale. "It was like making a picture in Pompeii with all the lava coming down. Khrushchev was even faster than me and Diamond." Wilder's sense of chronology is a little off, but the mood he describes is not. On the nights of August 12 and 13, with location work on *One, Two, Three* not yet complete after a little over a month of shooting, the Soviets and their East German deputies sealed off the border and erected a makeshift barrier of barbed wire and cinder blocks. (The fifteen-foot-high concrete walls, watchtowers, gun turrets, electric fences, and land mines came later.) The Berlin Wall was now in place. Not only was the production of *One, Two, Three* thrown into turmoil, but the already fragile premise of the comedy suddenly became a great deal shakier. If Billy wanted to make the most nervous comedy of his career, his timing couldn't have been better.

Tension in Berlin was extreme. Even before the Wall went up Billy was calling the city "Splitsville." Now members of families were separated from one another. Subway and surface-rail service between East and West was halted. Berliners wondered if the superpowers would use their divided city as an excuse to set off an atomic World War III. More disturbing to Billy, perhaps, was the fact that he had to change his screenplay: "We had to make continuous revisions to keep up with the headlines. It seemed to me that the whole thing could have been straightened out if Oleg Cassini had sent Mrs. Khrushchev a dress."

Other exteriors were constructed in Munich as well as the Gate, and the whole production shifted to Bavaria sooner than scheduled, just to be on the safe side of international conflict. They hadn't been able to film on location at Tempelhof airport, owing to the noise of real air traffic, so Trauner supervised the building of a replica in Munich. The Unter den Linden quarter of East Berlin—the embassy district, located on the first mile of the boulevard on the other side of the Gate—had to be reconstructed as well, though in Billy's mind it still needed to be in ruins even though the East Germans had already renovated it as a showplace.

Wilder still hadn't filmed the final scene at the studio-reconstructed Templehof arrival gate when Horst Buchholz ran his motorcycle off the road and had to be hospitalized. The production shut down prematurely to give him time to recover, but since the Bavaria Studios soundstage on which Tempelhof was rebuilt was already booked for another production (John Huston's *Freud*), they had to take the set down and rebuild it again—at the Goldwyn Studios in Hollywood, where everyone had to reassemble weeks later. Buchholz's accident thus added $250,000 to the cost of *One, Two, Three.*

For Billy, *One, Two, Three* is as much a matter of conflicting styles of wit as it is a battle of ideologies. Wilder was impressed by what he saw as the Communists' complete lack of a sense of humor when he wrote *Ninotchka* in 1939. It hadn't improved by 1961. Still, as in *Ninotchka*, Billy draws individual comrades affectionately. The three trade commissars, the sons of Buljanoff, Iranoff, and Kopalski, are sufficiently mercenary to retain Wilder's respect.

On the surface, Cagney seemed content. He equaled Billy in bullhead-edness, but he kept his gripes to himself. Cagney was a consummate professional who recited his lines as often as Billy wanted, rehearsed his gestures and blocking well, practiced tap dancing during the break, and made it a point to help Pamela Tiffin with her scenes. Tiffin, young and inexperienced, was nervous to be working with a star of Cagney's stature, and Cagney, sensing her discomfort, patiently and generously coaxed her into a state of confidence.

Horst Buchholz, on the other hand, was a nagging problem for Cagney, who took a quick dislike to the headstrong young German. His contempt only grew as the filming proceeded. Cagney thought Buchholz was far too full of himself, especially for someone with so little experience. "I came close to knocking him on his ass," Cagney said later. One of the few things Cagney appreciated about Wilder was that he kept Buchholz in line himself, saving Cagney the need to follow through on his threat.

There was very little else about working with Billy Wilder that Cagney found enjoyable. "Billy Wilder was more of a dictator than most of the others I worked with," Cagney said later. "He was overly bossy—full of noise, a pain. Still, we did a good picture together. I didn't learn until after we were done that he didn't like me, which was fine as far as I was concerned, because I certainly didn't like him. He didn't know how to let things *flow*, and that matters a great deal to me." But Cagney kept his thoughts to himself, even after *One, Two, Three* wrapped. His close friend Ralph Bellamy later described the gentlemanly way Cagney handled it: "He was not happy with Wilder at all, and the pace of the film got to him, too. . . . When he finished, he came back and told me the experience had disturbed him, but he wasn't all that specific."

When the production returned to Los Angeles to shoot the final scenes at the Goldwyn Studios, Cagney, who loved to sail for relaxation, loaned his yacht to some friends. They sent him a photo of themselves standing on the deck drinking a toast to their absent host; the photo was inscribed, "Thank God you are gainfully employed." On a break between setups, the star of sixty-one previous films over the course of thirty-one years was standing in the warm Southern California sunshine when an assistant director called for him. "We're ready for you now, Mr. Cagney," he said. "That's it, baby," Cagney thought to himself, and he never made another film until *Ragtime* (1981).

One, Two, Three had been grueling for Cagney. One shot in particular required fifty-two takes. Unfortunately, a reporter watched every last one of them. Cagney's MacNamara is spitting out dialogue while trying to select clothes for Buchholz's Piffl. The shot begins as a tailor wheels in a rack of suits and sportcoats:

MacNAMARA: Now what do we have here?

TAILOR: Very distinguished styles. All fabrics imported!

MacNAMARA: They look more like they were *de*ported. *(Grabbing the jackets, one by one)* Too loud, too quiet, all right but take the padding out of the shoulders, that's not bad . . . *(in disbelief)* belt in the back*!*? I thought that went out with high button shoes!

SHOEMAKER: High button shoes? I have some right here!

MacNAMARA: Never mind! Take that stuff into the conference room! I want these ready in twenty-four hours!

TAILOR: Twenty-four hours?!

MacNAMARA: And where's the morning coat and striped pants?

TAILOR: My assistant is bringing them!

MacNAMARA: Those I want fitted right away!

JEWELER: *Schmuck!*

MacNAMARA: *(threateningly) What* did you say?

JEWELER: *Schmuck!* Jewelry!

MacNAMARA: Oh.

Like Monroe with her bourbon, Cagney simply could not remember to say the "morning" in "And where's the morning coat and striped pants?" Over and over Billy called for new takes, losing more of his temper each time. "Take it a little slower, Jimmy," Billy said. "Let's try it again." On the eighteenth take, Cagney got it out, after which the jeweler failed to make his entrance on cue; thus no *"schmuck."* *"Damn it!"* Billy roared. *"Too late!* You're supposed to come in on 'twenty-four hours!' " Wilder recovered his composure and said, "Let's go again. With emphasis, Jimmy."

Cagney blew it once more. "Isn't it a lovely day?" he cried after take twenty-five.

On take fifty-two, everything worked. "Okay, print it," Billy said in a rancid tone. But he still wasn't happy and insisted that he would have to reshoot it. "This is the worst day I've had in thirty-two years of making pictures. It's the *fohn*." The *what?* the reporter asked. "The *fohn*," Billy explained. "It's a wind that comes down from the Alps and drives everyone crazy. Really. People get depressed. Kill their wives. Commit suicide. Forget their lines."

Billy makes fun of Cagney's screen image, of course, but for Billy this kind of joke is a sign of respect. There's a grapefruit gag, straight from *Public Enemy*; the cuckoo clock plays "Yankee Doodle"; one of the MPs does a Cagney impersonation; *Cagney* even performs a self-impersonation— when things look particularly bleak for MacNamara, he cries "Mother of Mercy! Is this the end of Little Rico?" But these are just the obvious homages; the whole film is a tribute.

Unlike his earlier run-ins with major stars, Billy's experience with Cagney occurred at a time when he himself had achieved star status. Just after *One, Two, Three*'s release, Wilder told two interviewers from *Cahiers du cinéma* that the *politique des auteurs*, the polemical position held by *Cahiers*'s own critics, was responsible for directors' increasing prominence and fame: "Until these last few years, there were only two directors of value known to the general public: DeMille and Hitchcock. Even Lubitsch was known only in our milieu. The director wasn't recognized as an author; that fashion came about in Europe, it won over New York and then Hollywood, where the director too became a star. Ten days ago in New York I saw for the first time my name as big as that of the star, James Cagney. It's to European journalism that we owe that."

Not exactly. Billy himself hadn't coveted the name-above-the-title fame that others—Capra, Wyler, and DeMille—insisted upon in the 1940s, long before *Cahiers* began ranking directors on a steep ladder of talent and neo-Platonic moral value. By 1960, the ladder descended from Hitchcock and Hawks at the top to Wilder hanging somewhere below the middle and Fred Zinnemann, Carol Reed, and the whole French *cinéma de qualité* (Claude Autant-Lara, Jean Delannoy, Julien Duvivier . . .) clinging to the bottom rung, with Jean-Luc Godard stepping on their fingers. As the two *Cahiers* critics themselves put it, "Billy Wilder's words are famous in Hollywood. But, we must say, it's the man's verve that attracts us more than his work, which is not among those we place in the highest ranks (even if we would put it a hundred notches ahead of our compatriots whom Wilder admires)."

If anything, Wilder had even more control over his projects than Capra, Wyler, and DeMille did, for the simple reason that he wrote his films as well as produced and directed them, but until 1961 Wilder didn't seem to care all that much about his own name recognition. Now, with all those Oscars under his belt, Wilder saw himself as a selling point. He was aided by the *New York Times*, which noted that "in many respects Wilder is a bigger star on his own pictures than any of his actors." ("Something of an aggressive imp," the *Times* continued, "he achieves his results with a steady barrage of bubbling comments, most of them derogatory, many of them unprintable, but all of them highly quotable.") Wilder's success was now such that United Artists featured him on one of the posters for *One, Two, Three*. It shows Wilder—and Wilder alone—sitting with his chin resting glumly on his hand and holding three cartoon balloons. "This is Billy Wilder" the tag line explains. "He made *The Apartment* and *Some Like It Hot*. Now—his explosive new comedy, *One, Two, Three*." Practically as an afterthought, the ad continues: "It stars James Cagney, Horst Buchholz, Pamela Tiffin, Arlene Francis. . . ."

For the musical score, Wilder turned to André Previn, who at the age of thirty-one had already been working as a film scorer and composer for eleven years. A two-time Oscar winner (for the scores of *Gigi*, 1958, and *Porgy and Bess*, 1959) and seven-time nominee, Previn was literate, cultured, a bit arrogant, and very much an admirer of Billy Wilder. Previn soon grew to respect Wilder's musical tastes, not to mention his professionalism: "He was a far cry from the imperious producers who asked their composers to audition their 'themes' for them before they were recorded," Previn notes, "and who then demanded countless changes and rewrites, all stemming from an ignorance of music only outdone by an unending need to flaunt authority. Not so with Billy." According to Previn, Wilder would run the unscored print for him and offer an extensive running commentary—one that was restricted to the dramatic elements of the picture, not its musical demands. Previn found it refreshing. He went on to compose three more scores for Wilder.

One, Two, Three is Wilder's most abrasive comedy. Adding to the tension of the film's political farce is a smarmy overlay of mercenary sex. Wilder even makes orthography dirty. MacNamara greets his secretary by calling her "Frau-lein Ingeborg." "It's *Fräulein*," she corrects, "*mit* a umlaut!" This gives MacNamara the chance to remark that he's looking forward to his wife's departure so he can have the "chance to brush up on the *umlaut*." When MacNamara escorts Ingeborg into the Grand Hotel Potemkin, he greets the three Russians with the remark, "If it isn't my old friends Hart, Schaffner, and Karl Marx." Mishkin immediately grabs Ingeborg's ass. "I said *Karl* Marx, not Groucho." All the while, Ingeborg remains only too happy to be pimped—first for the West, then for the East. She embraces MacNamara's scheme as enthusiastically as she embraces the married MacNamara himself. Without any hesitation whatsoever, she jumps up on the table at the Potemkin and dances a lurid routine with flaming shish kebab skewers, all so that MacNamara will buy her a dress.

The ballroom, by the way, looks suspiciously like a Berlin dance hall from the 1920s—one that has gone through the war. Two couples dance, adrift. One acts like a gigolo forced to sway his stone-faced partner around in order to earn small change; the other two, equally stone-faced, are both women. The band's conductor, leading a rendition of "Yes, We Have No Bananas," seems to have years of experience behind him, and indeed he has: he's Frederick Hollander.

As the scene progresses, the camera, at high angle, stares down from a considerable distance at an American executive calmly biding his time as three leering Russians go wild watching a West German woman wearing a loud, tight polka-dot dress shove her beautiful rear end in their faces while waving a whip. She cracks it on the table, showing them who's in control, MacNamara all the while patiently sitting there waiting for them to sell out. It seems an accurate prediction.

Capitalizing on their *Some Like It Hot* reputation, Wilder and Diamond added a subplot involving Schlemmer donning Ingeborg's covetted polka-dot dress in order to distract the three Russians, thereby giving MacNamara extra time to spirit Piffl out of the East. This leads to a nervous gag when Schlemmer returns to West Berlin utterly bedraggled, the dress in ruins. "Did you have any trouble getting out of East Berlin?" MacNamara asks. "No," Schlemmer responds, "but I had a little trouble in West Berlin. I was picked up by an American soldier in a jeep. He was *very* fresh." One can only imagine, since even in the dress Schlemmer looks nothing like a woman. Schlemmer cleans the joke up a little in his follow-up explanation: "Wanted to take my picture for something called *Playboy*," he explains unconvincingly.

"Sorry, sir," says Schlemmer later, pulling up his pants and running into MacNamara's office. "I had difficulty getting out the girdle." "Schlemmer!" MacNamara barks. "I want all those people out there to drop everything and stand by for orders. General alarm! Complete mobilization!" Schlemmer is thrilled: "Ah, like the good old days! Yes, sir!"

Later, when Schlemmer's old SS commander resurfaces in the form of a seemingly respectable West German journalist, Schlemmer automatically heils him; Billy was scarcely willing to let the Germans forget their own history. Wilder told Ray Eames what one of the German actors in *One, Two, Three* had told him about the war. Wilder was fascinated: "He said to me, 'Billy, you know, during the war, we hid Jews.' And I said, 'You hid Jews?' 'Yes, we hid Jews.' 'And how many Jews did you hide?' 'Well, we only hid about two or three.' 'That's significant,' " Billy replied, " 'because of all the Germans I talked to—how many Germans are there?—fifty million, forty million, something? That's 120,000,000 Jews you hid.' "

Young American women may be as nubile as Ingeborg, but in *One, Two, Three* they're dumber. Played winningly by Pamela Tiffin, Scarlett is nevertheless an idiot. "You can forward my mail to American Express in Moscow," she confidently declares. "Do you realize that Otto spelled backwards is Otto?" In her finest moment, she casually executes her parents on her way out the door: "They're the ones I feel sorry for," she confides to MacNamara. "Otto says they'll have to be liquidated. 'Bye!"

Still, for all of Scarlett's inanity, MacNamara's cruelty, and the thoroughgoing prostitution of the West, communism ultimately fares worse than capitalism in *One, Two, Three*. Never one to pocket a windfall for writing and directing a paean to peasants or a venerating tribute to the working class, Billy is honest about his own sensibility. He respects the sellouts of the world:

> BORODENKO: Well, comrades, what are we going to do? He's got it, we want it. Are we going to accept this blackmailing capitalist deal?
> MISHKIN: Let's take a vote.
> BORODENKO: I vote yes!
> MISHKIN: I vote yes!
> BORODENKO: Two out of three—deal is on.
> PERIPETCHIKOFF: Comrades, before you get in trouble I must warn you—I am not really from Soft-Drink Secretariat. I am undercover agent assigned to watch you.
> MISHKIN: In that case, I vote no. Deal is off.
> PERIPETCHIKOFF: But I vote yes!
> BORODENKO: Two out of three again. Deal is on!

There is a difference between East and West, however. Inside the grim, imposing confines of the People's Police Station in East Berlin, the torture of the prisoner is conducted: Piffl is forced to listen to "Itsy Bitsy Teenie Weenie Yellow Polka Dot Bikini." Holding his ears and screaming in agony, Piffl breaks down. A confession is extracted, and, despite the ridiculous song, the East German police state doesn't seem very funny. On the other hand, when Piffl rushes into MacNamara's office in his boxer shorts, he declares, "I'm going to like this job! Do you know what the first thing is I'm going to do? I'm going to lead the workers down there in revolt!" "Put your pants on, Spartacus," says MacNamara. As Mrs. MacNamara says when she learns that Scarlett's parents are about to arrive later that day, "Now *that's* funny."

Wilder's moral vision hinges on expedience. His favorite characters are heroically glib. The little MacNamara boy is admirably matter-of-fact about Scarlett's putative illness: "If she dies can I have my room back?" For Billy, idealism isn't simply out-of-date. It's contemptible. "Maybe we should liquidate the whole human race and start all over again," Piffl cries in despair. It's at this point that Billy gives voice to his own concluding moral: "Look at it this way, kid," says MacNamara in close-up. "Any world that can produce the Taj Mahal, William Shakespeare, and Stripe toothpaste can't be all bad."

One, Two, Three came in at a cost of $2,927,628. This was hardly excessive. Still, the picture did not make its money back. The domestic gross was less than $2.5 million, its foreign gross was only $1.6 million, and after all the advertising and distribution expenses were figured in, the Mirisch Company and United Artists were stuck for a loss of $1,568,500. Jimmy Cagney never saw the film, and neither did most other potential audience members. The Germans were particularly unamused. It was Billy's first bomb since *The Spirit of St. Louis*. "I happen to think Coca-Cola is funny," Billy said later. "A lot of people didn't. Maybe that's why the picture bombed out. I still think it's funny. And when I drink it, it seems even funnier."

In London for the British opening in early February 1962, Billy was defensive. "If there's anything I dislike more than being taken too lightly, it's being taken too seriously," he griped. "After every drama people say, 'What do you want to give us all this bitterness and gloom for? Why don't you go back to comedies instead?' while after every comedy they say, 'Very nice, but isn't it now time for you to give us something really serious?' " He confessed that he was worried that audiences just couldn't keep up with the frenzied pace of the film. Perhaps they simply didn't "have the stamina to pay such close attention continuously," he mused. Maybe, he said, his little "experiment" in speed went a step or two too far.

Some American reviewers applauded *One, Two, Three*; others were lukewarm at best. Stanley Kauffmann called the film a "political satire with an air of daring but without daring anything." John Simon decried the "shallow, gratuitous cynicism which, somewhere in the back of Mr. Wilder's mind, seems to say, 'I laugh at the whole damned world—whether it's Shakespeare, striped toothpaste, or you.' " For Simon, this was wrong and immoral: "It's all right to laugh at striped toothpaste," Simon opined, "or us, or even Shakespeare, provided there is somewhere, at least by implication, something that one does not laugh at." Pauline Kael was simply disgusted: "*One, Two, Three* is overwrought, tasteless, and offensive—a comedy that pulls out laughs the way a catheter draws urine." Judging by the increasingly defensive tone he took whenever the subject of critics came up in the years to come, Billy noticed these jabs and was far more hurt by them than one might expect, given his own abrasive nature.

Still, life in Hollywood went on, with Billy and Audrey Wilder at the top of the social scene. There was a dinner party at Romanoff's on October 17, 1961. Randolph Churchill, Winston's son, was in town; a writer, he was working on a story about the production of Otto Preminger's *Advise and Consent* (1962). It was a typical evening in Hollywood—Preminger was there, along with Charles Laughton (who was starring in the film), Elsa, Iz and Barbara, and the Wilders—and it was fairly raucous. Then Churchill became radically drunk. The group turned anxious, then enraged, as Churchill loudly insulted everyone. "Somebody ought to hit that man!" Billy said to Preminger at one point. By the following day, all of Hollywood was buzzing: Audrey Wilder was said to have actually taken her husband up on the suggestion and slapped young Churchill across the face with a fish. According to the rumor mill, she had good reason. After someone made a joke that was well received by the crowd, Churchill observed that Audrey Wilder laughed like the soundtrack of *Make Room for Daddy*. The next thing anyone knew, "Billy's wife got him right in the kisser with a carp."

The Wilders both denied it, though Audrey did acknowledge having thrown her napkin vaguely in Churchill's direction.

A few months earlier, Billy himself was involved, in absentia, in a comical incident involving Stanley Kramer's earnest *Judgment at Nuremberg* (1961). Marlene Dietrich costarred as the widow of a Nazi general. She took the role to make the same point Schlemmer keeps making ridiculously in *One, Two, Three*: World War II was all Hitler's fault, nobody else's, and the Germans really had no idea what was going on. Dietrich found this notion to be a big historical fraud. She also found her dialogue to be a lot duller than Schlemmer's—or any other Billy Wilder characters'—so behind the backs of Kramer and screenwriter Abby Mann, Marlene asked Billy to do a little rewrite job. He did, all too gladly. Mann later recalled sitting with Dietrich as Spencer Tracy, her costar on *Judgment at Nuremberg*, kept "storming up and down and giving me dirty looks." Said Mann, "I went over and asked him, 'What's the matter?' and he said, 'Don't you know she has Billy Wilder rewriting all your lines?' " Mann, who thought he could write dialogue, was enraged. "So the next time when Marlene came in with her script with 'little changes' in it, I tore up the script and she had to go out and read my lines as written." Billy had the last laugh, as (almost) always. Later, when Mann chose the occasion of his guest appearance at the Moscow Film Festival to criticize Hollywood filmmaking, Wilder sent a message to *Variety* and the *Hollywood Reporter*. Referring to a well-known company in the business of leasing household items by the week, Wilder asked, "Who appointed Abby Mann as spokesperson for the American film world in Moscow? Personally, I'd rather be represented by Abbey Rents."

In the spring of 1962, Paul Kohner helped Billy acquire the rights to an Italian play called *L'Ora della Fantasia* (*The Dazzling Hour*). It concerned the emotional and spiritual virtues of mate swapping. Another project was offered to him as well. In October, Wilder was approached by Darryl Zanuck to direct one of Diamond's solo scripts—a comedy called *Goodbye Charlie*. "Dear Billy," Zanuck wrote. "I have been told that you like the script *Goodbye Charlie* which was written by Issie [*sic*] Diamond. Is it true? If it is, I will read it immediately and get in touch with you. In one way or another, I intend to talk you into working with me. Best always, Darryl."

"Dear Darryl," Billy replied. "Thank you very much for your invitation to do *Goodbye Charlie* for you. However, you've been too long and too far away to know that a wave of disgust has swept over this town since the brutal and callous dismissal of people even though they hold perfectly legal contracts. The 'let them sue' attitude is reprehensible. No self-respecting picture-maker would ever want to work for your company. The sooner the bulldozers raze your studio, the better it will be for the industry. Yours truly, Billy Wilder."

Wilder was angry at the way Zanuck had just fired two of Billy's oldest friends—Joseph Mankiewicz, whose lavishly messy *Cleopatra* was a long thorn in Zanuck's side, and Charles Brackett, an innocent bystander. Having been ousted from Fox and then returned to power, Zanuck was refusing to honor deals struck by the interim regime; that was his excuse for terminating Brackett's contract. Although he and Charlie had been anything but close since their breakup, Billy was infuriated by what he perceived as Zanuck's insensitively public cruelty to his old partner. His letter to Zanuck was widely reported in the trades, having almost certainly been leaked by Billy. Unfortunately, *One, Two, Three*'s disappointing box office tally left Wilder exposed to a sharp retort on Zanuck's part: "Reviewing Wilder's professional record since his statement, he obviously got in the way of his own bulldozers."

During this period, too, there were plans for a Broadway musical based on *Sunset Boulevard* to be written by Stephen Sondheim, but Billy didn't like the concept. Basking in the success of his latest hit, *A Funny Thing Happened on the Way to the Forum*, Sondheim began outlining the first act of his *Sunset Boulevard* and even started composing the first scene with his lyricist, Burt Shevelove, but a chance encounter with Billy at a cocktail party put an end to Sondheim's project. "I had never met him before," Sondheim recalls, "but I shyly advanced the proposition of writing a musical of *Sunset Boulevard*. His response was, 'But you can't write a musical of *Sunset Boulevard*—it has to be an opera. After all, it's about a dethroned queen.' " Years later, Hal Prince and Hugh Wheeler tried to talk Sondheim into writing a musical film of *Sunset Boulevard* for Angela Lansbury; in this scheme, Norma Desmond was to be a musical comedienne of the 1920s rather than a silent film star. "I demurred on Mr. Wilder's grounds," Sondheim says, "to which Hal replied 'Then let's make an opera out of it.' Since I don't much like opera as a form, I demurred again." Thus Andrew Lloyd Webber.

Billy himself had begun working on *Irma la Douce*, his first musical since *The Emperor Waltz*. Having been terribly disappointed with the way *The Emperor Waltz* turned out, particularly in terms of its visuals, Wilder's original idea was to film *Irma la Douce* in black and white. By 1962, color technology had been in wide use for over twenty years, and Billy still detested it. It wasn't only Technicolor that irritated him, of course. Many things rankled. One of Billy's recurrent offscreen themes during this period was the new emphasis on Hollywood deal making, particularly on the part of stars. He railed repeatedly against the proliferation of independent production companies, a trend from which he himself tended to profit. (*One, Two, Three* was coproduced by his own Pyramid company in association with the Mirisches, and even though it bombed, he was paid handsomely and retained complete artistic control.) Hollywood filmmakers don't talk about making movies anymore, Billy declared. Instead, it's all about whether to incorporate in Liechtenstein or Liberia. "Deals are so complicated it takes five lawyers eight weeks at Romanoff's to work them out. They ought to have an Academy Award for the 'Best Deal of the Year.' "

Jack Lemmon was different, or so Billy said. "Jack comes to a picture to do a job. He isn't spending months with his lawyers over billing clauses and whether or not he gets a chauffeur-driven Cadillac on the set and a masseuse every day." Jack Lemmon signed on to *Irma la Douce* in early February 1961. He let his lawyers do the talking for him, and they spoke impressively. For his participation, Lemmon got an unspecified salary up front, a hefty 15 percent of the profits, and a deferred salary of $100,000. Added to the deals already finagled by Wilder and MacLaine, United Artists and the Mirisches were left holding the bag. If *Irma la Douce* did poorly at the box office, the financiers would be out of luck but the stars and the director would still walk away with piles of cash in their various accounts. If the film was a hit, most of the profits would go to Wilder, Lemmon, and MacLaine. (By 1961, the fourth Mirisch brother had a sizable stake in the Mirisch Company itself. The Mirisches owned 86 percent of the capital stock, Wilder owned 10 percent, and the remaining 4 percent was divided among a few other employees.)

Commercial considerations (which is to say the Mirisch brothers' insistence) convinced Billy to scuttle his plans for a black-and-white musical. "I'm going to do *Irma la Douce* in color," he was forced to admit shortly before the film began to roll. "I hope to capture the gray and blue of Paris. I hate violent colors. I wish the cinema would find black and white once again."

A more drastic revision was forced upon him when his close friend Charles Laughton fell ill in August. Laughton pretended it was an ulcer. Wilder knew it was cancer. Back in Hollywood after an August trip to Paris, Wilder stopped by to visit Laughton every few days and sat by his bed, going over dialogue for *Irma la Douce*, though each of them knew that Laughton would never live to play the part. On December 15, 1962, Laughton died. Billy was supposed to be one of the pallbearers but at the last moment had to bow out; he was replaced by Jean Renoir.

Lou Jacobi took over the role of Moustache from Laughton, a decision announced on August 8. Unfortunately, *Irma la Douce* suffers for it. Jacobi is sometimes amusing delivering Billy's affably world-weary pronouncements, but without any of Laughton's exquisite timing and comportment he ultimately wears thin. Laughton would have been brilliant, and *Irma* would have been better.

As the start date loomed closer, Wilder filled in the gaps in casting. The role of a tubby, corrupt, dumb-looking policeman went to Dartmouth graduate Cliff Osmond. Billy saw him on TV; *Irma la Douce* was his first film role. Herschel Bernardi, recruited to play Inspector LeFevre, was currently playing a cop on the television series *Peter Gunn*. Billy didn't confess to watching *Peter Gunn*, but he did think Bernardi had been very funny in a Screen Writers Guild skit about a Spanish ambassador. Hippolyte, Irma's first *mec* (or pimp, the first in the course of the film's action, since she chronicles a string of *mecs* for an appalled Nestor), would also be played by a TV actor—Bruce Yarnell, of the series *The Outlaws*. And for the minor character role of the Hotel Casanova's concierge, Billy turned to *The Andy Griffith Show* for inspiration: fumbling, fussy Howard McNear, Mayberry's beloved barber Floyd, mans the desk at the Casanova.

One of the aspects Billy found lacking in the Broadway musical was the presence of other prostitutes. The show was overloaded with *mecs*, but it lacked whores. Irma is the only one with any significant lines in the show, and for Billy, one prostitute wasn't nearly enough. So he and Diamond added a number of women's roles, some of which were jokes on current events and movies. There is Lolita, a Sue Lyon look-alike complete with heart-shaped sunglasses and a frosted fall; she's played raucously by Hope Holiday (of Mrs. MacDougall fame). There is an Asian streetwalker, too—

Suzette Wong. Kiki the Cossack and Mimi the MauMau serve as political humor, and Amazon Annie was as good an excuse as any to rehire Joan Shawlee.

To prepare for her role, MacLaine personally got to know some Parisian working girls. In August, she spent four days in Les Halles talking to them in bars. "I always do this kind of research," she explained. On stage, Irma was brassy; Shirley and Billy saw her differently. "Irma is still a woman of the streets," MacLaine said, "but it is now a love story, and I am playing it straight—more humanly. You see, Irma is touched, really touched for the first time. Sure, she's all used up physically, but it's the first time she is touched emotionally by love."

As Nestor, Lemmon honed his skill at playing the jittery, butterfingered everyman most men wish they weren't. "He has the greatest rapport with an audience of anyone since Chaplin," Billy insisted. "Just by looking at him people can tell what goes on in his heart." Before teaming up with Lemmon, Wilder's connection to his comedy characters tended to be more detached. Now, with Lemmon, he could reveal (however hesitantly and cruelly) some of his own hidden sweetness and bumbling insecurity.

Shirley MacLaine remarked years later that she and Lemmon hadn't performed a single kiss in *Irma la Douce* but that the love they expressed on-screen scarcely required it. She also pointed out that "he was like my Aunt Bertie. I could depend on her completely, and that's the way it is with Jack."

Irma la Douce is a play about prostitutes, pimps, and johns, and yet there is little payoff; nobody really gets laid. As Billy once said of this movie, "We are doing it with taste and feeling. It will strike a happy medium between Tennessee Williams and Walt Disney." *Irma la Douce* is also a musical without songs. As Wilder and Diamond developed their adaptation, they gradually concluded that Marguerite Monnot's tunes only cramped their style. "I have nothing against music," says Wilder, "but the more I went into that story, the better I thought it was. And for me, the numbers got in the way. So, first, one of them went. Then another one went. And, one day, I made the decision, and we threw the whole score out and made it a straight picture."

When Wilder acknowledges that he "used some of the music for underscoring, but that was all," he underrates his own inspiration. There's a strained quality to *Irma la Douce*, one that the film's detractors tend to dwell upon at some length, and part of it results from the inability of any of the characters to let their emotions ring out through song. The wonderful (if often-remarked) thing about Hollywood musicals is that characters can tap immediately into their emotional lives by opening their mouths and singing. The drab constraints of everyday life give way to melody, and often the more sentimental the song the more affecting the moment. Wilder does not permit his characters such easy access. Love, joy, regret, despair, bliss, triumph—these are the mainstays of musical comedy, but for Billy they're too quick, easy, and pretty. In *Irma la Douce* he uses orchestral themes literally to underscore what's going on in his characters' hearts, but he doesn't give those hearts the freedom to express it directly.

Shirley MacLaine seems to have had mixed feelings about all of this. She is, after all, a musical comedienne—a dancer, too—and sparkling spontaneity is one of her trademarks. But Wilder kept her strictly under control. Although in recent years she has expressed some irritation about Wilder, in 1970 she said that "he directs every eyelash" and she meant it as a compliment: "I feel more secure with Wilder because he will be there as a finite judge of your performance. With Hitchcock you have to be your own editor." (This is a remarkable assertion.) William Wyler, on the other hand, "is totally inarticulate. If you ask him what the time is, he will be quite stuck for an answer—and that's the way he directs."

In some ways, *Irma la Douce* is the opposite of *One, Two, Three*. Contemplation, not speed, is Wilder's goal. There are long stretches of near silence as Wilder's camera explores characters' inner lives to a greater degree than ever. If box office success is any indication, he got a lot of laughs with *Irma la Douce*. But Billy was looking for something more—a peculiar mix of laughs and soft, languid romance. Until *Irma la Douce*, the mature, fully resolved love relationships Wilder created either began in the final moments of the film or else the characters shot or knifed each other. Having lived for almost sixty years, now Billy wanted to see how various not-so-young lovers behaved toward each other over the long haul.

Only a few shots were taken on location in Paris—the scenes on the banks of the Seine across from the rue des Saints-Pères, near Alexander Trauner's own residence, some master shots of Les Halles, and an aerial view, and the street cleaners. The markets of Les Halles, two Parisian streets, Moustache's bistro, and Irma's top-floor studio were constructed on a single Goldwyn set, courtesy of Trauner. "To a visitor, it could only look fake," Wilder said, "all the wrong proportions, the ridiculous perspectives, but on the screen, believe me, everything fell into place with a stupefying authenticity." As Trauner recalled, "I always ask directors to explain their film in a single sentence, and Wilder simply told me, 'It's a marvelous subject—it's the story of a man who is jealous of himself.'"

One of Wilder's most cherished images appears at the beginning of *Irma la Douce*—a set of street-washing trucks to express Wilder's abiding appreciation of the nighttime gutter and its dependable, every-morning cleansing. Marking the end of a long day and the simultaneous beginning of another, three street washers ride in a wide figure around the Arc de Triomphe. A young waiter from Maxim's hoses down the sidewalk (it's a glorified former bordello, after all); the narrator notes that the restaurant has been closed for many hours. Drawing an odd parallel, he goes on to note that "if you want to jump off the Eiffel Tower, it's too early." There's a pause. "So," the narrator explains, "if you're looking for a little action, forget the high-rent district. You better come into *our* neighborhood." Les Halles, "the stomach of Paris"—"vulgar, smelly, but alive."

He takes us on a tour of the meat market. Technicolor carcasses float by as the camera tracks lovingly along row after row of "brains and kidneys and tripe, pigs' feet and calves' heads waiting for sauce vinaigrette." Then fish and fruit and vegetables, a progression ending with a stack of cabbages. "But man does not live by cabbage alone." Billy cuts to a long line of cheap whores on the sidewalk. "And if that's what you're in the market for, just step around the corner into the rue Casanova."

At the local bistro, Wilder introduces us to his surrogate, the film's expedient moral arbiter, or arbiter of expedient morals: "This is the owner. He is known as Moustache. According to the police records, he is a Romanian chicken thief named Constantinescu." (This is a Wilder in-joke—a reference to *Was Frauen träumen*.) Still, perhaps because of the loss of Laughton, Wilder is less engaged with Moustache than he might have been. Moreover, Wilder's empathy lies, surprisingly, with Irma. She is a woman who first gives her johns what they think they want, then calculatingly extracts sympathy from them—and ups her income accordingly. Irma is literally a five-dollar hooker (a Texan pays her in dollars), but thanks to the pathos she inserts into her work she earns much, much more. For instance, she tells the Texan a phony story about the United States Air Force bombing her own little French village: "If you could see those poor little orphans sleeping on the floor, the rain coming in, there are no beds yet and no roof. . . ." He gives her the extra tip in traveler's checks. These men don't pay her tips *despite* the tales of woe she tells them. They pay her tips *because* of them. Irma knows what Billy knows: people like to feel guilty, sleazy, base, and bad, particularly when they're out to have a good time. Not only that, they enjoy paying for it.

The comic tone of *Irma la Douce* is quite peculiar, especially when it mixes with violence. At one point, Hippolyte yanks Irma's arm around behind her back because she tried to hold out on him for the Texan's ten-dollar traveler's check. Taunting her, Hippolyte cruelly invites her to find herself another *mec*: "Why don't you leave me *now*?" he snarls as he twists her arm tighter. That's when the one-armed midget pool player arrives on the scene. He strolls over from the pool table and, with a distinct swagger, says to Hippolyte, "I'd take her *any* time." Hippolyte yanks the dwarf up by the collar and holds him aloft. "It was just a joke, Hippolyte!" the midget cries. "A joke? Then how come nobody's laughin'?" he asks, whereupon he tosses the midget away. The little man flies out of the image. There is a thud—and a new shot of the midget, now unconscious, sliding across the floor. The camera pans with the body until it glides to a halt. Moustache sprays him with seltzer, ending the farce. Hippolyte immediately takes a swing at Irma's ass, hitting her squarely. "Now go back to work," he barks. "Ox," she snarls under her breath.

Dirty jokes provide ongoing amusement. Nestor meets Irma on the street as she walks her dog:

NESTOR: Pardon me, mademoiselle, but do you have a license?
IRMA: A license? No.
NESTOR: That's a violation of ordinance number fifty-six.
IRMA: Oh, well *(she giggles conspiratorially)*, usually they let us get away with it.
NESTOR: Not me. And another thing, according to the law you're supposed to keep it on a leash.
IRMA: *On a leash?!* Oh.

Irma la Douce is a sex comedy, but the jokes turn cold in the police van when Nestor attempts to arrest what appears to be the entire population of the rue Casanova. He is no match for these aggressive women, who turn on him. Lolita is particularly cruel: to the tune of "Alouette," she sings a mocking little song expressly for him: "Little birdie, pretty little birdie, little birdie, fly away with me." The meanest thing a woman can do in Billy's eyes is to call attention to a man's weakness. Nestor loses his gun in the struggle.

What Nestor finds with Irma, however, is a form of redemption—not only for her as a woman, but for him as a man. Blending jokes that aim lower while the emotions run deeper, Wilder begins the scene in which they spend their first night together with a throwaway, a minor Borscht Belt groaner, and moves on to one of the loveliest scenes of the film. (Irma refers to a poor painter who cut off his ear. "Van Gogh?" Nestor asks. "No, I think his name was Schwartz," says Irma.) Nestor begins fussing with newspapers, placing them demurely over the windows to shield Irma from the world's gaze, all to a delicate waltz on the soundtrack. Wilder raises Nestor's touching if pathetic gesture to a kind of nobility. Irma comments on his shyness. "Me? Shy? Not particularly. It's just, uh, the kind of world we live in. What I mean is, if you hate somebody you can do that any time, any place. But if you *like* somebody, you've got to hide in dark corners." He catches himself, knowing he's let something intimate slip out. Wilder knows it, too; there is a real delicacy to the moment. Irma then climbs into bed, pulls the covers up, takes a puff on her cigarette, and asks the man she is about to sleep with what his name is.

In a way, Wilder's quest is complete: from *The Major and the Minor*, in which a young, smart-alecky girl whips out a cigarette and signals the dawn of a new era of forthrightness, to *Irma la Douce*, where a somewhat older woman does the same thing, except that now she's a naked whore in bed with a former policeman standing by ready to climb in with her. "Well, don't take all night, Nestor Patou," she says, urging him in. For better or worse, American mass-culture morality had been transformed, and Billy Wilder led the charge.

Jack Lemmon in the act of undressing is indescribably graceful and sad, especially when he asks her to put on her eye mask. "You're really something," she says as she covers her eyes. He has a particularly sick look on his face as he pulls open his pants. At that point Irma's little dog, Coquette, begins to growl menacingly. He picks it up. It squeals. He puts it in the hall.

"Why do you have to have anybody at all?" Nestor asks (referring to Hippolyte). "Everybody needs somebody," Irma answers. "Like Coquette needs me. Who wants to be a stray dog? You've got to belong to someone, even if he kicks you once in a while."

Wilder's world is full of disguises. His characters are often flexible nearly to the point of schizophrenia; for Billy, some personalities are best revealed by the masks that cover them. In Nestor's case, this priggish failure of a policeman becomes a *mec* by accident and, since the role of neighborhood stud is such a fraud, he is compelled to concoct yet another persona—the half-castrated Lord X, who pays Irma, who then turns her earnings over to Nestor, who returns to Irma as Lord X, all to keep Irma happy as a wage earner. (Lord X's partial emasculation is said to have occurred during an accident at a Japanese prison camp on the River Kwai.)

Wilder and Diamond insert a bit of comedy dialogue that they each evidently found amusing, however different their perspectives may have been. Izzie was Billy's employee, after all:

IRMA: Let's see . . . five hundred francs each time, that's a thousand francs a week, fifty-two weeks in a year, so that would be . . . Darling, can I have a hundred francs?

NESTOR: Sure!

IRMA: For a hair dryer.

NESTOR: Here's another hundred. Get some curtains, too.

IRMA: Why are you so good to me?

NESTOR: I just believe in fair dealings between labor and management.

The comedy can be extremely broad and bloodthirsty at times. Wilder opens one sequence with a Panavision close-up of a side of beef, splayed, its legs pointing up in the air. A cleaver is falling as the shot fades in. The blade drops, splitting the beef right between the legs and well into the rib cage. Wilder dissolves to a row of pigs' heads with Nestor's face popping in the middle. At times, *Irma* is anything but *douce*. In one especially grim scene Irma and Nestor snipe at each other viciously, with Irma descending into shrill squawking. Nestor twists her arm behind her back, bullying her the way Hippolyte once did; she spits in his face, and it's not the least bit funny. Wilder fades to black, holds on the emptiness for a moment, then fades back in, the sound coming in before the image: "Here we are in the seventh inning, Maury Wills on first. . . ." A GI is walking with a whore, a transistor radio held to his ear. She leads him to the hotel and has to whistle at him to tear his attention away from the game. He grudgingly goes in with her.

In a remarkable bit of duplicity, Nestor comes to the bizarre realization that Irma's leaving him—for *him*. The other him, the fake him—Lord X. How unsettling it is for him to realize that the phony persona is more appealing to her than the real one, especially since he knows that the real one is so deficient:

NESTOR: How do you like that phony—he's been lying to her!
MOUSTACHE: What do you mean, *he*? There is no *he*—it's you!
NESTOR: Of course it's me. But she doesn't know that! And she doesn't know that I know. But I know that she likes him better than she likes me. See? She wouldn't even take any money from him.
MOUSTACHE: You'd better have a drink.

Nestor's only solution is to kill himself.

As if he were compelled to pay for his own sexual excesses, both on-screen and off, Wilder inserts a disingenuous moral near the end of the film. "I don't believe in miracles," Irma sighs, to which Nestor replies, "When I met you, you were a streetwalker. Now you're going to be a wife and mother. Isn't that a miracle?" Critics who deride Wilder's need to have it both ways could do no better than to cite this, the sappiest line in his career.

André Previn was recruited once more to score the film. Previn was surprised when Wilder asked him to "disregard all the pratfalls" and compose a sweet-tempered romantic score, especially for the scene in which Nestor and Irma spend their first night together. "Of course he was right," Previn recalls. "And the final result was curiously touching." After showing the composer the film he was about to score, Wilder left him alone.

Considering the subject matter of *Irma la Douce*, the lack of cuts demanded by the PCA and the Legion of Decency was extraordinary. Their laxness led directly to a violent backlash the following year, but in 1963 they dropped their guard. United Artists told the Legion in May 1963 that just a few cuts had been made to make the film acceptable. A shot of MacLaine naked to the waist was replaced by a shot showing only her head and shoulders. The sequence in which Lord X reacts to Irma's attempts to arouse him by spinning fantasies was revised to eliminate "as much as possible his body and pelvic contortions"; they were replaced with shots of his face. And the shot of an American soldier coming down the stairs of the Hotel Casanova with a whore on each arm was cut—but only from the U.S. and Canadian prints.

"Wilder has never shown less of his brassy film-engineering ability, and he and Diamond have never written so soggy a script," was Stanley Kauffmann's assessment. Kael thought the theme of prostitution was tired: "as a source of comedy I find it about as hilarious as muscular dystrophy." She seized particularly on the Schwartz joke as proof of Wilder's tin ear. "At that level of wit, the wonder is that Miss MacLaine and Mr. Lemmon consented to remain on the set." She didn't comment on the way the rest of the scene played, nor did she seem to care.

After *Irma*'s release, Geoffrey Shurlock of the PCA received a blistering letter from producer Hal Wallis, who was enraged and repulsed by everything *Irma la Douce* represented. The producer of various Lewis and Martin farces as well as the recent Elvis Presley hits *Blue Hawaii* (1961), *Girls! Girls! Girls!* (1962), and *Fun in Acapulco* (1963), Wallis was disgusted. He simply couldn't imagine "what this salacious, pornographic, distasteful, obscene, offensive, degrading piece of celluloid can mean to an audience." Possibly, Wallis went on, audiences respond to *Irma la Douce* "in the same way that [they do to] exhibitions in brothels and looking at stag films. . . . This is without a doubt the filthiest thing I have ever seen on the screen." But by this point, even Hollywood's chief censor found Wallis's objections to be wildly excessive. "It is mostly men who complain about it," Shurlock wrote back to Wallis. "Women generally seem to find it hilarious." Shurlock also noted that the Code Administration did convince Wilder to have the film reviewed by PCA, a practice that was no longer required, and that United Artists had assured them that it would be sold strictly as an adult movie. Only then did the PCA issue its certificate of approval.

Wallis was repulsed by the film's vulgarity, but worldwide audiences were delighted by it. *Irma la Douce* was a smash hit. In January 1964, *Variety* reported that the film had grossed $9,500,000 and was second only to *Around the World in 80 Days* as a comedy blockbuster. This was no New York/Chicago/Los Angeles urban hit with otherwise limited appeal.

In the American heartland *Irma* was raking it in. In Saint Paul, Minnesota, for example, the film set a long-run record—twenty-four weeks. As *Variety* noted, "This was accomplished by a picture with a prostitute as its principal feminine character in a predominantly Catholic community where foreign, sex, Legion-of-Decency-condemned and skin pix are boycotted by all exhibs in recognition of the fact that a considerable element of local citizenry frowns on them." (And what was the previous record holder in Saint Paul? *The Robe*.)

The 1960s were in full swing. *Irma la Douce* was Billy Wilder's greatest commercial success, far surpassing anything else he ever made. It grossed about $20 million and made him richer than ever. Lemmon and MacLaine were happy, too. "The truth is, I personally earned more out of that picture than any other picture I ever made," Wilder said. "That doesn't mean it was the best. It just means I made the most money. And I enjoyed making it, too." As for the film's quality, Billy wasn't especially happy with it: "If I had my way I'd reshoot ninety-five percent of that thing," he said. Phalanx and Pyramid, Billy's production companies, took in at least $1,200,000. (United Artists and the Mirisches, on the other hand, received $440,000 combined.)

Sex was selling—and selling big. Billy, an inveterate gambler flush with success, was compelled to up the ante.

26. KISS ME, STUPID

ZELDA (Felicia Farr): What have *you* done lately?
DINO (Dean Martin): How lately?
ZELDA: I bet the Singing Nun sells more records than you.
DINO: The Singin' *who*?
ZELDA: Let's face it—you haven't got it anymore. You're old-fashioned.
DINO: You sure know how to hurt a fella.

—*Kiss Me, Stupid*

When he began planning *Kiss Me, Stupid*, the first of his two back-to-back feel-bad comedies, Billy was in the catbird seat and could do most anything he wanted. He liked reaping profits. Asked which of his many films was his favorite, Wilder answered quickly: *Some Like It Hot*. His interlocutor objected, citing *The Lost Weekend* and *Sunset Boulevard*, but Billy dismissed them: "Nice little pictures," he admitted, "but in those days I wasn't getting a percentage of the gross." Thanks to *Irma la Douce*, should he decide to replace his Rolls-Royce, financing would not be a problem. Acting as his own agent, he signed an even sweeter directing deal. Under the new contract, the Mirisches agreed to pay him $400,000 for each film against 10 percent of the gross until the break-even point. After his films made their money back, Billy would receive a flabbergasting 75 percent of their profits.

And what was the first film he planned to make under this lucrative deal? As though deliberately tying to scuttle his own success, Billy chose a new project that was as foul as anything he ever conceived—at least on the surface. Giddy with the public's embrace of a comedy about prostitution, and itching to rub the public's noses in something that smelled worse than the backstreets and used mattresses of Les Halles, Wilder turned to smut. He saw it as redemptive. The script Billy and Iz produced is full of *entendres* so overtly coarse they can't be said to be double anymore. The comedy of *Kiss Me, Stupid* is purposefully low. Penises, breasts, pubic hair, religion, marriage, American small-town life—Billy holds everything in equal contempt. He was confident about his carnal goals. "Unlike David

Lean, who needs the desert for *Lawrence of Arabia*, my pictures are set in the bed, or under the bed, or in the bathroom," he told a British journalist in July 1964. "They need a minimum amount of Cinerama," though he did film *Kiss Me, Stupid* in Panavision, perhaps only to capture the dull emptiness of his characters' lives with even more expansive, vacuous space. At the dawn of the sexual revolution, Wilder set out to make sex seem filthy again.

He succeeded. *Kiss Me, Stupid* is about a husband and wife redeemed by adultery—the husband with a two-bit hooker, the wife with a sodden Las Vegas crooner who gets headaches if he doesn't get laid once a day (and it doesn't matter by whom). Movie reviewers have long taken *Kiss Me, Stupid* to be an artistic failure, as if the film's extraordinary sadness and muck were somehow inadvertent. *Kiss Me, Stupid* may not be Wilder's most finely wrought film, but its tone is so consistently depressing, its vision so assiduously dispirited, and its jokes so relentlessly bad, that the malaise it engenders in its audience becomes a kind of triumph. What the film's detractors miss is that the peculiar tenderness of the ending results from, not despite, the vulgarity of everything that precedes it. *Kiss Me, Stupid* is without doubt one of the most complicated comedies Billy ever made.

Kiss Me, Stupid marked the second time in Wilder's career that he used Ketti Frings as his source: *The Dazzling Hour*, Frings's and Jose Ferrer's adaptation of *L'Ora della Fantasia* (a farce by Anna Bonacci) enjoyed a short run at the La Jolla Playhouse in 1953. Frings and Ferrer transported Bonacci's characters to a quaint English village in 1838; as *Variety* observed, this was "an unlikely spot for the second act bordello scene." The comedy concerned the village composer, his prim wife, a worldly London nobleman who can further the composer's career, and the well-handled town prostitute. Wife and whore change places for the night, and everything works out in the end, though *Variety* was quick to note that the genteel housewife's surprising enthusiasm at the bordello was really just an extreme version of an old Hollywood pattern—the meek small-towner metamorphosing into a big-city glamour girl.

In 1953, *The Dazzling Hour* was ahead of its time. *Kiss Me, Stupid*, on the other hand, may seem in retrospect like a harbinger of the sexually liberating 1960s, but for all its effort to be sexually topical it was notably out of synch with its era. At a time when younger directors like Richard Lester were taking their increasingly lightweight cameras out of the soundstage and into the so-called real world (*A Hard Day's Night*, 1964), Billy stayed mostly indoors on sets. While his colleague George Cukor was filming the meticulously lavish *My Fair Lady* (1964), Billy focused his attentions on an all-but-dead town in the Nevada desert. MGM was making

The Unsinkable Molly Brown (1964); Disney was making *Mary Poppins* (1964). Meanwhile, at United Artists, Billy was forcing his characters to sit on a piano bench in a drab living room banging out seemingly tin-eared songs they can't sell.

Wilder's discreet camerawork worked against him, too. In the 1960s, after the French New Wave had begun to call candid, graphic attention to the plasticity of the image, to the shocks of editing, to irregularities on the soundtrack, and to all the other pleasing artifices of the cinema, Wilder's all-but-invisible style seemed to be a throwback: "I admire elegant camera work but not fancy stuff. The camera hanging off the chandelier—that's for children, to astonish middlebrow critics. I would like to have them forget there is a camera, a dolly, a crew of one hundred fifty." American high-culture mongers were trumpeting Brechtian distancing devices, but Wilder was still trying to pull his audience *in* to his fictions. The last thing he wanted to do was to force them to stand apart, watch the spectacle intellectually, and notice all the mechanics behind it. "If it was possible," he said, "I'd like to get them up on the screen working."

Again, this was not simple. *Kiss Me, Stupid* did mark a new appreciation of cinematic artifice, though on a decidedly starker plane. On a practical level, Wilder wanted to maintain his high degree of control by constructing his dreary little world on a soundstage, but there was an aesthetic consequence, too. For all its colorlessness, *Kiss Me, Stupid* is set in a fantasy world—a depressing, vulgar fantasy, but one no less fantastic for its baseness. There was some location filming in the dusty town of Twenty-Nine Palms, California, and the Moulin Rouge nightclub in Hollywood as well as in Las Vegas, but Joseph LaShelle's severely dark, noticeably filtered cinematography makes even these real locales seem hermetically sealed.

At Twenty-Nine Palms, special effects coordinator Milton Rice supervised the construction of an immense sign outside the local Elks Club, which the company transformed into a roadhouse-whorehouse called the Belly Button, where a gargantuan woman with a glamorous, electrified navel stands guard. (To give some idea of this billboard-woman's proportions, the piece of glass in the navel measured three inches across.) The sign works well to describe a chafing social reality—the Twenty-Nine Palms Elks Club became the Belly Button with such verisimilitude that a dozen women are said to have shown up looking for work. It serves as broad, bitter satire just as well. *Kiss Me, Stupid* is a most realistic-seeming nightmare.

For the most part, *Kiss Me, Stupid* was shot in soundstages at the Goldwyn Studios and the Universal backlot. Shooting took place in March through June of 1964. Even Barney's gas station and portions of the Belly Button exterior were rebuilt to order, though the canned quality was always part of the design. When Alexander Trauner took a research trip to scope out the way people lived in the Nevada desert, he was struck by the way their wooden framework houses reminded him of his own all-surface, no-substance movie sets.

The peculiar comic tone of *Kiss Me, Stupid* is like the long-lost Gershwin tunes Billy resuscitates in the film—a little off-key at first, but oddly sweet and increasingly tender after the initial shock wears off. Barney sings "I'm a Poached Egg" to Orville's piano accompaniment: "I'm a mousetrap—without a piece of cheese; I'm Vienna—without the Viennese! I'm da Vinci—without the Mona Lis', when I'm . . ." Orville stops playing, appalled: " '*Mona Lis'*?' " "That's what makes it," Barney explains. "Irregularity. That unexpected little twist. Keep playing."

Ironically, Billy's inspiration to use Gershwin to score his film about adultery occurred at a wedding anniversary party for Mr. and Mrs. William Wyler. Billy asked Ira Gershwin's wife, Leonore, what would convince her husband to work again, and she responded, "To be asked by someone he admires." Wilder evidently felt he fit the bill, and Ira concurred. Billy assumed that Ira would write lyrics to music composed by someone else, so he asked for suggestions for a suitable composer. He was surprised and thrilled when Ira suggested his late brother, George; there was a trove of unfinished work he could adapt. Billy initially said that he needed no more than three songs—two novelty songs and an Italian ballad—and Ira set to the task of figuring out how to write songs that could plausibly have been written by two amateur songwriters from Nevada but that would still work as refined Gershwin tunes.

Wilder suggested "Blah, Blah, Blah" (a song from the 1931 Fox musical *Delicious*), but Ira vetoed it on the grounds that it was already a Gershwin standard. (The world's idea of what constitutes a Gershwin classic is evidently different from Ira's.) Ira then asked for the screenplay-in-progress, which Billy helpfully provided. It was as yet incomplete. Wilder and Diamond hadn't even finished laying down the story line. With increasing discomfort, Ira Gershwin realized that Billy was asking him to compose the songs first, with Wilder and Diamond using them as the foundation of the script. He was stumped.

Enter Swifty Lazar, who represented not only Diamond but Ira Gershwin, too. Lazar went through the song list in *The Gershwin Years* and read each title out loud to Billy, Izzie, and Ira. When Swifty got to "Does a Duck Love Water," Billy and Izzie declared that it was precisely the kind of song they were looking for. Ira then revised a song he and his brother wrote for RKO's 1937 Astaire-Rogers musical *Shall We Dance* (though it didn't make it into the film); now it was reworked into "Sophia," an Italianesque ditty for the Las Vegas crooner. For "I'm a Poached Egg," Ira revived and expanded some lyrics and a tune he and George began in the 1920s but never finished, and it was Ira Gershwin rather than Billy who insisted on the title's cheap whimsy. Wilder and Diamond wanted him to call the song "When I'm Without You," but Ira refused. Finally, Ira combined two songs he and his brother wrote over a period of time—"Phoebe" and "Livelong Day" to create "All the Livelong Day (and the Long, Long Night)," a simple, graceful ballad.

As songwriters, the neurotic piano teacher Orville J. Spooner and his grease monkey sidekick, Barney Millsap, are only superficially bad. Scratch the surface, and you find the Gershwins. As "I'm a Poached Egg" is to " 'S Wonderful," so Billy's own early screenplays are to *Some Like It Hot* or *The Apartment* or *Kiss Me, Stupid* itself. This is a film about a writing team that hasn't made it yet. Even in the moment of his own greatest worldwide commercial glory, Billy relates to these unsung, small-town writers. He can't help but put them down, but he does it with love.

Kiss Me, Stupid was financed as a coproduction among the Mirisch Company, Phalanx, and Claude Productions. Dean Martin was Claude. Like other top-drawing stars, Martin had set up his own production company to ensure profit participation in his films. What was odd about *Kiss Me, Stupid* was that Dino, in addition to starring in and coproducing the film, was also its overt subject. As Martin's biographer Nick Tosches puts it, "He was to play himself: the singer of 'That's Amore,' consul of cool, holy ghost of tastelessness." He serves as his own point of reference.

Postmodern film theorists should be struck by the film's fascination with signs, most of them deteriorating. The film begins with an iris-in on a sign painted on the side of a truck (LAS VEGAS SIGN CO.). To the brassy opening fanfare of " 'S Wonderful," the camera tilts and pans right to a shot of the vast neon sign of the Sands hotel, ending in drastically low angle to further aggrandize the glitz. The camera tilts down to the Sands marquee announcing Dino's show. (Dino doesn't need a last name, his caricature and nickname signifying more than enough already.) This was the actual marquee of the Sands announcing Martin's performance there in July 1964. But in Wilder's vision, the sign is in collapse; the letter O has already been pulled off the marquee by a harnessed workman, who swings across the sign, removing the other letters as Wilder cuts inside to the stage, where Dino is singing " 'S Wonderful" with a line of befeathered Las Vegas chorus girls staring glumly into space behind him.

"You can't blame me for feeling amorous," Dino croons, then says with a cock of the head to the nearest showgirl, "Now is this a bit of terrific, hmm? Las' night she was bangin' on my door for forty-five minutes. I wouldn' let her out." He toasts his own terrible joke, sips his drink, and lets the laughter wash over him. Billy cuts to a line of five waiters stretched out across the Panavision screen. The one in the middle isn't laughing. The others are chortling raucously, but the guy dead center remains stone-faced. This is the tone of *Kiss Me, Stupid*—the sour joke, the half-failed communication. Out of this poverty Wilder finds redemption and love, and it's not terribly funny in the end.

Wilder makes fun of Dean Martin (as Dino graciously did to himself), but there's a sense of personal identification, too—the womanizing old pro always on the make. Billy had been something of an adjunct Rat Packer for years, but one incident secured his personal admiration for Martin. Three years before he approached Martin to play Dino in *Kiss Me, Stupid*, Billy let fly at a Hollywood Press Club dinner with a torrent of bad-tempered, well-publicized remarks: American theater owners were thoroughly uninterested in the movies they showed, they didn't keep up their movie houses, they made no effort to sell the films they screened, and, by the way, actors were totally irrelevant. "Stars don't mean a thing today," was how Billy put it. The story hit the trades, of course, and Martin was outraged. He quickly wrote Billy an angry letter in which he told Wilder off for being such an arrogant and self-important jerk. Billy appreciated it.

According to Wilder, Martin wasn't the slightest bit embarrassed to play this cruel, complicit self parody. "He's a delicious and adorable man who does what you ask him," Billy later said. "He's one of the most relaxed and talented men I know. With him, no intellectual discussions. 'Dean, we're making a film.' 'When?' 'We start in June.' 'What clothes? Thanks, 'bye.' "

Forced to detour off the highway between Las Vegas and Los Angeles after his Sands act closes, Dino asks the highway patrol where he'll end up. "You come out at Barstow—by way of Warm Springs, Paradise Valley, and Climax." "The only way to go," says Dino. Dry and dusty Climax, where there is little action and where Orville and Barney desperately try to sell Dino their own musical compositions. Peter Sellers was cast as Orville.

The thirty-eight-year-old Sellers was the kind of tension-provoking funnyman who upsets his way through the world, using his audiences' discomfort to nag them into helpless laughter. In Stanley Kubrick's *Lolita* (1962), Sellers's Clare Quilty is such a relentless adversary to James Mason's Humbert Humbert that he becomes a sort of torture device. In Kubrick's more recent *Dr. Strangelove* (1964), Sellers's triple role—Group Captain Lionel Mandrake, President Merkin Muffley, and the title character himself—were all menacing. Strangelove's mind-of-its-own arm, constantly shooting up in a Nazi heil, was like Sellers himself—unpredictable, out of control, hysterical. Sellers's latest antic screen persona, Inspector Clouseau (in Blake Edwards's *The Pink Panther* and *A Shot in the Dark*, both 1964) was a bungling idiot—a moron, and violently so. Casting him as a milquetoast piano teacher consumed by jealous rage was a stroke of genius.

Wilder knew that Sellers was a man of infinite masks. He also knew how difficult Sellers could be—the rotten times he'd given Edwards and Kubrick were fresh legends in Hollywood—but Wilder thought he could control him, at least to the extent of making Sellers say his lines the way Billy and Iz wrote them. *Kiss Me, Stupid* was not the only project Wilder had in mind for Sellers, either. Billy wanted him to play Dr. Watson in his Sherlock Holmes project, with Peter O'Toole as Holmes, and Sellers readily agreed. Both men saw *Kiss Me, Stupid* as a pleasant warm-up act to the more important comedy-drama to come.

Kiss Me, Stupid's star slate was completed by Kim Novak, who projects an image of luminous confusion on-screen. Her in-over-her-head quality is essential to her emotional appeal. As David Thomson writes, "There was a mute honesty in Novak: she did not conceal the fact that she was a broad drawn into a world capable of exploiting her. Filming itself was an ordeal for her; it was as if the camera hurt her. . . . Novak was stoical, obdurate, or sullen, like the stolid girls in Faulkner novels. She allowed very few barriers between that raw self and the audience."

By 1964, Novak had a reputation for causing trouble on the set. Like Sellers, her insecurities registered as defiance, especially to the men for whom she labored. "I was warned about Kim before I started to work with her," Billy admitted at the time. "They said she was difficult, so I said to her on the first day that if there were any difficulties *she* would be tossed out and not the director. The girl said with tears in her eyes that she was misunderstood, and in fact working with her has been a most pleasant surprise. She has the quality of Monroe and Dietrich, and that's remarkable because she was a studio-created star—a nylon artificial thing to be scraped off, something created as a threat to Rita Hayworth." (Novak was invented by Harry Cohn as competition for Hayworth, with whom Cohn had grown impatient in the mid-1950s.)

Novak's greatest, most disturbing film performance occurs in Alfred Hitchcock's *Vertigo*, in which she plays a woman playing another woman in the service of a disturbed man's morbid fantasy. As Thomson puts it, it's "less a performance than a helpless confession of herself." For *Kiss Me, Stupid*, Wilder cast her in a similar if more vulgar role—Polly the Pistol, a roadhouse whore hired to play Orville's wife for the night so Orville can pimp her off on Dino, the sale of his songs as his goal. If *Vertigo*'s Judy Barlton hadn't jumped off the mission bell tower at the end of the film but disappeared instead into the Nevada desert with nothing but the clothes on her back, she might well have ended up as Polly the Pistol.

For the role of Barney Millsap, Wilder needed a good-natured sharpie, a wiseacre slob. He chose Cliff Osmond, with whom Billy had been most impressed during the production of *Irma la Douce*. Osmond was an imposing man—six foot four and 260 pounds. As Wilder said at the time (with extraordinary hyperbole, even for Billy), "He is the only man in pictures today who, in my opinion, can come close to filling the shoes of the late Charles Laughton." Rounding out the bill was Felicia Farr, a relaxed and beautiful actress who could project an image of domestic allure with even greater ease than Arlene Francis. Farr also had an intimate personal connection to Billy and Audrey Wilder: she was now Jack Lemmon's wife, having married him in Paris during the production of *Irma la Douce*. Billy was one of Lemmon's two best men at the wedding. (The other was the director Richard Quine.)

In February 1964, right before the production of *Kiss Me, Stupid* was scheduled to begin, Peter Sellers married a twenty-one-year-old bombshell named Britt Ekland. She learned something quickly about her new husband: "His incredible affection soured rapidly into an habitual jealousy which filled the first few weeks of our marriage with despair." Possessive and weak, neurotic but highly energized, Sellers grilled Ekland relentlessly about her daily activities, convinced she was already cheating on him. He stationed spies on the set of *Guns at Batasi*, the film she was making at the time, and they dutifully reported her every move back to Sellers, whose jealousy was truly insane. As Sellers's biographer Roger Lewis notes, "instead of playing Orville J. Spooner, he *was* Orville J. Spooner."

There was some tension when Sellers began working with Wilder, but no more than the usual stress between a strong-willed director who demanded total control and a high-strung, erratic star with ego problems. Famous for his deft improvisations, Sellers found himself being told to confine his inventions to the sphere of gesture and business; the words he was to utter were unalterable. Sellers hated it. That Sellers wasn't happy was nothing new. He could be genial and charming if he cared to be, but other times he showed up at the studio late in the afternoon and the whole day was wasted. It was the price to be paid for his performance.

"The two directors I've always wanted to work with are Vittorio De Sica and Billy Wilder," Sellers said at the beginning of the production. "I think Wilder is one of the greatest, if not *the* greatest, comedy directors in the world." As late as March 20, after shooting began on the Goldwyn lot, Sellers was telling the press that he was really quite content: "It's proving to be very enjoyable indeed—a wonderful opportunity." There was an ominous note, however: "The trouble is, you find yourself trying all the time for satisfaction and then never really being satisfied with yourself. I suppose that's good for an actor, but sometimes it is awful—like a battle you can never win."

Privately, though, Sellers was upset by the casual bonhomie of Billy's set. For all of Wilder's autocratic control over his performers and crew, he seemed to exert no restraint whatsoever at the door of the soundstage. Some directors kept a closed set, but by the early 1960s, Billy was so relaxed in the role of supreme commander of the cinema that he turned his sets into the working equivalent of the Romanisches Café. Crowds strolled in and out at will. Stars, writers, poker buddies, Audrey's friends—a party atmosphere prevailed on Wilder's soundstages. As one of his camera operators put it, "When you leave a Wilder set at night, you feel you've enjoyed yourself, not as if you've finally dragged yourself through another day of miserable chores." The reclusive Sellers disagreed.

Sellers was living high at the time. Pot and poppers were his drugs of choice, and he consumed them with abandon. Already wound too tight for his own good, Sellers's self-medication pushed him further toward catastophe, though neither he nor his friends and family seemed to be aware of any danger. Sellers spent his days frantically tracking his bride, following Billy's demanding directions, and hating his own exposure to strangers' eyes on the set; at night he smoked weed, sniffed amyl nitrite, and wished he didn't have to show up the following morning to film any more scenes of Kiss Me, Stupid.

On Sunday, April 5, Sellers, Ekland, his children (by a previous marriage), and some friends spent the day at Disneyland. They returned to Sellers's house in the evening, the children were dispatched, and Sellers did some poppers and began having sex with Britt. Suddenly he felt terrible. A doctor was summoned. He examined Sellers and departed. When Sellers still didn't feel right he went to Cedars of Lebanon hospital. "You've got to have top billing to get into a five-star joint like this," the grinning actor told the staff as he checked in. He was soon diagnosed as having suffered a mild heart attack. One of the friends who accompanied them to Disneyland had to laugh when she found the scribbled note left at home by Ekland; having spent the day listening to Sellers bitch about Wilder and Kiss Me, Stupid, her first thought on learning that Sellers had been rushed to Cedars of Lebanon was, "Good God, the lengths he'll go to so he doesn't have to make this film."

Shortly after midnight on Tuesday, a nurse found Sellers lying in his hospital bed with no blood pressure and no pulse. He was rushed into the intensive care unit and, to everyone's surprise, revived. It happened several more times over the next few days—Sellers would die and then return to life, like a ghastly comedy routine. By the end of the week he'd suffered a total of eight separate heart attacks and lived through them all. He was taken off the critical list on Friday at 10:30 A.M., by which time Billy had already replaced him with Ray Walston. Walston began filming all of Orville's scenes from scratch on April 13.

The production of *Kiss Me, Stupid* proceeded with Walston having to reshoot all of Sellers's scenes with actors who had already been through Billy's extensive rehearsals and knew precisely how Billy saw everything. Walston felt like an outsider, but what could he do? On exceptionally short notice, he had to fill Sellers's closetful of shoes—the manic Sellers, the placid Sellers, the suspicious Sellers and the sly one, too; Sellers the wimp, the lothario, the fool. His task was difficult, to say the least.

Walston was currently starring as the alien title character of television's *My Favorite Martian*, complete with little rabbit-ear antennae that shot up from behind his head. "When I went in to see Wilder and talk to him," Walston says, "he had his entire crew in that office—there were fifty people there. And the first thing he did was say to me, 'Come over here by the window, I want to see your face.' I had been in an accident in one of the segments of the *Martian* show—we were working with a chimpanzee and the chimpanzee went berserk and attacked me and chewed me up quite a lot—but he said it was okay. Then I went home with the script, and I read it with my wife, and I said, 'It won't go. It's not good.' Everybody said, 'Don't be ridiculous, this is Billy Wilder, he doesn't make mistakes, he'll fix all that bullshit. . . .' I thought, 'Well, let's hope he does.' I couldn't say that I wouldn't do a picture with the great Billy Wilder because I don't like the script."

Walston's first day of shooting was not without comedy. With Dean Martin leaning against a nearby wall, Billy issued a long set of instructions to Walston on how to play the scene. As he stepped back to the camera, Dino loudly put his two cents in: "Tell the cocksucker to go fuck himself," Martin advised. "Do it your own way." Billy loved it. Walston also reports what Martin told Wilder after listening to a similar set of commands: "Well for Chrissake Jesus Christ Almighty what the fuck! I mean, if you wanted an actor what the fuck did you get me for? Why didn't you go get fucking Marlon Brando?"

Sellers was gone, but his shadow remained. It found its voice in June. By that point fully recovered and feeling his oats once more, Sellers decided to tell Alexander Walker of the *Evening Standard* that in Hollywood, the studios "give you every creature comfort except the satisfaction of being able to get the best work out of yourself." He complained about all the hangers-on on the set of *Kiss Me, Stupid*, and how distracting it had been for him. (As he described Billy's behavior later, "He was running a bloody Cook's Tour!") Sellers also made no bones about his dissatisfaction with Billy's exacting and thorough control.

Billy, Dean Martin, Felicia Farr, and Kim Novak sent him a collective wire. It read, in toto, "Talk about unprofessional rat finks."

Sellers's appearance in the Sherlock Holmes film was already in doubt, but by June 20, he officially pulled out. "I'm surprised they should be so sensitive," he added. "I made my criticisms in public and in America and I only told the truth." Sellers also defined "rat fink" for the British press: "Someone who says something you don't like."

Wilder responded with a famous quip: "Heart attack? You have to have a heart before you can have an attack."

Sellers took out an ad in *Variety* to make his position clear: "There appears to be a feeling getting around in Hollywood that I am an ungrateful limey or rat fink or whatever, who has been abusing everything Hollywood behind its back. . . . The creative side in me couldn't accept the sort of conditions under which work had to be carried out. . . . The atmosphere is wrong for me." While this unpleasant, well-publicized exchange between star and director didn't threaten to sink *Kiss Me, Stupid* entirely, it certainly didn't help.

Meanwhile, Kim Novak tripped over someone's stray foot and took a bad fall on the set. She resumed work immediately. Knowing all too well her own reputation for being difficult, Novak wanted to work through it without complaining: "I wouldn't go to the doctor because I'd started the picture. I kept thinking it would all work out." Ten days later she was rushed to the hospital in acute pain. Her doctor prescribed two weeks in traction, but Kim refused. So he administered pain pills and injections of novocaine and sent her back to the studio.

Visitors to the set continued to show up unannounced, and in one case Billy put one to work. On the day Novak and Walston were rehearsing their ridiculous dance of joy (after Dino agrees to buy "Sophia"), Gene Kelly stopped by to say hello. According to Walston, "Wilder had everyone in Hollywood at his beck and call on a friendly basis. He called Gene Kelly in to stage all that dancing and jumping around when I pull the Kleenex out of the box—that was Kelly's work." Before the day was over the dance steps between Orville J. Spooner and Polly the Pistol were laid out by the man who choreographed *On the Town* (1949) and *An American in Paris* (1951). "Your contribution will be unbilled and unpaid, naturally," Billy told him.

Walston, meanwhile, was taken aback by the seaminess of his new picture. He was struck in particular by the line, "Well, it's not very big, but it's clean," ostensibly made in reference to his house. Billy "wanted it done with a slight look from her as if it meant my cock," says Walston. As though the dialogue itself wasn't clear enough:

POLLY: Nice place you got here.
ORVILLE: Oh, you'll like it. It's not very big but it's clean.
POLLY: What is?
ORVILLE: What is *what*?
POLLY: I don't know—you brought it up.

The cast and crew of *Kiss Me, Stupid* were taken aback one day when Wilder pulled a prank. Walston recalls: "I had a scene where I was supposed to get under the sheets with Kim Novak—nude. You didn't actually see us nude, but you did see us taking off our clothes and then assumed the rest. So I got ready to do it, and Wilder said, 'Wait a minute, wait a minute, I'll show you how to do this.' So he took off his clothes and got into bed with her."

Billy was already needling Walston about the potential reaction of his TV audience to *Kiss Me, Stupid*. One day Walston snapped. "Eight or nine weeks into the shoot he said to me, 'What do you think the kiddies are going to say about you when they see this picture?' And I said, 'What do you think the public and the critics are going to say about *you*?' 'What do you mean?' he said. I said, 'You've got a lot of risqué bullshit in this.' 'Lemme tell you something,' he said. 'I'm going to tell you what's going to happen in pictures. You are going to see nudity. Profanity. Things that you are never going to believe in your life that you would see in movies.' Well, true to his word, all of those things started—in 1968, not 1964."

According to Walston, "Felicia Farr was really quite wonderful and very helpful. The fellow who played the big guy—he was a problem." As Walston describes it, Cliff Osmond "had become Wilder's favorite. In all of Wilder's pictures he latched on to someone he admired and liked and was very friendly with. Well, this guy took advantage of that and got in my way quite a lot."

Like all too much of life itself, *Kiss Me, Stupid* is a comedy of meager sex jokes and unfulfilling punchlines. Giant cacti serve as erections in the Spooners' front yard. One can't miss them; rudeness, not subtlety, is their point. Zelda's maiden name is Pettibone. (It makes more sense once you see her wizened parents.) Since Polly's talking parrot spends his days watching old westerns on television, the only thing he can say is "bang bang," a phrase he repeats when Dino starts to undress in front of Zelda. "No coaching from the audience," Dino tells the parrot.

Audiences were meant to get these jokes—and get them hard. Wilder and Diamond make no attempt to write slyly, nor is this comedy lighthearted. With a sick, sinking sensation, we are confronted by the everyday crumminess of being human. How can there be romance in a world of

bodily functions? The whole comedy has an unpleasant aroma—as when
Dino goes into the men's room at Barney's gas station and Barney forces
Orville to go in behind him (to chat Dino up about their songs). Orville,
of course, heads in singing what is at its core a love song: "I'm a haunted
house that hasn't got a ghost, when I'm without you. . . ." The door closes
behind him. A splashing sound is heard on the soundtrack. Wilder cuts to
the gas hose overflowing on the sidewalk. When he cuts back to the men's
room door, Dino is emerging; he shakes his dripping hands dry. Barney
tells him that there are paper towels in the ladies' room. Dino goes in, and
Orville, still singing his love song, follows him.

Barney suggests getting rid of Zelda temporarily and substituting a
whore from the Belly Button, all in order to please Orville's houseguest:

> ORVILLE: Just tell me one thing if you're so clever. How do I get rid of
> my wife?
> BARNEY: That's the easiest part. Hit her.
> ORVILLE: Hit her?!
> BARNEY: Start an argument. Get her sore at you. Shove a grapefruit in
> her face! There's lots of ways.

Kiss Me, Stupid turns especially bitter and dark when Polly gets
pinched, fondled, slapped, and clawed by Dino as Dino tells Orville an
especially rancid joke. Polly clearly hates being treated this way, but she's
used to it. Orville plays "All the Live Long Day" and lulls himself into a
romantic reverie that redeems him; he forgets entirely about his pimping
plans. Polly, who begins to feel for him, forces him out—because she loves
him. Just when the world seems as if it couldn't stink any worse, Orville
and Polly fall for each other, if only for the night. Orville throws Dino
bodily out the door, after which Wilder's camera traces a wistful path as
Orville locks the door, turns out the lights, and escorts Polly into the bedroom. That this tenderness occurs in the midst of such grossness is crucial.
It would be easy to find beautiful moments in a beautiful world, but since
Wilder sees life as unbearably ugly, any instance of redemption is all the
more powerful.

These flickers of tenderness don't preclude more raunchy humor. "Not
a bad lookin' dame, if ya like home cookin'," Dino slurs to Zelda in Polly's
trailer. "Me, I like to eat out." When he gropes Zelda in Polly's tiny bed,
it's particularly unpleasant. Then his back goes out. "I've always had back
trouble. It's an old football injury." Zelda replies in disbelief: "You played
football?" "No, I was watchin' the game on TV and this girl was sittin'
on my lap. . . ." Zelda gives him an alcohol rub, and Dino falls asleep—
or appears to. "You know something?" Zelda softly says; "If I weren't so

old-fashioned, and you weren't asleep. . . ." "Whadja say?" Dino pipes up. "Nothing. Go to sleep." Fade to black. Exterior: the Belly Button. Dawn. The neon signs go off. Wilder cuts to a high angle of Dino leaving the trailer, stretching. Orville's tryst with Polly bears a trace of sentimentality, whereas Dino's and Zelda's morning-after scenes are sweet but tough. When Zelda wakes up, obviously naked, and finds a wad of money stuffed in an empty bourbon bottle, her first reaction is a smile of pleasure. She clearly liked spending the night with Dino, and she likes getting paid for it.

For the marketing of *Kiss Me, Stupid*, caricaturist Al Hirschfeld was commissioned to create line drawings of Novak, Martin, and Walston, and novelty pins were produced and distributed. Spoofing the current campaign for Avis rental cars ("We try harder"), these buttons commanded "Kiss me, stupid" in English, Spanish, Portuguese, Italian, and German ("*Küss mich, dummkopf*"). In the theatrical trailer, the Mirisches retroactively awarded Billy name-above-the-title status for his previous UA films. "Remember Billy Wilder's *Some Like It Hot*?" a male voice asks above shots of Monroe, Lemmon, and Curtis in the train station sequence. "Who doesn't?" a female voice coos. "And Billy Wilder's *The Apartment*?" (Lemmon serving MacLaine spaghetti off his tennis racket). "Great, great," the woman sighs. "And Billy Wilder's *Irma la Douce*?" (Shirley dancing on the table). "Hilarious," the woman says. "But what's he done lately?"

Then, in a tone of disbelief, she says "*Kiss Me, Stupid*?! You're kidding. What could it *possibly* be about?"

The final shot of the trailer contained a written warning—"This picture is for adults only!" These words of caution appeared over a shot of Dino, in Las Vegas, spinning his Dual Ghia convertible to the left and looking guiltily over his shoulder as he makes the turn. At first, steering *Kiss Me, Stupid* past the censors didn't seem like much of a problem. By 1964, the Production Code Administration was strictly pro forma, and even the Legion of Decency was on the wane. The Legion continued to ask practicing Catholics to sign a pledge not to see films the Legion denounced, but the Legion hadn't issued a "C—condemned" rating to any American film since 1956, when it damned *Baby Doll* to perdition along with any Catholic who saw it and didn't confess. For Billy, the old battles seemed over. *The Apartment* passed with all its shack-ups and sex jokes, as did *One, Two, Three*, with its leering references to umlauts and tongues. ("I'm bilingual," says Ingeborg; "Don't I know it," says MacNamara). *Irma la Douce* slid by as well, complete with jokes about impotence and fellatio. ("What a night!" Irma exclaims. "Everybody seems to have the same idea! Always happens when there's a full moon—I haven't even had time to catch my breath!") Given *Irma*'s vast commercial success, Billy had no reason to expect a problem with *Kiss Me, Stupid*. The new film was darker-tempered, but Wilder's war over censorship and sexuality seemed to have been won. He saw himself as a victorious crusader.

In the fall, Billy met personally with Monsignor Little of the Legion of Decency, after which he agreed to reshoot several scenes. A less explicit denouement of Dino's encounter with Zelda in Polly's trailer would be filmed. Billy also agreed to take out some of the bedsprings' rhythmic squeaking in the Spooners' guest room; to change a Palm Sunday reference to Thanksgiving; and to remove one offensive line—"Give it both knees." Billy and Little did not reach an understanding on several other points, however. With reference to the screenplay, Billy told UA executives after his meeting that he was not at all disposed to changing the line about the organ on page 61, the word *screw* on page 68, and his little joke about families "that pray together" on page 84 (the family in question being the madam and her whores at the Belly Button). Billy also refused to reshoot the sequence on page 116 when Dino gets on top of Polly, nor was he about to cover up Kim Novak's cleavage, for reasons he found obvious. Finally, Wilder reported, "The use of any other vegetable other than parsley would satisfy them because several female members of the committee felt there was something particularly suggestive in the use of parsley," but Billy was recalcitrant. His parsley was there to stay.

Monsignor Little raised a pertinent point: he asked UA to reconsider releasing *Kiss Me, Stupid* at Christmastime. Not only was it a central holiday in the Catholic calendar, Little observed, but there was a practical matter. As the monsignor told Billy and United Artists, the nation's Catholics would be taking their Legion of Decency pledges in church on Sunday, December 13. Even Monsignor Little saw this as a significant marketing problem as far as *Kiss Me, Stupid* was concerned. Had UA, the Mirisches, and Billy listened to the clergyman's advice, *Kiss Me, Stupid* might not have bombed.

"United Artists Reedits Wilder Pic Though MPAA Gave It Clean Bill," *Variety* reported in late October after *Kiss Me, Stupid* was sneaked in New York. The drastically diminished power of the Hollywood censoring agency was duly noted. As *Variety* pointed out, the MPAA (the Motion Picture Association of America, under whose aegis the Production Code was administered) also approved that season's new James Bond thriller, *Goldfinger*, even though it featured a character named Pussy Galore, a joke few English-speaking adults or children failed to get. By that point, *Variety* reported, Wilder had reshot the new sequence between Farr and Martin so that the sexual culmination was left to the audience's imagination, but as Harold Mirisch explained, the Legion demanded so many changes that they would have had to bring Kim Novak back for extensive reshooting, and she couldn't return, since she was in Britain filming *The Amorous Adventures of Moll Flanders*.

Kiss Me, Stupid remained under the editing knife, and by late November, *Variety* reported (under the headline "Billy Wilder in Grip of Reticence as His *Kiss Me, Stupid* Scrubbed") that the latest round of revisions "involved more than just a few cuts." It wasn't simply the fault of the Legion of Decency, *Variety* noted. By then, preview audiences had been reacting most "unfavorably to some of the bluer aspects of the Wilder film, both in Gotham and Hollywood." Billy himself was in New York for these previews earlier that week, but he declined *Variety*'s request for an interview.

The cast and crew's expectations ran as high as the preview audiences' responses ran low. "When you were on a set with that man, you knew why," says Walston. "It's difficult to this day for me to express, but you knew you were working for someone who had this aura about him. I was absolutely flabbergasted with his technique with the camera. And yet, on the other hand, there was a preview of the picture in Westwood, and I was surrounded by several agents from the William Morris office, and I was very down, and they said to me, 'Don't give up, don't be stupid, Wilder will take this thing into the cutting room, and he'll pull Wilder wonders.' And I said to them, 'Did you see the picture I just saw? Did you see the manner in which it was shot? He doesn't have any coverage.' He shot the picture in continuity—that was the way he shot everything. That's all he had. Once the picture bombed he had nowhere else to go."

As the ill-timed Christmas release of *Kiss Me, Stupid* approached, the story of sex, censorship, morality, and the cinema began to grow into a national affair. It wasn't being covered in the mainstream press yet, but every movie reviewer in the country had heard about it, and this exposure proved decisive. "Although it has a Code seal," *Variety* commented, "the gag going around UA in past weeks has been that in order for the pic to get by more strenuous censor groups like the Legion of Decency, *Stupid* would have to be cut into a fifteen-minute silent short." More serious discussions involved the removal of UA's corporate label from *Kiss Me, Stupid*. Arthur Krim and his team were in no mood to have their company's name sullied by a dark, dirty sex farce released at yuletide. The film would now be released under the imprimatur of Lopert Films, UA's art house subsidiary. This was not an insignificant shift, since Lopert had never handled a Wilder film before, nor a Mirisch film, though the company did have success with the Legion-condemned *Never on Sunday* (1960). *Kiss Me, Stupid*'s advertising campaign was rethought and toned down. References to Climax, Nevada, were eliminated from the ads.

The Legion then issued its rating: C—condemned. In a remarkable commentary accompanying the rating, the Legion set the tone for most of the nation's film critics by calling *Kiss Me, Stupid* "a thoroughly sordid piece of realism which is esthetically as well as morally repulsive. Crude and suggestive dialogue, a leering treatment of marital and extramarital sex, [and] prurient preoccupation with lechery compound the film's condonation of immorality." As *Variety* pointed out, this was "some of the sharpest criticism that the Roman Catholic reviewing organization has ever leveled at a major American film." *Variety* went on to note that the Legion was astonished "that a film that is 'so patently indecent and immoral' should receive a Production Code seal." Ironically, the Legion of Decency cited *The Apartment* as an example of effective social satire—the kind of film Hollywood *should* be making instead of filth like *Kiss Me, Stupid.*

Kiss Me, Stupid was no longer just a tasteless movie. It had become a symbol of everything that was wrong with American entertainment, a threat to American families, a moral blight and an embarrassment, and— worst of all—the harbinger of a sex-ridden future. In retrospect, the backlash seems only natural, given the film's holiday-season release. For the Legion, it was "a commercial decision bereft of respect for the Judeo-Christian sensibilities of the majority of the American people."

Ironically, the *Kiss Me, Stupid* furor erupted, as if on cue, immediately before a nine-week retrospective of Wilder's films opened at the nation's best-known bastion of contemporary highbrow taste—the Museum of Modern Art in New York. The museum's auditorium was categorically unlike a Loews, a Roxy, a Pantages, or a Grauman's (not to mention the Bijou in Butte). Despite MoMA's embrace and promotion of American mass culture, the Rockefeller-funded museum was the essence of upscale urban elitism. When the retrospective's curator, Richard Griffith, applauded Wilder for being "the most precise, indeed relentless chronicler of the postwar American scene, in shade as well as in light," he was subtly, unwittingly damning him in the eyes of mainstream moviegoers. Billy himself felt the need to set the record straight at the press conference announcing the retrospective: "I'm just a pop artist, not Rembrandt," he insisted. He added this choice observation: "I've been compared to Lubitsch and von Stroheim. Does that mean I specialize in cruel bedrooms?"

Billy was his usual voluble, phrase-making self at the press conference, but it was Audrey Wilder who got the day's biggest laugh. At one point she put up her hand and, when called upon, instructed her husband to talk louder. After that, the Wilders fled to Europe.

When they returned in early January, Billy saw for himself how the American press treated his movie. He reacted with paranoia. "Dear Geoff," he wrote to Shurlock. "I have just returned from Europe and have been briefed on the uproar the picture has caused. It is obvious that the Legionnaires have been lying in the bushes, biding their time until they could waylay some picture-maker of import and use him as a whipping boy for the entire industry. At this late date it would be both pointless and useless for me to stand up and defend myself against this vicious onslaught of bigotry. However, I am aware that I must have caused you considerable trouble, and for this I am genuinely sorry. Let me assure you that I am resolved never to put you on the spot again. Affectionately, Billy Wilder."

Shurlock responded: "My warm thanks for your kind and generous letter. Basically, I have no right to object to being put on the spot by any of my friends in the business, because after all this is, among other things, what I get paid for. But in your case, I was motivated primarily by my esteem and affection for you, over and above the normal call of duty. And I hope I can oblige again some day. Affectionately, Geoffrey Shurlock."

The critics, of course, had already attacked:

"Wilder, usually a director of considerable flair and inventiveness (if not always impeccable taste), has not been able this time to rise above a basically vulgar, as well as creatively delinquent, screenplay." "A jape that seems to have scraped its blue-black humor off the floor of a honky-tonk nightclub." "A painful, loud-mouthed, two-hour recitation of . . . the dirty jokes the boy down the street used to tell." One critic went so far as to wonder about Billy's mental health: "Is senility setting in or has he always been, beneath his satiric grin, not quite bright?"

Even with this onslaught of bad notices, *Kiss Me, Stupid* played well for a few weeks in America's biggest cities—Los Angeles, Chicago, New York—but died soon thereafter. The hinterlands were an insurmountable problem. For example, after Loews canceled its scheduled run in Columbus, Ohio, *Kiss Me, Stupid* was picked up by the RKO Grand, which promptly canceled it as well after a deluge of protests. Across the nation the film was officially boycotted by the Council of Catholic Women, United Church Women, and the Christian Family Movement. With all these boycotts, cancellations, bad press, and worse reviews, *Kiss Me, Stupid* hadn't a prayer.

Wilder remained bitter and defensive on the subject for years. He was unable to see why audiences rejected his dark-tempered farce-drama about the positive moral value of adultery. In his eyes, *Kiss Me, Stupid* is a quest for dignity in an ugly and humiliating world. And yes, the film does bear a certain moral message: only by fucking strangers may a husband and wife renew their love for each other. "I don't know why the film shocked people," Billy maintained. "It's the most bourgeois film there is. A man wants a career and the person who wants to help him wants to sleep with his wife. He replaces his wife with another, but when he is nearest to success, he refuses it and throws the guy out. . . . The public accepted it better in *The Apartment* because it was better conceived, better written, better lubricated."

The film fared much better in Europe. "British Critics Hail Billy Wilder's *Stupid* for its 'Cheery Bad Taste' " ran one *Variety* headline. The British in particular and Europeans in general tended to applaud the film, using it (in *Variety*'s opinion, at least) as a well-earned chance to make fun of hypocritical American sexual mores. As the *London Times* put it, "In a world all too obsessively infected with the cult of ghastly good taste, thank heavens for Mr. Billy Wilder."

The only American critic who praised *Kiss Me, Stupid* was Joan Didion. Her venue served as its own irony: the one magazine in the United States that applauded Billy's movie was *Vogue*. Didion loved Wilder's dark realism, she wrote in her "minority report": "*Kiss Me, Stupid* shows Wilder doing exactly what only he can do. It is a profoundly affecting picture, as witnessed by the number of people who walk out on it.

"They walk out, I suspect," Didion continued, "because they sense that Wilder means it. . . . The Wilder world is one seen at dawn through a hangover, a world of cheap double entendres and stale smoke and drinks in which the ice has melted: the true country of despair." Billy was sufficiently moved that he sent Didion a thank-you note: "I read your piece in the beauty parlor while sitting under the hair dryer, and it sure did the old pornographer's heart good. Cheers, Billy Wilder."

The failure of *Kiss Me, Stupid* had a profound impact on Wilder's sense of himself and his place in the world of American mass culture. He began work on the film envisioning himself as a brave pioneer ushering in a new era of frankness and honesty in regard to sex, and he ended it as a martyr— an out-of-touch martyr at that. Walter Reisch summed it up: "Billy was spoiled lately with success. He asked me not to see the picture. It is the one thing about which he has no sense of humor."

Wilder snarled about the aftermath of *Kiss Me, Stupid*: "When I was lying in the gutter, a number of people came along and administered a kick in the groin. But in that period of depression and self-doubt, there was an element of beauty. My office is a clearing house usually for my chums— maybe they have third-act troubles, maybe they have actor troubles, and I work with them. Well, they stayed away in droves. They don't even put the bite on me right now. It's like the Ford plant after the Edsel was made. And it's wonderful. I have some time for the first time."

It wasn't pleasant for Diamond, either. As Billy put it, "After the picture came out, I went to Europe and walked through the snow and got it out of my system and came back and sat down with my esteemed colleague,

I. A. L. Diamond. For twelve weeks we sat and stared at each other. He said we were like parents who have produced a two-headed child and don't dare to have intercourse." (One doubts whether "have intercourse" is the precise term Billy used.) Diamond himself remarked that "Nobody ever made a fast buck by telling people they're no damned good." "But we shall survive," Billy insisted. "We shall now come out with the Mustang and sweep the market."

There were no hard feelings as far as the Mirisch brothers were concerned. Five months after *Kiss Me, Stupid* opened and died they extended Billy's contract.

Wilder bought art to distract himself. In 1964 alone, he added to his collection Aristide Maillol's *Jeune Baigneuse debout,* a terra-cotta sculpture cast around 1914; Edouard Vuillard's *Femme coupant le pain;* Braque's *Nature morte sur un guéridon,* a watercolor over pencil on paper done in the mid-1920s; Miró's oil on canvas *L'Etoile,* painted in 1927; Klee's *Haus am Wasser,* a watercolor and pen and black ink on paper laid down by the artist on board in 1930; and Picasso's *Deux nus,* a colored wax crayons and pen and black ink over pencil on paper. The following year, he bought yet another Picasso—*Femme au bras gauche levé,* a crayons and pen and brown ink on board, drawn in Barcelona in 1902, in the same series as the ones Wilder bought in 1962.

He needed a big hit more than ever before, so he turned his attention in three directions—his cherished Sherlock Holmes, a comedy about insurance fraud, and a successful Broadway play starring Walter Matthau and Art Carney. As far as the third idea was concerned, he may have first read about it under the hair drier—the March 1965 issue of *Vogue* in which Joan Didion wrote about *Kiss Me, Stupid* featured a two-page fashion spread with a chicly dressed model cavorting Avedon-style with Carney, Matthau, and *The Odd Couple*'s director, Mike Nichols.

The play was enjoying a long run on Broadway, and there would be no film version until the play closed. But in the meantime, Matthau expressed great interest in appearing in the film, as did Jack Lemmon; both thought of teaming up with Billy as director, and Billy agreed. The story of two men who share a bond of animosity, *The Odd Couple* was perfect Wilder material, and it promised to be a huge moneymaker as well. Paramount owned the movie rights, and the combination of Lemmon and Matthau and Wilder seemed a surefire plan to all three. As Lemmon recalled, "Billy and Walter and I were going to be partners in this thing and split it three ways. But nobody had asked Mr. Paramount—[Charles] Bluhdorn. And they had not asked Neil Simon. First of all, Neil would hardly want anybody to start fucking around with his script. Billy, obviously, would want some changes. Number two: Mr. Bluhdorn personally hauls me into the studio and says, 'Why do I want Billy Wilder? Why should I *pay* Billy Wilder? I've got you and Walter and this great script—I don't *need* Billy Wilder.' That was it. And Billy just said to Walter and me while they were futzin' around, 'Look, you guys go to the dance without me.' " Which is exactly what they did.

27. FAKE

I didn't like the setup, I didn't like the characters involved—
especially me.
—Harry Hinkle (Jack Lemmon) in *The Fortune Cookie*

Before a fight, you know you can defend yourself. But I'm just going to get slugged, and there's nothing I can do." This is Billy Wilder speaking to a reporter right before a preview screening of his next film, *The Fortune Cookie* (1966). "If you're a producer, you make eighteen pictures a year. An actor makes three pictures a year. If Al Kaline strikes out, he gets up again two innings later. We get to bat once a year—and the suffering in the dugout is prolonged, believe me, when the people are booing. The thing one has to remember is, it's not going to be the greatest—not the greatest hit, not the greatest flop." Billy went on in this vein for a while and then cut himself short: "Look, it's just another picture. It'll be on the bottom half of a double bill soon."

Wilder turned to *The Fortune Cookie* after realizing that he had to postpone *Sherlock Holmes* indefinitely. In early 1965, Wilder had plans to film *Sherlock* that summer. *Variety* reported that Louis Jourdan was committed to a starring role, but no contracts had been signed yet for the roles of Holmes and Watson. Wilder still wanted Peter O'Toole as Holmes, and (incredibly) Peter Sellers was still being mentioned as Watson, at least in the press. But as 1965 rolled on, Wilder had to put the whole thing off. First it was pushed back to the fall, then to the following summer. The reason cited: Jack Lemmon was available for *The Fortune Cookie* immediately. A more likely explanation is the absence of both a Holmes and a Watson. Billy's *Sherlock* promised to be long, lush, and expensive, and it would have been foolhardy to proceed with preproduction work without the key performers in place.

The Fortune Cookie, an original story by Wilder and Diamond, concerns some of Billy's favorite subjects: avarice, self-contempt, a fallen woman, male bonding, and televised sports. By the mid-1960s, the Wilders' art-laden penthouse sported two televisions along with the Picassos, Klees, and Mirós, so that Billy could watch baseball and football games simultaneously during the crossover early-autumn season. He met with the owner of the Cleveland Browns in May to set up a crucial location shoot for *The Fortune Cookie*: he would film on the field during an actual Browns game in the fall.

In Billy and Iz's new comedy, an immorality tale, Lemmon would play Harry Hinkle, a cameraman for CBS Sports who gets accidentally tackled on the sidelines by a player during a Browns football game. His shyster-lawyer brother-in-law, Willie Gingrich (Walter Matthau), convinces him to feign injury and sue both CBS and the Browns for a million dollars. Given the history of American negligence litigation and damage awards, this sum probably doesn't register with quite the ridiculous force it did in 1966. Toward the end of the film, when Gingrich agrees to settle the case for $200,000, he chortles that it's "the biggest cash award ever made in a personal injury case in the state of Ohio." (That line alone is enough to get a laugh in the late 1990s.)

Billy once said that *The Fortune Cookie* is about greed, love, compassion, and human understanding, but not sex. This is not entirely true. For one thing, the film features one of the most repugnant chippies Wilder ever created. With *The Fortune Cookie*, Billy returns to the emotional and moral terrain of *Double Indemnity* and *Ace in the Hole*: when a man pulls a scam, the only person he despises more than himself is the rotten blonde who spurs him on. The difference is that *The Fortune Cookie* is a comedy. So instead of dying at the end, Wilder's protagonist ends the film by literally kicking the blonde in the ass, whereupon he proceeds to a football field and horses around with someone he can understand—another man.

Adding a bit of social tension to the comedy is the fact that the player who knocks him down is black. Luther "Boom Boom" Jackson would be played by a strapping newcomer, Ron Rich. The blonde was also a novice: *The Fortune Cookie* was Judi West's first film.

Like *Kiss Me, Stupid*, *The Fortune Cookie* was set up as a coproduction between United Artists, the Mirisches, Billy's Phalanx, and a star's own production company; this time it was Lemmon's Jalem. The budget hovered around $3.5 million; Phalanx advanced $450,000, and the terms of Billy's directing deal remained the same.

"Why are you doing this film?" Matthau asked Lemmon; "I have the best part." "Don't you think it's about time?" was Lemmon's response. Lemmon didn't mean that the two actors' roles were reversed. In fact, they'd never worked together before and hadn't even met until *The Fortune Cookie*. The idea of Jack Lemmon confined to a wheelchair and neckbrace, unable to fidget, is funny enough as it is, but in this film Billy's American Everyman would also be yielding to a surly, growling cutthroat with a decidedly Eastern European demeanor. (Matthau is the son of a Russian Orthodox priest who abandoned him as an infant, but as David Thomson observes, he "was brought up by the Daughters of Israel Day Nursery and must have absorbed timing with his Vitamin C.") Matthau was integral to *The Fortune Cookie* from the beginning. Matthau had done some movies, but his reputation rested on his theatrical success, most recently in *The Odd Couple*. As Diamond once explained, "before we put a word on paper we went to New York to see Mr. Matthau. We told him the story and got him committed to do it before we began to write. We thought he was ideal for the part of the shyster brother-in-law." As Wilder and Diamond describe Matthau's Willie Gingrich in their screenplay, "He is a tall, loose-jointed man of forty, with a brain full of razor blades and a heart full of chutzpah." This was not an original turn of phrase; it's what William Holden once said about Billy.

For Wilder, the personal cost of shooting a major-league sports film was that he was forced once again to film on location. He could fake the Paris Opéra and the markets of Les Halles, but since he wanted to use eighty-five thousand cheering football fans as a backdrop for the accident sequence, he was compelled to leave the soundstage. Filming began on Sunday, October 31, in Cleveland. The script called for a "gloomy, bone-chilling" day, and the writer-director couldn't have gotten a better one with all the special effects Hollywood had to offer. The world champion NFL Browns were playing the Minnesota Vikings before a packed Municipal Stadium. Three cameras were stationed around the arena. Wilder the sports fan and Wilder the director were each delighted by a spectacular punt return by the Browns' LeRoy Kelly in the third period. Kelly, in his number 44 uniform, took the ball on his own thirty-two-yard line and ran it all the way back to the Vikings' twenty-four. The crowd went wild. It was precisely the play Wilder needed. Boom Boom was now number 44.

Cleveland ended up losing; the fans turned so mean in the fourth quarter that they booed quarterback Frank Ryan off the field. There was a party/press conference later that day, and Billy chose the moment to say that "after my last picture I know how Modell feels. But he shouldn't worry. There'll be further disasters." The prediction proved correct.

If there were any catastrophes during the rest of the location shooting on *The Fortune Cookie*, however, they went unreported. LeRoy Kelly's triumphant rush was meticulously re-created and falsified the following day, with Browns halfback Ernie Green substituting as number 44. (At close range Kelly was simply too small to fake being Boom Boom.) This time, however, number 44 ran an extra 20 yards before being shoved out of bounds, at which point two stuntmen took over—one for number 44, one for the cameraman who gets creamed in the play. A few action shots were filmed, after which coach Wilder pulled the stuntmen out of the game and sent Lemmon and Rich in their places to film the conclusion of the sequence.

The following day, Ernie Green returned to the field, but the rest of the Cleveland Browns were off playing a real practice game, so the freshman team from nearby Kent State University took their place. They were joined by Lemmon, Rich, and about ten thousand extras who had been lured to the stadium with promises of over 5,600 prizes—televisions, transistor radios, a free trip to Hollywood, a 1966 Ford Mustang. . . . Suspiciously, the film's press kit claimed that the winner of the car was none other than Audrey Wilder. In any event, Billy was out-DeMilleing DeMille; it was reportedly the largest extras call in film history. Shots were set up and filmed; prizes were awarded; more shots were taken; Green ran; more prizes; ten thousand people were ordered to stand up and cheer, and they complied; Lemmon was hoisted out on a stretcher; the day was a success.

With the location footage in the can, Billy and his cast and crew returned to the relatively predictable safety of the Goldwyn Studios, where the rest of *The Fortune Cookie* was filmed on schedule—at first. Lemmon spent all but one day of the rest of the shoot in either a wheelchair or a hospital bed. Matthau ended up spending time in a hospital bed, too—the result of a heart attack he suffered with only ten days of shooting left. Replacing him the way Walston replaced Sellers was out of the question. The production of *The Fortune Cookie* had to shut down for three months while Matthau recovered.

The Fortune Cookie was sneaked at a Westwood theater in June 1966, with Wilder, Diamond, Lemmon, and Rich in attendance. Art Modell showed up, too; the Wilders had dinner with him beforehand. The first big laugh of the evening occurred when old lady Gingrich turns to a nun and says, "Thank you, sister," and Willie replies, "Shut up, mother." Billy thought the preview went pretty well, though a reporter found the crowd's reaction to be "spotty." All Billy planned to do with the film was to cut three minutes of baggage and revise the scoring at the end, changing the original waltz to a more playful tune for the sequence in which Harry Hinkle and Boom Boom play football under the lights of an empty stadium. Jack Lemmon, however, was troubled: "I thought it was a bomb—almost as bad as I thought *Irma La Douce* was at its preview. I thought it died every time Matthau was off-screen."

Wilder brought *The Fortune Cookie* in at $3,705,000. Domestically, the film grossed about $5 million, with an added $1.8 million coming in from abroad. This was not a bomb, but it was scarcely a vast success on the order Wilder craved. He blamed the schizophrenic zeitgeist: "I have been criticized for happy endings. The easiest ending is the unhappy ending—that you can write any time. It's become sort of a bromide now that they don't live happily ever after. . . . The question is whether you have a right to get people into the theater and they expect a cocktail and they get a shot of acid. People don't want to hear that they stink." (Having built his career on the fact that they did, Billy was now forced by his own recent disappointments to reassess the matter.) He added an observation so firmly grounded in the 1960s that it seems laughable today: "It's not like the theater," he said, comparing the high cost of Broadway with low-priced movie tickets. "For $7.70 you can give a message. For $1.25—no message."

But there *was* a message in *The Fortune Cookie*. As the film historian William Paul points out, this is a film concerned with image making. Its lead character is a cameraman, the opening sequence traces how television transforms real actions into broadcast images, and a good deal of the film deals with the way camera lenses transform private lives into public property. The film is divided into sixteen segments, each with its own title card, each a shot of acid: "1. The Accident"; "2. The Brother-in-Law"; "3. The Caper", "5. The Chinese Lunch". . . . Nobody is immune from modern decay. "The Caper" opens with a nun behind the desk at the hospital tiptoeing over to Boom Boom and saying in a whisper, "Can I ask you something? What do you think our chances are against the Philadelphia Eagles? Because Sister Veronica wants *thirteen points*."

Harry stretches in his hospital bed and starts to swing his legs out toward the side. Willie cuts him off. "Hate to break it to you, kid, but you got a spinal injury," he announces. "*What?*" "Your left leg is numb and you got no feeling in the first three fingers of your left hand." "You're crazy. I can move my hand *and* my leg." "Sure you can, if you want to blow a million bucks."

Willie Gingrich is amusingly contemptible; Sandy is inexcusable. When Wilder introduces her on the telephone to Harry, he has her dressed up in a tawdry feather-boa'ed negligee. Behind her lies a naked man in a disheveled bed. "And *stupid*," Harry goes on later to Willie. "Never read a book in her life." He corrects himself. "Uh, she read *one* book—*The Carpetbaggers*. End of six months she was on page nineteen. We had no life together. No dialogue, no laughs. . . ." When Harry and Willie go at each other in the scene in which Harry rips his back brace off, Willie snarls that Harry has no "guts," but Harry turns not on Willie but on Sandy, bitterly calling her "that cold-blooded little tramp." Then the phone rings. It's Sandy.

Harry climbs back into his wheelchair and reaches up for the receiver like a baby begging for its bottle. "Guess what?" Harry asks after hanging up. "Tinkerbell is coming back?" Willie asks in a particularly mean and sarcastic tone.

Wilder shows little mercy to Sandy, but he sympathizes thoroughly with Willie Gingrich. Note the craven twinkle in Walter Matthau's eyes when a nun arrives bearing a floral arrangement and asks if there is anything she can do; "Pray for him, sister," says Gingrich, dripping with phony concern. Unlike Sandy's, Willie's mendacity is something Wilder respects. Later, when Harry wheels himself speedily out the door, down the hall, and into the elevator, he crosses directly in front of the same elderly nun. "Doesn't it do your heart good?" she says. "I have a hunch he'll be up and around in no time!" "Heh heh," Willie chuckles, laying it on the line: "Look, sister, I asked ya to pray for him, but we don't want any miracles."

Then there is Boom Boom. In 1966 Stokely Carmichael terrified white America with his militant call for black power. But Wilder, intent on making a film about black victimization, chose the unknown Rich, who went on to appear in only one more film before changing careers. Wilder seems to have gone out of his way to cast the part of Boom Boom as innocuously as possible. Either he purposely created a cipher into whom audiences could pour their thoughts about black men, or else he simply couldn't deal with a magnetic black costar competing for attention with Lemmon and Matthau. Wilder did have other casting options, after all; Sidney Poitier was not the only black actor in Hollywood. In 1966, the muscular, eminently watchable Jim Brown had already costarred in his first film while continuing his professional football career. He played for Cleveland. (The team's star player, he was excused from having to show up to film *The Fortune Cookie*.)

Boom Boom's blandness gives way a bit when he turns to drink, but by that point he's already been emasculated by his own guilt. Two detectives, meanwhile, have staked out Harry's place from an apartment across the street. They spy directly in the window, thanks to a camera with a telephoto lens, and they've bugged the apartment for sound as well. The lead detective, Purkey (Cliff Osmond in a Hitler mustache), lies on the bed while his assistant peers through the viewfinder. He's bored, and not a little disgusted: "That colored guy has to dress him, shave him, feed him, put him to bed, *carry him to the toilet*, brush his teeth. . . . If that's an act then I'm Soupy Sales." His contempt applies to *both* performances; Boom Boom is no stronger than Lemmon. He's literally Lemmon's nursemaid. The detective is right: it's not very pretty to watch.

Wilder plays on contemporary racial issues without fully addressing any of them. The film's climax occurs when Purkey, the detective, starts making remarks about how "our black brothers—they've been getting a little out of hand lately." "Look, I'm all for equal," he says, echoing many barroom and country club conversations of the time. "What gets me is, I'm driving an old Chevy. And when I see a coon ridin' around in a white Cadillac . . ." Harry jumps out of his wheelchair and slugs him. His anger is all too easy—and all too white. Boom Boom himself never gets the chance to express anything more than guilt and, in the final moments of the film, forgiveness.

At its best, *The Fortune Cookie* is about how rotten it feels to be a fake. Wilder is dead right—it feels rotten, and it looks rotten, too. Wilder was less accurate in another respect: audiences enjoyed feeling rotten, but only to a point. Commercially, Wilder reached that level with *Irma la Douce*. By attempting to outdo himself with his own acidity, the two films that followed were difficult for most moviegoers to watch. There is little enobling about *The Fortune Cookie*. The emotions it chronicles most effectively range from maudlin or sour sentimentality to thudding embarrassment and grandiose self-abasement. It is purely pathetic to see Harry Hinkle spinning around his dingy apartment in an electric wheelchair anticipating the return of a woman who doesn't love him. Harry even does a little dance every time he moves. How elegant the gesture might be—if it weren't insurance fraud in the service of lovelessness.

Things go over the edge when Harry kicks Sandy. Wilder films the moment in its own separate shot, with Sandy, on her hands and knees looking for her missing contact lens, her body stretched out rump-up across the Panavision screen. Harry's foot comes in from the left and knocks her smack to the floor.

Wilder and Diamond explain the film's title (however obliquely) in the fifth segment of *The Fortune Cookie*, "The Chinese Lunch." Harry is watching a tiny television suspended from the ceiling of his hospital room. Willie enters, glances at the screen, and asks Harry what's on. "An old movie about Abraham Lincoln," Harry answers. Willie's response is terse: "Lincoln. Great president. Lousy lawyer." Willie's charlatan "doctor" arrives, wheeling in a cart full of platters—it's the Chinese food Willie has ordered for lunch. There's a quick track forward as the doctor pulls the domed metal lid off a Chinese soup dish to reveal a plateful of drugs. "This is Doc Schindler from Chicago," Willie explains. Harry is concerned: "You'll be careful, Doc?" "I better be," Schindler says in a singsong voice of experience, "because I'm on parole." (They caught him doping a horse.)

What happens next is very peculiar. Schindler, wielding a hypo, dives headfirst under the covers around Harry's crotch. "I'm looking for a freckle," he explains. Cut to Willie snapping his fingers in raw impatience, with Harry, offscreen, handling the punchline. (*"Ow."*) A hatchet-faced nurse arrives at Harry's bedside. She gasps in shock and horror as Schindler comes up for air. "He's, uh . . . ," says Harry, mortified. Willie steps in quickly and covers for everyone: "We lost a shrimp somewhere," he explains.

Willie slams the cover back on the Chinese soup dish and tries to end the matter, but he doesn't succeed. Harry says to the nurse, "I don't want that, would you take it away? Take *everything* away." "Are you sure?" she says with too much sympathy. "*You* eat it," he snaps. "Don't you even want the fortune cookie? *Come on*," she says, waving it right in his face. "You've *got* to open your fortune cookie." This seems more a taunt than an invitation. Harry cracks it open one-handed, reads it intently, then collapses against his pillow with a defeated expression on his face. "What does it say?" Harry quotes the fortune: " 'You can fool all of the people some of the time and some of the people all the time. . . .' "

The Fortune Cookie is about fakery and shame; putting one over—or better, *trying* to put one over—is a central theme of Wilder's career. But what is the nature of the pretense here? The overt subject is insurance fraud, but that's only part of the deception. For Wilder and Diamond, a fake spinal injury isn't funny enough on its own, so for comic discomfort they add a gag about sex and humiliation. Dr. Schindler appears as though he has just finished giving Harry a blow job; Willie's reference to a lost shrimp only deepens Harry's shame.

Immediately following the opening of Harry's disturbing cookie, Wilder cuts to a hospital room. Accompanied by the tense scream of a theremin, the camera cranes down as we reenter the terrain of Bellevue's drunk tank, except that now, instead of Don Birnam, it's Harry Hinkle under examination. And instead of nurse Bim, we find a group of doctors discussing nerve trauma and Hinkle's paralysis. The doctor in the background has his back to the camera. "And what is *your* learned opinion, Professor Winterhalter?" The camera tracks quickly forward as he turns around. It's Sig Ruman: "I have not formulated an opinion yet," says the familiar, thickly German-accented voice, "but I have formulated a hunch." "Oh?" says Hinkle. "*Fake*," says Winterhalter.

Ruman/Winterhalter takes his dark monocle off and announces with a tone of abject contempt: "All these newfangled machines. Fake! They prove nothing. In the old days ve used to do these things better! A man says he's paralyzed, ve simply threw him in the snake pit. If he climbs out then ve know he's lying." Wilder cuts to another doctor, who says in dawning horror, "And if he doesn't climb out?" Cut back to Winterhalter, the theremin still shrieking: "Then ve haff lost the patient. But ve haff found an honest man."

Hinkle replies: "Wait a minute you guys, you're not throwin' *me* into any pit. And you bring just one snake in here—just one little snake! . . ." He leans up on his examination table, looks directly into the camera, and screams.

The sixteenth and last chapter of *The Fortune Cookie* is called "The Final Score," and in a manner of speaking Harry ultimately does—with Boom Boom. Having punted his chippy ex-wife to the floor, Harry turns to the man he snookered and victimized for companionable forgiveness on a deserted football field, a kind of comic relief in male-bonded isolation. One might call Wilder's buddy-buddyism homoerotic—many critics do— but it's devoid of eros. Osgood Fielding's gaping mouth in *Some Like It Hot* is far more carnal than anything in the final scene of *The Fortune Cookie*.

For Wilder, Harry's erotic if pathetic attraction to the repulsive Sandy is as natural as his aching need for chaste absolution from Boom Boom. The sexlessness of these men's relationship is crucial; it's more antierotic than homoerotic. Wilder ends the film expressively with an extreme long shot—two tiny figures, set apart even from each other, engulfed in the vast emptiness of a floodlit stadium. This is not quite the evasion it seems. After all, Wilder is scarcely afraid of expressing homosexuality. Alone among directors of his stature, he gives voice to it methodically in his body of work, though it often seems designed more to rub Americans' faces in a topic he knew would shock them as to express his own inevitably private interior life. Unwaveringly heterosexual in fact, Wilder is far more eclectic in his art, in large measure because he knows a little polymorphous perversity will appall and titillate the middle-American audience he never stopped viewing as insufferably hung up. In a way, when Schindler emerges from the vicinity of Hinkle's penis, the look of horror on the nurse's face stands as an emblematic tableau of Wilder's rude goal with moviegoers. It's so much the case that Wilder replays the gag in *Avanti!* with a planeload of passengers aghast at the sight of two men emerging together from a cramped airplane bathroom.

It was in the context of *The Fortune Cookie* that the critic George Morris declared that Wilder simply couldn't face the homosexual implications of his work. (For Morris, "the virulent treatment of Judi West's Sandy reinforces this feeling," as though the love of men and the hatred of women went necessarily hand in hand.) But how could Wilder not have faced them? He wrote them. Still, Wilder's self-awareness is circumscribed. In his films, homosexuality tends to surface through and around symbology: Neff's matches and Keyes's cigar; Mrs. Minosa's guilt-inducing votive candles; Harry Hinkle's ridiculous lost shrimp and the threat of snakes.

What Leslie Fiedler wrote in 1948 in regard to the *Adventures of Huckleberry Finn* holds true for *The Fortune Cookie*, particularly since it represents the sole treatment of race in Wilder's career:

> The existence of overt homosexuality threatens to compromise an essential aspect of American sentimental life: the camaraderie of the locker room and ball park. . . . From what other source could arise that unexpected air of good clean fun which overhangs such sessions? It is this self-congratulatory buddy-buddiness, its astonishing naivete that breed at once endless opportunities for inversion and the terrible reluctance to admit its existence, to surrender the last believed-in stronghold of love without passion.

For Wilder, "good clean fun" is impossible, of course, since nobody is ever clean, least of all his protagonists. But the football toss at the end of *The Fortune Cookie* restores precisely the kind of passionless love that Wilder appears to need, if for no other reason than to countermand Sandy's despicable allure. If Fiedler's theory holds, Wilder's adoptive Americanism reaches its apotheosis in "The Final Score," as Harry and Boom Boom join a line of sexless, boyishly miscegenating couples that stretches back to Ishmael and Queequeg, Natty Bumppo and Chingachgook, and of course Huck and Jim: "Behind the white American's nightmare that someday, no longer tourist, inheritor, or liberator, he will be rejected, refused, he dreams of his acceptance at the breast he has most utterly offended. It is a dream so sentimental, so outrageous, so desperate, that it redeems our concept of boyhood from nostalgia to tragedy."

But the tragedy of *The Fortune Cookie* is compromised. This is the urban 1960s, not the romantic, woodsy or seaborne nineteenth century. Imagine Boom Boom responding to his dramatic ill use at the hands of his scheming white friend by embracing Stokely Carmichael's justifiable rage and you see how essentially fraudulent his and Harry's tragic romance becomes in *The Fortune Cookie*. As for Wilder himself, he scarcely got the nagging issue of male bonding out of his system. He returned to it in his very next film, and he did so much more overtly.

The Fortune Cookie fared well enough with the critics, with one consistent theme: a phony spinal injury in a neck brace, a shyster lawyer, a weeping and hysterical mother, a tacky blonde in big hair and a fur, a bet-laying nun, and the only decent human being is a black man, and the reviewers, all white, found him unbelievable. Vincent Canby, having taken over from Bosley Crowther at the *New York Times*, called Wilder "an unregenerate moralist," his film "a fine, dark, gag-filled hallucination peopled by dropouts from the Great Society." Pauline Kael admiringly found the film to be "very funny and very cruel," though she believed that Wilder took "repellent advantage" of Boom Boom's race. In a keener observation, Kael (sounding suspiciously auteurist) observed that "Mr. Wilder has a low opinion of mankind; when he scourges us, I suspect that it is not so much because he hopes to improve us as because he wishes to keep his own despair at bay." (Strangely, Kael changed her mind completely on *The Fortune Cookie* in the years to come. By the early 1980s she was calling it "a sour, visually ugly comedy . . . which gets worse as it goes along." As for the ending, Kael noted, "only Leslie Fiedler could care.")

Wilder himself is terse on the subject of *The Fortune Cookie*: "The film didn't impress the critics and didn't make money and it disappeared in the big garbage pit along with a year of my life." *The Fortune Cookie* was not a total loss, however: "But it was very amusing to make. We didn't lie, we said what we had to say, we didn't compromise to make it commercially viable. But it's forgotten."

Despite the commercial disappointment of his latest effort—and despite his own remarks about being cut off and shut out by his "old pals"— Billy Wilder was still one of the kings of Beverly Hills. Few directors could claim Billy's lifetime batting average, both artistically and commercially, and nobody was better suited to serve as an evening's entertainment in Hollywood. The Wilders were still at the top of the social ladder—among the highest-ranking members of an already elite group. He and Audrey were said to have "invented" The Bistro, then the most fashionable restaurant in Beverly Hills. "My pal Romanoff, you know, he closed," Billy said. "And I wanted there to be a restaurant I would go to."

Kurt Niklas, the former captain at Romanoff's who became the manager and principal stockholder in The Bistro, observed that "when you're a captain everybody tells you, 'If you ever want to open your own restaurant, come and see me.' It's all baloney. It never happens. Billy was the only one I knew would be as good as his word. So when Romanoff's closed, I went to him. Within twenty-four hours Billy had checks in the mail for $90,000." Audrey helped, too: "We have sixty stockholders," Niklas explained, "and the people Billy didn't get, his wife got." Originally, Wilder envisioned a rustic, casual sort of place with checkered tablecloths and sawdust on the floor. Audrey's tastes prevailed, aided by Alex Trauner's: The Bistro ended up with red carpeting, elegant dark paneling, some of the set pieces from *Irma la Douce*, and a lot of mirrors on the walls so that diners could spy on other tables. Billy was nonplussed. Recycling an old gag from *Sunset Boulevard*, he said that "the background starts out to be a flower shop and winds up as a PT boat."

Art and cards continued to be Billy's passions. A bridge game met every Saturday—and Sunday. Alfred Sheinwold, the professional bridge player and nationally syndicated columnist, was a recurrent guest. "Billy is a regular winner in that game, and not because he's a great technician," said Scheinwold in 1966. "He can't be bothered with that. He's a *good* technician, but more than anybody else, he plays the people. Bridge players use an expression, 'He always knows where the queen of spades is.' The expert may try all sorts of discovery plays to find that out. Billy just looks at the people and knows." MCA's Lew Wasserman was cajoled into joining one of these weekend matches, despite his demurral on the grounds of being out of practice. Billy was only too happy to teach him how to play again: "You know, for a fellow who hasn't played for a year, he certainly played badly."

Wilder mastered the game of chess as well, but it had one insurmountable problem: it took too long.

André Previn recounts a typical day at Billy's penthouse: "Once we arrived in his living room, he went to a closet and brought out his new Schiele watercolor. It was one of the master's more luridly explicit efforts: an emaciated young woman, green-tinged flesh, sunken cheeks, hopeless eyes, naked, and about to engage in what used to be called self-abuse. Billy contemplated the picture with total concentration. 'Isn't it great?' he said. At this moment, his wife Audrey came in the front door. Audrey is chic and dear and extremely funny. As she passed us, she gave a quick glance of horrified appraisal. 'Good God, Billy,' she said. 'Just once—buy a landscape!' " One gets the sense that the couple played this gag routinely for any new audience that came along.

Billy Wilder at sixty bore a great resemblance to Billy Wilder at twenty. As his old friend Walter Reisch observed in the mid-1960s, "Speed is absolutely of the essence to him. He cannot do anything slowly. If he enters a party, and everybody is talking slowly, he leaves. People who insist on finishing their sentences drive him crazy—he wants to write it himself. That's why he likes paintings—they don't talk back." Wealth, fame, and thirty-seven years of filmmaking hadn't quenched his impatience. "That's his only fear in life—to be bored," Reisch went on. "He cannot stand to be with people who bore him. Which doesn't mean he doesn't like them or respect them. He just doesn't mingle with them. He loves them and he avoids them." Reisch continued: "He has never gone 'Hollywood.' He makes everybody in his pictures feel important. Of course, he's also cruelly rude."

Being Billy Wilder, he needed something new to sink his teeth into— films to make, art to buy. In 1966 alone, while mulling over whether or not to make one or the other of two musicals as well as the Sherlock Holmes film, Billy bought a Klimt, three Roys, a Dufy, a Cornell, a Rivers, a Moore, and two Steinbergs, and in the fall he supervised an important exhibition of his collection at the University of California Santa Barbara. "You don't have paintings," one dealer told Billy; "You have hors d'oeuvres." The Santa Barbara exhibition was an especially rich array, featuring many of the best works in the collection: seven Picassos, four Klees, four Moores, five Steinbergs; a couple of Schieles and a Klimt; two Calders, three Braques, one Cornell, two Renoirs, one Giacometti, and sixty other works ranging from an anonymous French eighteenth-century eyeball and a wooden Bazangi mask to a 1962 Larry Rivers collage. He'd also begun collecting bonsai trees for his penthouse terrace and, of course, more fine, often custom-made clothes for his overstuffed closets and bureau drawers. He was still in the market for stories.

On Billy's behalf, Paul Kohner continued on the trail of Franz Lehár's *The Count of Luxembourg*; this, of course, was the project Billy had been talking about since January 1945, when he and Charlie Brackett told Louella Parsons that Danny Kaye would be starring in their own adaptation. Twenty-one years later, at the end of January 1966, Billy met with UA and the Mirisches in Beverly Hills after Wilder officially submitted a proposal. The film would cost $7.5 to $8 million, Billy estimated, and he'd like to see Brigitte Bardot in the lead opposite Rex Harrison, Cary Grant, or (Billy's first choice) Walter Matthau.

The Mirisches and UA seemed lukewarm at best, so Wilder agreed to proceed on a step-by-step basis, with United Artists reserving the right to turn the project down after seeing the screenplay (which was, needless to say, not written yet). Wilder also wanted the right to take *The Count of Luxembourg* elsewhere, should it go into turnaround at UA. If the Mirisches and UA didn't want to proceed, Billy added, he would be willing to do something else for them. This seems to have been the cue for Harold Mirisch to propose an idea that he, his brothers, and United Artists had already floated: *My Sister and I*, revived from the Hepburn-Holden proposal of the mid-1950s. Julie Andrews would assume the lead.

No problem. If the Mirisches and United Artists wanted a Julie Andrews picture he would certainly be able to give them one, Billy said, and departed.

Within moments of Billy leaving the room, the assembled executives put a quick end to *The Count of Luxembourg*. Moreover, the partners did not want to give Wilder the right to take it elsewhere if they did not proceed with it themselves. Harold Mirisch was given the task of informing Billy of their decision; he was also told to say that everyone preferred that Wilder go to work on the Julie Andrews picture. As for *Sherlock Holmes*, as far as the Mirisches were concerned Billy was off the project as director. It is most unclear whether Wilder was aware of this decision, though, since the discussion occurred only after Billy left the meeting. By this point, Wilder had presented the brothers with an idea for a Holmes picture, but the Mirisches were busily looking for the right director for the project. In their view, Billy was not the man to do it; the name on everyone's lips was Bryan Forbes. The Mirisches were attempting to strike a deal with Forbes whereby he would write an outline of his concept of the story based on Billy's original idea. If Forbes wasn't interested, the Mirisches told UA, they already had a back-up in mind: John Schlesinger.

Two years earlier, Billy Wilder had been full of enthusiasm about the new direction movies were taking. "Pictures will be better and better," Billy announced, "with more skill and fewer bromides. Anyone who says the movies of the past were great is out of his tiny mind." With a new film for Mary Poppins on the drawing board, perhaps he wasn't so sure anymore.

28. HEARTBREAK

I've often been accused of being cold and unemotional. I admit it. And yet, in my own cold, unemotional way, I'm very fond of you, Watson.

—Sherlock (Robert Stephens)
in *The Private Life of Sherlock Holmes*

Two of Billy Wilder's oldest friends died in 1967 while the sixty-one-year-old Billy was writing the second of the two most personal films of his life. During that year he lost Doane Harrison, his trusted editorial advisor, and Franz Waxman, who had been his chum as long ago as Berlin and Paris. Waxman's death was a personal blow; Harrison's was both personal and professional. Mild-mannered to the point of almost complete self-effacement, Harrison had been by Billy's side for all of his films since *The Major and the Minor*. The depth of Wilder's affection for Harrison is evident not so much in the fact that Billy eventually cut Harrison in on the profits, but in his response to Harrison's gratitude: "It's not because you have talent but because I'm used to you." Now Billy was on his own.

A third friend, one from whom he had been long estranged, suffered a debilitating stroke that year. At the age of seventy-four, Charlie Brackett was still suffering from the sting of Billy's rejection. He reminisced sadly with Garson Kanin about Billy, the films they wrote together, and the way their friendship had once mattered. Charlie mentioned *Ace in the Hole*, the first picture Wilder wrote and directed after they separated: "Billy used to say he thought it failed because it was too tough. I don't think he's right about that. Tough is all right. I admire toughness. I don't admire hardness. That picture wasn't tough. It was hard. But then, Billy's hard, isn't he?" Brackett died two years later—in March 1969, just before *The Private Life of Sherlock Holmes* went into production. Billy may not have been quite so hard anymore. Rather than further embittering him, the loss of friends to illness, anger, time, and ambition served, finally, to soften him—a little.

He continued to talk hard, however, and he always would. Emphatic declarations kept coming, fast and furious. Reporters all over the world knew he was ceaselessly good for a quote, and lucky for them, Billy remained untroubled by contradictions that arose between one announcement and another. "A movie is a star vehicle," Billy insisted in 1966. "What good is it to have a magnificent dramatic concept for which you must have Laurence Olivier and Audrey Hepburn if they're not available?" Thus, he explained, he and Diamond only wrote scripts with specific actors already signed up. Wilder reversed gears completely two years later, and he did so in a most flamboyant way. He was speaking to a British reporter about his upcoming Sherlock Holmes film. "The star thing is changing," he announced while on a location-scouting trip to England. He offered an example: "There was nobody of importance in *Bonnie and Clyde*."

Like the film itself, the saga of *The Private Life of Sherlock Holmes* is long, convoluted, and melancholy. Wilder briefly attempted a collaboration with Alan Jay Lerner, Frederick Loewe, and Moss Hart (the trio behind *My Fair Lady*) but nothing came of it. By 1964, Rex Harrison was out and O'Toole and Sellers were in, but then came the *Kiss Me, Stupid* imbroglio, and Sellers, too, was history. O'Toole was still Sherlock by the time *Kiss Me, Stupid* opened in London, but by 1967, when the film still hadn't come together, all the roles were once again wide open, and Wilder had to start casting from scratch. In addition to a Sherlock and a Watson, Billy needed a Mycroft Holmes and a mysterious and sexy French-speaking woman for his long-planned, pricey film. In March, Paul Kohner mentioned three film projects to Jeanne Moreau, one of which was Billy's; she replied that Wilder's idea was the one she was most interested in pursuing. Wilder was apparently not interested in pursuing Moreau in return.

Wilder and Diamond spent much of that year laying out what was still the first draft of *Sherlock Holmes*, though they'd been working on ideas for quite some time. Then, for the first time in their collaboration, Billy brought in a third collaborator. Billy and Iz had been kicking *Holmes* scenes around for ten years—almost their entire relationship—and it still wasn't what Billy envisioned. So Diamond went off to write *Cactus Flower* (1969) for Walter Matthau, Ingrid Bergman, and Goldie Hawn (as well as doing some uncredited rewrite work on *Sweet Charity*, also 1969). The man Billy selected to replace him had experience writing and shouting with Billy—Harry Kurnitz, whose appeal was that he loved British culture and was an accomplished crafter of detective stories; he was, of course, the already-broken-in cowriter of *Witness for the Prosecution*.

On January 10, 1968, Billy arrived in London, checked into the Connaught Hotel, and began looking for actors for *Holmes*, which he hoped to start filming that summer. Kohner did some of the legwork long-distance from Beverly Hills by sending advance word of Wilder's arrival to various British talent agents. "He is not looking necessarily for name actors but wants an excellent cast, even if the names are lesser known," Kohner told one.

Wilder was still at the Connaught in late February. "What I plan is a serious study of Holmes," he told the British press—"something in depth." Wilder had been fascinated with Sherlock, he said, ever since he was a boy. "After all, he was a most riveting character—a dope addict and a misogynist. Yet in all the movies made about him nobody has ever explained why." This would be Sherlock's 128th feature film appearance, and Billy planned to change his image—to fill in the blanks and reveal the private life of a public man. "He'll still be tall, ascetic, and cerebral, of course, but he'll be real." There was one aspect of Billy's Holmes that remained as yet unspoken to the British press. Billy's Sherlock Holmes was going to be homosexual.

Wilder expanded on his personal attraction to Sherlock:

I was interested by this bachelor misogynist—the way his brain worked. "The best of the century," as Watson said of his very dear friend. Was he just a thinking machine? An extraordinary eye with great intuition? With a great combination of talents? Or was there something in his life which wounded him, which gave him emotions? Did he hate women? Why did he take drugs? (You know that he took cocaine.) I had to explore all that as well as his marvelous relationship with Watson, a petit-bourgeois doctor retired from the Army. It's a situation like *The Odd Couple*, only with a Victorian backdrop—two bachelors living together. We made it funny and romantic. It's not a Freudian analysis.

It was 1968, the counterculture was in full swing, and Wilder, having swept past middle age, found himself careening toward an elder-statesmanship he never wanted. He was sixty-two. Given the box office performance of his last two films, he was feeling more intensely than ever the pressure of remaining contemporary and commercial. He had to find a way to stay on top of the rapidly changing culture without giving up his own style—a style he had honed for nearly forty years. As he said at the time, he was "neither *nouvelle vague* nor *ancienne vague* but *moyenne vague*"—an awkward position for an aging firebrand. "Some of these young guys coming up are goddamn good—and using brand-new styles.

What is one to do?" he went on. "When you're a painter of a certain school and you see the gallery across the way selling pop and doing well while your stuff is gathering dust, the worst thing you can do is change your style. One must try to keep up with the times, but in one's own style." In Billy's mind, the time couldn't have been more fit for an in-depth portrait of his own fictional hero—a brilliant, maladjusted, misogynistic gay drug addict.

Billy shuttled back to Hollywood but returned to England in mid-April. By the end of April he had his Sherlock. Robert Stephens, a key member of Olivier's National Theatre Company, had played several major, demanding, and diverse roles there—Horatio in *Hamlet*, the Incan god-king Atahualpa in Peter Shaffer's highly regarded *Royal Hunt of the Sun*, and Benedick in *Much Ado About Nothing*. Beatrice was played in that production by the incomparable Maggie Smith, whom Stephens had just married. When he signed onto *Sherlock Holmes*, Stephens was about to appear with Smith (albeit in a supporting role) in *The Prime of Miss Jean Brodie* (1969), after which he would be free to appear in Billy's film. "I'm one of Billy Wilder's greatest admirers," said Stephens at the time. "So is my wife. So is my dresser."

Billy had never seen Stephens perform onstage or on film before. He had barely set eyes on Stephens at all: "I'd never seen Stephens except for twenty minutes in the bar of the Connaught Hotel. But I thought, 'What's good enough for Larry Olivier is good enough for me.'" As Stephens recalled, "We had one drink. I didn't read anything or do an audition. We chatted, and I left. I had lunch with a playwright friend, and when I got home there was a message to ring my agent. Billy Wilder wanted me to play Sherlock Holmes. I was more elated than I had ever been in my life." Wilder told Stephens he didn't want the film to be good or even very good but perfect. According to Stephens, "He didn't care how long it took."

As Wilder and Diamond originally conceived it (with help from Kurnitz), *The Private Life of Sherlock Holmes* opened in the present day, with Watson's grandson arriving in London from his home in Saskatchewan. Young Watson is a veterinarian, and he has come to England to attend a hoof-and-mouth disease convention. He's Watson's grandson, all right, and he's tired of people constantly referring to the fact. At the bank in which the elder Watson had deposited a box of great secrecy and value—a box that young Watson is about to open—the banker Havelock-Smith (John Williams) describes himself as a charter member of the Sherlock Holmes Society. There has been a recent rush of new memberships, Havelock-Smith says, "in protest against that Secret Service chap—the one with the hairy chest. What's his number?"

"You mean 007? James Bond?" asks the thudding Cassidy of the legal department. Havelock-Smith continues on the theme: "It's trash. Cheap sensationalism. Totally witless. Berettas and bare bosoms. Sports cars with flamethrowers and booby-trapped attaché cases. Smersh. Now really! Give me a foggy night, a hansom cab drawing up to 221B Baker Street, a desperate knock on the door. . . ." The three men open the dusty strongbox, which contains photos of Watson and Sherlock, Holmes's famous deerstalker hat, a few hypodermic needles, and a manuscript, the first case of which is "The Curious Case of the Upside-Down Room." The tale begins on a train, with Holmes and Watson returning from some solved case or other. When a wounded Italian bursts into their compartment, Holmes deduces from the usual scant evidence that the man is a Neopolitan singing teacher who, after being caught trysting with a nobleman's wife, has injured himself in a hasty self-defenestration. Watson, disbelieving, urges Holmes to prove his bizarre deduction, whereupon Holmes pretends to be the nobleman and the Italian hurls himself off the train. Watson is deeply offended at Holmes's cold cruelty: "Of all the heartless, cynical, inhuman. . . . It's unworthy of you, Holmes—just to prove how clever you are." Holmes shuts him up: "I'm trying to get some sleep, Watson."

Billy's Holmes is an erudite, successful man—world renowned, in fact—but a bored one. His is a life of edgy ennui. The world, a dull disappointment, no longer engages him. He's momentarily distracted by a new case—the corpse of an elderly man has been found with a stuffed owl, a boomerang, a meat grinder, and a Bible, with all the furniture upside down on the ceiling. Holmes's interest soon dwindles, the solution so touchingly obvious. In the cadaver's clenched hand is a playing card—the seven of diamonds, to be precise. Holmes deduces the solution to "The Curious Case of the Upside-Down Room" but doesn't spell it out right away except to say that the case clearly involves narcotics. First of all, Sherlock notes, the corpse's clothes were buttoned by someone else (because they were buttoned in reverse). When they return to Baker Street they find Mrs. Hudson playing solitaire; Holmes gives her the seven of diamonds, which matches her deck. The person responsible has been in their own neighborhood, Sherlock declares, there being four shops between 221B and the bus stop—a hardware store, a bookstore, a sporting goods shop, and a taxidermist. (Meat grinder, Bible, boomerang, owl.) Holmes also knows that the corpse had been borrowed for the occasion, since its big toe bore the marks of an identification tag wire. Referring to the mysterious Mr. Fowler, who rented the room in which the corpse was found, Holmes announces to Watson that "he rigged up an elaborate puzzle, replete with red herrings, for the sole purpose of baffling the expert." "I'm sorry, Holmes, but you've lost me," says Watson. "Have I really, Mr. Fowler?" says Sherlock.

WATSON: What possible motive could I have?
HOLMES: I told you—narcotics. You wanted to involve me in an insoluble case, in order to wean me away from cocaine. You had me fooled for almost ten minutes.
WATSON: I guess I'm not very bright.
HOLMES: No, but you're most endearing. No one could ask for a better friend.

But friendship is not enough to get Holmes through the rest of the day, let alone the night. So he demands a new hypodermic needle from Watson. The old one, he says, is "getting rather blunt" from overuse. Watson, furious and hopeless, packs his bags and prepares to move out. Mrs. Hudson bursts into tears. "I know how it feels," she cries. "I went through a divorce once meself."

"I didn't want to remake *The Hound of the Baskervilles*," Wilder said just before filming began. "I don't think I'm being pretentious in saying that I structured my film in four parts, like a symphony: one for the drama, one for the comedy, one for the farce, and one for romance." *The Private Life of Sherlock Holmes* would be a multitextured study of a complicated, prickly man—too smart for contentment, too prodigious for sanity. "How I envy you your mind, Watson," Holmes reflects at one point. "It's placid, imperturbable, prosaic. My mind rebels against stagnation. It's like a racing engine tearing itself to pieces because it's not connected up with the work for which it was built." Only work and drugs make life tolerable. They are the only activities that soothe his breakneck nerves. "Aren't you ashamed of yourself?" Watson demands when Holmes prepares to shoot up. "Thoroughly," Holmes replies, "but this will take care of it."

Holmes's romantic life is the subject of two of the symphony's movements; in neither case is the romance fulfilled. Holmes begins "The Singular Affair of the Russian Ballerina" by describing his contempt for ballet: "It's not the music. What nauseates me is the sight of muscle-bound nymphs on tiptoe being pursued by dainty young men in tights who would much rather be chasing each other." In a series of slow revelations, Holmes discovers that the great Petrova wishes him to father her child. Holmes was not her first choice, the ballet master Rogozhin declares, speaking on Madame's behalf. She considered Tolstoy ("too old"), Nietzsche ("too German"), and most recently Tchaikovsky. Holmes asks what was wrong with Tchaikovsky. Rogozhin is circumspect: "Tchaikovsky . . . how shall I put it? Women not his glass of tea."

For reasons that Wilder and Diamond treat simply as a given, Holmes declines the chance to spend a week in Venice with this beautiful, elegant, and talented woman. Forced to come up with an excuse for the expression of amused revulsion on his face, he explains that he is not a free man: "A bachelor living with another bachelor for the last five years. Five very happy years. Some of us, through a cruel caprice of mother nature. . . ." "Get to point," says Rogozhin.

HOLMES: The point is that Tchaikovsky is not an isolated case.
ROGOZHIM: Surely you and Dr. Watson . . . ! He is your glass of tea?
HOLMES: If you want to be picturesque about it.

A visually elaborate but wordless sequence follows, as the news of Holmes's relationship with Watson spreads through the corps de ballet. A string of exquisite young women celebrating a wild Russian folk dance with an overjoyed Watson gives way to a line of dancing, leering men. Watson is confused. "No need to be bashful—we are not bourgeois!" Rogozhin explains. Watson becomes hysterically aghast at this slight on his manhood and storms home in a rage.

"So there'll be a little gossip about you in Saint Petersburg," Holmes says offhandedly. Watson snaps: "Obviously we cannot continue to live under the same roof. We must move apart." Holmes humors him: "Of course we can still see each other clandestinely, on remote benches in Hyde Park, and in the waiting rooms of suburban railway stations. . . ." Played for laughs, the episode nevertheless severely undermines Watson's faith in his friend. "I can get women from three continents to testify for me!" he shouts hopefully. "And you can get women to vouch for you too, can't you, Holmes?" He turns and approaches Sherlock, looking him in the eye in a two-shot. "Can you, Holmes?"

"Good night, Watson," says Holmes, whereupon Wilder pans with Sherlock as he walks away, alone. "Holmes?" asks Watson without his usual pedestrian stiffness. "Let me ask you a question. I hope I'm not being presumptuous, but there *have* been women in your life?" Holmes answers by receding into the isolated refuge Alexander Trauner designed for him, saying, "The answer is yes—you're being presumptuous. Good night."

Wilder and Diamond conclude "The Singular Affair of the Russian Ballerina" with a gag. Rogozhin shows up later at Baker Street bearing the gift of a violin. "I did nothing to deserve it," says Holmes, to which Rogozhin replies, "Neither did Tchaikovsky, but she gave him grand piano." Rogozhin then turns: "And these, Dr. Watson, are for you," he says, producing a bouquet of flowers.

WATSON: From Madame?
ROGOZHIN: No.

Rogozhin then whispers to Watson an invitation to meet him later at the Savoy Grill and exits happily. Watson, horrified, explodes in yet another rage.

Twelve years after its inception, *The Private Life of Sherlock Holmes* began filming at Pinewood studios in London in mid-May 1969, with a budget of $10 million, by far the largest of Billy's career. There were several elaborate sets to build, including a large expanse of Baker Street, an entire ocean liner built to sizable scale, and a working submarine shaped like the Loch Ness monster. United Artists and the Mirisches justified these pricey items by planning special treatment for *The Private Life of Sherlock Holmes*. Following the pattern of some of the biggest blockbusters of the 1960s, *Holmes* was devised as a special engagement "road show" picture. *The Sound of Music, My Fair Lady, Lawrence of Arabia, Dr. Zhivago*—these gargantuan, hugely popular productions were initially released in limited venues with reserved seating and inflated ticket prices for only two performances a day. They were sent into wide release later, by which time they had acquired a patina of class and exclusivity. The road show was a strategy for *important* pictures; it gave them even more weight.

Colin Blakely, a far cry from Peter Sellers, was cast in the role of Dr. Watson. Like Stephens, Blakely was a member of Olivier's National Theatre Company. For the role of Mycroft Holmes, Sherlock's authoritarian brother, Billy approached George Sanders, whose urbane and cynical screen persona reached its apotheosis in *All About Eve* nearly two decades earlier. The trouble was, Sanders was ailing and didn't know if he could withstand the rigors of filming a serious movie for a perfectionist. Sanders flew to London and met with Wilder, but he was uncertain he could do it. "I would rather do some crummy guest spot in a second-rate movie and take my time to get well," Sanders wrote to a friend. A few weeks later, the opportunity vanished. "I'm afraid that I lost the Billy Wilder picture. Was not able to get well quick enough." The part of Mycroft was taken instead by Christopher Lee.

The cast was rounded out by the marvelous Clive Revill as Rogozhin, Tamara Toumanova as the ballerina, and Genevieve Page as Gabrielle Valladon, a beautiful Belgian woman who seeks Holmes's aid in finding her missing husband. (Billy may have named her after Suzanne Valadon, the French painter of the early twentieth century whose work appeared in his collection.) Graceful, delicate, and thoroughly duplicitous, Gabrielle turns out to be a mercenary German spy named Ilse who thus breaks Holmes's otherwise callous heart. Intertwined with this romantic and devastating subplot is a lengthy business involving the Loch Ness submersible, six midgets on the lam from a circus act, a group of ominous Trappist monks, a flock of birds, and prim, plump Queen Victoria.

As filming continued throughout the summer of 1969, Wilder harped on details. A reporter caught him personally measuring out the exact amount of liquid he wanted in a particular glass. The shoot was originally supposed to last nineteen weeks but inflated to twenty-nine—an unusually long schedule for Billy. But then this was an unusually long and elaborate film, and it mattered to him more than most.

Dressed usually in the finest menswear accompanied by white tennis shoes, a scarf, and a small brown hat (indoors or out, it didn't matter), Billy paced around the set snapping orders and instructions, a cigarette inevitably hanging out of his lips. Diamond, reunited with Billy for the shoot, sat in a chair chewing gum and smoking, often simultaneously, mouthing the words as the actors spoke them during each take. If they were wrong he corrected them. Watching hawklike from the sidelines for violations, Iz was even empowered to say "Cut" if he didn't like what he heard. He used this power with some regularity.

The more footage Robert Stephens shot, the more exasperated he became with Wilder's and Diamond's demands for precision. Stephens's confidence eroded with each passing day as he struggled to give shape, sound, and gesture to what Billy kept calling his "love story between two men." When they were filming the scene in which Holmes, in a warehouse with Watson and Gabrielle, saws through some grillwork, slips through the passage, and jumps onto a mattress underneath, Wilder didn't like what he saw at all. Waving directions furiously with a handkerchief, Billy shouted, "Come on! There's brain and muscle there! Make it seem *difficult*!" They tried it again. "There's a lack of elegance in that sawing!" Billy yelled. The actors were shaken, particularly Stephens. Wilder headed off for a long pace around the set. Lucky for them all the next take was good. Still, Stephens felt like he was "being put through the meat grinder every day." Referring to the way he sometimes treats his actors, Wilder once said that "sometimes you just have to do it with a whip and they like you for it." Sometimes they don't.

Blakely wasn't happy either, but he dealt with the strain better than Stephens did. Both men were shocked by Billy's insistence on timing every gesture to the last syllable. "We would spend hours on a line such as 'If the study door was open . . .' which meant nothing at all," Stephens bristled, "changing the emphasis, banging a gavel or an ashtray on the desk just as we said one or other syllable until the whole thing was squeezed completely dry and you felt like running, screaming, off the set. Which is more or less what I did." Stephens had been warned about this in advance from a surprising source—Jack Lemmon. At a party the Wilders threw in Hollywood before shooting began, Lemmon privately confessed to Stephens that (as Stephens put it) "he adored Billy Wilder but that he drove him crazy with all that Germanic regimentation and matching of action to the slightest inflection."

When September rolled around, the company found itself in a cemetery. Billy was directing the sequence in which Holmes, Watson, and Gabrielle watch three coffins being buried. Touchy and diligent as ever, Wilder abruptly declared that the grass around the graves wasn't nearly green enough. The props crew was immediately dispatched to dig up some fresher clods and replant them around the pits Billy had ordered to be dug. On a more comical note, Billy welcomed one of the gravediggers, the actor Stanley Holloway, to the cast by singing "I'm getting buried in the morning." The film's publicist told reporters not to mention the name of the church because of the difficulty the production company had in getting permission to film on consecrated ground. "Difficulty? *Why?*" asked Billy. "We have no naked girls here. No marijuana, no orgies. Just four midgets praying. You can't get any humbler than that."

The naked girl came later. A scene involving Gabrielle waking up in Holmes's bedroom caused a bit of tension when Billy told Genevieve Page to slip the negligee off her shoulder. It would be difficult, the madam from *Belle de Jour* (1967) responded, since she wasn't wearing anything underneath. "Okay," Wilder snarled, "be Debbie Reynolds if you want to." He paced, grumbled, and smoked cigarettes until he won the point.

Of Trauner's production design, Wilder said, "I asked him to reconstruct the Victorian era, with its plush reds—but not *too* red. I like David Lean a lot, but do you remember that nightclub scene in *Dr. Zhivago?*" At first, Trauner thought about dressing up the real Baker Street for a location shoot, but as he found, "It has changed a lot and there are tons of cars there." In addition, the address where Conan Doyle places Holmes's house doesn't exist. Trauner and his staff looked around London and finally decided to build the interiors and some of the exteriors, particularly Baker Street, at Pinewood. It took four months. Characteristically, the 150 yards of Baker Street Trauner conceived was designed in forced perspective to exaggerate its length, but here, in addition to the elaborate facades, sidewalks, streetlamps, and road surface, there was an extra element: pipes were run overhead to produce special-effects rain on command.

The Loch Ness monster-submarine brought with it its own set of technical difficulties. Wally Veevers, who was in charge of special effects, came up with a long-necked, hump-backed contraption that slithered and plunged on command. They took it out for a test run. As Trauner described it, "I was watching our monster on the lake—it was superb. All of a sudden I see it plunge. I asked Wally if this was intentional. It wasn't." The one-of-a-kind monster had sunk to the bottom of the loch and couldn't be retrieved. Wilder may have been worried, but he didn't show it; instead he made it a point to console Veevers, who was truly upset. After the first Nessie's failure, Wilder, Trauner, and Veevers decided to shoot the monster scenes in the studio pool at MGM's facility in Elstree.

As for the scale-model ocean liner the Mirisch brothers paid to build for "Case of the Naked Honeymooners," the thing was too big to fit into the pool and instead had to be set afloat off the Isle of Wight. Wilder was putting this thunderingly expensive set to the service of a comedy scene in which Watson proves, all too redundantly, that he is an inept detective. (He offers to solve a case involving two corpses found in a stateroom, but after casing the wrong stateroom and deducing a farcical solution to a nonexistent crime, he succeeds only in waking up the passed-out wedding couple asleep in their bed.)

In mid-October, a tiny blurb appeared in *Variety*: "Robert Stephens, who has been emoting in *The Private Life of Sherlock Holmes* for Billy Wilder, has had to withdraw on doctor's orders from the cast of the film *The Three Sisters*, which Laurence Olivier is directing for Alan Clore Productions at Shepperton. Stephens has been replaced by Alan Bates." British newspapers reported later that Stephens had collapsed from exhaustion and stress, but in point of fact he nearly committed suicide. His nerves were shot. Billy wanted him to be rail thin, so he'd lost a lot of weight for the role, and he didn't feel very strong. He was working twelve-hour days, every day, for weeks on end while his wife, Maggie Smith, had gone off to Sussex with their two sons to star in a play. Incompetence, failure, fraudulence, loneliness, abject self-contempt—Wilder induced these raw feelings in the actor he'd chosen to play his on-screen surrogate. So in the middle of filming, his leading man ate a pile of sleeping pills and washed them down with a bottle of whisky.

Suicide wasn't Stephens's aim, at least not on a conscious level, or so he said. He came close to succeeding nonetheless. Laurence Olivier's personal intervention kept the story out of the newspapers, but the production had to shut down for a few weeks. Wilder blamed himself. How could he not, the way he'd been nagging him? As Stephens put it, "Billy was terribly upset and said that it was all his fault. But it wasn't, really. It was a culmination of things." Billy, shaken and contrite, told his star not to worry— "We'd carry on and finish the picture and we'd go a little slower and not hurry things," Stephens recalled Wilder saying. "But of course when I returned it was all exactly the same."

There were moments of levity along the way, of course. It was a Billy Wilder set, after all—exacting directions peppered by entertaining ad-libs. During the filming of the hilarious, dialogue-free balalaika dance between Watson and the ballet boys, Billy told Colin Blakely to "move like Nureyev and act like Laughton." After the first take, Wilder was disappointed:

"Colin, why did you act like Nureyev and move like Laughton?" For a scene in which Gabrielle breaks into tears, Genevieve Page managed to produce real teardrops right on cue, but Wilder wasn't satisfied with reality. Makeup! Billy cried. "Glycerine tears! Great, big, Hollywood false tears! You'd never see those in one of Godard's films," he added, "except on the face of his financier."

Even though Doane Harrison was no longer there to advise Wilder on editorial strategies during shooting, Wilder was still a master craftsman as far as setups were concerned. *Sherlock Holmes* was the twenty-first film he directed; he knew what he was doing. As Ernest Walter, the film's editor, puts it, "He shot the film in such a way that my work was relatively easy. It was a question of just taking the clappers off, more or less, and hooking it all together." Walter's memories of the personal side of Billy Wilder are typically limited: "You didn't find Mr. Wilder—and he was mostly called Mr. Wilder—a very easy man to get close to. We had a wonderful working relationship, there's no question about that. As long as you knew your job, there was no problem. But there were other people on that unit who either were a little bit confused about their job or tried to be the funny man. Mr. Wilder is a funny man, and to try and top him with funny stories wasn't the best thing to do."

Blakely and Stephens are said not to have known how *The Private Life of Sherlock Holmes* would end until they actually filmed it. Wilder had a melancholy conclusion in mind. In a cold British November and December, the Baker Street set was covered in artificial snow, and the sad, final scenes of *Sherlock Holmes* were shot.

As the critics Joseph McBride and Michael Wilmington astutely observe of Ilse von Hoffmannstahl, the character Wilder uses to explain why Holmes doesn't trust women, "We become aware of her deception of Holmes long before he does, and our attention is turned quickly from the ostensible spy plot to an exploration of the desperation and fragility which seem to lie beneath her disguise. And it is Holmes's gradual intuition of her desperation which, perversely, begins to attract him to her. . . . (Wilder) respects professionals because they do not attempt to conceal their corruption; and we respect Fräulein von Hoffmannstahl even though she is deceiving Holmes, because she is not deceiving us."

Wilder handles Sherlock's falling in love as a series of subtle glances and refined gestures. On the train to Scotland, with Holmes and Gabrielle sharing a sleeping compartment (posing as Mr. and Mrs. Ashdown), Holmes is clearly captivated by her, though he keeps himself safely separated from her by remaining in the top bunk. He trusts her, however tentatively. When she starts talking to him about women, he tells her a story. He was on the rowing team during his undergraduate days at Oxford, he recounts, and if his team won, someone's name would be pulled out of a hat and the winner would get a prostitute as his prize. Holmes, who was passionately attracted to a beautiful girl he kept seeing from afar, was the prizewinner one afternoon; the encounter was to take place in an Oxford boathouse. When the callow Sherlock arrived, he reports, he was shattered to discover that his real prize was knowledge, an end to innocence: the prostitute was the girl he loved. Sherlock's story, of course, bears more than a passing resemblance to the tale that so intrigued Maurice Zolotow: Vienna, Billie, the corrupted record-store girl whose name was Ilse. . . . Whether or not Billie's crushing disappointment in matters of love ever happened in fact, it certainly occupies a central place in his imagination.

By the time Sherlock and Gabrielle check into a Scottish inn, their phony identities as Mr. and Mrs. Ashdown have become more genuine than their real ones. They sleep in twin beds that have been built as a single unit, connected by one of Trauner's carved wooden arches. After Mycroft dashes his brother's tenderness by pointing out that he has been duped by a German spy, Wilder constructs this heart-rending sequence: Holmes walks to the rear of the image, where Gabrielle lies asleep, the covers pulled off her bare shoulders. Despite her deceit, his first reaction is tender: he lifts the covers higher to keep her warm. Then he rudely bangs the parasol on the metal chandelier. She wakes up with a start. "Sorry about that," he says, "but as long as you're up, what is the German word for castle? *Schloss*, isn't it?" "I think so," she says. "And how would you say 'under the castle'? *Unter das Schloss*? Or *die Schloss*?" He calls her by name— "Fräulein Hoffmannstahl"—and it is chilling when she responds in perfect German: "*Unter* dem *Schloss*," she says. It is a shocking revelation—not because she reveals that she is a spy (which we already know), but because her very voice reveals a more startling twist: Wilder sees himself in her. It's Gabrielle, the professional fraud, who bears the weight of Billy's empathy. Figuratively as well as literally, she speaks his language.

Their parting, as romantic a scene as Wilder ever filmed, is almost entirely wordless; Billy conveys the depth of his feelings through glances, lighting, and the placement of his camera. When Ilse crosses the length of the Ashdowns' bedroom toward Sherlock, Wilder pans with her, as if to capture a last embrace. All she wants is her parasol. "I'll take that," she says as she pulls it away from a perplexed Watson. Framed in the doorway, she departs with a single word of farewell ("Gentlemen"). With Watson pestering him for an explanation, Holmes watches from his window as she is driven away in a carriage. With the carriage receding farther and deeper into the image, surrounded by dappled sunlight in a bower of lush trees, Ilse sends Morse code signals by opening and closing her parasol; the carriage heads toward a blazing patch of sunlight in the far distance. Billy cuts to Ilse, staring ahead in the carriage, never looking back as she opens and closes the parasol over her shoulder. *"Auf wiedersehen,"* Holmes reads, at which point Wilder slowly dissolves from the Scottish highlands at the end of summer to London in the cold dead of winter, the point of light remaining over Baker Street for a few moments until it fades completely from view.

In a delicate, depressing coda, Holmes learns in a letter from Mycroft that Ilse has been killed. According to the letter, she had been caught spying against the Japanese and summarily executed by firing squad. Mycroft's postscript evinces a rare touch of brotherly love (or is it simply more cruelty?): she was living in Japan under the name Mrs. Ashdown. Holmes, drained, calmly asks Watson where he has hidden the cocaine. Watson tells him. ("You're getting better," Holmes says with real tenderness.) With Holmes having walked swiftly to his room, closing the door behind him, Wilder ends his personal film with a shot of Watson, no longer foolish, sitting in his chair by the fire, pulling his desk toward him, looking at a stack of blank paper, and beginning to write.

On December 13, after eleven solid months of intensive preproduction work, rewriting, and shooting, Billy was on his way back home. He did not return empty-handed, having purchased one more Henry Moore sculpture—*Maquette for Square Form with Cut*, a newly cast bronze he bought through the Gimpel Fils Gallery in London.

Miklós Rózsa's Concerto for Violin and Orchestra (Opus 24) had originally been commissioned, performed, and recorded in the 1960s by Jascha Heifetz, and according to Rózsa, Wilder approached him at Walter Reisch's annual Christmas party "and said he loved my violin concerto and that he had worn out his copy of the record and wondered if I had another one. I was as intrigued as much as flattered but all he would say was, 'I've got an idea.'" Later, Wilder revealed that he was writing *Sherlock Holmes* and (according to Rózsa, at least) "he had written it around my concerto, inspired by the fact that Holmes liked playing the fiddle." Billy didn't give Rózsa quite as much elbow room as he'd given André Previn. As Rózsa put it:

> For the scenes shot in the lovely Scottish highlands Wilder wanted Scottish music of some kind. As usual, I did my homework and wrote music based on some Scottish national tunes I had researched. Wilder complained that it was *too* Scottish. The scene itself was a happy one, with Holmes, Watson, and the "Belgian" girl scooting along on bicycles. Then Wilder, perhaps remembering "Bicycle Built for Two," asked for a waltz, but when he heard it he complained that it was too Viennese. There was only one session left, in two days' time, and he at last allowed

me to write something that I considered appropriate. I used the love theme, but with an urgent, pulsating rhythm underneath, and it worked well.

In March 1970, Wilder was back in London for an appearance at the National Film Theatre, where he reported to his audience that *Sherlock Holmes* was then being fitted with its musical score. Someone asked him if he would consider it an insult to be called a good commercial director, and Wilder's answer was characteristic and concise: "It depends on the percentage I have of the picture." Responding to a question of how *Holmes* turned out, Wilder answered, "It's like asking a pregnant woman what the baby's like. I haven't seen it yet, and I won't till I see it with an audience."

In point of fact, he had certainly seen the three-hour-and-twenty-minute cut he and his editor, Ernest Walter, had turned in to the Mirisches in Los Angeles. "To my astonishment, they were surprised," Walter recalls. "But having seen the script in the first place, it was obvious it was going to be a long movie." United Artists and the Mirisch brothers' anxiety over Billy's long, exorbitant, intimate movie heightened considerably after the initial previews: audiences found it dull. Alarmed, they demanded that Billy pare the picture down considerably. They also scuttled the road show plan. *The Private Life of Sherlock Holmes* would be released in a normal manner at a normal length, UA and the Mirisches announced, or it would not be released at all.

The Private Life of Sherlock Holmes was no longer simply *about* a famous man's devastating secret life; it had become its director's personal desolation. Billy raised objections to a level and a volume one can only imagine, but given his recent track record combined with *Holmes*'s extreme cost (not to mention the catastrophic failure of similarly overproduced films like *Doctor Doolittle*, *Star*, and *Darling Lili*), he had little choice but to accept the Mirisches' and UA's harsh decision. Wilder had the right of final cut, of course, but it did him no good if the cut he demanded remained coiled in its cans in a United Artists warehouse.

"I suggested that we remove the 'Upside-Down Room' completely," Ernest Walter reports. Wilder did so, and Walter returned to England. United Artists and the Mirisches were still displeased, so the prologue in the bank, the flashback to Oxford and the prostitute, and the entire "Case of the Naked Honeymooners" were cut out as well. Walter remained concerned about the downbeat ending of Holmes retreating into solitude and cocaine, and he suggested an alternative: "I said to Billy Wilder, 'Why don't we end with that scene with [Rogozhin and] the violin and the flowers?' He wouldn't have it at all."

Billy was brokenhearted. According to Trauner, the evisceration of

Holmes "wasn't done without resistance on his part. But Wilder thinks that if a film isn't an immediate success it's because he has failed. So he let them cut the two sequences, and it's really too bad."

The failure of *The Private Life of Sherlock Holmes*, however, owes as much to what Wilder left in as to what the Mirisches and United Artists took out. The tone is off. Having bared his own soul with such sweet delicacy in the scenes between Holmes and Gabrielle, Billy was compelled to subvert the romance by way of some peculiarly lame comedy. The scene between Mycroft and Holmes, in which one brother calmly delivers to the other his personal ruin, is exquisite; for Holmes, the revelation of Ilse's dishonesty is crushing, particularly because the news comes from his life-long rival. But Wilder is unwilling to sustain this mood, preferring to cut it short with the arrival of Queen Victoria. It's tacky. "I trust you had a pleasant journey, Ma'am?" Mycroft asks, to which the doughball queen responds: "It was long, and it was tedious, and it had better be worth our while, Mr. Holmes." There is an unpleasant ring to the line, since it also defines the film's structure and payoff. By interrupting two of the most heartfelt scenes he ever directed with a fakey Queen Victoria parading around an overly whimsical monster contraption, Wilder misfires so profoundly that the film can't recover. Then he throws the silly submersible scene itself away with a crass low-angle shot of Victoria uttering her greatest cliché, the inevitable "We are not amused."

Victoria was not alone. *The Private Life of Sherlock Holmes* opened at Radio City in the last week of October 1970, and it was gone before Thanksgiving. Its entire domestic gross was $1.5 million.

In the heat-seeking eyes of American reviewers, old Billy Wilder wasn't with it anymore. Pauline Kael was bored. For her, *Holmes* was "rather like the second-class English comedies of the fifties: it doesn't have enough bounce, and it isn't really very interesting, but it would be quite pleasant if it didn't dawdle on for over two hours." Wilder's critical fans surfaced only later, in journals. Writing in *Film Quarterly* the following spring, McBride and Wilmington began by remarking on a certain sea change: "It was only seven years ago (remember?) that the Legion of Decency condemned *Kiss Me, Stupid* in terms usually reserved for the Whore of Babylon; now it has slipped quietly into release with a GP rating. But Wilder is still harnessed with his old press agent's image of the bull let loose in the china shop of American Puritanism—and now, with the fragments of the china scattered all over the shop, the reviewers are ready to consign the old bull to the pasture." McBride and Wilmington saw the poignance with which Billy portrayed his detective hero: "Holmes appeals to Wilder for his human failings more than for his legendary qualities as a detective— *The Private Life* depicts a crushing humiliation which Dr. Watson has suppressed from public knowledge—but Wilder's tone is unusually subdued, even elegiac, perhaps because the film is set in a simpler, more gentlemanly era far from the barbarism of James Bond and Pussy Galore."

Wilder was bitterly disappointed in *The Private Life of Sherlock Holmes*, and he blamed himself. "I should have been more daring," Wilder mused to the director Chris Columbus in the mid-1980s; "I wanted to make Holmes a homosexual. . . . That's why he is on dope, you know. . . . Look," he continued, "we have been freed now from the Breen Office or the Johnson Office or that stupid thing. In many respects it's terrifying, because now any idiot and any pornographer can do anything. But for the ones who are a little bit discriminating, who do it delicately, a grand new thing is opened. But that was after *Private Life*. Just the saddest thing about it is that it was a waste of a year and a half of my life."

PART SEVEN
1971–1998

29. LOVE AND DEATH

REPORTER 1: Why the hell don't we chip in and get some new
  cards?
REPORTER 2: Don't look at me—I haven't won a hand since Leopold and Loeb.

—*The Front Page*

I n 1970 Charles Eames finally gave Billy the napping couch he'd asked
for in Nova Scotia fifteen years earlier during location shooting on *The
Spirit of St. Louis*. It was called, plainly, "the Chaise"—a long, narrow,
modernist plank made of aluminum and cushioned in black leather. Con-
forming to Billy's specifications, it is self-evidently not a casting couch, since
it's impossible to fit more than one person on it except in a most extreme
manner. (The Chaise is only 17.5 inches wide.) Copies soon went on sale
at $636 apiece. Wilder loved it, but he had to make a crack nonetheless:
"If you had a girlfriend shaped like a Giacometti it would be wonderful."

In need of a temporary getaway from the jangle of Hollywood, Billy
and Audrey bought a one-story bungalow on Broad Beach Road in Trancas, a slip of land off the Pacific Coast Highway just north of Malibu. The
house cost $70,000. The next-door neighbors were Jack and Felicia Lem-
mon. The Matthaus lived down the block, as did Carroll O'Connor, Goldie
Hawn, and Dustin Hoffman. This beach house in an exclusive, star-laden
enclave was as close to the model American dream as Billy Wilder got: it
featured a rose garden in the backyard and a white picket fence. Trancas
had none of the high-gear energy of Malibu—it was more mellow and
secluded. But then the Wilders used it only on weekends. The rest of their
time was spent in the thick of Beverly Hills and Westwood.

Holmes's failure was vast and symptomatic. Hollywood found itself
adrift in a jittery sort of way. The town had always been trendy, but now
the only trend was heightened confusion. The Best Director nominees for
1970 tell the schizophrenic story: Arthur Hiller for *Love Story*, Federico

Fellini for *Fellini Satyricon*, Ken Russell for *Women in Love*, Franklin J. Schaffner for *Patton*, and Robert Altman for *M*A*S*H*; Schaffner won. Trying to stay hip in Hollywood while imagining broad, bankable hipness for the rest of the country, nobody was quite sure what movie audiences wanted—especially not older directors who'd grown accustomed to a steady career. Casting about for another project, Billy turned to a play he'd considered and forgotten a few years earlier. Samuel Taylor's play *Avanti!* opened and closed on Broadway in 1968 to a cascade of terrible reviews. Even before opening night, however, Charles Feldman had purchased the film rights and announced that Billy was set to direct. Feldman and Wilder remained friendly after *The Seven Year Itch*, and in fact Billy did some uncredited script doctoring on Feldman's James Bond send-up, *Casino Royale* (1967). Julie Christie was mentioned as the top candidate for the leading lady, but perhaps because of the play's negative notices and the impending production of *Sherlock Holmes*, Billy put *Avanti!* on hold. He did take over the option from Feldman, but he didn't do anything about it until Taylor ran into Diamond one day and asked him to remind Billy about it.

When Wilder did pick up *Avanti!* again, Diamond wasn't part of the game plan. Instead, Billy chose a new old writing partner, Julius Epstein, to help him adapt the play for the screen. The Wilder-Epstein collaboration wasn't a particularly happy one, and it ended without a draft of *Avanti!* having been completed, though Epstein was paid $50,000 for his work. A new collaborator was brought in—once again, not Iz. Norman Krasna tried. He failed. Then Luciano Vincenzoni, the Italian playwright and screenwriter best known for his collaboration with Sergio Leone on *The Good, the Bad, and the Ugly* (1967), began working with Billy in the summer of 1971. *Avanti!*'s premise had shifted. No longer was it the story of a rich young American finding unlikely love in Italy. The protagonist was now an Italian-American trying to recapture his father's romantic past in their shared homeland. Wilder offered the lead to Nino Manfredi.

But Vincenzoni departed as well, as did Manfredi, and by January 1972, Billy was back to the old routine—a script with Diamond, a role for Jack Lemmon. Lemmon had a key virtue: like Diamond, he was not only a close friend but also an old one. "At first, I was thinking of casting someone around thirty years old," Billy explained. "Then I gave him, as a friend, the first half of the script to read, and he asked me to play it. So I adjusted the character to fit his age, and I wrote the second half." Familiarity, the comfort of habit, is key to *Avanti!*'s relaxed tone. What Billy said about Lemmon applied equally to Diamond: "I love working with him. We understand each other, and after all these years, we've developed a language between us—he understands my half-formed thoughts."

By the early spring *Avanti!* was mostly scripted. The film was now about a middle-aged man who finds redemption by cheating on his wife. Billy himself described it very differently: "It's basically a love story between a father and a son." The father, dead throughout, serves for Wilder as a kind of angelic bastard. Heartless toward his family in life (we're led to believe), he becomes a blessed figure in death—once, that is, his son discovers the old man has been flying to the glorious island of Ischia once a year to wine, dine, and screw a working-class British woman behind his wife's and family's back. Wendell Armbruster Jr., the forty-two-year-old head of a large corporation, discovers his father's secret, cherished life only after Senior drives over an Ischia cliff and spectacularly dies. Junior, having flown to Italy to retrieve one body, discovers two in the morgue, elderly Dad having gone out in a blaze of glory with his lower-class lover in the car beside him. For Junior this is a devastating blow.

Wilder and Diamond describe their protagonist in the opening pages of their screenplay: "He went to Cornell, he's a Young Republican, he occasionally plays a game of squash with S. Agnew. To him, W. Cronkite is a Maoist and R. Nader is a pain in the ass." As Billy told Michel Ciment, "He starts to have doubts and finally his false beliefs can't endure." For Billy, Armbruster's shifting beliefs have little to do with politics. Armbruster doesn't change his cold, corporation-man demeanor through the course of the film. *Avanti!* appreciates, as few other films do, that middle-age transformations are actually very limited in scope. Wendell leaves the film close to the way he entered it—a calculating corporate crud, every inch his father's son. The point of *Avanti!* is that Armbruster finally sleeps with someone he cares about, and it changes his life in a small but meaningful way.

Wilder once made a telling (if fleeting) analysis of his central character: "He starts to understand a father whom he'd barely thought about. . . . He's closer to his dead father than to the living one." Billy then changed the subject entirely: "It's a reevaluation of the Americans," Billy continued, "of their errors, of what counts and what doesn't count. But of course that sounds pompous, and it's not how I pitched the film to get $3 million. All that is the sauce and the vegetables. The meat is an affair between an American and a girl who is a bit too fat but who has a nice chest."

Juliet Mills, whom Billy cast in the role of chubby Pamela Piggott, is naturally petite. Wilder first saw her onstage in London in the play *Five Finger Exercise*—she was about sixteen years old at the time—and he made it a point to come backstage after the show. He told her not only that he loved the performance, Mills recalls, but also that he had something in mind for her—an enticing carrot on a long, thin string: "One day I'm going to work with you," he said. Making *Avanti!*, Mills says, was "the highlight of my life." Wilder later told her that he and Diamond had written the part of Pamela Piggott with Mills in mind. She was living in Los Angeles after her TV sitcom, *Nanny and the Professor*, went off the air, and to her enormous surprise and pleasure Billy just called her up and asked her to do the part. There was no auditioning, no calls to and from an agent— just Billy Wilder picking up the phone and asking her to play the lead in his next film. He did tell her that there was just one catch—she had to gain thirty-five pounds. "We were lucky to find Juliet Mills, a miraculous actress," Billy later said. "It's difficult to find a girl who weighs too much— who's teased about her weight but is still adorable, touching, and finally erotic. It's an enormous risk, and I might have looked fifty years without meeting the right actress. Now it's around her that the action turns. And she's perfect."

Mills's pedigree was impressive to Billy, if not her recent career: "She was raised in a family of actors. Her father is John Mills and her sister is Hayley Mills. She lived in California where she acted in a stupid television series called *Nanny and the Professor*." In terms of her casting, Wilder remembered a slightly different sequence of events than Mills does, but the outcome is quite the same: "I had found an actress in London who had a nervous breakdown," he notes. "Back in California, I met with an agent who spoke to me about one of his clients, Hayley Mills, as a great English actress. I asked him her weight, and he answered that she was skinny as a thread. I explained to him that the role demanded an actress twenty pounds overweight. When I said that (you know agents), he answered that she had a weight problem. Then I thought of her sister." "I was looking at her photo when she entered the office," Billy went on. "She was also thin, but she's more petite yet has a slightly larger build. I gave her the script; she read it; and she called me, saying, 'I want the role, I'm going to gain twenty pounds, give me eight weeks.' She showed such a desire to play the part, such an enthusiasm, that I believed in her. She ate day and night, was very disciplined, became very plump, and gave a superb performance." The script describes Pamela more succinctly: "Lovely, touching, warm, and let's face it, overweight. Pity, that."

Nino Manfredi returned, on the drawing board at least, for a supporting role—that of the gracious, worldly hotel manager who orchestrates Armbruster Jr.'s redemption. Billy considered two other Italian comedians, Alberto Sordi and Romolo Valli, as well, but their English was a problem— they spoke it, but not well enough. As Billy put it, "They wouldn't have returned the ball quick enough to Lemmon on the other side of the net. I would have had to post-dub them." At the time, Billy wouldn't consider such a drastic, half-baked solution—it would have looked and sounded terrible—so he chose someone whose speaking voice was as precise as his comedy style: Clive Revill. Judging purely by the evidence on-screen, Wilder adored Revill's performance in *Sherlock Holmes*, and his performance in *Avanti!* is so exquisitely wrought that one gets the sense that Billy wrote the role expressly for him.

Vincenzoni reappeared to help Wilder and Diamond with the Italian dialogue. Billy also took Vincenzoni's advice about Italian customs. "He's a very good friend," Billy reported, "and he was a bit of an expert for me in local color." To shoot *Avanti!*, Wilder's first deliriously colorful film after *The Emperor Waltz*, Billy picked another Italian, cinematographer Luigi Kuveiller. "I looked at the work of a dozen Italian directors of photography, all excellent," he said. But one particular film struck Wilder's fancy—*A Quiet Place in the Country*, by Elio Petri from a script by Vincenzoni. "I loved the lucidity, the lightness, the precision of his photography," Billy said admiringly. "I like him a lot, and not only does he direct lighting, he also directs the camera. . . . I was seduced by his work, and I love his charm and his personality which are very positive on a set."

Despite the troubled tedium of the *Sherlock Holmes* shoot in England, Billy was eager to return to Europe to shoot. His resistance to shooting on location was no match for the pull of European culture, especially as he approached his old age. "It's unconscious," he said, but maybe not. Wilder continued: "Maybe it comes from a deep desire to return here from time to time—to change my eating habits, to see the place I come from." The place he came from, of course, was pure fantasy, Ischia bearing little resemblence to Kraków, but it was a compelling reverie nonetheless, rooted as it was in a refugee's enduring sense of lack. With *Avanti!*, Billy Wilder was obliquely trying to come to terms with what he lost—the father he hadn't adored, the continental culture he abandoned in favor of Los Angeles.

Under Wilder's instructions, Kuveiller shot *Avanti!* in an aspect ratio of 1.85:1—the first time since *Some Like It Hot*. He filmed everything else in extrawide Panavision, all the better to keep his characters at a little distance from each other, but as George Morris notes, the comparatively tighter framing of *Avanti!* reflects the intimacy Wilder strives to create. More vitally, to capture the fresh, supersaturated colors and heart-speedingly romantic drama of the western Italian coast, Wilder had to go there. It wasn't something he could mimic on a Hollywood lot. He filmed *Avanti!* in Ischia itself, as well as Amalfi, Naples, and Portofino, with interiors shot in a studio in Rome. Even for studio work, the Safra Palatino complex in Rome offered something no well-equipped Los Angeles soundstage could: "The air is Italian. And if I moved the bed, the sofa, the vase of flowers to a Hollywood studio, they wouldn't have the same look." As always, he wanted to show his friends what Europe had over Southern California. On a fine, blistering day he escorted Audrey, Jack, Felicia, and Juliet to Pompeii. It was unbearably hot, Mills remembers, but "Billy was really in his element—the art, the history, the heat. It was like walking around with one of the emperors himself."

Having spent almost forty years in the United States, Billy still reveled in his foreign nature. In a markedly anti-American way, he and Diamond utterly ignore the future of Armbruster's marriage in the face of his budding affair with Pamela. "The play is very different," Billy noted. "The second part, for example, is dedicated to the dilemma of a man who wonders if he's going to stay in Europe with his lover or return to his wife. He asks himself questions about his children, about whether he belongs to society, and so on. We suppressed all that." As the critic Stephen Farber notes, "The film is something more than an escapist fantasy; it is about the importance of escape from the sterile, single-minded American workaday world—a tribute to the lazy, romantic holiday spirit that industrious Americans find immoral."

Pamela Piggott's chubbiness is equally central to Wilder's vision of *Avanti!*. "Ask fat-ass if she wants a ride," Armbruster says none too discreetly to the concierge, Carlucci. "Little girl?!" he snaps at another point; "She's built like a Japanese wrestler!" Beneath the cruelty of the dialogue, though, Wilder is on *her* side emotionally. The barbs sting because Pamela is the most lovingly written woman in all of Wilder's films. Then again, as if to compensate, he calls her Piggott.

Mills gained her weight by eating three huge, starchy, fat-laden meals a day—and a whole lot of Guinness, which she drank with her father. The regimen continued during the shoot, since Billy was afraid she'd start to slim down naturally. So much of the day was spent working, he knew, that there wasn't nearly enough time to eat too much, so he ordered a snack bar to be brought onto the set around four in the afternoon, with loads of ice cream especially for Juliet. Billy commented once on the sense of sybaritic regeneration he meant to suggest in the scene in which Pamela wanders through the streets of Ischia, amazed at how beautiful the world looks when self-indulgence is allowed to flourish: "It's a montage where I tried to evoke the magic of a countryside inundated with sun, the way it touches a young woman who lived all her life in a humid and cold country. We are preparing for her evolution—but without transforming the sequence into 'Debbie Reynolds Goes to Ischia,' since it has a certain bite. It's the girl who provides it when she buys four ice creams in front of three kids and she eats them all herself."

More bitingly, Armbruster Jr. begins his quest for his father's corpse with no discernible affection for the old man. When he composes the eulogy on his Dictaphone machine, he might as well be drafting a speech for some irrelevent chamber of commerce luncheon in suburban Baltimore. At the epicurean seaside resort to which his father retreated every summer, Junior is shocked to discover that the staff adored him—a depth of feeling he himself never felt. The spa, managed by the avuncular Carlucci, is unapologetically geriatric—a lush paradise for the aged. Populated by guests ranging from chic women of a certain age to a Methuselah-like geezer pushed around in his wheelchair by two stacked blonde nurses, it's a wellspring of rejuvenation meant for people past their prime. Wilder, finally allowing himself to film in blazing color again, clearly finds the whole place seductive. *Avanti!*'s narrative project is to teach Wendell Armbruster Jr. to appreciate it as well. "Sonofa*bitch*!" Armbruster snarls upon discovering his father's longtime affair. "Do you know how old he was?! Sixty-seven! A grandfather—with a bad back yet!" For Wilder, sixty-six at the time, advancing age was clearly no obstacle to pleasure.

The disaster of *The Private Life of Sherlock Holmes* didn't stop Wilder from trying to work out close, intimate themes in *Avanti!*. Max Wilder was fifty-six when he died in Billy's arms on the way to the hospital in 1928; he died a younger man than Billy was when he made *Avanti!*. Armbruster, like Billy, ends up burying his father in a foreign land, and to a great extent the whole film is a meditation on death—not the abstracted, comical morbidity of *Sunset Boulevard* and *Some Like It Hot*, but real death, the mystifying absence of his parents, who cared about him.

For the scene in which Armbruster and Pamela identify their parents' bodies at the morgue, Wilder chose to film on location in a church high over the sea, a whitewashed chapel set against a clear blue sky. According to Mills, when she and Lemmon walked inside to begin shooting, there was a reverential hush to the place as natural light streamed through the windows, especially the roundel over what would have been the altar, where the sheet covered bodies lie. And there was a song in the air. To enhance the mood, Billy had arranged for music to be softly piped in, the way silent film directors used to do—not to record, but simply to stir his actors' hearts.

Avanti! was widely slammed by American reviewers upon its release in December 1972. Most critics were unable to see beyond a failed attempt at political topicalism. *Avanti!*'s admirers surfaced later in film journals, but at the time, the film's few current events jokes—references to Kissinger and Nader—were said to fall flat, as if Billy was aiming much higher. For Wilder, America in 1972 was itself flat and thudding, a pleasureless country administered by bureaucrats. That is why the film is set elsewhere—a gorgeous European spa. The United States is never seen in *Avanti!*—except as a colorless airport in the opening sequence.

The film came in at about $2,750,000, grossed only $4,500,000 world-wide, and even after the sale of television rights *Avanti!* ended up losing about $700,000.

Juliet Mills recalls that Billy was "very, very upset" by *Avanti!*'s failure. "It was close to his heart." Billy concluded that *Avanti!* was "just too gentle. The way the picture would have aroused interest is that the son of the chairman of that enormous corporation goes to claim the body of the father and finds out that the father and a naked bellhop have been found dead in that car. The father was a fag. But it's just a young girl. So who cares? So he got laid. So big fuckin' deal, right?"

The cinema he loved was dead, and it wasn't likely to resurrect itself. "All of that is gone—Lubitsch, Leisen, *Love in the Afternoon*. It's too soft, you know." Ernst Lubitsch and Mitchell Leisen in the same breath? Billy Wilder must have been morose indeed.

"Today you obviously have to come at people with a sledgehammer," he told an interviewer. "You have to get to the point as fast as possible. People aren't patient anymore. They're not willing to sit and watch. . . . What bothers me is the fact that I'm a very strict critic of my own movies, and with this movie I expected more. I think it's one of my better films. But obviously it's too tame today, too contemplative. Audiences nowadays want something juicier. Today, when there are movies like Brando's *Last Tango in Paris*, it's obviously not perverted enough."

A more self-betraying set of remarks came spewing out when Billy spoke with the author Kenneth Geist the week after *Avanti!*'s seemingly successful preview in October 1972. The audience had enjoyed the film, but Wilder knew it was doomed, and he wanted to explain why, as much to himself as to everyone else. Geist was interviewing Wilder on the subject of Joseph Mankiewicz, but as usual, Billy kept straying. "Our ears have been dulled by the onslaught of television," he mused. "This is not Noel Coward's era now. They just kind of whack at you with television situation comedies. It is all more or less on the level of Lucille Ball." Pressed on the subject of Joseph Mankiewicz, Wilder reacted personally. Mankiewicz had moved from Los Angeles to New York, and Billy had a few snide things to say about it: "He was one who kept some class in this wretched town. [But] he abandoned it." Even with the wretchedness, moving from Hollywood to Manhattan didn't make any sense to Billy: "What normal man except an Eskimo wants to live in the Arctic and have his balls frozen off?" On his own career, he was blunt: "It's so tiny, minuscule in comparison to Lubitsch." People were not being kind to him, he said: " 'You think that you are in the mold of Lubitsch,' " Wilder claims he was being told, " 'but you're really in the mold of Stroheim'—meaning ambitious." And he was feeling very out-of-date: "They are not dancing this kind of gavotte anymore—they're beyond the twist and the frug, or whatever the damn thing is. What the hell is the use of writing it if they aren't going to come and dance? . . . *For what?* But then I say, *what else?* It's not easy. Maybe the proper thing would be to abandon it altogther."

Why then did he keep working? Geist asked him. "If only to get away from the vacuum cleaner, I come and work the typewriter." But he had to be more careful than ever about the projects he chose to work on, he said, "now that there are not so many bullets left in the elderly gun. Even if you pointed me to a target, I'd still miss. . . .

"I will kill myself after this interview," Billy declared. "I have just come to the conclusion that it is no use."

Adding insult to injury, *Esquire* dubbed him an "old director" even before *Avanti!* died at the box office. The writer Noel Berggren asked some of Hollywood's elder statesmen what they thought of contemporary American cinema, and Wilder was only too happy to be rude. Recent trends bored him: "I certainly will not see pictures that deal once more with the colored question, once more with Woodstock youths, with motorcycles and heroin, all of that—unless, like in *Taking Off*, there is a new point of view." A certain French straw man and his American cousin were trotted out for their daily whallop: "I'm looking back with great nostalgia to the well-made picture—not the Godard-type pictures which bore me totally, no matter how many *Village Voice* Andrew Sarrises tell me that this is indeed the new art form. I think it's baloney." (Billy may have been snarling, but John Ford was even more terse. Asked if he kept up with what was going on in the motion picture business, Ford answered, "No." Asked if he saw any new movies, Ford answered, "No." Asked if he had seen *Midnight Cowboy*, Ford replied, "No! Especially not that. I don't like porn—these easy liberal movies. A lot of junk. I don't know where they're going. They don't either.")

As Billy looked forward to seventy, the pull of the past grew stronger. He found himself dreaming of Germany as he grew old. "Of course I was bitter after the war," he told a German interviewer in 1973, "but today it's a closed chapter. I have buried my anger and my hate. The wounds are healed. It is absolutely, totally forgotten. I even miss Germany again today. I'm homesick for Berlin and the Kurfürstendamm. . . . I see with great pleasure that a new generation is growing up in Germany. It is, I believe, unthinkable that something like what happened in the 1930s will happen again in Germany." The terrorist attack on Israeli athletes at the 1972 Munich Olympics disturbed him deeply. He felt particularly sorry for the host nation: "It was as if Germans were haunted by a curse. It affected me greatly."

European culture offered him breathing room of a sort the American way of life did not. He did what he wanted in Los Angeles, of course, but it was better on the Continent. Other countries were like the past—they did things differently there, and Billy found it comforting. In Rome in 1974, Billy was seen picking up a whore on the Via Veneto. He was placid when confronted with it. "There was a strike on at the Grand Hotel where I was staying," he explained. "And no hot water. After a few days I was desperate for a bath—so I went and picked up a girl on the Via Veneto and went back to her place. I had a nice hot bath, paid her, and went on my way. Cheap at the price, I thought. I did it several times while the strike was on."

Despite his last two bombs, Billy Wilder wasn't about to quit making pictures. His work was his life. *The Front Page* was originally announced in June 1973 as a project for Joseph Mankiewicz, but his actual involvement was practically nonexistent. By the end of July, Mankiewicz was out and Wilder and Diamond were on their way in. Talks were being held with Universal's Jennings Lang, the producer whose aggrieved testicles had served as an early inspiration for *The Apartment*, and by mid-August it was official: *The Front Page* would be Wilder's next film. On the surface it sounded perfect: two seasoned, bantering reporters, Walter Burns and Hildy Johnson; Billy Wilder and Izzie Diamond; Walter Matthau and Jack Lemmon.

"We felt we should go back to one of the classic farces of the 1930s," Diamond said, implicitly acknowledging a retreat after the twin debacles of *Sherlock Holmes* and *Avanti!*. "We thought of *Roxie Hart, Libeled Lady, Nothing Sacred.* It just so happened that these were all newspaper stories. Nobody has made this kind of picture recently." This might have been a reason *not* to remake *The Front Page* again, especially when younger, hotter directors were dazzling audiences with visually au courant films like *Chinatown* and *The Godfather Part II* (both 1974), but Wilder and Diamond thought they were being topical and, hopefully, commercial. In their view, the current Watergate scandal had made heroes out of journalists once more.

So in the fall of 1973, Wilder and Diamond set to work on a complete rewrite of one of the most popular American plays of the twentieth century. Adolphe Menjou and Pat O'Brien starred in the 1931 film version, and Cary Grant and Rosalind Russell took over the roles in Howard Hawks's gender-switched 1940 remake *His Girl Friday*. Wilder and Diamond kept the plot but sharpened the vulgarity, Billy apparently convinced that the way to appeal to mid-1970s audiences was to give these hard-bitten characters lines that he himself would use. "Listen, you lousy baboon," Wilder's Hildy barks to Walter, "you better start wearing cast-iron shorts because the next time I see you I'm going to bury my shoe up your ass, so help me."

By mid-February 1974, Wilder and Diamond had produced a complete draft. A shooting script was ready by mid-March, by which time nearly the entire film had been cast. A pretty young actress, Susan Sarandon, would play Hildy's fiancée, Peggy Grant; Austin Pendleton would play the sniffling, neurotic anarchist Earl Williams; and the television comedy star Carol Burnett would play Mollie the whore. In 1961, Burnett, then appearing as a featured comedienne on *The Garry Moore Show*, told an interviewer that she would work for free in a movie if Billy Wilder directed and Jack Lemmon starred. But Burnett had to be honest: "You don't see them knocking down my doors." She got her chance in 1974. Burnett didn't work for free, certainly, but she did donate her salary to the Jonas Salk Institute.

On April 2, 1974, just as *The Front Page* was going in front of the cameras, Billy's friend Armand Deutsch and his wife threw an Oscar-night party. It was a particularly exciting night for the Wilders, since Jack Lemmon was nominated for *Save the Tiger* (1973) and stood a good chance of winning. Deutsch mailed out ballots for an Oscar pool beforehand—$50 a pop with the winner getting all the money, the only stipulation being that everybody had to vote for Lemmon. When Billy and Audrey showed up, Billy surprised his host by carting in his own six Oscars, which he kept at his office on the Goldwyn lot. He lined them all up on a table—three on one side, three on the other, with an open space in the center. "Lemmon will walk in later and put his in the middle," Billy announced.

On the television set, Liza Minnelli and Gregory Peck opened the Best Actor envelope. Lemmon won. Billy, overwhelmed, beamed in pride—but only until the other guests turned and looked at him, at which point he quickly wiped the grin off his face and resumed his usual look of vague perturbation. "I had a speech prepared in 1959," Lemmon said from the TV. "I've forgotten it." After the televised ceremonies concluded, Lemmon showed up at the party and immediately rushed to Billy's side. "Congratulations," Wilder brusquely offered, "but remember, don't be late to work tomorrow. Actors are apt to take these things too seriously." Lemmon's face fell. Having achieved his aim of deflating the winner, Wilder then grinned and gave his close friend a big bear hug—a most uncharacteristic response for a man who disliked physical contact with others. He took Lemmon's Oscar and put it in the place of honor at the center of the family stash. Walter Matthau, who witnessed the whole interchange, thought the happy outcome was a bit of a toss-up; "It could have gone either way," he said. For his part, Lemmon made it a point to tell reporters in the next few days that "If Billy Wilder tries to give me any direction, I'll hit him right over the head with both my Oscars."

This was a merry group, by and large—egotistical and competitive but fun. These men knew each other very well and usually enjoyed themselves in their joint company. Lemmon, Matthau, and Deutsch had a standing date at the Wilders' apartment on Monday nights to watch football and lay large bets. Everyone wagered $100 per game—except for Matthau, who tended to have thousands of dollars at stake on any given evening. It was boys' night out, even if the boys were all Hollywood millionaires. The men watched TV; Audrey cooked. Other than to thank her when she served the meal at halftime, they paid her no attention. She once complained to Billy that she might as well be serving them naked because none of them would look up long enough to notice. Just as Walter Reisch described her years earlier, Audrey Wilder remained every bit as hard as her husband. "Yes, I think she's tough," agrees someone who knows them both; "You'd have to be to be married to Billy." It stands to reason. To field Billy's endless, tasteless, often cruelly personal wit, and even just to withstand the force of his larger-than-life personality, one would have to be pretty resilient. One would also have to enjoy it, and by all accounts Audrey Wilder always did. "There aren't many men like Billy, I can tell you that," she said. "And he's difficult. But all great men are difficult, you know. So? It goes with the territory. He may have been a headache, but he never was a bore. Ever. *Ever*."

Principal photography on *The Front Page* began on April 3, at the Universal Studios on the hills between Hollywood and Burbank. "He fired someone the first day of shooting," Susan Sarandon recalls. "That got everybody very much on their toes. One of the reporters was having trouble getting his lines right. The more pressure he felt, the worse it got, and that was it. Mr. Wilder wasn't particularly nasty about it, but it definitely set a standard. We knew he was serious." Sarandon, whose career was just beginning, was amazed by Wilder's precision, not to mention his commanding presence: "I had a wardrobe test; we were due to shoot in two days. He said, 'Her neck is beautiful. Get rid of that costume and do something that shows more of her neck.' I was flabbergasted. I'd never even noticed that I *had* a neck. And to expect a costume to appear the day after tomorrow. . . . And it did." Sarandon goes on:

> I was pretty inexperienced at the time, so he was a shock to me. He directed with a stopwatch. He didn't "cover" in the traditional way—master, two shot, single. He knew exactly what he wanted, and that's all he shot. It was a great lesson for me. That was a time when people were encouraged to indulge themselves; he was of an era when the script still meant something. So he had this little stopwatch, and he'd count down—'Three more seconds,' and then we'd do it. He also insisted on everyone going to dailies in the afternoon. Everyone would eat lunch

together and watch them. It was a very social gathering, but I was not comfortable seeing myself on film—I *still* don't go to dailies—and Mr. Wilder found it personally upsetting that I didn't join in with everyone else. I tried to explain it, and he eased up a little bit, but he kept kidding me about it throughout the shoot.

After a lifetime of smoking, Billy Wilder had finally quit; *The Front Page* was his first production without cigarettes and cigars. To keep himself distracted he stuffed his mouth with chewing gum.

Much to the dismay of Helen Hayes, Charles MacArthur's widow and the owner of his share of the rights, Wilder and Diamond rewrote about 60 percent of the original dialogue. Part of this transformation, as Joseph McBride notes, was due to the fact that the play takes place entirely in a pressroom, whereas the film is opened up to an outside world. Wilder and Diamond's script describes Walter Burns as falling in "the great tradition of Machiavelli, Rasputin, and Count Dracula." And, for that matter, Billy Wilder, a fact acknowledged by Matthau. "I *always* play Wilder," Matthau said at the time; "*Wilder* sees me as Wilder."

"Billy Wilder said I like to humiliate directors. That's not true." This is Walter Matthau in the 1990s, explaining his reputation for impromptu rewriting during a shoot. Matthau went on to say that he always knows the story of the film he's making, and as a result, he knows best what his character should say at any given point. Jack Lemmon was always more accommodating to Billy's direction. Even when Matthau speaks with open admiration of Wilder, there's conflict. Referring to one of their many conversations on the set, Matthau reports that Billy wanted every scene to crackle: "He said, 'Each scene that you do must have some dramatic explosion, some astonishing thing about it. Otherwise it falls down.' I said, 'How about if I *build* to that.' He said, 'No, forget about building. Building is for architects.'"

Austin Pendleton, thrilled to be in a Wilder picture, was nevertheless a nervous wreck. It wasn't Billy's fault. As Pendleton describes it, "He came over to me the first day on the set and said, 'I made up my mind I would not die without having you in a film of mine.' I mean, this is serious charm we have going here. I was overwhelmed." Pendleton continues: "We started shooting, and he said—very kindly but firmly—that he wouldn't print it because I wasn't truthful enough. He didn't want to embarrass me artistically by releasing across the country anything less than the truth—the absolute vulnerability of the character. He said it as if he was just concerned for my well-being. It wasn't sharp or embarrassing. He had a kind of courtly concern for my reputation."

"For some reason, the part [of Earl Williams, the neurotic killer] was very frightening and threatening for me," Pendleton goes on.

Now, he's easily smart enough to use that. You don't make a lot of really great films without having figured *that* out. I have a feeling that part of the reason people think the performance does work is that he decided to photograph my own turbulence, as opposed to trying to correct it or edit it out. Sometimes I would just get overwhelmed and be all but unable to do the scene. One time I was doing a scene with Martin Gabel, and I just couldn't do it. [It's the scene in which Williams undergoes a psychiatric examination by a German-accented Freudian, played by Gabel.] "We did a couple of takes, and then Billy came over to me and simply put his hand on my shoulder. That's all he did. And then I did it. I felt very protected by him, and yet I felt he wasn't going to let me get away with anything bad.

Carol Burnett was also nervous and insecure even though, unlike Pendleton's, her part didn't particularly call for it. Wilder didn't bother to soothe her very much, and she was too embarrassed to ask him what she was doing wrong. Confused by Wilder's tendency not to rehearse much before each take, Burnett also felt like an outsider in the blustering, boys-club world of Billy, Izzie, Jack, and Walter. Moreover, she was a successful TV star then, one of the most recognizable and popular women in American entertainment, but it didn't matter a whit to Billy as far as her scheduling was concerned. Wilder kept her waiting on the set all day long, requiring her to be there in the morning but not filming anything with her until late at night. Mollie Molloy is not one of her best performances. Later, after the film was released, Burnett and her husband were on a plane on which *The Front Page* was shown during the flight. Burnett was aghast and hid under her coat, but after it was over she asked the flight attendant if she could make an announcement. Grabbing the mike, Burnett said, "Ladies and gentlemen, this is Carol Burnett. I didn't know that this movie was going to be shown on this flight, and I would sincerely like to apologize to each and every one of you."

The Front Page was still in production when, on May 6, 1974, at around 4:15 P.M., an electrical switch shorted out on Goldwyn's Soundstage 5 on the set of *Sigmund and the Sea Monsters*, a children's television program. A flash fire erupted, and soon two other Goldwyn soundstages, the Writers Building, and several executive offices were engulfed in flames and acrid smoke. Firefighters were quick to respond. So was Steve McQueen, who explained to the boys and girls of the press that he was researching his upcoming role as the fire chief in the Fox-Warners coproduction of *The Towering Inferno* (1974). When the flames were finally put out, Billy's office in the Writers Building lay completely destroyed. All the papers, correspondence, contracts, script drafts, notes, doodles, and poker chits collected over the course of his long career were gone, along with some paintings and sculptures he'd been storing in a loft space tucked away in a secluded area of Soundstage 5. He did not, however, lose his six Oscars. He simply hadn't gotten around to bringing them back from Armand Deutsch's place. Walter Mirisch was not as lucky. The Academy Award he won for *In the Heat of the Night* was decapitated.

Austin Pendleton describes Billy's state of mind just after the fire: "We were preparing the lighting for a scene, and he got a call that his office burned down, and all these expensive and beloved paintings had been destroyed. I went over and told him how sorry I was. He kind of shrugged. I was astounded." The art Billy lost was very disturbing but not devastating; they weren't the key works in his collection. (He kept many of those stacked in closets and behind furniture at home.) Moreover, the destruction of his screenplay drafts, notes, deal memos, and correspondence may even have been something of a relief to such a private man. But whatever he lost, and however much the items meant to him, Wilder's steely reaction to the fire went beyond mere grace under pressure; perhaps he didn't react with shock because the fire only confirmed once again the way the world worked. "Things could have been worse," he told a journalist. "Hitler could have won World War II."

The Front Page wrapped after a two-and-a-half-month shoot. For all its amusing, even endearing moments—Eggelhoffer's examination of Williams, the smoky camaraderie of the pressroom, the hatchet-faced janitress (Doro Merande in her third appearance for Wilder)—*The Front Page* is Wilder's slightest work. Its themes are so integral to his worldview that he doesn't have anything new to say about them. Competence and deceit, uneasy male bonding, the distracting pleasure of chopping words out of thin air, a hooker—Wilder and Diamond had little need to remake and rewrite Ben Hecht and Charles MacArthur's play other than to use it as a gimmick to get financing. It's not that they were disinterested in the film they made. If anything, they cared too much about making the film, *any* film, in order to keep working, and they ended up settling for less rather than accepting the early retirement to which Hollywood was otherwise consigning them. Wilder actually begins his film with a montage of an antiquated system—one that he and Diamond clearly loved: a newspaper is made from hand-set type. The headline, a Wilder-Diamond addition, is revealing in its morbid logic: "Cop Killer Sane, Must Die."

With all its burnished nostalgia for a more accommodating (if not especially simpler) era, *The Front Page* contains some of Billy's most unpleasant interchanges. More heartless by far than *Kiss Me, Stupid*, *The Front*

Page dwells (as does the play) on the gallows being built outside the press-room window in the deep pit of a jailhouse courtyard. Wilder's camera stares down on it from above and zooms back to become a point of view that is shot from the perspective of an annoyed reporter, who calls for quiet. When the tubby cop who supervises the construction (Cliff Osmond) calls for a halt, looks up, yells "Screw you," and waves the builders back to work, it's not very nice on any level. Billy introduces his surrogate with similar coarseness. Hunched over with his back to the camera, Walter Burns shouts into the telephone: "That dumb sonofabitch bastard, who does he think he is?! I'm sorry. I didn't mean to yell at you. Well look, if Hildy shows up will you be so kind as to tell that dumb sonofabitch bastard to get his ass over here? Thank you."

With *The Front Page*, Wilder and Diamond wrote their first practicing homosexual, the effeminate Bensinger (David Wayne), who seems to have been designed to distract audiences from the male bonding on which *The Front Page* has always stood and on which Wilder and Diamond had themselves been dwelling since *Some Like It Hot*. Their attempt to create a gay Sherlock Holmes having ended in ambivalent disappointment, they now strove to create a classic mincing fag. "Never, *never* get caught in the can with Bensinger," is Hildy's central piece of advice to the callow novice-reporter Rudy Keppler (Jon Korkes), and sure enough, not only does Bensinger insinuate his hand onto Keppler's shoulder in a later scene, a comical epilogue finds the two men having moved to Cape Cod together to open an antique shop. But unlike Wilder's and Diamond's earlier (and funnier) gay jokes, homosexuality in *The Front Page* is all about incompetence. "Jesus, Hildy, you're a newspaperman, not some faggot writing poetry about brassieres and laxatives." That's Walter Burns trying to convince Hildy not to get married and become an advertising copywriter. "Nobody but fairies go into advertising," another reporter underscores. All of this is meant to explain why Jack Lemmon should ditch Susan Sarandon and stick with Walter Matthau.

The film's leisurely pacing is more damaging than a few callous fairy jokes. Overlapping dialogue, one of the play's best-known devices, was such an anathema to Wilder that he eliminated it, and the film suffers greatly for its absence. As much as *One, Two, Three, The Front Page* has always been a play of speed. Since George S. Kaufman first staged it on Broadway in 1928, actors were instructed to step on each other's lines to create a breakneck whirl of words. But as Lemmon said, "I think that the idea of overlapping is repugnant to Billy, because you're going to lose some of the dialogue. And he *really* stopped us from overlapping." *The Front Page* never played so slow.

In 1974, Universal's big films were *Airport 75* and *Earthquake*. This in itself might have told Billy that his character-driven, language-loving brand of filmmaking would be a hard sell for the studio's publicity department. *The Front Page* premiered on December 19 at the Plitt Century Plaza theater, with a supper served afterward at the Century Plaza Hotel. Guests included Ross Hunter, Mitzi Gaynor, and then-governor Ronald Reagan and his wife, who was clad in a bugle-beaded Galanos gown. (Audrey Wilder countered with a silver fox coat.) The film quickly bombed. *The Front Page* "sure looks good on paper," *Variety* opined. "But that's about the only place it looks good." "Wilder is out of touch with the temper of the times," said *Newsweek*. *Time* was crueler: "This is a movie conceived with indifference and made with disinterest, like a piece of occupational therapy."

Even the praise of Wilder's critical admirer George Morris rings with inadvertent dismay. Noting that the property had already been filmed twice before, Morris observes that Wilder gives it "a predictably distinctive interpretation." The very predictability of its distinctiveness was precisely the problem. Ironically, what a host of hostile critics wrote wrongheadedly about *Sherlock Holmes* and *Avanti!* was actually true of *The Front Page*: despite its moments of humor and affection, particularly in regard to Pendleton's Earl Williams, the film is old and tired and out of touch. With sickening accuracy, something Wilder once said of Preston Sturges was suddenly true of himself: "His was the case of the strikeout fear. You go to bat and you hit singles, doubles, you hit them out of the ballpark—and then comes a series of strikeouts. You strike out, and you can't even bunt anymore. There was a loss of self-confidence and a sense that the money men were dealing with a burnt-out but enormous talent. And, of course, bad luck."

Hollywood had changed, and Billy, who hadn't missed an issue of the trades since he learned English, knew it as well as anyone in town. He'd always been for sale, with all the accompanying gigolo guilt, but it had been over a decade since audiences bought him. He wasn't the agile young dancer anymore. If anything, he'd become one of the old ladies he used to guide around the Hotel Eden ballroom—the ones who couldn't get dates unless they paid for them. After the failure of his fifth film in a row, Billy Wilder seemed to be truly out of time. Audiences were to blame. "The subtlest comedy you can get right now is *M*A*S*H*," he complained. "They don't want to see a picture unless Peter Fonda is running over a dozen people or unless Clint Eastwood has got a machine gun bigger than 140 penises."

Still, another one of Universal's 1974 releases caught his attention and admiration—a Goldie Hawn/William Atherton/Ben Johnson road movie that stirred genres in a manner Wilder could appreciate better than anyone. This slick but quirky film combined comedy and drama, adventure and emotion, action and soul, and Billy loved the mix. *The Sugarland Express* wasn't all that well received by the critics—in England, it was such a bomb that it only played on the bottom half of a double bill with *The Front Page*. But Wilder knew genius when he saw it. "The director of that movie is the greatest young talent to come along in years," Billy said at the time. Then he added a personal remark: "I was Steven Spielberg—once."

30. *FEDORA*

It's a whole different business now. The kids with beards have taken over. They don't need scripts. Just give 'em a handheld camera with a zoom lens. For two years I've sweated blood to get this project off the ground; now I've finally found me some tax-shelter guys. They're willing to finance it, but only if I can deliver Fedora. Without her there's no picture.

—Barry Detweiler (William Holden) in *Fedora*

In March 1977, Billy and Paul Kohner met in Munich to negotiate a whole new deal for Wilder's latest project, a film about the impossibility of recovering the past. The first deal had completely and demeaningly fallen apart. But thanks to what Billy called the German "money boys," *Fedora* was revived, and with unusual efficiency it was scheduled to go before the cameras two months later in Corfu. Seven weeks at Munich's Bavaria Studio would follow, after which the production would shift to Paris. The budget was $4,250,000, 47 percent of which was cobbled together from tax-shelter sources in Germany. *Fedora* would be a warped elegy to a world that no longer existed except in the minds of those who once loved it.

A year earlier, none of this multinational bean-counting would have been necessary. *Fedora* was a Universal project then. *The Front Page* had spooked the studio, but not enough to prevent another go-round with Wilder. *The Front Page* hadn't been botched; it just bombed, and like any studio in the 1970s, Universal was used to releasing money losers, the hope being that for every ten *Front Pages* there might be one *Jaws* (1975). After the best-selling author (and former actor) Tom Tryon signed his own four-picture deal with Universal, the studio announced that Wilder and Diamond would adapt and film one of the novellas in Tryon's collection, *Crowned Heads*. The film, now called *Fedora*, was soon scheduled to roll in the fall of 1976. Jennings Lang would produce, and Billy would direct.

There was one new element on which the studio insisted, however. This time, Universal demanded what was called a "step deal." The fact that

Wilder and Diamond were hired to write the screenplay, with Wilder signing to direct, did not mean that *Fedora* would be made. No, *this* deal would be structured in stages, based on the executives' continuing approval. Universal had forty-five days after receipt of Billy and Izzie's completed script to decide whether or not to green-light the production. Wilder hadn't been treated like this since the early 1940s, but given his commercial track record over the last dozen years, he was in no position to argue the point. "I'm going through a dry spell, that's all," he snapped. "I did not suddenly become an idiot." It was the mid-1970s, and Billy, age seventy, was not much impressed with the world he was forced to inhabit. In his view, he hadn't changed at all. It was the pictures that got small. "They say Wilder is out of touch with his times," he admitted, but "frankly I regard it as a compliment. Who the hell wants to be in touch with *these* times?"

When Universal executives read the script Wilder and Diamond created, they summarily put *Fedora* in what they called "turnaround," a popular Hollywood euphemism for garbage can. Billy was stunned—and enraged. "I don't know who they are, the mysterious people up there," he said. "It's Kafka. From what I gather—I didn't even talk to them because I was pissed off, as they say—I gather that they didn't think that it had a chance. What hurts the most is that they may be proven right." Universal's decision makers, led by Sidney Sheinberg, were motivated not only by concern over the script's defiantly loopy quality—it was a long, lovingly sick joke on Hollywood—but also by a string of past flops about the golden age of American cinema. Two of these money losers were Universal pictures—*Gable and Lombard* (1976) and *W. C. Fields and Me* (1976). Like *The Front Page* two years earlier, both were bits of burnished Hollywood nostalgia, both were major box office disappointments, and the studio saw no need to make it three in a row.

Billy was immediately on the phone shopping *Fedora* to all the other studios in town. One after another they turned him down. Universal's step deal was degrading enough. Now Wilder found himself hurled back to the 1930s, peddling a screenplay nobody wanted to buy.

Depending on the loyalty of friends, Wilder turned to Kohner. Thirty-six years earlier, the honorable agent knew Billy had gotten too big for him to represent. When he congratulated Wilder on the success of *Hold Back the Dawn*, Kohner concluded by noting, "I don't know why I am writing you such letters since I know I can't get you as a client anyhow." Now that Kohner could get Billy again, he did, and together the two old refugees found support from the Germans. Universal still wanted the right of first refusal as far as distribution was concerned, but Billy, holding a grudge, put enough of his own money into the project to prevent that double humiliation. It was the last-minute infusion of muscular German marks, though, that was his salvation. "Look, I can't lose," Billy declared as *Fedora* approached its release, "because if this picture is a big hit, it's my revenge on Hollywood. If it's a total financial disaster, it's my revenge for Auschwitz."

Fedora is the story of a reclusive, foreign-born movie star who has remained ineffably beautiful despite her advancing years. When an on-the-skids Hollywood producer tracks her down at her remote villa on a tiny island off Corfu, his pestering, belligerent attention sets off a chain of events that results in suicide. The Hollywood rumor mill had it that Wilder was trying to convince Greta Garbo to come out of seclusion to play the role of Fedora, but Billy denied it. He did, however, ask Marlene Dietrich, with an eye toward casting Faye Dunaway as her daughter. Marlene declined— "for various reasons," according to Billy. "She thought there was some kind of similarity with her own life, which it certainly is not. And she is not well." More to the point, Dietrich despised the screenplay. "I hated the book, I hated the script, and I don't know why you want to do it," the cantankerous recluse told Billy by letter.

Artistically, the seventy-year-old Billy was in a reflective and morose mood. By 1976, when Universal threw *Fedora* into turnaround, he had spent more than ten years planning, writing, and directing a series of beloved failures. It is hardly surprising that he found himself musing on the theme of Hollywood's cruelty to has-beens.

Fedora wasn't his only idea with a Tinseltown motif. He claims to have been working on an original story about a multigenerational, Mayer-like Hollywood family. Its title was the punchline: *The Foreskin Saga*. "I had another idea," he said, "a film about a retirement home for movie stars. It's one of the rare successes that the community can be proud of. They take out a percentage of your salary for this institution, which is located in the valley on land that used to belong to Warner. . . . My plan was to make a film about a child star à la Shirley Temple, whose career is over at age seven and who argues that she should have the right to live there since she filled all the conditions. So this little monster arrives in the world of the aged, and they have only one wish—to kill her."

Fedora held more appeal, though the property brought with it a difficult problem: "What attracted me was what I finally wasn't able to resolve: would it be the same actress playing the mother and the daughter? Could I find someone who can appear both twenty years old and eighty, decrepit in a wheelchair, without revealing my secret? It was a big problem and if I had only partially solved it, I would have been very happy." Wilder describes the tale as one of reverence: "The story is the old homosexual dream of admiration for strong women—Garbo, Dietrich, Mae West—at whose feet they throw flowers. . . . I needed an actress with the force of Bette Davis at her peak. But at the same time—and this increased the difficulties—I wanted her to be an imported star, with a vague air of Dietrich, Garbo, or Pola Negri." He settled on Marthe Keller.

Sydney Pollack planted the notion when he invited Billy to a prescreening of *Bobby Deerfield* (1977). The Swiss actress was glamorous, refined, and lightly accented. The camera adored her cheekbones and creamy-velvet complexion. He delivered a script to her on January 28, Keller's thirty-second birthday. At first, Keller was to play both parts—the aged Fedora as well as her daughter, Antonia. Hildegard Knef, who ultimately took the role of Fedora, was an afterthought—a kind of human Band-Aid. "Keller had been in a very bad automobile accident," Wilder explained. "Her face was smashed up, and she had a bad cut. It's all fixed up, but the nerve ends are such that when you try heavy makeup, with rubber and stuff like that, she couldn't tolerate the pain when they took it off." That was the practical excuse. More salient was the fact that the magnitude and presence of the elderly Fedora, said to have been one of the greatest movie stars of the century, was more than Keller could handle.

William Holden provided Billy with a firmer foundation, not to mention a more resonant icon. Wilder cast his old friend in the role of Barry Detweiler, film producer manqué. Said Wilder, "My only problem was that it would reinforce the parallel with *Sunset Boulevard*," an echo Billy seems not to have wanted to create quite so self-evidently. "But he has a seriousness, a presence, a maturity, a solidity which makes him indispensable. You know he's maybe the only actor in Hollywood his age who hasn't had face-lifts. It's remarkable in a city where, with the pieces of skin that have been cut from the face of one star you could make five or six new ones." Holden was cagey about accepting the role, which required extensive time in Greece, Paris, and Munich. He played some money games through his agent, but Billy knew he'd do it in the end: "You know why? Because he had ordered a new BMW and he told them he would pick it up personally."

The most striking change from novella to film lies in Holden's character. In the book, he's a successful writer who searches for Fedora out of a romantic nostalgia; he and Fedora had once been lovers. Wilder and Diamond keep their past tryst, but they make Barry Detweiler older and more bitter, an aging producer on the skids. Detweiler introduces his brief affair with Fedora in voice-over: "It was 1947. We were shooting something called *Leda and the Swan*. I was the second assistant. You didn't even know I was around—until we started on the big pool scene—the handmaidens, and the water lilies, and you in the nude." A flashback begins. "I'm afraid we're going to have a little problem with the censors," says *Leda*'s thickly German-accented director. "You mean the boobs," his assistant clarifies, at which point young "Dutch" Detweiler (Stephen Collins) is ordered into the studio tank to rearrange the water lilies on Fedora's bare breasts. He slaps them on and yawns.

Later, in her dressing room, she confronts him: "Tell me, Mr. Detweiler, are you a faggot?" "A *what?*" he answers with a look of shock. "A queer. A fairy," she reiterates, biting on both expressions hard enough to wound him all the more deeply. "Don't tell me you're normal. Because no normal man would yawn if he saw me without my clothes." "I had a very rough night last night," he explains. "Doing what?" she answers. "Picking up sailors at the bus station?" "Boy have you got the wrong number. Ask any of the girls on the set! Or in wardrobe. Or makeup!" They proceed to enjoy a romantic night together on the beach in Santa Monica, but the only moment of this lovemaking Wilder shows on-screen is a brief, morning-after sequence with the couple, fully clothed, huddled together for warmth in the front seat.

Fedora herself changed subtly in the adaptation as well. In the novella, she's a nearly fantastic character of almost eighty years. Wilder and Dia mond make her younger and more plausible, and the film explains her secret more pragmatically than does the novella. As the critic Christian Viviani points out, Tryon doesn't detail what Fedora's career was like or what made her a star. He "shows us how the legend survives, but not what it's based on. Wilder's approach is diametrically opposite: the foundation of the legend is what interests him, but he doesn't really evoke it in the script. He prefers to let images play with all their hypnotic power." The trouble was, late 1970s audiences were less willing to be hypnotized by images of old, demented movie stars. They preferred young Jedi knights and voracious sharks.

In Wilder and Diamond's *Fedora*, another character plays a pivotal (some might say reeling) role—Doctor Vando (José Ferrer). The secret of Fedora's persevering beauty—her plastic surgeon—is dead in Tryon's novella, but Wilder and Diamond keep him very much alive and center screen. This, too, was problematic for audiences, since Vando's perseverence turns comical. Finally, there are profound differences between Tryon's and Wilder's visions of Fedora's daughter. She's called Ophelia in the book, but Wilder and Diamond rechristen her Antonia. In the book, Ophelia is more responsible for her precarious state of mind. She believes in the star myth and tries to become it herself, whereas Antonia is a confused pawn driven to madness by her own victimization. Ophelia drugs herself; Antonia gets dosed by Dr. Vando. Viviani picks up on the more subtly allusive name change: "In giving her a first name that evokes Hoffmann via Offenbach, Wilder and Diamond make her a sister of the unhappy heroines of the poet: dancers who fly into pieces, singers who can only sing by accepting death, victims of a fatality that annihilates them." If only *Fedora* sustained this degree of operatic grandeur.

Wilder expands on the morbid texture and theme he wished to create: "My original idea was an impressionistic quest like Böcklin's *The Isle of the Dead*. That took place in Greece, but I wanted something Wagnerian— like on Lake Como. But I would have had to wait three weeks to have the necessary light or use a fog machine to envelop the island. Then I told myself that the murder could be much more interesting in full sun. Another difficulty was finding a sufficiently imposing and isolated villa." In terms of its peculiar comico-mythic tone, *Fedora*, clearly, was one of Billy Wilder's most ambitious pictures.

Topicality was originally provided by Barbara Walters, who was written into the script as a newscaster in an early sequence; the role was eventually taken by Arlene Francis. Michael York was to play himself, the movie star with whom Antonia falls tragically in love. The role of the president of the Academy, who travels to Fedora's secluded villa to bestow a belated prize, was initially to go to Gregory Peck; Henry Fonda ended up playing the part (using Alex Trauner's own Oscar as his prop).

Shooting began on June 1 on Corfu, with a pack of old and new buddies serving as Billy's production team. His closest German friend, Willy Egger, was made production supervisor; his pal Harold Nebenzal (the grandson of *Menschen am Sonntag*'s producer Heinrich Nebenzahl) served as production coordinator. And a young writer, Rex McGee, came aboard as *Fedora*'s historian and archivist on behalf of the Directors Guild. A grant from Jack Lemmon financed McGee's project, which was widely announced in the press as the first time an entire Hollywood production would be chronicled from inception to release. A film student who wrote a fan letter to Billy after *Avanti!* was released, McGee was shocked to get a personal phone call from Wilder, who invited him over to his office. "I can still remember the first time I heard that unique voice over the phone in my tiny dorm room," McGee recalls. Low-key and smart, the young Texan quickly became one of Wilder's trusted chums. He was invited to hang around the set of *The Front Page* and watch Billy work at close range, and the two spent countless hours over tables at Johnny Rockets eating burgers, discussing moviemaking, writing, and politics. Billy even asked him to appear on-screen in *Fedora*; McGee plays a news photographer. No one was in a better position than Rex McGee to document the production of *Fedora*. It's too bad the Directors Guild ultimately lost all of the material he assembled.

After four days of exterior filming in Corfu, the company moved to the islands of Lefkás and Madouri, the latter being the site of Fedora's villa.

As always, Trauner was intrigued by the technical design problems he faced: "To show the isolation in which Fedora lived, we had to provide an immediate physical dimension, so we found a small island on the Greek coast—in that region of personal fortresses where people buy islands to slip away to. A difficult place to approach, where there's only one house and not even a road." They found what they were looking for at the village of Nydri on the tiny island of Lefkás, which (purely by chance) is located immediately next to Skorpiós, Onassis's retreat. Trauner and his production design team softened the crusty old house with some extra trees, a wide terrace, and two headless Greek goddesses, all of which were fine with Billy. But the homey porch swing Trauner added was too much. Billy was appalled. "Take it out!" he insisted. "It looks cheap—like something from Glendale."

A jumble of reporters, visitors, and photographers stood by on Trauner's terrace, clicking and chatting as Billy prepared to direct a scene in which Antonia and Fedora learn of the Academy's award—a scene in which Antonia reminds Fedora of the role she'd played in the (fictitious) film *East of Suez* in 1956. Charmingly and intimately, the daughter was to do a little impersonation of the mother making her famous entrance in the film. The script describes the scene: "With one tug she has unfurled the turban from her head. She now tosses it around her neck like a feather boa, starts singing 'C'est Si Bon' in a low sexy voice—an outré parody of yesterday's screen sirens. Swiveling her hips, she moves over to Vando." "Cheer up, Reverend," Antonia was supposed to purr, quoting her mother's film performance; "Let's sin some and gin some. East of Suez there are no Ten Commandments."(This prompted Billy to make up a plaque for his beach house; it reads "North of Zuma there are no Ten Commandments." He claimed to have given copies to his neighbors Herbert Ross and Dinah Shore.)

The scene reads simply enough. But Keller simply could not perform it. Over and over Billy rehearsed the shot—to no avail. Knef and Frances Sternhagen (as Fedora's assistant/nursemaid, Miss Balfour) were edgy as well, with a horde of onlookers standing on the sidelines. The ever-social Billy saw no need to clear the set. Keller grew increasingly clumsy and exasperated as Billy habitually fed her particular line readings, the rhythms just so. "Please don't tell me any more," she finally snapped. Her English regressed. Her lines were no longer clear. She was beginning to shift her beturbaned shoulders like a clumsy drag queen, and the crowd of reporters, sensing the mounting tension, grew increasingly rapacious until Keller's performance completely fell apart. Izzie Diamond, grouchy on the sidelines, grew mystified at the way a very good actress was able to mangle his and Billy's lines. "I know what it says, and *I* didn't understand it," he muttered.

They reshot the "C'est Si Bon" scene on a Munich soundstage one month later, transposing it from the terrace to a bedroom, but Keller still couldn't get it right, and the whole business ended up being cut.

Keller was in tears on the plane from Greece to Munich. "I can't work with a director like that!" she wailed to William Holden. "He treats me just like a puppet!" Holden told her that he commiserated, but he made it a point to note that every time he made a Billy Wilder film he got an Oscar nomination. Keller wasn't soothed. "He wouldn't even give me the chance to be wrong, to find out for myself," she later declared. "I just had to do as he said. I said, 'Can I try it this way?' He said, 'Of course, but I'll cut it out later.' " She became most distressed: "In the end I went a bit crazy and had to see a doctor." Reporters were quick to seize on the drama. Wilder responded to their insistent questions by saying that he didn't have time to engage in a public debate with Marthe Keller. But, he noted, "She's marvelous in the picture."

Keller may have been difficult, but Wilder didn't make things any easier for her when he started ridiculing her current boyfriend, Al Pacino, who visited her while she shot *Fedora*. The sticking point was Pacino's taste in food: there he was in Europe, and Pacino kept ordering hamburgers. Billy was his usual merciless self on the subject, and Keller grew even more perturbed. For her part, Keller found Holden a bore and avoided socializing with him. She complained privately that all he did was repeat stories she'd already heard. She got along no better with Hildegard Knef. "Knef and Keller are not exactly at war but they are avoiding each other," a reporter breathlessly revealed in the *Los Angeles Times*. This was especially sad, since Keller was said to have suggested Knef for the role in the first place. Knef, meanwhile, was telling receptive interviewers that she was the leading lady in the picture and that her costars were Jose Ferrer and William Holden. Keller's name wasn't even mentioned.

Billy gave up on his chewing gum. He started smoking again—three especially pungent French stogies every day.

In late July, after nearly two months of shooting, Billy and Izzie saw an hour's worth of a rough cut and promptly fired the editor. No replacement was in sight. The production team hobbled from Munich to Paris, where interior shooting continued at the now-fairly-decrepit Studios de Boulogne, on the same soundstages where they had shot *Love in the Afternoon*. Billy, who once enjoyed shooting in France, was no longer content there. He was used to his baseball games on television, his poker and bridge buddies, his routine. Besides, he said, "It's not a vacation, believe me. It's a punishment to film in Paris. Being closed up in the Boulogne Studios and not being able to walk down the street is like being a pianist in a bordello while hearing the people screwing on every floor. It makes you crazy."

Fedora wrapped on August 31, the budget having soared to over $6,727,000. A few days later, Billy was back in Hollywood with a lot of shaky footage and no editor. Ralph Winters, who had cut both *Avanti!* and *The Front Page*, was already booked on another project, but he recommended Fritz Steinkamp, who agreed to take on the task. By the beginning of October, Steinkamp pulled together a little more than half the film. Looking at the footage again and again, Wilder found himself muttering a mantra: "Rózsa, Rózsa, Rózsa." The composer was summoned, and the two old friends resumed their typically prickly exchange. "I'm sorry, Miklós, I didn't mean to hurt you," Billy said after hurling a characteristic barb. "It's not my style. Kill, yes; but hurt, never." "Then you've changed," Rózsa counterpunched. "Before it was always hurt first, then kill."

By the end of October, Steinkamp and Wilder produced the first complete rough cut. It was a little over two hours long, but it felt even longer. As Steinkamp observed, the rhythms Wilder achieved within each scene were magnificent—"Other directors would give their left arms to be able to stage scenes like this," he said, but his transitions from scene to scene had become ungainly. Doane Harrison had been gone for a decade, and nobody else could take his place. Moreover, Billy hamstrung himself with his own exactitude. Had he not precut the film so elegantly with the camera while shooting, any proficient editor might have had more room to maneuver.

A more drastic problem loomed. Marthe Keller's voice didn't work on film. There was still another obstacle: neither did Hildegard Knef's. They simply did not sound enough alike to sustain the myth of Fedora, and without that conceit there was no picture. Both voices—the two central performances in the film—would have to be looped in postproduction.

It was one thing for Marni Nixon to have been hired to sing for Audrey Hepburn in *My Fair Lady* (1964). It was quite another to bring a German actress named Inga Bunsch into a sound studio to rerecord more than four hundred lines of dialogue that make up the two most important roles in the film. Knef was disgusted: "First he destroys my face, now he takes away my voice. What else is left?" Keller hadn't heard the news yet, but her agent had, and he wasn't happy about it. Under some duress, Billy agreed to tell Keller the news personally, which he did. Much to his surprise Keller wasn't entirely horrified, though she may simply have been resigned to fate. "She sounds a lot like me," Keller acknowledged. Still, the actress had one inflexible demand: that her own voice be kept for the last four scenes of the film—the ones in which she is no longer masquerading as Fedora. Diamond fretted. "If we use the Keller and Bunsch voices back to back, we'll lose our credibility," he said. He and Billy knew they were in a double bind, since the voices of the two Fedoras needed to be looped precisely because of a total lack of credibility. Thus Marthe Keller was brought back in to loop her own performance.

When Keller saw the film for the first time right before New Year's, she was shocked. She blew into Wilder and Diamond's office at the Goldwyn Studios in such a state of high energy that both men feared catastrophe. "I was knocked out!" she blurted. "It was beautiful! I loved it!" "God bless you, dear," Billy said with relief. Keller had but one request: "I want you to use my voice where it is appropriate," she said with a distinctly threatening edge.

More looping followed. Keller's voice was sufficiently familiar in France that she looped both Antonia's and Fedora's voices for the French release. Hildegard Knef, famous in Germany, then looped *her* voice in for both characters as well. The tone of already strained credulity on which this cinematic tale stood was now wobblier. Rózsa, meanwhile, ended up with a total of three weeks to score the film. *Fedora*, which had once been carefully planned, had somehow turned slapdash. Never before had Rózsa composed anything so quickly, and he was not pleased about it. After an orchestra recorded the score in mid-December, he and Billy listened to a playback. "I can't hear anything," said Rózsa, disturbed at the low volume. Billy was unmoved: "The mere fact that you didn't hear anything doesn't necessarily make you Beethoven."

The mood was even glummer after *Fedora*'s sound mixing in January, when it became apparent that Inga Bunsch's voice worked no better than Keller's or Knef's. Lines that sounded fine when she recorded them became deadening when laid onto the image. Rózsa pronounced it "fatal." Steinkamp was equally blunt. "You've lost a whole performance," he told Billy; "Knef's is *the* performance of the picture." Diamond was forced to admit a crucial fact: "If we use Hilde's voice we're asking for a lawsuit. It will look like we lied to Marthe." "The agents are ready to pounce," Billy acknowledged. He had no choice but to use Bunsch's monotonous loops. "Forget Knef's voice," he told the others. "*You* have heard it, and *you* know the difference, but the audience doesn't. They will never miss it." As it happened, they did.

Adding to *Fedora*'s woes in late February, Allied Artists dropped its deal to distribute the film in the United States. Allied still had the film on February 18, when *Fedora* was screened in New York at a Myasthenia Gravis Foundation benefit, but a few days later the film was free-floating. The issues under dispute were distribution patterns and advertising and publicity expenditures. Allied wanted a gradual, exclusive run, while the film's distributor, Lorimar, favored the kind of broad national release they were used to providing. The complexities of postclassical American cinema are grimly illustrated by *Variety*'s account of the deal's collapse: "Informed sources say Allied had reached a verbal distribution deal with Lorimar, the U.S. agent for the film's German production financiers, but contract talks broke down about two weeks ago. Pic has been returned to Lorimar, which has reportedly concluded a network TV sale of *Fedora* to CBS-TV." Eventually, United Artists picked up *Fedora* and released it in only a few select, limited markets, with UA (in Wilder's words) "releasing it in a perfunctory and insulting way and spending about $625 on an advertising campaign."

In mid-March, *Fedora* was shown to Lorimar executives Merv Adelson and Lee Rich at the Burbank Studios in what had once been Jack Warner's personal screening room. Wilder sat in the back smoking. "I'm watching you, Merv," he said. "If you want to sleep, sit behind me." Rex McGee reports the uncomfortable exchange that occurred when the lights came back up:

RICH: How much are you going to take out, Billy?
WILDER: A couple of minutes, maybe three.
ADELSON: It's strong.
RICH: Very strong.
WILDER: It's different.
ADELSON: Yes, it is.
RICH: It *is* different.

Rich went on to observe that the print was really quite good. "You should see some of the stuff we get in here," he noted.

Paul Kohner saw the film for the first time a few days later, and the agent, a master of discretion and tact, knew precisely how it should be handled. "The beautiful thing about *Fedora* is that nobody knows about it," Kohner pointed out. "The film should be treated as a precious jewel. I think it is a masterpiece. It must be treated as an important picture. Otherwise, it gets around that the film is problematic and I think maybe you are sunk."

Wilder, Diamond, and Steinkamp set about making what were (to Billy, at least) some fairly drastic cuts—twelve minutes' worth. The film was ready for previews in May. Billy picked Santa Barbara. He'd wanted to preview *Fedora* with one of two current films then in release—*The Turning Point* or *Julia*, either of which would have drawn an appropriate audience. Neither was playing in Santa Barbara at the time. *Annie Hall* was in release, but the 1,200-seat theater in which it was playing was far too cavernous to sustain an intimate film like *Fedora*. He ended up at the State Theater, which was showing *House Calls* (1978), a broad comedy starring Walter Matthau and Glenda Jackson.

Fedora's first real audience was receptive for the first half. Then they started laughing. This in itself might not have been a problem, but they laughed at places that weren't supposed to be funny. When they roared with derision at a pivotal scene between Keller and Michael York, Billy and Iz felt slapped by their own failure. Rózsa suggested a few more cuts, but Billy was tired of *Fedora* and decided to leave it alone. "In this time I could have made *three* lousy pictures instead of one," he griped.

Fedora found its world premiere at the Cannes Film Festival on May 30, 1978. Keller was so thrilled with its reception and the initial European reviews that she actually hosted a party for Billy in Paris a short time later. The Cannes crowd was primed to receive the film well. A small but important retrospective of Billy's work was included in the Festival, and Billy himself was chosen to bestow the prestigious Palme d'Or at ceremonies before his new film's premiere. As *Variety* reported, "European critics liked it at the Cannes Fest though Yank appraisers sneered. . . . Pic can be summed up as a well made but flawed tale." *Variety*'s critic, at least, appreciated the effort. He admired Wilder's "directorial flair" as well as Holden's and York's performances. But, he went on to note, "missing are needed hints at Fedora's true star quality, which are not there from past clips or inherent in Keller's performance or that of Knef as her ruthless mentor, and which mar pic with disbelief."

The *Hollywood Reporter* was nastier. The critic was unable to resist noting the scornful laughter of audiences, who are said to have hooted in disbelief when Antonia doesn't recognize Dr. Vando on the telephone when she thinks she's talking to Michael York. Richard Schickel, writing in *Time*, was simply rude. Under the cute headline "Old Hat," Schickel found Billy Wilder to be laughably over the hill: "Finally, because this movie invokes director Wilder's earlier *Sunset Boulevard*, we are asked to accept a melodramatic manner of storytelling and characterization that is outmoded by at least a quarter of a century. Settings, dialogue, the very looks on the faces of everyone in Fedora's household teeter on the ludicrous."

One of the clearest, best reviews of *Fedora* came from Wilder's old nemesis, Andrew Sarris. Having penned in the 1960s the damning line "Billy Wilder is too cynical to believe his own cynicism," Sarris pulled a guilty about-face in the 1970s. Noting the drumbeat of gossip-column chronicles of the film's poor reception at various prerelease screenings, Sarris was sharply incensed—and all too accurate: "The usual collection of freeloading trend-seekers were reportedly laughing at all the wrong places. There is nothing quite so hideously heartless as the idiot cackle of the incrowd when it senses that a career may be on the skids." Sarris added a dry rebuke: "It is not as if high aesthetic standards were being upheld in the process." (One can see the shadow of Sarris's guilt here; it was Sarris, after all, who paused in his rave review of *Lord Love a Duck* (1966), to remark, "One shudders to think of Billy Wilder running amok in this material.") Acknowledging that Keller and Knef weren't up to their roles, Sarris was still impressed by the way in which Billy appeared to be speaking directly from his heart through the intermediary of William Holden. "If memory serves me correctly," Sarris added, "Wilder was even wearing the same jaunty hat in Cannes that Holden sported in *Fedora*." Wilder courted disaster with *Fedora*, and Sarris applauded him for it: "Long before noir was a critical catchword," he continued, "Wilder's characters seemed to walk on the dark side of the street out of a natural predilection for peril. Even Wilder's comedies—*The Apartment, Sabrina, Avanti!*, most notably— have been shadowed by death and self-destruction. But in *Fedora* the cinema itself ends up in a coffin of Wilder's own design. And one can hardly expect 1979 screening audiences to join Wilder at the wake."

Janet Maslin got it right in the *New York Times*: "It is rich, majestic, very close to ridiculous, and also a little bit mad. It seems exactly what Mr. Wilder wants it to be, perfectly self-contained and filled with the echoes of a lifetime." Thanks in no small measure to Maslin, Sarris, and Vincent Canby (who expanded on Maslin's appreciation in a Sunday Arts and Leisure essay), *Fedora* beat all expectations in New York. Its cruelest reviews notwithstanding, the film performed well at the Gotham box office.

With *Fedora*, Wilder and Diamond strove to achieve an offbeat, comical-tragic tone—a precarious goal, since the danger of filming a character who descends from gracious, distant self-confidence to delusional paranoia is specifically that she will look funniest when she is at her most vulnerable. Antonia asks who Detweiler has in mind for the part of Vronsky. "Oh, we can get Jack Nicholson, Warren Beatty, Steve McQueen. . . ." "You know Michael York?" she asks enthusiastically. Even in 1978 her devotion to York seemed immoderate. She has met the actor already and fallen in love with him; the two have costarred in a film called *The Last Waltz*, a Technicolor musical set in Schönbrunn Palace in Vienna. In the film (which looks suspiciously like the extravagant musical Wilder wrote and filmed with Brackett), she plays a general's wife who falls in love with her son-in-law.

Antonia's breakdown occurs when she realizes that she is trapped in a false persona—that of her mother, who has herself constructed an enduring public identity to mask the lack of a secure private one. But the seeds of her emotional instability are planted in a flashback of Antonia's childhood. "We don't have to go anywhere," Fedora's daughter begs her mother during one of her infequent visits. "We can have dinner right here in the room. Nobody has to see us." "It's not that, darling," Fedora responds, "but a friend of mine—you've heard of Noel Coward?—he's leaving tomorrow for Jamaica, and I haven't seen him in six months."

ANTONIA: You haven't seen *me* for a year!
FEDORA: I brought you some presents. Open them.
ANTONIA: All you ever give me is things. I don't want things!

Like *Avanti!*, *Fedora* blazes with colorful cascades of flowers, but this time the vital reds, blues, purples, pinks, oranges, and whites aren't the paradisiacal flora of Ischia but rather funeral bouquets, too-late tributes offered to a corpse. *Fedora* spends even more time with characters standing around dead bodies, confronting the overwhelming distance that separated them in life, though in *Fedora*'s case it's a daughter, not a father, who got too little love. "You've been around this business long enough," the ancient Fedora explains to Detweiler; "You know it's all special effects, painted backdrops, glycerine tears." "Magic time," he says with an ironic smirk.

Wilder was philosophical about *Fedora* after its release, at least in public: "Like all my other films, I'd like to remake this one. In fact, one should only remake one's own films. That said—and contradictorily—I don't want to touch it again. I want to move ahead to new errors." Still, he couldn't help but dwell on his mistakes:

Now that the film is finished, I wake up at night and I think of each scene in my head and I shoot it differently. For example, the first time that Holden sees the countess, the hearth next to which she's sitting should be much farther from us, and around her there should be eight electric radiators instead of two; she would look like a Buddha seated in a wheelchair surrounded by lamps and darkness. She should be more paralyzed, and only a side of her face should be visible. . . . What a chance the playwrights and theater directors have—those who try out their work in Pittsburgh, Boston, Toronto, and finally New York, and who can constantly make changes. We work with a puzzle, and the first time the pieces are joined together is the last. The star's gone to Yugoslavia and the sets have been destroyed. You have to be sure not to make mistakes.

31. "NICE WORKING WITH YOU"

Is it all ashes, or is there still a spark?
—Victor Clooney (Jack Lemmon) in *Buddy Buddy*

On May 12, 1980, after an absence of forty-one years, Billy returned to work at MGM's studios in Culver City. He hadn't been employed there since *Ninotchka*, though he did do some shooting for *Some Like It Hot* on one of MGM's soundstages. But now he and Diamond were gearing up to write a new comedy for MGM, and they set up a working suite for themselves on the lot—one floor above Billy's old *Ninotchka* office. There they began rewriting a seven-year-old French farce. David Begelman, MGM's head of production, had an ambitious lineup of thirty-eight films in mind for the next two years. Five were already completed, ten were in active preproduction, and twenty-three more queued in varying stages of development. They included Dennis Potter and Herbert Ross's extravagant musical, *Pennies from Heaven*; Francis Ford Coppola's equally lavish and ambitious *One from the Heart*; and a musical comedy for Luciano Pavarotti called *Yes, Giorgio*. Begelman was striving to return a bit of class to Hollywood filmmaking, and, two months later, the greatest writer-director in American film history and his loyal collaborator finished the first draft of their screenplay. It was called *Buddy Buddy*.

Wilder and Diamond's screenplay concerns a hit man bent on assassinating all the witnesses in a Palm Springs land fraud scandal. It's business as usual in Southern California, a fact the writers both knew very well, since they were making the film for a convicted felon. Begelman, a former talent agent, had launched his own firm, Creative Management Associates, with Freddie Fields in 1960, and together they pioneered the movie "package"—stars, writers, and director, all sharing the same representation, bundled together for speedy sale to a studio. In 1973 Begelman was hired to head production at Columbia Pictures. The studio was nearly bankrupt when Begelman took charge, but a few years later, Columbia roared back with a string of big hits such as *Close Encounters of the Third Kind*, *Shampoo*, and *Funny Lady*. Some inconvenience arose in 1977 when Begelman forged $40,000 worth of checks and had to be let go, but after insisting on a rehabilitative two-month suspension, Columbia reinstated him. Unluckily for Begelman, though, nobody forgot about his forgery, and he was forced out of Columbia again in February 1978. Three months later he pleaded no contest to charges of felony grand theft. Begelman blamed his crime on drugs (pills and cocaine), and after a period of dignified convalescence he was hired to be head of production at MGM. This was a bit of an inside job, since MGM/UA's chairman, Frank Rothman, served as Begelman's lawyer on the check-forging case.

Wilder found a few changes on the MGM lot. For one thing, the soundstage on which he shot the *Some Like It Hot* sequences had been torn down to build a condo. This was not surprising; across town in Hollywood, the Goldwyn stages on which he shot *The Apartment* and *Irma la Douce* were demolished in favor of a parking lot. "But you know," he mused to the critic Stephen Farber, "if you visit the Parthenon today it's not quite the way it was in the old days. Everything in this world changes, with the one exception of Dolores Del Rio." Or himself. His remarks about aging stars have a personal ring: "Look at Joan Crawford, dying alone in her apartment. Before her death she actually went down in the elevator; two women saw her. One said to the other, 'You know, that used to be Joan Crawford.' That is very difficult to take, especially when you are on your own and were so beautiful. . . . When the rapture and the ecstasy comes to an end for the big star, they just cannot cope. They become drunks or take pills or live tucked away in the Arizona desert." Billy Wilder compelled himself to keep working.

Wilder and Diamond based *Buddy Buddy* on *L'Emmerdeur*, a 1973 French film written by Francis Veber and directed by Edouard Molinaro. Veber's *Pardon Mon Affaire* (1977) had been an art-house hit; Veber and Molinaro's *La Cage aux Folles* (1978) was a smash. *L'Emmerdeur* was far less successful in the States, where it was released as *A Pain in the A–*, *L'Emmerdeur* translating neither well nor cleanly, falling somewhere between *The Asshole* and *The Fuckhead*. (Even in the sex-laden 1970s there was no chance of using either the *a*-word nor the *f*-word in an American title.) In any case, Lino Ventura starred as Ralph, a contract killer. Jacques Brel played his nemesis, Pignon, the eponymous jerk, a suicidal shirt salesman whose life Ralph uselessly preserves.

Alain Bernheim had been Molinaro's agent at one time, and according to his *Buddy Buddy* coproducer Jay Weston, "he showed the film to Lemmon on Tuesday, Matthau on Thursday, Wilder on Friday, and had a package on Friday." Like *The Front Page*, *Buddy Buddy* works best on paper; the deal memo must have looked great. Budgeted around $10 million—"less than the average advertising campaign," Billy knew—*Buddy Buddy* was to be "something between *Stir Crazy* and George Bernard Shaw," by which Wilder seems to have meant that it was a comic social satire about two men. Begelman responded to both the pitch and the package; a William Morris agent put it together for Lemmon and Matthau, and the two stars brought Billy on board to complete the deal. "I didn't have to audition for the studios and pass through Checkpoint Charlie before they would approve the project," Billy noted.

Filming began on February 4, 1981, in Agoura, California. The central location, however, was at the Riverside County courthouse. The film's location manager had scouted Utah, Colorado, New Mexico, and much of Southern California before arriving in Riverside and finding this sun-baked, gingerbready hall of justice. The building was perfect, but there was no hotel across the street, as the script demanded, so production designer Dan Lomino built a whole hotel facade and suspended it on top of the row of stores facing the courthouse. Wilder and company shot in Riverside through February, then moved back to MGM Soundstages 11 and 12, and finally finished up on a secluded Hawaiian beach on April 27.

That *Buddy Buddy* is morbid is no surprise. That its morbidity is so lifeless is shocking. The film's tone goes so far beyond resignation that it achieves a kind of flat despair. "In this Donner Pass expedition known as Hollywood," Wilder once said, "many people fall by the wayside. People eat people. Very few make it. Lately I've been going to more funerals than openings to pictures. Sometimes you have a funeral and an opening on the same day, and you don't feel very good when you see a comedy after you've put somebody to rest or watched the Neptune Society blow his ashes into the Pacific Ocean." One loss was especially bitter. On Saturday, November 14, a weekend that fell in the middle of *Buddy Buddy*'s scripting, Billy and Audrey packed some clothes and prepared to set off for Palm Springs to spend the weekend with Bill Holden. Their chum had been inviting the Wilders to visit for some time. They still hadn't seen his new desert retreat, and finally they found a weekend that worked for all of them. Billy phoned Holden before setting off, but the housekeeper who answered the phone said that Holden wasn't there, and nobody knew where he was. Billy and Audrey unpacked and spent the weekend at home.

On Monday, back at work on *Buddy Buddy*, Billy learned that Holden was dead. He'd fallen, drunk, in the bedroom of his apartment in Santa Monica, hit his head on a table near the bed, and bled to death. There was no funeral. Later Billy and Audrey attended a memorial service at Stefanie Powers's place in Benedict Canyon. Wilder said he wouldn't have been surprised had his old friend been gored on an African game preserve or killed in a plane crash in Hong Kong. It would even have made sense if "a crazed, jealous woman had shot him and he drowned in a swimming pool." But Holden's death was doubly depressing for Billy: "To be killed by a bottle of vodka and a night table—what a lousy fadeout for a great guy."

Buddy Buddy is one of the very few Wilder scripts that takes place in something approaching real time, and it drags. Although it is based on *L'Emmerdeur*, its earlier antecedent is *Der Mann, den seinen Mörder sucht*—a suicidal schlepp, a hit man, bonding, death jokes. Fifty years, millions of dollars, six Oscars, and a very thick scrapbook of international attention later, Billy still couldn't think of any reason to remain alive other than the pleasure one derives from one's profession. In both films, killing people serves as an honest day's work, and the hell of it is simply that some worthless asshole keeps getting in the way.

There are noteworthy revisions from *L'Emmerdeur*. As the film historian Richard Parker Hadley Jr. notes, *L'Emmerdeur* opens ominously with a zoom-in and zoom-out to a car, which explodes seconds later, killing an innocent man. The killer is then summarily shot in the head by the hit man. Wilder and Diamond not only give the pleasure of *both* murders to their assassin, Trabucco, but they make them both maliciously comical. *Buddy Buddy*, unlike *L'Emmerdeur*, is full of disguises. Death comes in various mundane forms—a mailman, a milkman, a Roman Catholic priest. *L'Emmerdeur* ends with Ralph and Pignon in a prison yard; *Buddy Buddy* ends with the killers retiring together on a secluded beach in the South Seas.

Jack Webb was originally considered for the role of Hubris, the chief of police, but the part ultimately went to a less recognizable actor, Dana Elcar. The film's romantic complication, apart from Clooney-Lemmon's nagging affection for Trabucco-Matthau, takes the form of Victor's wife, Celia; Wilder cast the comedienne Paula Prentiss in the part. (For the first shot of Prentiss, Wilder instructed the cinematographer, Harry Stradling Jr., to "make her look very beautiful." "She's no Garbo," Billy added, "but that shouldn't be too difficult.") For the repulsive Dr. Zuckerbrot, the head of the sex clinic to which Celia has fled and whom she is deliriously screwing, Wilder chose Klaus Kinski, best known for his portrayal of Nosferatu in Werner Herzog's 1979 remake of the Murnau classic. And with a certain loyal honor, Wilder cast Joan Shawlee as the clinic's mean-spirited receptionist, for whom Celia ultimately ditches Zuckerbrot.

At the age of seventy-five, Billy claimed to be the object of strange women's romantic attentions. A plucky Riverside resident was said to have been calling the studio daily, trying to invite Wilder over for a home-cooked meal. Billy graciously refused, saying, "I told her I was a homosexual on a diet." One day on the set, the talk turned to Wilder's predilection for evil women and his fondness for pairing two men. Walter Matthau asked Billy in front of the whole cast and crew why it was that Jack Lemmon kept ending up either with a rotten dame or Matthau at the end of their joint films. (Matthau may not have gotten the plots right, but he did pinpoint a certain tendency.) Billy, mildly annoyed, dismissed the remark out of hand, but Matthau couldn't bear to let the point drop. "Look to your own misogyny," the actor advised.

Matthau seems to have enjoyed teasing his old friend. "Why don't you think that actors are smart?" Matthau asked Billy one day. "Robert Redford directs his first film and he wins an Academy Award." "Okay," Billy replied, "Rod Steiger will direct your next picture."

When someone asked him what the next setup was, Billy was direct: "None of your fucking business." Still, he only lost his temper once during the production—when a publicist brought her squalling infant onto the set and ruined a take.

Directing Lemmon before filming the sequence in which Clooney gets dressed to visit his wife, Wilder told Lemmon, "You are dancing on clouds. You're going back to your wife, you schmuck." Sing "Cecilia," he advised, and snap the towel like a matador. One more thing: "Jackie-poo, a slight smile of anticipation."

The three pros had been through a lot together over the years, Lemmon in particular. They enjoyed their private language, over two decades of shared work and play. Matthau and Lemmon, driving toward a rock in rear projection, were directed to be casual but slightly tense. "The attitude is a very simple one," Billy coached, "nervous expectation." "Please don't talk to me," Lemmon snapped, quoting Marilyn Monroe. "I'll forget how I'm going to play it."

As always, Lemmon was the more accommodating, while Matthau was a needler. During each take of the shot in which he administers last rites to the guy on the courthouse steps, Matthau kept changing the dialogue, but by that point in the production neither Diamond nor Wilder corrected him. "I used to do that, sure," Diamond confessed to the critic Adrian Turner, "but perhaps I'm getting lazy or older." Diamond admitted that Matthau was a special case: "With Walter we allow a little flexibility." They had to; bitching over little lines had grown tiresome. One day Wilder and Matthau argued for twenty minutes over whether Trabucco should say "What kind of shit is *this*?" or "What kind of shit is *that*?" It no longer seemed worth it, especially after Matthau had to be hospitalized in early April after filming the scene in which he and Lemmon slide down a laundry chute. Matthau was supposed to land on a mattress, and he did, only to bounce off and hurt his neck. Everyone feared it was broken, but it turned out to be only bruised, and he returned to work the following week, albeit with a neck brace. One of Billy's remarks has a poignant ring: "For all the trouble and aggravation he puts me through, I wish I could have him for my next fifty pictures."

Wilder's camera operator was noticeably intimidated at working for the master. Asked to make a small adjustment in the framing of a particular shot, he turned to Billy and began, "With your kind permission, sir. . . ." "This is a Spanish court ceremony?" Billy replied. "Permission granted. I can see what your sex life is like."

Klaus Kinski, on the other hand, was not overawed by his director. The German star kept his feelings to himself in public, but he didn't hold back in his journal: "That piece of Hollywood shit with Billy Wilder is over, thank God," he wrote after *Buddy Buddy* wrapped. "No outsider can imagine the stupidity, blustering, hysteria, authoritarianism, and paralyzing boredom of shooting a flick for Billy Wilder. The so-called 'actors' are simply trained poodles who sit up on their hind legs and jump through hoops. I thought the insanity would never stop. But I got a shitload of money." Kinski, a sexual blowhard, should have gotten along well with Billy, but he held his director in total contempt. This was nothing new: " 'From now on you'll do serious movies with Herzog and comical ones with me.' That's what Billy Wilder told me when we first met at the La Scala restaurant. But I think the reverse is true. For a long time Billy Wilder's so-called comedies have been uptight and anything but funny, and your laughter freezes in the corners of your mouth. And Herzog's so-called serious flicks would be unintentionally funny if I did what he wanted me to do."

Kinski is crude but correct; *Buddy Buddy* is joyless. Billy ended this, his twenty-fifth and final film, with a freeze-frame. Held in icy stasis, Walter Matthau puffs on a big stogie, and that's the end of it. After directing the last take of his life, Billy turned to his friend and partner and said, simply, "Izzie, nice working with you."

Wilder's warped romanticism died a hard death with *Fedora*. *Buddy Buddy* is by far the meanest movie of his life. *Ace in the Hole* looks loving by comparison. When Kirk Douglas's head bangs on the floor at the end of that film, Wilder tempers the harshness with a sense of innocence lost. Chuck Tatum acts like he's on top of the world when the film opens, but fate and his own flaws cut it tragically out from under him. But in *Buddy Buddy*, even tragedy is too sweet for Wilder. All hope has been exterminated, even in the opening scenes, and the result is the lowest of farces coupled with the least forgiving of moral judgments.

Lemmon and Matthau's well-honed screen personalities served as the basis of the film's marketing campaign—the *Odd Couple* was back, the ads declared—but Wilder made no effort to follow through on that idea. This is not a comedy about a slob forced to share living quarters with a priss; the jokes don't hinge on dirty laundry on the floor and rotten food in the refrigerator. This is a nasty comedy in which Matthau escorts Lemmon out into the middle of a sagebrush wasteland, urges him to vomit behind a rock, and, to the sound of Lemmon's gagging up his last meal, pulls out a revolver and tries to shoot him.

Lemmon's Victor Clooney is an uncompromisingly sniveling pest; Matthau's bulb-nosed venality has never been cruder. *The Fortune Cookie*'s Willie Gingrich is adorable by contrast. There is no moral awakening, no redemption, no honor. The wretched Clooney's single moment of triumph occurs when he successfully murders the star witness in a hearing on organized crime. His suicide attempts are laughably inept, but the laughs are mirthless. In a bare hotel bathroom, he stands perched, one foot on the bathtub, the other on the can, as he ties a knot around an overhead pipe. Then he stops to take a leak.

However unfulfilled they may be, Wilder's other failures bear traces of affection and wistful regret. Here, there's nothing—no hope, no grace. In the opening sequence a mailman delivers a letter bomb, blows his victim to bits, emerges as the film's protagonist, and lights a cigar in celebration of his little triumph. When Trabucco calmly rounds the corner after his bomb goes off, Wilder gives us shrieking suburbanites rushing past him heading eagerly toward the calamity. With underworld stool pigeons living inside these bright, bleak tract houses and a hired killer on the sidewalk, Wilder's America ceases to offer any good cheer whatsoever. Even the lines are sullen, colorless, miserable. "Premature ejaculation means always having to say you are sorry," says Dr. Zuckerbrot. Cruelty still provides a spark of pleasure: "You know what your problem is, Victor?" Celia observes. "You should have been born a man." By the time Matthau snarls, "You better drive, shithead," one begins to dream of the glory days of the Hays Office. On the other hand, Wilder and Diamond still have a bit of fun, however obvious it may be. When Trabucco puts on his clerical collar to effect his escape toward the end, Clooney has a good question: "You wouldn't have a spare dickie, would you?"

Trabucco, for one, has dispensed with his wife:

CLOONEY: You ever been married, Mr. Trabucco?
TRABUCCO: Once, but I got rid of her. Now I just lease.

The second Mrs. Clooney runs off with the monstrous Zuckerbrot, the Nosferatu of Southern California, a man who wears around his neck the melted-down metal from Mrs. Clooney's wedding ring reshaped into an erect cock. The creatures who populate Zuckerbrot's clinic, meanwhile, stare sadly at projected transparencies of sex organs in a doomed attempt to rekindle the spark of their long-lost desire. Like the patient who wanders aimlessly bearing the deflated corpse of his inflatable woman, *Buddy Buddy* is cinema in which love and passion have evaporated, and in Wilder's view, neither audiences nor directors can revive it by sheer force of will.

Happily bringing in a bottle of milk from his doorstep, Trabucco's second victim, Mr. Pritzig, departs to fix himself breakfast. Detectives surround his house trying to protect him, but just as the chief begins to ask him questions, Pritzig loudly chokes offscreen. The chief runs into the kitchen to find Pritzig facedown in his cereal bowl. He lifts Pritzig's head, looks at the milk-dripping face, then drops it back into the dish with a splash. The embarrassing ways in which people die serve as the film's biggest laugh getters. Later, Clooney triumphantly announces to the exasperated Trabucco, "I'm going to set myself on fire!" With the only joy generated in this world coming from inspirations on how to commit suicide, the vision offered by Billy Wilder at the end of his career is so much blacker, so much harsher than any of his younger filmmaking colleagues that such hostility, coming as it does from the last master of the Hollywood cinema, is sobering indeed.

The world premiere of *Buddy Buddy* was held at the Avco Cinema Center in Westwood on December 8, 1981. A celebratory dinner was held afterward at the Beverly Wilshire, where the Wilders, Lemmons, Matthaus (Walter still in a neck brace), and Begelmans joined Swifty and Mary Lazar for a meal of chicken marinara and smoked salmon.

"A comedy of sustained mirthlessness" was *Variety*'s assessment. Sadly, the review was penned by Wilder's longtime admirer Todd McCarthy. "The tone is so off and comic imagination is so surprisingly absent that one must wonder what the rationale for the package was beyond an attractive-sounding deal." The *Hollywood Reporter* deemed it better than *The Front Page* but detested it nonetheless. *Time*'s Richard Corliss declared that "Wilder's antique vehicle is no more than serviceable" but applauded the effort, however failed he found it. Vincent Canby in the *New York Times* also put the best face on things: "slight but irresistible. . . ." Canby was most impressed by the film's small scale; compared to *1941* and *The Blues Brothers*, *Buddy Buddy* was a relief. David Ansen, writing in *Newsweek*, saw Wilder and Diamond as two confused dinosaurs: "From the evidence of their shrill and unfunny gags, they stopped listening to how people talk about ten years ago, when it was still barely possible to make hippie jokes and get a laugh from the line 'go with the flow.' " As Diamond put it all too accurately, "I think if *Buddy Buddy* had starred John Belushi and Dan Aykroyd and was directed by a young filmmaker it would have had a totally different critical reception."

Andrew Sarris, still feeling guilty, took Wilder's last film more seriously than anyone else. "François Truffaut once made the bizarre criticism of Wilder that he was too much the Lubitsch-style comedy director to handle a Germanic melodrama like *Double Indemnity*," Sarris wrote. "I think it has always been the other way around in that there was too much shame and guilt in Wilder for him to fashion a comedy without dramatic infusions of humiliation and regeneration. In this context, the material furnished in *Buddy Buddy* is essentially too light for the glorious gravity of Wilder to take hold."

Earlier, Jay Weston had had the idea of remaking *Love in the Afternoon* with Nastassia Kinski, Klaus's beautiful daughter. Wilder and Diamond liked the idea, Weston reported, but they worried about who could play the male lead. "They're aware it didn't really work the first time with Gary Cooper," Weston told the *Hollywood Reporter* while *Buddy Buddy* was shooting, "but I'm hoping I can convince them we can cast it properly now." Then *Buddy Buddy* brought in a mere $3,014,230 at the box office. There would be no *Love in the Afternoon*. Billy Wilder's career was over.

And his friends had no choice but to keep on dying. Walter Reisch went in March 1983, a victim of pancreatic cancer, thus ending yet another fifty-year friendship. A few weeks later, after Billy presented the Best Director Oscar (to Richard Attenborough, for *Gandhi*), he was characteristically morose when he faced the reporters backstage: "I'm doing this so my relatives in Vienna will know I'm still alive." There were, perhaps needless to say, no more relatives in Vienna. Susan Sarandon recalls another remark: "I ran into him at the Academy Awards, and I said, 'Mr. Wilder! Why are you here?' And he said, 'People think I'm dead.' "

At a Film Society of Lincoln Center tribute in New York on May 3, Billy was irascible but charming. Toasters included Izzie, John Huston, Ginger Rogers, Austin Pendleton, Shirley MacLaine, Horst Buchholz, and Pamela Tiffin; Lemmon and Matthau sent their tributes in on film. The two-hour-plus event was telecast on PBS. "Hollywood has changed a lot," Billy told the crowd in his acceptance speech. "Today, half the people you run into are on the way to China to set up a coproduction deal, the other half are on their way to Cedars-Sinai for a quadruple bypass. As a matter of fact, the entire industry is in intensive care." Billy maintained an air of optimism, though: "What then about our industry?" he asked. "Is it really dying? Not at all. I wouldn't worry. It has survived so much—the advent of sound and the advent of television and the Hays Office and 3–D glasses and Cinerama and Smell-o-rama—and it *will* survive inflation and insane interest rates and cable and satellites and Betamax and Atari and the Beverly Hills Diet. They can't kill it; it's too big, it's absolutely essential—like water or oxygen or sex."

"As for myself," Wilder concluded, "I have absolutely no intention of retiring. As far as I'm concerned, this here ball game is going into extra innings. And I'm ready. I played winter ball in the Dominican Republic, I changed my stance, I shortened my grip, and I got me some contact lenses. There are still a few hits left in me—maybe even a triple or a home run. An evening like this is like a shot of adrenaline. And for this I am most grateful. So thank you indeed, you beautiful people out there in the dark." Owing to the many technical misfires that marred the evening, the last part was cut off the telecast.

"Medals, they're like hemorrhoids," he once said: "Sooner or later every asshole gets one." The Austrians gave him one in October. Billy was awarded the Grand National Prize, which included a hefty honorarium of $10,000; he donated it to USC's Max Kade Institute for Austrian-German-Swiss Studies.

Billy had taken a trip to Europe in the early summer of 1982. He spent three days in Rome, where he received an award from the journal *Filmcritica*. The mayor of Rome showed up at the Campidoglio for the ceremony; so did Audrey Hepburn, who presented Billy with the plaque and a kiss. Some of the Italian cinema's leading lights—Antonioni, Cottafavi, Rosi, Scola—paid homage and enjoyed a glorious buffet in the gardens of the Caffarelli villa. The next day, Billy was escorted on a tour of the Centro Sperimentale, the Italian film school. A trip to Cinecittà followed; Billy spoke for a few minutes with Franco Zeffirelli on the set of *La Traviata*. He was then introduced to first-time director Francesco Laudadio, who was shooting something called *Grog*. Fellini followed.

By the following day, June 4, Billy's mood was strained. He was in no mood to listen to the series of papers delivered at the *Filmcritica* symposium held in his honor. When asked his opinion of the earnest exegeses on his work, Billy was blunt: "It is like listening to a funeral oration." The guest of honor elaborated: "I'm annoyed when I hear names like Oedipus and Narcissus mentioned regarding my films. If I had proposed such a script to Hollywood I wouldn't have received five dollars." He was enjoying himself, in a mean sort of way. He invited the audience to listen to the notes he took during the presentations. With his notepad in hand, Billy read: "Go get shoes from Gucci. Tell my wife that the Bulgari jewelry is really too expensive this year. Don't forget to steal two ashtrays from the Cafe Greco." Having warmed up, Billy moved in for the kill: "Are you still translating?" he asked the interpreters. "I was waiting for more reactions and bigger laughs. Maybe the simultaneous translation isn't fast enough, or maybe my jokes aren't funny, or maybe your skill leaves something to be desired." The guest of honor finished up: "It bothers me to always have to answer the same questions, so I'll vary the responses: Bogart was gay, Wayne was a Soviet agent and Sylvester Stallone will be the next president of the United States. And to conclude: An homage at Lincoln Center in New York, a trophy at Cannes, now a colloquium in Rome. All that in the same year. This kind of vacation can kill you."

32. IN TURNAROUND

The only thing that would break my heart would be if they took the camera away from me and wouldn't let me make films anymore.

—Billy Wilder

I t was all about his bad English. That was the reason Billy cited in 1986 for continuing to work with a writing partner. "I've been here for fifty-plus years," he told the up-and-coming director Chris Columbus in an interview for *American Film*, "but I still do not trust my hanging participles or where to put the verb." Billy mentioned another excuse as an afterthought: "Writing is also very, very lonely."

He mused further on the subject of stringing words together into scripts: "Somebody asked me one day, 'Is it really important that a director also knows how to write?' And I said, 'No, but it helps if he knows how to read.'" Wilder also took the occasion to offer some personal advice to Columbus: "Don't slit your throat, as you will want to do when you see the rough cut. That is the most depressing thing in your life. Whether it was *Ninotchka*, sitting there with Lubitsch, or hits like *Some Like It Hot* or *Sunset Boulevard*, I always wanted to slit my throat because there was no rhythm there. You just think, 'My God, my God! Is that all there is? It's so bad!' So I warn you. Don't have a razor blade or fifteen Nembutals on you when you see that."

For years Billy liked to say he wasn't interested in working anymore—the system was too awful, current films too "mezzo-pornographic." "They are also afraid that I will demand things they don't agree with—afraid I'm going to make a fool of them. But I'd never do that, no matter how ignorant they are. I'm nice and gentle." True, the newest New Hollywood—that of the 1980s—held little appeal for Billy, but the feeling was mutual.

He regarded the modern, independent-production industry he helped to create with a sense of depressed contempt: "In the olden days you went to see an MGM picture. It had its own handwriting. Or you knew it was a Warner Bros. picture—Cagney and Bogart and the small actors that were under contract there. Now studios are nothing but the Ramada Inn—you rent space, you shoot, and out you go." He'd inaugurated this system himself with the Mirisch brothers in the late 1950s, when it worked to his advantage, but thirty years later, with no new movie deals anywhere in sight, the studio system against which he once railed looked better and better. "Nobody talks about the picture, just about what kind of deal: Who presents? Whose picture is it? And all that totally idiotic crap! It's a world with ugly, ugly, terrifying words like *turnaround* and *negative pickup*. Although I think the two ugliest words in the world are *root canal*, with the possible exception of *Hawaiian music*."

He wasn't finished: "And only a fool would think that by kissing ass you will make it," Billy announced, "because you are kissing the ass that's going to be out on *his* ass a week from today and there's going to be a new ass coming in."

As he approached his eightieth year, Wilder maintained his office at the Artists and Writers Building in Beverly Hills and still kept trying to find work wherever he could. In October 1985, Steve Sohmer, the new president of Columbia, took Billy to lunch at Le Dome. Ignoring the fact that *Pam-Pam*, his first Hollywood screenwriting job, was at Columbia, and that the studio had paid for his one-way ticket out of Europe, Wilder told Sohmer that he'd dealt with Columbia only once before—when Harry Cohn supposedly sent him a bill to cover the lunch he'd eaten when pitching the Marlon Brando–Mae West *Pal Joey*. A few days later, Sohmer sent Wilder a note saying that a corporate audit had uncovered an instance of improper billing: "Accordingly, pursuant to Columbia Pictures Internal Audit Procedures Directive No. 417 (Correction of Misallocations), enclosed herewith please find check No. 229387 in the amount of Four Dollars ($4.00) hereby correcting said improper assessment." It was a nice joke, but the lunch didn't give Billy what he really wanted. He still didn't have anything to work on.

In January 1986, with his eightieth birthday in sight, Billy landed a job: he was made special assistant to the new chairman and CEO of United Artists, Jerry Weintraub. The idea was for Wilder to provide wise, experienced counsel to an art industry run increasingly by twenty-five-year-olds waving business degrees. Weintraub began by screening one of UA's upcoming releases for his new assistant. After the lights came up again, Billy proffered his wisdom in capsule form: "This picture is a big pile of shit," he told the head of the studio. "Perhaps I could tell you how to make it into a smaller pile, but it will still be shit." Ten months later, Weintraub was out of UA, and so was Billy.

In March, he appeared at the Oscars as one of three presenters of the Best Picture award. John Huston, Akira Kurosawa, and Billy made their entrance to a standing ovation, though Huston, suffering from advanced emphysema, had to be wheeled onto the stage on a strict timetable. As Wilder recalls, "They had the presentation carefully orchestrated so they could have Huston at the podium first, and then he would have forty-five seconds before he would have to get back to his wheelchair and put the oxygen mask on." The plan was for Huston to open the envelope and then hand it to Kurosawa, who, according to Billy, "was to fish the piece of paper with the name of the winner out of the envelope and hand it to me, then I was to read the winner's name." But there was a problem. "Kurosawa was not very agile, it turned out, and when he reached his fingers into the envelope, he fumbled and couldn't grab hold of the piece of paper with the winner's name on it. All the while I was sweating it out; three hundred million people around the world were watching and waiting. Mr. Huston only had about ten seconds before he needed more oxygen." A quip came to mind. According to Billy (who went on to tell the joke as often as possible), he wanted to turn to Kurosawa—and the microphone— and say, "Pearl Harbor you could find."

The following month, a reporter from the Austrian monthly *Profil* got Billy on the phone and asked him about the current Kurt Waldheim scandal. No longer the secretary general of the United Nations, Waldheim was running for the presidency of Austria, and his Nazi past had surfaced. (Until then, Waldheim simply lied about having been an intelligence officer for the German army unit that dispatched most of the Jews of Salonika to Nazi death camps in 1943.) The young Viennese reporter wanted to know what the old one's impressions were. "We are living on the other side of the world," Billy explained. "People here still think that Beethoven is Austrian and Hitler German." Americans have their own problems, Wilder continued, though he didn't much care what they were: "How the vox populi is, I really have no idea. First, I don't think people are very interested in Waldheim, and second, I don't see the populi." As for Waldheim's shady past, "We have bigger problems than what he did fifty years ago," Billy said impatiently. But then, he added, the Holocaust itself was no big deal either: "I was embarrassed during the time of Hitler. It was a huge shame. Now it's a small detail—a postscript."

He turned eighty in June. "For a while I felt either morose or suicidal," he confessed in a letter to Miklós Rózsa the following year (on the occasion of Rózsa's own eightieth birthday), "but then I came up with a little trick.

I started lying about my age. No, I'm not making myself younger. Now I'm telling everybody I'm ninety-five. Suddenly they all wonder at my youthful appearance. For eighty I look slightly moldy. For ninety-five I'm a remarkable specimen."

In May 1987, he and Audrey traveled to Europe for a well-received revival screening of *One, Two, Three* in Berlin. They stopped off in Paris, where they tried to get in touch with Marlene Dietrich, to no avail. Dietrich had become more reclusive than ever. Billy called her on the phone: "After pretending to be her own masseuse or a cook, she admitted it was herself. At first Marlene had agreed to see my wife and me. We offered to take her out for dinner or to bring food to her apartment—anything that would please her. But then she changed her mind, saying that she had to go to an eye doctor. It was obvious she just didn't want to see anyone. Or anyone to see her." She died in 1992.

When he received the American Film Institute Life Achievement Award later that year, he knew there was only one reason. As he told Armand Deutsch, "I'm getting it because Lubitsch is dead." Billy was publicly grateful but privately disturbed; as Deutsch later described it, Billy saw the award as "simply another marker to the grave." Interviewed by Lubitsch's biographer Scott Eyman around this time, Wilder waxed morose. He continued to be haunted by the past—in particular, his own inability to measure up to it. "You know," he mused, "if one could *write* Lubitsch touches, they would still exist, but he took that secret with him to his grave. It's like Chinese glass blowing. No such thing exists anymore. Occasionally, I look for an elegant twist and I say to myself, 'How would Lubitsch have done it?' And I will come up with something and it will be *like* Lubitsch but it won't *be* Lubitsch. It's just not there anymore."

Still, Wilder's trip to Berlin had gotten him thinking; now he was talking to Jackie Mason about remaking *One, Two, Three*—in China. Billy didn't express the desire to direct the picture himself—by this point even he was forced to admit that he just didn't feel up to it anymore—but he was interested in supervising the project for *Buddy Buddy*'s coproducer, Jay Weston. Arthur Hiller was asked to direct. The film never got made.

On April 11, 1988, the Academy of Motion Picture Arts and Sciences presented Billy Wilder with its Thalberg Award at ceremonies at the Shrine Auditorium. Jack Lemmon introduced the winner, noting that the award had only been given to twenty-five people in its fifty-year history. "Mere mortals need not apply," he said. Calling Billy "a master of the art of the movie, unfailingly true to himself and his audience," Lemmon presented the heavy award to Wilder, who immediately handed it right back to him. "I have a feeling it is going to break," he said. Billy then made a five-minute acceptance speech before a worldwide audience. He thanked the

Academy and "all the millions of fans I have all over the world—the *civilized* world," he made sure to add. The grateful Wilder also made a point of saluting "one specific gentleman without whose help I would not be standing here tonight. I have forgotten his name but I have never forgotten his compassion." It was the American consul in Mexicali who in 1934 granted him permanent entry into the United States, but only after finding out that he was a movie writer. At the end of the speech, Billy added one final, personal remark to an ailing friend: "I hope you're watching, I. A. L., because part of this is yours. So get well, will you?" The *Los Angeles Times* opined that Billy's acceptance speech "about his career lasted almost as long as his career."

In the backstage pressroom, Wilder was in fine form. First he ripped into the Coca-Cola Company for interfering in the operations of its subsidiary, Columbia Pictures: "It would never occur to a filmmaker to go to Atlanta and tell them how to make a soft drink. I worked at Paramount for eighteen years. They were making fifty pictures a year. Now they're making four or five, and they're always looking over your shoulder. In the old days, we had the moguls. At least you knew whose ass to kiss." A reporter then asked him how he most wanted to be remembered. "As a great lover," he said, after which Jack Lemmon whisked him away. "Mr. Wilder has to point his peter at the porcelain," Lemmon explained.

Izzie Diamond was ill, and gravely so, when Billy wished him well over the airwaves. He was far sicker than Wilder was able to acknowledge, even to himself. Ten days later, Billy's closest friend and most intimate professional associate was dead. Diamond, true to form, had steadfastly refused to tell Billy the truth—it was multiple myeloma—until very late in the course of his illness, preferring to keep it to himself and work on, unencumbered by emotion. As one of Wilder's friends put it, Billy was "flattened" by Diamond's death. "He knew he had that disease four years," Wilder told David Freeman later. "He never said a word. Finally, when we were talking about something I thought we could do, he said, 'I better tell you, I guess.' " A month later, Billy was in his office with an interviewer but more alone than ever. "He used to sit in that chair there, the Eames chair," Wilder reflected. "Raymond Chandler said in one of his books, 'Nothing is as empty as an empty swimming pool.' Well, nothing is as empty as this Eames chair now. I feel very sentimental about it. The way we had plotted this script—the script about our lives—was that being twelve or fourteen years older I was supposed to go first. And as you see, that didn't happen."

There was still no work, though as late as 1994 he was telling the press of his latest filmmaking schemes. The book he most wanted to make into a film was *Josefine Mutzenbacher*, he announced to a British magazine that year. A porno novel by Felix Alten, "it is the diary of a prostitute whose father was a janitor," said Billy. There were always trade papers to read, gossip to spread, industry news to bemoan. Having arrived in Hollywood in 1934 in the midst of a war between scripters and studio executives, Billy followed the Writers Guild strike of 1988 with interest. He supported the strikers, of course, and he did so publicly in a letter read aloud at a Studio City rally in late July. He was currently resting at the beach house on doctor's orders, Billy wrote, but that was the only reason he didn't make a personal appearance. The strike was then twenty weeks old. "We are all writers together," Billy declared, "from those of us fortunate enough to have the Academy Award to the WGA member so new that he or she hasn't yet heard the joke about the Polish actress."

He still considered himself a working writer, and he always would. In November, Doubleday announced a new book deal: Billy Wilder had finally agreed to write his memoirs. He had the chance to set the record straight— about his youth, about his films, about that cockamamie Ilse story. . . . Billy's book was scheduled for publication in 1990. He brought in cowriter Herman Gollub, who soon departed. That book was never completed, but in 1998, the film director Cameron Crowe announced that he was working with Wilder on *Conversations with Billy*, a series of film-by-film interviews modeled after the book-length dialogue François Truffaut conducted with Alfred Hitchcock in 1966.

At home with Audrey, life proceeded as a ceaseless string of purchases (art, clothing, knickknacks, books) and attempts to increase the apartment's storage capacity. The Wilders' penthouse had long been a marvel of juxtaposition, not to mention capacity. Above an autographed picture of Marilyn Monroe hung a Renoir. Frank Stella paintings graced the bathroom. Saul Steinberg drew Billy one of his famous scribbled diplomas; Billy hung it in a place of honor over the desk in his den. In a small powder room were Matisse drawings. The bar featured six Henry Moore maquettes. Billy and Audrey shared their quarters with Kirchner, Rouault, Vuillard, Caillebotte, Münter, Nicholson, Braque, Miró, Hockney, Hartung, Marini, Manzu, Hepworth, Maillol, Calder, Giacometti, Lachaise, Graham, Jawlensky, Klee, Vivin, Rimbert, Bombois, Perennet, Botero, Balthus. . . . "You start collecting material objects," Billy reflected, "so you wind up having to buy a house at the beach."

As a senior curator at the Los Angeles County Museum of Art once said, "There's nothing like it in Los Angeles. It's the kind of personal collection that is rare now, with a taste for the small and felt work of art and a sense of wit and humor. Billy bought at a time when he had a tremendous amount of choice, and he's always had an exquisite eye." Literally, as it happened: one of his favorite works was an anonymous French oil painting of a single human eyeball—in Billy's description, "a cross between Magritte and CBS." "I don't have a collection," Wilder said. "I have accumulations, like a squirrel."

Several years earlier, Wilder commented on the fact that the art in his office was almost completely nonrepresentational: "I prefer to look at abstract works when I work, rather than landscapes, portraits, or still lifes. You look around a lot when you write a script, when you try to resolve a narrative problem or find a good reply, and if you fix on a landscape or a cup of fruit, it quickly becomes annoying. But an abstract canvas can signify different things at different times. It can become a portrait or a still life. It stimulates my imagination and lets me invent my own story." Wilder also said that he bought what he liked, without caring about its projected future value, and that when he was really crazy about something he would never consider selling it: "I never collected paintings, sculptures, African or Oceanic art to protect me against inflation. When I'm crazy about a canvas, I could never envision selling it. Nor would I separate myself from a dog I love." "It's a sickness," Billy went on. "I don't know how to stop myself. Call it bulimia if you want—or curiosity, or passion. I have some Impressionists, some Picassos from every period, some mobiles by Calder. I also collect tiny Japanese trees, glass paperweights, and Chinese vases. Name an object, and I collect it."

In the 1980s Billy Wilder became an avant-garde artist himself. His plastic-artistic creations were, characteristically, both witty and crowd pleasing. One of his sculptures, for example, was called *Stallone's Typewriter*. The work, constructed in the immediate post-*Rambo* period, consisted of an old Underwood that Billy painted in camouflage colors and appliquéd with bullets and little toy guns. The stars and stripes wrapping the platen provided additional political irony. Several years later, in December 1993, Wilder curated a show of his own work at his longtime friend and art dealer Louis Stern's gallery in Beverly Hills. The exhibition included *Variations on the Theme of Queen Nefertete I,* a sculpture Wilder co-created with Bruce Houston; the ravishing Egyptian queen sported a Campbell's soup can on her head. A necklace made of smaller red-and-white tins graced her throat. *This Fish Needs a Bicycle* and *Marble Salesman's Sample Case* were also featured in the exhibition.

Because his tastes ran toward "good examples of painters I love," and because he was always a shrewd deal maker, Billy was known for trading up in the art world. For example, he once swapped a minor Cézanne watercolor for Kirschner's *Two Nudes*. Lesser oil paintings by Roualt and Miró were also swapped—for five small Picassos in crayon and watercolor. He once traded Charles Eames two Yoruba tribal sculptures (a jaguar and a leopard) for a rare Calder stabile that Eames had acquired from Joseph Cornell.

In 1989, Billy decided to part with some of it. The art market had skyrocketed in the giddy, greedy 1980s, and Billy, having been out of the public eye (except for all the awards ceremonies he didn't enjoy), was curious to know what ninety-four of his choicest pieces would pull in on the grossly inflated market. Christie's handled the sale. "I wanted to test my willpower," he said. "I kept reading about those fantastic sales, those incredible prices. So one day I said to my wife, 'Let me call their bluff.' " After a series of small, sample showings in Tokyo, Zurich, Geneva, and Paris, the Billy Wilder Collection was shown for two days in September at the Beverly Hills Hotel's Crystal Room.

Asked why he decided to sell, Wilder cited several factors: "An art collection is a living thing, like a river," he said. "If you don't keep developing it, it becomes a silent pond. Algae starts to grow. It starts to smell." In addition, Billy noted, the idea of completing his collection at current prices was impossible: "Fifty years ago, of course, you paid just a small fraction of today's prices. Moreover, I didn't have enough room in my apartment, which is quite big, but not as big as a whole house. The walls weren't long enough. Finally, I didn't want to pay the huge insurance premiums." He tried out another metaphor on someone else: "A collection needs to grow with the times or it becomes like an old suit—you love it, but the moths have eaten it." Moreover, he allowed, "We worried that the people in the apartment above ours would let the bathtub overflow." Finally, he claimed that he didn't want Audrey, whom he had begun calling the "widow-to-be," to have to deal with the whole thing after his death.

David Hockney, Tony Bennett, Walter Matthau, Victoria Principal, Peter Falk, Betty White, and Henry Mancini all showed up at the Crystal Room for the preauction viewing. Hockney was most impressed by Balthus's *La Toilette*; "It's magnificent," he marveled. Billy was enormously pleased and surprised by the crowd's seriousness of purpose. "Amazing," he said. "People didn't just run for the cocktails and for friends to talk about their private lives. They actually talked about the paintings." He had no plans to maintain a discreet distance from the auction itself: "I want to be present at the fight. Money is of less importance than the inner satisfaction that I was on the right Lotto numbers. . . . I'd like to give a little advice to the purchasers," he declared: " 'This Matisse drawing needs to be in the shade,' or 'That Braque needs to be watered three times a week.' I had those things for twenty, thirty, forty years. Now they'll just have to leave their parents' house and see whether they can stand on their own two feet."

At the auction itself, held on November 13, Billy paced the floor of the sale room while Audrey watched from the safety of Christie's boardroom, where she was joined by Claudette Colbert, Angie Dickinson, and Dominick Dunne. The sale progressed smoothly, and a short time later Billy's collection was dispersed to collectors and museums all over the world. The take: $32.6 million.

The highest price—$4,840,000—was paid for Picasso's 1921 pastel, *Classic Head of a Woman*. As high as the price may seem, however, it was actually disappointing. Before the auction the work was estimated to be worth as much as $7,000,000; Christie's low estimate was $160,000 more than the final bid. Kirchner's *Two Nudes on a Blue Sofa* brought in $1,540,000. The Balthus pulled in $2,090,000. An American dealer bought Miró's 1936 gouache *The Farmer and His Wife* for $2,700,000, while Miró's 1927 oil painting *The Star* brought in $2,600,000. Giacometti's painted bronze sculpture *Standing Woman II* took in $1,100,000. "It was less nerveracking than a film preview," said Billy. Also, as Wilder made sure to point out, he paid about $14 million in taxes.

Billy sold only the most valuable pieces in his collection, which meant that the Wilders' penthouse still hosted drawings, paintings, sculptures, and a wide array of African-primitive and pre-Columbian art, not to mention a library of over two thousand books. Thus the anxiety the following month when two explosions and a fire broke out at a construction site next door. Billy and Audrey had to be evacuated along with the other residents. Four hundred firefighters arrived to battle five separate blazes, which spread into the lower floors of the Wilders' building. Twenty-two of the building's apartments were destroyed or severely damaged. The Wilders', fortunately, was not among them, though there was considerable smoke damage. Billy noted with relief that while his current policy would cover the costs of conservation, he and Audrey would have been vastly underinsured if the fire had happened before the auction.

It was no simple matter to clean up the mess, though, especially since their apartment was still crammed to the brim. For instance, all of Billy's and Audrey's clothes had to be inventoried by the insurance company before they were sent out to be cleaned to remove the smell of smoke. Forced by circumstance to chronicle his ridiculous array of material possessions, the compulsive clotheshorse was shocked at what his closets and dresser drawers contained. As Armand Deutsch reported later, "Billy was stunned to learn that he owned sixty cashmere sweaters."

Billy Wilder in his old age became even more of a surly cherub than he had been in his youth. Gracious one minute and bitter and rude the next, he spent his time shopping, shmoozing, going into the office, receiving admiring visitors, and accepting major international awards given by groups who kept wanting to applaud him. In 1990 it was the Kennedy Center Honors. When he found messages in his office to call a number with a Washington area code, he called Audrey and told her to start packing: "I'm being appointed to the Supreme Court." In 1991 it was the Preston Sturges Award from the Writers Guild. In his acceptance speech, Billy confessed to being testy because he had to miss the televised Florida State–Michigan game to attend the ceremony.

Another award was more trying for him. In 1991, Billy Wilder was given the Golden Order, First Class, for Meritorious Services Rendered to the Republic of Austria. The award was bestowed upon him at the Austrian consul's house in Los Angeles. One of Billy's favorite Austrians, the chef Wolfgang Puck, was in attendance; the Wilders were regulars at Spago, Puck's restaurant overlooking the Sunset Strip. Given the prominence of the award and his harsh ambivalence about those who would have been his fellow countrymen had they not denied his father citizenship, Billy chose the occasion to be unforgiving of Kurt Waldheim. Wilder made it a point to tell the Austrian press just how offensive he found their unrepentant president. Still, he told the magazine *Profil*, he was grateful for the award: "I'm sure I'll get a better table at the Hotel Sacher."

Germany was far less tormenting to him than Austria. In 1992, he planned two trips—first to the Frankfurt Book Fair in September to celebrate the publication of *Billy Wilder: Eine Nahaufnahme (A Close-Up)*, Hellmuth Karasek's biography, and then again in December to receive another Lifetime Achievement award—this time at the Felix awards held at Babelsberg Studios in Potsdam. He relished all the attention at the Book Fair, though he later said privately that he didn't much like Karasek's book. "Why go to the trouble of writing a book if you're going to write a stupid one?" he asked a friend. Once again, having revealed some of himself to an admiring biographer, Billy detested the final result. (And curiously, Wilder's family receives even less attention from Karasek than from Zolotow; his wife has little to say, his daughter nothing at all.)

He was still raging about politics, culture, Congress, baseball teams. . . . When he would launch into one of his regular diatribes about America, Audrey would try valiantly to cut him off. "Billy," she'd begin. "Yes, yes, I know," he'd answer, "if I don't like it here I should go back where I came from."

Ill health prevented his attendance at Babelsberg, though he announced his intention to travel to Berlin for the Film Festival two months later, where he was to receive yet another award—an honorary Golden Bear. "Personally, I'd prefer a Volkswagen," he said. A bizarre sight greeted him upon his arrival: a troop of American-style cheerleaders waving pompons. He was quite perplexed by it all, and as the guest of honor, he saw little need to hide his displeasure. More to his liking was the commemorative plaque that had been installed on the face of his old apartment building at Viktoria-Luise-Platz 11. It was a belated effort to make up for a past slight; on a 1987 visit to the building, Billy mistook another plaque (for composer Ferruccio Busoni) for his own.

A film idea had been tugging at him, and even though he knew he was too frail to withstand the rigors of directing it, he was compelled to try—at least to pitch the notion. He continued to feel "fury, tears, reproaches" over his mother's death at Auschwitz. "Why didn't I take my parents with me?" he kept asking himself well into his old age. "I left the day after the Reichstag fire and I left my mother in Vienna. What is done is done and cannot be undone." So when Thomas Keneally's novel *Schindler's List* came out in 1982, Billy's immediate response was to try to buy the rights and direct it.

The story spoke to him: a self-serving, amoral bastard finds redemption by saving helpless Jews from the gas chambers. He got as far as talking to Universal about the idea, only to find that the studio had already bought the rights for Steven Spielberg. According to Billy, Spielberg actually considered letting Wilder direct it, with Spielberg producing it on his behalf; another plan, said Billy, was to let Wilder produce the film so Spielberg could direct it himself. Spielberg himself has acknowledged that Wilder's intense drive was what convinced him to make the film after years of procrastination. "He made me look very deeply inside myself when he was so passionate to do this," Spielberg said. "In a way he tested my resolve." Wilder wrote Spielberg a long letter of appreciation after seeing *Schindler's List*. "They couldn't have gotten a better man," Wilder said. "The movie is absolutely perfection."

Wilder had a great deal more to say about the film, and he chose his audience with the precision of a sharphooter: he bypassed American readers entirely and published his essay, written in German, in the *Süddeutsche Zeitung Magazin*. He told his former countrymen (particularly those in conservative southern Germany, where the magazine was headquartered):

Yesterday I saw *Schindler's List* for the third time, and next week I will go again with my wife. Actually, she doesn't like war movies, but this movie, my God, is no movie. It is an event—a document of the truth. I was so moved afterwards that for an hour I couldn't utter a single word. It was the same with the others in the theater—everywhere you looked you saw handkerchiefs. Even after the first ten minutes I had forgotten it was a movie. I didn't care about camera angles and all that technical stuff—I was only enthralled with the total realism. It starts like a newsreel from the period—very difficult to stage, to make real.

And believe me, these scenes are so authentic it makes you shiver. I lost a big part of my family at Auschwitz—my mother, my stepfather, my grandmother—and the whole agony came up again. I sat there and saw on the screen how the Jews were driven together into the trains on which they were deported to the gas chambers, and I looked at the line of people, thinking—my mother has to be somewhere in that crowd. But I couldn't find her.

Wilder laid an early bet on the Academy Awards: "I am convinced that he'll finally get the Oscar this year. I always voted for him, but this time nobody will be able to avoid it. *The Piano* is also a wonderful movie, too, though I did fall asleep a little bit in the middle. Don't pass that on." (Spielberg took Billy to Spago some time along the way, and the younger, more famous man was immediately surrounded by autograph hounds, only one of whom approached Billy. "Could you autograph three times?" Wilder's fan asked. "Sure," Billy answered, "but why?" The hound's answer was simple: "Because for three Wilders I can get one Spielberg.")

"The most important function of this movie is this," Wilder concluded: "It manifests for all time that these unbelievable cruelties really happened. We need not forget that. With each year dust lays itself on this history; it is pushed away, forgotten. The young people, growing up today without the awareness of it, are already doubting that such a horror really could happen in the cultivated country of Goethe. 'The Auschwitz myth.' Nonsense, more and more people are saying—concentration camps, gas chambers, all that exists only in a Jewish fantasy. I venture to ask in each case: if the concentration camps and the gas chambers were all imaginary, then please tell me—where is my mother? Where can I find her?"

Wilder returned to Vienna in May 1994. It was his first visit since the disastrous 1958 trip when, feeling snubbed by the Viennese press, he let fly with his growling remarks about how his old colleagues used to call him "the bootlicker," and how the kids always called him the Polak. Billy had returned to Germany several times since then, but Austria remained a kind of forbidden zone; it was too painful. But Vienna had gradually but essentially yielded; Wilder finally became more or less Viennese in the eyes of the Viennese.

As his international stature grew, the city began tentatively to embrace him. But it took a lot of cajoling for him to return the hug. In 1981, for instance, on the occasion of Billy's seventy-fifth birthday, there was an article in the Austrian press touting "the Viennese Billy Wilder." One of Wilder's Austrian émigré friends, Dr. Robert H. Austerlitz, read the piece and reacted with outrage: Wilder was being called "Viennese" by the very people who had dismissed and denied him. So Austerlitz wrote from Los

Angeles to the newspaper *Die Presse* in Vienna: "Vienna was, as is well known, only one of his stations during his life; it is where he came with his parents from Kraków. He himself has never called himself nor has he viewed himself as Viennese, nor has he even been proud of being Viennese. I am certain of this." Austerlitz quoted Billy himself: "All of a sudden, they're calling me Viennese, even though in 1938, together with the other Jews, they wanted to send me to hell."

In 1992, Chancellor Franz Vranitzky of Austria issued a personal invitation to Wilder to return to Austria. He repeated the invitation in 1993. And again in 1994. Billy was finally talked into it that year, thanks to the intervention of the Austrian film director Wolfgang Glück. Chancellor Vranitzky met him personally at the airport and whisked him to Fleischmarkt 7, where Vienna's cultural minister, Ursula Pasterk, unveiled a new plaque commemorating Wilder's old home. (The city managed to mount the plaque a matter of hours before Wilder's arrival.) This ceremony and the state dinner at which Wilder was the guest of honor were all covered closely by Austrian television. Special screenings of *Double Indemnity* were arranged at one of the movie houses. Vranitzky offered a discreet but poignant toast at the state dinner—he said he hoped Wilder would see "a new Austria." Billy, visibly moved, responded graciously. He offered to cast Vranitzky in the role of the dashing diplomat in his next picture.

In October 1993, Billy won the National Medal of Arts at ceremonies held at the White House; in November, he won the first Lifetime Achievement Award in Screenwriting given by PEN Center USA West. He received a more unusual honor in 1996, when, on the occasion of his ninetieth birthday, School Street in the heart of Sucha Beskidzka was renamed Ulica Billy Wildera. As Wilder noted in a letter to town officials, it was "one of the highest points in my life." "They wouldn't just grab anybody and name a street after him," he said.

In the early 1990s, Billy learned about the proposed musical adaptation of *Sunset Boulevard* being written by Andrew Lloyd Webber, the composer of various operatic extravaganzas. Lloyd Webber seems to have been more appealing a musical translator of his work than Stephen Sondheim had been, though only mildly so. "I'm not saying he writes great music," Billy declared; "He'll have one good song." As for Lloyd Webber's theatrical style, Billy was precise: he "provides a kind of whole special atmosphere, a kind of magic for enveloping you. That's originality. People pay for that, because it is different from the neighbor's house." Billy claims to have heard of the project first from some Paramount lackey, who called him up to say that the studio wanted to take a picture of him standing with Lloyd Webber at the famous Bronson Avenue Gate. "Tell me," Billy snapped, "who is this good for? This is good for Paramount, right? Because I'm not going to see a single penny from this show, because the picture was made before 1960 and Paramount owns it. So why should I go and be photographed with Mr. Lloyd Webber? Have Mr. Webber come to my office and photograph me here. Preferably with the Twentieth Century–Fox sign in back of me."

To librettist Christopher Hampton, Billy was less nasty. He simply said that he held no claim to the property: "Call it injustice or a cruel boo-boo of the capitalist system, the sole possessor of the property is Paramount Pictures." Hampton's play, *Tales of Hollywood*, about German refugees in the movie colony, hadn't impressed him much, but as Billy put it, "He seems an okay guy." *Sunset Boulevard* proceeded without Wilder's official input, though the Wilders dined with Lloyd Webber and his wife, Madeleine, while Webber was in town working on the Los Angeles opening. Shirley MacLaine had once been considered for the role of Norma Desmond—a nice resonance, but it wasn't to be. The role was ultimately taken by Patti LuPone in London and Glenn Close in Los Angeles and New York.

In November 1993, Billy and Audrey flew to London for the West End premiere, where they were joined in the reunion by Nancy Olson. Billy later said he and Audrey each had tears in their eyes; "It was like seeing old friends." "The best thing they did was leave the script alone," Billy observed after the show. "I thought the director did a good job, considering." He had no love for the immense, gaudy set: "It looks more a palace built by some Arab sheik for his ladies." About Patti LuPone, Wilder had nothing but praise: "She's a star from the moment she walks on the stage." As for Kevin Anderson as Joe Gillis, Billy said, "I just wish he'd change his hair style."

The Wilders later traveled to New York for the Broadway opening of *Sunset Boulevard*, and Billy actually appeared onstage for the curtain call, though it took quite a bit of talking before he agreed to do so. Glenn Close greeted his entrance with a curtsey low to the ground. But it was at the earlier Los Angeles opening that Billy was in his finest form. Peter Bart recalls the scene. *Tout* Beverly Hills appeared at the opening night party, including Nancy Reagan and her socialite friends, and as Bart puts it, "Everyone was being very civil and polite until one woman asked, 'Billy, why does the show open with this, this monkey?' " "Don't you understand?" Billy replied; "The Glenn Close character was fucking the monkey before Joe Gillis came along." Bart reports that "Nancy Reagan looked like she was about to pass out."

In case anyone thought he'd gone reassuringly soft in his old age, Billy made it a periodic point to disabuse them of the notion. When Tony Curtis's son Nicholas died of a heroin overdose in the summer of 1994, Curtis was devastated. He climbed into bed and stayed there for a week or so, until he decided to venture out into the world of greater Beverly Hills once more. Curtis chose Spago for his first night out; there he ran into Billy at his usual table. "I knelt down by him for a moment," Curtis remembers, "and he said, 'How are you, Tony?' I said, 'Billy, my son died. My son Nicholas died. He died of an overdose of heroin.' " Wilder's response was terse: "He learned it from you."

In 1995, Billy told *Sight and Sound* the story of his recent conversation with a studio executive who told him that they were interested in remaking *Love in the Afternoon*. The studio was prepared to offer him $2,500 immediately and $25,000 if they actually made the film. "You must be crazy!" Billy said he told him. The executive said he'd think about it, to which Billy replied, "While you are thinking, remember that Mr. Eszterhas just got $3 million for *Natural Instincts*, I mean *Basic Instinct*. *Three million dollars,* do you hear?" Then he hung up on him. Billy said they called back soon thereafter and offered $100,000, and he told them that whatever he got, half would go to Barbara Diamond. The sale appears not to have gone through.

Sydney Pollack got a taste of Wilder's grumpiness when he invited Billy to an advance screening of his 1995 remake of *Sabrina*. According to Pollack, Wilder was not happy about the film being made at all. If they had to remake it, he told Pollack, they should make the Larrabee family's company bankrupt, and Sabrina's competition for the younger Larrabee should be the daughter of a Japanese prospective buyer. Pollack ignored Billy's advice and made a more faithful update. When the new *Sabrina* was finally complete—with Harrison Ford in Bogart's role, Julia Ormond in Hepburn's, and Greg Kinnear in Holden's—Pollack invited Wilder to watch the film at a Paramount Studios screening room. The two men were the only audience in the small theater. The lights went down, the 1990s *Sabrina* began, and in the middle of the opening scene—with Ormond assuming Hepburn's perch in the tree—Billy barked, "Why is it so dark? Who was the cinematographer?" Pollack told him. "An Italian!" Billy snapped. "He should know better!"

It went downhill from there, though Billy made a few pleasant remarks at the end. Then they went out to lunch. Pollack noticed that the room suddenly hushed when they walked in, everyone holding Billy in awe. When they sat down at their table, Billy promptly turned to Pollack and said, "How many Oscars you got?" "Two," Pollack replied. "I've got six," said Billy.

Wilder also took the opportunity to offer a capsule review of another one of Pollack's films: "That African movie you made—classy but boring."

Billy continued working. He had moved out of the Artists and Writers Building into a second-story office a few blocks away, a cozy space over some Beverly Hills boutiques. In a 1993 interview with *Buzz* magazine, he talked about his daily routine. He was still speaking in the present tense, though it had been a dozen years since *Buddy Buddy*: "When I'm shooting a picture I have a large suite at the studio. But once the picture is finished,

I come back here to my little office on Brighton Way. It's not like the old days when we were all under contract and lived on the lot. But at least this way I don't have to worry about running into a studio executive."

His secretary came in once a week on Fridays to type and make phone calls. "I usually have several scripts in the works at once, so I'm always rewriting something," he said. "When I don't feel like writing, I sit by the window and wait for the muses to fly in and kiss my brow. If they don't, I go shopping."

At the age of eighty-nine, Billy was approached to make his Hollywood feature film debut. It wasn't his brow that was being kissed when Cameron Crowe, preparing *Jerry Maguire*, tried valiantly to convince Wilder to play the role of Jerry's mentor, an aging sports agent called Dicky Fox. After much plotting and planning, Crowe was told by a mutual friend that Billy had agreed to meet with him. After mistaking the boyish Crowe for a messenger, Wilder invited him into his paneled Brighton Way office; after much conversant fawning, Crowe said, "There is a part I want you to play in my movie." "I don't act," Billy answered. "I won't do it." "It's just a small part," Crowe persisted. "Then I *definitely* won't do it," said Billy.

Crowe, having been around the Hollywood block a few times himself, kept right on pitching until finally Wilder agreed to read the script. According to Crowe, Billy was rather positive about the idea over the next few months, but when Crowe called to cinch the deal, Wilder only grunted, "Why are you doing this to me? I said, 'No.' I'm too old. Leave me alone." Then he hung up on him.

Crowe proceeded to Wilder's office; this time, Tom Cruise accompanied him. With Cruise fidgeting in one chair, Crowe kept on pitching from another. Billy was unmoved. "And why do we care about this sports agent to begin with?" he inquired. Crowe had no answer. Cruise took over, explaining how important it was to both of them, and so on, and as Crowe reports, "Suddenly, the chemistry of the room shifted, and Wilder knew it. He snapped back to attention. The cloudiness in his eyes disappeared. Earnestly, the globe's best-known male actor explained that it was not so much an acting job as a documentary-style appearance. The room was suddenly filled with hope." Then: "No. I am too old to be in front of the camera." Billy concluded the meeting by criticizing Cruise's outfit (black jeans and a dress shirt). "Nice to meet you," Billy said to Crowe as he rose out of his chair. Then he turned to Cruise: "And nice to meet you. Especially you."

Billy did end up onscreen in 1998 after being approached by one of his shoe salesmen. Steven Proto, an aspiring filmmaker, worked in a boutique under Wilder's office on Brighton Way. "He came in a lot and tried on shoes," said Proto. "He never bought anything. He just wanted company and to bust chops." Proto didn't even know who Billy was until the cantankerous old man started griping about Woody Allen's Oscars. "I still have more than he does," said Billy. Proto, who wanted to make a documentary called "The Shoe Store," suddenly saw possibilities. After much begging, he convinced Wilder to sit for a short interview. "I've always been depressed," Billy confessed to Proto's camera, "even to the point of suicide. . . . My chums that I used to hang around with, most of them, are dead. I live a sincere, orderly life, and I wait for things to happen."

Hollywood youth are still impressed by the master's wit. They keep telling "Billy" stories, as well they should. Billy Bob Thornton, for instance, tells the story of how he worked as a caterer's assistant when he first moved to Los Angeles. At one of the parties he helped cater, he met Billy. "You want to be an actor, don't you?" Billy asked the young waiter. Thornton admitted that he did, to which Wilder replied, "Let me give you a piece of advice. You're not handsome enough to be a leading man, so write yourself a good part and play the hell out of it." Thornton won a screenwriting Oscar for *Sling Blade* (1996) as well as a Best Actor nomination.

Paramount Pictures named a building after him, but Wilder was unmoved: "I was on the lot for its seventy-fifth anniversary. All the old-timers were there. I said, 'There's a building named after me, can I see it?' Nobody had heard about it. But then, somebody told me, 'It's not on the Paramount lot, it's on the RKO lot,' which they bought and never built on. I never worked at RKO. I think my name must be crowning a latrine someplace. So much for glory."

At the 1994 Oscars, Fernando Trueba, the director of *Belle époque*, the year's Best Foreign Language Film, accepted his award by saying, "I would like to believe in God so that I could thank him, but I just believe in Billy Wilder. So thank you, Billy Wilder." "I was just mixing myself a martini and I heard it on the television," Billy said. "The bottle of gin falls out of my hand." When Trueba's phone rang the following day, the voice on the other end said, simply, "It's God." Billy told the *Los Angeles Times* that he wished Trueba "hadn't said that. People start crossing themselves when they see me."

On June 22, 1996, Billy Wilder turned ninety. He spent the day at home in bed because he wasn't feeling well—his persistent vertigo was acting up—but he was back in his office again two weeks later, reworking sentences, repeating dirty jokes, planning his lunch, and, as he has been doing since the age of two, telling stories and hurling insults at anyone lucky enough, and resilient enough, to listen.

A joke: "An elderly man goes to see a doctor, and the doctor asks him, 'What is your problem?' And he says, 'I can't pee.' And the doctor asks him, 'How old are you?' He says, 'I'm ninety.' And the doctor says, 'You peed enough.' "

NOTES

***

CHAPTER 1

3 Sucha Beskidzka: Dean F. Murphy, "Wilder Honored by Hometown in Poland," *Pittsburgh Post-Gazette*, May 29, 1996, p. D4.

3 On Galicia: Klinkenborg, p. 44: citing Piotr S. Wandycz, *The Lands of Partitioned Poland, 1795–1918* (Seattle: University of Washington Press, 1979), p. 11, and Victor Greene, "Poles," in *The Harvard Encyclopedia of American Ethnic Groups*, Stephan Thernstrom, ed. (Cambridge: Belknap Press, 1980), p. 791.

4 Nine percent of Galicia's population: McCagg, p. 27.

4 "In Galicia . . .": McCagg, p. 115.

4 Wilder's parents: Zolotow, p. 21.

4 Zakopane: Hutter, pp. 65–67.

4 Nowy Targ: Lally, p. 1.

4 Reich family: Zolotow, p. 21.

5 Railway stops: Karasek, pp. 27–28; Freeman, p. 72.

5 Checking under the bed: Karasek, p. 29.

5 Galician peasants: Klinkenborg, pp. 45–46: citing "Emigration Conditions in Europe," in *Reports of the Immigration Commission, 1907–1910*, vol. 4 (Washington: Government Printing Office), p. 381, and *Our Slavic Fellow Citizens, 1910*, by Emily Greene Balch (New York: Arno, 1969, reprint of 1910 edition), pp. 308–309.

5 Anti-Semitism in Galicia: Golczewski, Frank. *Polnisch-jüdische Beziehungen, 1881–1922*. Wiesbaden: Franz Steiner Verlag G.m.b.H., 1981, pp. 68–74.

5 "Lion Phillimore . . .": Klinkenborg, p. 46.

6 "Long before Billy Wilder . . .": Wood, p. 2.

6 "They beat the shit . . .": Zolotow, pp. 21–22.

6 The Wilders' marriage certificate: Karasek, p. 33.

7 The Hapsburg empire: McCagg, p. 181, and Janik and Toulmin, p. 13.

7 Karl Lueger: Janik and Toulmin, p. 54.

7 Jewish emigration from Galicia: McCagg, pp. 182–87.

7 Billie's aunt: Lally, p. 2.

7 Buffalo Bill, Coney Island, and the wooden Indian: Zolotow, p. 21.

8 Moving to Vienna: Zolotow, p. 23; "Billy Wilder: The Human Comedy," *American Masters*, PBS, 1998; Karasek, p. 28; Lally, p. 2; Hutter, in conversation with the author.

8 Horse-drawn carriage and Billie's grandmother: Karasek, p. 29.

10 "He was my dream prince . . .": Karasek, pp. 23–24.

11 "Foreign legion . . .": Hutter, pp. 71–72: citing a letter from Billy Wilder to Andreas Hutter dated May 25, 1990.

11 Billie's coursework and grades: Hutter, pp. 71–72; Zolotow, p. 24; BW to Donald Albrecht, May 20, 1994.

11 "We were flexible . . .": Lally, p. 4.

12 Motorcycle story: Zolotow, p. 24.

12 "Pornography . . .": Carter, p. 60; Lally, p. 6.

12   The dachshund and masturbation, Karasek, pp. 36–37.

13   Stenography and half-brother stories: Karasek, pp. 34–35.

14   "But he was not as old . . .": Lally, p. 5.

14   David Baldinger: Karasek, p. 39. Note: Haller's Army, also known as the Blue Army, fought in World War I on the side of the Allies against the Hapsburgs and the other Central Powers.

14   Rotenturm Kino: Hutter, p. 74, and Zolotow, p. 24.

15   Walther Rathenau: Heilbut, p. 10, citing Rathenau, *Schriften* (Berlin, 1965).

15   Denial of citizenship: Optionsakten Max recte Hersch Mendel Wilder, Z. 175693/21, I 1461 VI, Bundesministerium für Inneres, Österreichisches Staatsarchiv, Archiv der Republik, unearthed by Andreas Hutter.

15   Billie and Greta: Lally, p. 6.

16   "I thought to myself 'Patience, patience . . .": Karasek, pp. 41–42.

16   Billie's grades: Hutter, p. 74.

16   Moving to Billrothstrasse: Hutter, pp. 77–79.

17   The Ilse story: Zolotow, p. 26.

17   "No! Bullshit! Total bullshit! . . .": McBride and McCarthy, p. 43.

17   Wilder himself admitted to Andreas Hutter . . . : Hutter, pp. 74–77, citing a letter from Billy Wilder to Andreas Hutter dated May 25, 1990.

17   Jazz lyrics: Zolotow, p. 25.

CHAPTER 2

18   Billie thinks about journalism: Karasek, p. 43.

19   "We cannot employ . . .": Hutter, pp. 80–81.

19   On *Die Bühne* and *Die Stunde*: Hutter, pp. 77–88.

19   "Or at least one of them is a dentist," and the Liebstöckl story: Lally, p. 10 and Karasek, p. 44.

20   "I made up crossword puzzles . . .": Hutter, pp. 80–81.

20   Sari Fedak and the bananas: Hutter, pp. 80–84, citing *Die Bühne* no. 11, p. 15.

20   "Space rates": Gehman, p. 90.

21   "Dead bodies in the Danube . . .": Karasek, p. 44, and Zolotow, p. 27.

21   "I would do the dirty work,": "Billy Wilder: The Human Comedy," *American Masters*, PBS, 1998.

21   Crime reporting research, and "Get up and write some anecdotes,": Hutter, pp. 137–144, citing Paul Erich Marcus, "B. W. will immer originell sein: Ein Gespräch mit Billy Wilder," *Die Kultur* (Munich) 141, Oct. 1, 1959, p. 12.

21   "Billie always had an alibi . . .": Hutter, Andreas, and Klaus Kamolz, "Plötzlich ein Wiener," *Profil*, May 9, 1994, pp. 90–94; and "Billie und Barkassy," *Profil*, Sept. 1992, pp. 82–85.

21   Hoffenreich on Billie: "Filmregie: So gut, wie das Publikum will." *Die Wochen-Presse: Das österreichische Nachrichtenmagazin*, Nov. 23, 1957, pp. 1–2.

21   The "bootlicker" nickname: "Filmregie: So gut, wie das Publikum will"; *Österreichisches Wörtbuch* (Vienna: Österreichisches Bundesverlag, 1993), p. 374.

21   "May he become as light . . .": Karasek, p. 44.

22   "An artist in vignettes . . .": Schorske, p. 9.

22   The nature of Wilder's feuilletons: Hutter, pp. 132–37, and Zolotow, p. 28.

22   Friedrich Porges: Hutter, pp. 150–52.

22   "This is no profession . . .": Billie, "Der Rosenkavalier am Rosenhügel," *Die Stunde*, Aug. 1, 1925, p. 6.

22   "Film is the future . . .": Hutter, pp. 154–58.

22   "The size of a city's pawn industry . . .": Billie, "Das Dorotheum steigt!" *Die Stunde*, Aug. 29, 1925.

22   Interview with Molnár: Zolotow, p. 28.

23   "Billy Wilder wants his biography . . .": Hutter, p. 179, citing Paul Erich Marcus, "B. W. will immer originell sein: Ein Gespräch mit Billy Wilder," *Die Kultur* (Munich) 141, Oct. 1, 1959, p. 12.

23 "Strauss and Adler talked their heads off . . .": "Billy Blows the Bugle," *Evening Standard* (London), Dec. 6, 1974, and Zolotow, pp. 28–29.

23 Wilder's admission about the four interviews: Hutter, pp. 175–79, citing a letter from Billy Wilder to Andreas Hutter dated May 25, 1990.

23 "The most successful scrounger . . .": Andreas Hutter in conversation with the author.

24 On Löwenstein's career: Youngkin, p. 23; on his relationship with Wilder: Hutter, pp. 159–160.

24 Letter from Fulda and Wilder's response: Hutter, pp. 168–75.

24 "A suitable Christmas present . . .": "Gezeichnet 'Billie,' " *Profil*, Sept. 28, 1992: quoting Billie, "Passendes Weihnachtsgeschenk für 12– bis 14 jährige Knaben," *Die Stunde*, 1925.

25 On Asta Nielsen: Kracauer, p. 26; Kleimeier, p. 41: citing Béla Balázs, *Der Film: Werden und Wesen einer neuen Kunst* (Vienna, 1961), p. 307ff.

25 "Like a schoolgirl . . .": Wilder, Billie, "Asta Nielsen's theatralische Sendung," *Die Bühne*, Feb. 4, 1926, pp. 6–8.

25 "It is all the result . . .": Zolotow, p. 28.

25 Wilder's residences: Hutter, pp. 181–87.

26 On Wilder, Békessy, and Spitz: Hutter, pp. 201–08; Hutter and Kamolz, "Billie und Barkassy," pp. 82–85; letter from Billy Wilder to Andreas Hutter dated May 25, 1990.

27 Currying favor: Hutter, pp. 207–11.

27 "The man is called 'Nicky' . . .": Billie, "Der Hungerkünstler Nicky beginnt heute in Wien zu fasten," *Die Stunde*, April 4, 1926, p. 9.

27 "Out of the train . . .": Billie, "Die Tiller-Girls sind da! Sie sind heute vormittags auf dem Westbahnhof angekommen," *Die Stunde*, April 3, 1926, p. 7.

28 Békessy flees: Hutter, pp. 209–11.

28 On Whiteman: DeLong, pp. 88–100.

29 On Katscher and Whiteman: Zolotow, p. 29; DeLong, p. 94, and Hutter, pp. 213–16.

30 "You add the most delightful mustache . . .": Wilder, Billie, "Paul Whiteman, sein Schnurrbart, der Cobenzl, und der Heurige: Ein Nachmittag mit Amerikas zweitberühmtesten Mann." *Die Stunde*, June 13, 1926, p. 7.

30 Billie accompanies Whiteman to Berlin: DeLong, p. 94; Zolotow, p. 30; "Filmregie: So gut, wie das Publikum will," pp. 1–2.

CHAPTER 3

31 "I left Vienna . . .": Kanin, p. 176.

31 "I persuaded him . . .": Ciment, *Positif* 269/270, pp. 15–28.

32 Jazz in Berlin: Gill, p. 104; Heilbut, p. 127; DeLong, p. 95; unsourced clippings in the Paul Whiteman Collection, Williams College, reel 1, vol. 3.

32 "His body vibrates . . .": Wilder, Billie, "Whiteman feiert in Berlin Triumphe," *Die Stunde*, June 29, 1926.

32 Letter from Krienes: Lally, p. 14.

32 On the "Berliner Schnauze": Heilbut, p. 3; Gill, p. 100.

33 "We called her proud . . .": Friedrich, *Before the Deluge*, p. 273.

33 "Berlin tasted of the future . . .": Gay, *Freud, Jews, and Other Germans*, p. 178.

33 "A real snotty Berliner . . .": Author's interview with Robert Lantz, July 25, 1995.

33–35 Newspapers and cafés in Berlin: Gill, pp. 190–93; Friedrich, *Before the Deluge*, p. 148.

34 "Then the shy young man . . .": Hutter, pp. 219–22: citing Pem (Paul Erich Marcus), *Heimweh nach dem Kurfürstendamm: Aus Berlins glanzvollsten Tagen und Nächten* (Berlin: Blanvalet, 1952), p. 77.

34 Békessy aftermath: Hutter, pp. 224, 542–43.

35 Billie's rooms and early career in Berlin: Hutter, p. 223: citing Pem (Paul Erich Marcus), "B.W. will immer originell sein: Ein Gespräch mit Billie Wilder," *Die Kultur* (Munich) no. 141, Oct. 1, 1959, p. 12; Lally, pp. 14–15; Zolotow, pp. 31–32. Note: *Buletten* are meatballs.

35 On the *Berliner Nachtausgabe* and Wilder's early reportage in Berlin: Hutter, pp. 229–33, citing Géza von Cziffra, "Kauf dir einen bunten Luftballon: Erinnerungen an Götter und Halbgötter," (Berlin: Herbig, 1975), pp. 144–45.

36 "That other fellow Wilder . . .": Lemon, p. 36.

36 "Hello, Billie!": Karasek, p. 53.

36 "Since I was a gifted enough dancer . . .": Ciment, *Positif* 269/270, July/Aug. 1983, pp. 15–28.

36 On Klabund: Hutter, pp. 240–41; Gill, p. 193.

36–37 On Billie's dancing career: Hutter, pp. 235–36.

37 "I dance with young ones . . .": Wilder, *Der Prinz von Wales geht auf Urlaub*, pp. 23–24: taken from "Der tägliche Dienst" ("The Daily Service"), *Berliner Zeitung am Mittag*, Jan. 24, 1927.

37 "I feel something . . .": Wilder, *Der Prinz von Wales geht auf Urlaub*, p. 20: taken from "Die Kollegen" ("The Colleagues"), *Berliner Zeitung am Mittag*, Jan. 22, 1927.

37 "Dark blue, finely-made . . .": Wilder, *Der Prinz von Wales geht auf Urlaub*, pp. 24–25: taken from "Der tägliche Dienst," *Berliner Zeitung am Mittag*, Jan. 24, 1927.

37 On Billie and Margerie: Lally, p. 18.

38 "In between, we dance . . .": Wilder, *Der Prinz von Wales geht auf Urlaub*, pp. 26–27: taken from "Der tägliche Dienst," *Berliner Zeitung am Mittag*, Jan. 24, 1927.

38 "The one beside me, Kurt . . .": Wilder, Billie, "Herr Ober, Bitte einen Tänzer!," *Die Buhne*, Sept. 1927.

39 "Served as a tea-time partner . . .": Anon. "Interview: Billy Wilder," *Playboy* 10, no. 6, June 1963, p. 57.

39 "The Hotel Eden was an international center . . .": Lemon, p. 36.

39 "It was a tabloid . . .": Gay, *Freud, Jews, and Other Germans*, p. 170.

39 "Who, with his hat tilted on his head . . .": Hutter, pp. 231–33: citing *Memoiren eines Moralisten: Erinnergungen I, Gesammelte Werke*, Hg. Klaus Schöffling (Zurich: Ammann, 1983), p. 109.

40 "I was not very serious . . .": Hutter, 231–33: citing Alfred Starkmann, "Billie Wilder: Es läuft ein grosses Drama über die Bühne," *Die Welt*, no. 300, Dec. 27, 1989, p. 7.

40 "I remember that my father . . .": Gill, p. 206.

40 "Women are guilty . . .": Wilder, *Der Prinz von Wales geht auf Urlaub*, p. 43: taken from "Renovierung" ("Renovation"), *Berliner Börsen Courier*, July 13, 1927.

40 " 'Mostly death and ruin . . .' ": Wilder, *Der Prinz von Wales geht auf Urlaub*, p. 93: taken from "Interview mit ener Hexe" ("Interview with a Witch"), *Berliner Börsen Courier*, Dec. 23, 1927.

40 Wilder on Faktor: Karasek, p. 53.

41 Wilder's poem: Lally, p. 15.

41 "A fantastic knack for getting interviews . . .": Lemon, p. 36.

41 The trip to Monte Carlo: Zolotow, p. 36.

41 The real Zaharoff story: Hutter, pp. 254–55.

41 On Chamberlin and Levine: Hutter, pp. 269–70; Zolotow, pp. 31–32.

41 Wilder and Remarque: Zolotow, p. 36.

42 On Chaliapin: Wilder, *Der Prinz von Wales geht auf Urlaub*, p. 99.

42 On Youssopoff: Zolotow, p. 33.

42 "Kisch used the Romanisches . . .": Gill, pp. 191–92.

43 On Col. Redl: Morton, pp. 72–75.

43 "Nothing is more imaginative . . .": Willett, pp. 107–08.

43 "Egon Erwin Kisch formed a completely new . . .": Hutter, pp. 241–43: quoting Horowitz, "Fussball, Beuschel und Nackt-Tänzerinnen: Gespräch zwischen Billie Wilder und Michael Horowitz," in *Ein Leben für die Zietung: Der rasende Reporter Egon Erwin Kisch* (Vienna: Orac, 1985), p. 159.

43 "He lived on the third floor . . .": Hutter, pp. 225–229, citing Horowitz, pp. 158–160.

44 "We were young and dreamed . . .": Domarchi and Douchet, p. 2.

44 Wilder on the number of ghostwritten scripts he wrote: "Billy Wilder: The Human Comedy," *American Masters*, PBS, 1998.

44 On Lustig, Reisch, and Kuh: McGilligan, *Fritz Lang*, p. 190; Hutter, pp. 225–26, 273.

44 "His father gave me my first job": Author's interview with Robert Lantz, July 25, 1995.

45 Reisch on Mayer: Zolotow, p. 37. Mayer's biography: Kracauer, pp. 61–62 and p. 256, citing a letter from Paul Rotha to Kracauer, Sept. 3, 1944.

45 "Mayer was a politically thoughtful . . .": Kreimeier, p. 143.

46 "Two Jews from Kraków . . .": Hutter, pp. 278–79, quoting von Cziffra, pp. 145–46.

46 Schulz's stinginess and black eyes: Lally, pp. 19– 20.

46 On Mr. and Mrs. Dwan's tour: Lally, p. 21; Zolotow, p. 34. Note: One fishy element of the tale is that Wilder spoke very little English at the time, and the American-born Dwan was probably not fluent in German.

47 "Of course it was way above my means . . .": Carter, p. 63.

47 The Chrysler: Zolotow, p. 38.

47 Max Wilder's death: Hutter, pp. 290–95; Zolotow, p. 42. Note: Zolotow, Karasek, and Lally all place the grave at the Jewish cemetery on the Schönhauser Allee, but it is not there; it is in Weissensee.

CHAPTER 4

49 Heinz, Lulu, and Galitzenstein: Zolotow, pp. 39–40; "Interview: Billy Wilder," *Playboy* 10, no. 6, June 1963, p. 58; Milland, pp. 5–7.

50 Typing at the Romanisches Café: Lally, p. 23.

50 Pasternak's and Kohner's remarks: Zolotow, p. 40.

50–51 Production details of *Der Teufelsreporter*: Hutter, pp. 290–95.

52 "It was bullshit . . .": McBride and McCarthy, pp. 42–43.

52 "Do I have to talk . . .": Lally, p. 44.

52 Wilder on the Dietrich film: Wilder, *Der Prinz von Wales geht auf Urlaub*, pp. 143–44, taken from "Spaziergang durch die Ateliers. Man dreht stumme Film" ("Walk through the Studios—They're Filming Silent Movies"), *Berliner Zeitung am Mittag*, June 21, 1929.

52 Wilder on Coca-Cola: Wilder, *Der Prinz von Wales geht auf Urlaub*, p. 117, taken from "Hallo, Herr Menjou?" ("Hello, Mr. Menjou?"), *Tempo*, Aug. 5, 1929.

52 Wilder on Klabund: Wilder, *Der Prinz von Wales geht auf Urlaub*, p. 123, taken from "Vor einem Jahr starb Klabund" ("A Year Ago, Klabund Died"), *Tempo*, Aug. 12, 1929.

52–53 Wilder on von Stroheim: Wilder, *Der Prinz von Wales geht auf Urlaub*, p. 134, taken from "Greed—In the Camera," *Berliner Zeitung am Mittag*, July 10, 1928; and Wilder, "Stroheim, der Mann den man gern hasst" ("Stroheim—the Man You Love to Hate"), *Der Querschnitt*, April 1929, pp. 293–95.

53 On Erich von Stroheim and *Greed*: Koszarski, p. 4; Saunders, pp. 134–36.

54 "It was a shallow time . . .": Lally, p. 29.

54 On Ufa in Berlin: Gill, p. 94.

54–55 "As we all know . . .": Kreimeier, p. 122: citing Stefan Grossmann, "Erich Pommers Sturz," *Das Tage-Buch*, Jan. 30, 1926.

55 On Parufamet: Kreimeier, pp. 127–28.

55 On *Metropolis*: Bock, p. 145.

55 On Pommer: Saunders, pp. 69, 82, 210, and 248.

55 On Hugenberg: Friedrich, *Before the Deluge*, p. 276; Kreimeier, p. 172.

56 On Berlin's parks: Gill, p. 89.

56 On Joe May: Murray, p. 81; Kracauer, p. 56.

58 On Schüfftan: Eisner, p. 31.

58 On the production of *Menschen am Sonntag*: Hutter, pp. 328–60.

58 On Curt Siodmak: McBride, "Kurt Siodmak . . . ," p. 15.

58–59 On the making of *Menschen am Sonntag*: Hutter, pp. 328–60; Lally, pp. 26–30; Brigitte Borchert, *Stiftung Deautsche Kinemathek Newsletter* no. 4, June 1993; Zinnemann, p. 16; Siodmak and Blumenberg, p. 42.

59 Wilder's reportage on *Menschen am Sonntag*: Wilder, Billie, "Wir vom Filmstudio 1929," *Tempo*, July 23, 1929; Wilder, Billie, "Wie wir unseren Studio-film drehten," *Montag Morgen*, Feb. 10, 1930.

62 On Brodnitz: Kreimeier, pp. 113–14, 196–97.

62 "When the movie begins . . .": Wilder, Billie, "Wie wir unseren Studio-film drehten," *Montag Morgen*, Feb. 10, 1930.

62 On *Menschen am Sonntag*'s opening night: Hutter, pp. 328–60; Lally, pp. 33–37; Siodmak and Blumenberg, p. 45; Kreimeier, p. 197.

63 On the sardine can: Zolotow, p. 42.

CHAPTER 5

64 German film statistics and "Ufa started concentrating . . .": Lally, pp. 36–37.

65 "One day Billie Wilder was inveighing . . .": Hutter, pp. 358–36: citing Pem (Paul Erich Marcus), *Heimweh nach dem Kurfürstendamm: Aus Berlins glanzvollsten Tagen und Nächten* (Berlin: Blanvalet, 1952), p. 87; variation: Zolotow, pp. 40–41; Liebmann's eye: McGilligan, *Fritz Lang*, p. 193.

65 Curt Siodmak on *Der Kampf*: Lally, pp. 37.

66 "Please invent . . .": Kreimeier, p. 104.

66 "Pommer was not a man . . .": Lally, p. 40.

66 "Billie was the life . . .": Lally, p. 46.

66 "A very quick thinker . . .": Zolotow, p. 44.

67 The German economy, Spender quotation, and 1930 election: Friedrich, *Before the Deluge*, pp. 300–2, 323, and 363.

67 "If there was any influence on me . . ." and remarks about Brecht: Anon. "Interview: Billy Wilder," *Playboy* 10, no. 6, June 1963, p. 57.

68 History of *Der Mann, der seinen Mörder sucht*: Hutter, pp. 360–65.

68 Quotations about *Der Mann, der seinen Mörder sucht*: Hutter, pp. 380–83: citing *Zwischen Berlin und Hollywood. Erinnerungen eines grossen Filmregisseurs*, ed. Hans C. Blumenberg (Munich: Herbig, 1980), pp. 48–49; Rühmann, p. 124.

68–69 Note on the remakes of *Der Mann, der seinen Mörder sucht*: The extent to which any of these films is a true "remake" is quite debatable, though many film reference books make the claim.

69 "Siodmak and I . . .": McDonald, p.66.

69 On the release of the three films in March: Hutter, p. 384.

70 On Willy Fritsch: Kreimeier, p. 147.

70 "Little does the handsome soldier . . .": Zolotow, p. 45.

70 Note: *Adorable* was released in 1933.

70 Note: screenplay credit for *Seitensprunge* went to Lajos Biro, Bobby E. Lüthge, and Karl Noti.

70 On *Emil*: McDonald, pp. 74–75; Hutter, pp. 393–94, citing Rasner and Wulf, " 'Ich nehm' das alles nicht so ernst . . . ,' " p. 20.

73 "Already in Berlin he was a man . . .": Zolotow, p. 48.

73–74 On Hitchcock: Kirkham, p. 19.

74 On *Es war einmal ein Walzer*: Hutter, pp. 402–3.

74 "Only interfered with the development . . .": Lally, p. 45.

74 Marta Eggerth recollections: interview with the author, Sept. 2, 1997, and letter to the author, Sept. 9, 1997.

74 Note: According to Hans Feld, with whom Wilder worked at Aafa, Billie also wrote a script called *Aus dem Tagebuch einer schönen Frau* (*From the Diary of a Beautiful Woman*). It was eventually released as *Das Abenteuer der Thea Roland* (*The Adventure of Thea Roland*) and was directed by Hermann Kosterlitz (later Henry Koster), but Wilder's name is nowhere to be found in the credits.

74–75 On the writing of *Ein blonder Traum* and the Austrians in Berlin: Hutter, pp. 405–6: citing Rasner and Wulf, " 'Ich nehm' das alles nicht so ernst . . . ,' " p. 25.

75 On Peter Lorre: Youngkin, p. 31.

75–76 On *Ein blonder Traum*, Pommer, and Harvey: Zolotow, pp. 42–45.

76 Kracauer on *Ein blonder Traum*: Kracauer, p. 212.

77 On *Der Sieger*: Hutter, pp. 402–8; Kreimeier, p. 188.

77 On *Scampolo*: Hutter, pp. 414–15.

77–78 Note: It's what Scampolo represents to these aging men as much as who she is herself that makes her seem so charming, and in this way she prefigures the hoyden-heroines of *Sabrina* and *Love in the Afternoon*. Indeed, Dolly Haas rather resembles Audrey Hepburn.

78 On *Das Blaue vom Himmel*: Hutter, pp. 424–26.

79 "Yes, the story of *Das Blaue vom Himmel* . . .": Marta Eggerth letter to the author, Sept. 9, 1997.

79 On censorship of *Das Blaue vom Himmel*: Film-Oberprüfstelle file #5865, dated Dec. 14, 1932, on file at the Bundesarchiv-Filmarchiv, Berlin.

80   On Billie and Wachsmann: Zolotow, p. 47; Lally, p. 44.

80   "Berlin was the city . . .": Gay, *Freud, Jews, and Other Germans*, p. 174.

80   "German workers . . .": Kreimeier, p. 198.

80   Note: an adaptation of Clément Vautel's novel *Madame ne veut pas d'enfants, Madame wünscht keine Kinder* was another Austrian coproduction by Lothar Stark G.m.b.H. and was probably written during a trip Wilder made with Kolpe to the Baltic Sea.

80   "We were only a few kilometers . . .": Hutter, pp. 426–28.

81   On *Madame*: Hutter, pp. 433–36; Lally, pp. 49–50.

81   "He was a turd . . .": Hutter, pp. 428–29; Rasner and Wulf, " 'Ich nem' das alles nicht so ernst . . . ,' " p. 21

81   On *Hitlerjunge Quex*: Kracauer, p. 262: citing Gregory Bateson, "Cultural and Thematic Analysis of Fictional Films," *Transactions of the New York Academy of Sciences*, Feb., 1943, p. 76; Leiser, pp. 35–39.

81   "He's the biggest asshole . . .": Hutter, pp. 428–29: citing Géza von Cziffra, *Ungelogen: Erinnerungen an mein Jahrhundert* (Berlin: Herbig, 1988), p. 259; Kreimeier, pp. 339–40.

81–82   "Political power in Germany . . .": Shirer, p. 163.

82   Note: Levassor turns out to be an internationally wanted jewel thief named John Constantinescu. Romanian jewel thieves were popular that year—Lubitsch's *Trouble in Paradise* features Herbert Marshall as Gaston Monescu.

83   Wilder on Hella: Zolotow, pp. 48–49.

84   Wilder on dominoes and liverwurst: McDonald, p. 83.

84   On Wilder's wages: Hutter, pp. 440–44: citing Claus Preute, "Playboy Interview: Billy Wilder: Ein offenes Gespräch mit dem Mann, der an Hollywoods Legende mitwirkte und sie schliesslich überlebte." *Playboy* (Munich), no. 9, Sept. 1978, p. 51.

84   "At night we went to the El Dorado . . .": Hutter, pp. 440–44: citing Preute, p. 51.

84–85   On Wilder, Dietrich, and Waldoff: Zolotow, pp. 31–32; Gill, pp. 85, 104–5; Bach, p. 73.

85   "Ladies who carried a bit . . .": Author's interview with Robert Lantz, July 25, 1995.

85   "They were eating . . .": Hutter, pp. 440–44: citing Pem, "Heimweh . . . ," p. 91.

85   On *Der Frack*: Zolotow, pp. 45–46.

85   Note: Wilder and Reisch ended up giving the idea for *Der Frack* to Sam Spiegel for *Tales of Manhattan* (1942); see Chapter 10.

85   "I think it's time to leave . . .": Zolotow, p. 49.

85   "It wasn't my idea . . .": Kanin, p. 177.

85   "To an Aryan friend . . .": Reed and Bacon, p. 157.

85   Wilder's flight to Paris: Zolotow, p. 49; Hutter, p. 446; Ciment, *Positif* 269/270, p. 18.

86   "One day I watched them . . .": Hutter, p. 446: citing Preute, p. 52.

86   On Kisch: Hutter, p. 446: citing Horowitz, "Fussball . . ." p. 160.

86   On *Brennendes Geheimnis* and Siodmak: Hutter, pp. 447–48.

86   On Wilder and the detectives: Lally, p. 54.

86–87   Note: Special thanks go to Andreas Hutter for compiling most of this shocking list of refugees. See Hutter, pp. 447–48; Kreimeier, pp. 212–13; Jelavich, p. 231; McGilligan, *Fritz Lang*, pp. 190–93; Symonette, p. 60.

87   "What happened to the novelists . . .": Author's interview with Robert Lantz, July 25, 1995.

87–88   "But what happened then was one . . .": Lally, pp. 51–52.

88   "That's finished . . .": Fromm, p. 61.

88   The premiere of *Was Frauen träumen*: Hutter, p. 451.

CHAPTER 6

89   "Hitler took over Berlin . . .": Lemon, p. 36.

89   "One suitcase and a bunch . . . ," posters, and passport information: Gehman, p. 90; Zolotow, pp. 49–50; Murphy, p. D4.

90   "Rather louche hotels . . .": Zolotow, p. 51.
90   On *apatrides*: Heilbut, p. 28.
90   On Wachsmann: Thomas, Tony, *Music*, pp. 76–77.
90   "It was located on the rue de Saigon . . .": Ciment, p. 18.
90–91 Holländer's recollections: Holländer, pp. 293–99.
91   On Billie and *die Spinne*: Holländer, p. 304.
93   "An elusive personality . . .": Jeancolas, pp. 30–31.
94   "I directed it with another cineaste . . .": Ciment, *Positif* July/Aug. 1983, p. 17.
94   "For lack of money . . .": Ciment, p. 17.
95   On the cheapness of the production: Lally, p. 56.
97   On *Pam-Pam* and Wilder's emigration: Zolotow, p. 52; Gehman, p. 60.
98   On Genia's remarriage: Karasek, p. 39.
98   On the Nazis' increasing power: Heilbut, p. 23.
98   On Wilder's voyage: Lally, p. 60.

CHAPTER 7

101   Quotation from *Hold Back the Dawn*: AMPAS, Paramount Collection, *Hold Back the Dawn* screenplay file. The scene was cut during shooting.
101   "It is a fantastic commentary . . .": Wyman, *Paper Walls*, unpaginated epigram.
101   "We had no first impressions . . .": Heilbut, p. 17.
102   On the Chief: Marshall, p. 301; Beebe, p. 57.
102   On Cohn: Gabler, p. 152.
102   On the Screen Writers Guild and Zanuck: Hamilton, pp. 94–96.
102–3 On Wilder's first day at Columbia: Lally, pp. 61–62.
103   Note: Max Kolpe, who moved from Paris to Vienna, made a musical of *Pam-Pam* along with two composers, Fritz Spielmann and Weiss. It premiered on Nov. 3, 1937, in Vienna. In 1940, Jan Lustig wrote the script for *Dancing on a Dime*, a Paramount film that appears to have been based on *Pam-Pam*, though Wilder received no credit. Hutter, pp. 453–54.
104   "Never got beyond a draft . . .": Lally, pp. 62–63.
105   On American immigration in the 1930s: Thatcher, pp. 63–64; Divine, pp. 78, 92; Wyman, *Abandonment of the Jews*, pp. 3–15, and *Paper Walls*, pp. 4–8.
105   On Wilder and the official: Wiley and Bona, p. 720; *Playboy*, Dec. 1960, p. 145.
105   On Wilder, the Chateau Marmont, and his art collection: Gehman, p. 145; Lemon, p. 36; Columbus, p. 24; Alleman, p. 167; Barnett, p. 104; Hitchens, p. 216; Friedrich, pp. 44–45.
106   "When I could not sleep . . .": Friedrich, pp. 44–45.
106   "I doubt if he dated . . .": Balasz, p. 43.
106   On Pommer and the pool: Lemon, p. 33; Friedrich, pp. 44–45.
106–7 "You know, when you are a writer . . .": Michel Ciment and Annie Tresgot, *Portrait d'un homme parfait à 60%*.
107   "I learned by not associating . . .": *Playboy*, June 1963, p. 60.
107   "An imported exporter . . .": Heilbut, p. 29.
107   "But he had a wonderful ear . . .": *Playboy*, June 1963, p. 60.
107   On the differences between English and German: Heilbut, pp. 57–58.
107   "When you start a sentence in German . . .": Friedrich, *Before the Deluge*, p. 344.
108   "Gee but I'd give the world . . .": McDonald, p. 121.
108   On *Music in the Air*: Hanson, 1931–1940, pp. 1449–450 and 2553; *Music in the Air* final cutting script (undated), UCLA Arts Library—Special Collections, Twentieth Century–Fox script collection, file folder 3.
109   *Lottery Lover*'s credits: UCLA Arts Library—Special Collections, Twentieth Century–Fox legal files collection, 095 MC 4834861.
110   Wilder's wages for *Lottery Lover*: Hamilton, p. 260.
110   Description of *Under Pressure*: Hanson, 1931–1940, p. 2301.
110–11 On the censors and *Mauvaise Graine*: AMPAS, Paramount Collection, *Mauvaise Graine* MPAA file.
112   On the approaching Anschluss: Shirer, pp. 279, 284.

112 Wilder's lodging in Vienna: hotel registration for Samuel "Billie" Wilder, Nov. 17, 1935, Austrian National Archives, Vienna.

112 "I remember how embarrassing . . .": Karasek, p. 33.

113 Wilder returns to the Chateau: Balasz, p. 43.

113 "I was so impressed . . .": Hitchens, p. 217.

113 Parrish and Brecht: Robert Parrish interview with the author, July 25, 1995.

113 "She was one of the few . . .": Reinhardt, pp. 303–4.

114 "Knowing so much already . . .": Heilbut, p. viii.

114 On Judith Coppicus: Zolotow, pp. 97–98.

115 Note: Originally, *Champagne Waltz* was the title of a treatment—by two *other* writers—that had to do with bookies and an orphanage in New York City; Paramount lifted the title and left the rest of the treatment well enough alone.

115 On Wilder's contract at Paramount: Zolotow, pp. 60–61; Hanson, 1931–1940, p. 315.

115 On Manny Wolfe's idea: Zolotow, p. 62.

CHAPTER 8

117 Note: *Ghost Music* is the original title Wilder and Jacques Théry gave to what would become *Rhythm on the River*. The quotation describes the character of Prescott, the composer, and is found in Wilder and Théry's first (undated) treatment. AMPAS, Paramount Collection, *Rhythm on the River* screenplay file.

117 On Brackett's biography: AMPAS, Paramount Pictures press sheet dated 1948 and various other clippings in the "Brackett, Charles" biographical file; *Variety*, March 12, 1969; Barnett, pp. 102–3; Zolotow, p. 63.

118 Brackett at RKO: Barnett, pp. 104–5.

119 Brackett's salary at Paramount: AMPAS, Paramount Collection, Charles Brackett legal briefs file.

119 Note in regard to *Angel*: *Bluebeard's Eighth Wife* was ultimately not a hit either. Eyman, p. 256.

119 "We fought a lot . . .": Freeman, p. 74.

120 "Lubitsch was one of the great ones . . ." and "*The Smiling Lieutenant* deals with . . .": Domarchi and Douchet, pp. 2–4.

120 "Lubitsch could do more . . .": Freeman, p. 74.

120 "Didn't notice, for months, that he was a short man . . .": Raphaelson, p. 25.

120 Lubitsch's background: Kreimeier, p. 56.

120 "If the truth were known . . .": Eyman, p. 259.

121 "Lubitsch was not what a writer . . .": Raphaelson, pp. 22–25.

121 "Mental slapstick": Paul, p. 128.

122 "What if when Gary Cooper . . .": Linville, pp. 51–52.

122 "The emptiest movie [Lubitsch] ever made": Eyman, p. 260.

123 Living with Judith's mother: Zolotow, p. 99.

123 Brackett's credits: AMPAS, Paramount Collection, Charles Brackett legal briefs file.

123 On *That Certain Age*: Hanson, 1930–1939, p. 2157.

123–24 "Pasternak didn't do anything memorable . . .": Domarchi and Douchet, pp. 5–6.

124 Wilder's representation: Sammlung Paul Kohner, Stiftung Deutsche Kinemathek, h. ss-88/1h-6, file 1.

124 On Kohner's agency: "Paul Kohner: Hollywood's Gentleman Agent" (exhibition), Goethe-Institut, Los Angeles, April 10–May 31, 1997.

124 On the European Film Fund: "Paul Kohner: Hollywood's Gentleman Agent" (exhibition), Goethe-Institut, Los Angeles, April 10–May 31, 1997.

124–25 On the Nazis in Vienna: Gilbert, pp. 58–59.

126 On the National Labor Relations Board and the Guild: Slide, pp. 2, 296.

127 On Wilder, Brackett, Hornblow, and Englund: Barnett, pp. 108–9.

128 Censorship of *Midnight*: AMPAS, Paramount Collection, *Midnight* MPPA file.

128 "I've never known John . . .": Barnett, pp. 108–9

128 On the "idiot cards": Chierichetti, p. 123.

129 Bridge instructions: Roth and Rubens.

130 "One of the most important things to learn about bridge . . .": Sheinwold, p. 295.

CHAPTER 9

131   On *Kristallnacht*: Shirer, pp. 430–31.
131   "In a political age . . .": Heilbut, p. x, pp. 110–11.
132   On the shoeshine stand: Eyman, p. 250; on the parking space: Zolotow, p. 70.
132–33 On *What a Life*: Hanson, 1930–1939, pp. 2388–389.
133–34 "Russian girl saturated . . ." and *Ninotchka*: Eyman, pp. 265–68; Zolotow, p. 80.
134   On Reisch: AMPAS, Walter Reisch biographical file.
134   "A movie and operetta writer, Walter Reisch . . .": Symonette, p. 427.
135   "Boys, I've got it . . .": Linville, p. 53.
135   "We worked weeks wondering . . .": Domarchi and Douchet, pp. 2–4.
135   "We communists, we will change . . .": Zolotow, pp. 83–84.
135–36 Petitioning for screenwriting credit: Eyman, p. 267.
136   "He would look at our stuff . . .": Eyman, p. 267.
136   "I think that all the pictures . . .": Columbus, p. 25.
136   "The most inhibited person . . .": Eyman, p. 268.
136   "As incongruous in Hollywood as Sibelius . . .": Paris, p. 550.
136   "Like a loving father . . .": Eyman, p. 269.
136–37 Casting *Ninotchka*: Swindell, p. 213; Eyman, p. 274.
137   Possible titles of *Ninotchka*: Eyman, p. 272.
137   "What would the directors . . .": Barnett, p. 109.
137   "The only way . . .": *Edinburgh Evening News*, Aug. 29, 1958.
137   "I remember going . . .": Clive Hirschorn, "The Billy Wilder Way with Women," *Sunday Express*, Sept. 14, 1969.
137   "Lubitsch's cinema is not a cinema of revolt . . .": Kreimeier, p. 55: quoting Enno Patalas, "Ernst Lubitsch: Eine Lektion in Kino," in *Lubitsch*, Hans Helmut Prinzler and Enno Patalas, eds. (Munich and Lucerne, 1987), p. 113.
137–38 "In a universe of playful . . .": Paul, p. 213.
139   "Absolutely stunning screenplay . . .": Ferguson, p. 401.
140   "He had this very serious expression . . .": Eyman, p. 271.
141   "A Hardy picture cost $25,000 less . . ." and box office figures: Eyman, p. 274.
141   MGM's purchase of *Heil Darling!*: Sammlung Paul Kohner, Stiftung Deutsche Kinemathek, h. ss-88/1h-6, files 1 and 3.
141–43 Details of *Heil Darling!*: AMPAS, Special Collections, William Wyler Collection, *Heil Darling!* treatment by Billy Wilder and Jacques Thery (undated).
144   Wilder becomes a citizen: Zolotow, p. 57.
144   Purchase of property on Tarcuto Way: Deed, Los Angeles County Registrar, lot 3, tract 11067, book 198, pp. 19 and 20.
144   The birth of the twins: Standard Certificates of Birth, State of California Department of Health Services, W-436 39-099416 and W-436 39-099417. Note: one curious detail contained in the birth certificates of Wilder's children is that they each indicate that Judith had given birth to another child previous to the twins, but the State of California appears to have neither a birth certificate nor a death certificate for that infant.
144   Birth announcement: on file at the Sammlung Paul Kohner, Stiftung Deutsche Kinemathek, h. ss-88/1h-6, file 3.
145   Note on Vincent's death: As Fritz Keller wrote to Paul Kohner on April 4, 1940: "Notified Rosenberg of the death of the Wilder boy. Both children were examined about a week ago and were in perfect health." Sammlung Paul Kohner, Stiftung Deutsche Kinemathek, h. ss-88/1h-6, file 3.
145   The biblical source of *Arise, My Love*: *The New Scofield Reference Bible* (New York: Oxford University Press, 1967), p. 706.
146   The tale of Hornblow and the synopsis: Barnett, p. 109.
147   "This whole sequence [of] Milland in the bathtub . . .": AMPAS, Paramount Collection, *Arise, My Love* MPAA file.
148   Hornblow's advice about war news: AMPAS, Paramount Collection, *Arise, My Love* production file.
148   Colbert's claim about Gusto: *Saturday Evening Post*, March 6, 1948.

149 Wilder's art purchases: *People,* Nov. 13, 1989, p. 157; Christie's catalogue, pp. 104, 118.

149–50 FBI surveillance of refugees: Schöllhammer, Georg. "FBI—oder die Dialektik der Aufklärung," *Der Standard,* April 10–12, 1993, p. 8.

150 On the new émigrés: Heilbut, pp. 110–11.

150–51 On *Polonaise:* AMPAS, Paramount Collection, *Hold Back the Dawn* production file; AMPAS, Paramount Collection, *Polonaise* MPAA file.

151 On the Bob Hope film: Sammlung Paul Kohner, Stiftung Deutsche Kinemathek, h. ss-88/1h-6, file 1.

151 "Just before Paulette Goddard . . .": Louella Parsons syndicated column of Oct. 7, 1940.

151 Wilder and Brackett claim not to have read Frings's treatment: Barnett, p. 110.

152 Questions about Kurt Frings: AMPAS, Paramount Collection, *Hold Back the Dawn* production file.

152 On Jaray and Maibaum: AMPAS, Paramount Collection, *Hold Back the Dawn* production files.

153 "A onetime classical actor . . .": Friedrich, *City of Nets,* p. 44.

153 On de Havilland and MacMurray: Tony Thomas, *The Films of Olivia de Havilland,* p. 173; Kass, pp. 65–66.

155 "Brackett and I are having lunch . . .": Columbus, p. 26.

155 "I do not wish to have these discussions . . .": Zolotow, p. 91.

155 "What we wrote was a bit of toilet paper . . .": Ciment, *Positif,* July/Aug. 1983.

155 Colbert's revision of the *Midnight* script: AMPAS, Paramount Collection, *Midnight* production file.

155 Salaries for *Hold Back the Dawn:* AMPAS, Paramount Collection, *Hold Back the Dawn* production file.

156 "Leisen was too goddamn fey . . .": Zolotow, p. 69.

156 "He hated writers . . .": Freeman, p. 74.

156 "Billy would scream . . .": Kelly, p. 94.

156 "It was very funny . . ." and "He would referee . . .": Chierichietti, pp. 120–21.

156 "Charlie hated him . . .": Zolotow, p. 69.

CHAPTER 10

158 "I considered how I should address him . . .": Karasek, pp. 24–25. Note: Wilder makes fun of Otto von Hapsburg for speaking at places other than the top American universities in 1941, but the joke is on Billy: in the 1990s Mr. von Hapsburg became one of the most active (and most senior) members of the European Parliament.

159 The Spiegel, Wilder, and Reisch story: Zolotow, p. 95.

159–60 The Henie story: Zolotow, p. 92.

160 "His ineptitude was often his appeal . . .": Peary, p. 498.

161 "You know, Bill . . .": Berg, p. 361.

161 "I found in my trunk . . .": Ciment, "Interview with Billy Wilder," *Positif* 120, Oct. 1970, pp. 5–17; "Happiest Couple in Hollywood," p. 110.

161 Wilder on Goldwyn: Berg, pp. 362–63.

161 "I stayed constantly on the set . . .": Domarchi and Douchet, p. 4.

162 "You tell Ginger Rogers . . .": Barnett, p. 110.

162 On Lombard: Berg, p. 362.

162–63 Cooper on *Ball of Fire:* Swindell, pp. 236–37.

164 Note on "She jives by night!": *They Drive by Night,* Warner Bros., 1940.

166 Note on the telephone: *The Story of Alexander Graham Bell* starred Don Ameche.

167 Wilder was never fully paid: Berg, p. 363.

167 "Taking that suit . . .": Barnett, p. 110.

167 The Nijinsky story: Berg, p. 364.

CHAPTER 11

171 "Finally, I pissed them off . . .": Domarchi and Douchet, p. 2.

171 On Brackett and Wilder fighting in the office: Zolotow, pp. 91–92.

172   On Sistrom and the origins of *The Major and the Minor*: Zolotow, pp. 103–5; AMPAS, Paramount Collection, *The Major and the Minor* production files 5 and 7. "Would you work in a picture . . .": Zolotow, p. 105.

173   "Met your daughter on the train . . .": AMPAS, Paramount Collection, *The Major and the Minor* MPAA file.

174   "To be accused of lack of taste . . .": Eyman, 302; Swindell, p. 296.

174   Budget of *The Major and the Minor*: AMPAS, Paramount Collection, *The Major and the Minor* production files 2 and 4.

174–75   Rogers's costuming: Head, pp. 59–60.

175   "We had Ginger's marvelous tits . . ." etc.: Zolotow, pp. 105–7.

175   History of the "dry martini" joke: Altman, p. 345.

176   The split-screen shots: AMPAS, Paramount Collection, *The Major and the Minor* production file 6.

176   "A director must be a policeman . . .": Anon., "Policeman, Midwife, Bastard," p. 75.

176   "Look, I have made sixty pictures . . .": Columbus, p. 26.

176   Purchase of Hidden Valley estate: Room 208, Los Angeles County Registrar and Recorder of Deeds, Norwalk, California.

177   Sturges's gift: Jacobs, p. 244.

177   Wilder's first complete take as a director: AMPAS, Paramount Collection, *The Major and the Minor* production file 4; Zolotow, p. 106. Note: Zolotow cites March 4 as the day on which the directors appeared on the set to give Wilder moral support, but if they appeared on the first day of shooting, they appeared on March 12.

177   "I would like to give the impression . . .": Domarchi and Douchet, p. 7.

177   "When somebody turns to his neighbor . . .": *Playboy*, Dec. 1960, p. 147.

178   On Harrison: Zolotow, p. 106.

178   Wilder on Benchley: Zolotow, p. 107.

179   Ginger's gift to Billy: *Los Angeles Examiner*, April 27, 1942.

179   On *Bundles for Freedom*: AMPAS, Paramount Collection, legal briefs file on Charles Brackett. The film appears never to have been made.

179   Lela Rogers's retakes: AMPAS, Paramount Collection, *The Major and the Minor* production file 5.

180   Announcement of *Women's Wear*: *Los Angeles Examiner*, June 3, 1942.

181   Wilder, Brecht, and the hypnosis story: Brecht, *Arbeitsjournal* entries dated Jan. 16 and April 11, 1942; Friedrich, *Nets*, p. 127; AMPAS, Paramount Collection, *The Major and the Minor* production file 6; Brecht, *Gesammelte Werke*, vol. 10, p. 858; Lyon, p. 54; Friedrich, *Nets*, p. 127; Hayman, p. 260.

181–82   Announcement of *Five Graves*: *Los Angeles Examiner*, Aug. 14, 1942; *Hollywood Reporter*, *Variety*, and *Motion Picture Daily*, Aug. 28, 1942.

182   Assignment to *Five Graves*: AMPAS, Paramount Collection, *Five Graves to Cairo* production file 1.

182   "I just needed something to keep my hands busy . . .": Linville, p. 58.

182   Suggestions for retitling *Five Graves* and Brackett and Wilder's response: AMPAS, Paramount Collection, *Five Graves to Cairo* production file 1.

182   History of the war in North Africa: Shirer, pp. 827–29, 911–14, 919–22; Weinberg, pp. 222–25, 360–63.

182   Box office records for *The Major and the Minor*: AMPAS, *Five Graves to Cairo* production file; *Hollywood Reporter*, Oct. 19, 1942.

183   The 1942 poll of popular films: Koppes and Black, p. 222.

184   Wilder and crew go to the desert and other production details: AMPAS, Paramount Collection, *Five Graves to Cairo* production files.

184   Cary Grant declines to appear in *Five Graves*: American Film Institute Oral History with John F. Seitz, p. 102.

184–85   Billy sweeps the desert: Zolotow, p. 108.

185   Costuming for *Five Graves*: *Paramount News*, Feb. and April, 1943.

186   On von Stroheim: Koszarski, p. 164.

186   "It's especially Stroheim . . .": Domarchi and Douchet, p. 12.

186   "In regard to sex perversions . . .": Zolotow, p. 109.

187 Seitz's techniques: AFI Oral History with John F. Seitz, pp. 109–10.

187 "Wilder's ability to wear the many masques . . .": Allen, p. 30.

188 Stroheim's ideas about costuming: Koszarski, pp. 286–87.

189 Final costs of *Five Graves*: AMPAS, Paramount Collection, *Five Graves to Cairo* production files.

189 Scoring of *Five Graves*: Rózsa, pp. 130–131; Lipstone's early career: AMPAS, biographical clippings file on Lipstone.

189 "The volatile Wilder . . .": Rózsa, p. 130.

191 Note on Dunkirk: Of the more than 330,000 troops evacuated from the beaches of Dunkirk in May 1940, about 120,000 were French. Weinberg, pp. 130–31.

CHAPTER 12

193 *Double Indemnity* and the telephone number: AMPAS, Paramount Collection, *Double Indemnity* production file 3.

194 "Keep it quiet . . .": *Double Indemnity* pressbook.

194 "I realized that no matter . . .": *Los Angeles Times*, Aug. 6, 1944.

194 Cain's tale of *Double Indemnity*: "Hays Censors Rile Jim Cain" by David Hanna, *Paramount News*, Feb. 14, 1944.

194–95 The story of Wilder's secretary: Friedrich, *Nets*, p. 161.

195 Details of the Snyder-Gray murder: "In Cold Blood: Murders that Shocked New York," New York Historical Society exhibition, Jan. 24—April 7, 1996.

196–97 "You bet that your house will burn down . . .": Cain, p. 29.

197 "1944 was 'The Year of Infidelities' . . ." and "Billy got so despondent . . .": Kanin, pp. 177–78.

197 "I wanted James M. Cain . . .": Columbus, p. 25.

198 "This is shit . . .": Zolotow, p. 114.

198 "It's the only picture I ever saw , , ,": Brunette and Peary, p. 55.

198 "We had no problems whatsoever . . .": Madsen, p. 170.

198 The censors' objections to *Double Indemnity*: AMPAS, Paramount Collection, *Double Indemnity* MPAA file.

199 "To begin with, there was my German accent . . .": Hamilton, p. 257; Miriam Gross, ed., *The World of Raymond Chandler*. (London: Weidenfeld & Nicolson, 1977), p. 50.

199 Wilder hates Chandler: Zolotow, pp. 114–15; "Billy Wilder: The Human Comedy," *American Masters*, PBS, 1998.

199 "Chandler, an older man . . .": Jensen, p. 21.

200 "Chandler was typical . . .": Columbus, p. 25.

201 Wilder and Brackett's "bedroom": Barnett, p. 103.

201 "Sex was rampant . . .": Linville, p. 61.

202 Wilder approaches Raft and Wilder's comment to the press: Zolotow, p. 117; Friedrich, *Nets*, p. 164; *Los Angeles Times*, Aug. 6, 1944.

202 Wilder approaches MacMurray: Zolotow, p. 117.

203 Wilder approaches Stanwyck: *Double Indemnity* pressbook; Wiley and Bona, p. 144.

203 "We hire Barbara Stanwyck . . .": Friedrich, *Nets*, p. 165.

203 Derlinger: AMPAS, Paramount Collection, *Double Indemnity* production file 3.

204 Note on Keyes: I thank John Simons for countless observations about the Promethean Barton Keyes.

204 "A wolf on a phony claim": Cain, p. 12.

205 The ending of *Double Indemnity*: AMPAS, Paramount Collection, *Double Indemnity* screenplay file.

206 The anklets: AMPAS, Paramount Collection, *Double Indemnity* production file 2.

206 "He was ready for anything . . .": Ciment, *Positif*, Oct. 1970, p. 16.

207 Neff's apartment based on the Chateau Marmont: Alleman, p. 167.

207 The insurance office resembles Paramount's own corporate office: *Paramount News*, Aug. 1944.

207 Rationing in force on the set: AMPAS, Paramount Collection, *Double Indemnity* production file 3.

208 "I was doing it fast . . .": Friedrich, *Nets*, p. 164.

208 "I have always felt that surprise . . .": *Los Angeles Times*, Aug. 6, 1944.
208 "I just wanted to be sure . . .": *Double Indemnity* pressbook.
208 "A notorious line-muffer . . .": *Los Angeles Times*, Aug. 6, 1944.
209 "Memo to Wilder . . .": *Double Indemnity* pressbook.
209 Final shot of principal photography: AMPAS, Paramount Collection, *Double Indemnity* production file 3.
209 The sole surviving genius remark: *Los Angeles Examiner*, Jan. 10, 1944.
209 MacMurray's execution scene: AMPAS, Paramount Collection, *Double Indemnity* production file 3; Friedrich, *Nets*, p. 165.
209 "Very questionable in its present form": AMPAS, Paramount Collection, *Double Indemnity* MPAA file.
210 Note on the ending of *Double Indemnity*: James Naremore understands the "alternate ending" as really being two endings: a final fade-out after Neff's line "Will you, Keyes?," and a fade-out/fade-in to the gas chamber sequence. Naremore, pp. 29–30.
210 On the proposed score for *Double Indemnity*: *Paramount News*, May 1944.
210 On Rózsa's score: Palmer, p. 197; on Lipstone's and Wilder's responses, Rózsa, p. 142.
211 Final cost of *Double Indemnity*: AMPAS, Paramount Collection, *Double Indemnity* production file 1.
211 *Boxoffice*'s marketing suggestion: AMPAS, general collection, *Double Indemnity* production file.
211 "How did you like the picture . . .": *Los Angeles Examiner*, Aug. 23, 1944.
211 Cigar idea: *Double Indemnity* pressbook. Note on the cigar: See Frank Krutnik, "Desire, transgression, and James M. Cain," in *Screen* 23, 1, 1982, pp. 31–44, and the more extensive treatment of the issue in *In a Lonely Street: film noir, genre, masculinity*.
212 Preview and "There goes my picture . . .": *Los Angeles Times*, July 23, 1944; *People*, Dec. 9, 1991.
212 "The two most important words . . .": Schumach, p. 48; *Los Angeles Times*, Aug. 6, 1944.
212 The Oblath's ad: Zolotow, p. 122.
213 Cain on Kate Smith: Brunette and Peary, p. 56.
213 Chandler on his experiences in Hollywood: Freeman, pp. 74–75; Jensen, p. 20.
213 "How could we . . .": Zolotow, p. 121.

CHAPTER 13

214 "It is evident to me . . .": Zolotow, p. 129.
214 Note on Brackett and alcohol: The extent of Brackett's own drinking is unclear. Nearly every entry that refers to the Bracketts in Christopher Isherwood's diary reports a lot of drinking, and Mrs. Brackett was not the only one participating. *Life* magazine also reported that after a rough-cut screening, Brackett took some of the cast and crew across the street to Lucey's and ordered a round of drinks for everybody. He caught a glimpse of himself in the mirror at the bar, a drink in his hand, and he froze; the whole group was staring at him. One gets the sense that their stares were not simply because *The Lost Weekend*'s producer was holding a single drink on a single occasion. See Jensen, pp. 17–23.
214 The epigraph: *Hamlet*, III, i.
215 Wilder telephones Brackett: Wiley and Bona, p. 150.
215 Brackett's alcoholic friends: Friedrich, *Nets*, pp. 416–17.
215 Note on the Hacketts: Albert Hackett and his wife, Frances Goodrich, who cowrote *The Thin Man*, *After the Thin Man*, and *Another Thin Man*, all based on Hammett's characters and stories. Hamilton, pp. 253–54; Johnson, p. 151.
215 "All the woeful errors . . .": Jackson, pp. 48–49.
215 "Larmore was an actor . . .": Zolotow, pp. 128–129. Note: Larmore does appear in a bit part in *A Foreign Affair.*.
216 Note on Larmore's relationship with Brackett: Isherwood himself does not state the

rumor in the course of his published diary entries; the editor of the volume does, however, in the glossary entry for Larmore. Isherwood, p. 966.

216 The Joan Fontaine project: AMPAS, Paramount Collection, *The Lost Weekend* production file 1.

216 On *Olympia*: AMPAS, Paramount Collection, *Olympia* production file 2.

216 Silence in *Lost Weekend*: *New York Times*, July 16, 1944.

216 Hepburn in *Lost Weekend*: *Los Angeles Examiner*, July 7, 1944.

217 Censors respond to *Lost Weekend*: AMPAS, Paramount Collection, *The Lost Weekend* production file 4.

218 Scheduling of *Lost Weekend* and Fidler broadcast: AMPAS, Paramount Collection, *The Lost Weekend* MPAA file.

218 "But the head of Paramount . . .": Columbus, p. 27.

218 "At the time, alcoholism . . .": Ciment, *Positif* July/Aug. 1983.

218 Stanwyck in *Lost Weekend*: Madsen, *Stanwyck*, p. 220.

218 "That drunk film": Quirk, p. 79.

218 Wilder, Terry, and Fontaine: *The Lost Weekend* pressbook.

218 Production meeting on *Lost Weekend*: AMPAS, Paramount Collection, *The Lost Weekend* production file 4.

219 The Met's demand: AMPAS, Paramount Collection, *The Lost Weekend* production file 4.

219 "Will you please see . . .": AMPAS, Paramount Collection, *The Lost Weekend* production file 4.

219 Sale and purchase of properties: Room 208, Los Angeles County Registrar and Recorder of Deeds, Norwalk, California.

219 "Increasingly snappish and morose": Milland, p. 215.

220 October 5 memo: AMPAS, Paramount Collection *The Lost Weekend*, production file 4.

220 On the hidden cameras: Milland, p. 217; American Film Institute Oral History with John F. Seitz, p. 152.

221 Filming at and around Bellevue: Jensen, March 11, 1946; Erskine Johnson, "Billy Wilder's Trail of Whims," *Los Angeles Mirror*, July 12, 1961.

221 Completing shooting in New York and traveling back to Los Angeles: AMPAS, Paramount Collection, *The Lost Weekend* production files 3 and 4.

221–22 Censorship problems, Allied Liquor Industries, Jackson, and Brackett's remarks to the press: AMPAS, Paramount Collection, *The Lost Weekend* MPAA file.

222 On Doris Dowling and Audrey Young: Freeman, p. 75.

223 "I almost went crazy with excitement . . .": Creelman, Eileen, "Doris Dowling Discusses Her First Movie, 'The Lost Weekend,' Due Soon at the Rivoli," *New York Sun*, Nov. 24, 1945.

224 "Brilliant, beautiful, and as hard . . .": Lemon, p. 37.

224 Note on Audrey Young's singing career: Young's splendid recordings include "Sentimental Rhapsody," "On the Painted Desert," "Sunlight Souvenirs," and "Where Is the One?" all with Tommy Dorsey in 1947.

224 "With her reed-slim figure . . .": Vilidas, p. 154.

224 Audrey calls Billy on the phone: Karasek, p. 327.

224–25 Seitz's technical achievements: *Paramount News*, June 1945; AFI Oral History with John F. Seitz, pp. 56, 152–53; *The Lost Weekend* pressbook.

225 Note on the stunt: It has been reported that the camera was strapped to Milland's own chest, but it is unlikely that he would have performed such a dangerous stunt on his own.

225 Synchronization of raindrops: *Paramount News*, July 1945.

225 Cigarette rationing: *Paramount News*, Feb. 1945.

225–26 History of the war in the fall of 1944: Weinberg, p. 752.

226 Reporting the Holocaust: Heilbut, p. 113; Wyman, pp. 324–25.

226 "A bit like the old court Jews . . .": Heilbut, p. ix.

226 "Is that all you got to do . . ." and family photographs on the set: *The Lost Weekend* pressbook.

228 "A long ululating howl": Milland, pp. 215–16.

228 "The stronger ego kills the weaker" and "Birnam's hallucination . . .": *The Lost Weekend* pressbook; Scheuer, Philip K., "Die Cast on Doings of Drunk," *Los Angeles Times*, Dec. 3, 1944.

228 On *Olympia*: *Los Angeles Examiner*, Nov. 11, 1944.

228 Censors respond to Gloria and the bat: AMPAS, Paramount Collection, *The Lost Weekend* MPAA file.

229 Production schedule and budget of *Lost Weekend*: AMPAS, Paramount Collection, *The Lost Weekend* production file 2.

229 Announcement of *Count of Luxembourg*: *Los Angeles Examiner*, Jan. 19, 1945.

229 Budget of *Count of Luxembourg*: AMPAS, Paramount Collection, *The Count of Luxembourg* file.

229 Announcement of *Around the World*: *Los Angeles Examiner*, Jan. 31, 1945.

230 Luise Rainer story: Zolotow, p. 123; Lally, p. 140.

231 "The studio was against it . . .": *Variety*, April 14, 1954.

231 "Told me it was a great movie . . .": Hitchens, p. 217.

231 Rumor about Costello, story about De Sylva and Freeman: Friedrich, pp. 416–17.

232 Hope's joke about Freeman: Zolotow, p. 127.

232 Freeman and the word *homosexual*: Chierichietti, p. 16.

CHAPTER 14

233 Note on the "Beast of Belsen" line: This line, delivered by Johnny to Erika, appears in Wilder's earliest treatment of *A Foreign Affair* but was deleted thereafter.

234 On McClure: Pogue, p. 86.

234 On Davis: Laurie, p. 114.

235 "One of the greatest honors . . .": *Los Angeles Examiner*, March 5, 1945.

235 "According to CNDI LA 2718 . . .": Lyon, *Brecht*, p. 284.

235 Fisk Building meeting on VE Day: Zolotow, p. 135; Karasek, p. 303. Note: Wilder was probably already in London by VE Day, since British newspapers reported his presence there as early as April 18.

235 Note on Wilder's rank: The National Archives in College Park, Maryland, house many boxes of documents pertaining to the Psychological Warfare Division offices at Bad Homburg and Berlin and the activities of PsyWar employees. None of these documents refer to Billy Wilder as an officer of the United States Army. Instead, they refer to him as "Mr. Wilder," in contrast, for example, to Colonel William Paley.

236 Wilder's vision of London: Karasek, p. 304.

236 "I can say very little now . . .": Ernest Betts, "Little Man, Long Title," *Daily Express*, April 18, 1945.

236 On Voss: Lally, p. 152.

237 Reporting the Holocaust: Heilbut, p. 113.

237 "There was an entire field . . .": "Billy, How Did You Do It?": Billy Wilder in Conversation with Volker Schlöndorff, BBC-TV, 1988.

238 "A kind of dog food": Karasek, p. 304.

238 Bad Homburg compound: Paley, p. 169.

238 Sally Taylor's recollections: Interview with the author, Feb. 11, 1997.

238 "Over and over we would fix . . .": Smith, p. 224.

239 Exploding champagne story: Lemon, p. 36.

239 "Which ones were the least . . .": Freeman, p. 75.

239 On Werner Krauss: Lally, p. 152.

239 Anton Lang story: Lemon, p. 36.

240 Holocaust documentary plans: National Archives at College Park, Record Group 260, Box 290.

241 "The preview occurred . . .": Lally, pp. 154–55.

242 Note on *Todesmullen*: In November, two months after Billy returned to the States, an almost-final version of *Todesmullen* was screened—first to an audience comprised of Information Control Division (ICD) staffers in Bad Homburg, and later, with assistance

from intelligence officers, to a German audience in Frankfurt. One version of the film had been screened in Erlangen, but it was greeted so unfavorably that it was abandoned—this may be the night of the stolen pencils, but no memos of that particular screening seem to have survived. According to records in the National Archives, the final (or perhaps *a* final) version of *Todesmullen* was put together in London by Ivor Montagu and various assistants from ICD and OWI, with narration written and recorded in Munich by Lieutenant Oskar Seidlin. After the Frankfurt screening, the decision was made to cut only a single image—a body thrown off a wagon. Based on the success of the screening, 114 prints of the film were ordered so that *Todesmullen* could be exhibited widely beginning in January. Later, the military government in parts of Bavaria did make screenings of *Todesmullen* mandatory and attached an attendance record to the Germans' ration cards so they couldn't obtain food unless they saw it, but because this practice was strictly against policy it was soon halted. By that point Billy Wilder had been back in Hollywood for several months.

242   *Todesmullen* postponed: National Archives at College Park, Record Group 260, Box 290.

242   German audience polls: National Archives at College Park, Record Group 260, Box 289, "Film Test Screening" file.

242   Note: *KZ* is German shorthand for *Konzentrationslager*, or concentration camp.

242   "Except three women . . .": National Archives at College Park, Record Group 208, "OB Motion Picture Bureau—June, 1945" file.

242   "The atrocity film we now . . ." and other memos: National Archives at College Park, Record Group 260, Box 290.

242   Reediting of footage: National Archives at College Park, Record Group 260, Box 280, "Film Production" file.

243   "I never met a single Nazi . . .": Karasek, p. 313.

243   "I know the decent ones . . .": Lally, p. 153; "Billy, How Did You Do It?: Billy Wilder in Conversation with Volker Schlöndorff," BBC-TV, 1988.

244   The nun story: Zolotow, pp. 137–38.

244   "The summer of '45 . . .": Karasek, p. 310.

244–45   The cemetery story: Karasek, p. 312; Lally, p. 153; Zolotow, p. 138. Note: Wilder had a new gravestone erected at the Jewish cemetery in Weissensee (Field H6, Row 16) to honor his father's memory after the original stone was destroyed in the war.

246   The *Mrs. Miniver* story: Lally, pp. 155–56.

247   Wilder's and Paley's memos: National Archives at College Park, Record Group 260, Box 280, "Film Production" file.

249–50   Gin rummy story: Karasek, p. 321.

250   Grosz painting: *People*, Nov. 13, 1989, p. 157.

CHAPTER 15

251   Divorce settlement: *Judith Wilder v. Billy Wilder*, Case #D292642, Los Angeles County.

251   Moving in with Lubitsch: *Los Angeles Examiner*, Oct. 4, 1945.

251   On Victoria: Zolotow, pp. 141–48.

251   Divorce finalized: *Judith Wilder v. Billy Wilder*, Case #D292642, Los Angeles County.

251   Judith's engagement: *Los Angeles Examiner*, March 5, 1947.

252   *Glass Alibi* announcement: *Los Angeles Examiner*, Aug. 7, 1945.

253   Kohner represents Willie and discussion of *Emil* remake: Sammlung Paul Kohner, Stiftung Deutsche Kinemathek, William Wilder file.

253   "A dull son of a bitch": "Dialogue on Film," p. 45.

253   Brackett contacts Jackson: AMPAS, Paramount Collection, *The Lost Weekend* production file 1.

253   Rózsa exchange with Selznick: Rózsa, p. 148.

254   Escalated cost of *Lost Weekend*: AMPAS, Paramount Collection, *The Lost Weekend* production file 4.

254   "As things finally developed . . .": *Variety*, April 14, 1954.

254   "Once we make a picture . . .": Wiley and Bona, p. 150.

254   "Take no steps . . .": AMPAS, Paramount Collection, *The Lost Weekend* MPAA file.

254–55 Censorship concerns: AMPAS, Paramount Collection, *The Lost Weekend* MPAA file.

255 "London is on a praise binge . . ." and "Even with the paper shortage . . .": Wiley and Bona, p. 150.

255 "Paramount found the courage . . .": *The Lost Weekend* pressbook.

255–56 Critics on *Lost Weekend*: *New York Herald Tribune*, Dec. 3, 1945; *Hollywood Reporter*, Aug. 14, 1945; John McCarten in the *New Yorker*, quoted in *Motion Picture Daily*, Dec. 6, 1945; Louella Parsons, *Los Angeles Examiner*, undated clipping in AMPAS, Paramount Collection, *The Lost Weekend* MPAA file; *New York Times*, Dec. 3, 1945.

256 "Paramount has succeeded . . .": Wiley and Bona, pp. 150–53.

256 *Times* interview: Thomas Pryor, "End of a Journey," *New York Times*, Sept. 23, 1945, Sec. II, p. 3.

256 The jeep: *Los Angeles Examiner*, Dec. 13, 1945, and Feb. 12, 1946.

257 Oscar details: Wiley and Bona, pp. 150–56.

258 Bottles hanging from the windows: Zolotow, p. 140.

CHAPTER 16

259 Nicknames for Brackett and Wilder: Milland, p. 213.

259 Louella Parsons's broadcast: Transcript of radio show, Feb. 17, 1946, on file at the Archives of the Performing Arts, Doheny Library, University of California.

260 "TO ALL CONCERNED . . .": AMPAS, Paramount Collection, *The Emperor Waltz* screenplay file.

262 Zweig quotation: Heilbut, p. 34.

262 On Bing Crosby: Osterholm, p. 34.

263 Note on Fontaine's deal: On the other hand, Fontaine's biographer Marsha Lynn Beeman claims that Paramount paid Selznick $225,000 for Fontaine, of which Selznick paid Fontaine herself $75,000 minus her agent's commission. Beeman, p. 22; AMPAS, legal briefs file on Joan Fontaine.

263 Censorship concerns: AMPAS, Paramount Collection, *The Emperor Waltz* MPAA file.

264 Budget figures: AMPAS, Paramount Collection, *The Emperor Waltz* production file 4.

265 Joan Fontaine recollections: Interview with the author, May 22, 1996.

265 On Barney Dean: Osterholm, p. 34.

267 Crosby yells at dog: Osterholm, p. 265.

267 Costuming: Head, pp. 71–72.

267 "Stinkers," etc.: Kanin, p. 179.

267 "That's my story . . .": Eyman, p. 350.

268 "Ice cream parlor . . .": Karasek, p. 340.

268 "It's always better to go to a hunting lodge . . .": Prelutsky, p. 174.

269 *Love in the Air*: AMPAS, Paramount Collection, *A Foreign Affair* production file 1.

270 Note on Breens: Richard Breen was no relation to Joseph Breen, the censor.

270 Title suggestions: AMPAS, Paramount Collection, *A Foreign Affair* production file 1.

270 Laughton in *Galileo*: Freidrich, *City of Nets*, p. 291; Callow, pp. 187–90.

271 Wilder and crew to Berlin: AMPAS, Paramount Collection, *A Foreign Affair* production file 13.

271 Pommer at ICD: National Archives at College Park: Record Group 260: Records of United States Occupation Headquarters, World War II; OMGUS, Records of the Information Control Division, Motion Picture Branch, Records Re: Motion Picture Production and Distribution, 1945–1949; stack area 390; row 42; Record Group 260, Box 280: "Foreign Affairs" file and Box 278: "Location work Bad Nauheim" file.

271 Raw film stock: National Archives at College Park: Record Group 260, Box 278, "Location work Bad Nauheim" file.

271 Location shooting details: National Archives at College Park: Record Group 260: Records of United States Occupation Headquarters, World War II; OMGUS, Records of the Information Control Division, Motion Picture Branch, Records Re: Motion Picture Production and Distribution, 1945–1949; stack area 390; row 42; Record Group 260, Box 280: "Foreign Affairs" file; AMPAS, Paramount Collection, *A Foreign Affair* production file 14; *Paramount News*, Sept. 1, 1947.

272 "After viewing aerial shots . . .": Woodcock, p. 15.

272 Dietrich details: Bach, p. 330; Dietrich, p. 226; Spoto, *Blue Angel*, pp. 212–13.

272 Dietrich's fee: AMPAS, Paramount Collection, legal briefs file on Marlene Dietrich.

272 Arthur details: Pierce, p. 71.

273 Arthur's fee: AMPAS, Paramount Collection, legal briefs file on Jean Arthur.

274 HUAC details and Wilder's remarks: Navasky, p. 79; Ceplair and Englund, pp. 275–76; Berg, pp. 434–35; Friedrich, p. 304; Goodman, p. 419.

275 Kohner and the Mays: Sammlung Paul Kohner, Stiftung Deutsche Kinemathek, h. ss-88/ 1h-6, file 1.

276 Death of Lubitsch: Friedrich, p. 417; Eyman, pp. 357–60.

276 *Robe* rumor: *Los Angeles Examiner*, Dec. 1, 1947; *Hollywood Reporter*, Oct. 26, 1953.

276 Goldwyn story: Berg, p. 426.

276 Censorship problems with *Foreign Affair*: AMPAS, Paramount Collection, *A Foreign Affair* MPAA file.

277 Dietrich vs. Arthur: Bach, p. 335.

277 "Absolutely frenzied . . .": "Dialogue on Film," p. 37.

277 "What a picture . . .": Bach, p. 335.

277 *Foreign Affair* wraps: AMPAS, Paramount Collection, *A Foreign Affair* production files 13 and 14.

278 Denunciation in Congress: Heilbut, p. 244.

278 "Berlin's trials and tribulations . . .": Bach, p. 334, quoting Stuart Schulberg, who vetted American films for German consumption in the postwar era; Schulberg, p. 435.

278 Critics on *Emperor Waltz*: *Hollywood Reporter*, May 3, 1948; *Variety*, May 3, 1948; *Motion Picture Daily*, May 3, 1948.

279 Palestine project: *Los Angeles Examiner*, May 13, 1948.

279 Wilder on marrying Dowling: Karasek, p. 325.

279 Wilder's affair with Lamarr: *Los Angeles Examiner*, April 17, 1949.

279 Wilder meets Eames: John Neuhart interview with the author, Dec. 4, 1997.

279 "We asked them one day . . .": Billy Wilder to Donald Albrecht, May 20, 1994.

279 "The morning we were leaving . . .": "Billy Wilder: The Human Comedy," *American Masters*, PBS, 1998.

279 Louella announces marriage: *Los Angeles Examiner*, July 1, 1949.

279 "She was the worst . . .": Karasek, p. 328.

280 Goldwyn and Griffith: Berg, p. 447.

280 European Relief Fund: "Paul Kohner: Hollywood's Gentleman Agent" (exhibition), Goethe-Institut, Los Angeles, April 10–May 31, 1997.

280–81 Art purchases: Deutsch, "Scenario," p. 84.

281 "Sitting in the living room . . .": Berg, p. 446.

281 Meeting with Garbo: Paris, pp. 419–20.

282 The Blue Danube: "Paul Kohner: Hollywood's Gentleman Agent" (exhibition), Goethe-Institut, Los Angeles, April 10–May 31, 1997; *Los Angeles Examiner*, April 6, 1949.

CHAPTER 17

284–85 Clift's fee: AMPAS, Paramount Collection, legal briefs file on Montgomery Clift.

285 Clift goes skiing: LaGuardia, pp. 78–79.

285 "You must remember . . .": *Playboy*, June 1963, p. 65.

285 Swanson details: *Saturday Evening Post*, July 22, 1950, pp. 31, 56.

286 "For a long time . . ." Linville, p. 55. Note: West would have been a reasonable option, since her last film, a flop, had been in 1943. Brando, however, is less likely to have been considered at the time. Unlike Clift, Brando hadn't yet made any movies at all.

286–87 Wilder and Cukor: Levy, p. 175.

287 "Joseph, you'd better get out here . . .": Koszarski, p. 220.

287 "There was something great . . .": Ciment, *Positif*, Oct. 1970, pp. 5–17.

287 "I don't have to tell you . . .": Erich von Stroheim to Paul Kohner, November 21, 1948, "Paul Kohner: Hollywood's Gentleman Agent" (exhibition), Goethe-Institut, Los Angeles, April 10–May 31, 1997.

288 Marshman hired: *Entertainment Today*, Oct. 10, 1975.

288 "Bullshit!" and "I like it, I'll do it . . .": Bob Thomas, pp. 59–60.

289 Holden's fee: AMPAS, Paramount Collection, *Sunset Boulevard* production file 2.

289 Note on Hispano-Suiza: The line is from Wilder's script for *Scampolo*.

289 "Suppose the old dame . . .": Friedrich, pp. 418–19.

289 "Billy once showed Axelrod . . .": Deutsch, pp. 155–56.

290 Brackett's and Wilder's earnings: AMPAS, Paramount Collection, *Sunset Boulevard* production file 2.

290 "It won't be Schwab's . . .": Sidney Skolsky, "Hollywood Is My Beat," *Hollywood Citizen-News*, Aug. 29, 1949.

291 "I thought Billy Wilder was a friend . . .": Paris, p. 431; AMPAS, Paramount Collection, *Sunset Boulevard* production file 13.

291 "I wanted two gossip columnists . . .": "A New Turn for *Sunset Boulevard*," *Los Angeles Times* (undated clipping in AMPAS, Paramount Collection, *Sunset Boulevard* production file 13).

291 Swanson's makeup: Bob Thomas, p. 61; *Sunset Boulevard* pressbook.

291 "Do you know Bill Holden . . .": Bob Thomas, p. 61.

291 Getty mansion: Alleman, p. 94; Friedrich, pp. 418–19.

292 Censors' response: AMPAS, Paramount Collection, *Sunset Boulevard* MPAA file.

292 Swanson's costuming: Head, p. 89.

293 Production schedule: AMPAS, Paramount Collection, *Sunset Boulevard* production file 3.

293 Instructions to Seitz: Goodman, p. 202; Lightman, p. 319.

295 Haines quotation: *New York Times*, June 5, 1949, Sec. II, p. 5.

295 Note on the waxworks: To be fair, all three former stars did play small roles in a number of other films of the 1940s and 1950s, though never, humiliatingly, as themselves.

295 Stroheim's suggestions: Freeman, p. 77; Koszarski, p. 289.

296 "He was shooting *Samson* . . .": Freeman, p. 77.

296 On DeMille's appearance: *Motion Picture Herald*, June 4, 1949; *Hollywood Citizen-News*, June 1, 1949; *New York Times*, May 29, 1949; *Sunset Boulevard* pressbook.

297 "The night shot where Holden . . .": Freeman, p. 77.

297 "Darling, it's late . . .": Karasek, p. 328.

297 Holden and Olson kissing: Bob Thomas, p. 62.

297 Weather problems: Ursini, p. 62.

298 The snoring corpse: *Paramount News*, Aug. 22, 1949.

298 Von Stroheim's driving: Swanson, p. 482; Freeman, p. 77.

298 Shooting Gillis in the pool: AMPAS, Paramount Collection, *Sunset Boulevard* production file 3; Meehan, pp. 6–8; Lightman, p. 318.

300 DeMille's retakes: Freeman, p. 77; AMPAS, Paramount Collection, Legal briefs file "DeMille Productions, Cecil B."

300 "Strauss for the rehearsal . . .": Freeman, p. 77.

300–1 Final shot of *Sunset*: AMPAS, Paramount Collection, *Sunset Boulevard* production file 12.

301 Budget of *Sunset*: AMPAS, Paramount Collection, *Sunset Boulevard* production file 7.

301 Gifts: *Playboy*, Dec. 1960, p. 147.

301 Wilder on the previews: Ciment, *Positif*, July–Aug., 1983, pp. 15–28. Note: I found no written record of when these previews occurred. Based on the reshooting schedule, they probably took place in late September or early October.

301 Balaban's response to morgue: Ursini, p. 61.

302 Waxman's career and style: Thomas, Tony, *Music for the Movies*, pp. 41, 78–79; Palmer, pp. 97, 104–5, 109–10.

302 *Sunset*'s ads: AMPAS, Paramount Collection, *Sunset Boulevard* production file 1; *Sunset Boulevard* pressbook.

303 *Sunset*'s industry screening: *Hollywood Reporter*, Aug. 3, 1950.

303 Stanwyck kneels: Wiley and Bona, p. 202.

303 "Fuck you": Zolotow, p. 168.

303 "Go shit in your hat": Freeman, p. 76.

303–4 "That this completely original work . . .": *Hollywood Reporter*, April 17, 1950.

304   Sarris remark: Sarris, "Romanticist," p. 8.
304   Oscar details: Wiley and Bona, p. 205.
304   Mankiewicz's remark: Geist, pp. 6–7.
304–05 Wilder and Holden's interchange: Bob Thomas, p. 65.
305   "Screwing you're getting . . .": Madsen, *Stanwyck*, p. 286.
305   The Wilders' house: Neuhart, Neuhart, and Eames, p. 137; Billy Wilder to Donald Albrecht, May 20, 1994.
305   Brackett and Wilder divorce: *Los Angeles Examiner*, Nov. 2, 1949.
306   "Billy had outgrown . . .": *Time*, June 27, 1960, p. 75.
306   "I never knew what happened . . .": Kanin, pp. 178–79.
306   "It's like a box of matches . . .": Linville, p. 58.
306   Billy says nothing: Zolotow, p. 171.

CHAPTER 18

309   "Paramount feels their combined salaries . . .": *Los Angeles Examiner*, Aug. 13, 1949.
309   Brackett's new deal: *Los Angeles Examiner* Oct. 30, 1950; *Los Angeles Examiner*, Nov. 7, 1950.
309   Note on Brackett: *The Mating Season* was Brackett's final Paramount film, *The Model and the Marriage Broker* his first film for Fox.
310   Carlson plagiarism suit: *Stephanie Joan Carlson v. Paramount Pictures et al.*, Superior Court file #C591411, Los Angeles County Hall of Records.
310   Note on Carlson suit: Court records terminate with a dismissal; whether or not the dismissal was accompanied by a settlement is unclear, and to my knowledge the principals have never discussed the details in public.
311   Buckler suit: *Variety*, July 20, 1954; *Hollywood Reporter*, Aug. 4, 1955.
311   Newman's recollections: Zolotow, p. 174.
311   Laughton idea: Zolotow, pp. 174–75.
312   Note on the title: An "ace in the hole" is an ace kept facedown during a game of stud poker.
313   "Sure, they called it cynical . . .": *Playboy*, Dec., 1960, p. 145.
313   "The dramatist who sets out . . .": *Los Angeles Daily News*, Sept. 1, 1950.
314   "Do not give out . . .": AMPAS, Paramount Collection, *Ace in the Hole* screenplay file.
315   Douglas's fee: AMPAS, Paramount Collection, legal briefs file on "Douglas, Kirk."
315   Jan Sterling's recollections: Interview with the author, Oct. 29, 1997.
316   Note on "and another thing . . .": By the time Wilder filmed this sequence he had deleted Lorraine's final remark about getting to like it.
316   Douglas's letter to Wilder: State Historical Society of Wisconsin, Kirk Douglas Collection, Box 1: Correspondence, May 2–Aug. 31, 1950.
316   "Give it both knees . . .": Douglas, p. 178.
316   Censors' response: AMPAS, Paramount Collection, *Ace in the Hole* MPAA file.
317   Note on Samuels's payment: Because these transactions appear to have been private contracts between Wilder and his writers, Paramount's budgets do not reveal what they each earned. AMPAS, Paramount Collection, *Ace in the Hole* production file 1.
317   Cave set details: *Ace in the Hole* pressbook.
318   Weather problems: AMPAS, Paramount Collection, *Ace in the Hole* production file 2.
318   Censors' response: AMPAS, Paramount Collection, *Ace in the Hole* MPAA file.
318   Medical advice: AMPAS, Paramount Collection, *Ace in the Hole* production file 3.
318   Douglas chokes Sterling: Douglas, p. 178.
322   "He didn't 'direct' . . .": Jan Sterling interview with the author, Oct. 29, 1997.
325   *Ace*'s score: Thomas, *Music for the Movies*, pp. 150–55; and Thomas, *Film Score*, pp. 213–14.
325   "Well, you had the circle of stars . . .": Newman, p. 39.
326   Note on Wilder's box office failures: *The Emperor Waltz* was a failure only by virtue of its exorbitant cost.
326   "Ruthless and cynical . . .": *Hollywood Reporter*, May 7, 1951.
326   Venice Award: *Paramount News*, Sept. 24, 1951.
326–27 "Fuck them all . . .": Zolotow, p. 176.

327 Desny plagiarism suit: *Victor Desny v. Billy Wilder et al.*, Superior Court file #C591207, Los Angeles County Hall of Records.

327 Tippy's lawsuit: *Quick*, Jan. 8, 1951.

327 Hernandez departs: Zolotow, p. 176.

328 Note on Desny suit: The *Ace in the Hole* settlement was not widely covered in the press and may only have come to light when a trade paper covered the settlement of another plagiarism suit launched by Desny. In the 1960s, Desny successfully sued Fox for plagiarizing the Shirley MacLaine film *What a Way to Go!* (1964). Desny was awarded $50,000 in that case. According to an unsourced, undated clipping on file at the Academy library, "Judgement marks second time the writer has gone to court over a disputed story. In 1957, he won a suit against Paramount on charge his idea for a film script was pirated in studio's 1951 feature, *The Big Carnival*. Suit was settled out of court for a reported $14,350." Zolotow mentions the suit but claims the settlement was for $25,000. AMPAS clippings file, "Desny, Victor"; Zolotow, p. 176.

CHAPTER 19

329 "Talk is that Billy Wilder . . .": *Los Angeles Examiner*, Nov. 2, 1950.

329 Note on the studio system: See Douglas Gomery's *The Hollywood Studio System* for an unusually lucid discussion of the studios and their collapse.

330 Wilders' trip to Europe: Sammlung Paul Kohner, Stiftung Deutsche Kinemathek, h. ss-88/1h-6, file 1.

331 New contract: *Paramount News*, Dec. 4, 1950.

331 *The Loved One* and *Dr. Knock*: *Los Angeles Examiner*, Dec. 21, 1950; AFI Oral History with John F. Seitz; Sammlung Paul Kohner, Stiftung Deutsche Kinemathek, h. ss-88/1h-6, file 1.

331 *A New Kind of Love*: Bret, p. 151; *Los Angeles Examiner*, March 11, 1951.

331 Mankiewicz and DeMille furor: Geist, pp. 185–86; *Billy Wilder (et al.) v. Screen Directors Guild of America*, case #578838, Los Angeles County Hall of Records. I also thank Kenneth Geist for making his audiotaped interview available to me: Geist interview with Billy Wilder, Oct. 11, 1972.

331 On Chevalier: Behr, p. 295.

331 Note on *A New Kind of Love*: Paramount did make a film with that title in 1962; it starred Paul Newman, Joanne Woodward, and Chevalier, who played himself. That film boasts a plot that would likely have appealed to Billy Wilder. Chevalier is the host of the Festival of St. Catherine, where women who want husbands parade to the saint's statue to pray for a man. Samantha (Woodward) is a frigid fashion buyer for a New York department store; she meets Greg (Newman), a sports writer, on a trip to Paris. Samantha goes to St. Catherine, gets glamorized, and turns herself into Mimi, a wild Parisian. Greg falls in love with Mimi. After many complications owing to her disguise, Greg figures out that Mimi is really Samantha, and they get together in the end. Freedland, p. 206; *Variety*, April 25, 1951; and various clippings in the AMPAS file on Maurice Chevalier.

333 On Rossen: Ceplair and Englund, p. 383; Sammlung Paul Kohner, Stiftung Deutsche Kinemathek, h. ss-88/1h-6, file 1.

333 Note on the Laurel and Hardy project: Unlike Jou-Jou in *Ein blonder Traum*, the woman who comes between Laurel and Hardy would be rich—a widow visiting her husband's grave. She falls in love with Ollie but hates Stan.

333 "They were sharp wisecracks . . ." Zolotow, pp. 177–78.

334 On *Camille*: Zolotow, pp. 177–78.

334 Blum's fee: AMPAS, Paramount Collection, legal briefs file on "Blum, Edwin."

334 "Along with *Sunset Boulevard* . . .": Andres, pp. 1–2.

334 Paramount's financial expectations: Lemon, p. 36.

335 Parsons's announcement: *Los Angeles Examiner*, May 29, 1951.

335 Note on *Stalag 17*: Paramount's purchase of the rights was reported in *Variety* on Aug. 29, 1951. However, Wilder claims that he bought the rights himself for $50,000 and then took it to Paramount. Zolotow, p. 179.

335 Don Taylor recollections: Interview with the author, Aug. 14, 1995.

335 Cy Howard's casting: *Los Angeles Examiner*, Oct. 17, 1951.

336 Holden cast: Thomas, *Golden Boy*, p. 79.

336 Holden walks out: Douglas, p. 179; Thomas, *Golden Boy*, p. 79.

336 "If I were you . . .": Thomas, *Golden Boy*, p. 64.

336 "The kind of leading man . . .": Goodman, p. 255.

336 Location shooting: Andres, pp. 1–2.

337 Costs: A preliminary budget dated Feb. 4, 1952, sets the price tag at $1,315,000, of which $250,000 went to Wilder; the final cost was $1,661,530. AMPAS, Paramount Collection, *Stalag 17* production file 2.

337 Preminger's fee: AMPAS, Paramount Collection, *Stalag 17* production file 2.

337 Production meeting and shooting schedule: AMPAS, Paramount Collection, *Stalag 17* production files 3 and 4.

337 "He's making me anti-Semitic": Don Taylor interview with the author, Aug. 14, 1995.

338 "Goddamn it . . .": Thomas, *Golden Boy*, p. 80.

338 Escalating costs: AMPAS, Paramount Collection, *Stalag 17* production file 3.

339 Original ending: AMPAS, Paramount Collection, *Stalag 17* screenplay file.

340 Note on the Eisenhower era: True, the popular World War II general had not yet been elected when Wilder wrote the script for *Stalag 17*, but I think the 1950s can still be said to be the Eisenhower era.

341 "Little more than his butler . . .": Zolotow, pp. 180–81.

341 "Proving the essential rightness . . .": Denby, p. 52.

341 Note on Laszlo: He was a camera operator on *The Major and the Minor* and a competent if undistinguished cinematographer since 1944.

343 Box office returns: Thomas, *Golden Boy*, p. 82.

343 Cy Howard in the whorehouse: *New York Herald-Tribune*, May 4, 1951.

344 "Well, you know, Bill . . .": Thomas, *Golden Boy*, p. 82.

344 On *Catcher in the Rye*: Don Taylor interview with the author, Aug. 14, 1995. Note: of course the novel's reclusive author has steadfastly refused to sell the film rights.

344 Wilder's travel plans: *Los Angeles Examiner*, May 6, 1952.

344 Note on Epstein: He cowrote *Casablanca* with his brother Philip and Howard Koch.

345 Memo on *A New Kind of Love*: AMPAS, Paramount Collection, *A New Kind of Love* MPAA file.

345 "We find Audrey Hepburn . . .": Deutsch, p. 156.

CHAPTER 20

347 Parsons's announcement: *Los Angeles Examiner*, May 7, 1953.

347 "She looks as if she could spell . . .": Walker, p. 84.

348 "After so many drive-in . . .": Goodman, p. 271.

349 Actors' fees: AMPAS, Paramount Collection, legal briefs files on Humphrey Bogart, Audrey Hepburn, and William Holden; *Sabrina* production file 2.

349 Bogart's Warners contract, Committee for the First Amendment, and relationship with the Wilders: Hyams, pp. 125, 141, 163.

350 "Look, let's just shake hands . . .": Bogart, pp. 179–81.

350 "Audrey is a tall girl . . .": Goodman, p. 271.

350 Lehman's hiring: Walker, pp. 86–87.

350 Cast and crew in New York: AMPAS, Paramount Collection, *Sabrina* production files 3 and 4.

351 All-night writing sessions: Walker, pp. 86–87.

351 Hartman's nervousness: AMPAS, Paramount Collection, *Sabrina* production file 4.

351 "More likely . . .": Walker, p. 90.

351 Costuming details: Harris, p. 103; Collins, p. 282.; AMPAS, Paramount Collection, *Sabrina* production file 4.

351–52 Givenchy and Balenciaga story: Collins, p. 282.

352 Cost of cocktail dress: AMPAS, Paramount Collection, *Sabrina* production file 4.

353 Bogart's churlishness: Walker, pp. 86–88.

353 "Get them to do something . . .": Gehman, p. 90.

353 Drinks after work: Walker, p. 88.

353   "Bogart gave me . . .": Anon., *Playboy*, June 1963, p. 65.

353   Bogart walks out: Bogart, p. 179–81.

353   "Did *she* write this?": Thomas, *Golden Boy*, p. 85.

353   Holden and Hepburn in love and Clifton Webb remark: Maychick, pp. 98–100.

354   "Dumb prick": Woodward, p. 117.

354   "Kraut bastard Nazi son of a bitch": Bogart, pp. 179–81; Harris, p. 105.

354   "I examine your face . . .": Walker, p. 88; Zolotow, p. 253.

354   Holden written out: Walker, p. 88.

354   "Crock of shit": Collins, p. 287.

354   Lehman's doctor: Zolotow, pp. 183–84; Lally, pp. 234–35.

355   Cost of *Sabrina*: AMPAS, Paramount Collection, *Sabrina* production files 3 and 5.

355   "Fuck you": Zolotow, p. 187.

355   "Billy has to take over . . ." and "all kinds of names . . .": Zolotow, pp. 182–84.

355   Drastic retouching of Heburn's physique: *Sabrina* pressbook.

359   Retreat to Badgastein and Holden's painting: Thomas, *Golden Boy*, pp. 88–89, 95.

359   Wilder leaves Paramount: "Billy Wilder: The Human Comedy," *American Masters*, PBS, 1998.

360   Wilder signs with Allied Artists: *Los Angeles Examiner*, May 26, 1954.

CHAPTER 21

362   Censorship issues: AMPAS, MPAA file on *The Seven Year Itch*.

362   Censors report on *Itch*: *Hollywood Reporter*, Feb. 2, 1953; AFI, Charles K. Feldman Collection, folder 263.

362   French and Spanish versions of *Itch*: AFI, Charles K. Feldman Collection, folder 263.

362   Notes on negotiations: Wilder's share was 48.25 percent. By the way, Maurice Zolotow reports a very different transaction, the story of which Kevin Lally repeats practically verbatim. According to Zolotow, Wilder was a friend of superagent Swifty Lazar. At a party in Bel-Air, Lazar is said to have overheard an MGM executive telling someone that the studio was about to close a deal on *The Seven Year Itch*. The executive said that Axelrod wanted Wilder to direct the film adaptation. Lazar is then said to have called Billy and asked if he wanted to direct the movie, and, by the way, could he be Billy's agent on the deal? Billy said that he could. Lazar then went to New York and mentioned to Axelrod that he could get Billy Wilder to direct the film as long as he could represent Axelrod on the transaction. Thus Lazar is said to have gotten 10 percent from Billy's end and 10 percent from Axelrod's. Then Charles Feldman approached Swifty, saying that he wanted *The Seven Year Itch* for his client, Monroe. Swifty said that he could persuade Billy, "who had personally bought the play with his own money, for $255,000—to sell the property to Twentieth Century–Fox, Marilyn's studio." Thus Lazar got 10 percent of Feldman's deal, too, with Feldman reselling the film rights to Fox for $500,000. The name of Swifty Lazar does appear in a few of the many memos describing the deal on file at the American Film Institute and the UCLA Arts Library, but the story of his agenting for everyone seems entirely fictitious. Why would Charles Feldman, himself an agent, yield an agent's commission to Swifty Lazar? Why would MCA's Lew Wasserman do the same, as well as Axelrod's agent, Edward Colton? In any event, Wilder did not buy the film rights himself. The Feldman Group did. Zolotow, pp. 189–90; Lally, pp. 239–40; UCLA Arts Library, Special Collections, Twentieth Century–Fox legal files on *The Seven Year Itch*; AFI, Charles K. Feldman Collection.

362   Axelrod hired: *New York Herald-Tribune*, April 2, 1954.

363   "He sees the worst . . .": Anon., *Playboy*, June 1963.

363   "I thought we might use . . .": Gehman, p. 70.

363   "Bosoms a thing of the past": Head, p. 103.

363   Monroe's participation: UCLA Arts Library, Special Collections, Twentieth Century–Fox legal files on *The Seven Year Itch*.

363   Note on Wilder's deal: Later, Fox paid Wilder's share to him directly. UCLA Arts Library, Special Collections, Twentieth Century–Fox legal files on *The Seven Year Itch*.

364   Neckties: Zolotow, p. 190.

364 Lemmon in *Itch*: *Hollywood Reporter*, Aug. 3, 1954; AFI, Charles K. Feldman Collection, folder 272.

364 "He was so funny . . ." and "I was not powerful enough . . .": Kirkham, p. 20.

364 Casting decisions: AFI, Charles K. Feldman Collection, folder 263.

364 *Itch* finances: UCLA Arts Library, Special Collections, Twentieth Century–Fox legal files on *The Seven Year Itch*; AFI, Charles K. Feldman Collection, folder 274.

364 The title song lyrics: AMPAS, MPAA file on *The Seven Year Itch*.

365 *Ariane* and *Love* plans: Sammlung Paul Kohner, Stiftung Deutsche Kinemathek, h. ss-88/1h-6, file 1.

365 Yankee Stadium: AFI, Charles K. Feldman Collection, folder 272.

365 "Personally I prefer . . .": Ciment, *Positif*, July/Aug. 1983.

365 Note on George W. Davis: Davis shares screen credit with Lyle Wheeler on the production design of *The Seven Year Itch*, but that was simply studio politics; Wheeler was the head of Fox's design department but had nothing to do with this film's actual design.

365 Monroe details: Guiles, pp. 154–57.

366 "There were a good 5, people . . .": Ciment, *Positif*, July/Aug. 1983.

367 "I controlled nothing . . .": Ciment, *Positif*, July/Aug. 1983.

367 Feldman's advice: AFI, Charles K. Feldman Collection, folder 263.

367 "In medium shots he is very likable . . ." and Wilder's refusal to use second unit: AFI, Charles K. Feldman Collection, folder 270.

367 "I had no problems with Monroe . . .": Ciment, *Positif*, July/Aug. 1983.

368 "Didn't realize what a disorganized . . .": James Thomas, "Wilder's winning ways," *London Daily Express*, April 19, 1961.

368 Zanuck's remarks, Monroe's absence, the song, and the duet: AFI, Charles K. Feldman Collection, folders 263, 270, and 272.

369 "Billy's a wonderful director . . .": Zolotow, p. 256.

369 "Apparently I wasted . . .": AFI, Charles K. Feldman Collection, folder 270.

369 Cuts for Code approval: AMPAS, MPAA file on *The Seven Year Itch*.

369 Wilder and Bass: Kirkham, p. 20.

369 Axelrod's bonus: UCLA Arts Library, Special Collections, Twentieth Century–Fox legal files on *The Seven Year Itch*.

369 *Itch* premiere: AFI, Charles K. Feldman Collection, folder 266.

369 "I do not have the reputation . . .": AFI, Charles K. Feldman Collection, folder 269.

370 "I could have done it . . .": Richard Brown interview with Billy Wilder, aired on American Movie Classics, 1993.

370 Gross of *Itch*: UCLA Arts Library, Special Collections, Twentieth Century–Fox legal files on *The Seven Year Itch*.

370 Truffaut on *Itch*: Truffaut, p. 159.

370 "My theory about collaborators . . .": McDonald, p. xiii (from the foreword by Billy Wilder).

370 *A New Kind of Love* announcement: *New York Times*, June 19, 1955.

371 Preparing *Ariane*: Sammlung Paul Kohner, Stiftung Deutsche Kinemathek, h. ss-88/1h-6, file 1.

371 Plans for *The Bad Seed*: AMPAS, MPAA file on *The Bad Seed*.

372 Meeting with Cohn: Zolotow, pp. 196–97.

372 Wilder's first day at Warners: *Hollywood Reporter*, Dec. 20, 1954.

372 Lederer's fee: USC, Jack L. Warner Collection, *Spirit of St. Louis* file 2.

372 "For surgery . . .": Lemon, p. 37.

373 Kerr's refusal: Zolotow, pp. 314–15.

373 "I always regarded the fuss . . .": Mosley, pp. 218–35.

374 "I need a star . . .": Pickard, pp. 129–30.

374 Dinner with the Stewarts: Lally, p. 249.

374 Sharing *Spirit* profits: *Variety*, March 23, 1955.

374 Meeting with Lindbergh: *Beverly Hills Citizen*, Feb. 26, 1957; Lally, p. 248.

374 "I couldn't get into his private life . . .": Zolotow, p. 194.

375 Research questions: USC, Warner Bros. Archives, *Spirit of St. Louis* file 1.

375 Travel to Paris and lone gendarme scene: USC, Warner Bros. Archives, *Spirit of St. Louis* unnumbered research file.

376 "There were three thousand extras . . .": Trauner, p. 4 (from the introduction by Billy Wilder).

376 "No children": USC, Warner Bros. Archives, *Spirit of St. Louis* Special Material file and unnumbered research file.

376 Eames and second unit filming: USC, Warner Bros. Archives, *Spirit of St. Louis* unnumbered research file; Billy Wilder to Donald Albrecht, May 20, 1994.

377 Stewart's difficult behavior: USC, Jack L. Warner Collection, *Spirit of St. Louis* file 2.

378 Skyrocketing costs: USC, Warner Bros. Archives, *Spirit of St. Louis* unnumbered research file.

378 Script not yet completed: USC, Warner Bros. Archives, *Spirit of St. Louis* unnumbered research file.

378 Note on locations: there was also a Santa Ana location used for some *Spirit* in-flight sequences.

378 Difficulties with planes: USC, Warner Bros. Archives, *Spirit of St. Louis* file 393.

378 Script still incomplete: USC, Warner Bros. Archives, *Spirit of St. Louis* file 393.

378 "God, it was horrendous . . .": Zolotow, p. 275.

379 Shooting on *Spirit*, abandonment of *Love*: USC, Warner Bros. Archives, *Spirit of St. Louis* file 393; Sammlung Paul Kohner, Stiftung Deutsche Kinemathek, h. ss-88/1h-6, file 2.

379 Production log, process shots, accident, and circus rehearsals: USC, Warner Bros. Archives, *Spirit of St. Louis* file 393, Special Material file, unnumbered research file.

379 "I never got tired . . .": AMPAS, *Spirit of St. Louis* clippings file. Note: Lindy was being disingenuous; his book describes his exhaustion in some detail, though not as extensively as Stewart portrays it.

379 "Mr. Stewart did not object . . .": Zolotow, p. 195.

379 On the fly: Wilder to Donald Albrecht, May 20, 1994; *Los Angeles Mirror-News*, April 11, 1957; *Variety*, March 23, 1955.

379 Production log: USC, Warner Bros. Archives, *Spirit of St. Louis* file 393.

379–80 Sullivan show and aftermath: USC, Warner Bros. Archives, *Spirit of St. Louis* unnumbered research file.

380 Cutting of scenes from *Spirit* and new footage shot: USC, Jack L. Warner Collection, *Spirit of St. Louis* file 1; USC, Warner Bros. Archives, *Spirit of St. Louis* file 393.

380 *One, Two, Three*; *Ariane*; *Spionage*; and the Wilders' voyage: Sammlung Paul Kohner, Stiftung Deutsche Kinemathek, h. ss-88/1h-6, files 1 and 2.

380 Sturges takes over: USC, Warner Bros. Archives, *Spirit of St. Louis* file 393.

381 "Warner would have given everything . . .": Thomas, Bob, *Warner*, p. 5.

381 Note on Wilder's sense of religion: In the final moments of his descent into Le Bourget, Lindbergh, fearing a crash, exclaims "Oh God help me!" There's a cut to a St. Christopher medal. Though I could not verify it, my guess is that these shots were among the ones filmed by John Sturges. Whoever shot them, they defy the spirit of everything that comes before them. If Wilder did write and shoot them, they would mark the only moment of religious conversion in his career.

381 "Cum Dio": Columbus, p. 24.

381 Hunter's tour: *Variety*, March 23, 1955; *Motion Picture Herald*, March 23, 1957.

381 Stewart's departure: USC, Warner Bros. Archives, *Spirit of St. Louis* Special Material file.

382 Premiere and promotion: AMPAS, *Spirit of St. Louis* clippings file; USC, Warner Bros. Archives, *Spirit of St. Louis* unnumbered research file and Special Material file.

382 "I asked Billy Wilder . . .": An unsourced clipping on file at AMPAS claims that Wilder did appear at the premiere, but this item may have been planted by Warner Bros. to save embarrassment. USC, Warner Bros. Archives, *Spirit of St. Louis* unnumbered research file; AMPAS, *Spirit of St. Louis* clippings file.

382 *New Yorker* cartoon: Mosley, p. 351.

382 Gross of *Spirit*: USC, Warner Bros. Archives, *Spirit of St. Louis* Special Material file; Pickard, p. 135.

382 Note on *The Bad Seed*: That film was released in 1956 but continued to make money well into 1957.

382 "I felt sorry . . .": Pickard, p. 136.

382 "The picture should have . . .": Pickard, p. 127.

382 "I succeeded with some good moments . . .": Domarchi and Douchet, p. 7.

383 "I should confine . . .": Pickard, p. 133.

383 Awards for *Spirit*: USC, Warner Bros. Archives, *Spirit of St. Louis* unnumbered research file.

CHAPTER 22

387 Note on I. A. L.: This is the more colorful explanation of Diamond's initials. A somewhat more pedestrian explanation appeared in 1960, when the *Los Angeles Examiner* reported that the initials first appeared when Diamond was writing for the *Jester*, a humor magazine. The *Jester*'s editor gave him a made-up first name—"Ian." Diamond hated it, complained, and was told to make up some initials. He picked I. A. L. *Los Angeles Examiner*, June 19, 1960.

387 Diamond's biography: McCarthy, *Variety*, April 27, 1988; Rodman, pp. 71, 78.

387 "I wanted a *goyische* . . .": Rodman, pp. 71, 78.

388 Diamond and *Monkey Business*: McCarthy, *Hawks*, p. 495.

388 Guild skits: Rodman, pp. 71, 78.

389 "I was married to him . . .": Schumach, "Diamond," p. 80.

389 "The highest compliment . . .": Freeman, p. 78.

389 "In the top 10 percent . . .": *Los Angeles Examiner*, June 19, 1960.

389 Final polish on *The Apartment*: Rodman, pp. 71, 78.

389 "The two men complement . . .": Morris, p. 34.

390 Note on the *Omaha* story: Maurice Zolotow tells the same story, though not as well as the friend of Billy's who told it to me. In Zolotow's version, Broidy suggests "Meanwhile, Back at the Ritz"—admittedly a more likely recommendation, given the subject of *Love in the Afternoon*, but far less successful as a punchline. Zolotow, p. 199.

390 "I bought a painting . . .": Reed and Bacon, p. 157.

390 Note on *Ariane*: Mayer's *Ariane* was itself a remake of a silent 1926 film; both were adaptations of Claude Anet's novel. Kracauer, p. 255; Behr, p. 301.

390 The train sequence: Zolotow, p. 197.

390 "*Ariane* without you . . .": Sammlung Paul Kohner, Stiftung Deutsche Kinemathek, h. ss-88/1h-6, file 1.

391 Note on Hepburn's roles for Wilder: Thanks to Adam Orman for this observation.

391 *War and Peace*: Walker, p. 119.

391 Relationship with Frings: Walker, p. 140; Harris, p. 119.

391 Aly Khan story: Arce, p. 258; Zolotow, p. 198.

391 "Coopsy": Annie Tresgot interview with the author, Oct. 11, 1997.

391 "A little more French" and no singing: Behr, pp. 108, 301; Bret, p. 173.

392 Note on street rioting: Reportedly, the man died of his injuries, but this could not be confirmed. In fact, Annie Tresgot told me she remembered nothing of the sort occurring—no rioting, no injury, no death. Annie Tresgot interview with the author, Oct. 11, 1997.

392 Evacuation and "How proud I would be . . .": Walker, pp. 140–43.

393 Note on the parties: Annie Tresgot, on the other hand, makes the point that Chevalier left early because he lived outside of Paris and simply wanted to get home. Behr, p. 301; Freedland, p. 218.

393 On Henri Betti: Freedland, p. 218.

393 Retakes: Walker, p. 140.

394 "Somebody wake up Coop . . .": Anon., "Why Not Be in Paris?" *Newsweek*, Nov. 26, 1956, pp. 106–8.

394 On Trauner: Jerry Carlson interview with the author, May 29, 1996.

394 "It was exactly thirty . . .": Trauner and Berthomé, p. 4 (from the introduction by Billy Wilder). Note: according to Annie Tresgot, Lina Trauner was a basset hound, not a dachshund.

395 Chandelier story: Trauner and Berthomé, p. 4 (from the introduction by Billy Wilder).

395 *Love*'s release: Harris, p. 146.

395 Censorship problems: *Variety*, July 10, 1957.

395 "There isn't a sweatshirt . . .": Anon., "Why Not Be in Paris?" *Newsweek*, Nov. 26, 1956, pp. 106–8.

396 "Lecherous old chansonnier . . .": Eisenschitz, p. 106.

397 Foreign rights sale: Balio, p. 165.

397 "It was a flop . . .": Roderick Mann, "The Man Who Hated Marilyn Cools Down," *London Sunday Express*, July 31, 1960.

397 Hawks in Paris: McCarthy, *Hawks*, p. 545.

397 Sturges in Paris: Jacobs, p. 435.

397 Stroheim's headstone: Sammlung Paul Kohner, Stiftung Deutsche Kinemathek, h. ss-88/ 1h-6, file 1.

397 Apartment purchase: Schumach, p. 38.

397 Eames design: Anon., *Time*, Jan. 5, 1970.

398 Redl project: Sammlung Paul Kohner, Stiftung Deutsche Kinemathek, h. ss-88/1h-6, file 2.

398 Note on *Amok*: See Stephen Spender's essay on Zweig, "Guilty Pleasures," in *New York Review of Books*, March 18, 1982, pp. 7–8, 10.

398 Note on unproduced projects: This project was based on the play by Louis Verneuil. *The Catbird Seat* may have been Wilder's working title for the Colonel Redl story, or it may have been based on the short story of the same name by James Thurber, which served as the basis for the 1960 Peter Sellers comedy *The Battle of the Sexes*. State Historical Society of Wisconsin, Center for Film and Theatre Research, United Artists Collection, Box 5, folder 3.

398 "Wilder is planning to stage . . .": *Los Angeles Examiner*, July 16, 1957.

398 Deal on *Sherlock*: *Variety*, Aug. 18, 1957.

398 On the Mirisch brothers: State Historical Society of Wisconsin, Center for Film and Theatre Research, United Artists Collection, Box 5, folder 3.

399 *Fanfaren das Liebe*: State Historical Society of Wisconsin, Center for Film and Theatre Research, United Artists Collection, Box 5, folder 3.

399 "I wish I knew": *New York Times*, Dec. 8, 1957.

399 Christie's opinion: *Listener*, Dec. 19, 1974.

399 Sale of rights: *Hollywood Reporter*, June 23 and Aug. 17, 1955; *Variety*, January 30, 1956; USC, Jack L. Warner Collection, *Witness for the Prosecution* file 1.

399 Wilder's deal: USC, Jack L. Warner Collection, *Witness for the Prosecution* file 2.

400 Kirk Douglas idea: USC, Jack L. Warner Collection, *Witness for the Prosecution* file 2.

400 On Power: Guiles, *Power*, p. 281.

400 Channel hopping: USC, Jack L. Warner Collection, *Witness for the Prosecution*, misc. correspondence file.

400 Gardner, Lemmon, Kelly, and Moore: USC, Jack L. Warner Collection, *Witness for the Prosecution* file 2.

401 Power's salary: USC, Jack L. Warner Collection, *Witness for the Prosecution*. misc. correspondence file.

401 The monocle: Scheuer, "Outcome," July 14, 1957; Callow, p. 182.

401 Shooting begins: USC, Jack L. Warner Collection, *Witness for the Prosecution* file 1.

402 The Old Bailey set: *London Herald Express*, July 6, 1957; Pryor, "Hollywood Canvass," July 7, 1957.

403 "He took the dark load . . .": From an unpublished interview Joshua Harrison conducted with Billy Wilder for a documentary on Alexander Trauner.

403 Laughton as Cockney coach: Dietrich, p. 127.

403 "Not easy to teach Cockney . . .": Spoto, *Blue Angel*, p. 264.

403 Shooting ends: USC, Jack L. Warner Collection, *Witness for the Prosecution* file 1.

403 "As if she thought her career . . .": Spoto, *Blue Angel*, p. 263.

403 "You'll never win . . .": Dietrich, p. 127; Spoto, *Blue Angel*, p. 264.

404 "To give an Academy Award . . .": Wiley and Bona, p. 285.

404 Dietrich's lovers: Spoto, *Blue Angel*, pp. 264–65.

404 Dietrich's cooking: *Los Angeles Times*, Aug. 27, 1957.

404 Withholding the ending: *London Herald Express*, July 6, 1957.

404 On the surprise ending: *Variety*, July 11, 1957. Note: Readers accustomed to the thundering avalanche of publicity that accompanies nearly every film released in the 1990s may wonder how a hit West End and Broadway play could keep its secret ending when adapted into a Hollywood movie. But the fact that many theatergoers in London and New York knew how *Witness for the Prosecution* ended did not mean that the rest of the population did. Moreover, it appears that in those days entertainment reporters felt less of a need to give away the plot.

404 Royal family's pledge: Wiley and Bona, p. 281.

405 "Everybody had a crush . . .": Arce, *Power*, p. 270.

405 "For health reasons": *Variety*, July 11, 1957.

405 "I'm fully aware . . .": Arce, *Power*, p. 270.

405 Travel itinerary: Hutter and Kamolz, *Profil*, May 9, 1994, pp. 90–94.

405 On Badgastein: Wechsberg, pp. 116–29.

405 Wilder in Vienna: "Filmregie. So gut, wie das Publikum will," *Die Wochen-Presse* 12, no. 47 (Nov. 23, 1957), pp. 1–2; Hutter and Kamolz, *Profil*, May 9, 1994, pp. 90–94.

CHAPTER 23

408 "In jazz, we must distinguish . . .": Panassié, pp. 22–23.

408 "I have an idea . . .": Gehman, p. 69.

409 "Heavy-handed and Germanic . . ." and "The next morning . . ." Diamond, p. 132. Note: As Lotte Eisner puts it, *Mädchen in Uniform* (1931) "is the last word on the slavery and starvation to which the aristocracy subjected its daughters." Eisner, p. 325.

409 Casting options: Curtis and Paris, pp. 154, 158; Diamond, p. 132.

410 Sinatra budget and Wilder's deal: UA box 5, folder 4; Balio, pp. 168–70.

410 "Billy Wilder stopped by . . .": Winecoff, p. 163.

410 "It's you, Marilyn, Sinatra . . .": Curtis and Paris, p. 169.

410 "He was quite vehement . . ." and "I think this . . .": Kelley, pp. 252, 347.

411 Note on casting: Curtis's own account contains a contradiction: According to Curtis, Wilder saw Jack Lemmon in *Operation Mad Ball* and realized he could pair him with Curtis, but *Operation Mad Ball* was released before Billy started writing *Some Like It Hot*. Curtis and Paris, p. 158.

411 "The weakest part . . .": Anon., "In the Picture," p. 134.

411 Curtis and Monroe: Curtis and Paris, p. 166.

411 Mirisch party: Diamond, p. 135; Curtis and Paris, p. 157.

411 "Within three to four weeks . . .": Holtzman, p. 73.

411 "Kept asking me . . .": Widener, p. 167

411 "Lemmon had to be an actor . . .": Holtzman, p. 15

412 "Tony's pants . . ." and "The trouble with you . . .": Gehman, p. 70.

412 "Hi, I'm Daphne!": Diamond, p. 135.

412 "You create a shell . . .": New York Center for Visual History interview with Jack Lemmon circa 1993, unpublished transcript.

412 On Barbette: Steegmuller, pp. 130–31.

412 Barbette's instructions: Curtis and Paris, p. 154.

413 Barbette walks out: Curtis and Paris, p. 162–63; Widener, p. 169.

413 Curtis's resemblances: *Los Angeles Mirror-News*, Sept. 18, 1958; Curtis and Paris, p. 154.

413 Lemmon's resemblances: New York Center for Visual History, interview with Jack Lemmon circa 1993, unpublished transcript.

413 Jazz band names: Dan Morgenstern, "Hot Jazz on Blue Note," liner notes to the CD set of the same name. Washington: Smithsonian Institution Press, 1996.

414 Urine contraption: Curtis and Paris, p. 168.

415 "We had our dresses on . . .": New York Center for Visual History interview with Jack Lemmon circa 1993, unpublished transcript.

415 "Audiences will be laughing . . .": *Los Angeles Mirror-News*, Sept. 18, 1958.

415 Writing schedule: *New York Times*, Nov. 2, 1958.

415 "You want machine guns . . .": Curtis and Paris, p. 170.

416 Preliminary budget, Krim's concerns, and the title: State Historical Society of Wisconsin, Center for Film and Theatre Research, United Artists Collection, box 5 folders 3 and 14.

416 "Miss Wiggle Hips . . .": *Los Angeles Mirror-News*, Sept. 18, 1958.

416 Wilder kicks Charlie: Yablonsky, p. 218.

417 "I want the world . . .": *New York Post*, Aug. 15, 1958.

417 "Don't you want your audience . . .": *New York Post*, Sept. 10, 1958.

417 "There are very few . . .": *This Week*, Oct. 5, 1958.

417 "One morning . . .": Diamond, p. 135.

417 "The whole idea . . .": *New York Journal American*, Oct. 24, 1958.

417 "After each scene . . .": Diamond, p. 135.

418 "One day she walked . . .": Wilmington, p. 12.

418 "I knew we were in mid-flight . . .": Curtis and Paris, p. 162.

418 "Relax . . .": Curtis and Paris, p. 167.

418 "Naive purity": *Los Angeles Mirror-News*, Sept. 18, 1958.

418 "How was that . . .": Curtis and Paris, p. 168.

418 "We were filming the scene . . .": "Marilyn Monroe: 30 Jahre nach ihrem Tod—die letzten Bilder eines Idols," *Stern*, Aug. 1992, p. 34.

418 "He doesn't have tits . . .": Curtis and Paris, p. 167.

419 "Marilyn, possibly . . .": Curtis and Paris, pp. 162–63.

419 Forty-seven takes: Diamond, p. 135.

419 Negative cost: State Historical Society of Wisconsin, Center for Film and Theatre Research, United Artists Collection, box 5 folder 14.

419 "I never felt . . .": Curtis and Paris, p. 168.

419 "I walked in all excited . . .": New York Center for Visual History interview with Jack Lemmon circa 1993, unpublished transcript.

419 "It was twenty minutes . . .": Wilmington, p. 16; Lemon, p. 38.

420 Cary Grant's response: Curtis and Paris, p. 160.

420 On Grant's masculinity: See Steven Cohan's analysis in *Screen*.

420 "May well be the best scene . . .": Widener, p. 174.

421 "Billy handed me a set . . .": Widener, p. 174.

421 Tinkering with maracas scene: Curtis and Paris, pp. 160–61.

421 "Movies should be like amusement parks . . .": *Los Angeles Mirror-News*, Sept. 18, 1958.

421 "Flaming faggot": Zolotow, p. 201.

421 "The whole trick . . ." and "But when he forgot . . .": "Dialogue on Film," p. 43.

421 Those thin-magazine people . . .": Anon., *Playboy*, June 1963, p. 62.

421 Note on why drag comedy can be funny: This is largely the subject of the *Some Like It Hot* chapter and other sections of my book *Laughing Hysterically: American Screen Comedies of the 1950s*.

421 "One can hardly play . . .": Panassié, pp. 22–23.

422 Wilder and his radio: Deutsch, p. 160.

422 "It's a habit of his . . .": Ciment, *Positif*, Jan. 1974, p. 8.

422 Curtis's response to "magic time": Curtis and Paris, p. 167.

423 Writing Sugar out of the ending: Turner, p. 18.

423 Wilder and the stripper: Curtis and Paris, p. 170; Wood, p. 7.

423 Raft's story: Yablonsky, p. 217.

423 "Diamond and I were in our room . . .": Linville, pp. 59–60.

423 Diamond's idea for "nobody's perfect" and Wilder's nervousness: Freeman, p. 78.

424 Purple Heart: *New York Herald Tribune*, Feb. 10, 1959.

424 "In the United States . . .": Gehman, p. 70.

424 Note on "Stairway to the Stars": The song was cowritten by Malneck, Mitchell Parish, and Frank Signorelli.

425 Monroe on the telephone: Diamond, p. 136.

425 "She had to run upstairs . . .": *Newark Evening News*, Dec. 18, 1958.

425 Wilder's telegram: Curtis and Paris, p. 162.
425 "I am able for the first time . . .": *New York Herald Tribune*, Feb. 10, 1959.
425 "Who says stars . . .": *New York Post*, Feb. 12, 1959.
425 "I would make a picture . . ." *Pictorial Review*, March 8, 1959.
425 "Better Marilyn late . . .": Gehman, p. 70.
425 "Breasts like granite . . .": Goodman, p. 231.
426 Preview story: Curtis and Paris, p. 170.
426 New York sneak: Curtis and Paris, p. 170.
426 Train sequence claim: Curtis and Paris, pp. 160–61.
426 "I have no prejudice . . ." etc.: *Life*, April 20, 1959, p. 104.
426 "I suppose Billy Wilder . . .": Ellen Patrick, *Films in Review*, quoted in Baltake, p. 100.
427 Grosses and Wilder's share: *Variety*, Jan. 6, 1960; State Historical Society of Wisconsin, Center for Film and Theatre Research, United Artists Collection, Box 5, folder 3; Balio, p. 170.
427 Note on art purchases: Specifically: Klee's *Felsenkamer*, a watercolor over pencil on paper laid down by the artist on board in 1929; Nicholson's *Two Forms,* a gouache on board painted in 1940; Matisse's *Femme aux bras croisés*, a 1935 pencil on paper; Schwitters's *Apollo im Februar,* a collage on board made in 1945; and de Stael's *Footballeurs,* an oil on board painted in 1952.
427 "We should all thank God for TV . . .": *Hollywood Close-Up*, March 26, 1959.
427 Television series idea: State Historical Society of Wisconsin, Center for Film and Theatre Research, United Artists Collection, box 5 folder 14.
427 On the *United States*: Diamond, p. 136.

CHAPTER 24

428 Cigarettes: Gehman, p. 147.
429 Proposed titles: J.R., p. 3.
429 Unproduced film ideas. Sammlung Paul Kohner, Stiftung Deutsche Kinemathek, h. ss-88/1h-6, files 1, 2, and 3.
429 *Nijinksy Story*: *Los Angeles Examiner*, Sept. 10, 1959.
429 *Imitation of Life* bet: Sammlung Paul Kohner, Stiftung Deutsche Kinemathek, h. ss-88/1h-6, file 3. Note: By the first week of 1960, *Imitation of Life* had pulled in $6.2 million.
429 "You won a prize . . .": Robinson, p. 105.
430 Paley screening: Lally, p. 296.
430 "What I had written was . . .": Linville, p. 55.
430 Note on Wilder's losers: Richard Sherman in *The Seven Year Itch* is the antecedent.
430 "I started with this character . . .": Ciment, *Positif*, July/Aug. 1983.
430 "This is about a young fellow . . .": Gehman, p. 69.
430 "I would have done it in 1948 . . .": Ciment, *Positif*, Oct. 1970.
431 Skolsky's story: Curtis, p. 179.
431 Wanger's walk: Bernstein, pp. 274–75.
431 "Originally Billy wanted . . .": *Los Angeles Examiner*, June 19, 1960.
431 Stars' fees: State Historical Society of Wisconsin, Wisconsin Center for Film and Theatre Research, United Artists Collection, Box 5, folder 14.
432 "Take Shirley MacLaine . . .": Anon., *Playboy*, June 1963.
432 "I am listed as a coproducer . . .": *Los Angeles Examiner*, June 19, 1960.
432 "The only one willing . . .": Todd McCarthy, "I.A.L. Diamond" (obituary), *Variety*, April 27, 88, pp. 6, 23.
432 MacLaine's research and wardrobe: *Los Angeles Times*, Sept. 10, 1993; AMPAS, General Collection, *The Apartment* clippings file—microfiche, from the United Artists press kit for *The Apartment*.
432 "There were only twenty-nine . . .": "Billy Wilder: The Human Comedy," *American Masters*, PBS, 1998.
432 "In the last four days . . .": Gehman, p. 90.
432 *The Apartment* occurred to me . . .": Lemon, p. 38.
432 Note on CinemaScope and Manhattan: Thanks to William Paul for this observation.

432 Note on terminology: Here and elsewhere I use "CinemaScope" to refer to any extra-widescreen process, including Panavision.

433 *The Sound of Music*: Lemon, p. 38.

433 "We weren't making progress . . .": Trauner and Berthomé, pp. 152–54.

433 "I met him at the Warwick . . .": Ray Waltson interview with the author, Oct. 27, 1997.

433 Shooting schedule: State Historical Society of Wisconsin, Wisconsin Center for Film and Theatre Research, United Artists Collection, Box 5, folder 14.

434 "Wilder copied the scene . . .": Dowd and Shepard, p. 245.

434 "Take the big office set . . .": Trauner and Berthomé, p. 5 (from the introduction by Billy Wilder).

435 Groucho: Lally, p. 304.

436 "He kind of peered at me . . .": Zolotow, pp. 278–79.

436 "She hated rehearsals . . .": *Variety*, Oct. 22, 1975.

437 "I wished Billy Wilder . . .": MacLaine, p. 258.

437 Pinball machine: State Historical Society of Wisconsin, Wisconsin Center for Film and Theatre Research, Walter Mirisch Collection, Box 17.

438 "We came out of a restaurant . . .": Jan Sterling interview with the author, Oct. 29, 1997.

438 MacMurray at Disney's Magic Kingdom: *People*, Nov. 7, 1988.

439 "Baxter is a study . . .": Denby, p. 52.

439 "I read Axel Madsen's book . . .": Ciment, *Positif*, Oct. 1970, pp. 5–17.

440 "In my opinion it is a highly moral . . .": Gehman, p. 147.

440 "For me, there is nothing . . .": Schlöndorff, *Premiere*, p. 127.

440 Note on *Manhattan*: Woody is racing to see Mariel Hemingway.

442 "You don't usually do that . . .": Lally, p. 305.

442 Advertising line: Wiley and Bona, p. 316.

442 Personal appearance tour: State Historical Society of Wisconsin, Wisconsin Center for Film and Theatre Research, United Artists Collection, Box 5, folder 14.

442 Note on Albert Zugsmith: He was known for producing such exploitation films as *Sex Kittens Go to College* (1960), though he also produced more respectable films such as *Touch of Evil* (1958).

442 Grosses: State Historical Society of Wisconsin, Wisconsin Center for Film and Theatre Research, United Artists Collection, Box 5, folder 3.

442 Critics' comments: Balio, p. 170; Kauffmann, p. 149 (originally published in the *New Republic*, June 27, 1960); Macdonald, pp. 280–283.

443 "Editorial cooperation": State Historical Society of Wisconsin, Wisconsin Center for Film and Theatre Research, United Artists Collection, Box 5, folder 14.

444 Script ideas: *Time*, June 27, 1960, p. 75.

445 Price of *Irma*: AMPAS, General Collection, *Irma la Douce* clippings file.

446 "I'm possibly mad . . .": *Sunday Express* (London), July 31, 1960.

447 "You know how it is . . .": *London Daily Mail*, June 27, 1961.

447 Bardot and MacLaine: *New York Herald-Tribune*, Aug. 7, 1960.

447 Diamond's deal and first production schedule: State Historical Society of Wisconsin, Wisconsin Center for Film and Theatre Research, United Artists Collection, Box 5, folders 5 and 14.

447 Taylor controversy: *Variety*, Nov. 7, 1961.

447 MacLaine's deal: State Historical Society of Wisconsin, Wisconsin Center for Film and Theatre Research, United Artists Collection, Box 5, folder 5.

CHAPTER 25

453 "Burnt pneumatic tires . . .": Wilder, *Der Prinz von Wales geht auf Urlaub*, p. 117, published originally as "Hallo, Herr Menjou?" ("Hello, Mr. Menjou?"), *Tempo*, Aug. 5, 1929.

454 "Pamela, dear . . .": *Los Angeles Mirror*, Sept. 2, 1961. Note: The line does appear more or less intact in Molnár's play; precious few others remain unchanged.

454 "I'm tired of clichéd typecasting . . .": Francis, p. 169.

455 Edith Mayer Goetz story: Linville, p. 67.

455 Production team: *Los Angeles Times*, July 14, 1961; Sammlung Paul Kohner, Stiftung Deutsche Kinemathek, h. ss-88/1h-6, file 3.

455 "THIS PIECE MUST BE . . .": State Historical Society of Wisconsin, Wisconsin Center for Film and Theatre Research, I. A. L. Diamond Collection, Box 7, folder 4.

456 On Cagney: Cagney, p. 155; Warren and Cagney, p. 120; *Los Angeles Mirror*, Aug. 17, 1961.

457 "Okay, get your steel helmets . . .": *New York Times*, July 16, 1961.

457 East German border police: *Los Angeles Mirror*, Aug. 17, 1961; Eichhof, Joachim, "Architekten betrügen das Auge," *Filmspiegel*, Oct. 6, 1961.

458 "It was like making a picture . . .": *Playboy*, June 1963, p. 62.

458 "We had to make continuous . . .": *Playboy*, June 1963, p. 62.

459 Buchholz's accident and rebuilding: AMPAS, *One, Two, Three* clippings file; *One, Two, Three* press book.

459 Cagney, Tiffin, and Buchholz: Francis, p. 172; Warren and Cagney, pp. 192–93; Cagney, p. 155.

459 "He was not happy . . .": White, Timothy, p. 24.

460 Cagney's decision to quit acting: McGilligan, *Cagney*, p. 244.

461 The *fohn*: *Los Angeles Mirror*, Aug. 18, 1961.

461 "Until these last few years . . ." and "Billy Wilder's words . . .": Domarchi and Douchet, pp. 1, 5.

462 "Something of an aggressive imp . . .": *New York Times*, July 16, 1961.

462 "This is Billy Wilder . . .": State Historical Society of Wisconsin, Wisconsin Center for Film and Theatre Research, Walter Mirisch Collection, Box 17; Pressbooks.

462 "He was a far cry . . .": Previn, p. 117.

463 Hidden Jews story: John Neuhart interview with the author, Dec. 4, 1997.

465 Grosses: State Historical Society of Wisconsin, Wisconsin Center for Film and Theatre Research, United Artists Collection, Box 5, folder 3.

465 "I happen to think . . .": Kanin, p. 185.

465 "If there's anything I dislike . . .": *London Times*, Feb. 8, 1962.

465 "Have the stamina . . .": *New York Times*, March 4, 1962, sec. 2 p. 7.

465 Critics' responses: *New Republic*, Dec. 11, 1961; *Theatre Arts*, July 1962; Kael, p. 150.

466 Churchill story: *Hollywood Reporter*, Oct. 27, 1961; *Los Angeles Examiner*, Oct. 19, 1961.

466 Mann story: Davidson, p. 188.

467 ". . . Abbey Rents": Lemon, p. 32.

467 *L'Ora della Fantasia* rights: Sammlung Paul Kohner, Stiftung Deutsche Kinemathek, h. ss-88/1h-6, files 1 and 2.

467 "Dear Darryl . . ." etc. American Film Institute, Charles K. Feldman Collection, folder 792; Gussow, p. 252; Geist, p. 331.

467 *Sunset Boulevard* musical: Stephen Sondheim, letter to the author, July 21, 1997. Note: As Sondheim acknowledges, these "may not be his exact words, but the phrase 'dethroned queen' is accurate and has remained in my mind to this day."

468 "Deals are so complicated . . .": *Variety*, June 8, 1960.

468 "Jack comes to a picture . . .": State Historical Society of Wisconsin, United Artists Collection, Box 5, folder, 3.

469 "I'm going to do *Irma* . . .": Domarchi and Douchet, p. 7.

469 Laughton's illness and death: Zolotow, p. 240; Bergan, p. 327.

469 Casting *Irma*: State Historical Society of Wisconsin, Wisconsin Center for Film and Theatre Research, Walter Mirisch Collection, Box 17.

469 Note on Howard McNear: To be fair, McNear was a well-known character actor in films for many years before *The Andy Griffith Show*.

470 Note on Suzette Wong: In other words, *The World of Suzie Wong* (1960).

470 "I always do this . . .": *Evening Standard* (London), Dec. 7, 1962.

470 "He has the greatest rapport . . .": *Sunday Express* (London), Jan. 6, 1963.

470 "He was like my Aunt Bertie . . .": *Variety*, March 16, 1988.

470 "We are doing it with taste . . .": Wood, p. 196.

470 "I have nothing against music . . .": Kanin, pp. 185–86.

470 Note on the lack of music: Wilder followed the lead of his friend Joshua Logan, who deleted all the songs from his own stage musical *Fanny* (with a score by Harold Rome) when adapting the show for the screen in 1961. Logan, too, uses orchestral themes drawn from the score as background music for the film.

471 "I feel more secure . . .": *London Times*, Sept. 25, 1970.

471 "To a visitor . . .": Trauner and Berthomé, p. 5 (from the introduction by Billy Wilder).

471 "I always ask directors . . .", "Our big problem . . .", and "It was a rather . . .": Trauner and Berthomé, pp. 160–65.

473 Note on Nestor: As a policeman, the moralistic Nestor makes such a mess of his job that he is fired. He turns to Irma out of desperation; she's his only friend. Nestor takes over the role of Irma's *mec* after knocking Hippolyte out more or less by accident. To keep Irma happy, however, he decides to masquerade as Lord X and become her regular client; thus she may continue to earn her own living.

475 "Of course he was right . . .": Previn, p. 118.

476 Censorship cuts: State Historical Society of Wisconsin, Wisconsin Center for Film and Theatre Research, United Artists Collection, Box 5, folder 14.

476 Wallis letter and response: AMPAS, *Irma la Douce* MPAA file.

477 "This was accomplished . . .": *Variety*, Jan. 8, 1964.

477 "The truth is . . .": Kanin, pp. 185–86.

477 "If I had my way . . .": Lemon, p. 37.

477 Financial returns on *Irma*: State Historical Society of Wisconsin, Wisconsin Center for Film and Theatre Research, United Artists Collection, Box 5, folder 14; Balio, p. 171; *Hollywood Reporter*, April 13, 1966.

CHAPTER 26

478 "Nice little pictures . . .": Kurnitz, p. 94.

478 Wilder's new deal: Balio, p. 182.

478 "Unlike David Lean . . .": *Daily Mail* (London), July 31, 1964.

479 Review of *The Dazzling Hour*: *Variety*, Aug. 5, 1953, p. 58.

480 "I admire elegant . . .": Lemon, p. 38.

480 Trauner's sets: Trauner and Berthomé, p. 166.

483 "Stars don't mean a thing . . .": *Film Daily*, Jan. 19, 1962; Tosches, p. 361.

483 "He's a delicious and adorable . . .": Ciment, *Positif*, Oct. 1970, pp. 5–17.

484 "There was a mute honesty . . .": Thomson, pp. 412–13.

484 "They said she was difficult . . .": *Daily Mail* (London), July 31, 1964.

485 "He is the only man in pictures . . .": *Kiss Me, Stupid* pressbook, on file at the British Film Institute.

485 On Sellers: Simon, p. 183.

485 "The two directors I've always . . .": Lewis, pp. 672–74.

486 "When you leave . . .": Schumach, "The Wilder—and Funnier—Touch," p. 30.

486 Sellers's heart attack: *Sun Telegraph* (London), April 12, 1964.

487 "Well for Chrissake Jesus Christ . . .": Tosches, p. 362.

487 "He was running . . .": Wiley and Bona, p. 368.

488 "You have to have a heart . . .": Simon, p. 183.

488 Ray Walston interview with the author, Oct. 27, 1997.

488 "Your contribution . . .": Kleno, p. 209.

488 "Wanted it done with a slight look . . .": Tosches, p. 363.

489 "Felicia Farr was really quite wonderful . . .": Ray Walston interview with the author, Oct. 27, 1997.

491 Ad campaign: *Kiss Me, Stupid* pressbook, on file at the British Film Institute.

492 Meeting with Little, etc.: State Historical Society of Wisconsin, Wisconsin Center for Film and Theatre Research, United Artists Collection, Box 5, folder 14.

492 "United Artists Reedits Wilder Pic . . .": *Variety*, Oct. 21, 1964.

492 Novak cannot return: *Variety*, Dec. 9, 1964.

493 Further cuts: *Variety*, Nov. 25, 1964.

493 "Although it has a Code seal . . .": *Variety*, Nov. 25, 1964.

493 On Lopert: Balio, p. 183.

493 Note on *Never on Sunday*: Although it was released in the States by Lopert/UA, *Never on Sunday* was still a Greek film, not a Hollywood film.

493 The Legion's commentary and *Variety* coverage: Balio, p. 182; *Variety*, Dec. 9, 1964.

494 The press conference: *Hollywood Reporter*, Dec. 8, 1964.

494 "Dear Geoff" and response: AMPAS, MPAA Collection, *Kiss Me, Stupid* file.

495 Critics' responses: *Variety*, Dec. 16, 1964; *Time*, Jan. 1, 1965; *Christian Century*, Feb. 3, 1965; *New York Journal-American*, Dec. 23, 1964; *New York Herald Tribune*, Dec. 23, 1964; *New York Times*, Dec. 23, 1964; *New Yorker*, Dec. 26, 1964.

495 Cancellations and boycotts: *Exhibitor*, June 2, 1965.

495 "I don't know why the film shocked . . .": Ciment, *Positif*, Oct. 1970, pp. 5–17.

496 "British Critics Hail . . .": *Variety*, March 31, 1965.

496 "*Kiss Me, Stupid* shows Wilder . . .": Didion, p. 97.

496 Wilder's response to Didion: Lemon, p. 30.

496 "When I was lying in the gutter . . ." etc.: Lemon, pp. 30–32.

497 Wilder's contract extension: *Time*, Jan. 1, 1965.

CHAPTER 27

499 "Before a fight . . .": Lemon, pp. 38–39.

499 *Sherlock* reporting: *Variety*, May 19, 1965.

500 Wilder's televisions: Lemon, p. 33.

500 About greed, love, etc.: Holtzman, p. 108.

500 Budget information: State Historical Society of Wisconsin, Wisconsin Center for Film and Theatre Research, United Artists Collection, Box 5, folder 14.

500 "Why are you doing . . .": Todd McCarthy, "AFI Lauds Jack Lemmon," *Variety*, March 16, 1988, p. 6.

501 "Daughters of Israel Day Nursery . . .": Thomson, p. 369.

501 "Before we put a word on paper . . .": Turner, p, 20.

501 "He is a tall, loose-jointed man . . .": Lemon, p. 34.

501 The Browns' game: AMPAS, General Collection, *The Fortune Cookie* file, United Artists press kit.

501 "After my last picture . . .": Lemon, p. 38.

502 Lemmon in the wheelchair: AMPAS, General Collection, *The Fortune Cookie* file, United Artists press kit.

502 "I thought it was a bomb . . .": Lemon, pp. 38–39.

503 Cost and grosses: State Historical Society of Wisconsin, Wisconsin Center for Film and Theatre Research, United Artists Collection, Box 5, folder 3.

503 "I have been criticized . . .": Lemon, p. 38.

503 William Paul on image-making: In conversation with the author and in unpublished lecture notes from Paul's film classes at the University of Michigan.

507 "The virulent treatment . . .": Morris, p. 36.

508 "The existence of overt homosexuality . . .": Fiedler, p. 414–20.

508 Critics responses: *New York Times*, Oct. 20, 1966; *New Yorker*, Oct. 29, 1966; Kael, *5001 Nights*, p. 197.

509 "The film didn't impress the critics . . .": Ciment, *Positif*, Oct. 1970, pp. 5–17.

509 On the Bistro and Sheinwold: Lemon, pp. 32–33.

510 " 'Once we arrived . . .' ": Previn, pp. 118–19.

510 "Speed is absolutely . . .": Lemon, pp. 34–36.

510 Note on the new art: Specifically: Gustav Klimt's *Brustbild einer Dame im Profil nach links*; Pierre Roy's *Physique amusant* and *Les papillons No. 1 and No. 2*; Raoul Dufy's *Nature morte au poisson*; Joseph Cornell's "The Puzzle of the Reward #1"; Ben Nicholson's *Dec 61 (clay green)*; Larry Rivers's *Parts of the Body: Italian Vocabulary Lesson*; Henry Moore's *Maquette for Head and Hand*; and Saul Steinberg's *Government Regulations on Landscape Painting #5* and *The Treaty of Accaonac Partition-Exile Regions-Forbidden Areas*.

511 Note on *The Count of Luxembourg*: Wilder was not yet through with this idea. Kohner

and Billy's lawyer, Marvin Meyer, discussed the purchase of the rights in July on behalf of Phalanx for $100,000; there is no record of the sale having gone through, however. State Historical Society of Wisconsin, Wisconsin Center for Film and Theatre Research, United Artists Collection, Box 5, folder 3; Sammlung Paul Kohner, Stiftung Deutsche Kinemathek, h. ss-88/1h-6, file 2.

512   Note on Bryan Forbes: He is the British writer-director of *King Rat* (1965) and *Of Human Bondage* (1964), among other films.

512   Note on John Schlesinger: He had recently directed *Darling* (1965), which was nominated for a Best Picture Oscar. State Historical Society of Wisconsin, Wisconsin Center for Film and Theatre Research, United Artists Collection, Box 5, folder 3.

512   "Pictures will be better . . .": *Daily Mail* (London), July 31, 1964.

CHAPTER 28

513   "It's not because you have talent . . .": Tom Wood, p. 10.

513   "Billy used to say . . .": Kanin, p. 180.

514   "A movie is a star vehicle . . .": Lemon, p. 37.

514   "The star thing is changing . . .": Roderick Mann, "Why Billy Wilder Forgets His Feuds," *Sunday Express*, Feb. 18, 1968. Note on *Bonnie and Clyde*: The 1967 film catapulted Faye Dunaway into stardom, but Warren Beatty was already there—so much so that he could produce the film himself as well as star in it.

514   Lerner, Loewe, Hart collaboration: Zolotow, p. 323.

514   Kohner and Moreau: Sammlung Paul Kohner, Stiftung Deutsche Kinemathek, h. ss-88/1h-6, file 2.

514   Diamond departs: Zolotow, p. 324.

514   Kurnitz announced: *Variety*, Oct. 9, 1967.

515   Kohner and the agents: Sammlung Paul Kohner, Stiftung Deutsche Kinemathek, h. ss-88/1h-6, file 2.

515   "What I plan . . .": Roderick Mann, "Why Billy Wilder Forgets His Feuds," *Sunday Express*, Feb. 18, 1968.

515   "Neither *nouvelle vague* . . .": Michael Billington, *The Times* (London), July 19, 1969.

515   "Some of these young guys . . .": Roderick Mann, "Why Billy Wilder Forgets His Feuds," *Sunday Express*, Feb. 18, 1968.

516   "I'm one of Billy Wilder's greatest . . .": *The Times* (London), April 30, 1968.

516   "We had one drink . . .": Stephens, pp. 96–97.

518   Four movements: Cohn, pp. 49–50.

520   Budget of *Holmes*: *Hollywood Reporter*, May 5, 1969.

520   On Sanders: VanDerBeets, p. 192.

521   Diamond on the set: Gillett, *Sight and Sound*, p. 26; Interview with Ernest Walter, *The Private Life of Sherlock Holmes* collector's edition laserdisk, MGM/UA Entertainment, 1994.

521   "Love story between two men . . .": Michael Billington, *The Times* (London), July 19, 1969.

521   "Come on! . . .": Gillett, *Sight and Sound*, p. 26.

521   "Being put through the meat grinder . . .": Stephens, p. 96.

521   ". . . do it with a whip . . .": "Billy Wilder: The Human Comedy," *American Masters*, PBS, 1998.

521   "We would spend hours . . .": Stephens, p. 98.

522   Planting new grass: Clive Hirschorn, *Sunday Express* (London), Sept. 14, 1969.

522   Note on Stanley Holloway: He played Mr. Doolittle in *My Fair Lady*, in which he sings "I'm Getting Married in the Morning."

522   "I asked him to reconstruct . . .": Ciment, *Positif* 120, Oct. 1970, pp. 5–17.

523   Stephens's illness announcement: *Variety*, Oct. 14, 1969.

523   "Billy was terribly upset . . .": Stephens, p. 101.

524   Laughton and tears anecdotes: Iain Johnstone, "Billy Wilder in London," *The Listener*, Nov. 13, 1969.

524   Withholding of ending: Mark Shivas, "Holmes with Vinegar," *Manchester Guardian*, Nov. 24, 1969.

524   "We become aware of her deception . . .": McBride and Wilmington, p. 48.

526   Wilder leaves England: *Evening Standard*, Dec. 11, 1969.

526   Rózsa and the score: Thomas, Tony, *Music for the Movies*, pp. 96–97; Rózsa, pp. 208–209.

527   "It depends on the percentage . . .": The *Times* (London), March 16, 1970.

528   "Wasn't done without resistance . . .": Trauner and Berthomé, p. 184.

528   Gross: Lally, p. 373.

528   Kael on *Sherlock*: *New Yorker*, Nov. 14, 1970.

528   "It was only seven years ago . . .": McBride and Wilmington, p. 46.

529   "I should have been more daring . . .": Columbus, p. 28.

CHAPTER 29

533   Eames Chaise: Anon., "Anti-Casting Couch." *Time* 95, Jan. 5, 1970, p. 37; Neuhart, Neuhart, and Eames, p. 339.

534   *Avanti!* plans: *Hollywood Reporter*, Feb. 6, 1968.

534   Taylor and Diamond: Turner, p. 19.

534   Epstein comes and goes: *New York Times*, Nov. 15, 1970; State Historical Society of Wisconsin, Wisconsin Center for Film and Theatre Research, United Artists Collection, Box 5, folder 5.

534   Vincenzoni and Manfredi: *Variety*, Aug. 4, 1971.

534   "At first . . ." and "It's basically . . .": Ciment, *Positif*, Jan. 1974, pp. 4, 8.

535   "He went to Cornell . . .": State Historical Society of Wisconsin, Wisconsin Center for Film and Theatre Research, I. A. L. Diamond Collection, Box 14, folder 2.

535   "He starts to have doubts . . ." and "He starts to understand . . .": Ciment, *Positif*, Jan. 1974, p. 5.

535   "One day I'm going to work with you . . ." and other Mills recollections: Juliet Mills interview with the author, July 2, 1997.

536   "We were lucky to find . . .": Ciment, *Positif*, Jan. 1974, p. 5.

536   "Lovely, touching . . .": State Historical Society of Wisconsin, Wisconsin Center for Film and Theatre Research, I. A. L. Diamond Collection, Box 14, folder 2.

537   "He's a very good friend . . .": Michel Ciment, "Entretien avec Billy Wilder," *Positif* 155, Jan. 1974, pp. 6–8.

537   On intimacy of aspect ratio: Morris, p. 38.

537   "The air is Italian . . .": Ciment, *Positif*, Jan. 1974, p. 6.

538   "The play is very different . . .": Ciment, *Positif*, Jan. 1974, p. 6.

538   "The film is something more . . .": Farber, *Film Quarterly*, p. 51.

538   "It's a montage . . .": Ciment, *Positif*, Jan. 1974, p. 6.

540   *Avanti!* losses: State Historical Society of Wisconsin, Wisconsin Center for Film and Theatre Research, United Artists Collection, Box 5, folders 3 and 5.

540   "Just too gentle . . .": McBride and McCarthy, p. 44.

540   "Today you obviously . . .": Voss, Feb. 7, 1973.

540   "Our ears have been dulled . . ." etc.: Wilder to Kenneth Geist, Oct. 11, 1972.

541   Wilder and Ford in *Esquire*: Berggren, pp. 134–35.

541   "Of course I was bitter . . .": Voss, Feb. 7, 1973.

542   "There was a strike on . . .": Roderick Mann, "Why Billy Wilder Went Out to Pick Up a Girl," *Sunday Express* (London), Dec. 8, 1974.

542   Mankiewicz and *The Front Page*: Geist, p. 11.

542   Preparation of *The Front Page*: State Historical Society of Wisconsin, Wisconsin Center for Film and Theatre Research, I. A. L. Diamond Collection, Box 15, folders 3 and 4.

543   On Carol Burnett: Taraborelli, pp. 116, 300; *Variety*, April 25, 1974.

543   Lemmon, the Oscars, and poker: Wiley and Bona, pp. 492–93; Deutsch, p. 161.

544   "There aren't many men . . .": "Billy Wilder: The Human Comedy," *American Masters*, PBS, 1998.

544   "He fired someone . . .": Susan Sarandon interview with the author, Feb. 4, 1998.

545   "I *always* play Wilder . . ." etc.: McBride, *Sight and Sound*, p. 212.

545   "Billy Wilder said . . .": *Larry King Live*, CNN, Dec. 7, 1996.

545 "Each scene that you do . . .": "Billy Wilder: The Human Comedy," *American Masters*, PBS, 1998.

545 Pendleton recollections: Austin Pendleton interview with the author, Jan. 27, 1998.

546 Note on Burnett story: Burnett said later that she liked the movie well enough, just not her own performance. Taraborelli, pp. 300–1.

546 On the Goldwyn fire: *Variety*, May 8, 1974.

547 "Things could have been worse . . .": *New Times*, May 31, 1974.

548 Lemmon on overlapping dialogue: Wilmington, p. 18.

549 Critics' responses: *Variety*, Dec. 9, 1974; *Newsweek*, Dec. 23, 1974; *Time*, Dec. 23, 1974.

549 "Predictably distinctive . . .": Morris, p. 38.

549 "His was the case . . .": Curtis, p. 197.

549 ". . . 140 penises": McBride, *Sight and Sound*, p. 212.

550 "I was Steven Spielberg . . .": Baxter, p. 115.

CHAPTER 30

551 *Fedora* announced: *Los Angeles Times*, May 15, 1976.

552 "They say Wilder is out of touch . . .": McGee, p. 18.

552 "It's Kafka . . .": McBride and McCarthy, p. 42.

552 "I don't know why . . .": Sammlung Paul Kohner, Stiftung Deutsche Kinemathek, h. ss-88/1h-6, file 1.

552 Wilder invests in *Fedora*: McGee, p. 18.

553 "Look, I can't lose . . .": McBride and McCarthy, p. 42.

553 Garbo and Dietrich: Thomas, *Golden Boy*, p. 213; McBride and McCarthy, p. 44.

553 *Foreskin Saga*: McBride and McCarthy, p. 41.

553 "I had another idea . . .": Ciment, *Positif*, Sept. 1978, p. 29.

553 "The old homosexual dream . . ." etc. : Ciment, *Positif*, Sept. 1978, pp. 30–31.

554 Script to Keller: *Los Angeles Times*, March 28, 1977.

554 "Her face was smashed up . . .": McBride and McCarthy, p. 44.

554 "My only problem . . .": Ciment, *Positif*, Sept. 1978, p. 34.

554 "You know why? . . .": McGee, p. 19.

555 Viviani analysis of *Fedora*: Viviani, pp. 25–27.

556 "My original idea . . .": Ciment, *Positif*, Sept. 1978, p. 33.

556 Walters and Peck: State Historical Society of Wisconsin, Wisconsin Center for Film and Theatre Research, I. A. L. Diamond Collection, Box 14, folders 6 and 7.

556 McGee's research: From McGee's tribute to Wilder at the 1991 Directors Guild awards dinner.

557 "With one tug . . ." etc.: State Historical Society of Wisconsin, Wisconsin Center for Film and Theatre Research, I. A. L. Diamond Collection, Box 14, folder 6; McGee, pp. 19–20.

558 Keller, Holden, and Wilder: Mann, Roderick. "Wilder Tips His Hat to 'Fedora's' Keller," *Los Angeles Times*, March 16, 1978; Thomas, *Golden Boy*, p. 213.

558 Stogies: Mary Blume. " 'Fedora': Walking on the Wilder Side," *Los Angeles Times*, Oct. 2, 1977, p. 39.

558 Editor fired: McGee, p. 30.

559 Rising cost of *Fedora*: *Variety*, Aug. 10, 1977.

559 Wilder and Rózsa: McGee, p. 31.

560 "Forget Knef's voice . . .": McGee, p. 31.

560 "Informed sources say . . .": *Variety*, Feb. 28, 1979.

561 "Perfunctory and insulting way . . .": Harmetz, "At 73 . . . ," p. C12.

561 Adelson, Kohner, and preview: McGee, p. 32.

562 Cannes: Roderick Mann, "Wilder Tips His Hat to 'Fedora's' Keller." *Los Angeles Times*, March 16, 1978.

562 Critics' responses: *Hollywood Reporter*, Nov. 28, 1978; *New Yorker*, April 23, 1979, p. 123; Sarris, *Confessions*, p. 242; *Village Voice*, April 16, 1979.

564 "Like all my other films . . ." etc.: Ciment, *Positif*, Sept. 1978, pp. 29–33.

CHAPTER 31

565 *Buddy Buddy* announced: *Variety*, May 12, 1980; State Historical Society of Wisconsin, Wisconsin Center for Film and Theatre Research, I. A. L. Diamond Collection, Box 14, folders 3 and 4.

565 On Begelman: *Los Angeles Times*, August 9, 1995; see also McClintick's book-length discussion.

566 ". . . Dolores Del Rio": Farber, "Wilder: A Cynic . . . ," p. 21.

566 "Look at Joan Crawford . . .": *Daily Mail* (London), Sept. 8, 1978.

567 ". . . *Stir Crazy* and George Bernard Shaw": Adrian Turner, "Walk on the Wilder Side," unsourced clipping on file at the BFI.

567 "I didn't have to audition . . .": Farber, "Wilder: A Cynic . . . ," p. 21.

567 Hotel set: *Hollywood Reporter*, Feb. 17, 1981.

567 "In this Donner Pass . . .": Farber, "A Cynic . . . ," p. 21.

567 Holden's death: Thomas, *Golden Boy*, pp. 3–8; Farber, "Wilder: A Cynic . . . ," p. 21.

568 On changes from L'Emmerdeur: Hadley, p. 99, and throughout.

568 Jack Webb: State Historical Society of Wisconsin, Wisconsin Center for Film and Theatre Research, I. A. L. Diamond Collection, Box 14, folder 3.

568 "She's no Garbo . . .": Hadley, p. 196.

569 ". . . Homosexual on a diet": Byrne, p. 10.

569 Wilder's "misogyny": Hadley, p. 80.

569 "Rod Steiger . . ." and other quotations: Hadley, pp. 108–27.

570 "For all the trouble . . .": *Buddy Buddy* press kit.

570 "Permission granted . . .": Hadley, p. 173.

570 "That piece of Hollywood shit . . .": Kinski, p. 299.

570 "Izzie, nice working . . .": Hadley, p. 186.

572 Critics' responses: *Variety*, Dec. 9, 1981, p. 20; Turner, p. 20; *Village Voice*, Dec. 16–22, 1981, p. 73.

573 *Love in the Afternoon* remake: Hollywood *Reporter*, Feb. 17, 1981.

573 Box office figures: Hadley, p. 1, citing *Variety*, Jan. 12, 1982, p. 46.

573 "I'm doing this . . .": Wiley and Bona, p. 626.

573 Film Society speech: Wilder, "Movies Forever!" p. 23.

574 "They're like hemorrhoids . . .": *Los Angeles* magazine, June 1982.

574 *Filmcritica* symposium: Ciment, *Positif*, July/Aug. 1983, pp. 4–7.

CHAPTER 32

576 "The only thing that would break . . .": *The Times* (London), Feb. 8, 1962.

576 "I've been here for fifty-plus . . ." and "Nobody talks about the picture": Columbus, pp. 24–26.

576 "They are also afraid . . .": Kirkham, p. 21.

577 Note on the Columbia debt: $5? $4? What's the difference? (See p. 372.) *Los Angeles Herald-Examiner*, Feb. 26, 1986.

577 Wilder's new job: Mike Thomas, pp. 1–12.

577 "This picture is a big pile of shit . . .": "Running Wilder: H'w'd needs a dose of the master," by Peter Bart, *Daily Variety*, April 22, 1996, p. 19.

578 Wilder on Waldheim: *Profil*, April 7, 1986.

578 Letter to Rózsa: Rózsa, p. 229.

579 Dietrich in Paris: Spoto, *Blue Angel*, p. 300.

579 "Lubitsch is dead": Deutsch, p. 158.

579 "If one could write Lubitsch touches . . .": Eyman, p. 368.

579 Note on *One, Two, Three*: *Variety* reported that the idea was proposed by Mason's manager, Jill Rosenfield. *Variety*, April 5 and 13, 1988.

579 Thalberg Award: Wiley and Bona, p. 720; Mike Thomas, p. 1.

580 Empty chair: Rodman, pp. 71, 78.

580 *Josefine Mutzenbacher*: The *Times* (London), June 7, 1994.

581 Wilders' penthouse and art: Vilidas, p. 154; Carter, p. 60; Deutsch, p. 82; Arce, "At home . . . ," p. 22.

582 "I prefer to look . . .": Ciment, *Positif*, July/Aug. 1983, pp. 15–28.

582 Wilder's artistic creations: Freeman, p. 79; *Vanity Fair*, April 1989, p. 126; *Variety*, Dec. 21, 1993.

583 "An art collection is a living thing . . .": Starkmann, Alfred. "Billy Wilder: Es Läuft ein grosses Drama über die Bühne," *Die Welt*, Dec. 27, 1989, p. 7.

583 "A collection needs to grow . . ." and other auction quotations: Reed and Bacon, pp. 154–57; *Los Angeles Times*, Nov. 14, 1989, p. A4.

584 "It was less nerve-wracking . . .": Kirkham, p. 21.

585 On the fire: Muchnic, Suzanne, "Art Conservators: Even Where There's Smoke, There's Hope," *Los Angeles Times*, Jan. 5, 1990, pp. F1, 12, 13; Deutsch, p. 164.

585 "I'm being appointed . . .": Deutsch, p. 158.

585 "I'm sure I'll get a better . . .": Amberger, pp. 88–90.

585 Note on the other biographies: My guess is that *no* book about Billy Wilder would be any better in Billy's eyes—even (or especially) the present one.

585 Cheerleaders: James Ulmer, "In Transit," *Hollywood Reporter*, Feb. 19, 1993.

586 The plaque: *Berliner Zeitung am Mittag*, Feb. 19, 1993.

586 "I left the day after . . .": Kakutani, p. 14.

586 Spielberg on Wilder: Baxter, p. 362.

586 Wilder on *Schindler's List*: McBride, *Steven Spielberg*, p. 427.

587 Autograph story: David Gritten, "Sunset Days," *Telegraph* (London), June 24, 1993, pp. 14–20.

587 Wilder on *Schindler's List*: Wilder, Billy, "Man sah überall nur Taschentücher," pp. 18–19.

587 Wilder in Vienna: Hutter and Kamolz, pp. 90–94.

588 Sucha Beskidzka: "Wilder Honored by Hometown in Poland," by Dean E. Murphy, *Pittsburgh Post-Gazette*, May 29, 1996, p. D4.

588 Wilder on *Sunset Boulevard*, Webber, and Hampton: Stephen M. Silverman, "Oscar Wilder," *Times* magazine (London), July 10, 1993, pp. 10–12; "A New Turn for 'Sunset Boulevard'," by David Gritten, *Los Angeles Times* Calendar, p. 8; David Gritten, "Secrets of *Sunset Boulevard*," *Mail on Sunday* (London), Nov. 4, 1993; *Variety*, Oct. 20, 1993; Richard Brooks, "Close-up on show of memories," *Observer* (London), July 18, 1993, p. 52.

589 "Everyone was being very civil . . .": Bart, p. 19.

590 "He learned it from you": Junod, p. 250.

590 *Love in the Afternoon* remake: Kirkham, p. 21.

591 "When I'm shooting . . .": "Where I Work: Billy Wilder," anon., *Buzz*, Jan./Feb. 1993, p. 36.

591 Wilder and *Jerry Maguire*: Crowe, pp. 137–42.

592 "The Shoe Store": Anthony Scaduto, "Then the Story Gets Wilder," *Newsday*, June 15, 1998, p. A12. Note: As of July 1998, "The Shoe Store" had not enjoyed commercial release

592 Thornton on Wilder: *Larry King Live*, March 1997.

592 "So much for glory": Stephen M. Silverman, "Oscar Wilder," *Times* magazine (London), July 10, 1993, pp. 10–12.

592 Wilder on Trueba: Kirkham, p. 21; Sragow, p. 143.

592 "An elderly man . . .": "Billy Wilder: The Human Comedy," *American Masters*, PBS, 1998; he told the joke at the age of ninety, when he received the 1997 Golden Laurel Award.

BIBLIOGRAPHY

A Selection of Paintings, Drawings, Collages, and Sculpture from the Collection of Mr. and Mrs. Billy Wilder. Santa Barbara, California: University of California, 1966.

ALBRECHT, DONALD, ed. *The Work of Charles and Ray Eames: A Legacy of Invention.* New York: Harry N. Abrams, Inc., 1997.

ALLEMAN, RICHARD. *The Movie Lover's Guide to Hollywood.* New York: Harper Colophon, 1985.

ALLEN, TOM. "Bracketting Wilder." *Film Comment* 18, May/June 1982, pp. 29–31.

ALPERT, HOLLIS. "Billy, Willy, and Jack." *Saturday Review* 49, Sept. 24, 1966, p. 30.

ALTMAN, BILLY. *Laughter's Gentle Soul: The Life of Robert Benchley.* New York: Norton, 1997.

AMBERGER, HERMI. "Die beste Landschaft." *Profil,* April 2, 1991, p. 88–90.

AMES, K. "Funny Money." *Newsweek,* Oct. 9, 1989, p. 75.

ANDRES, ALAN. "Antihero: William Holden Gambles on *Stalag 17.*" *American Movie Classics* magazine, Dec. 1993, pp. 1–2.

ANOBILE, RICHARD, ed. *Ernst Lubitsch's Ninotchka.* New York: Avon, 1975.

ANON. "An Endowed Boswell Follows Billy Wilder While Filming *Fedora.*" *Variety,* May 25, 1977, p. 35.

ANON. "Anti-Casting Couch." *Time* 95, Jan. 5, 1970, p. 37.

ANON. "Billy Wilder Doffs 'Fedora' to Bavaria Studios in Munich." *Variety,* Aug. 10, 1977, p. 20.

ANON. "Dialogue on Film: Billy Wilder and I. A. L. Diamond." *American Film,* July/Aug. 1976, pp. 33–48.

ANON. "Epic in Alcohol." *Newsweek* 26, Dec. 10, 1945, p. 112–15.

ANON. "Filmregie: So gut, wie das Publikum will." *Die Wochen-Presse* 12, no. 47 (Nov. 23, 1957), pp. 1–2.

ANON. "In the Picture: Bergman and Wilder." *Sight and Sound* 28, no. 3, Summer/Autumn 1959, p. 134.

ANON. "Interview: Billy Wilder." *Playboy* 10, no. 6, June 1963.

ANON. "It's Really Rollicking." *Newsweek* 55, June 20, 1960, pp. 110–111.

ANON. "Moral or Immoral?" *Newsweek* 64, Dec. 28, 1964, pp. 53–54.

ANON. "Policeman, Midwife, Bastard." *Time* 75, June 27, 1960, pp. 75–77.

ANON. "Putting *Life* into a Movie: *Ace in the Hole.*" *Life* 30, Feb. 19, 1951, pp. 57–60.

ANON. "Rome's Billy Wilder Retro Features All Pix, Primal Prints." *Variety* 307, June 16, 1982, p. 40.

ANON. "Walk Like This, Marilyn." *Life,* April 20, 1959, pp. 101–4.

ANON. "Why Not Be in Paris?" *Newsweek* 48, Nov. 26, 1956, p. 106–8.

ANSEN, DAVID. "Movies: Some Like It Not." *Newsweek,* Dec. 14, 1981, p. 124.

APPIAH, KWAME ANTHONY, AND HENRY LOUIS GATES JR. *The Dictionary of Global Culture.* New York: Alfred A. Knopf, 1997.

ARCE, HECTOR. "At Home with Billy Wilder." *California Living,* Sept. 14, 1969, pp. 22–24.

———. *Gary Cooper: An Intimate Biography.* New York: William Morrow, 1979.

———. *The Secret Life of Tyrone Power*. New York: Bantam, 1980.

ASPREY, ROBERT. *The Panther's Feast*. New York: Carroll & Graf, 1986.

BALASZ, ANDRÉ, ed. *Hollywood Handbook*. New York: Rizzoli, 1996.

BALIO, TINO. *United Artists: The Company That Changed the Film Industry*. Madison: University of Wisconsin Press, 1987.

BALTAKE, JOE. *The Films of Jack Lemmon*. Secaucus, New Jersey: Citadel Press, 1977.

BARNETT, LINCOLN. "The Happiest Couple in Hollywood: Brackett and Wilder." *Life* 17, Dec. 11, 1944, pp. 100–9.

BART, PETER. "Backtalk." *Variety*, April 22, 1996, p. 19.

BAXTER, JOHN. *Steven Spielberg—The Unauthorised Biography*. London: HarperCollins, 1996.

BECKERMANN, RUTH, ed. *Die Mazzesinsel: Juden in der Wiener Leopoldstadt, 1918–1938*. Vienna: Löcker Verlag, 1992.

BEEBE, LUCIUS, AND CHARLES CLEGG. *The Trains We Rode*, vol. I. Berkeley: Howell North, 1965.

BEEMAN, MARSHA LYNN. *Joan Fontaine: A Bio-Bibliography*. Westport, Conn.: Greenwood Press, 1994.

BEHR, EDWARD. *Thank Heaven for Little Girls*. London: Hutchinson, 1993.

BERG, A. SCOTT. *Goldwyn: A Biography*. New York: Ballantine Books, 1989.

BERGAN, RONALD. *Jean Renoir—Projections of Paradise*. London: Bloomsbury, 1992.

BERGGREN, NOEL. "Arsenic and Old Directors." *Esquire* 77, no. 4, April 1972, pp. 132–35.

BICHHOL, JOACHIM. "Architekten betrügen das Auge." *Filmspiegel*, Oct. 6, 1961.

The Billy Wilder Collection (catalogue). New York: Christie's Publications, 1989.

BLOWEN, MICHAEL. "The Art of Billy Wilder." *Boston Globe*, Oct. 22, 1989, pp. 81–83.

BLUME, MARY. " 'Fedora': Walking on the Wilder Side," *Los Angeles Times*, Oct. 2, 1977, p. 39.

BOCK, HANS-MICHAEL. "Erich Pommer." In *The Oxford History of World Cinema*, ed. Geoffrey Nowell-Smith. New York: Oxford University Press, 1996.

BOGART, STEPHEN HUMPHREY. *Bogart: In Search of My Father*. New York: Dutton, 1995.

BRACKETT, CHARLES. "Counsel of the Ungodly." *Saturday Evening Post*, Jan. 31, 1920, pp. 3–4; Feb. 7, 1920, pp. 24–27; Feb. 14, 1920, pp. 26–27.

BRECHT, BERTOLT. *Arbeitsjournal*. Frankfurt am Main: Suhrkamp Verlag, 1973.

BRET, DAVID. *Maurice Chevalier: Up on Top of a Rainbow*. London: Robson Books, 1992.

BROWN, GEOFF. "A Bite as Fierce as His Bark." *The Times* (London), June 18, 1996, p. 34.

BRUNETTE, PETER, AND GERALD PEARY. "Tough Guy." *Film Comment* 12, no. 3, May/June 1976, pp. 50–57.

BRUYNINCKX, WALTER. *60 Years of Recorded Jazz*. Mechelen, Belgium: 1980.

BYRNE, BRIDGET. "Eyeview: Wilder Ways." *Women's Wear Daily*, April 2, 1981, p. 10.

CAGNEY, JAMES. *Cagney by Cagney*. Garden City, N.Y.: Doubleday and Co., 1976.

CAIN, JAMES M. *Double Indemnity*. New York: Vintage Books, 1978.

CANBY, VINCENT. "Critic's Notebook: The Wonders of Wilder, the Movies' Master Wit." *New York Times*, May 10, 1991, pp. C1, 32.

———. "Film View: Fedora Is Vintage Wilder." *New York Times*, May 6, 1979, sec 2, pp. 15–16.

———. "Screen: Wilder's *Buddy Buddy*." *New York Times*, Dec. 11, 1981, C12.

CANETTI, ELIAS. *The Torch in My Ear*. New York: Farrar, Straus & Giroux, 1982.

CARROLL, HARRISON. "London's Old Bailey Built Here for Murder Movie," *Los Angeles Herald Express*, July 6, 1957.

CARTER, MALCOLM N. "Great Private Collections: The Obsessions of Billy Wilder." *Saturday Review*, Dec. 1980, pp. 60–64.

CEPLAIR, LARRY, AND STEVEN ENGLUND. *The Inquisition in Hollywood: Politics in the Film Community, 1930–1960*. Berkeley: University of California Press, 1979.

CHIERICHIETTI, DAVID. *Mitchell Leisen: Hollywood Director*. Los Angeles: Photoventures Press, 1995.

CIMENT, MICHEL. "Billy Wilder urbi et orbi," *Positif* 269/270: pp. 4–7 July/Aug. 1983.

———. "Entretien avec Billy Wilder (sur Fedora)." *Positif* 210, Sept. 1978, pp. 28–35.

———. "Entretien avec Billy Wilder." *Positif* 269/270: 15–28, July/Aug., 1983.

————. "Entretien avec Billy Wilder." *Positif* 120, Oct. 1970, pp. 4–17.

————. "Nouvel Entretien avec Billy Wilder (sur *Avanti!*)." *Positif* 155, Jan. 1974, pp. 3–9.

CIMENT, MICHEL, AND ANNIE TRESGOT. *Portrait d' un homme parfait à 60%* (motion picture). Paris: 1983.

CLARKE, GERALD. "Portrait: Billy Wilder: Sunset Boulevard's Creator Talks of the Town." *Architectural Digest* 51, no. 4, April 1994, pp. 22–23.

COHAN, STEVEN. "Cary Grant in the Fifties: Indiscretions of the Bachelor's Masquerade." *Screen* 33, no. 4, 1992, pp. 394–412.

COHN, BERNARD. "Wilder, Billy (Tournage)." *Positif* 109, Oct. 1969, pp. 49–50.

COLLINS, AMY FINE. "When Hubert Met Audrey." *Vanity Fair*, Dec. 1995, pp. 278–94.

COLUMBUS, CHRIS. "Wilder Times." *American Film* 11, March 1986, pp. 22–28.

CROWE, CAMERON. "The *Jerry Maguire* Journal." *Rolling Stone*, Dec. 26–Jan. 9, 1997, pp. 137–42.

CULBERT, DAVID. "Hollywood in Berlin, 1945: A Note on Billy Wilder and the Origins of *A Foreign Affair*." *Historical Journal of Film, Radio, and Television* 8, no. 3, 1988, pp. 311–16.

CURTIS, JAMES. *Between Flops—A Biography of Preston Sturges*. New York: Harcourt Brace Jovanovich, 1982.

CURTIS, TONY, AND BARRY PARIS. *Tony Curtis: The Autobiography*. New York: William Morrow, 1993.

DAVIDSON, BILL. *Spencer Tracy—Tragic Idol*. London: Sidgwick and Jackson, 1987.

DELONG, THOMAS A. *Pops: Paul Whiteman, King of Jazz*. Piscataway, N.J.: New Century Publishers, Inc., 1983.

DENBY, DAVID. "Always Making Wisecrackers." *Premiere* 4, Nov. 1990, pp. 48–49.

DEUTSCH, ARMAND. *Me and Bogie*. New York: G. P. Putnam's Sons, 1991.

DEWEY, DONALD. *James Stewart—A Biography*. Atlanta: Turner Publishing, 1996.

DIAMOND, I. A. L. "The Day Marilyn Needed 47 Takes to Remember to Say, 'Where's the Bourbon?' " *California*, Dec. 1985, pp. 132, 135–36.

DICK, BERNARD F. *Billy Wilder*. New York: Da Capo, 1996.

DIDION, JOAN. "*Kiss Me, Stupid*: A Minority Report." *Vogue* 145, no. 5, March 1, 1965, p. 97.

DIETRICH, MARLENE. *Marlene*. New York: Grove Press, 1987.

DIVINE, ROBERT A. *American Immigration Policy, 1924–1952*. New Haven: Yale University Press, 1957.

DIXON, WHEELER W. *The 'B' Directors: A Biographical Directory*. Metuchen, N.J.: Scarecrow Press, 1985, pp. 502–03.

DOMARCHI, JEAN, AND JEAN DOUCHET. "Entretien avec Billy Wilder." *Cahiers du Cinema* 23, no. 134, Aug., 1962, pp. 1–16.

DOUGLAS, KIRK. *The Ragman's Son: An Autobiography*. New York: Simon & Schuster, 1988.

DOWD, NANCY, AND DAVID SHEPARD. *A Director's Guild of America Oral History—King Vidor*. Metuchen, N.J.: Scarecrow Press, 1988.

EISENSCHITZ, BERNARD. "Pardon My French." In *Frank Tashlin*, ed. by Roger Garcia and Bernard Eisenschitz. London: British Film Institute, 1994.

EISNER, LOTTE H. *The Haunted Screen*. Berkeley: University of California Press, 1973.

ELLEY, DEREK. "The Film Composer: Miklós Rózsa (Part 2)." *Films and Filming* 23, no. 9, June 1977, pp. 30–34.

ELSAESSER, THOMAS. "Germany: The Weimar Years." In *The Oxford History of World Cinema*, ed. Geoffrey Nowell-Smith. New York: Oxford University Press, 1996.

EYMAN, SCOTT. *Ernst Lubitsch: Laughter in Paradise*. New York: Simon & Schuster, 1993.

FARBER, STEPHEN. "The Films of Billy Wilder." *Film Comment* 7, no. 4, Winter 1971, pp. 8–22.

————. "Two Old Men's Movies." *Film Quarterly* 26 no. 4, Summer 1973.

————. "Wilder: A Cynic Ahead of His Time." *New York Times*, Dec. 6, 1981, C1, 21.

FARRINGTON, SELWYN KIP. *The Santa Fe's Big Three*. New York: McKay, 1972.

FERGUSON, OTIS. *The Film Criticism of Otis Ferguson*. Philadelphia: Temple University Press, 1971.

FIEDLER, LESLIE. "Come Back to the Raft Ag'in, Huck Honey!" *Partisan Review*, June 1948. Reprinted in: Samuel Langhorne Clemens, *Adventures of Huckleberry Finn*, New York: W. W. Norton and Co., 1977, pp. 413–20.

FRANCIS, ARLENE, WITH FLORENCE ROME. *Arlene Francis: A Memoir*. New York: Simon and Schuster, 1978.

FREEDLAND, MICHAEL. *Maurice Chevalier*. New York: William Morrow, 1981.

FREEMAN, DAVID. "Sunset Boulevard Revisited: Annals of Hollywood." *The New Yorker*, June 21, 1993.

FRIEDRICH, OTTO. *Before the Deluge: A Portrait of Berlin in the 1920s*. New York: Harper & Row, 1972.

———. *City of Nets: A Portrait of Hollywood in the 1940s*. New York: Harper and Row, 1986.

FROMM, BELLA. *Blood and Banquets: A Berlin Social Diary*. New York: Harper and Bros., 1942.

GARCIA, ROGER, ed. *Frank Tashlin*. London: British Film Institute, 1994.

GARDNER, PAUL. "Is Art Good for You?" *ARTnews*. March 1994, pp. 118–22.

GAY, PETER. *Freud, Jews, and Other Germans: Masters and Victims in Modernist Culture*. New York: Oxford University Press, 1978.

GEHMAN, RICHARD. "Charming Billy." *Playboy* 7, no. 12, Dec. 1960, pp. 69–70, 90, 145–148.

GEIST, KENNETH L. *Pictures Will Talk: The Life and Films of Joseph L. Mankiewicz*. New York: Charles Scribner's Sons, 1978.

GENSLER, HOWARD. "Call of the Wilder." *Premiere* 5, no. 11, July 1992, p. 96.

GILBERT, MARTIN. *The Holocaust: A History of the Jews of Europe During the Second World War*. New York: Henry Holt, 1985.

GILL, ANTON. *A Dance between Flames: Berlin between the Wars*. New York: Carroll & Graf, 1993.

GILLETT, JOHN. "In Search of Sherlock." *Sight and Sound* 29, no. 1, Winter 1969/1970, pp. 26–27.

———. *Billy Wilder*. John Player Celebrity Series (pamphlet).

GOLCZEWSKI, FRANK. *Polnisch-jüdische Beziehungen, 1881–1922*. Wiesbaden: Franz Steiner Verlag G.m.b.H., 1981. NYPL *PXV82–2740

GOODMAN, EZRA. *The Fifty Year Decline and Fall of Hollywood*. New York: Simon & Schuster, 1961.

GUIDO BAUMANN, "Ein Oscar sieht nur peinlich aus." *Rheinischer Merkur/Christ und Welt*, Dec. 21, 1985, p. 17.

GUILES, FRED LAWRENCE. *Norma Jean: The Life of Marilyn Monroe*. New York: McGraw-Hill, 1969.

———. *Tyrone Power—The Last Idol*. Garden City, N.Y.: Doubleday, 1979.

GUSSOW, MEL. *Don't Say Yes Until I Finish Talking: A Biography of Darryl Zanuck*. New York: Doubleday, 1971.

GYÖRGYEY, CLARA. *Ferenc Molnár*. Boston: Twayne, 1980.

H. T. S. "*Das Blaue vom Himmel*" (review), *New York Times*, Sept. 8, 1934, p. 18.

———. "*Der falsche Ehemann*" (review), *New York Times*, Oct. 17, 1932, p. 18.

———. "*Ein Maedel der Strasse*" (review), *New York Times*, April 6, 1933, p. 22.

———. "*Emil und die Detektive*" (review), *New York Times*, Dec. 21, 1931, p. 28.

———. "*Es war einmal ein Walzer*" (review), *New York Times*, Oct. 15, 1934, p. 10.

———. "*Ihre Hoheit befiehlt*" (review), *New York Times*, Nov. 7, 1931, p. 16.

———. "*Madame wünscht keine Kinder*" (review), *New York Times*, June 2, 1933, p. 22.

HADLEY, RICHARD PARKER, JR. *Billy Wilder and Comedy: An Analysis of Comedic and Production Techniques in "Buddy Buddy"* Ph.D. dissertation, University of Southern California, 1989.

HAMILTON, IAN. *Writers in Hollywood: 1915–1951*. London: Minerva, 1991.

HANSON, PATRICIA KING, ed. *The American Film Institute Catalog: Feature Films, 1931–1940*. Berkeley: University of California Press, 1993.

HARMETZ, ALJEAN "American Film Institute Honors Billy Wilder." *New York Times* March 8, 1986, 135: 13.

———. "Seven Years without Directing, and Billy Wilder Is Feeling Itchy." *New York Times*, Oct. 3, 1988, C21.

———. "At 73, Billy Wilder's Bark Still Has Plenty of Bite." *New York Times*, June 29, 1979.

HARRIS, WARREN G. *Audrey Hepburn*. New York: Simon and Schuster, 1994.

HAYMAN, RONALD. *Brecht: A Biography*. New York: Oxford University Press, 1983.

HEAD, EDITH, AND PADDY CALISTRO. *Edith Head's Hollywood*. New York: E. P. Dutton, Inc., 1983.

HEILBUT, ANTHONY. *Exiled in Paradise: German Refugee Artists and Intellectuals in America from the 1930s to the Present*. Boston: Beacon Press, 1984.

HIGHAM, CHARLES. *Merchant of Dreams: Louis B. Mayer, MGM, and the Secret Hollywood*. New York: Donald Fine, 1993.

HILBERG, RAUL. *The Destruction of the European Jews*. New York: Holmes & Meier, 1985.

HITCHENS, CHRISTOPHER. "It Happened on Sunset." *Vanity Fair*, April 1995, pp. 215–22.

HOLLÄNDER, FRIEDRICH. *Von Kopf bis Fuss: Mein Leben mit Text und Musik*. Munchen: Kindler, 1967.

HOLTZMAN, WILL. *A Pyramid Illustrated History of the Movies*. New York: Pyramid, 1977.

———. *Jack Lemmon*. New York: Pyramid, 1977.

HOROWITZ, MICHAEL. *Ein Leben für die Zietung: Der rasende Reporter Egon Erwin Kisch*. Vienna: Orca, 1985.

HUTTER, ANDREAS WOLFGANG. *Vom Tages Zum Filmschriftsteller: Der Junge Billy Wilder als Reporter und Drehbuchautor im Wien und Berlin der Zwischenkriegszeit, 1925–1933*. Master's thesis, University of Vienna, 1992.

HUTTER, ANDREAS, AND KLAUS KAMOLZ. "Billie und Barkassy." *Profil*, Sept. 28, 1992, pp. 82–85.

———. "Plötzlich ein Wiener." *Profil*, May 9, 1994, pp. 90–94.

HYAMS, JOE. *Bogart and Bacall*. New York: David McKay Co., 1975.

Impressionist and Modern Paintings and Sculpture: Highlights of the Season. New York: Christie's, 1989.

ISHERWOOD, CHRISTOPHER. *Diaries: Volume One: 1939–1960*. New York: HarperCollins, 1996.

J.R. "Billy Wilder: Cum Deo." *Hollywood Close-Up*, March 26, 1959, p. 3.

JABLONSKI, EDWARD, AND LAWRENCE D. STEWART. *The Gershwin Years*. New York: Da Capo, 1996.

JACKSON, CHARLES. *The Lost Weekend*. New York: Farrar and Rhinehart, 1944.

JACOBS, DIANE. *Christmas in July—The Life and Art of Preston Sturges*. Berkeley: University of California Press, 1992.

JANIK, ALLAN, AND STEPHEN TOULMIN. *Wittgenstein's Vienna*. New York: Touchstone, 1973.

JEANCOLAS, JEAN-PIERRE. "Delicieuse . . ." *Positif* 271, Sept. 1983, pp. 30–31.

JELAVICH, PETER. *Berlin Cabaret*. Cambridge: Harvard University Press, 1993.

JENSEN, OLIVER. "*Lost Weekend* Hangover." *Life*, March 11, 1946, pp. 17–23.

JENSEN, PAUL. "Raymond Chandler and the World You Live In." *Film Comment* 10, no. 6, Nov./Dec. 1974, pp. 18–27.

JUNOD, TOM. "The Last Swinger." *GQ*, April 1996, pp. 220–27, 250–52.

KAEL, PAULINE. *5001 Nights at the Movies*. New York: Holt, Rinehart and Winston, 1982.

———. *Deeper into Movies*. Boston: Little, Brown and Co., 1973.

———. *I Lost It at the Movies*. Boston: Little, Brown and Company, 1965.

KAKUTANI, MICHIKO. "Billy Wilder Honored at Lincoln Center Gala." *New York Times* 131: C9, May 4, 1982.

———. "Ready for His Close-Up." *New York Times Magazine*, July 28, 1996, p. 14.

KANIN, GARSON. *Hollywood*. New York: Viking Press, 1974.

KARASEK, HELLMUTH. *Billy Wilder: eine Nahaufnahme*. Hamburg: Hoffman und Campe, 1992.

KASS, JUDITH M. *Olivia de Havilland*. New York: Pyramid, 1976.

KÄSTNER, ERICH. *Emil und die Detektive*. Zurich: Atrium Verlag, 1994. 139th edition. Originally published: Berlin: Williams & Co. Verlag, 1928.

KAUFFMANN, STANLEY. *A World on Film*. New York: Harper and Row, 1966.

KELLEY, KITTY. *His Way—The Unauthorized Biography of Frank Sinatra.* New York: Bantam, 1986.

KELLY, JAMES B., AND JOHN SCHULTHEISS. "Deux vases de fleurs fraîches dans la loge: Entretien avec Mitchell Leisen." *Positif* 434, April 1997, pp. 90–94.

KINSKI, KLAUS. *Kinski Uncut.* Trans. Joachim Neugröschel. New York: Viking, 1996.

KIRKHAM, PAT. "Saul Bass and Billy Wilder: In Conversation." *Sight and Sound,* June 1995, pp. 18–21.

KLENO, LARRY. *Kim Novak on Camera.* New York: A. S. Barnes, 1980.

KLINKENBORG, VERLYN. *The Last Fine Time.* New York: Vintage Books, 1990.

KOPPES, CLAYTON R., AND GREGORY D. BLACK. *Hollywood Goes to War: How Politics, Profits and Propaganda Shaped World War II Movies.* Berkeley: University of California Press, 1987.

KOSZARSKI, RICHARD. *The Man You Loved to Hate: Erich von Stroheim and Hollywood.* New York: Oxford University Press, 1983.

KOTANKO, CHRISTOPH. " 'Der Brandauer is Viel Interessanter.' " *Profil,* April 7, 1986, p. 43.

KRACAUER, SIGFRIED. *From Caligari to Hitler: A Psychological History of the German Film.* Princeton: Princeton University Press, 1974.

KREIMEIER, KLAUS. *The Ufa Story: A History of Germany's Greatest Film Company, 1918–1945.* New York: Hill and Wang, 1996.

KRUTNIK, FRANK. "Desire, Transgression, and James M. Cain." *Screen* 23, no. 1, 1982, pp. 31–44.

———. *In a Lonely Street: Film Noir, Genre, Masculinity.* New York: Routledge, 1991.

KURNITZ, HARRY. "Billy the Wild." *Holiday,* June 1964, pp. 93–95.

LAGUARDIA, ROBERT. *Monty.* New York: Avon, 1978.

LALLY, KEVIN. *Wilder Times.* New York: Henry Holt, 1996.

LAURIE, CLAYTON D. *The Propaganda Warriors: America's Crusade against Nazi Germany.* Lawrence, Kansas: The University Press of Kansas, 1996.

LEAMING, BARBARA. *Orson Welles: A Biography.* New York: Viking, 1985.

LEGRAND, G. "Deux ou trois comtesses." *Positif* 210, Sept. 1978, pp. 21–23.

LEISER, ERWIN. *Nazi Cinema.* Trans. Gertrud Mander and David Wilson. London: Secker and Warburg, 1974.

LEMON, RICHARD. "The Message in Billy Wilder's Fortune Cookie." *The Saturday Evening Post* 239, Dec. 17, 1966, pp. 30–35, 67–83.

LEVIN, NORA. *The Holocaust: The Destruction of European Jewry, 1933–1945.* New York: Schocken Books, 1973.

LEVY, EMMANUEL. *George Cukor: Master of Elegance.* New York: William Morrow, 1994.

LEWIS, ROGER. *The Life and Death of Peter Sellers.* London: Century, 1994.

LIGHTMAN, HERB. "Old Master, New Tricks." *American Cinematographer,* 31, no. 9, Sept. 1950, pp. 318–19.

LIMBACHER, JAMES L. *Film Music: From Violins to Video.* Metuchen, N.J.: Scarecrow Press, 1974.

LINDBERGH, CHARLES A. *The Spirit of St. Louis.* New York: Charles Scribner's Sons, 1953.

LINVILLE, JAMES. "Billy Wilder: The Art of Screenwriting." *The Paris Review* 138, Spring 1996, pp. 47–71.

LUFT, HERBERT. "A Matter of Decadence." *Quarterly of Film, Radio and Television* 7, no. 1, fall 1952.

LYON, JAMES K. *Bertolt Brecht in America.* Princeton: Princeton University Press, 1980.

MACDONALD, DWIGHT. *Dwight Macdonald on Movies.* New York: Berkeley, 1969.

MACLAINE, SHIRLEY. *My Lucky Stars.* New York: Bantam, 1996.

MACSHANE, FRANK. *The Life of Raymond Chandler.* New York: E. P. Dutton, 1976.

MADSEN, AXEL. *Billy Wilder.* Bloomington: Indiana University Press, 1969.

———. *William Wyler.* New York: Thomas Crowell, 1973.

———. *Stanwyck.* New York: HarperCollins, 1994.

MANN, RODERICK. "Wilder Tips His Hat to 'Fedora's' Keller." *Los Angeles Times,* March 16, 1978.

MARSHALL, JAMES. *Santa Fe: The Railroad that Built an Empire.* New York: Random House, 1945.

MASLIN, JANET. "Film View: Missing the Many Moods of the Durable Billy Wilder." *New York Times*, May 16, 1982, sec. 2, pp. 21, 37.

———. "Wilder's Movie 'Fedora' Opens." *New York Times*, April 15, 1979, p. 35.

MCBRIDE, JOSEPH. "In the Picture: *The Front Page*." *Sight and Sound* 43, no. 4, Autumn 1974, p. 212.

MCBRIDE, JOSEPH, AND THOMAS MCCARTHY. "Going for Extra Innings" (interview), *Film Comment*, 15: 40–48, Jan/Feb 1979.

———. "Kurt Siodmak: From Horror to Hollywood Honors." *Variety*, Oct. 1, 1992, p. 15.

MCBRIDE, JOSEPH, AND MICHAEL WILMINGTON. "*The Private Life of Sherlock Holmes*" (review). *Film Quarterly*, Spring 1971, pp. 45–49.

MCCAGG, WILLIAM O., JR. *A History of Habsburg Jews: 1670–1918*. Bloomington: Indiana University Press, 1989.

MCCARTHY, TODD. "AFI Lauds Jack Lemmon." *Variety*, March 16, 1988, pp. 6, 28.

———. *Howard Hawks: The Grey Fox of Hollywood*. New York: Grove Press, 1997.

———. "I. A. L. Diamond" (obituary). *Variety*, April 27, 1988, pp. 6, 23.

MCCLINTICK, DAVID. *Indecent Exposure*. New York: Dell, 1982.

MCDONALD, KEVIN. *Emeric Pressburger—The Life and Death of a Screenwriter*. Boston: Faber and Faber, 1994.

MCGEE, REX. "The Life and Hard Times of *Fedora*." *American Film*, Feb. 1979, pp. 17–32.

MCGILLIGAN, PATRICK. *Cagney: The Actor as Auteur*. San Diego: A. S. Barnes and Co., 1982.

———. *Fritz Lang: The Nature of the Beast*. New York: St. Martin's Press, 1997.

MEEHAN, JOHN. "Death Goes to a Party." *The Society of Motion Picture Art Directors' Bulletin*, 1, no. 5, May/June 1951, pp. 6–8.

MILLAND, RAY. *Wide-Eyed in Babylon*. New York: William Morrow and Company, 1974.

MOLNÁR, FERENC. *Romantic Comedies: Eight Plays by Ferenc Molnár*. New York: Crown, 1952.

MORRIS, GEORGE. "The Private Films of Billy Wilder." *Film Comment* 15, Jan./Feb. 1979, pp. 33–39.

MOSLEY, LEONARD. *Lindbergh: A Biography*. Garden City, N.Y.: Doubleday, 1976.

MUCHNIC, SUZANNE. "A Wilder Nefertete," *ARTnews* 93, no. 3, March 1994, p. 21.

———. "Art Conservators: Even Where There's Smoke, There's Hope." *Los Angeles Times*, Jan. 5, 1990, pp. F1,12, 13.

———. "Auction of Billy Wilder's Art Fetches $32.6M." *Los Angeles Times*, Nov. 14, 1989, p. A4.

MUNDY, ROBERT. "Some Notes on Billy Wilder," in the pamphlet *The Billy Wilder Movie Marathon*. Los Angeles Film Exhibition, Nov. 1972.

MURRAY, BRUCE. *Film and the German Left in the Weimar Republic*. Austin: University of Texas Press, 1990.

NAREMORE, JAMES. "Straight Down the Line." *Film Comment*, Jan./Feb. 1996, pp. 22–31.

NAVASKY, VICTOR S. *Naming Names*. New York: Penguin Books, 1981.

NEUHART, JOHN, MARILYN NEUHART, AND RAY EAMES. *Eames Design: The Work of the Office of Charles and Ray Eames*. New York: Harry N. Abrams, Inc., 1989.

NEWMAN, WALTER. "Writing for the Movies—An Interview with Walter Newman." *Focus on Film*, no. 11, Autumn 1972.

NORDEN, MARTIN F. *John Barrymore: A Bio-Bibliography*. Westport, Conn.: Greenwood Press, 1985.

OLSEN, TILLIE, AND BILLY WILDER. "The '30s: A Vision of Fear and Hope." *Newsweek*, Jan. 3, 1994, p. 24.

OSTERHOLM, J. ROGER. *Bing Crosby: A Bio-Bibliography*. Westport, Conn.: Greenwood Press, 1994.

Österreichisches Wörtbuch. Vienna: Österreichisches Bundesverlag, 1993.

PALEY, WILLIAM S. *As It Happened: a Memoir*. Garden City, N.Y.: Doubleday, 1979.

PALMER, CHRISTOPHER. *The Composer in Hollywood*. New York: Marion Boyars, 1990.

PALMER, JACK. "*Menschen am Sonntag* Sparked Careers of Film Luminaries." *Variety*, Feb. 8, 1989.

PANASSIÉ, HUGUES. *Hot Jazz*. Trans. Lyle and Eleanor Dowling. Westport, Conn.: Negro University Press, 1970.

PARIS, BARRY. *Garbo: A Biography*. New York. Alfred A. Knopf, 1995.

PAUL, WILLIAM. *Ernst Lubitsch's American Comedy*. New York: Columbia University Press, 1983.

PEARY, GERALD, ed. *Close-Ups: The Movie Star Book*. New York: Workman, 1978.

PICKARD, ROY. *Jimmy Stewart—A Life in Film*. New York: St. Martin's Press, 1992.

PIERCE, ARTHUR, AND DOUGLAS SWARTHOUT. *Jean Arthur: A Bio-Bibliography*. New York: Greenwood Press, 1990.

POGUE, FORREST C. *United States Army in World War II: The European Theater of Operations: The Supreme Command*. Washington, D.C.: Dept. of the Army, 1954.

PRELUTSKY, BURT. "An Interview with Billy Wilder," in *The Movies: Texts, Receptions, Exposures*, ed. Laurence Goldstein and Ira Konigsberg. Ann Arbor: University of Michigan Press, 1996.

PREVIN, ANDRÉ. *No Minor Chords: My Days in Hollywood*. New York: Doubleday, 1991.

PRYOR, THOMAS. "End of a Journey." *New York Times*, Sept. 23, 1945, sec. 2, p. 3

———. "Hollywood Canvass," *New York Times*, July 7, 1957.

QUIRK, LAWRENCE. *Jane Wyman: The Actress and the Woman*. New York: Dembner Books, 1986.

RAPHAELSON, SAMSON. *Three Screen Comedies by Samson Raphaelson*. Madison: University of Wisconsin Press, 1983.

RASNER, HEINZ-GERD, AND REINHARD WULF. " 'Ich nehm' das alles nicht so ernst . . . ," in *Billy Wilders Filme* by Neil Sinyard and Adrian Turner. Berlin: Spiess, 1980.

REED, SUSAN, AND DORIS BACON. "Director Billy Wilder Puts his Legendary $22 Million-or-so Art Collection on the Auction Block." *People*, Nov. 13, 1989, pp. 154–55.

REGENTS OF THE UNIVERSITY OF CALIFORNIA. *The Billy Wilder Art Collection: A Catalogue*. Santa Barbara: University of California Press, 1966.

RENTSCHLER, ERIC, ed. *German Literature and Film: Adaptations and Transformations*. New York: Methuen, 1986.

ROBBINS, J. "Wilder Bites the Hand that Barely Feeds Him at Lincoln Center Gala." *Variety* 307, May 5, 1982, p. 4.

ROBBINS, JHAN. *Yul Brynner: The Inscrutible King*. New York: Dodd, Mead & Company, 1987.

ROBINSON, ANDREW. *Satyajit Ray—The Inner Eye*. London: Andre Deutsch Ltd., 1989.

RODMAN, HOWARD. "I. A. L." *Village Voice*, June 14, 1988, pp. 71, 78.

ROSENBERG, EMILY S. " 'Foreign Affairs' after World War II: Connecting Sexual and International Politics." *Diplomatic History* 18, no. 1, Winter 1994, pp. 59–70.

ROTH, ALVIN, AND JEFF RUBENS. "The Mechanics of Bridge." *The Bridge World* Home Page, www.bridgeworld.com.

RÓZSA, MIKLÓS. *Double Life*. New York: Wynwood Press, 1989.

SARRIS, ANDREW. *Confessions of a Cultist*. New York: Simon and Schuster, 1970.

———. "Billy Wilder: Closet Romanticist." *Film Comment* 12, no. 4, July/Aug. 1976, pp. 7–9.

———. "Films in Focus: Billy Wilder and the Holocaust." *Village Voice*, May 4, 1982, p. 57.

———. "Films in Focus: Pieces of my Mind." *Village Voice*, May 18, 1982.

———. "Films in Focus: Western Movies." *Village Voice*, July 1, 1986, p. 71.

———. "Why Billy Wilder Belongs in the Pantheon." *Film Comment* 27, July/Aug. 1991, pp. 9–14.

SAUNDERS, THOMAS J. *Hollywood in Berlin: American Cinema and Weimar Germany*. Berkeley: University of California Press, 1994.

SCHEUER, PHILIP K. "Die Cast on Doings of Drunk." *Los Angeles Times*, Dec. 3, 1944, p. 22.

———. "Outcome of Christie Play Kept Dark Secret for Film." *Los Angeles Times*, July 14, 1957, p. V2.

SCHICKEL, RICHARD. "Old Hat: *Fedora*." *Time*, May 21, 1979, p. 125–26.

SCHLÖNDORFF, VOLKER. " 'Nobody Is Perfect:' Billy Wilder zum 85. Geburtstag," *Süddeutsche Zeitung*, June 21, 1991.

———. "The Apartment" (review), *Premiere*, April 1992, p. 127.

———. *Billy, How Did You Do It? Billy Wilder in Conversation with Volker Schlöndorff*. Arena series, BBC-TV, 1988.

SCHORSKE, CARL. *Fin-de Siècle Vienna: Politics and Culture*. New York: Vintage Books, 1981.

SCHULBERG, STUART. "A Letter about Billy Wilder." *Quarterly of Film, Radio and Television,* 7, no 4, Summer 1953.

SCHUMACH, MURRAY. "The Wilder—and Funnier—Touch." *The New York Times Magazine,* Jan. 24, 1960, pp. 30, 35, 38, 43.

———. "Bright Diamond." *New York Times Magazine,* May 26, 1963, pp. 80–81.

SELDIS, HENRY. "In the Galleries: Wilder Collection Astute." *Los Angeles Times,* Oct. 14, 1966, p. 14.

SHEINWOLD, ALFRED. *Five Weeks to Winning Bridge.* New York: Pocket Books, 1960.

SHIRER, WILLIAM. *The Rise and Fall of the Third Reich: A History of Nazi Germany.* New York: Simon and Schuster, 1960.

SHIVAS, MARK. "Yes, We Have No Naked Girls." *New York Times,* Oct. 12, 1969, p. D15.

SIMON, JOHN. "Belt and Suspenders." *Theater Arts,* no. 46, July, 1962, pp. 20–21, 70–73.

SIMON, NEIL. *Rewrites: A Memoir.* New York: Simon & Schuster, 1996.

SLIDE, ANTHONY. *The American Film Industry.* New York: Limelight, 1990.

SMITH, SALLY BEDELL. *In All His Glory: The Life of William S. Paley.* New York: Simon and Schuster, 1990.

SPOTO, DONALD. *Blue Angel: The Life of Marlene Dietrich.* New York: Doubleday, 1992.

———. *Madcap—The Life of Preston Sturges.* Boston: Little, Brown and Company, 1990.

SRAGOW, MICHAEL. "The Wilder Bunch." *Gentlemen's Quarterly* 84, no. 10, Oct. 1994, pp. 143–46.

STARKMANN, ALFRED. "Billy Wilder: Es Läuft ein grosses Drama über die Bühne." *Die Welt,* Dec. 27, 1989, p. 7.

STEEGMULLER, FRANCIS. "Onward and Upward with the Arts." *New Yorker,* Sept. 27, 1969, pp. 130–43.

STEPHENS, ROBERT, WITH MICHAEL COVENEY. *Knight Errant: Memoirs of a Vagabond Actor.* London: Hodder & Stoughton, 1995.

SWANSON, GLORIA. *Swanson on Swanson.* New York: Random House, 1980.

SWINDELL, LARRY. *Screwball: The Life of Carole Lombard.* New York: William Morrow and Co., 1975.

———. *The Last Hero: A Biography of Gary Cooper.* Garden City, N.Y.: Doubleday and Co., 1980.

SYMONETTE, LYS, AND KIM H. KOWALKE, eds. *Speak Low (When You Speak of Love): The Letters of Kurt Weill and Lotte Lenya.* Berkeley: University of California Press, 1996.

TARABORELLI, J. RANDY. *Laughing Till It Hurts: The Complete Life and Career of Carol Burnett.* New York: William Morrow and Co., 1988.

THATCHER, MARY ANNE. *Immigrants and the 1930s.* New York: Garland, 1990.

THOMAS, BOB. *Clown Prince of Hollywood: The Antic Life of Jack L. Warner.* New York: McGraw-Hill, 1990.

———. *Golden Boy: The Untold Story of William Holden.* New York: St. Martin's Press, 1983.

THOMAS, MIKE. "Bewitched, Bothered and BeWildered: A Conversation with the Great American Filmmaker." *Los Angeles Reader,* March 21, 1986, pp. 1, 8, 10–13.

THOMAS, TONY. *Film Score: The Art and Craft of Movie Music.* Burbank, Calif.: Riverwood Press, 1991.

———. *Music for the Movies.* New York: A. S. Barnes, 1973.

———. *The Films of Olivia de Havilland.* Secaucus, N.J.: Citadel Press, 1983.

THOMPSON, THOMAS. "Wilder's Dirty Joke Film Stirs a Furor." *Life* 58, Jan. 15, 1965, pp. 51–58.

THOMSON, DAVID. *A Biographical Dictionary of Film.* New York: William Morrow and Co., 1976.

TRASK, C. HOOPER. "Film Notes from Berlin." *New York Times,* March 15, 1931, sec. 9, p. 6.

TRAUNER, ALEXANDER, AND JEAN-PIERRE BERTHOMÉ. *Alexander Trauner: Décors de cinéma.* Paris: Jade-Flammarion, 1988.

TRUFFAUT, FRANÇOIS. *The Films in My Life.* New York: Simon and Schuster, 1975.

TURNER, ADRIAN. "Interview with I. A. L. Diamond." *Films and Filming,* May 1982, pp. 16–21.

UNITED STATES HOLOCAUST MEMORIAL MUSEUM. *Historical Atlas of the Holocaust.* New York: Simon & Schuster and Macmillan, 1996.

URSINI, JAMES. "AFI Oral History with John Seitz." Beverly Hills: American Film Institute, 1975.

VANDERBEETS, RICHARD. *George Sanders: An Exhausted Life.* New York: Madison Books, 1990.

VILIDAS, P. "A Life in Pictures." *House and Garden,* April 1989, pp. 154–60.

VIVIANI, CHRISTIAN. "Les Deux Fédora." *Positif* 210, Sept. 1978, pp. 24–27.

VOSS, HELMUT. "Billy Wilder hat Heimweh nach dem Kurfürstendamm." *Bonner Rundschau,* Feb. 7, 1973.

WALKER, ALEXANDER. *Audrey: Her Real Story.* London: Weidenfeld & Nicolson, 1994.

WARREN, DOUGLAS, WITH JAMES CAGNEY. *James Cagney: The Authorized Biography.* New York: St. Martin's Press, 1983.

WATTS, STEPHEN. "Noted on Britain's Screen Scene." *New York Times,* March 4, 1962, sec. 10, p. 7.

WECHSBERG, JOSEPH. *The Lost World of the Great Spas.* New York: Harper and Row, 1979.

WEINBERG, GERHARD L. *A World at Arms: A Global History of World War II.* New York: Cambridge University Press, 1994.

WHITE, SUSAN M. *The Cinema of Max Ophuls.* New York: Columbia University Press, 1995.

WHITE, TIMOTHY. "Looking Backward: James Cagney's Armchair Tour of Fifty Years in Showbiz." *Rolling Stone,* Feb. 18, 1982, pp. 21–24.

WIDENER, DON. *Lemmon: A Biography.* New York: Macmillan Publishing, 1975.

WILDER, BILLY. "Man sah überall nur Taschentücher." *Süddeutsche Zeitung Magazin,* July 1994, pp. 18–19.

———. "Movies Forever!" *The New Republic,* June 9, 1982, p. 23.

———. "One Head Is Better Than Two." *Films and Filming,* Feb. 1957.

———. *Der Prinz von Wales geht auf Urlaub: Berliner Reportagen, Feuilletons unk Kritiken der zwanziger Jahre.* Ed. Klaus Siebenhaar. Berlin: Fannet & Walz Verlag, 1996.

———. [Signed "Billie Wilder."] "Asta Nielsen's theatralische Sendung: ein Interview." *Die Bühne,* Feb. 1926, pp. 6–8.

———. [Signed "Billie Wilder."] "Bücher an den Mann bringen." *Der Querschnitt,* March 1930, pp. 192–94.

———. [Signed "Billie Wilder."] "Herr Ober, Bitte Einen Tänzer!" *Die Bühne,* June 9, 1927, pp. 34–36.

———. [Signed "Billie Wilder."] "Stroheim, der Mann, den man gern hasst." *Der Querschnitt,* April 1929, pp. 293–295.

———. [Signed "Billie Wilder."] "Whiteman feiert in Berlin Trimphe." *Die Stunde,* June 29, 1926.

———. [Signed "Billie Wilder."] "Wie wir unseren Studio-Film drehten." *Montag Morgen,* Feb. 10, 1930.

———. [Signed "Billie Wilder."] "Wir vom Filmstudio 1929." *Tempo,* July 23, 1929.

———. [Signed "Billie."] "Das Dorotheum steigt!" *Die Stunde,* 1925.

———. [Signed "Billie."] "Der Hungerkünstler Nicky beginnt heute in Wien zu fasten." *Die Stunde,* April 4, 1926, p. 9.

———. [Signed "Billie."] "Der Rosenkavalier am Rosenhügel." *Die Stunde,* August 1, 1925, p. 6.

———. [Signed "Billie."] "Die Kunst, sich umsonst anzuziehen." *Die Stunde,* Dec. 20, 1925, p. 5.

———. [Signed "Billie."] "Die Tiller-Girls sind da!" *Die Stunde,* 1926.

———. [Signed "Billie."] "Henry Barbusse in Wien." *Die Stunde,* Dec. 10, 1925, p. 4.

———. [Signed "Billie."] "Momentaufnahmen vom Bezirksgericht." *Die Stunde,* 1926.

———. [Signed "Billie."] "Passendes Weignachtsgeschenk für 12-bis 14 jährige Knaben." *Die Stunde,* 1925.

———. [Signed "Billie."] "Paul Whiteman, sein Schnurrbart, der Cobenzl, und der Heurige." *Die Stunde,* June 13, 1926, p. 7.

WILEY, MASON, AND DAMIEN BONA. *Inside Oscar: The Unofficial History of the Academy Awards.* New York: Ballantine Books, 1993.

WILLETT, JOHN. *Art and Politics in the Weimar Period.* New York: Da Capo Press, 1996.

WILMINGTON, M. "Saint Jack." *Film Comment* 29, March/April 1993, pp. 10–22.

WINECOFF, CHARLES. *Split Image—The Life of Anthony Perkins.* New York: Dutton, 1996.

WOOD, ROBIN. *Howard Hawks.* London: British Film Institute, 1981.

WOOD, TOM. *The Bright Side of Billy Wilder, Primarily.* Garden City, N.Y.: Doubleday and Co., 1970.

WOODCOCK, J. M. "The Name Dropper." *American Cinemeditor* 39, no. 4, Winter 1989/1990, p. 15.

WOODWARD, IAN. *Audrey Hepburn.* New York: St. Martin's Press, 1984.

WYMAN, DAVID. *Paper Walls: America and the Refugee Crisis, 1938–1941.* Amherst: University of Massachusetts Press, 1968.

———. *The Abandonment of the Jews: America and the Holocaust, 1941–1945.* New York: Pantheon, 1984.

YABLONSKY, LEWIS. *George Raft.* San Francisco: Mercury House, 1974.

YARROW, A. L. "Billy Wilder Decides to Sell Some of His Art Collection." *New York Times,* Aug. 30, 1989, p. C19.

YOUNGERMAN, JOSEPH. *My Seventy Years at Paramount Studios and the Directors Guild of America.* Los Angeles: Directors Guild of America, Inc., 1995.

YOUNGKIN, STEPHEN D., JAMES BIGWOOD, AND RAYMOND G. CABANA JR. *The Films of Peter Lorre.* Secaucus, N.J.: Citadel Press, 1982.

ZIEMKE, EARL F. *The U.S. Army in the Occupation of Germany, 1944–1946.* Washington, D.C.: Center of Military History, United States Army, 1975.

ZINNEMANN, FRED. *Fred Zinnemann: An Autobiography.* London: Bloomsbury, 1992.

ZINTZ, KARIN. "Verstand voller Rasierklingen." *Ostsee-Zeitung Rostock*, Sept. 15, 1992.

ZOGLIN, RICHARD. "The Class of the 20th Century," *Time,* Jan. 13, 1992.

ZOLOTOW, MAURICE. *Billy Wilder in Hollywood.* New York: Limelight Editions, 1987.

FILMOGRAPHY

DER TEUFELSREPORTER: IM NEBEL DER GROSSSTADT (1929). Deutsche Universalfilm Verleih. Black and white. Director: Ernst Laemmle; screenplay: Billie Wilder; cinematographer: Charles J. Stumar. Cast: Eddie Polo (Eddie, the reporter); Maria Forescu (Madame Lourdier); Jonas Garrison (Jonas); Fred Grosser (Maxe); Gritta Ley (Bessie). 65 minutes.

MENSCHEN AM SONNTAG (1929). Filmstudio Berlin. Black and white. Director: Robert Siodmak; screenplay: Billie Wilder, with Curt Siodmak; cinematographer: Eugen Schüfftan; lighting: Moritz Seeler; assistant: Fred Zinnemann. Cast: Brigitte Borchert (salesgirl); Christl Ehlers (would-be actress); Annie Schreyer (housewife); Erwin Splettstösser (taxi driver); Wolfgang von Waltershausen (wine salesman); with Kurt Gerron, Valeska Gert, and Ernst Verebes. 74 minutes.

DER MANN, DER SEINEN MÖRDER SUCHT (1931). Ufa. Black and white. Director: Robert Siodmak; producer: Erich Pommer; screenplay: Billie Wilder, Curt Siodmak, and Ludwig Hirschfeld, based on the play *Jim, der Mann mit der Narbe* by Ernst Neubach and the novella *The Tribulations of a Chinaman in China* by Jules Verne; cinematographers: Otto Baecker and Konstantin Irmen-Tschet; musical score: Friedrich Holländer and Franz Wachsmann; sound: Fritz Thiery. Cast: Heinz Rühmann (Hans Herfort); Lien Deyers (Kitty); Raimund Janitschek (Otto Kuttlapp); Hermann Speelmans (Jim); Gerhard Bienert (Schupo); Friedrich Holländer (conductor); Hans Leibelt (Adamowski). 98 minutes.

IHRE HOHEIT BEFIEHLT (1931). Ufa. Black and white. Director: Hanns Schwarz; screenplay: Paul Frank, Robert Liebmann, Billie Wilder; cinematographers: Konstantin Irmen-Tschet and Günther Rittau; music and lyrics: Richard Heymann, Ernst Neubach, and Robert Gilbert. Cast: Willy Fritsch (Lt. von Conradi); Käthe von Nagy (Princess Marie-Christine); Paul Hörbiger (Pipac); Reinhold Schünzel (Minister of State). 96 minutes. Note: *Ihre Hoheit befiehlt* was remade by Fox as *Adorable* (1933), directed by William Dieterle and starring Janet Gaynor; Wilder received story credit.

SEITENSPRÜNGE (1931). Ufa. Black and white. Director: Stefan Székely; screenplay: Ludwig Biro, Bobby E. Lüthge, and Karl Noti, from an idea by Billie Wilder; cinematographer: Walter Robert Lach; music and lyrics: Karl M. May, Fritz German, and Karl Brüll. Cast: Oskar Sima (Robert Burkhardt); Gerda Maurus (Annemarie); Paul Vincenti (Carlo); Jarmila Marton (Lupita). 81 minutes.

DER FALSCHE EHEMANN (1931). Ufa. Black and white. Director: Johannes Guter; screenplay: Paul Frank and Billie Wilder; cinematographer: Carl Hoffmann; musical score: Norbert Glanzberg; editor: Constantin Mick. Cast: Johannes Riemann (Peter and Paul Hanneman); Maria Paudler (Ruth Hannemann); Tibor Halmay (Maxim Tartakoff); Fritz Strehlen (Maharaja); Jessie Vihrog (Ines); Gustav Waldau (H.H. Hardegg); Martha Ziegler (Fraülein Schulze). 85 minutes.

EMIL UND DIE DETEKTIVE (1931). Ufa. Black and white. Director: Gerhard Lamprecht; producer: Günther Stapenhorst ; screenplay: Billie Wilder, based on the novel by Erich Kästner; cinematographer: Werner Brandes; musical score: Allan Gray. Cast: Rolf Wenkhaus (Emil); Käthe Haack (Emil's mother); Fritz Rasp (Grundeis); Rudolf Biebrach (policeman); Olga Engl (Emil's grandmother); Inge Landgut (Pony Hütchen); Hans Herrmann Schaufuss (Gustav); Hubert Schmitz (Professor); with Hans Richter, Hans Loehr, Ernst-Eberhard Reli, and Waldemar Kupczyk. 75 minutes. Note: *Emil und die Detektive* was remade by Gaumont-British Picture Corporation as *Emil and the Detectives* (1935), directed by Milton Rosmer; Wilder received credit for writing the original screenplay.

ES WAR EINMAL EIN WALZER (1932). Aafa Film. Black and white. Director: Victor Janson; screenplay: Billie Wilder; cinematographer: Heinrich Gärtner; musical score: Franz Lehár; editor: Ladislas Vajda Jr. Cast: Marta Eggerth (Steffi Pirzinger); Rolf von Goth (Rudi Möbius); Hermann Blass (Sauerwein); Fritz Greiner (coachman); Paul Hörbiger (Franz Pirzinger); Lizzi Natzler (Lucie Weidling); Albert Paulig (Pfennig); Ernst Verebes (Gustl Linzer); Lina Woiwode (Mrs. Zacherl); Ida Wüst (Mrs. Weidling). 79 minutes.

EIN BLONDER TRAUM (1932). Ufa. Black and white. Director: Paul Martin; producer: Erich Pommer; screenplay: Walter Reisch and Billie Wilder; cinematographers: Otto Baecker, Konstantin Irmen-Tschet, and Günther Rittau; musical score: Werner Richard Heymann and Gérard Jacobson. Cast: Willy Fritsch (Willy I); Willi Forst (Willy II); Lilian Harvey (Jou-Jou); Paul Hörbiger (Scarecrow); C. Hooper Trask (Mr. Merryman); Hans Deppe (secretary); Trude Hesterberg (Ilse). 84 minutes.

SCAMPOLO, EIN KIND DER STRASSE (1932). Bayerische Filmgesellschaft. Black and white. Director: Hans Steinhoff; screenplay: Max Kolpe and Billie Wilder, based on the play by Dario Niccodemi; cinematographes: Hans Androschin and Curt Courant; musical score: Franz Wachsmann and Artur Guttmann; editor: Ella Ensink. Cast: Dolly Haas (Scampolo); Karl Ludwig Diehl (Maximillian); Paul Hörbiger (Gabriel); Hedwig Bleibtreu (Mrs. Schmidt); Oskar Sima (Phillips, the banker). 87 minutes.

DAS BLAUE VOM HIMMEL (1932). Aafa Film. Black and white. Director: Victor Janson; screenplay: Max Kolpe and Billie Wilder; cinematographer: Heinrich Gärtner; musical score: Paul Abraham; editor: Else Baum. Cast: Marta Eggerth (Anni Mueller); Hermann Thimig (Hans Meier); Jakob Tiedtke (U-Papa); Ernst Verebes (Hugo); Fritz Kampers (Tobias); Hans Richter (Tommy); Margarete Schlegel ("Zigaretten-Cilly"); Walter Steinbeck (Piper). 82 minutes.

MADAME WÜNSCHT KEINE KINDER (1933). Director: Hans Steinhoff; screenplay: Max Kolpe and Billie Wilder, based on the book by Clément Vautel; cinematographers: Willy Goldberger and Hans Androschin; editor: Ella Ensink; music and lyrics: Bronislau Kaper, Walter Jurmann, Fritz Rotter, and Max Kolpe. Cast: Georg Alexander (Dr. Felix Rainer); Erika Glässner (Frau Wengert); Liane Haid (Madelaine Wengert); Lucie Mannheim (Luise); Hans Moser (Schlafwagenschaffner); Will Stettner (Adolf); Otto Wallburg (Herr Balsam). 86 minutes.

WAS FRAUEN TRÄUMEN (1933). Bayerische Filmgesellschaft. Black and white. Director: Géza von Bolváry; screenplay: Franz Schulz and Billie Wilder; cinematographer: Willy Goldberger; musical score: Robert Stolz. Cast: Nora Gregor (Rina Korff); Gustav Fröhlich (Walter König); Peter Lorre (Füssli); Kurt Horwitz (Levassor, alias John Constaninescu); with Kurt Lilien, Hilde Maroff, Erik Ode, Eric Steinbeck, and Otto Wallburg. 81 minutes. Note: *Was Frauen träumen* was remade by Universal as *One Exciting Adventure* (1934), directed by Ernst Frank and starring Binnie Barnes; Wilder received story credit.

MAUVAISE GRAINE (1934). Pathé Consortium Cinéma. Black and white. Directors: Billie Wilder and Alexander Esway; producers: Edouard Corniglion-Molinier and Georges Bernier; screenplay: Billie Wilder, Max Kolpe, Hans G. Lustig, and Claude-André Puget; cinematographers: Paul Cotteret and Maurice Delattre; musical score: Allan Gray and Franz Wachsmann. Cast:

Danielle Darrieux (Jeanette); Pierre Mingand (Henri Pasquier); Raimond Galle (Jean-la-Cravate); Paul Escoffier (Dr. Pasquier); Michel Duran (the Boss); Jean Wall (Zebra); Marcel Maupi (man in panama hat); Paul Velsa (man with peanuts); Georges Malkine (secretary); Georges Cahuzac (Sir); Gaby Héritier (Gaby). 77 minutes.

MUSIC IN THE AIR (1934). Fox Film Corporation. Black and white. Director: Joe May; producer: Erich Pommer; screenplay: Robert Liebmann, Billie Wilder, and Howard Irving Young, based on the musical by Oscar Hammerstein II and Jerome Kern; cinematographer: Ernest Palmer; musical adaptation: Franz Waxman. Cast: Gloria Swanson (Frieda); John Boles (Bruno Mahler); June Lang (Sieglinde); Al Shean (Dr. Lessing); Reginald Owen (Weber); Joseph Cawthorn (Uppman); Hobart Bosworth (Cornelius); Sara Haden (Martha); Marjorie Main (Anna); Roger Imhof (Burgomaster); Jed Prouty (Kirschner); Christian Rub (Zipfelhuber); Fuzzy Knight (Nick). 85 minutes.

UNDER PRESSURE (1935). Fox Film Corporation. Black and white. Director: Raoul Walsh; producer: Robert T. Kane; screenplay: Borden Chase, Noel Pierce, and Lester Cole, with revisions and additional dialogue by Billie Wilder, based on the novel *East River* by Borden Chase and Edward Doherty; cinematographers: Hal Mohr and L. W. O'Connell; art direction: Jack Otterson; costumes: William Lambert. Cast: Edmund Lowe (Shocker); Victor McLaglen (Jumbo); Florence Rice (Pat); Charles Bickford (Nipper); Ward Bond (fighter); Sig Rumann (doctor). 70 minutes.

LOTTERY LOVER (1935). Fox Film Corporation. Black and white. Director: Wilhelm Thiele; screenplay: Franz Schulz, Billie Wilder, and Hanns Schwartz, based on a story by Siegfried Herzig and Maurice Hanline; cinematographer: Bert Glennon; art direction: William Darling; costumes: Rene Hubert; music and lyrics by Jay Gorney and Don Hartman; editor: Dorothy Spencer. Cast: Lew Ayres (Frank Harrington); Pat Paterson (Patty); Peggy Fears (Gaby); Reginald Denny (Capt. Payne); Sterling Holloway (Harold Stump). 82 minutes.

CHAMPAGNE WALTZ (1937). Paramount Pictures. Black and white. Director: A. Edward Sutherland; producer: Harlan Thompson; screenplay: Frank Butler and Don Hartman, from a story by Billy Wilder and H. S. Kraft; cinematographer: William C. Mellor; editor: Paul Weatherwax; costumes: Travis Banton; music: Johann Strauss. Cast: Gladys Swarthout (Elsa Strauss); Fred MacMurray (Buzzy Bellew); Herman Bing (Max Snellinek); Jack Oakie (Happy Gallagher); Fritz Leiber (Franz Strauss); Rudolph Anders (Franz Joseph); Stanley Price (Johann Strauss). 85 minutes.

BLUEBEARD'S EIGHTH WIFE (1938). Paramount Pictures. Black and white. Director: Ernst Lubitsch; producer: Ernst Lubitsch; screenplay: Charles Brackett and Billy Wilder, based on the play by Alfred Savoir; cinematographer: Leo Tover; musical score: Werner R. Heymann and Frederick Hollander; costumes: Travis Banton; editor: William Shea; art directors: Hans Dreier and Robert Usher. Cast: Claudette Colbert (Nicole de Loiselle); Gary Cooper (Michael Brandon); Edward Everett Horton (Marquis de Loiselle); David Niven (Albert de Regnier); Elizabeth Patterson (Aunt Hedwige); Herman Bing (M. Pepinard); Warren Hymer (Kid Mulligan); Franklin Pangborn (hotel manager); Rolfe Sedan (floorwalker); Lawrence Grant (Prof. Urganzeff); Lionel Pape (M. Potin); Tyler Brooke (Clerk). 80 minutes.

THAT CERTAIN AGE (1938). Universal Pictures. Black and white. Director: Edward Ludwig; producer: Joe Pasternak; screenplay: Bruce Manning, from a story by F. Hugh Herbert, with uncredited contributions by Charles Brackett and Billy Wilder; cinematographer: Joseph A. Valentine; musical score: Harold Adamson and Jimmy McHugh; costumes: Vera West; editor: Bernard W. Burton; art director: Jack Otterson; musical director: Charles Previn. Cast: Deanna Durbin (Alice Fullerton); Melvyn Douglas (Vincent Bullitt); Jackie Cooper (Ken); Irene Rich (Mrs. Fullerton); Nancy Carroll (Grace Bristow); John Halliday (Fullerton); Jack Searl (Tony); Juanita Quigley (the pest); Peggy Stewart (Mary Lee); Charles Coleman (Stevens); Grant Mitchell (jeweler). 95 minutes.

MIDNIGHT (1939). Paramount Pictures. Black and white. Director: Mitchell Leisen; producer: Arthur Hornblow Jr.; screenplay: Charles Brackett and Billy Wilder, from a story by Edwin Justus Mayer and Franz Schulz; cinematographer: Charles Lang; musical score: Frederick Hollander; art directors: Hans Dreier and Robert Usher; editor: Doane Harrison; special effects: Farciot Edouart. Cast: Claudette Colbert (Eve Peabody); Don Ameche (Tibor Czerny); John Barrymore (Georges Flammarion); Francis Lederer (Jacques Picot); Mary Astor (Helene Flammarion); Elaine Barrie (Simone); Hedda Hopper (Stephanie); Rex O'Malley (Marcel); Monty Woolley (Judge); Armand Kaliz (Lebon); Eddie Conrad (Prince Potopienko); Billy Daniels (Roger). 94 minutes.

WHAT A LIFE (1939). Paramount Pictures. Black and white. Director: Jay Theodore Reed; producer: Jay Theodore Reed; screenplay: Charles Brackett and Billy Wilder, based on the play by Clifford Goldsmith; cinematographer: Victor Milner; editor: William Shea; art directors: Hans Dreier and Earl Hedrick. Cast: Jackie Cooper (Henry Aldrich); Betty Field (Barbara Pearson); James Corner (George Bigelow); Hedda Hopper (Mrs. Aldrich); John Howard (Mr. Nelson); Janice Logan (Miss Shea); Dorothy Stickney (Miss Wheeler); Sidney Miller (Pinkie Peters); Roberta Smith (Gertie); Lionel Stander (Ferguson). 75 minutes.

NINOTCHKA (1939). MGM. Black and white. Director: Ernst Lubitsch; producer: Ernst Lubitsch; screenplay: Charles Brackett, Billy Wilder, and Walter Reisch, from a story by Melchior Lengyel; cinematographer: William H. Daniels; musical score: Werner R. Heymann; art director: Cedric Gibbons; costumes: Adrian; editor: Gene Ruggiero. Cast: Greta Garbo (Ninotchka); Melvyn Douglas (Count Leon d'Algout); Ina Claire (Grand Duchess Swana); Béla Lugosi (Commissar Razinin); Sig Rumann (Iranoff); Felix Bressart (Buljanoff); Alexander Granach (Kopalski); Gregory Gaye (Rakonin); Rolfe Sedan (hotel manager); Edwin Maxwell (Mercier); Richard Carle (Gaston); Mary Forbes (Lady Lavenham); Peggy Moran (French maid); George Tobias (Russian visa officer). 110 minutes.

RHYTHM ON THE RIVER (1940). Paramount Pictures. Black and white. Director: Victor Schertzinger; producer: William LeBaron; screenplay: Dwight Taylor, from a story by Jacques Théry and Billy Wilder; cinematographer: Ted Tetzlaff; musical score: Johnny Burke, James V. Monaco, and Victor Schertzinger; costumes: Edith Head; editor: Hugh Bennett; art directors: Hans Dreier and Ernst Fegté; musical director: Victor Young. Cast: Bing Crosby (Bob Sommers); Mary Martin (Cherry Lane); Basil Rathbone (Oliver Courtney); Oscar Levant (Billy Starbuck); Oscar Shaw (Charlie Goodrich); Charley Grapewin (Uncle Caleb); Lillian Cornell (Millie Starling); William Frawley (Mr. Westlake); Jeanne Cagney (country cousin); Helen Bertram (Aunt Delia); John Scott Trotter (himself); Ken Carpenter (announcer); Charles Lane (Bernard Schwartz); Harry Barris (bass player). 92 minutes.

ARISE, MY LOVE (1940). Paramount Pictures. Black and white. Director: Mitchell Leisen; producer: Arthur Hornblow Jr.; screenplay: Charles Brackett and Billy Wilder, from a story by Benjamin Glazer and John S. Toldy, with additional contributions by Jacques Théry; cinematographer: Charles Lang; musical score: Victor Young; art directors: Hans Dreier and Robert Usher; costumes: Irene; editor: Doane Harrison. Cast: Claudette Colbert (Augusta Nash); Ray Milland (Tom Martin); Dennis O'Keefe (Shep); Walter Abel (Mr. Phillips); Dick Purcell ("Pinky" O'Connor); George Zucco (prison governor); Frank Puglia (Father Jacinto); Esther Dale (secretary); Paul Leyssac (Bresson); Ann Codee (Mme. Bresson); Stanley Logan (Col. Tubbs Brown); Lionel Pape (Lord Kettlebrook); Aubrey Mather (Achille); Cliff Nazarro (Botzelberg). 110 minutes.

HOLD BACK THE DAWN (1941). Paramount Pictures. Black and white. Director: Mitchell Leisen; producer: Arthur Hornblow Jr.; screenplay: Charles Brackett and Billy Wilder, based on a treatment and novel by Ketti Frings; cinematographer: Leo Tover; musical score: Victor Young; art directors: Hans Dreier and Robert Usher; costumes: Edith Head; editor: Doane Harrison. Cast: Charles Boyer (Georges Iscovescu); Olivia de Havilland (Emmy Brown); Paulette Goddard (Anita); Victor Francen (Van Den Luecken); Walter Abel (Inspector Hammock); Curt Bois (Bonbois); Rosemary De Camp (Berta Kurz); Eric Feldary (Josef Kurz); Nestor Paiva

(Flores); Eva Puig (Lupita); Micheline Cheirel (Christine); Madeleine Lebeau (Annie); Billy Lee (Tony); Mikhail Rasumny (mechanic); Charles Arnt (Mr. MacAdams); Arthur Loft (Mr. Elvestad); Mitchell Leisen (Mr. Saxon); Brian Donlevy (movie actor); Veronica Lake (movie actress); 115 minutes.

BALL OF FIRE (1941). Samuel Goldwyn. Black and white. Director: Howard Hawks; producer: Samuel Goldwyn; screenplay: Charles Brackett and Billy Wilder, based on a story by Billy Wilder and Thomas Monroe; cinematographer: Gregg Toland; musical score: Alfred Newman; costumes: Edith Head; editor: Daniel Mandell; art director: Perry Ferguson. Cast: Gary Cooper (Prof. Bertram Potts); Barbara Stanwyck (Sugarpuss O'Shea); Oskar Homolka (Prof. Gurkakoff); Henry Travers (Prof. Jerome); S. Z. Sakall (Prof. Magenbruch); Tully Marshall (Prof. Robinson); Leonid Kinskey (Prof. Quintana); Richard Haydn (Prof. Oddly); Aubrey Mather (Prof. Peagram); Allen Jenkins (garbage man); Dana Andrews (Joe Lilac); Dan Duryea (Pastrami); Ralph Peters (Asthma); Kathleen Howard (Miss Bragg); Mary Field (Miss Totten); Alan Rhein (Horseface); Eddie Foster (Pinstripe); Aldrich Bowker (justice of the peace); Addison Richards (district attorney); Pat West (bum); Kenneth Howell (college boy); Tommy Ryan (newsboy); Tim Ryan (cop); William A. Lee (Benny the Creep); Geraldine Fissette (hula dancer); Gene Krupa (himself). 111 minutes.

THE MAJOR AND THE MINOR (1942). Paramount Pictures. Black and white. Director: Billy Wilder; producer: Arthur Hornblow Jr.; screenplay: Charles Brackett and Billy Wilder, based on the story "Sunny Goes Home" by Fanny Kilbourne and the play *Connie Goes Home* by Edward Childs Carpenter; cinematographer: Leo Tover; musical score: Robert Emmett Dolan; art directors: Roland Anderson and Hans Dreier; costumes: Edith Head; editor: Doane Harrison; assistant director: Charles C. Coleman Jr.; makeup: Wally Westmore. Cast: Ginger Rogers (Susan Applegate); Ray Milland (Major Philip Kirby); Rita Johnson (Pamela Hill); Robert Benchley (Mr. Osborne); Diana Lynn (Lucy Hill); Edward Fielding (Colonel Hill); Frankie Thomas (Cadet Osborne); Raymond Roe (Cadet Wigton); Charles Smith (Cadet Korner); Larry Nunn (Cadet Babcock); Billy Dawson (Cadet Miller); Lela Rogers (Mrs. Applegate); Aldrich Bowker (Reverend Doyle); Boyd Irwin (Major Griscom); Byron Shores (Captain Durand); Richard Fiske (Will Duffy); Norma Varden (Mrs. Osborne); Gretl Sherk (Miss Shackleford). 100 minutes.

FIVE GRAVES TO CAIRO (1943). Paramount Pictures. Black and white. Director: Billy Wilder; producer: Charles Brackett; screenplay: Charles Brackett and Billy Wilder, based on the play *Hotel Imperial* by Lajos Biró; cinematographer: John F. Seitz; musical score: Miklós Rózsa; costumes: Edith Head; editor: Doane Harrison; art directors: Hans Dreier and Ernst Fegté; makeup: Wally Westmore. Cast: Franchot Tone (John J. Bramble); Anne Baxter (Mouche); Erich von Stroheim (Field Marshal Erwin Rommel); Akim Tamiroff (Farid); Fortunio Bonanova (General Sebastiano); Peter Van Eyck (Lieutenant Schwegler). 96 minutes.

DOUBLE INDEMNITY (1944). Paramount Pictures. Black and white. Director: Billy Wilder; producer: Joseph Sistrom; screenplay: Raymond Chandler and Billy Wilder, based on the novel by James M. Cain; cinematographer: John F. Seitz; musical score: Miklós Rózsa; costumes: Edith Head; editor: Doane Harrison; art directors: Hans Dreier and Hal Pereira; makeup: Wally Westmore. Cast: Fred MacMurray (Walter Neff); Barbara Stanwyck (Phyllis Dietrichson); Edward G. Robinson (Barton Keyes); Porter Hall (Mr. Jackson); Jean Heather (Lola Dietrichson); Tom Powers (Mr. Dietrichson); Byron Barr (Nino Zachette); Richard Gaines (Mr. Norton); Fortunio Bonanova (Sam Gorlopis); John Philliber (Joe Pete); Bess Flowers (Norton's secretary); Kernan Cripps (conductor); Harold Garrison (redcap); Oscar Smith (Pullman porter); Betty Farrington (maid); Sam McDaniel (Charlie). 107 minutes.

THE LOST WEEKEND (1945). Paramount Pictures. Black and white. Director: Billy Wilder; producer: Charles Brackett; screenplay: Charles Brackett and Billy Wilder, based on the novel by Charles R. Jackson; cinematographer: John F. Seitz; musical score: Miklós Rózsa; costumes: Edith Head; editor: Doane Harrison; sound: Stanley Cooley and Joel Moss; art directors: Hans Dreier and A. Earl Hedrick; special effects: Farciot Edouart and Gordon Jennings; makeup:

Wally Westmore. Cast: Ray Milland (Don Birnam); Jane Wyman (Helen St. James); Phillip Terry (Wick Birnam); Howard Da Silva (Nat); Doris Dowling (Gloria); Frank Faylen (Bim); Mary Young (Mrs. Deveridge); Anita Sharp-Bolster (Mrs. Foley); Lillian Fontaine (Mrs. St. James). 101 minutes.

THE EMPEROR WALTZ (1948). Paramount Pictures. Technicolor. Director: Billy Wilder; producer: Charles Brackett; screenplay: Charles Brackett and Billy Wilder; cinematographer: George Barnes; musical score: Johnny Burke and Victor Young; costumes: Edith Head and Gile Steele; editor: Doane Harrison; art directors: Hans Dreier and Franz Bachelin; assistant director: Charles C. Coleman Jr.; set decorators: Sam Comer and Paul Huldschinsky; sound: Stanley Cooley and John Cope; choreography: Billy Daniels; process photography: Farciot Edouart; special photographic effects: Gordon Jennings; makeup: Wally Westmore. Cast: Bing Crosby (Virgil Smith); Joan Fontaine (Johanna Augusta Franziska von Stoltzenberg-Stoltzenberg); Roland Culver (Baron Holenia); Lucile Watson (Princess Bitotska); Richard Haydn (Emperor Francis-Joseph); Harold Vermilyea (chamberlain); Sig Rumann (Dr. Zwieback); Julia Dean (Archduchess Stephanie); Bert Prival (chauffeur); Alma Macrorie (inn proprietor); Roberta Jonay (chambermaid); John Goldsworthy (officer); Doris Dowling (Tyrolean girl). 106 minutes.

A FOREIGN AFFAIR (1948). Paramount Pictures. Black and white. Director: Billy Wilder; producer: Charles Brackett; screenplay: Charles Brackett, Billy Wilder, and Richard L. Breen, based on a story by David Shaw and Robert Harari; cinematographer: Charles Lang; musical score: Frederick Hollander; art directors: Hans Dreier and Walter H. Tyler; costumes: Edith Head; editor: Doane Harrison; assistant director: Charles C. Coleman Jr.; set decorators: Sam Comer and Ross Dowd; process photographers: Farciot Edouart and Dewey Wrigley; sound: Hugo Grenzbach and Walter Oberst; special effects: Gordon Jennings; makeup: Wally Westmore. Cast: Jean Arthur (Phoebe Frost); Marlene Dietrich (Erika von Schlütow); John Lund (Capt. John Pringle); Millard Mitchell (Col. Rufus J. Plummer); Peter von Zerneck (Hans Otto Birgel); Stanley Prager (Mike); Raymond Bond (Pennecot); Boyd Davis (Giffin); Robert Malcolm (Kramer); Charles Meredith (Yandell); Michael Raffetto (Salvatore); Damian O'Flynn (lieut. colonel); Frank Fenton (Major Mathews); James Larmore (Lieut. Hornby); Harland Tucker (Gen. McAndrew); William Neff (Lieut. Thompson); George M. Carleton (Gen. Finney); Gordon Jones (M.P.); Freddie Steele (M.P.). 116 minutes.

SUNSET BOULEVARD (1950). Paramount Pictures. Black and white. Director: Billy Wilder; producer: Charles Brackett; screenplay: Charles Brackett, Billy Wilder, and D.M. Marshman Jr.; cinematographer: John F. Seitz; musical score: Franz Waxman; costumes: Edith Head; editors: Doane Harrison and Arthur P. Schmidt; assistant director: Charles C. Coleman Jr.; set decorators: Sam Comer, Ray Moyer, and John Meehan; sound: John Cope and Harry Lindgren; art director: Hans Dreier; process photographer: Farciot Edouart; special effects: Gordon Jennings; makeup: Wally Westmore and Karl Silvera. Cast: William Holden (Joe Gillis); Gloria Swanson (Norma Desmond); Erich von Stroheim (Max von Mayerling); Nancy Olson (Betty Schaefer); Fred Clark (Sheldrake); Lloyd Gough (Morino); Jack Webb (Artie Green); Franklyn Farnum (mortician); Larry J. Blake (repo man); Charles Dayton (repo man); Cecil B. DeMille (himself); Hedda Hopper (herself); Buster Keaton (himself); Anna Q. Nilsson (herself); H. B. Warner (himself); Ray Evans (himself); Jay Livingston (himself). 110 minutes.

ACE IN THE HOLE (1951). Paramount Pictures. Black and white. Director: Billy Wilder; producer: Billy Wilder; screenplay: Billy Wilder, Walter Newman, and Lesser Samuels; cinematographer: Charles Lang; musical score: Hugo Friedhofer; costumes: Edith Head; editors: Doane Harrison and Arthur P. Schmidt; set decorators: Sam Comer and Ray Moyer; process photographer: Farciot Edouart; sound: Gene Garvin and Harold C. Lewis; art directors: Hal Pereira and A. Earl Hedrick; makeup: Wally Westmore. Cast: Kirk Douglas (Chuck Tatum); Jan Sterling (Lorraine); Robert Arthur (Herbie Cook); Porter Hall (Jacob Q. Boot); Frank Cady (Mr. Federber); Richard Benedict (Leo Minosa); Ray Teal (sheriff); Lewis Martin (McCardle); John Berkes (Papa Minosa); Frances Domingues (Mama Minosa); Gene Evans (deputy sheriff); Frank Jaquet (Smollett); Harry Harvey (Dr. Hilton); Bob Bumpas (radio announcer); Geraldine Hall (Mrs. Federber); Richard Gaines (Nagel); Paul D. Merrill (Federber boy); Stewart Kirk Clawson (Federber boy); John Stuart Fulton (boy); Bob Kortman (digger); Edith Evanson (Miss Deverich); Ralph Moody (miner); Claire Du Brey (spinster); William Fawcett (sad-faced man); Basil Chester (Indian). 111 minutes. Note: The film was released as *The Big Carnival*.

STALAG 17 (1953). Paramount Pictures. Black and white. Director: Billy Wilder; producer: Billy Wilder; screenplay: Billy Wilder and Edwin Blum, based on the play by Donald Bevan and Edmund Trzcinski; cinematographer: Ernest Laszlo; editorial advisor: Doane Harrison; musical score: Franz Waxman; editor: George Tomasini; associate producer: William Schorr; art directors: Franz Bachelin and Hal Pereira; set decorators: Sam Comer and Ray Moyer; sound: Gene Garvin and Harold C. Lewis; special effects: Gordon Jennings; makeup: Wally Westmore. Cast: William Holden (Sefton); Don Taylor (Lieut. Dunbar); Otto Preminger (von Scherbach); Robert Strauss (Stosh "Animal" Krusawa); Harvey Lembeck (Harry Shapiro); Richard Erdman (Hoffy); Peter Graves (Price); Neville Brand (Duke); Sig Rumann (Schulz); Michael Moore (Manfredi); Peter Baldwin (Johnson); Robinson Stone (Joey); Robert Shawley (Blondie); William Pearson (Marko); Gil Stratton Jr. (Cookie); Jay Lawrence (Bagradian); Erwin Kalser (Geneva man); Edmund Trzcinski (Triz); Tommy Cook (prisoner). 120 minutes.

SABRINA (1954) Paramount Pictures. Black and white. Director: Billy Wilder; producer: Billy Wilder; screenplay: Billy Wilder, Samuel A. Taylor, Ernest Lehman, based on the play *Sabrina Fair* by Taylor; cinematographer: Charles Lang; musical score: Frederick Hollander; costumes: Edith Head; editor: Arthur P. Schmidt; assistant director: C. C. Coleman Jr.; editorial advisor: Doane Harrison; art directors: Hal Pereira and Walter H. Tyler; set decorators: Sam Comer and Ray Moyer; sound: John Cope and Harold Lewis; special effects: John P. Fulton; process photographer: Farciot Edouart; makeup: Wally Westmore. Cast: Humphrey Bogart (Linus Larrabee); Audrey Hepburn (Sabrina Fairchild); William Holden (David Larrabee); Walter Hampden (Oliver Larrabee); John Williams (Thomas Fairchild); Martha Hyer (Elizabeth Tyson); Joan Vohs (Gretchen Van Horn); Marcel Dalio (Baron St. Fontanel); Marcel Hillaire (professor); Nella Walker (Maude Larrabee); Francis X. Bushman (Mr. Tyson); Ellen Corby (Miss McCardle); Nancy Kulp (maid). 113 minutes.

THE SEVEN YEAR ITCH (1955). Twentieth Century–Fox. Color by DeLuxe. Director: Billy Wilder; producers: Charles K. Feldman and Billy Wilder; screenplay: Billy Wilder and George Axelrod, based on the play by Axelrod; cinematographer: Milton Krasner; musical score: Alfred Newman; costumes: Travilla; editor: Hugh S. Fowler; associate producer: Doane Harrison; title design: Saul Bass; art directors: George W. Davis and Lyle R. Wheeler; special effects: Ray Kellogg; sound: Harry M. Leonard and E. Clayton Ward; makeup: Ben Nye and Whitey Snyder; set decorators: Stuart A. Reiss and Walter M. Scott; assistant director: Joseph E. Rickards. Cast: Marilyn Monroe (The Girl); Tom Ewell (Richard Sherman); Evelyn Keyes (Helen Sherman); Sonny Tufts (Tom MacKenzie); Robert Strauss (Mr. Kruhulik); Oskar Homolka (Dr. Brubaker); Marguerite Chapman (Miss Morris); Victor Moore (plumber); Roxanne (Elaine); Donald MacBride (Mr. Brady); Carolyn Jones (Miss Finch); Butch Bernard (Ricky Sherman); Doro Merande (waitress); Dorothy Ford (Indian girl). 105 minutes.

THE SPIRIT OF ST. LOUIS (1957). Warner Bros. Warnercolor. CinemaScope. Director: Billy Wilder; producer: Leland Hayward; screenplay: Billy Wilder, Wendell Mayes, and Charles Lederer, based on the book by Charles A. Lindbergh; cinematographers: Robert Burks and J. Peverell Marley; musical score: Franz Waxman; editor: Arthur P. Schmidt; assistant director: Charles C. Coleman Jr.; associate producer: Doane Harrison; art director: Art Loel; makeup: Gordon Bau; technical advisors: Harlan A. Gurney and Major General Victor Bertrandias; special effects: Hans F. Koenekamp; set decorator: William L. Kuehl; special effects: Louis Lichtenfield; aerial supervisor: Paul Mantz; sound: M.A. Merrick; aerial photographer: Tom Tutwiler. Cast: James Stewart (Charles Lindbergh); Murray Hamilton (Bud Gurney); Patricia Smith (mirror girl); Bartlett Robinson (B. F. Mahoney); Marc Connelly (Father Hussman); Arthur Space (Donald Hall); Charles Watts (O. W. Schultz). 135 minutes.

LOVE IN THE AFTERNOON (1957). Allied Artists. Black and white. Director: Billy Wilder; producer: Billy Wilder; screenplay: Billy Wilder and I. A. L. Diamond, based on the novel *Ariane* by Claude Anet; cinematographer: William C. Mellor; musical score: Franz Waxman; art director: Alexander Trauner; editor: Léonide Azar; associate producers: Doane Harrison and William Schorr; songs: Henri Betti, Matty Malneck, F. D. Marchetti, André Hornez, and Maurice De Feaurdy; sound: Jean De Bretagne; assistant director: Paul Feyder; second-unit director: Noel Howard. Cast: Gary Cooper (Frank Flannagan); Audrey Hepburn (Ariane Chavasse); Maurice Chevalier (Claude Chavasse); Van Doude (Michel); John McGiver (Monsieur X); Lise Bourdin (Madame X); Bonifas (commissioner of police); Claude Ariel (existentialist); Olivia Chevalier (child in garden); Alexander Trauner (artist); Audrey Wilder (brunette). 130 minutes.

WITNESS FOR THE PROSECUTION (1957). United Artists. Black and white. Director: Billy Wilder; producers: Arthur Hornblow Jr. and Edward Small; screenplay: Billy Wilder and Harry Kurnitz, based on the play by Agatha Christie; cinematographer: Russell Harlan; art director: Alexander Trauner; musical score: Matty Malneck; costumes: Edith Head and Joe King; editor: Daniel Mandell; set decorator: Howard Bristol; assistant director: Emmett Emerson; associate producer: Doane Harrison; sound: Fred Lau; makeup: Gustaf Norin, Harry Ray, and Ray Sebastian. Cast: Tyrone Power (Leonard Vole); Marlene Dietrich (Christine Vole); Charles Laughton (Sir Wilfrid Robarts); Elsa Lanchester (Miss Plimsoll); John Williams (Brogan-Moore); Henry Daniell (Mayhew); Ian Wolfe (Carter); Torin Thatcher (Mr. Myers); Norma Varden (Mrs. French); Una O'Connor (Janet McKenzie); Francis Compton (judge); Philip Tonge (Inspector Hearne); Ruta Lee (Diana). 116 minutes.

SOME LIKE IT HOT (1959). United Artists/Mirisch Company/Ashton Productions. Black and white. Director: Billy Wilder; producer: Billy Wilder; screenplay: Billy Wilder and I. A. L. Diamond, based on the film *Fanfaren des Liebe*, written by M. Logan and Robert Thoeren; cinematographer: Charles Lang; musical score: Adolph Deutsch; art director: Ted Haworth; costumes: Orry-Kelly; editor: Arthur P. Schmidt; associate producers: I. A. L. Diamond and Doane Harrison; set decorator: Edward G. Boyle; makeup: Emile LaVigne; sound: Fred Lau; song supervisor: Matty Malneck; assistant director: Sam Nelson; special effects: Milt Rice. Cast: Marilyn Monroe (Sugar Kane); Tony Curtis (Joe); Jack Lemmon (Jerry); George Raft (Spats); Pat O'Brien (Mulligan); Joe E. Brown (Osgood Fielding); Nehemiah Persoff (Little Bonaparte); Joan Shawlee (Sweet Sue); Billy Gray (Sid Poliakoff); George E. Stone (Toothpick Charlie); Dave Barry (Beinstock); Mike Mazurki (henchman); Harry Wilson (henchman); Beverly Wills (Dolores); Barbara Drew (Nellie); Edward G. Robinson Jr. (Paradise). 119 minutes.

THE APARTMENT (1960). United Artists/Mirisch Company. Black and white. Panavision. Director: Billy Wilder; screenplay: Billy Wilder and I. A. L. Diamond; cinematographer: Joseph LaShelle; art director: Alexander Trauner; musical score: Adolph Deutsch; editor: Daniel Mandell; producer: Billy Wilder; associate producers: I. A. L. Diamond and Doane Harrison; set decorator: Edward G. Boyle; sound: Gordon Sawyer and Fred Lau; assistant director: Hal W. Polaire; makeup: Harry Ray; special effects: Milt Rice; script supervisor: May Wale. Cast: Jack Lemmon (C. C. "Bud" Baxter); Shirley MacLaine (Fran Kubelik); Fred MacMurray (J. D. Sheldrake); Jack Kruschen (Dr. Dreyfuss); Ray Walston (Joe Dobisch); Frances Weintraub Lax (Mrs. Lieberman); Hope Holiday (Margie MacDougall); Johnny Seven (Karl Matuschka); Naomi Stevens (Mrs. Dreyfuss); Willard Waterman (Mr. Vanderhof); Joan Shawlee (Sylvia); Edie Adams (Miss Olsen); David Lewis (Mr. Kirkeby); David White (Mr. Eichelberger); Hal Smith (Santa Claus); Joyce Jameson (blonde). 125 minutes.

ONE, TWO, THREE (1961). United Artists/Mirisch Company/Pyramid Productions. Black and white. Panavision. Director: Billy Wilder; producer: Billy Wilder; screenplay: Billy Wilder and I. A. L. Diamond, based on the play by Ferenc Molnár; cinematographer: Daniel L. Fapp; art director: Alexander Trauner; associate producers: I. A. L. Diamond and Doane Harrison; musical score: André Previn; editor: Daniel Mandell; sound: Basil Fenton-Smith; assistant director: Tom Pevsner; special effects: Milt Rice. Cast: James Cagney (MacNamara); Horst

Buchholz (Otto Ludwig Piffl); Pamela Tiffin (Scarlett Hazeltine); Arlene Francis (Phyllis MacNamara); Howard St. John (Mr. Hazeltine); Hanns Lothar (Schlemmer); Leon Askin (Peripetchikoff); Ralf Wolter (Borodenko); Peter Capell (Mishkin); Karl Lieffen (Fritz); Hubert von Meyerinck (Count von Droste-Schattenburg); Lois Bolton (Mrs. Hazeltine); Til Kiwe (reporter); Henning Schlüter (Dr. Bauer); Lilo Pulver (Ingeborg); Christine Allen (Cindy MacNamara); John Allen (Tommy MacNamara); Ivan Arnold (M.P.); Klaus Becker (policeman); Max Buchsbaum (tailor); Werner Buttler (policeman); Red Buttons (M.P.); Paul Bos (Krause); Jacques Chevalier (Pierre); Ingrid DeToro (stewardess); Otto Friebel (interrogator); Werner Hessenland (shoe salesman); Jaspar von Oertzen (haberdasher). 115 minutes.

IRMA LA DOUCE (1963). United Artists. Technicolor. Panavision. Director: Billy Wilder; producer: Billy Wilder; screenplay: Billy Wilder and I. A. L. Diamond, based on the musical by Alexandre Breffort and Marguerite Monnot; cinematographer: Joseph LaShelle; art director: Alexander Trauner; musical score: André Previn; costumes: Orry-Kelly; editor: Daniel Mandell; associate producers: I. A. L. Diamond and Doane Harrison; assistant director: Hal W. Polaire; special effects: Milton Rice. Cast: Jack Lemmon (Nestor Patou); Shirley MacLaine (Irma); Lou Jacobi (Moustache); Bruce Yarnell (Hippolyte); Herschel Bernardi (Inspector Lefevre); Hope Holiday (Lolita); Joan Shawlee (Amazon Annie); Grace Lee Whitney (Kiki the Cossack); Paul Dubov (Andre); Howard McNear (concierge); Cliff Osmond (Police Sergeant); Diki Lerner (Jojo); Herb Jones (Casablanca Charlie); Ruth Earl (one of the Zebra twins); Jane Earl (one of the zebra twins); Tura Satana (Suzette Wong); Lou Krugman (first customer); James Brown (Texan); Bill Bixby (tattooed sailor); Harriette Young (Mimi the MauMau); Sheryl Deauville (Carmen); James Caan (uncredited extra). 147 minutes.

KISS ME, STUPID (1964). Mirisch Company/Lopert Pictures. Black and white. Panavision. Director: Billy Wilder; producer: Billy Wilder; screenplay: Billy Wilder and I. A. L. Diamond, based on the play *L'Ora della Fantasia* by Anna Bonacci; cinematographer: Joseph LaShelle; musical score: André Previn, George Gershwin, and Ira Gershwin; art director: Alexander Trauner; costumes: Wesley Jeffries; editor: Daniel Mandell; producer: Billy Wilder; associate producers: I. A. L. Diamond and Doane Harrison; set decorator: Edward G. Boyle; assistant director: Charles C. Coleman Jr.; makeup: Loren Cosand and Emile LaVigne; art director: Robert Luthardt; sound: Clem Portman; special effects: Milton Rice. Cast: Dean Martin (Dino); Kim Novak (Polly the Pistol); Ray Walston (Orville J. Spooner); Felicia Farr (Zelda Spooner); Cliff Osmond (Barney Milsap); Barbara Pepper (Big Bertha); James Ward (milkman); Doro Merande (Mrs. Pettibone); Howard McNear (Mr. Pettibone); Bobo Lewis (waitress); Tommy Nolan (Johnnie Mulligan); Alice Pearce (Mrs. Mulligan); John Fiedler (Rev. Carruthers); Arlen Stuart (Rosalie Schultz); Cliff Norton (Mack Gray); Mel Blanc (Dr. Sheldrake); Eileen O'Neal (showgirl); Susan Wedell (showgirl); Bernd Hoffmann (bartender); Henry Gibson (Smith); Alan Dexter (Wesson); Henry Beckman (truck driver). 124 minutes.

THE FORTUNE COOKIE (1966). United Artists/Mirisch Company/Phalanx/Jalem. Black and white. Panavision. Director: Billy Wilder; producer: Billy Wilder; screenplay: Billy Wilder and I. A. L. Diamond; cinematographer: Joseph LaShelle; musical score: André Previn; costumes: Chuck Arrico and Paula Giokaris; editor: Daniel Mandell; associate producers: I. A. L. Diamond and Doane Harrison; special effects: Sass Bedig; set decorator Edward G. Boyle; makeup: Lauren Cosand; art director: Robert Luthardt; sound: Robert Martin; assistant director: Jack N. Reddish; makeup: Robert J. Schiffer. Cast: Jack Lemmon (Harry Hinkle); Walter Matthau (Willie Gingrich); Ron Rich (Luther "Boom Boom" Jackson); Judi West (Sandy); Cliff Osmond (Purkey); Lurene Tuttle (Mother Hinkle); Harry Holcombe (O'Brien); Les Tremayne (Thompson); Lauren Gilbert (Kincaid); Marge Redmond (Charlotte Gingrich); Noam Pitlik (Max); Harry Davis (Dr. Krugman); Ann Shoemaker (Sister Veronica); Maryesther Denver (nurse); Ned Glass (Doc Schindler); Sig Rumann (Prof. Winterhalter); Archie Moore (Mr. Jackson); Howard McNear (Mr. Cimoli); William Christopher (intern); Don Reed (newscaster). 125 minutes.

THE PRIVATE LIFE OF SHERLOCK HOLMES (1970). United Artists/Mirisch Company. Color by DeLuxe. Panavision. Director: Billy Wilder; producer: Billy Wilder; screenplay: Billy Wilder and I. A. L. Diamond, based on characters created by Arthur Conan Doyle; cinematographer: Christopher Challis; musical score: Miklós Rózsa; art director: Alexander Trauner; costumes: Julie Harris; editor: Ernest Walter. Cast: Robert Stephens (Sherlock Holmes); Colin Blakely (Dr. John Watson); Genevive Page (Gabrielle Valladon); Christopher Lee (Mycroft Holmes); Tamara Toumanova (Patrova); Clive Revill (Rogozhin); Irene Handl (Mrs. Hudson); Mollie Maureen (Queen Victoria); Stanley Holloway (gravedigger); Catherine Lacey (old woman); Peter Madden (Von Tirpitz); Michael Balfour (cabbie); James Copeland (guide); George Benson (Inspector Lestrade); Michael Elwyn (Cassidy); Miklós Rózsa (conductor). 125 minutes.

AVANTI! (1972). Mirisch Corporation/Phalanx/Jalem. Color by DeLuxe. Director: Billy Wilder; producer: Billy Wilder; screenplay: Billy Wilder and I. A. L. Diamond, with contributions by Luciano Vincenzoni, based on the play by Samuel A. Taylor; cinematographer: Luigi Kuveiller; musical score: Carlo Rustichelli; art director: Ferdinando Scarfiotti; costumes: Lino Coletta; editor: Ralph E. Winters. Cast: Jack Lemmon (Wendell Armbruster); Juliet Mills (Pamela Piggott); Clive Revill (Carlo Carlucci); Edward Andrews (J. J. Blodgett); Gianfranco Barra (Bruno); Francesco Angrisano (Arnoldo Trotta); Pippo Franco (Mattarazzo); Franco Acampora (Armado Trotti); Giselda Castrini (Anna); Raffaele Mottola (passport officer); Lino Coletta (Cipriani); Harry Ray (Dr. Fleischmann); Guidarino Guidi (maître d'); Giacomo Rizzo (bartender); Antonino Di Bruno (concierge); Yanti Sommer (nurse); Janet Agren (nurse). 144 minutes.

THE FRONT PAGE (1974). Universal International. Technicolor. Panavision. Director: Billy Wilder; producers: Jennings Lang and Paul Monash; screenplay: Billy Wilder and I. A. L. Diamond, based on the play by Ben Hecht and Charles MacArthur; cinematographer: Jordan Cronenweth; musical score: Billy May; costumes: Burton Miller; editor: Ralph E. Winters; art director: Henry Bumstead. Cast: Walter Matthau (Walter Burns); Jack Lemmon (Hildy Johnson); Susan Sarandon (Peggy Grant); David Wayne (Bensinger); Carol Burnett (Mollie Malloy); Austin Pendleton (Earl Williams); Vincent Gardenia (sheriff); Allen Garfield (Kruger); Herb Edelman (Schwartz); Charles Durning (Murphy); Martin Gabel (Dr. Eggelhofer); Harold Gould (mayor); Jon Korkes (Rudy Keppler); Dick O'Neill (McHugh); Cliff Osmond (Jacobi); Lou Frizzell (Endicott); Paul Benedict (Plunkett); Doro Merande (Jennie); Noam Pitlik (Wilson); Joshua Shelley (cabdriver); Allen Jenkins (telegrapher); John Furlong (Duffy); Biff Elliot (police dispatcher); Barbara Davis (Myrtle); Leonard Bremen (Butch). 105 minutes.

FEDORA (1978). Geria-Bavaria. Color. Panavision. Director: Billy Wilder; producer: Billy Wilder; screenplay: Billy Wilder and I. A. L. Diamond, based on the story by Tom Tryon; cinematographer: Gerry Fisher; musical score: Miklós Rózsa; art director: Alexander Trauner; costumes: Charlotte Flemming; editors: Stefan Arsten and Fredric Steinkamp; associate producer: I. A. L. Diamond; assistant director: Jean-Patrick Constantini; production supervisor: Willy Egger; production coordinator: Harold Nebenzal; makeup: Tom Smith. Cast: William Holden (Barry "Dutch" Detweiler); Marthe Keller (Fedora); Hildegard Knef (Countess Sobryanski); Jose Ferrer (Dr. Vando); Frances Sternhagen (Miss Balfour); Mario Adorf (hotel manager); Stephen Collins (young Barry); Henry Fonda (president of the Academy); Michael York (himself); Hans Jaray (Count Sobryanski); Gottfried John (Kritos); Arlene Francis (newscaster); Jacques Maury (usher); Christine Mueller (young Antonia); Ellen Schwiers (nurse); Bob Cunningham (assistant director); Christoph Künzler (clerk); Mary Kelly (Gladys); Elma Karlowa (maid); Panos Papadopoulos (bartender); Rex McGee (photographer). 113 minutes.

BUDDY BUDDY (1981). MGM. Metrocolor. Panavision. Director: Billy Wilder; producer: Jay Weston; screenplay: Billy Wilder and I. A. L. Diamond, based on the film *L'Emmerdeur*, screenplay by Francis Veber; cinematographer: Harry Stradling Jr.; musical score: Lalo Schifrin; art director: Daniel A. Lomino; editor: Argyle Nelson; makeup: Stephen Abrums and Ron Snyder; costumes: John A. Anderson and Agnes G. Henry; executive producer: Alain Bernheim; associate producer: Charles Matthau; set decorator: Cloudia; assistant director: Gary Daigler; set design: William J. Durrell; special effects: Milt Rice; sound: Don Sharpless. Cast: Jack Lemmon (Victor Clooney); Walter Matthau (Trabucco); Paula Prentiss (Celia Clooney);

Klaus Kinski (Dr. Zuckerbrot); Dana Elcar (Hubris); Miles Chapin (Eddie, the bellhop); Michael Ensign (assistant manager); Joan Shawlee (receptionist); Fil Formicola (Rudy "Disco" Gambola); C. J. Hunt (Kowalski); Bette Raya (maid); Ronnie Sperling (husband); Suzie Galler (wife); John Schubeck (newscaster); Ed Begley Jr. (policeman); Frank Farmer (policeman); Tom Kindle (patrolman); Biff Manard (patrolman); Charlotte Stewart (nurse). 96 minutes.

ACKNOWLEDGMENTS

Like filmmaking, the writing of a biography is a collaboration. Hundreds of people wrote this book with me, and to them I am inexpressibly grateful. The list of names that follows is a sorry attempt to reflect my thanks; its curtness embarrasses me, and I can only hope that everyone who finds his or her name on the roster knows how much their help and support really means to me. I thank my parents, Irving and Betty Sikov, for loving me no matter what. I have a very patient family. Christopher Bram, Mary Alexander, and Matthew Mirapaul waded through hundreds of thousands of words and told me, with affection and wisdom, which ones stank. I couldn't ask for better friends. I'm particularly grateful to Patrick Merla, for performing the difficult task of pre-editing the book, checking facts, pointing out the boring parts, and convincing me to delete them. I didn't know Dino Heicker at all when I asked him to wade through and translate a lot of German for me, and I'm indebted to him not only for his brilliant work but for his friendship as well. Adam Orman, Michael Wilson, Alex Volk, Michael Greenblatt, and Catherine Pagès researched and translated and held my hand, all at the same time, and they stayed friends with me even after they finished their tasks. Joe Smith and Tom Rhoads housed and fed me in Los Angeles and kept me from falling completely to pieces in a very strange city, and I'm grateful they still like me.

Of the many people who provided information and support, none were more unstinting than Andreas Hutter, whose diligent research is only surpassed by the generous spirit with which he shares it. He and Klaus Kamolz made my stay in Austria enormously productive and surprisingly comforting, and his master's thesis on Wilder's early life proved to be an invaluable source of information and criticism. The first five chapters of this book are indebted to him. Janet Malcolm steered me to Peter Swales, who steered me toward Klaus, who introduced me to Andreas; I thank them all. Howard Prouty, Sandra Archer, Sam Gill, Robert Cushman, Stacey Behlmer, Scott Curtis, Steve Garland, Sue Guldin, Jonathan Wahl, Norman Brennan, and the entire staff of the Margaret Herrick Library of the Academy of Motion Picture Arts and Sciences were inordinately kind to me as well as being supremely knowledgeable. Rosemarie van der Zee, Peter Latta, and Gerrit Thies at the Deutsche Stiftung Kinemathek were gracious and accommodating as well. Rebecca Collier at the National Archives could not have been more helpful; the time she spent sorting through old army records on my behalf was extraordinary. I'm also grateful to Wil Mahoney and David Pfeiffer, also at the Archives. Kenneth Geist, Donald Albrecht, and Molly Ornati and the New York Center for Visual History provided me with marvelous interview transcripts. Heartfelt thanks, too, to Howard and Ron Mandelbaum at Photofest. Charles Silver and Ron Magliozzi at the Museum of Modern Art; Ned Comstock and Stuart Ng at USC; Brigitte Keuppers at UCLA; and Gladys Irvis and her staff at the AFI—each of these heroic librarians responded to my persistent research requests with yeoman tact and expert care, and if I had any sense of honor I'd give them all a percentage of my royalties because they deserve it.

Particular thanks go to Don Albinson, Jerry Carlson, George W. Davis, Richard Deinler, Marta Eggerth Kiepura, Joan Fontaine, Joshua Harrison, Robert Lantz, Juliet Mills, John and Marilyn Neuhart, Alfred Paddock Jr., the late Robert Parrish, Austin Pendleton, Susan Sarandon, Robert Staples, Jan Sterling, Don Taylor, Sally Rice Taylor, Annie Tresgot, and

Ray Walston, all of whom agreed to share their thoughts and memories of Billy Wilder on the record. I am almost as grateful to those people who spoke with me on the condition that I keep their identities to myself. In addition, I drew inspiration, insight, and a life's worth of raw data from a host of writers who profiled Billy Wilder and analyzed his films over the years. My deepest thanks go to Michel Ciment and the late Maurice Zolotow, but everyone named in this book's bibliography should know that I am thoroughly indebted to them.

These friends, associates, colleagues, and correspondents provided help, support, and information in crucial and countless ways: Troy Alexander, Bevan Alexander, James Ireland Baker, Rudy Behlmer, John Belton, Martin Blumenson, Damien Bona, Bill Condon, George Custen, Jay Derrah, Bruce Finlayson, Mort and Sue Frishberg, Joseph Haddon, Ira Hozinsky, Michael Kaniecki, Howard Karren, Peter Koplan, Michel Lerner, Bill Mann, Graham Morgan, Peter Pappas, Bill Paul, Sean Philips, Scott Savaiano, Draper Shreeve, Anthony Slide, Sean Smith, Melanie Wallace, and Andrea Weiss.

On Sunset Boulevard would not exist without Rick Kot, who had enough confidence in me to buy the book for Hyperion and to see it through the midway point, and Jennifer Barth, who pared it down with a sharp eye and tough, demanding taste, and shepherded it with superb skill and commitment. Gratitude also goes to Lesley Krauss and her production team at Hyperion as well as my copy editor, Shelly Perron, and indexer, Nancy Wolff. My agents, Edward Hibbert and Neil Olson at Donadio and Ashworth, remain true champs. Bless them for keeping alive the graceful spirit of their friend and mentor, Eric Ashworth.

INDEX